THE PATH OF FREEDOM ... IGGA

Amupubbena medhāvī thokathokaṁ khaṇe khaṇe
kammāro rajatass' eva niddhame malam attano.
Dh. 239.

Gradually should the perspicacious one,
Momentarily, little by little, expel
His own dross, as would the smith
That which is in silver.*

* Soma Thera's Translation.

The Sinhalese translation of this work is being made by the Venerable Maḍihē Paññāsīha Mahā Nāyaka Thera of Vajirārāma, Colombo, Ceylon.

THE PATH
OF
FREEDOM

BY

THE ARAHANT UPATISSA

Translated into Chinese (*Gedatsu Dō Ron*)
by
Tipiṭaka Sanghapāla of Funan

Translated from the Chinese
by
The Rev. N. R. M. Ehara, Soma Thera and Kheminda Thera

Published by
Dr. D. Roland D. Weerasuria,
Balcombe House, Balcombe Place,
Colombo 8, Ceylon.
1961

PRINTED AT:
THE SAMAN PRESS,
MAHARAGAMA,
CEYLON

Sole Distributors: M. D. Gunasena & Co., Ltd. — Colombo, Ceylon

DEDICATED

to

the memory of

The Venerable Mahā Nāyaka Thera,

Paeḷāēnē Siri Vajirañāṇa of Vajirārāma,

Colombo, Ceylon

and

The Venerable Myin Mu Myo Sayadaw,

Pāṇḍava Mahā Thera of the Satipaṭṭhāna Monastery,

Moulmein, Burma.

In Memoriam

SOMA MAHĀ THERA

(1898 — 1960)

Aciraṁ vat' ayaṁ kāyo paṭhaviṁ adhisessati
Chuddho apetaviññāṇo, niratthaṁ va kalingaraṁ.[1]

Truly it will not be long before this body lies in the earth, bereft of consciousness, like a useless piece of wood, which is thrown away.

— Soma Thera's translation in "Words Leading to Disenchantment", *Bosat*, Oct. 1959.

Truly, indeed, it was not long after—just four months since he wrote this article—that he suddenly passed away. Often he used to say that this was the sort of death he preferred.

It is fitting to record here the life and work of the Venerable Soma Mahā Thera, for, but for his indomitable energy and earnestness this work would not have been undertaken, persisted in, and brought to a conclusion in just four months. Whenever any difficulty arose it was to him that the others turned. When we were tempted to give up the work on encountering really hard patches, he was always ready with encouragement and with a way out of the difficulty. He loved to work hard, and half-hearted effort was unknown to him. Not infrequently he used to say, "Better wear out than rust out".

Soma Mahā Thera was born on December 23, 1898, in Kotahena, Colombo, and passed away at Vajirārāma, Bambalapitiya, Colombo, Tuesday, February 23, 1960. His father was Emmanuel Marian Perera Pulle, and his mother, Theresa Rodrigo Babapulle. His name was Victor Emmanuel Perera Pulle. He received his education at St. Benedict's College, Kotahena.

Once at the age of eleven, when he was told by his teacher that God made man, he promptly asked him, "Who made God?". The teacher, apparently unused to this sort of question from his pupils, snapped back, "Do not question the antecedents of God". However, this incident pleased neither the teacher nor the pupil. He began to read and think for himself. One day his mother gave him one rupee as pocket-money, and Victor walked about three miles to a bookshop in the Fort, Colombo, looking out for a book priced at one rupee or less, as that was all he had. Finding an English translation of the Dhammapada being sold for a rupee he quickly bought and read it again and again. This was his introduction to the *Buddhadhamma*. From that day on he

1. Dh. 41.

eagerly attended lectures and sermons on the *Dhamma*, the while reading what literature came his way on philosophy, art, archaeology, history—in fact anything that would add to his knowledge. And thus he moved further and further away from the faith of his fathers. During these years, as his mother objected to his reading late into the night, he would, after she had gone to sleep, begin reading by candle light under the bed. Sometimes he found that when he had finished reading it was already day. Such was his thirst for knowledge.

Sometime in 1920 he had met Mr. W. Joseph Soysa, one of the founder-members of the Servants of the Buddha, the well-known association which has its headquarters at Lauries Road, Bambalapitiya, and of which the Venerable Kassapa Thera is the founder-patron. After being actively engaged for sometime in the publication of the "Blessing" which was edited by the then president of the association, Dr. Cassius A. Pereira, he, along with Mr. Soysa, joined the Colombo Buddhist Union in the early twenties, and presented a large collection of books to the Union library. He composed "A formula of associate worship"[1] to be used by members of the Union at their monthly joint flower-offering at one of the many shrines in the city.

Shortly after this, once again with his equally keen friend Mr. Soysa, he founded the Fort Study Circle and was elected its organizing secretary. Later, as work increased, assistance was needed and Mr. W. Don Michael was elected joint secretary.

The following extracts are from Mr. Michael's article entitled "Apostle of the Dhamma", written on the passing away of Soma Mahā Thera:

> 'The sudden death of Soma Thera has uprooted from our midst a personality distinguished at once by the versality of his talents, self-sacrifice, personal sanctity, and crusading apostleship of the *Dhamma*. A deep understanding of human nature and the human problem of suffering had mellowed him and bred in him, in an unusual degree, qualities of tolerance, patience, restraint and sympathy with fellow-beings. Opposition and frustration left in him no sense of defeat or bitterness. He was the working bee in the Master's hive and, in His service, the very juice of the bitter thyme turned into honey at his touch. No wonder that, in the Augustan age of Buddhist renascence in Ceylon, Soma Thera was considered to represent the fine flower of Buddhist culture. He shed its fragrance wherever he moved. As scholar, preacher, organiser, monk and friend it may be aptly said of him: "*Nihil tetigit quod non ornavit*".

1. *Associate Offering Of Flowers, Incense And Light To The Buddha.*

We have gathered here to pay homage to the Blessed One, who found the way to Happiness for all beings. With these flowers we honour the mainfold purity of the Master; with incense, his compassion; with the light of these lamps, his perfect enlightenment.

By our joint worship of the Buddha, may we gain the strength to work together in friendliness, sympathising with those in trouble, rejoicing with those who are are fortunate, and avoiding all the evil courses of action, namely, the evil courses of selffish desire, hate, fear and delusion.

'These sterling qualities of Soma Thera were happily blended in a character in which humility and service formed the keynote. He never spared himself. He gave till it hurt. He gave UNTO THIS LAST—unto death. Overwork, fatigue, were the proximate causes of the dire malady which struck down this mighty oak of the *Dhamma* which was a shade and refuge of many a seeker after Truth. Today a void is left standing which may take years to fill.

'To those of us who knew him and enjoyed his friendship and affection for nearly four decades both as the dashing young layman Victor E. P. Pulle, and as a monk of blessed memory, Soma Thera presents a remarkable character study. The child was the father of the man, Thera. Yet in his twenties, he was a rebel from the faith of his fathers and questing for the knowledge of the truth. In the 1930's, still hot on the pursuit, he was the leader of a band of young men who formed the Fort Study Circle under the Presidency of Mr. J. Tyagarajah, with Dr. L. A. (now Sir Lalita) Rajapakse and the late Mr. R. Nadarajah as Vice-Presidents.

'Their motto was sacrifice and service and their main object was the economic and cultural development of the country. The regular weekly programme of the Circle, all planned by Victor, included classes in Pali, Hindi, Layman's Law, History, Economics and politics. With what resourcefulness, with what prevision of judgement and success, he organised and directed its activities towards the cultural and literary formation of the day are now matters of history...

'Young Victor's reputation for literary and critical scholarship was such that Dr. Lucian De Zilwa prefaced his talk by saying that he accepted the invitation for a lecture with the major object of making the acquaintance of Mr. V. E. P. Pulle; and Mr. K. P. S. Menon, one of the most graceful and eloquent public speakers this country has ever had, began his lecture by saying that he was always anxious to see the set of young men who could produce an annual report of such literary excellence as that turned out by the Fort Study Circle.

'For Victor Pulle reason was the touchstone of truth. In this quest, he studied comparative religion, logic, philosophy—Dahlke and Schopenhauer had a particular appeal to him—art, sculpture, archaeology, history, music and even astrology. Indeed, like Bacon, he took all knowledge for his province. There was not a single individual in the Fort of his day who

---

Service of the world is the highest homage we can pay to the Buddha, the friend and helper of all beings. Let this act of homage with flowers, incense and light, be the symbol of the homage of service of the world every Buddhist has to fulfil. Let us dedicate ourselves anew today to tread the Path of Service trodden by the Master—the Path of Charity, Virtue and Clear Thought.

Let us remind ourselves now and frequently that the greatest charity is in giving the gift of fearlessness (*abhaya dāna*) to the world by refraining from killing, stealing, unchastity, lying and drink. Thus we shall be able to become merciful, honest, chaste, truthful and sober, and make the society in which we live a noble one.

May right understanding and right thought grow in the world!

combined in himself such a vast amalgam of knowledge. Literary and economic studies, however, could not satisfy his ardent mind and he joined the Sangha. It was in this august calling that his scholarship ripened and Buddhist revival throughout the World received from the results of his labour a new life and orientation.

'Meditation, study, teaching the *Dhamma*, canonical research and his own trials and tribulation in the process produced a vast transformation in Soma Thera. The *élan* and impulsiveness of the layman turned into serene calm. The combative debater of yesteryear became the sedate teacher and friendly adviser. The glint of battle which earlier rose to his eyes when argument waxed high grew into sparks of sympathy and compassion. The chiselled square jaws which hurled challenge softened their contours. Above all, the terrific right fist which characteristically swung menacingly in debate would swing no more. It was obvious even to us his old boon companions to whom he still accorded the privilege of "ragging" him once in a way, that this great pioneer and savant, by a terrific ordeal of trial and error, had at last subdued himself and that he had not only found the Middle Path but had established himself so firmly in it that he was a fitting exemplar of his Master's Way of Life.

'As a writer, Soma Thera belongs to the *genre* whom Buffon's dictum "*Le style est l'homme meme*" is perfectly applicable. In his Study Circle days, he had a massive style. The exposition and argument would at times be obscured by the weight of movement. He used his pen as a tomahawk. When Carthage had to be destroyed, he made no bones about it but went and destroyed. As a Thera, the old asperity and venom disappeared and the style assumed a precision, clarity, mellowness and gentle movement which reflected the repose and sureness of his own mind. It is significant that, in recent years, his thoughts turned to poetry. They all centre on the *Dhamma*. One of them recalls so naturally the self-abnegation of the bees in Virgil's lines "*Sic vos, non vobis, mellificatis, apes*"—not for yourself, ye bees, your cells ye fill—that the verses "Giving Up" deserve quotation'.[1]

One day, towards the end of 1928, our common friend, Mr. W. Joseph Soysa (Oliver as we call him), introduced me to Victor. But it was hardly necessary. Simultaneously Victor and I knew that we had been friends before, in an earlier life.[2] But we were always grateful to Oliver for this. Later I was happy to find that the Buddha taught that it was not easy to find a being, who, during the vast period of time covered in the process of birth and death, and birth again and death, had not, at one time or another, been a mother, a father, a brother, a sister, a son, a daughter. The Blessed One then asks the question, "What is the reason for this"? and himself answers: "Not to be known is the

1. See page xvi.
2. Since writing this the Ven. Vinita Thera of Vajirārāma was kind enough to draw my attention to a sonnet in which Lord Tennyson describes how he recognised a friend o

start of beings enmeshed in ignorance and fettered by craving, running on, speeding on through interminable births and deaths. Nor can it be said of the running on and the speeding on of ignorant and craving beings that they are tending to an end. And in this interminable process, for long have you all experienced grief bitter and sharp and made the graveyards bigger and bigger. Because of that you should turn away from the formations (*sankhāras*), cut them off, and become free of them"—S. II, 190 (Soma Thera's translation). This is no poetic fancy, as at first sight it may appear to be. This is the word of the Supremely Enlightened One who has done with poetic fancy. His is the vision of things as they are (*yathābhūtañāaṇdassana*). And this vision he describes without exaggeration; for exaggeration the Buddhas do not indulge in.

In the late twenties, Victor and I had heard from the late Mr. Wong Mow Lam, the Chinese scholar, who was in Ceylon for sometime, that there were great possibilities for spreading the *Theravāda* in his country and that there was much that could be translated from the *Mahāyāna* literature of China. So when we went to Burma in 1934, remembering the words of our scholar friend, we decided after careful thought to go to the Far East and return later to Burma for ordination. We began our journey to China by way of Kawkerik, over the misty Dawna Mountains and across the border for four days on foot to Raehaeng in Thailand, and thence by bus, river boat and train through Svankaloke (Svargaloka—heaven world), Pisaloke (Viṣṇuloka — Viṣṇu's world), we arrived in Krum Teb (Deva Nagara — the city of the gods) which is Bangkok. Then again, after travelling by train to Penang, and by ship to Singapore and Hong Kong, we arrived in Shanghai. Finding there no facilities for study we proceeded to Tokyo. There we met Prof. Nichiki Kimura of Rissho University, who invited us to attend his English lectures on *Mahāyāna*. Towards the end of 1935, through his good offices, we were invited to Jozaiji, the Nichiren temple in Kawatana-Machi, Nagasaki-ken. The head of that temple, the Rev. N. R. M. Ehara, had been a lecturer at Rissho for sometime. He was the perfect host—a most understanding, patient, pleasant, witty character with abundant laughter, and he was young. He did everything within his power to make our stay as comfortable as possible.

---

an earlier life, thus:

"*As when with downcast eyes we muse and brood,*
And ebb into a former life, or seem
To lapse far back in some confused dream
To states of mystical similitude;
If one but speaks or hems or stirs his chair,
Ever the wonder waxeth more and more,
So that we say, 'All this hath been before,
All this hath been, I know not when or where'.
So, friend, when first I look'd upon your face,
Our thought gave answer each to each, so true—
Opposed mirrors each reflecting each—
That tho' I knew not in what time or place,
Methought that I had often met with you,
And either lived in either's heart and speech".

In Memoriam

When we arrived at Kawatana-Machi, Jozaiji was being rebuilt. By the end of April, the building operations over, our host set apart the new guest-house for our use and called it the Lion Hall, "in honour", as he said, "of the Lion Isle, the home of my friends". We spent a most pleasant and fruitful year in our Lion Hall, for, it was here that the whole of the *Gedatsu Dō Ron* (the Chinese translation of the *Vimuttimagga*) was translated into English for the first time. Perhaps it will not be out of place to mention here that when the late Ven. Nyāṇatiloka Mahā Thera was in Japan during the years that followed the First World War, he tried, but failed, to persuade any Japanese scholar to undertake this translation. So when we sent him a copy of our translation he heartily welcomed it. The word for word translation the draft translation, copying, cyclostyling, binding, packing for the post, were all done by the three of us and that during the brief space of four months. Besides, the section on virtue had to be cyclostyled thrice before Victor was satisfied with it.

This is how the translation began. Some days after we went into residence in the Lion Hall, our friend showed us around his new library. Pointing to three thin volumes he said that that was the Chinese translation of the *Vimutti-magga*, and that originally it was supposed to have been written in Pali in Ceylon by a Sinhalese Thera. With one voice both of us exclaimed that we were ready to begin translating it that very instant,—of course, with his help. And our friend, with his great big ringing laughter, readily agreed. And we immediately translated the first few pages though he had much to do, it being very close to *Hanamatsuri*, the Flower Festival, which corresponds to Vesak in *Theravāda* lands. Working incessantly we managed to issue the translation of the first fascicle on *Hanamatsuri*, May 28, 1936. Continuing to work even up to twenty hours a day sometimes we were able to post the last copy of the last section of the translation to fifty scholars by the last day of September, 1936. During this period Victor knew no fatigue in that most agreeable climate of South Japan.

Jozaiji is beautifully situated a third of the way up the hill which rises abruptly from the broad paddy fields that stretch right up to the sea. In front is the river Kawa, the beauty of which they sing in *Kawa-no-Kawatana*, the song of the Kawa of Kawatana. Behind, the hill rises higher and higher and is level at the top. The temple was here in ancient times, and here Victor and I used to stroll under those attractively twisted and gnarled *suñgi* trees, the cypresses, that adorn the grounds of Japanese temples. One summer day while walking there our attention was drawn to some plants we seemed to recognize. At first we thought they were well-grown violets. But soon found they were *goṭukola* (*Hydrocotyle Asiatica*). Their stalks were nearly eighteen inches long with large leaves. We took a handful of them to the temple, and our host was agreeably surprised to hear that this was eaten in Ceylon. He liked it so much that he introduced it to the whole village. They call it horseshoe.

In Memoriam

During these four months of translation work the thought that repeatedly arose in our minds was how soon could we return to Burma for ordination and put into practice the teaching of the Sambuddha so clearly set forth in the *Vimuttimagga*. It was plain, open, and easy to understand. What it said reached the heart direct — *hadayangama* seemed to be the correct word to describe one's reaction on reading the *Vimuttimagga* for the first time. There was no point in delaying.

So we left Jozaiji with our friend the Rev. N. R. M. Ehara and a few others, went to Nagasaki and took ship to Rangoon. Our friend was much grieved that we were leaving so soon and repeatedly said as the ship was leaving, "Come back, come back again". That was the last time we were to see him. For, though we had hoped some day to see him again, word came shortly after the Second World War that he had suddenly passed away. This was sometime after he had been appointed head of the Nichiren sect for the district of Omura.

Before we decided to translate the *Vimuttimagga* our host was keen on translating some of the smaller treatises of Nichiren Shonin which Victor did. Some of them were published in the *Young East*, the journal of the Japanese Buddhist Associations, Tokyo.

We reached Moulmein by the end of October, and found that U. Chit Swe, our *dāyaka*, had made all arrangements for our ordination in an *araññāvāsa* (forest residence), as requested by us, and had gone over to India on pilgrimage. His close friend, U. Chit Su, deputised for him. And on November 6, 1936, Victor and I received our higher ordination with the Venerable Pāṇḍava Mahā Thera of Taungwainggyi Shewgyin Kyaung Taik, Moulmein, as teacher. Here we came to hear of the Venerable Nārada Mahā Thera, also known as Jetavana Sayadaw. As he was then living in nearby Thaton, we visited him. A lay pupil of his who had earlier instructed us in the practice of the *Satipaṭṭhāna* method of meditation, too, accompanied us to see the Sayadaw. His method was strictly in accordance with the *Satipaṭṭhāna Suttas* of the *Dīgha* and *Majjhima Nikāyas* and their commentaries. He said that the necessary instruction was found in them and no new interpretation was necessary; the Buddha called it the sole way and that there was no other 'sole' way to the purification of beings.

On reaching Ceylon by way of India in the middle of 1937, Bhikkhu Soma met a companion of his childhood days who became so attached to him that he would not leave him till his death — that distressing thing called asthma. It would have rendered many a strong man useless for work quite early. But asthma or no asthma, he worked on and on up to the end with increasing vigour. Hearing that we were returning to Ceylon, a *dāyaka*, the late Mr. W. M. Barnes de Silva, had set apart a small house for our use in a quiet place at Belihuloya. We could not stay there long as the Venerable Soma fell ill and had to go to Colombo for treatment and we stayed at the Vidyālankāra Oriental College, Kelaniya, for a time.

After he recovered from his illness, and wishing to live in quiet surroundings for a while, we were able to go into residence at the Mahānadī Ārāma at Gampolawela. Then at the invitation of the late Sir Baron Jayatilaka we visited Bangalore in 1939 with the Venerable Nārāvila Dhammaratana Mahā Thera, as leader of the Mission of Goodwill to India. There the mission was able to secure from the Government of Mysore a site for a Buddhist Centre, and both of us returned to Ceylon in 1940 owing to illness.

As Bhikkhu Soma needed rest for sometime, Mr. A. B. C. de Soysa placed his bungalow, in his estate in Kurunegala, at our disposal. After a few months' stay there we were invited by the Venerable Nyāṇaponika Mahā Thera to the Island Hermitage, Dodanduwa. As the Second World War had begun, all the German Theras of the Hermitage were interned and the Venerable Nyāṇāloka Mahā Thera, the present *adhipati* (chief resident Thera) was then in charge of the place. During this period the attacks of asthma were most severe. At one time the only available medicament was Himrod's Asthma Cure. It had to be lit with a match and the fumes inhaled. Bhikkhu Soma could hardly walk two yards without this Himrod's cure, and could not sleep at night without filling the room with these fumes. One night even this failed to help. So about 2 a.m. he sat at his table and scribbled these verses:

Out of the womb of sightless night
Rang out a word of healing strong,
And put to flight the evil throng
That stood betwixt the eye and light.

Where lies, friend, the golden mean?	*In giving up.*
Where's the heart forever clean?	*In giving up.*
Where is life at its best seen?	*In giving up.*
Where reaches one Peace Serene?	*In giving up.*
When does one always see things clear?	*In giving up.*
When is one to all beings dear?	*In giving up.*
When does one wipe away all fear?	*In giving up.*
When does one to Truth adhere?	*In giving up.*
How does one give full measure?	*By giving up.*
How, end poverty's pressure?	*By giving up.*
How, come to rarest treasure?	*By giving up.*
How, know the purest pleasure?	*By giving up.*
Why on self a tight hand keep?	*For giving up.*
Why the heart in culture steep?	*For giving up.*
Why turn on to wisdom deep?	*For giving up.*
Why care not to sow or reap?	*For giving up.*

In Memoriam

He lived in this "our little island home", as he liked to call the Hermitage, from 1940-45 and from 1948-54. These were years he treasured much. For it was here that the first edition of *The Way of Mindfulness* (1941) and *His Last Performance* (1943) were written. He also edited here in 1943 *Ānāpāna Sati* of Dr. Cassius A. Pereira. In spite of his failing health he wrote unceasingly. He contributed articles to various Buddhist journals regularly. The quiet of the Hermitage appealed to him a great deal. Frequently he sat beneath the trees by the water's edge in deep thought, and the following verses might indicate some of the thoughts that occupied his mind then:

Away against the lip of sea and sky
A tiny fisher craft tanned brown by sun,
Pops up and down, like monk in russet clout,
Upon the choppy sea of doubt and lust.

The tender palms of gold and light green fronds
Remind me of my youth and boyhood's days.
Amidst their plumy, wavy forms I throve
Imbibing nature's simple silent ways.

Once it was thought that his asthma might improve if he had a change and so he stayed at Asokārāma in Nuwara Eliya for sometime. There, walking along in Moon Plains once, he was absorbed in the beauty of a waterfall. He used to watch the water rushing down in a silver streak, and very often the asthma left him on those occasions or he forgot it. This tiresome friend, Asthma, has a peculiar trait. He wants attention. And, sometimes, if no attention is paid to him, he sharply retorts in return by paying no attention. These were the times when Soma Thera would say, "I am thoroughly fit. I can work even the whole day", reminiscent of the Lion Hall days when he really worked almost the whole day. It is about this waterfall in Nuwara Eliya that he wrote:

E'er let me live and die where waters flow
From hidden springs on heights that probe the sky,
And come to light as white foam falling by
The negro face of rocks that shine and glow.

Childlikeness was a prominent characteristic of his, and perhaps the following verses illustrate some aspect of it:

E'er let me live and die with childlike sight,
Beholding elfin gold and jewels bright,
And dream-made treasure in the silent night
Of travel on and on the Path of Light.

In Memoriam

At the invitation of the late Venerable Tai Tsu, the well known Buddhist leader of China, the Venerable Maḍihē Paññāsīha Thera (now Mahā Nāyaka Thera), the Venerable Soma Thera, and I, went to China to establish a Pali College at Sianfu, the ancient Buddhist Centre in Shensi Province, the home of Fa Hsien the famous pilgrim. Arriving in Shanghai in early July, we found that fighting had broken out in Shensi between the Nationalist and the Communist forces. There was no possibility of proceeding further. The *Vassa-vāsa*, the rainy season residence, was spent in Shanghai after which the mission returned. During this period Soma Thera's radio sermons were much appreciated. Besides, he addressed many gatherings in various parts of the city. The Shanghai Y.M.B.A. which he founded had, by the time the mission left, nearly three hundred members. He also conducted a Pali class, which was well attended. In November that year the Mission returned to Hong Kong where, too, Soma Thera addressed various groups of Buddhists. Arriving in Singapore in January 1947, the mission had to wait two months for a boat. Meanwhile Soma Thera delivered sermons and lectures to large gatherings both in Singapore and Kuala Lumpur. The Mission returned to Ceylon in March that year. Soma Thera returned to the Island Hermitage at the end of 1948 and remained there till 1954. After his return from China, on his initiative, two important Buddhist associations in Colombo, The Sāsanādhāra Kāntā Samitiya and The Banks' Asoka Society, were formed in 1950 and 1956 respectively. He was the founder-patron of the latter.

With the approach of the *Buddha Jayanti* celebrations, it was suggested that a bi-monthly called '*Buddha Jayanti*' be published for the duration of these celebrations for the benefit of the English reading public. When in 1953 the organizers came to ask Soma Mahā Thera for his help, he threw himself wholeheartedly into the work, for half-hearted effort was alien to his nature. Most of the editorials on the *Dhamma* in the '*Buddha Jayanti*' and a large number of translations from the Pali and the German, besides original articles, and the *Jayanti Miscellany*, were from his versatile pen. His masterly articles on 'The Greatest Mahānāyaka Thera of Our Time' and the editorial 'A Maker of Good Men' on the passing away of the Venerable Paelāēnē Siri Vajirañāṇa Mahā Nāyaka Thera, were written at a time when he was much harassed by asthma. Finding that the long stay at the Island Hermitage had worsened his asthma and seeing the advantage of being with the Venerable Paelāēnē Siri Vajirañāṇa Mahā Nāyaka Thera at Vajirārāma with its well equipped library, Soma Thera came to reside once more at Vajirārāma. Both the Mahā Nāyaka Thera and Soma Thera were happy to meet; for, as far back as 1919, the former had inspired the latter by his great knowledge, understanding, and kindness. Soma Thera's regard and respect for him kept on increasing during the years. They used to converse on the *Dhamma* and on allied subjects such as literature, history, grammar, folk-lore, and so on, for hours at a time. The Mahā Nāyaka Thera, too, was always ailing, but when both of them began to converse they forgot their ailments. It might be wondered how it was possible for one to get so interested in such a theme as grammar. But the Mahā Nāyaka Thera was such a master of the subject and an accomplished conversationalist that he was able to make even a subject like grammar interesting. I remember in the early thirties how the Mahā Nāyaka Thera discoursed on the *Dhamma* to a group of us young men whose leader was Victor. Once the questions put by Victor so interested the Mahā Nāyaka Thera that he continued the conversation till three o'clock in the morning.

This early earnestness he maintained to the very end. How this long and earnest practice of the *Dhamma* moulded Soma Mahā Thera's character is briefly shown in the following extracts from an article by Ceylon's Director of Education, Mr. S. F. de Silva: 'I came to know the Venerable Soma Thera as Mr. Victor Pulle some thirty years ago....My first impression was of a remarkably earnest man who was determined to seek and find out the Truth. His face was an index to his earnestness and I often listened to him arguing a point....We became very good friends and week in and week out I used to watch and realise that of the band that gathered together, he was one of the most earnest and untiring in his study of the *Dhamma*....As a member of the Order he became a changed man. I noticed a strength of character and calmness of demeanour in everything he said and wrote. I used to visit him in his room and talk things over many an evening. Occasionaly the eye would flash and I could see the old time fighter but there was an unmistakable sense of toleration of others and a remarkable kindliness in everything he said. The Venerable Soma Mahā Thera was very well known to English speaking audiences in the Island. Many may remember his thoughtful talks over Radio Ceylon. I am aware how deeply he was respected by Buddhist students in schools all over thc island....To me his translation, edition and notes of the *Satipaṭṭhāna Sutta* is characteristic of the man. He was one who wanted to practise the *Dhamma*, and the *Satipaṭṭhāna Sutta* was to him 'the one way for the ending of unhappiness'. I can see his mind in his introductory notes and his interpretations of the text. The Venerable Soma Thera's edition of the *Satipaṭṭhāna Sutta* is a part of his own life because he was one who wanted to practise the *Dhamma.* I miss him very much as a friend but those who knew him have no cause to grieve for a life that had been so nobly spent. He had acquitted himself heroically in all things he did to the end....Alert and intensely alive in the search and practice of the Truth, it is of these that the Buddha has said that 'those who are heedful do not die'. His life is an example to all those who knew him, that there is nothing nobler for a Buddhist than to live the life that the Buddha has preached, to walk the way He had walked and to follow Him on the Noble Quest. May the Venerable Soma Thera attain the Noble Quest he started some forty years ago'.

When one happens to be the only person in a powerful group to accept another teaching, much opposition may be expected. This Victor had in plenty. At these times he resorted to the calm atmosphere of Vajirārāma, where the late Venerable Mahā Nāyaka Thera and the Venerable Nārada Mahā Thera always found the time to speak with him, sometimes for hours, and he went away stimulated. Later, as a *bhikkhu*, when the Venerable Soma, while residing at the Vidyālankāra Oriental College, Kelaniya, found that the opposition had grown into hostility, he had the ready sympathy and unstinted support of the late Venerable Lunupokunē Dhammānanda Nāyaka Thera, the Venerable Kirivattuḍuvē Siri Paññāsāra Nāyaka Thera (now Vice-Chancellor) and the other venerable theras of the College. It is also fitting to record here the help readily given by the late Mr. Sāgara Palansuriya and Mr. K. M. W. Kuruppu during this difficult period. But both as layman and as monk his attitude to those who were opposed to him, and who later became hostile, was one of kindness and understanding. True follower of the Master, he bore his sufferings without rancour, like the fragrant sandal wood tree which perfumes the axe that lays it low, and like the sugarcane which sweetens the mouth where it is being crushed.

Soma Thera participated in the making of the *sīmā*, chapter house, at the Mahabodhi Society's Centre in Bangalore during the *Buddha Jayanti* celebrations in 1956. Some of the older members of the Buddhist Association there were pleasantly surprised to see him, for this was the site that the Mission of Goodwill had, in 1940, secured from the Government of Mysore for a Buddhist Centre. On his return to Ceylon in early 1957, Soma Thera was invited by the German Dharmadūta Society to lead the first Buddhist Mission to Germany in June that year, the other members being Vinīta Thera, Mr. W. Joseph Soysa and myself. But though he underwent a serious operation just two weeks before the mission was due to leave, he insisted on not altering the travel arrangements. Actually he went on board ship direct from the hospital. The wound had not healed completely then, and the dressing had to be continued for another five weeks. At the end of this period he could not move his left arm. It was after a further three months' treatment that he recovered. Yet during all this time Soma Thera worked with a fortitude which evoked the admiration of all around him. Though the dry climate of Berlin helped his asthma he was not entirely free of attacks. Referring to his fortitude, a friend wrote, "No other monk except another Soma Thera would have ventured forth on such a mission after the serious operation he had to stand only a couple of weeks before".

Yet the work which he had undertaken absorbed all Soma Thera's time and attention. He met the leading Buddhists in Berlin, who were anxious to co-operate with the mission's work, and soon there began a series of weekly meetings at which Soma Thera read a paper in German which was followed by answering questions that the audience liked to ask. The interpreting at these meetings was done by Mr. F. Knobelock, the then President of the Congress of German Buddhist Associations, or by Mr. Guido Auster. This programme was continued till the mission left Berlin. Meanwhile

Soma Thera addressed schools in various parts of the city. The children listened to him with the greatest interest. Just before leaving Berlin, the mission received an invitation from the Municipality of Iserlohn to conduct a Meditation Seminar during the "Indian Week" which was a part of the 'Sauerland Cultural Season'. About one hundred people from all walks of life attended it. The late Mr. Egon Vietta was the organiser of the Seminar. On the last day of the Seminar he announced that he had brought a few questions from his teacher, the well-known Existentialist philosopher, Prof. Heidegger, who was ill and unable to travel. When these questions were put to the Ven. Soma Mahā Thera his answers were prompt and so convincing that Mr. Vietta said that these same questions had been put by him to European scholars, individually and in groups, but he had not received such satisfying answers as had been given by Soma Mahā Thera.

Another invitation that the mission accepted was that of the Buddhists of Hamburg. They were anxious to have us with them during Vesak time. So from Islerlohn the mission left for Hamburg, where Mr. W. Stegemann, the President of the Buddhist Society of Hamburg, welcomed us. From here, after making a brief visit to London, Oxford, and Cambridge, the mission returned to Hamburg where Soma Thera conducted classes in meditation, and delivered lectures and led discussions on the *Dhamma*. These meetings were well attended. He much liked working among the Hamburg Buddhists because, as he said, they were well informed, organized, and greatly interested in their work as a body. In response to numerous requests, all the addresses delivered in Germany by Soma Mahā Thera were published by the Hamburg Buddhist Society in their Bulletin the *Mitteilungsblatt*.

With all this incessant work and travel Soma Thera grew weak, and when he returned to Ceylon from Germany in June 1958 he was very tired; but with skilful medical attention and another operation he regained his former vigour and worked hard which he loved to do. Then again he fell ill—this time with renal colic—and after another spell in hospital he was once more in a fit condition to continue his work. This time he slept hardly four hours a day, from about midnight to 4 a.m. When told that he tired himself overmuch, he used to say, "I have gathered enough now but I have not time enough to give". So he worked on to the end never caring for his health. Yet he was happy doing it.

He was held in affectionate and highest regard by all those who knew him for his qualities of heart and head. One of them wrote from England thus: "I was mentioning to the Dons of the Faculty of Eastern Religions at Oxford that there was in Ceylon a monk (referring to Soma Thera) who was eminently qualified by way of knowledge and learning to fill the Chair of Eastern Religions which is now vacant". Mr. Guido Auster, the Director of the Oriental Department of the German State Library, Berlin, hearing of his death wrote, "He contacted many personalities of the religious and intellectual life in Berlin and Germany. He delivered lectures at various places.

among them—most important in my opinion—several to pupils in our schools. He had an especially lucky hand in dealing with children and young people who admired him. He was most patient towards enquirers and beginners". Again, he says, "This impressive personality, reminding me in his dignity of a high prelate during the Middle Ages, weilding not only spiritual but also temporal power, has dissolved".

The President of the Servants of the Buddha, Mr. Ānanda Pereira, who, long before his 'teens, knew Soma Thera wrote thus of him in the Ceylon Daily News of February, 27, 1960.

'With the death of the Venerable Soma Thera, Lanka loses one of her noblest sons. Born of Roman Catholic parents on December 23, 1898, duly baptised and brought up in the faith of his parents, the youthful Victor Pulle began asking questions—deep, simple, direct questions—the answers to which as given by his parents and spiritual advisors did not satisfy him.

'His inquiries in due course led him to Buddhism, where at last he found the answers, or at least the hope of satisfactory answers to his questions.

'He plunged into the study of the Buddha *Dhamma*. It was at this period that he laid the foundation of that sure grasp of the Teachings that served him so well in later years as a missionary. He was associated with Dr. Cassius A. Pereira (later Ven. Kassapa Thera) in the preparation of the Blessing. He was an enthusiastic and hard-working member of the Servants of the Buddha. He made many friends.

'Never one to be satisfied with half measures, he was ordained as a Bhikkhu in 1936. From the day he joined the Sangha, he adorned it. As scholar, translator, writer, preacher and missionary, he strove mightily in the Buddhist cause. He never spared himself.

'But those who knew him, will remember him most for his humanity. His was not the cold way of the anaemic academician. He lived his Buddhism with every beat of his warm generous heart. Sometimes he seemed impulsive, sometimes even a shade pugnacious, but never, *never*, did he say or do a mean, false, or deliberately unkind thing.

'He was generous—with his advice, with his time, with himself. Though to outward appearance he was strong, his health was never particularly robust. But he never let ill-health interfere with his work, and his work was always giving. I have seen him preaching sermons or reciting *Pirith* at times when the mere act of breathing was acutely difficult because of asthma.

'Soma Thera was a genuine monk. He observed the *Vinaya* rules with absolute strictness, never permitting himself the slightest infringement, His standards were the highest. His life was a shining example to others, Bhikkhus and lay-folk alike.

'One does not need to feel sorrow on his behalf. His road is the road of the Buddha, the Arahats, the mighty ones. He lived here a while and has gone on, strong and assured, brave and smiling, kind, gentle, untiring. The story is not done. We too must fare onward when our time comes. We shall meet again'.

During the last few months of his life he often spoke and wrote on death, quoting from the *Suttas* and other writings, for instance, his own translations from the Sanskrit of Viṣṇusarman thus:

In him who ever and again,
Reflects on death's hard hand of pain,
The drive for gross material gain
Grows limp like hide soaked through with rain;

and from the commentary to the *Dhammapada:* "Uncertain is life, certain is death; it is necessary that I should die; at the close of my life there is death. Life is indeed unsure but death is sure, death is sure" — Dh.-a. III, 170; and from the *Sutta*—S. IV, 211: "Mindfully and with complete awareness should a bhikkhu meet his end. This is the advice I give you".

'I knew the Venerable Soma Mahā Thera intimately for nearly thirty-two years. During this period if the number of days we were absent from each other be added up it will not amount to more than a few months. Yet during all these years our interests centred round the *Dhamma* only. When I met him I knew very little *Dhamma*, having but recently accepted the Teaching of the Buddha. What *Dhamma* I now know was gleaned from him or in his company. So when he passed away suddenly the blow was difficult to bear. Before this event "the separation" referred to in the words of the Buddha: *Piyehi vippayogo dukkho*, "the separation from the loved is ill", did not seem so difficult a thing to bear. Now it appeared in a different light.

The passing away of the Venerable Sāriputta Thera caused in the Venerable Ānanda Thera, who was then only *Sotāpanna*, Stream-entrant (he became *Arahat* later), great agitation of mind, in spite of his having been with the Buddha and learned the *Dhamma* from him for twenty-five years. How he served the Buddha during those years is shown in the following verses, beautifully rendered by Mrs. C. A. F. Rhys Davids, thus:

For five-and-twenty years a learner I;
No sensual consciousness arose in me.
O see the seemly order of the Norm!
For five-and-twenty years a learner I;
No hostile consciousness arose in me.
O see the seemly order of the Norm!
For five-and-twenty years on the Exalted One
I waited, serving him by loving deeds,
And like his shadow followed after him.
For five-and-twenty years on the Exalted One

In Memoriam

I waited, serving him with loving speech,
And like his shadow followed after him.
For five-and-twenty years on the Exalted One
I waited, serving him with loving thoughts,
And like his shadow followed after him.
When pacing up and down, the Buddha walked,
Behind his back I kept the pace alway;
And when the Norm was being taught, in me
knowledge and understanding of it grew.[1]

And it is this 'knowledge and understanding' that he refers to as being confused' for him in the following verses, when the Venerable Sāriputta Thera passed away:

The firmament on every hand
Grows dim, yea, all confused stand
The truths I seemed to understand.
Gone is the noble friend we love,
And dark is earth and heaven above.[2]

The following is a description by Soma Thera (*Bosat*, October 1959, pp. 170-71) of how the Buddha comforted the Venerable Ānanda Thera on this occasion:

'When the Buddha was told of the passing away of the Venerable Sāriputta Thera, who was considered to be the Commander of the Army of Righteousness, the Blessed One said this to the Venerable Ānanda Thera, who was upset, "Tell me Ānanda, did Sāriputta take the aggregate of virtue along with him and become extinct? Or did he take the aggregate of concentration along with him and become extinct? Or did he take along with him the aggregate of wisdom and become extinct? Or did he take along with him the aggregate of freedom and become extinct? Or did he take along with him the aggregate of the knowledge and insight of freedom and become extinct?'—'No Venerable Sir'.—'Have I not, indeed, told you before that with all that is dear, pleasing, involved are change, separation, and variation?"

'The Buddha shows that it is not possible to stop the breaking up of what is born, produced, and put together, and of what has the nature of breaking, and compares the Venerable Sāriputta Thera to one of the greater branches of the mighty tree of the Community of Bhikkhus. Comparable to the breaking of a bigger branch of a mighty tree, says the Buddha, is the Venerable Sāriputta Thera's passing away and no one can stop the breaking of what is breakable by ordering that thing not to break'.

But when this peerless comforter, the Blessed One himself, passed away

1. Psalms of the Brethren, 1039-44.

2. Psalms of the Brethren, 1034.

shortly afterwards the Venerable Ānanda Thera uttered the following verses:

And is the comrade passed away,
And is the Master gone from hence?
No better friend is left, methinks,
Than to mount guard o'er deed and sense.
They of the older time are gone;
The new men suit me not at all.
Alone to-day this child doth brood,
Like nesting-bird when rain doth fall.[1]

Thus did the Venerable Ānanda Thera find comfort, and we, too, find solace at the feet of the Teacher of divine and human beings.

Sometimes birds fly into houses and, staying a while, sing and cheer those there; but suddenly they fly away, casting no glance behind, none knowing where. In like manner even as it is said: *Anavhāto tato āga, anuññāto ito gato*[2]— 'uncalled he hither came, unbidden soon to go', Soma Mahā Thera, too, came uninvited and unbidden went away, the while having cheered some weary traveller on the way.

To me Soma Mahā Thera was a *kalyāṇamitta*. In life he blessed me with the friendship extolled by the Blessed One in no uncertain terms: *Sakalam eva h-idam Ānanda brahmacariyaṁ yad idaṁ kalyāṇa-mittatā kalyāṇa-sahāyatā kalyāṇa-sampavaṅkatā*,[3]—'the whole of this holy life consists in noble friendship, in association, in intimacy with what is noble'. And in death he has drawn me ever near to the *Dhamma*, that sure refuge and support, as has been sung by the ancients, thus:

Dhammaṁ vinā natthi pitā ca mātā
Tameva tāṇaṁ saraṇaṁ patiṭṭhā
Tasmā hi bho kiccamaññaṁ pahāya
Suṇātha dhāretha carātha dhamme.[4]

Except the Dhamma of the Perfect One,
There is no father and no mother here;
The Dhamma is your refuge and support,
And in the Dhamma is your shelter true,
So hear the Dhamma, on the Dhamma think
And spurning other things, live up to it.[5]

May that 'trusty, staunch, true friend', the Venerable Soma Mahā Thera, attain to that happiness, higher than which there is none — *Nibbāna*, the Happiness Supreme!

Vissāsaparamā ñātī, nibbānaṁ paramaṁ sukhaṁ.[6]

Vajirārāma,
Bambalapitiya,
Colombo, September 3, 1960.

KHEMINDA THERA

1. Psalms of the Brethren, 1035-36.
2. J. III, 165 (Uraga Jātaka).
3. S. I, 87-8.
4. Rasavāhini.
5. Soma Thera's translation.
6. Dh. 204.

Prefatory Note to Original Draft Translation

In the following pages is a draft translation of the first fascicle of Gedatsu Do Ron (Vimuttimagga), No. 1648 *of the Taisho Edition of the Chinese Tripiṭaka (No.* 1293 *in Nanjio's Catalogue). The pages of the text are given in square brackets.*

This is circulated with the hope of receiving suggestions and criticisms helpful towards bringing out a complete translation of the Vimuttimagga.

We have derived much help from Prof. R. Higata's Japanese translation of the Gedatsu Do Ron, and Prof. Pe Maung Tin's English Translation of the Visuddhimagga.

N. R. M. Ehara
V. E. P. Pulle
G. S. Prelis

Jozaiji,
Kawatana-Machi,
Nagasaki-Ken. Japan.

Hanamatsuri, the eighth day of the fourth lunar month, May 28, 1936.

Acknowledgments (Original Draft Translation)

Jozaiji,
Kawatana-Machi,
Nagasaki-Ken,
Japan.
August 29, 1936.

For having encouraged us, we offer our hearty thanks to Dr. C. A. F. Rhys Davids, J. F. McKechnie Esq., (England); Prof. Dr. Wilh, Geiger (Germany); Dr. B. C. Law, Ven. Nyāṇatiloka Mahā Thera, Ven. Nārada Thera (India and Ceylon); Dr. Unrai Woghihara, Dr. Makoto Nagai, Prof. Nichiki Kimura, Prof. Giokei Umada, Dr. Baiye Henmi, Prof. Chotatsu Ikeda, Prof. Kaijo Ishikawa, Prof. Kairyu Yamamoto, Prof. Yukio Sakamoto, Rev. Sho-on Mizuno (Tokyo); Dr. Giei Honda, Prof. Chizen Akanuma (Kyoto); Prof. Ryusho Higata (Fukuoka).

N. R. M. Ehara
V. E. P. Pulle
G. S. Prelis

PREFACE

As stated elsewhere (In Memoriam (p. xv) the draft translation of the *Gedatsu Dō Ron* (being the Chinese name for the *Vimuttimagga*) was completed in four months. Therefore it was thought that it needed some revision. This the Venerable Soma Thera intended to do on his return to Ceylon in 1937. But he fell ill and by the end of 1939 the Second World War was already three months old. All hope of publishing the revised edition of the Original Draft Translation during the war had to be given up. With the end of the war, however, conditions were even less favourable. Meanwhile, though the Venerable Soma Thera wished to complete the revision and await a favourable occasion to publish it, other work he had undertaken prevented him from doing so. Further, asthma robbed him of much of his time. Thus the work he intended to do on the *Vimuttimagga* translation had to be postponed each time he took it up.

When he passed away many venerable theras and *dāyakas* were much interested in publishing, at least, the Original Draft Translation as it was, and they requested me to prepare it for publication. Knowing my own limitations, I was at first rather disinclined to undertake this work, but later acceded to their earnest request for the following reasons.

The Venerable Soma Thera had originally wished to have the English translation of the *Vimuttimagga* (The Path of Freedom) revised and published some day. But later, seeing difficulties, he modified the idea and was even content with merely revising the Draft Translation, leaving the publication itself to some future time. He said that the important thing, the Draft Translation, had been done, and that if people felt that they needed it they would see to its publication.

It was a work that had inspired both the Venerable Soma Thera and me, and there were many who welcomed its publication.

Dr. D. Roland D. Weerasuria of Balcombe House, Balcombe Place, Colombo, invited the Venerable Soma Thera sometime in 1959 to write an abridged version of the *Visuddhimagga* as he felt that such an edition would supply a long felt want. But shortly after he began writing it death intervened. Dr. Weerasuria then requested the Venerable Ñāṇamoli Thera to take up the work which, after some hesitation, he agreed to finish within a year. But he, too, passed away within a week. Sometime after this Dr. Weerasuria, having seen the Original Draft Translation of the *Vimuttimagga*, was keen on its publication.

This was a fitting occasion to pay a tribute to the memory of the two senior co-translators of the *Vimuttimagga*, the Reverend N. R. M. Ehara and the Venerable Soma Mahā Thera.

And finally the urgent personal need to keep myself immersed in the *Dhamma* throughout the waking hours during this period of stress prompted me to take up the work.

From the above it will be seen that this work was taken up due to sheer force of circumstances and not because of any special qualification on my part. Therefore, perhaps, some things stated here could have been said in other and better ways. Inexpert as I am in scholarly persuits there is bound to be many a lack in my portion of this work and so I ask the reader to bear with me should he detect any errors of commission or omission here.

In preparing this work for printing I have made a few alterations in the rendering of certain terms and passages, as they appeared in the Original Draft Translation, in accordance with notes and instructions left by the Venerable Soma Thera. The lacunae in the Draft Translation were filled, as far as possible, with the help of the word for word translation in consultation with Soma Thera's notes. All the longer Pali quotations in the footnotes, except a few from the *Visuddhimagga* and some from the *Dhammasaṅgaṇi* etc., were inserted by me. They are given in full mainly with the idea of helping the general reader conversant with the Pali but to whom reference books are not easily accessible. By this attempt of mine if but just a few readers happen to be benefitted, to any extent, I should consider myself amply rewarded.

Since the Introduction had already been sent to the Printers by the time the 'Encyclopaedia of Buddhism' (1961 Government of Ceylon, Fascicule A-Aca) was out, the following is included here. In his article, Abhidharma Literature, Dr. Kōgen Mizuno makes three statements on page 78 of the Encyclopaedia regarding the *Vimuttimagga*: (1) that the *Vimuttimagga* (along with the *Dhammapada*, the *Aṭṭhakavagga* of the *Suttanipāta* etc.) "probably belonged to the Abhayagiri sect and not to the Mahāvihāra sect" (paragraph B continued from the previous page); (2) that "He (i. e., the Venerable Buddhaghosa Thera) evidently studied the *Vimuttimagga*, which was a manual of the Abhayagirivihāra sect" (paragraph C); and (3) "That the *Vimutti-magga*, was Upatissa's work and belonged to the Abhayagirivihāra sect is mentioned in the ṭīkā (sub-commentary, i.e., Dhammapāla's Paramattha-mañjūsā) of the *Visuddhimagga*" (paragraph C).

The first statement, (1) above, says that the *Vimuttimagga* "probably belonged to the Abhayagiri sect", while the second, (2) above, says "*Vimutti-magga*, which was a manuel of the Abhayagirivihāra sect". How, precisely, did probability in paragraph B became certainty in paragraph C? As for the third statement, (3) above, the *Paramatthamañjūsā* does not say that the *Vimuttimagga* "belonged to the Abhayagirivihāra sect" as is claimed here. What it says is that the *Vimuttimagga* is the work of the Venerable Upatissa Thera. The fact that certain teachings are common to both the Abhayagirivihāra and the *Vimuttimagga* does not prove that the latter belonged to the Abhayagirivihāra sect. For details see Introduction pp. XXXVI, XXXVII and n. 2, p. 57 of the present translation.

I have derived much help from Prof. Dr. P. V. Bapat's *Vimuttimagga* and *Visuddhimagga—a Comparative Study*, and the Venerable Ñāṇamoli Thera's translation of the *Visuddhimagga—The Path of Purification.* The Pali Text Society's Pali-English Dictionary 1921, and Trenchner's Critical Pali Dictionary, Copenhagen 1924-1948 have been equally helpful.

It is with great pleasure that I make the following acknowledgements to all those whose help and encouragement made my work less difficult.

To the Venerable Maḍihē Paññāsīha Mahā Nāyaka Thera of Vajirārāma for his kindly and ready help and advice at all times lacking which this work would not have been completed.

To all those venerable monks who encouraged me by word and deed when that encouragement was most needed.

To the Venerable Ñāṇavīra Thera for his welcome suggestions and the readiness with which he helped in many ways.

To Mr. W. Joseph Soysa who helped in reading over some of the proofs. He has always been much interested in the *Vimuttimagga* and in its publication.

To Mr. Lakshman de Mel who read through the type-script and made valuable suggestions.

To Mr. R. D. Piyasena and those who helped him for taking a great deal of trouble in preparing the English Index.

Lastly, to Dr. D. Roland D. Weerasuria who has generously borne the entire cost of publishing this translation. Provision has been made by him to keep the price of this book within reach of the modest purse. He has performed this meritorious act (*puññakamma*) with great faith (*saddhā*) wishing his father, Mudaliyar D. D. Weerasuria J.P., who passed away on 25. 5. 1949. the happiness of *Nibbāna*. May the result of this pure deed redound in full measure to his lasting happiness.

The Printers have to be thanked for their patience and high quality of work.

Vijirārāma, KHEMINDA THERA.
Colombo. Ceylon. October 2505/1961.

INTRODUCTION

IN the Journal of the Pali Text Society of 1919, there appeared an article by Prof. Dr. M. Nagai on "The Vimutti-Magga, 'The Way to Deliverance' ". Referring to it Mrs. C. A. F. Rhys Davids in a letter dated September 20, 1936 to the translators of the *Gedatsu Dō Ron* (*Vimuttimagga*) said, "Then as to the issuing of the book (referring to the Path of Freedom) in a volume of print: Were this society in easier circumstances enjoyed by it up to the Great War, when we were immensely helped by the princely donations of your wealthy men, I would undertake at once to publish the work with Prof. Nagai's excellent article in our Journal, 1919, as preface, with anything he liked to add. Or, if you objected, I should ask you three to write your own preface, making such references to his article as you thought fit".

This article of Prof. Nagai took the Buddhist world by surprise; for, according to the *Cūḷavaṁsa* chapter XXXVII, 236-39, when the Venerable Buddhaghosa Thera had written the *Visuddhimagga* at the behest of the *Mahāsangha*, the *devas* had hidden it and he had to write it afresh. When this was done, it too was hidden by the *devas*. So, when he wrote it for the third time and presented it to the *Mahāsangha*, it is said, the *devas* produced the first two copies. It was then found that the three copies agreed in every detail. The record goes on to say (Cv. Ch. XXXVII, 241-43): 'Then the bhikkhus read out all the three books together. Neither in composition and content, nor also as regards the sequence (of the subjects), in the teaching of the Theras, in the quotations, in words, and sentences was there any kind of deviation in all three books. Then the community satisfied and exceedingly well pleased, cried again and again: "without doubt, this is Metteyya!" and handed over to him the books of the three Piṭakas together with the commentary' — Dr. Geiger's translation. By this statement it was, perhaps, only intended to stress the Venerable Buddhaghosa Thera's great ability, which is amply borne out by this (i.e., the *Visuddhimagga*) and his later works. No other view seems to be warranted, or else it has to be conceded that the Mahāvihāra Theras knew very well that the Bodhisatta Metteyya could not have been born in this world at this time; — see, for instance, the earlier statement of the *Mahāvaṁsa* at Ch. XXXII, 73: 'Awaiting the time when he shall become a Buddha, the compassionate Bodhisatta Metteyya dwells in the Tusita-city'— Dr. Geiger's translation. Further, that the Venerable Buddhaghosa Thera and the Bodhisatta Metteyya are two different persons has been established by the Venerable Buddhaghosa Thera himself in his Postscript to the *Visuddhimagga* (found only in the Sinhalese texts and translated by Ñāṇamoli Thera):

'. . .
So may I in my last becoming
Behold the joys of Tāvatiṁsā,
. . .
And having in my last life seen
Metteyya, Lord of Sages, Highest
Of persons in the World, and Helper
Delighting in all beings' welfare,
And heard that Holy One proclaim
The Teaching of the Noble Law,
May I grace the Victor's Dispensation
By realizing its Highest Fruit'.

And this, too, the Mahāvihāra Theras would have known. But in thus stressing his ability, the *Cūḷavaṁsa* account seems to make out that the *visuddhimagga* was written without recourse to other works. There is a discrepancy in this account of the *Cūḷavaṁsa*. It will be noted that 'the three *Piṭakas* together with Commentary' were handed over to the Venerable Buddhaghosa Thera by the Mahāsangha only after he had written the *Visuddhimagga*, which is correctly designated the General Commentary to the three *Piṭakas*. Now, if he had access to the three *Piṭakas*, and the Commentary only after he had written this General Commentary to the three *Piṭakas*, how did he do it? This is difficult to comprehend. Here is where the article of Prof. Dr. Nagai appears to fit in.

Bearing No. 1293 in Prof. Nanjio's Catalogue is a work in Chinese called *Cié-to-tāo-lun*. It is also called *Gedatsu Dō Ron*. Prof. Nanjio has rendered the title of this work in Sanskrit as 'Vimokṣa-Mārga', the author being Arahant Upatissa. In trying to identify him with a Ceylon Thera, Prof. Nagai adduces the following reasons:

1. It cannot be the Venerable Sāriputta Thera, who was also called Upatissa, because he is often quoted in the Venerable Upatissa Thera's text.

2. In the *Samantapāsādikā* (I, p. 263), it is said that there were two elders, named Upatissa Thera and Phussadeva Thera, pupils of the same teacher who was proficient in the *Vinaya*. Upatissa Thera was superior to the other; and he had two pupils named Mahāpaduma Thera and Mahāsumana Thera. The latter learned the *Vinaya Piṭaka* nine times from his teacher, while Mahāpaduma Thera learned it eighteen times and was, therefore, the superior. When the former left his teacher to live elsewhere Mahāpaduma Thera remained with his teacher saying that as long as one's teacher was alive one should be with him and learn the *Vinaya* and the Commentaries many times more. The teacher, the Venerable Upatissa Thera, and his pupil the Venerable Mahāpaduma Thera, recited the *Vinaya* in this manner for many years more. During this period they expounded the *Vinaya* and on one occasion the Venerable Upatissa Thera, at the request of the Mahāsangha in assembly, pronounced a ruling on a question that arose regarding the first *Pārājika*.

3. A teacher such as the Venerable Upatissa Thera was the most appropriate person to be the author of a work of such importance as the *Vimuttimagga*. Then he goes on to mention the account of the gift of King Vasabha's queen to the Venerable Mahāpaduma Thera who accepted it as his teacher's share.

4. To show that the Venerable Buddhaghosa Thera was aware of the existence of the *Vimuttimagga*, Prof. Nagai refers to the comments of the Venerable Buddhaghosa Thera regarding the "fourteen *cariya's*" of the *Vimuttimagga*.

It is quite probable that the Venerable Buddhaghosa Thera had the *Vimuttimagga* in mind when he made this comment; for there is the definite statement of the Venerable Dhammapāla Thera in his commentary to the *Visuddhimagga* (*Paramatthamañjūsā*, Venerable Morontuḍuvē Dhammānanda Nāyake Thera's Sinhalese ed. p. 103) which says: *Ekacce ti Upatissattheraṁ sandhāyāha. Tena hi Vimuttimagge tathā vuttaṁ*,—" 'Some' is said with reference to the Venerable Upatissa Thera. It is said thus by him in the *Vimuttimagga*". From the foregoing it is clear that the Venerable Buddhaghosa Thera had the *Vimuttimagga* of Venerable Upatissa Thera before him when he wrote the *Visuddhimagga*.

In his Pali Literature of Ceylon, Dr. G. P. Malalasekera has this to say on the subject:

(*a*) "The *Vimutti-magga* is an Abhidhamma exegesis, serving as a compendium for that portion of Buddhist literature . . . , and in some points the Chinese work seems to have been influenced by the Mahāyāna doctrine" (p. 86).

(*b*) He says, further, that if it is granted that the *Vimuttimagga* was taken to China by some of the schools of approximately the same tradition, "it would not be difficult to conclude that the *Visuddhi-magga* and *Vimutti-magga* are more or less independent works, written by men belonging to much the same school of thought — the *Thera-vāda*" (pp. 87-88).

Regarding the statement (*a*) above, it will be seen that very little *Abhidhamma* is found in the *Vimuttimagga*, though of course, it begins by saying that he who wishes to "lead those on the other shore to perfection, should be versed in the *Sutta*, *Abhidhamma* and *Vinaya*". Here, the late Venerable Ñāṇamoli Thera's opinion on the subject will be of interest: "However the *Vimuttimagga* itself contains nothing at all of the Mahayana, its unorthodoxies being well within the 'Hinayana' field". Again he says: "Also Abhidhamma, which is the keystone of Bhadantācariya Buddhaghosa's exegesis, is not used at all in the *Vimuttimagga* (Aggregates, Truths, etc., do not *in themselves* constitute Abhidhamma in the sense of that Pitaka). There is, for instance, even in its description of the Consciousness Aggregate, no reference to the *Dhammasaṅgaṇī's* classification of 89 types, and nothing from the *Paṭṭhāna*; and though the 'Cognitive Series' is stated once in its full form (in Ch. II) no use is made of it to explain conscious workings. This *Vimuttimagga* is in fact a book of practical instruction, not of exegesis" (Path of Purification Introduction pp. XXVII-XXVIII). The statement of the Venerable Dhammapāla Thera in the *Paramatthamañjūsā* quoted earlier seems to disallow (*b*) above.

The Venerable Buddhadatta Mahā Nāyaka Thera in the Pali Text Society's edition of the *Saddhammappajotikā* refers to Prof. Nagai's view that the author of the *Vimuttimagga* was the Venerable Upatissa Thera who flourished during King Vasabha's reign, 66-109 A. C. He says, "However, there is no such great difference as cannot be bridged between his supposition and mine" (Introduction p. VIII).

Regarding the view that the *Vimuttimagga* was a work written at the Abhayagiri Monastery, the late Venerable Ñāṇamoli Thera rightly says, "That it (the *Vimuttimagga*) contains some minor points accepted by the Abhayagiri Monastery does not necessarily imply that it had any special connection with that centre. The sources may have been common to both. The disputed points are not schismatical. Bhadantācariya Buddhaghosa himself never mentions it" (Introduction, XXVIII).

Prof. Dr. P. V. Bapat in the Introduction (p. liv) to his careful work "Vimuttimagga and Visuddhimagga, A Comparative Study" (1937), has examined a great deal of material. In support of his theory that the *Vimuttimagga* originated in India, he puts forward, among others, the following reasons (p. liv): (*a*) "It is very likely that Vimuttimagga was one of the books brought over from India. From the internal evidence of the book we may say that there is no reference to any name[2] or place in Ceylon". If the view of

"2. Unless the name Nārada (p. 134) referred to any high personage from Ceylon, which seems to be very improbable". This name is found at S. II, 117-18. See p. 321.

the late Venerable Ñāṇamoli Thera, that the "*Vimuttimagga* is in fact a book of practical instruction, not of exegesis" — which is also the view of the late Venerable Soma Thera and myself — is accepted, and if it is recognized that the whole style of the *Vimuttimagga* makes for brevity — it is even abrupt sometimes —, then it will be seen that the exclusion of any 'name or place in Ceylon' is not surprising.

(*b*) "We find in this book many words which are transliterations of Indian words. The list of worms residing in different parts of the body gives names which are transliterations of Indian names. These names must have been taken by Upatissa from some old work or works on medical science" (p. liv). This is as it should be, seeing that the Dhamma is of Indian origin, and when medicine or anything related to medical science is mentioned it is natural for Ceylon writers to use Indian terms: for what medical knowledge Ceylon possessed at the time was of Indian origin. The standard Ayurvedic medical works in use even now are Suśruta and Vāgbhaṭa. Caraka is not unknown.* The first two works have been in use in Ceylon through the ages. But if the list of worms is not derived from the first two works or one of them, then the *Vimuttimagga* most probably bases itself here on some other medical work of Indian origin known in Ceylon at the time.

Regarding the statement, "We find Upatissa going into the details of the development of the foetus week by week" (p. lvi), it will be seen from pp. 173-74, n. 3 that here the *Vimuttimagga* follows the *Sutta* and its commentary.

(*c*) "Besides, the reference to a *Caṇḍāla*, which we have already noticed, also points to the origin of the book in India,[3] particularly, in South or Dravidian India where there is a very strong prejudice against Caṇḍālas" (p. liv). References to *Caṇḍālas* are found eslewhere, in the texts and commentaries. For instance, as pointed out by Prof. Bapat himself (p. xlvi), at A. I, 107 and A. III, 214, *caṇḍāla* is mentioned. Here it should be borne in mind that in the society of the time, and also later, the *caṇḍāla* was a person looked down upon. To illustrate certain points in a way that the large mass of the people would understand, appropriate similes were used by the Buddha and his Disciples, and the commentators who came after them. It does not mean that they thereby endorsed some of the statements made in their similes. For instance, when the Buddha, in the *Satipaṭṭhāna Suttas*, says, "Just as if a clever butcher or butcher's apprentice, having slaughtered a cow and divided it into portions were sitting at the main cross-road," and so on, it does not follow that the Buddha upheld the buchers' profession. If the word *caṇḍāla* was used in a simile, the motive behind it was nothing else than to facilitate the understanding of the point under discussion. The upholding of the caste system does not come in here. On the contrary, the Buddha and his disciples were opposed to it as we see in the use of the word *caṇḍāla* in a different context referring to an *upāsaka* (i.e., one who has gone to the Buddha, the Dhamma, and the Sangha for refuge) but who does not observe the *sīlas* etc. — he being called *upāsakacaṇḍāla* (A. III, 206). The *Vasala Sutta* (Sn. 116-42) may also be mentioned here. Further, these sentences occur in the *Vimuttimagga* itself, thus: "Virtue is called excellent joy, the highest of all castes . . . This is to

*Since writing the above the *Caraka Saṁhitā* has been translated into Sinhalese by Āyurveda Śāstri R. Buddhadāsa, Colombo.

"3. Upatissa's change of the 'yellow' colour of the earth for *kasiṇa* (as said by B.) into 'black' (p. 43) may be considered as significant. Can it suggest the black soil of the country of origin of Upatissa?" The soil in many parts of Ceylon, too, is black.

wear the thread which must be worn. This is the sacred caste" (p. 8).

What has largely prompted Prof. Bapat to protest seems to be the statement found in Chapter III dealing with the Austerities, and his objection runs thus: "Let us note one peculiar fact about Upatissa. He seems to have some kind of contempt for, or low opinion of, a *Caṇḍāla*" (p. xlvi). Then on the same page he goes on to say the following, which are possibly the reasons for the statement mentioned above.

(1) "In one place, there is a reference to a *Caṇḍāla* where we are told in a simile that he has no desire for a princely throne" (p. xlvi). The relevant passage is, "As an outcast has no desire for a king's throne" (p. 25 of the present translation). The same idea is found in the *Visuddhimagga* too, namely, "*Nirāso saddhamme caṇḍālakumārako viya rajje*" (p. 54) — "He is desireless for the Good Law as a *caṇḍāla* (outcast) is for a kingdom". It is therefore not a statement peculiar to the Venerable Upatissa Thera.

(2) With regard to the next objection: "At another place, to see a *Caṇḍāla* on the way is considered to be a sufficient reason for the laxity in the observance of the practice of *sapadāna-cārikā* (going from house to house in succession for begging one's food)" (p. xlvi). This is not quite what the text says, as will be seen later. There is no question of laxity. Then the next sentence continues, "Upatissa says that if a mendicant sees a *Caṇḍāla* on the way, he should cover his begging-bowl and may skip over some houses and go further. In the third place we find a lack of conscientiousness (*ahirika*) is compared to a *Caṇḍāla*" (pp. xlvi-xlvii). Further, at p. 23, "Even if he has taken up the practice of a *sapadānacārika*, he should avoid elephants or horses that may be coming in his way. Seeing a *caṇḍāla*, he should cover his begging-bowl. 'Following one's *ācariya* or *upajjhāya*' is also mentioned as an occasion for exception". Here is the relevant passage from the present translation (p. 36): "What is the teaching as regards expedience in the observance of 'regular almsround'? If a bhikkhu on seeing elephants or horses fighting or in rut, at the gate, avoids them, or on seeing an outcast (*caṇḍāla*, transliteration) covers his bowl, or goes behind his preceptor, teacher or a visiting bhikkhu, and thus commits certain faults for expedience' sake, he does not fail in 'regular almsround' ".

Now let us consider why the expedience in regard to elephants and horses may be resorted to. It is plain that it is to avoid being hurt or even killed. Regarding the preceptor or teacher — it is out of respect due to them. It is an offence not to do so. Again, covering the bowl on seeing a *caṇḍāla* is for self-protection. The society at that time was very much caste-conscious. If the people objected to, or did not favour, the receiving of alms from one they considered an outcast, the support from the large majority of the people would be liable to be withdrawn and the life of the bhikkhu rendered difficult, to say the least. Here the story of the son and heir of the King Duṭṭhagāmaṇi comes readily to mind. It is said that the people were prosperous and happy during his reign and that he had a son named Sālirājakumāra, concerning whom the following is recorded.

"Greatly gifted was he and ever took delight in works of merit; he tenderly loved a caṇḍāla woman of exceedingly great beauty. Since he was greatly enamoured of the Asokamālādevi, who already in a former birth had been his consort, because of her loveliness, he cared nothing for kingly rule" (Mv. Ch. XXXIII, 2-4). Therefore King Duṭṭhagāmaṇi, after his death, was succeeded by his brother, Saddhātissa, who reigned for eighteen years.

"He cared nothing for kingly rule", — *So rajjaṁ neva kāmayi.* Surely there is something similar in this statement and the simile which is common to both the *Vimuttimagga* and the *Visuddhimagga*, namely, *Nirāso saddhamme caṇḍālakumārako viya rajje*; — *Vimuttimagga* p. 25: He has no desire for the Noble (Law), as an outcast has no desire for a king's throne"; *Visuddhimagga* p. 54: "He is desireless for the Good Law as an outcast (*caṇḍāla*) is for a kingdom"! Have not both the *Vimuttimagga* and the *Visuddhimagga* been making some sort of allusion to this event, which would, no doubt, have shocked the whole land? Might it not seem that here was an actual story well-known in the land and even recent history as far as the Venerable Upatissa Thera of King Vasabha's reign was concerned (King Duṭṭhagāmaṇi reigned from 161-137 B.C. and King Vasabha from 66-110 A.C.)? If our author is in fact this Upatissa Thera, this story will provide him with the most appropriate material for a simile to illustrate the regardlessness of an unvirtuous man for the Good Law. How appropriate the background provided by the prince's story is for purposes of the simile, which was perhaps even inspired by it, can be seen from the present translation, p. 25.

That the author of the *Vimuttimagga*, whoever it was, knew such passages as

1. *Mā jātiṁ puccha caraṇañ ca puccha.*
   Kaṭṭhā have jāyati jātavedo;
   nīcākulīno pi munī dhitīmā
   ājāniyo hoti hirīnisedho — Sn. 462

   Judge not by birth but life.
   As any chips feed fire
   Mean birth may breed a sage
   Noble and staunch and true*

2. *Na jaccā 'vasalo' hoti; — na jaccā hoti brāhmaṇo;*
   kammanā 'vasalo' hoti kammanā hoti brāhmaṇo — Sn. 136

   No birth a wastrel — or a Brahmin — makes;
   *'tis conduct wastrels makes — and Brahmins too**

is beyond doubt. And it is inconceivable that he had a prejudice which he put down in writing knowing full well that it was entirely against the Teaching of the Buddha.

As for the statement that the *Vimuttimagga* "reveals no special mastery of the Vinaya which is claimed by Prof. Nagai for that Upatissa who lived in the first century A.D. in Ceylon" (p. lvi), the *Vimuttimagga* is hardly the place to display such special knowledge.

Finally, to this following statement: "My discovery of the Tibetan version of the third chapter on '*dhutas*' is also important . . . This Tibetan text provides an additional evidence to show the Indian origin of the book. It does not appear to be probable that a text from Ceylon was taken over to India and there it was studied in Buddhist schools and that it assumed such importance as to be translated, in part at least, in Tibetan" (pp. liv - lv). An article which the late Lama Geshe La Gedum Chomphell originally contributed

* Lord Chalmers' translation.

to *The Buddhist*, the journal of the Y.M.B.A., Colombo, and which was reprinted in the *Buddha Jayanti* of July 22, 1956, begins — 'The horse of Buddhism is dead in India; only the tops of the horse's ears are still visible in the east and the west of the land'. This saying which had gained currency in Tibet once, perhaps originated with the monk Vanaratana, known, in Tibetan history, as the last great Indian *Mahāpaṇḍita* who came to live and teach in Tibet. A native of Bengal, he was ordained young, as a *sāmaṇera*, in a monastery of one thousand monks. He received full ordination in Ceylon, with two well-known Theras, the Venerable Buddhaghosa and the Venerable Dhammakitti as preceptor and teacher respectively. He studied the *Vinaya Prabhā* (Splendour of the Discipline), a *Sarvāstivāda* work. Then he returned to his native country and, after studying the *Kālacakra*, went to Tibet by way of Assam. The Lama says: "During the journey he is believed to have remembered his Sinhalese preceptor, and inscribed on a wayside rock these words: 'I salute Buddhaghosa the teacher of thousands of beings' ". And he says further that in the middle of the seventeenth century the lama king of Bhutan, when at war with the Central Tibet government, had seen and mentioned it in one of his writings. On reaching Tibet his interpreter died, and so after a short stay there he returned to Bengal. "Vanaratana's second visit to Ceylon lasted six years; during that time he studied all branches of Buddhism", says the lama. The Venerable Vanaratana in his account of a pilgrimage he made to Śrī Padā in Ceylon states that he received two bone relics there. Then again the lama goes on to say, "With the relics and some books he had collected, Vanaratana returned to his country and not long afterwards re-entered Tibet. This time he was able to speak Tibetan well; he made many lamas his disciples through his preaching. The chief of Vanaratana's disciples was Rong-Thong-Pa, the founder of a new sect; to him Vanaratana gave one of the relics he had got in Ceylon. Rong-Thong-Pa built near Lhasa a monastery called Nālandā". The Venerable Vanaratana died fifteen years after he re-entered Tibet "at a monastery in Singpori in Tsang province; his tomb can still be seen in that monastery . . . The full admission of Vanaratana to the Sangha by Ceylon theras, and the long stay here, point to the existence of cordial relations between the Indian and Ceylon Sangha of his time. Tibetan books show that Ratnākara Gupta of Vikramaśīla stayed in Ceylon for seven years on his way to Dhanyakaṭaka; and Atīśa (Dīpaṁkara Śrī Jñāna), who became abbot of Vikramaśīlā, was here in the eleventh century". Further, I myself remember the late lama, when he was preparing this article, mentioning to the Venerable Soma Thera that he had seen in a monastery in Tibet a Sinhalese manuscript which, he said, probably dated back to the Venerable Vanaratana Thera's time.[1]

In view of the above we are entitled to say that, while it is not proved that the *Vimuttimagga* was written in Ceylon, it has been shown that the very reasons put forward to support the view that it must have been written in India, support equally well the view that it may well have been written in Ceylon. To this can be added the idea that the simile of the outcast having no desire for a king's throne, possibly drew inspiration from the story of Sālirājakumāra, which must certainly have been current at the time, though

1. Since writing the above, the Ceylon Daily News reported, in its issue of September 9, 1960, of the discovery of a Singhalese manuscript in a Buddhist monastery of Saiskya in Tibet by Prof. Rāhula Sankrityāyana of the Vidyālankāra University, Kelaniya, in the years between 1929 and 1938. This manuscript has been assigned to the twelfth, or the thirteenth, century and is now deposited in the library of the Vidyālankāra University.

the account of it in the *Mahāvaṁsa* came to be written later. Yet the *Mahāvaṁsa*, according to Dr. Geiger (Introduction, Mv. translation p. IX), was "based upon older material", the "*Aṭṭhakathā-Mahāvaṁsa*", as he calls it, and "existed as did the Aṭṭhakathā generally, in different monasteries of the Island, in various recensions which diverged only slightly from one another" (p. x). He further says, "The chronicle must originally have come down only to the arrival of Mahinda in Ceylon. But it was continued later, and indeed to all appearance, down to the reign of Mahāsena (beginning of the fourth century A.D.)".

Tipiṭaka Sanghapāla Thera of Funan

Below is given the Life of Tipiṭaka Sanghapāla Thera of Funan, being a translation from *Kosoden*, Biographies of Famous Clerics, in Vol. 50, No. 2059, Taisho edition of the Chinese *Tripiṭaka:*

In the early years of the Ryo dynasty there was Sanghapāla; he was a foreign scholar. His bearing was noble and he was handsome of feature. He was a skilful debater. Coming to the capital he stayed at Shōkwanji (Mahāvidarṣanārāma). The Emperor Bū honoured and respected him, and treated him with great consideration. He was requested by the emperor to translate Buddhist scriptures in Jūkoden (Āyus-prabhā vihāra) and Sen-un-kwan (. . . megha-vihāra). He translated the *Mahā Aśoka Sūtra*, *Vimokṣa-Mārga-śāstra*, and others. Hōsho, En-don-u and others assisted (lit. wrote).

This occurs under the Biography of Guṇavṛddhi of Mid-India who built Shōkwanji and died in Shōkwanji in the second year of Chūko (p. 345).

The following is from *Zokukosoden*, Further Biographies of Famous Clerics, number 2060, volume 50 of the Taisho edition of the Chinese *Tripiṭaka*. Here the life of Sanghapāla is given first. Sanghapāla: In the language of Ryo his name may be translated thus: *Sō:* Order; and *Yō:* Nurse. Or *Sō:* Order; and *Gui*: Protector. He was a Funan-man. From his youth, he was very clever. Having mastered the Law, he became a monk. He was expert in the knowledge of the *Abhidharma*, and was famous in the lands of the Southern Sea. After completing (possibly the study of the *Abhidhamma*), he studied the *Vinayapiṭaka*. He was zealous in the propagation of the Vanquisher's Faith, and hearing that the time was propitious for the spreading of the Truth in the country of Sai (Canton), he took ship and came to the capital. He stayed in Shōkwanji and became a disciple of Guṇabhadra, a *śramaṇa* of India and studied *Vaipulya* under him. Sanghapāla's knowledge was wide and deep and he was conversant with the languages and books of several countries . . . Pāla was clean of body and of mind and was reluctant to engage in conversation. In the seclusion of his room he stayed and worked, taking very simple fare.

In the 5th year of Tenkwan, he was offered by the emperor these five places of residence: Jukoden, Karinenden (Flower-forest-garden), Shōkwanji Senunkwan and Funānkwan of the Capital Yoto (Sun City). He translated for seventeen years. His translations amounted to eleven cases of forty-eight fascicles. They are the great *Aśoka sūtra*, the *Vimokṣa-Mārga-śāstra* and others. When the translations began the Emperor Bū himself came to Jukoden, attended to the exposition of the Law by Sanghapāla and himself wrote (down the translations). After that he handed them over to the writer who was to make the printing blocks. The emperor commanded the *śramaṇa* Hōsho, the *śramaṇa* Echo and the *śramaṇa* Sochi to assist Sanghapāla. His translations were in elegant Chinese and faithful to the original. The emperor treated him most cordially and respectfully and made him the court chaplain. It is said that he altered many customs of the people. Pāla did not hoard treasure. With offerings that were made to him Pāla built the Ryujūji (Ārabdha-vīryārāma). The minister Rinsenoko was deeply attached to him. In the fifth year of Futsu, he died at Shōkwanji. He was sixty five years old.

About the beginning of the Ryo dynasty another *śramaṇa* of Funan named Maṇḍara came to China. He brought many Sanskrit texts and presented them to the emperor. The emperor ordered him to translate them together with Pāla. They translated *Hō-ung-hō-kai-taisho-monju-haññā-kyo: Ratna-megha-dharma-dhātu-kāya-svabhāva-mañjuśrī-prajñā-sūtra*. Though he translated, he could not understand Chinese well. So in his translations there are many vague renderings (p. 426, fascicle 1).

The Visuddhimagga

Much has been written about the *Visuddhimagga* from the earliest times right down to the present day. King Parākrama-Bāhu II (1236-68 A.C.) is reported to have written the paraphrase to the *Visuddhimagga* after he had handed over the kingdom to his son Bodhisatta Vijaya-Bāhu (1271-72 A.C.). During the last century Pandit M. Dharmaratna revised this work. Of him and his work on the Visuddhimagga, the Venerable Soma Thera wrote in the *Buddha Jayanti* of April 5, 1955 thus: "Had he not written any of the works mentioned above and not edited the paper, still people of this country would have been obliged to remember him for his great gift of the translation of the *Visuddhimagga*, with his edition of the *Visuddhi* Text, and the revised version of the ancient paraphrase of the *Visuddhi* by Parākrama-Bāhu II, a comprehensive work which is of never-failing interest and great usefulness to all students of the Dhamma and the Sinhalese language". Then again there is the late Venerable Paṇḍita Mātara Śrī Dharmavaṁsa Mahā Stavira's more recent translation which was completed by his pupil the Venerable Paṇḍita Baṭuviṭa Nandārāma Māha Thera in 1957. There is also the English translation of the Pali Text Society by Prof. Pe Maung Tin of Rangoon, completed in 1931, and that of the late Venerable Ñāṇamoli Thera of the Island Hermitage, Dodanduwa in 1956. The German translation is by the late Venerable Nyāṇatiloka Mahā Thera, founder of the Island Hermitage, Dodanduwa, the publishers being Verlag Christiani, Konstanz, 1952.

The *Visuddhimagga* is a household word in all *Theravāda* lands. No scholar of Buddhism whether of *Theravāda* or of *Mahāyāna* is unacquainted with it. Therefore there is no need of repeating what has already been said at one time or another. But an introduction to the *Vimuttimagga*, can hardly avoid all mention of the *Visuddhimagga*, and I may be excused if I go over ground already covered by others. An endeavour, however, is made to present some of these facts briefly and with a slightly new approach. It is for the reader to assess how far this has been achieved.

In the introduction to his translation of the *Visuddhimagga*, The Path of Purification, the late Venerable Ñāṇamoli Thera, after carefully sifting a large collection of material, points out that the influence of Sanskrit Buddhism, the centre of which was the Abhayagiri monastery in Anuradhapura, was so great in the first century A.C. that it became a threat to the Mahāvihāra's position as the central authority of orthodox Pali Buddhism in Ceylon. Indeed that threat grew into open rivalry and even enmity between these two institutions, culminating in King Mahāsena's (277-304) giving protection to Sanghamitta, "a Cola monk, follower of Vetullavāda", and driving away the monks of the Mahāvihāra from Anuradhapura for nine years. Then, Mahāsena, repenting of his deeds, restored the Mahāvihāra to its former position and burnt the Vetulyan books. But by then Sanghamitta had got the Lohapāsāda destroyed, and he and his friend, the minister Soṇa, were killed by a labourer on the orders of the queen when they attempted to destroy the Thūpārāma. The efforts of the Mahāvihāra monks since the beginning of the dispute with those of the Abhayagiri in the first century A.C. were solely directed to the establishment, says the Venerable Ñāṇamoli Thera, of "Pali as the language for the study and discussion of Buddhist teachings, and the founding of a school of Pali literary composition" (Intro. p. xiv). He then goes on to say, "It is not known what was the first original Pali composition in this period; but the *Dīpavaṁsa* (dealing with historical evidence) belongs here (for it ends with Mahāsena's reign and is quoted in the *Samantapāsādikā*), and quite possibly the *Vimuttimagga* (dealing with practice—see below) was another early attempt by the Great Monastery in this period (4th cent.) to reassert its supremacy through original Pali literary composition: there will have been others too. Of course, much of this is very conjectural" (Intro. p. xiv). It will be noted here that the Venerable Nāṇamoli Thera does not place the *Vimuttimagga* during the reign of King Vasabha, but in the 4th century. Still it does not contradict the fact that the Venerable Buddhaghosa Thera had access to the *Vimuttimagga* of the Venerable Upatissa Thera when he wrote the *Visuddhimagga*.

If the suggestion that the *Vimuttimagga* "was another early attempt by the Great Monastery in this period to reassert its supremacy through Pali composition" is acceptable, it would then not be difficult to suppose that the Venerable Buddhaghosa Thera, with what knowledge he had already acquired of the *Dhamma* in India—(for he had written the *Ñāṇodaya*, the *Atthasālinī* and had begun "to compose a commentary to the *Paritta*", Cv. Ch. XXXVII, 225-26—), was able to write the *Visuddhimagga*, perhaps with the assistance of the Mahāvihāra Theras. This work is more comprehensive than the *Vimuttimagga* and in every sense more scholarly, with a wealth of material drawn from every imaginable source and interspersed with numerous Ceylon stories. Thus, not only did it provide instruction for those needing it in the practice of the *Dhamma*, but it was also capable of holding its own as a work of literary composition.

Two things seem to have played an important part in making available for later generations, even up to the present day, a work of such excellence as is the *Visuddhimagga*. They are: (1) The desperate need of the Mahāvihāra for a work which would prove its claim to be the centre of Buddhist learning in Ceylon; (2) the equally urgent need of the Venerable Buddhaghosa Thera to prove his ability as a worthy scholar in the eyes of the Theras of the Mahāvihāra. Without this recognition he could not have obtained from them the commentaries and the expositions of the teachers (*ācariyavāda*) for translation into Pali as required by his teacher in India, the Venerable Revata Mahā Thera, and for which express purpose he came to Ceylon (Cv. Ch. XXXVII, 227-32). That this dual need was supplied to the complete satisfaction of both parties is amply borne out by the recorded history of the centuries that followed.

Introduction

The Vimuttimagga and *the Visuddhimagga.*

On certain points the *Vimuttimagga* and the *Visuddhimagga* hold contrary views. For instance, the latter says that by developing the *Buddhānussati* (the recollection of the Buddha) the factors of meditation, *jhāna,* arise in a single moment; that as the qualities of the Buddha are unfathomable or else owing to reflection on his numerous qualities *appanā* (fixed meditation) is not attained, and only *upacāra* (access-concentration) is reached. The *Vimuttimagga* on the other hand says that "from the recollection of the Buddha the four meditations, *jhānas* arise". This statement seems to agree with the *sutta* and its commentary quoted in note 3 on pp. 148-49.

They agree that in practising *Ānāpānasati* (mindfulness of respiration) the breath should not be followed inside or outside because it distracts the mind. This causes the body and the mind to waver and tremble. The simile of the man sawing wood illustrating where the breath should be noted (i.e., at nose-tip or on the lip) is common to both works. The *Visuddhimagga* quotes other similes in illustration. It also quotes (p. 280) the *Paṭisambhidāmagga* (I, p. 165) which warns against the practice of trying to follow the inhaled breath to the heart (*hadaya*) and the navel (*nābhi*) and the outgoing breath back from the navel to the heart and nose-tip, for, both the mind and the body become 'disquieted and perturbed and shaky' if this practice is resorted to. The *Visuddhimagga* (p. 278) says that there are eight stages in the practice of *Ānāpānasati,* the first four of which are (1) counting, (2) connection, (3) touching, and (4) fixing. Here the Venerable Buddhaghosa Thera does not quote authority for this statement as he usually does. The *Vimuttimagga* (p. 159) supplies this omission by saying that 'certain predecessors' taught these four ways. Here both base themselves on authority outside the texts and the commentaries.

In discussing the earth *kasiṇa,* the *Visuddhimagga* (p. 123) says, 'The four blemishes of the earth *kasiṇa* are due to the intrusion of blue, yellow, red, or white'. But it does not give any reason. The *Vimuttimagga* (p. 72) says, 'By dwelling on white, black, or red, he practises colour *kasiṇa*'. It is seen here that by practising one subject of meditation another cannot be developed — for instance, when one practises *Ānāpānasati* one does not become proficient in, say, *Buddhānussati,* though this is sometimes imagined to be possible. If, for instance, one sees the form of the Buddha or a Buddha statue while developing any other meditation, then it is a clear case of failure in the practice of that particular meditation, though the seeing of these signs in itself is a good thing. The proper occasion for these signs to appear is when *Buddhānussati* is practised.

That the *Vimuttimagga* is an inspiring work is stated elsewhere. It is confirmed by the spontaneous testimony of those who have read the original draft translation. It has inspired men of ancient times. That is shown by the fact that the people of Ryo in the early years of the sixth century A.C. called the author of the *Vimuttimagga* 'Great Light'.

What connection there is between these two works has been shown, though briefly, in the foregoing pages. No more can be expected in an introduction. For a detailed study the reader may consult the thorough investigation made by Prof. Bapat in his "*Vimuttimagga* and *Visuddhimagga*, a comparative Study", Poona 1937.

BIBLIOGRAPHY

Visuddhimagga

Text — 1. Edition of the Pali Text Society, London 1920.
2. Edition of the Harvard Oriental Series, Vol. 41, Cambridge, Mass., 1950.

Translations — **English**
1. The Path of Purity (3 Vols.) by Prof. Pe Maung Tin, P.T.S., London, 1922, 1928, 1931.
2. The Path of Purification by the Venerable Bhikkhu Ñāṇamoli, Colombo, 1956.

German:
1. Der Weg zur Reinheit, 1 Band, by the Venerable Nyāṇatiloka Mahā Thera (Vorwort pp. IV-VII), Benares Verlag, Munchen Neubiberg, 1931.
2. Der Weg zur Reinheit, complete edition, by the Venerable Nyāṇatiloka Mahā Thera (Vorwort pp. VIII-X, XII), Verlag Christani, Konstanz, 1952.

Sinhalese:
1. The Ancient Paraphrase by King Parākramabāhu II (1236-68 A.C.).
2. Sinhala Visuddhimārgaya by Paṇḍita Mātara Śrī Dharmavaṁsa Sthavira, Mātara, 1953.

Paramatthamañjūsā (*Vidsuddhimagga* commentary) by Bhadantācariya Dhammapāla — Venerable Morontuḍuvē Dhammānanda Nāyaka Thera's Sinhalese edition, 1908.

Mahāvaṁsa

Text — Edition of the Pali Text Society, London, 1908.

Translation — **English:** The *Mahāvaṁsa* or The Great Chronicle of Ceylon by Dr. Wilhelm Geiger, Ceylon Government Information Department, Colombo, 1950 (Reprint).

Cūḷavaṁsa

Translation – **English:** *Cūḷavaṁsa*, being the more recent part of the *Mahāvaṁsa* by Dr. Wilhelm Geiger and Mrs. C. Mabel Rickmers, (2 Parts). P.T.S London 1929, 1930.

Bibliography

The Pali Literature of Ceylon by Dr. G. P. Malalasekera, Royal Asiatic Society's Prize Publication Fund Vol. X, London, 1928.

History of Indian Literature by Dr. M. Winternitz, English translation by Mrs. S. Ketkar and Miss H. Kohn, University of Calcutta, 1933.

Early History of Buddhism in Ceylon by Dr. E. W. Adikaram, Colombo, 1953 (Second Impression).

Vimuttimagga and Visuddhimagga, a Comparative Study by Prof. P. V. Bapat, Poona, 1937.

Vimuttimagga

Translation — **Chinese:** *Cié-to-tāo-lun* or *Gedatsu Dō Ron* by Tipiṭaka Sanghapāla of Funan (6th cent. A.C.).

ABBREVIATIONS

A.	Anguttara Nikāya
Abhms.	Abhidhammattha-Saṅgaha
Abhmv.	Abhidhammāvatāra
Ap.	Apadāna of the Khuddaka Nikāya
As.	Atthasālinī=Dhammasaṅgaṇi Aṭṭhakathā
It.	Itivuttaka
It.-a.	Itivuttaka Aṭṭhakathā=Paramattha-Dīpanī
Ud.	Udāna
Ud.-a.	Udāna Aṭṭhakathā
C.Pit.	Cariyā-piṭaka
Cv.	Cūḷavaṁsa
J.	Jātaka (Fausböll's ed.)
Th.	Thera-gāthā
Thī.	Therī-gāthā
D.	Dīgha Nikāya
Dh.	Dhammapada
Dh.-a.	Dhammapada Aṭṭhakathā
Dhs.	Dhammasaṅgaṇi
Nd[1] (and Nidd. I)	Mahā Niddesa
Netti.	Netti-Pakaraṇa
Pts.	Paṭisambhidāmagga
Pts.-a.	Paṭisambhidā Aṭṭhakathā=Saddhammappakāsinī
Peṭaka.	Peṭakopadesa
Pm.	Paramatthamñjūsā=Visuddhimagga Aṭṭhakathā=Mahā Ṭīkā
Ps.	Papañcasūdanī=Majjhima Nikāya Aṭṭhakathā
M.	Majjhima Nikāya
Mv. (and Mhv.)	Mahāvaṁsa
Mil.	Milindapañha (V. Trenckner's ed.)
M. Vyut.	Mahāvyutpatti
Rūpārūp.	Rūpārūpavibhāga
Lal.V.	Lalitavistara
Vin.	Vinaya
Vis. Mag.	Visuddhimagga
Vbh.	Vibhanga
Vbh.-a.	Vibhanga Aṭṭhakathā=Sammoha-vinodanī
S.	Saṁyutta Nikāya
Saddh.	Saddhammopāyana
Sn.	Sutta-nipāta (Harvard Oriental Series)
Sn.-a.	Sutta-nipāta Aṭṭhakathā=Paramatthajotikā
Sp.	Samantapāsādikā=Vinaya Aṭṭhakathā
Spk.	Sārattha-ppakāsinī=Saṁyutta Nikāya Aṭṭhakathā
Sv.	Sumaṅgala-vilāsinī=Dīgha Nikāya Aṭṭhakathā

CONTENTS

FASCICLE I, CHAPTER I

INTRODUCTORY DISCOURSE

CHAPTER II

ON DISTINGUISHING VIRTUE

FASCICLE II, CHAPTER III

ON AUSTERITIES

CHAPTER IV

ON DISTINGUISHING CONCENTRATION

CHAPTER V

ON APPROACHING A GOOD FRIEND

FASCICLE III, CHAPTER VI

THE DISTINGUISHING OF BEHAVIOUR

Contents

CHAPTER VII

THE DISTINGUISHING OF THE SUBJECTS
OF MEDITATION

FASCICLE IV, CHAPTER VIII, SECTION I

ENTRANCE INTO THE SUBJECT OF MEDITATION

FASCICLE VI, CHAPTER VIII, SECTION III

THE TEN PERCEPTIONS OF PUTRESCENCE

Contents

FASCICLE VII, CHAPTER VIII, SECTION IV

FASCICLE VIII, CHAPTER VIII, SECTION V

Contents

FASCICLE IX, CHAPTER IX

THE FIVE FORMS OF HIGHER KNOWLEDGE

CHAPTER X

ON DISTINGUISHING WISDOM

FASCICLE X, CHAPTER XI, SECTION I

THE FIVE METHODS

Contents

PAGE

Contents

PAGE

FASCICLE XI, CHAPTER XI, SECTION II

THE FIVE METHODS

CHAPTER XII, SECTION I

ON DISCERNING TRUTH

Contents

FASCICLE XII, CHAPTER XII, SECTION II

ON DISCERNING TRUTH

Contents

[399] **THE PATH OF FREEDOM**[1]

FASCICLE THE FIRST

WRITTEN

BY

THE ARAHANT UPATISSA

WHO WAS CALLED

GREAT LIGHT IN RYO

TRANSLATED IN RYO

BY

TIPIṬAKA SANGHAPĀLA OF FUNAN

INTRODUCTORY DISCOURSE

CHAPTER THE FIRST

SALUTATION

Homage to the Blessed One, the Consummate One, the Supremely Enlightened One.[2]

INTRODUCTORY STANZA

Virtue, concentration,
Wisdom and the peerless freedom:
To these verities awoke
Illustrious Gotama.[3]

He who wishes to be released from all trouble, wishes to be unloosed from all attachment, wishes to gain the pre-eminent mind, wishes to be rid of birth, old age and death, wishes to enjoy bliss and freedom, wishes to achieve the yet unachieved extinction, Nibbāna, and lead those on the other shore to perfection, should be versed in the Sutta, Abhidhamma and Vinaya. This is the Path of Freedom.

Now will I expound. Hearken.
Question: What is 'virtue'?

Answer: 'Virtue' means restraint.[4] 'Concentration' means non-distractedness. 'Wisdom' means comprehension. 'Freedom' means freedom from bondage. 'Peerless' means canker-free. 'Awoke' means realized and understood through wisdom. 'These verities' means the four noble verities.[5] 'Gotama'

---

1. *Vimuttimagga*
2. *Namo tassa bhagavato arahato sammāsambuddhassa.*
3. A. II, 2; D. II, 123: *Sīlaṁ samādhi paññā ca vimutti ca anuttarā Anubuddhā ime dhammā Gotamena yasassinā.*
4. *Saṁvara.*
5. *Cattāro ariyadhammā.*

is the name of a family. 'Illustrious' means blessed. Through the excellent merits: virtue, concentration, wisdom and freedom, he gained boundless and highest fame.

PATH OF FREEDOM DESCRIBED

What is the meaning of the Path of Freedom? 'Freedom' means the five kinds of freedom: freedom of suppression,[1] freedom of parts,[2] freedom of eradication,[3] freedom of tranquillity,[4] and freedom of emancipation.[5]

What is 'freedom of suppression'? It is the suppression of the passions through the practice of the first meditation.[6] This is called 'freedom of supression'. 'Freedom of parts' is the freedom from views through the practice of concentration which partakes of penetration.[7] This is called 'freedom of parts'. 'Freedom of eradication' is the destruction of the fetters through the practice of the supramundane path.[8] This is called 'freedom of eradication'. 'Freedom of tranquillity' is (to be understood) as the happy heart of a man who acquires fruit. This is called [400] 'freedom of tranquillity'. 'Freedom of emancipation' is extinction without residue of the substratum of being.[9] This is called 'freedom of emancipation'. This Path of Freedom is for the attainment of liberation. This perfect path is called the Path of Freedom through virtue, concentration and wisdom.

Now will I preach concerning the Path of Freedom. *Q*. For what reason is the Path of Freedom taught? *A*. There is a good man. He is like a blind man who wanders to a distant land without guidance, because, although he wishes to gain freedom, he does not listen to the teaching of freedom; because he does not acknowledge freedom and because he wrongly acknowledges freedom. Since he is hemmed in by much suffering he cannot gain freedom. Although he wishes to gain freedom, he has not the means. To gain freedom means are necessary. The Buddha has declared: "There are beings covered with but a little dust. They will fall away unless they hear the Truth".[10] Again the Buddha has declared: "O bhikkhus, through two occasioning causes can one arouse Right Understanding. Which two? Hearing from others is the first. Intelligent attention is the second".[11] Therefore do I preach freedom.

I preach freedom to those who do not acknowledge freedom in order to produce in them the feeling of detachment. This is like a traveller to a distant land getting a good guide.

MERITS OF ACKNOWLEDGEMENT OF THE PATH

If a man acknowledges this Path of Freedom, he fulfills three groups.[12] What are the three? They are the group of virtue,[13] the group of concentration,[14] and the group of wisdom.[15]

---

1. *Vikkhambana-vimutti*. 2. *Tadanga-vimutti*. 3. *Samuccheda-vimutti*. 4. *Paṭippassaddha-vimutti*. 5. *Nissaraṇa-vimutti*. 6. *Paṭhamajjhāna*. 7. *Nibbedhabhāgiya-samādhi*. 8. *Lokuttara-magga*. 9. *Anupādisesanibbāna*. 10. S. I, 105-6: *Santi sattā apparajakkha-jātikā assavaṇatā dhammassa parihāyanti*. 11. A. I, 87: *Dve'me bhikkhave paccayā sammādiṭṭhiyā uppādāya. Katame dve? Parato ca ghoso yoniso ca manasikāro*. 12. *Khandhā*. 13. *Sīlakkhandha*. 14. *Samādhikkhandha*. 15. *Paññakkhandha*.

What is the group of virtue? It is Right Speech, Right Action, Right Livelihood and the like. Or the group of virtue is the merit-mass of diverse virtues.

What is the group of concentration? It is Right Effort, Right Mindfulness, Right Concentration and the like. Or (the group of concentration is) the merit-mass of diverse forms of concentration.

What is the group of wisdom? It is Right Understanding, Right Thought and the like. Or (the group of wisdom is) the merit-mass of diverse kinds of wisdom. Thus these three groups are completed.

THREE TRAININGS

A man who acknowledges the Path of Freedom should be versed in the triple training: the training of the higher virtue,[1] the training of the higher thought,[2] and the training of the higher wisdom.[3]

(It is said:) Virtue is the training of the higher virtue; concentration is the training of the higher thought; wisdom is the training of the higher wisdom.

And again (it is said:) There is virtue which is the training of virtue and there is virtue which is the training of the higher virtue. There is concentration[4] which is the training of thought and there is concentration which is the training of the higher thought. There is wisdom which is the training of wisdom and there is wisdom which is the training of the higher wisdom.

Q. What is the training of virtue? *A.* Indicated virtue[5] — this is called the training of virtue. Virtue partaking of penetration[6] — this is called the training of the higher virtue. Again, the virtue of the commoner — this is called the training of virtue. Ariyan virtue — this is called the training of the higher virtue.

Q. What is the training of thought? *A.* It is concentration pertaining to (the) sense (plane)[7]. *Q.* What is the training of the higher thought? *A.* It is concentration pertaining to (the) form (plane)[8] and (the) formless (plane)[9]. This is called the training of the higher thought. And again, indicated concentration[10] is the training of thought. Concentration partaking of penetration and concentration of the Path are called the training of the higher thought.

What is the training of wisdom? Worldly knowledge — this is called the training of wisdom. The four truths, (enlightenment) factors' knowledge[11] and the knowledge of the Path — these are called the training of the higher wisdom.

The Blessed One expounded the training of the higher virtue to a man of the lower type, the training of the higher thought to a man of the middle type and the training of the higher wisdom to a man of the higher type.

---

1. *Adhisīlasikkhā.* 2. *Adhicittasikkhā.* 3. *Adhipaññāsikkhā.* 4. Lit. *Samādhisikkhā.* 5. The virtue that can be appreciated by ordinary men. 6. *Nibbedhabhāgiya.* 7. *Kāmāvacara samādhi.* 8. *Rūpāvacara samādhi.* 9. *Arūpāvacara samādhi.* 10. The concentration that can be appreciated by ordinary men. 11. *Bodhipakkhiyadhamma ñāṇa.*

THE MEANING OF TRAINING

Q. What is the meaning of training? *A*. To be trained in the things wherein training is necessary, to be trained in the excellent training and to be trained to transcend all training. Thus to be trained in these three trainings is called the acknowledgement of the Path of Freedom.

REMOVAL OF THE IMPURITIES

Through these three kinds of training one attains to purity: purity of virtue,[1] purity of thought,[2] and purity of views.[3] Thus virtue is purity of virtue, concentration is purity of thought, and wisdom is purity of views.

Virtue cleanses away the impurities caused through transgression of precepts (— this is called the purification of virtue). Concentration cleanses away the encompassing impurities—this is called the purification of the mind. Wisdom removes the impurities of ignorance—this is called the purification of views. And again, virtue removes the impurities of demeritorious action. Concentration removes the encompassing impurities. Wisdom removes the impurities of the latencies.[4] Through these three purities a man acknowledges Freedom's Path.

THE THREE KINDS OF GOOD

Again, a man acknoweldges the path through three kinds of good: the initial good, the medial good, the final good.[5] Virtue is the initial (good); concentration is the medial (good); wisdom is the final (good). Why is virtue the initial good? There is a man who is energetic; he attains to the stage of non-retrogression; on account of non-retrogression, he is joyful; on account of joy, he becomes buoyant; on account of buoyancy, his body is thrilled; on account of his body being thrilled, he is happy; on account of happiness, his mind is at ease — this is called 'the initial good'. 'Concentration is the medial good' thus: Through concentration a man understands things as they are — this is called the medial good. 'Wisdom is the final good' thus: Understanding things as they are, a man is disgusted; through disgust he separates from passion; through separation from passion, he frees himself; having freed himself, he knows it (the nature of his freedom).[6] Thus a man accomplishes the Path of the triple good.

---

1. *Sīlavisuddhi*. 2. *Cittavisuddhi*. 3. *Diṭṭhivisuddhi*. 4 Cp. Vis. Mag. 5, 6: *Tathā sīlena kilesānaṁ vitikkamapaṭipakkho pakāsito hoti; samādhinā pariyuṭṭhānapaṭipakkho; paññāya anusayapaṭipakkho. Sīlena ca duccaritasankilesavisodhanaṁ pakāsitaṁ hoti; samādhinā taṇhāsankilesavisodhanaṁ; paññāya diṭṭhisankilesavisodhanaṁ.*

5. *Ādi-, majjha-, pariyosāna-kalyāṇa*. 6. Cp. A. V, 2: *Iti kho Ānanda kusalāni sīlāni avippaṭisāratthāni avippaṭisārānisaṁsāni, avippaṭisāro pāmujjattho pāmujjānisaṁso, pāmujjaṁ pītatthaṁ pītānisaṁsaṁ, pīti passaddhatthā passaddhānisaṁsā, passaddhi sukhatthā sukhānisaṁsā, sukhaṁ samādhatthaṁ samādhānisaṁsaṁ, samādhi yathābhūtañāṇadassanattho yathābhūtañāṇadassanānisaṁso, yathābhūtañāṇadassanaṁ nibbidavirāgatthaṁ nibbidavirāgānisaṁsaṁ, nibbidavirāgo vimuttiñāṇadassanattho vimuttiñāṇadassanānisaṁso.*

THE THREE KINDS OF HAPPINESS

After acknowledging the Path of Freedom, a man acquires three kinds of happiness: the happiness of the fault-free, the happiness of tranquillity and the happiness of Enlightenment. He acquires the happiness of the fault-free through virtue; he acquires the happiness of tranquillity through concentration; and he acquires the happiness of Enlightenment through wisdom. Thus a man acquires the three kinds of happiness.

PERFECTION OF THE MIDDLE WAY

After a man acknowledges the Path of Freedom, he attains to the perfection of the middle way[1] rejecting the two extremes. Through this virtue he removes well the attachment to diverse sense-desires and arouses within him the joy of the fault-free. Through concentration he removes the weariness of the body. In the case of tranquillity he increases joy and bliss. Through wisdom he understands the four noble truths[2] reaches the middle way and deeply cherishes the delectable happiness of Enlightenment. Thus, he, rejecting the extremes,[3] attains to the perfection of the middle way.

After acknowledging the Path of Freedom, through virtue he transcends the way to states of regress;[4] through concentiation he transcends the sense plane;[5] through wisdom he transcends all becoming.[6] If he practises virtue to the full and practises little of concentration and wisdom, he will reach the stage of the Stream-entrant[7] and the stage of the Once-returner.[8] If he practises virtue and concentration to the full and practises little of wisdom, he will reach the stage of the Non-returner.[9] If he pracıises virtue, concentration and wisdom to the full, he will reach the peerless freedom of the Consummate One.[10]

1. *Majjhimā paṭipadā.* 2. *Cattāri ariya-saccāni.* 3. *Antā.* 4. *Apāya.*
5. *Kāmāvacara.* 6. *Sabba bhava.* 7. Cp. A. IV, 381: *Puna ca paraṁ Sāriputta idh' ekacco puggalo sīlesu paripūrakārī hoti samādhismiṁ mattasokārī paññāya mattasokārī. So tiṇṇaṁ saṁyojanānaṁ parikkhayā sattakkhattuparamo hoti.*
8. Cp. Ibid. 380: *Puna ca paraṁ Sāriputta idh'ekacco puggalo sīlesu paripūrakārī hoti, samādhismiṁ na paripūrakārī paññāya na paripūrakārī. So tiṇṇaṁ saṁyojanaṁ parikkhayā rāgadosamohānaṁ tanuttā sakadāgāmi hoti.*
9. Cp. Ibid. *Puna ca paraṁ Sāriputta idh'ekacco puggalo sīlesu paripūrakārī hoti, samādhismiṁ paripūrakāri paññāya na paripūrakārī. So pañcannaṁ orambhāgiyānaṁ saṁyojanānaṁ parikkhayā.... uddhaṁsoto hoti akaniṭṭhagāmī.* 10. *Arahaṁ.*

ON DISTINGUISHING VIRTUE

CHAPTER THE SECOND

Q. What is virtue? What is its salient characteristic?[1] What is its function?[2] What is its manifestation?[3] What is its near cause?[4] What are its benefits?[5] What is the meaning of virtue? What is the difference between virtue and mode of life?[6] How many kinds of virtue are there? What produces (virtue)? What are the initial, medial and final stages in virtue? How many states[7] are obstacles to progress in virtue? How many are the causes of virtue? How many groups of virtue are there? What purifies virtue? Owing to how many causes does one dwell in virtue?

VIRTUE DEFINED

A. 'What is virtue?' It is virtue of volition,[8] virtue of abstention[9] and virtue of non-transgression.[10] What is 'virtue of volition'? It is this resolve: "I will do no evil, because, if I do evil, I shall have to suffer for it". What is 'virtue of abstention'? It is keeping away from occasions of evil. What is 'virtue of non-transgression'? (Here) a virtuous man has no fault of body and speech. Again, the meaning of cutting is 'abstention'. All good activities[11] are virtue. It is said in the Abhidhamma[12] thus: "The destruction of sense desires by renunciation (is virtue). This virtue can remove evil. It is the 'virtue of volition', the 'virtue of restraint'[13], the 'virtue of abstention'. The destruction of ill will by not-ill will, the destruction of rigidity and torpor by the perception of brightness, the destruction of agitation and anxiety by non-distraction, the destruction of uncertainty by the determination of states, the destruction of ignorance by knowledge, the destruction of discontent by gladness, the destruction of the five hindrances by the first meditation, the destruction of initial and sustained application of thought by the second meditation, the destruction of happiness by the third meditation, the destruction of bliss by the fourth meditation, the destruction (of perceptions ranging) from the perception of form to (the perception of) sense-reaction and the perception of diversity by the concentration of the sphere of the infinity of space,[14] the destruction of the perception of the sphere of the infinity of space by the

---

1. *Lakkhaṇa*. 2. *Rasa*. 3. *Paccuppaṭṭhāna*. 4. *Padaṭṭhāna*. 5. *Ānisaṁsa*
6. *Vata*. 7. *Dhammā*. 8. *Cetanā sīla*. 9. *Veramaṇī sīla*. 10. *Avītikkama sīla*.
11. *Sabbe kusalā dhammā*. 12. Cp. parallel passage in the Vis. Mag. 49-50, beginning with "*Vuttaṁ h'etaṁ Paṭisambhidāyaṁ*". The beginning of the quotation from "*Abhidhamma*" in the Vim. Mag. is confused, possibly due to copyist's error. The repetition of 'destruction' or 'severance' (or is it 'rejection'?) is perhaps due to the needs of Chinese composition. 13. *Saṁvara sīla*.
14. The ideograph for '*paṭigha*' is 'hatred'.

concentration of the sphere of the infinity of consciousness, the destruction of the perception of the sphere of the infinity of consciousness by the concentration of the sphere of nothingness, the destruction of the (perception of the) sphere of nothingness by the concentration of the sphere of neither perception nor non-perception, the destruction of the perception of permanence by the view of impermanence, the destruction of the perception of bliss by the view of ill, the destruction of the perception of self by the view of not-self, the destruction of the perception of the pure by the view of the impure,[1] the destruction of the perception of craving by the view of tribulation,[2] the destruction of the perception of passion by the view of the stainless, the destruction of origination by the view of cessation,[3] the destruction of density by the view of evanescence, the destruction of union by the view of separation, the destruction of fixity by the view of change, the destruction of the sign by the view of the signless, the destruction of yearning by the view of non-yearning, the destruction of adherence by the view of the void, the destruction of clinging and adherence (to essence?) by the view of the higher wisdom, the destruction of the adherence to delusion by the knowledge and discernment of things as they are, the destruction of adherence to dwelling[4] by the view of tribulation, the destruction of non-reflection by the view of reflection, the destruction of adherence to fetters by the view of the rolling back (of delusion), the destruction of adherence to the cankers of views by the path of the Stream-entrant, the destruction of the gross cankers by the path of the Once-returner, the destruction of the subtle cankers by the path of the Non-returner, and the destruction of all cankers by the path of the Consummate One" — these are called the 'virtue of non-transgression', the 'virtue of volition', the virtue of restraint' and the 'virtue of abstention'. These are called virtue.

SALIENT CHARACTERISTIC OF VIRTUE

'What is the salient characteristic of virtue'?: The removal of non-dignity by dignity. What is called 'non-dignity'? *A*. It is transgression of virtue. There are three kinds of transgression of virtue: transgression of the virtue pertaining to the rules of the Community of Bhikkhus;[5] transgression of the virtue pertaining to the requisites;[6] transgression of the virtue pertaining to the faculties.[7] What is 'transgression of the virtue pertaining to the Community of Bhikkhus'? [401]. It is loss of faith in the Tathāgata owing to immodesty[8] and indecorum.[9] What is 'transgression of the virtue pertaining to the requisites'? When a man's life is concerned with the adornment of the body, he loses contentment. What is 'transgression of virtue pertaining to the faculties'? It is separation from wise attentiveness through not closing the six sense doors. These three constitute 'non-dignity'. This is called the 'salient characteristic of virtue'.

1, 2. Not in Vis. Mag. And, '*nibbidānupassanāya nandiyā*' of Pts. I, 46, quoted in Vis. Mag., is not here.
3. After this Vis. Mag. has '*paṭinissaggānupassanāya ādānassa*'.
4. *Ālaya*. 5. Lit. *Pātimokkha dhamma*. 6. Lit. *Paccaya dhamma*.
7. *Indriya dhamma*. 8. *Ahiri*. 9. *Anottappa*.

FUNCTION, MANIFESTATION AND NEAR CAUSE OF VIRTUE

What are its 'function', 'manifestation' and 'near cause'? Excellent joy is its 'function'. Non-repentance is its 'manifestation'. The three meritorious activities are its 'near cause'. And again, excellent delight is its 'function'. Non-repentance is its manifestation. The shielding of all faculties is its near cause.

BENEFITS OF VIRTUE

What are the 'benefits' of virtue? Non-repentance is the benefit of virtue. This is in accord with the words of the Blessed One addressed to (the Venerable Elder) Ānanda: "Non-repentance is the benefit and gain of virtue."[1] And again, virtue is called excellent joy, the highest of all castes, the treasure[2] and the noble. This is the ground of the Buddhas. This is to bathe without water.[3] This is to permeate with fragrance.[4] This is the shadow accompanying form. This is to wear the thread which must be worn. This is the sacred caste. This is the peerless training. This is the course of well-faring. If a man practises virtue, on account of that virtue, he will become fearless, ennoble his friends and be dear to the holy ones. This is the good ornament.[5] This rules all conduct. This is the place of merit. This is the field of offering. This is the ground of growth in noble companionship.

(He who practises virtue) will be steadfast in all good. He will fulfil purity of aspiration. Even in death he will be self-possessed.[6] Accomplishing the freedom of suppression he will experience the bliss of artifice (?). Thus there are many merits of virtue.

MEANING OF VIRTUE

'What is the meaning of virtue'? *A*. It means coolness, the higher excellence, action, nature and natural condition of the nature of suffering and joy. Again, it means the head, coolness[7] and peace. Why is it said that virtue is the 'head'? *A*. If a man has no head he cannot get rid of the dust of passion from his faculties. Then it is called death. Thus the virtue of the bhikkhu is the head. Beheaded, (he) loses all good qualities. Thus in the teaching of the Buddha it is called death. This is the meaning of 'head' in virtue. Why is it said that virtue means 'coolness'? *A*. Just as the exceedingly cool sandal allays the fever-heat of the body, just so does virtue allay the fever of the mind that fears after breaking the precepts, and induce joy. This is the meaning of virtue as 'coolness'. Why is it said that 'peace' is the meaning

---

1. A.V,1: *Avippaṭisāratthāni kho Ānanda kusalāni sīlāni avippaṭisārānisaṁsāni.*
2. *Dhana.* 3. Th. 613: *Titthañ ca sabbabuddhānaṁ tasmā sīlaṁ visodhaye.*
4. Cp. Th. 615: *Sīlaṁ vilepanaṁ seṭṭhaṁ.* 5. Cp. Th. 614: *Sīlaṁ ābharaṇaṁ seṭṭhaṁ.*
6. D. II, 86: *Sīlavā sīlasampanno asammūḷho kālaṁ karoti.* 7. See Vis. Mag. 8: *Aññe pana sirattho sītalattho ti evam ādinā pi nayen' ev' ettha atthaṁ vaṇṇayanti.*

of virtue? *A.* If a man practises viitue he will be quiet of behaviour. He will not arouse fear. This is the meaning of virtue as 'peace'.

VIRTUE AND MODE OF LIFE

'What is the difference between (virtue) and mode of life'?[1] Practice,[2] energy,[3] resolution,[4] austerities.[5] These are modes of life, not virtue. Virtue is also called mode of life. Virtue is called dignity. Feeling (?) is also called mode of life.

THREE KINDS OF VIRTUE

'How many (kinds of) virtue are there'? There are three kinds of virtue: skilful virtue, unskilful virtue and non-charactriezable virtue.[6] What is skilful virtue? Bodily and verbal meritorious activities and right livelihood. (Here), because of absence of tribulation, good result ensues. What is unskilful virtue? Bodily and verbal demeritorious activities and wrong livelihood. (Here), because of tribulation, good result does not ensue. What is 'non-characterizable virtue'? It is bodily and verbal canker-free activities and spotless livelihood. (Here) there is neither tribulation nor good result.

WHAT PRODUCES VIRTUE

'What produces virtue'? Virtue produced in a good heart is skilful virtue. Virtue produced in an evil heart is unskilful virtue. Virtue produced in a non-characterizable heart is non-characterizable virtue.[7]

STAGES IN VIRTUE

'What are the initial, medial, and final (stages in) virtue'? The keeping of precepts is the initial (stage), non-transgression is the medial (stage) and rejoicing is the final (stage) in virtue.[8]

How many are the 'obstacles' to and how many are the 'causes' of virtue? *A.* Thirty-four states[9] are 'obstacles'. Thirty-four states are 'causes' of virtue.

IMPEDIMENTS AND CAUSES OF VIRTUE

Anger, malice, hypocrisy, agitation, covetousness, jealousy, wile, craftiness, resentment, disputatiousness, pride, self-conceit, arrogance, negligence, idleness, lust, non-contentment with little, not following the wise, non-mindfulness, harsh speech, evil companionship, evil knowledge, evil views, impatience, want of faith, immodesty, indecorum, indulgence of body mouth and palate,

---

1. *Vata, Vatta.* Cp. Nd[1] 66, 92, 104, 106, 188. 2. *Paṭipatti.* 3. *Viriya.* 4. *Adiṭṭhāna.* 5. *Dhutanga.* 6. Lit. Indescribable virtue. Pts. I, 44: *Kati sīlāniti? Tīṇi sīlāni, kusalasīlaṁ, akusalasīlaṁ abyākatasīlaṁ.* 7. and 8. Not in Vis. Mag. 9. *Dhammā.*

vulgarity, contact with women, not honouring the teacher, non-practice of restraint of the senses, non-practice of concentration in the first and last watches of the night, not reciting the discourses in the first and last watches of the night — these thirty-four states are 'obstacles'. A man impeded by any one of these cannot perfect his virtue. If his virtue is not perfected he will surely retrogress. The thirty-four states which counteract these ('obstacles') are the 'cause' of virtue.[1]

FIRST GROUP OF TWO IN VIRTUE

'How many groups of virtue are there'? Group of two, group of three and group of four. What is the group of two? Precepts governing usage[2] and precepts governing prohibitions.[3] Those decisions of the Buddha which indicate what ought to be done by body and speech are 'precepts governing usage'. Those decisions of the Buddha which indicate what ought not to be done by body and speech are 'precepts governing prohibitions'. 'Precepts governing usage' are accomplished through the effort of faith. 'Precepts governing prohibitions' are accomplished through being mindful of faith.

SECOND GROUP OF TWO IN VIRTUE

And again, there is a group of two in virtue: the virtue of discarding[4] and the virtue of undertaking.[5] What is called 'discarding'? It is the destruction of non-virtue. What is called 'undertaking'? It is the undertaking to keep many good precepts. Just as light dispels darkness, just so a man who discards non-virtues, by the discarding of those non-virtues, will be freed from ill-faring. Through undertaking to keep good precepts he can enter the path of merit. Through the destruction of non-virtue he fulfils steadfastness.[6]

THIRD GROUP OF TWO IN VIRTUE

And again, there is a group of two in virtue. Mundane virtue[7] and supramundane virtue.[8] What is 'supramundane virtue'? The virtue which is fulfilled together with the fruit of the noble Path — this is 'supramundane virtue'. The rest is 'mundane virtue'. Through the fulfilment of 'mundane virtue' pre-eminence is accomplished. Through the fulfilment of 'supramundane virtue' freedom is accomplished.

1. Not in Vis. Mag. 2. *Cāritta sīla.* 3. *Vāritta sīla.* 4. *Pahāna.*

5. *Samādāna.* Cp. with reference to both (1 and 2) D. I, 63: *Kathañ ca mahārāja bhikkhu sīla-sampanno hoti? Idha mahārāja bhikkhu pāṇātipātaṁ pahāya pāṇātipātā paṭivirato hoti, nihita-daṇḍo nihita-sattho lajjī dayāpanno sabba-pāṇa-bhūta-hitānukampī viharati. Adinnādānaṁ pahāya....*

6. Not in Vis. Mag. 7. *Lokiya sīla.* 8. *Lokuttara sīla.*

FOURTH GROUP OF TWO IN VIRTUE

And again, there is a group of two in virtue: measurable virtue[1] and immeasurable virtue.[2] Incomplete virtue — this is called 'measurable virtue'. Complete virtue — this is called 'immeasurable' (virtue), according to the declaration of the Buddha.

FIFTH GROUP OF TWO IN VIRTUE

And again, there is a group of two in virtue: with limit and without limit.[3] What is 'with limit'? If a man undertakes to keep any precept but transgresses it for the sake of worldly welfare, for the sake of fame, for the sake of friends*, for the sake of the body** and for the sake of life, then his virtue makes worldly welfare its limit, makes fame its limit, makes the body its limit, makes life its limit. What is 'without limit'? Here a bhikkhu undertakes to keep a precept rightly and does not entertain even the thought of transgressing (the precept) for the sake of worldly welfare, for the sake of fame, for the sake of the body and for the sake of life. How then will he transgress it? This is called virtue 'without limit'.

SIXTH GROUP OF TWO IN VIRTUE

And again, there is a group of two in virtue: dependent and non-dependent.[4] Virtue that is connected with becoming is dependent on craving. The virtue that is connected with addiction to rites and ceremonies is dependent on opinions. The virtue that is connected with self-praise and blame of others is dependent on pride.[5] These are 'dependent' virtues. Virtue that is for the sake of freedom is 'non-dependent' virtue. 'Dependent' virtue is not for wise men. 'Non-dependent' virtue is for the wise.

SEVENTH GROUP OF TWO IN VIRTUE

And again, there is a group of two in virtue: the virtue of the fundamentals of the holy life[6] and the virtue of enhanced practice.[7] What is 'the virtue of the fundamentals of the holy life'? The virtue comprising purified bodily

---

1. *Pamāṇa sīla.* 2. *Appamāṇa sīla.*

3. *Pariyanta-°*, *apariyanta-sīla.* Cp. Pts. I, 43-44: *Atthi sīlaṁ pariyantaṁ, atthi sīlaṁ apariyantaṁ. Tattha katamaṁ taṁ sīlaṁ pariyantaṁ? Atthi sīlaṁ lābhapariyantaṁ, atthi sīlaṁ yasapariyantaṁ, atthi sīlaṁ ñātipariyantaṁ, atthi sīlaṁ aṅgapariyantaṁ, atthi sīlaṁ jīvitapariyantaṁ. Katamaṁ taṁ sīlaṁ lābhapariyantaṁ? Idh' ekacco lābhahetu lābhapaccayā lābhakāraṇā yathāsamādiṇṇaṁ sikkhāpadaṁ vītikkamati — idaṁ taṁ sīlaṁ lābhapariyantaṁ.... Katamaṁ taṁ sīlaṁ na aṅgapariyantaṁ? Idh' ekacco aṅgahetu aṅgapaccayā aṅgakāraṇā yathāsamādiṇṇaṁ sikkhāpadaṁ vītikkamāya cittaṁ pi na uppādeti kiṁ so vītikkamissati; idaṁ taṁ sīlaṁ na aṅgapariyantaṁ. Katamaṁ taṁ sīlaṁ na jīvitapariyantaṁ? Idh' ekacco jīvitahetu jīvitapaccayā jīvitakāraṇā yathāsamādiṇṇaṁ sikkhāpadaṁ vītikkamāya cittaṁ pi na uppādeti, kiṁ so vītikkamissati; idaṁ taṁ sīlaṁ na jīvitapariyantaṁ.*

* Pts. passage quoted above reads *ñāti* (relatives), ***aṅga* (limb).

4. *Nissita, Anissita.* 5. *Māna.* 6. *Ādibrahmacariyaka.* 7. *Ābhisamācārika.*

action, purified verbal action and pure livelihood[1] is called 'the virtue of the fundamentals of the holy life'. The remaining virtue of training is called 'the virtue of enhanced practice'.

EIGHTH GROUP OF TWO IN VIRTUE

And again, there is a group of two in virtue: connected with mind and not connected with mind. What is 'connected with mind'? It is 'the virtue of the fundamentals of the holy life'. What is 'not connected with mind'? The other, 'the virtue of enhanced practice'. In observing 'the virtue of the fundamentals of the holy life' the hearer[2] accomplishes the austere and the lofty virtue. By this 'virtue of enhanced practice' one does evil. Because the Buddha did not declare that (i.e., the virtue of enhanced practice), it is a hindrance to Enlightenment. (Therefore one does evil).

NINTH GROUP OF TWO IN VIRTUE

And again, there is a group of two in virtue: inviolable virtue and spotless virtue.[3] What is 'inviolable'? It is hearer's virtue. What is 'spotless'? It is the virtue of the Buddhas and the Paccekabuddhas.

TENTH GROUP OF TWO IN VIRTUE

And again, there is a group of two in virtue: virtue practised within a time-limit[4] and virtue practised till the dissolution of the body.[5] What is practised for a short time and is not connected with life is called 'virtue practised within a time-limit'. What is practised to the end of life from the time a man follows his teacher and undertakes the precepts is called the 'virtue practised till the dissolution of the body'. There is time in the reward of virtue practised within a time-limit. There is no time in the reward of virtue practised till the dissolution of the body.

FIRST GROUP OF THREE IN VIRTUE

What (is the group of) three (in virtue)? It is (the virtue of) quelling evil and not transgressing, experiencing and not transgressing, extirpating and not transgressing.[6] What is 'quelling evil and not transgressing'? Though hitherto not experienced feelings not belonging to one's practice arise, yet one does not suffer even the thought of transgression, in his mind—this is called 'quelling evil and not transgressing'.

---

1. *Sammā kammanta, sammā vācā, sammā ājīva.* 2. *Sāvaka.* 3. Not in Vis. Mag.
4. *Kālapariyanta.* 5. *Āpāṇakoṭika.* 6. Not in Vis. Mag.

What is 'experiencing and not transgressing'? Having experienced a feeling one does not on that account transgress ever after — this is called 'experiencing and not transgressing'.

What is 'extirpating and not transgressing'? The noble individual[1] extirpates various causes of evil through the noble Path — this is called 'extirpating and not transgressing'.

SECOND GROUP OF THREE IN VIRTUE

And again, there is a group of three in virtue thus: tarnished virtue,[2] not-tarnished virtue,[3] tranquillized virtue.[4]

What is 'tarnished virtue'? One clings to the appearance of a put-together-thing at first sight—this is called 'tarnished virtue'.

The virtue of the commoner[5] which is also the means of entering into the Path—this is called 'not-tarnished' virtue.

What is 'tranquillized virtue'? It is the virtue of the Consummate One.

THIRD GROUP OF THREE IN VIRTUE

And again, there is a group of three (in virtue) thus: the virtue swayed by the world,[6] the virtue swayed by the body and life,[7] the virtue swayed by the Law.[8]

What is virtue swayed by the world'? A man, through fear, removes various evils following the will of the world — this is called 'virtue swayed by the world'.

What is 'virtue swayed by the body and life'? A man, through fear, removes various evils in order to protect his life—this is called 'virtue swayed by the body and life'.

What is 'virtue swayed by the Law'? A man, through reverence, removes various demeritorious states for the sake of the True Law — this is called 'virtue swayed by the Law.'

FOURTH GROUP OF THREE IN VIRTUE

And again, there is a group of three in virtue [402] thus: virtue allied to disparate desires, virtue allied to like desires, virtue allied to no desires.[9]

---

1. *Ariya puggala.* 2. *Parāmaṭṭha sīla.* Cp. S. II, 94: *Dīgharattaṁ hetaṁ bhikkhave assutavato puthujjanassa ajjhositaṁ mamāyitaṁ parāmaṭṭhaṁ etaṁ mama eso 'ham asmi eso me attāti.* 3. *Aparāmaṭṭha sīla.* Cp. A. II, 56-7: *Puna ca paraṁ bhikkhave ariyasāvako ariyakantehi sīlehi samannāgato hoti akkhaṇḍehi acchiddehi asabalehi akammāsehi bhujissehi viññuppasaṭṭhehi aparāmaṭṭhehi samādhisaṁvattanikehi.*
4. *Paṭippassaddha sīla.* 5. *Puthujjana.*
6, 7, 8. A. I, 147: *Tīṇ' imāni bhikkhave adhipateyyāni. Katamāni tīṇi? Attādhipatteyyaṁ lokādhipateyyaṁ dhammādhipateyyaṁ.* 9. Not in Vis. Mag.

What is 'virtue allied to disparate desires'? (A man, while) tormenting others, undertakes to observe the precepts — this is called 'virtue allied to disparate desires'.

What is 'virtue allied to like desires'? A man undertakes to observe the precepts for the sake of happiness in the present life and for the sake of the happiness of freedom in the future — this is called 'virtue allied to like desires'.

What is 'virtue allied to no desires'? A man undertakes to observe the precepts, does not repent and benefits others — this is called 'virtue allied to no desires'.

FIFTH GROUP OF THREE IN VIRTUE

And again, there is a group of three in virtue thus: pure virtue,[1] impure virtue,[2] doubtful virtue.[3]

What is 'pure virtue'? Through two causes 'pure virtue' is fulfilled: the first is non-transgression; the second is confession after transgression — this is called 'pure virtue'.

Through two causes 'impure virtue' is fulfilled: the first is wilful transgression; the second is non-confession after transgression — this is called 'impure virtue'.

What is 'doubtful virtue'? Through three causes 'doubtful virtue' is fulfilled: the first is the non-distinguishing of place; the second is the non-distinguishing of transgression; the third is the non-distinguishing of wrongful deeds — this is called 'doubtful virtue'.

If a yogin's virtue is impure he confesses and experiences the bliss of the purified. If he had doubt, he presently finds out the blemish and acquires peace.

SIXTH GROUP OF THREE IN VIRTUE

And again, there is a group of three in virtue: learner's virtue,[4] learning-ender's virtue,[5] neither learner's nor learning-ender's virtue.[6]

What is 'learner's virtue'? It is the virtue of the seven learner-individuals.[7]

What is 'learning-ender's virtue'? It is the virtue of the Consummate One.

What is 'neither learner's nor learning-ender's virtue'? It is the virtue of the commoner.

SEVENTH GROUP OF THREE IN VIRTUE

And again, there is a group of three in virtue thus: fearful virtue, anxious virtue, fatuous virtue.[8]

1. *Visuddha sīla.*
2. *Avisuddha sīla.*
3. *Vematika sīla.* Cp. Vis. Mag. 14.
4. *Sekha sīla.*
5. *Asekha sīla.*
6. *Nevasekhanāsekha sīla.* Cp. Vis. Mag. 14.
7. *Sattasekhiyapuggala sīla.*
8. Not in Vis. Mag.

What is 'fearful virtue'? There is a man who through fear does not commit evil — this is called 'fearful virtue'.

What is 'anxious virtue'? A certain man, remembering an intimate friend from whom he is separated, is troubled with anxiety; owing to anxiety he does not commit evil — this is called 'anxious virtue'.

What is 'fatuous virtue'? There is a man; he observes the precepts of cow-asceticism[1] or dog-asceticism[2] — this is called 'fatuous virtue'.

If a man fulfils 'fatuous virtue', he will become a cow or a dog. If he does not fulfil, he will fall into hell.[3]

EIGHTH GROUP OF THREE IN VIRTUE

And again, there is a group of three in virtue: inferior,[4] middling,[5] superior.[6]

What is 'inferior'? (A certain man) is affected with much passion, excessive passion, great passion and is impregnated with non-paucity of wishes — this is called 'inferior' virtue.

What is 'middling'? (A certain man) is affected with subtle passion and is impregnated with paucity of wishes — this is called 'middling' virtue.

What is 'superior'? (A certain man) is not affected with passion and is impregnated with paucity of wishes — this is called 'superior' virtue.

Through the fulfilment of 'inferior' virtue, one is reborn as a man; through the fulfilment of 'middling' virtue, one is reborn as a god; through the fulfilment of 'superior' virtue, one attians to freedom.

FIRST GROUP OF FOUR IN VIRTUE

And again, there is a group of four in virtue: partaking of deterioration,[7] partaking of stagnation,[8] partaking of excellence,[9] partaking of penetration.[10]

What is 'partaking of deterioration'? A certain man does not remove what shuts out the attainment of the Path; he is not energetic; and he wilfully transgresses (the precepts) and thereafter conceals (his fault) — this is called 'partaking of deterioration'.

What is 'partaking of stagnation'? A certain man keeps the precepts and is not heedless, but he does not arouse aversion — this is called 'partaking of stagnation'.

---

1. *Go Sīla.* 2. *Kukkura sīla.* For details of 1 and 2, see M. I, 388 f. (note 3).
3. M. I, 388-9: *So go vataṁ bhāvetvā paripuṇṇaṁ abbokiṇṇaṁ... kāyassa bhedā parammaraṇā gunnaṁ sahavyataṁ uppajjati. Sace kho panassa evaṁ diṭṭhi hoti: iminā 'haṁ sīlena vā vatena vā tapena vā brahmacariyena vā devo vā bhavissāmi devaññataro vāti sāssa hoti micchādiṭṭhi. Micchādiṭṭhikassa kho ahaṁ Seniya dvinnaṁ gatīnaṁ aññataraṁ gatiṁ vadāmi: nirayaṁ vā tiracchānayoniṁ vā.* A similar result follows in the case of dog-asceticism.
4. *Hīna sīla.* 5. *Majjhima sīla.* 6. *Paṇita sīla.* Cp. Vis. Mag. 13.
7. *Hānabhāgiya.* 8. *Ṭhitibhāgiya.* 9. *Visesabhāgiya.*
10. *Nibbedhabhāgiya.* For 7-10; see A. III, 427, Vis. Mag. 15.

A certain man fulfils virtue and concentration, is not heedless, but does not arouse aversion — this is called 'partaking of excellence'.

A certain man fulfils virtue and concentration, is not heedless and arouses aversion — this is called 'partaking of penetration'.

SECOND GROUP OF FOUR IN VIRTUE

And again, there is a group of four in virtue: the precepts for bhikkhus, the precepts for bhikkhunīs, the precepts for the not-yet-ordained,[1] and precepts for the white-clothed householders.[2]

What are 'the precepts for bhikkhus'?[3] The *Pātimokkha*-restraints— these are 'the precepts for bhikkhus'.

(What are) 'the precepts for bhikkhunīs'?[4] The *Pātimokkha*-restraints— these are 'the precepts for bhikkhunīs'.

The ten precepts for male and female novices[5] and the precepts for female probationers[6]—these are called 'the precepts for the not-yet ordained'.

The five precepts and the eight precepts for lay-disciples, male and female— these are 'the precepts for the white-clothed householders'.

THIRD GROUP OF FOUR IN VIRTUE

And again, there is a group of four in virtue thus: Virtue that is natural,[7] virtue that is good manners,[8] virtue that is law[9] and virtue that is (the result of) former conditions.[10]

What is 'virtue that is natural'? The virtue of the people of Uttarakuru— this is called 'virtue that is natural'

What is 'virtue that is good manners'? Conduct conforming to rules of clan, caste, country, beliefs and the like—this is called 'virtue that is good manners'.

What is 'virtue that is law'? The virtue (of the mother of the Bodhisatta) when he enters the womb — this is called 'virtue that is law'.

What is 'virtue that is (the result of) former conditions'? The virtue of the Bodhisatta and the Venerable Elder Mahā Kassapa—this is called 'virtue that is (the result of) former conditions'.

FOURTH GROUP OF FOUR IN VIRTUE

And again, there is a group of four in virtue: virtue as virtue, virtue as accumulation, virtue as ending, virtue as complete path of ending.[11]

---

1. *Anupasampanna sīla.* 2. *Odāta-vasana gahaṭṭha sīla.* Cp. D. III, 125: *Santi kho pana me Cunda etarahi upāsakā sāvakā gihī odāta-vasanā brahmacārino.* 3. *Bhikkhu sīla.*
4. *Bhikkhunī sīla.* 5. *Sāmaṇera-sāmaṇerī dasa sīla.* Cp. Vis. Mag. 15.
6. *Sikkhamānā sīla.* 7. *Pakati sīla.* 8. *Ācāra sīla.* 9. *Dhammatā sīla.* D. II, 13: *Dhammatā esā bhikkave, yadā Bodhisatto mātu kucchiṁ okkanto hoti, na Bodhisattamātu purisesu mānasaṁ uppajjati kāmaguṇūpasaṁhitaṁ, anatikkamaniyā ca Bodhisattamātā hoti kenaci purisena ratta-cittena. Ayaṁ ettha dhammatā.*
10. *Pubbahetuka sīla.* Cp. Vis. Mag. 15.
11. Not in Vis. Mag.—*Kusala sīla, samuṭṭhāna sīla, nirodha sīla, nirodha paṭipadā sīla.*

What is 'virtue as virtue'? Two kinds: skilful and unskilful virtue — these are called 'virtue as virtue'.[1]

What is 'virtue as accumulation'? A good heart accumulates skilful virtue; a bad heart accumulates unskilful virtue.[2]

What is 'virtue as ending'? A man ends unskilful virtue through the acquisition of skilful virtue; a man ends skilful virtue through the accomplishment of sanctity.[3]

What is 'virtue as complete path of ending'? Namely, the four-fold right effort[4] — this is called 'virtue as complete path of ending'. The four-fold activity is to be understood thus: It is called energy and is not real observance of virtue — this is named 'right effort'.

FIFTH GROUP OF FOUR IN VIRTUE

And again, there is a group of four in virtue: virtue of the rules-of-the-order restraint,[5] virtue of the purity of livelihood,[6] virtue of faculty restraint,[7] virtue connected with the requisites.[8]

What is 'virtue of the rules-of-the-order-restraint'? Here a bhikkhu dwells, being restrained by rules-of-the-order restraint, is endowed with good behaviour and lawful resort, fears even a small fault and well trains himself in the precepts in which he should be trained.[9] 'Here' means in this Master's teaching. 'Bhikkhu' means good commoner. Also it means learner, learning-ender, unshakable one.[10] 'Rules-of-the-order-restraint' means virtue, manifestation, beginning, activities, protection, restraint, sloughing and unbinding. This is the entrance into the doctrines. By this the Good Law[11] is accepted. This is the meaning of 'rules-of-the-order'. Not transgressing through bodily and verbal action is 'restraint'. 'Restrained' means accomplished in the rules-of-the-order-restraint. 'Dwells' means guards the four postures. 'Is endowed with good behaviour and lawful resort':— (In this) there is good behaviour[12] and there is misbehaviour.[13]

---

1. Cp. (a) M. II, 27: *Katame ca, thapati, kusalasīlā? Kusalaṁ kāyakammaṁ, kusalaṁ vacīkammaṁ, ājīvapārisuddhiṁ pi kho ahaṁ, thapati, sīlasmiṁ vadāmi. Ime kho, thapati, kusalasīlā;* (b) M. II, 26: *Katame ca, thapati, akusalasīlā? Akusalaṁ kāyakammaṁ, akusalaṁ vacīkammaṁ, pāpako ājīvo, — ime vuccanti, thapati, akusalasīlā.*
2. Cp. (a) M. II, 27: *Yaṁ cittaṁ vītarāgaṁ vītadosaṁ vītamohaṁ, itosamuṭṭhānā kusalasīlā,* (b) M. II, 26: *Sacittaṁ sarāgaṁ sadosaṁ samohaṁ, itosamuṭṭhānā akusalasīlā.*
3. Cp. M.II,26 (a): *Idha, thapati, bhikkhu kāyaduccaritaṁ pahāya kāyasucaritaṁ bhāveti... manoduccaritaṁ pahāya manosucaritaṁ bhāveti, micchā-ājīvaṁ pahāya sammā-ājīvena jīvikaṁ kappeti. Etth'ete akusalasīlā aparisesā nirujjhanti,* (b) M. II, 27: *Idha, thapati, bhikkhu sīlavā hoti, no ca sīlamayo, tañ ca cetovimuttiṁ paññāvimuttiṁ yathābhūtaṁ pajānāti, yatth'assa te kusalasīlā aparisesā nirujjhanti.*
4. Cp. M. II, 27: *Idha, thapati, bhikkhu anuppannānaṁ pāpakānaṁ akusalānaṁ dhammānaṁ anuppādāya chandaṁ janeti vāyamati viriyaṁ ārabhati cittaṁ paggaṇhāti padahati, uppannānaṁ akusalānaṁ dhammānaṁ pahānāya—pe—anuppannānaṁ akusalānaṁ dhammānaṁ uppādāya, uppannānaṁ kusalānaṁ dhammānaṁ ṭhitiyā asammosāya bhiyyobhāvāya vepullāya bhāvanāya pāripūriyā chandaṁ janeti vāyamati viriyaṁ ārabhati cittaṁ paggaṇhāti padahati. Evaṁ paṭipanno kho, thapati, kusalānaṁ sīlānaṁ nirodhāya paṭipanno hoti.*
5. *Pātimokkhasaṁvara sīla.* 6. *Ājīvapārisuddhi sīla.* 7. *Indriyasaṁvara sīla.*
8. *Paccayanissita sīla.* 9. D. I, 63-70. 10. *Sekha, asekha, akuppaṁ.* 11. *Saddhamma.*
12. *Ācāra.* 13. *Anācāra.*

What is 'misbehaviour'? "Here a bhikkhu gives someone bamboo staves, or flowers, leaves and fruits, or tooth-sticks and bath-powder; or he courts favour, speaking well or ill of others; or he is given to fawning; or he runs hither and thither and to far off places contrary to the rule, in order to invite folk to an assembly; or does such other actions censured by the Buddha and thus subsists by wrong livelihood—this is called 'misbehaviour'.[1]

And again, there are two kinds of 'misbehaviour': bodily and verbal misbehaviour. What is 'bodily misbehaviour'? A certain bhikkhu goes to the midst of the assembly of the Order with pride in his heart, brushing past the venerable ones; he recklessly pushes them, or goes forward, or haughtily stands, or sits on a high seat before the venerable ones (sit), or keeps back the venerable ones, or sits pompously, or disdainful of the venerable ones disposes himself on a seat; or patting them (the venerable ones) on the shoulder, he speaks lightly to them. While the venerable ones go barefooted, he wears sandals. When aged and venerable ones walk on the path below, he walks on the high and broad road above. In various ways he slights and troubles (others). He withholds what is good from the younger bhikkhus. He gives what is mean to the venerable ones. Without permission, he burns fuel in the bath-room and opens and shuts the door. Or when he goes to the water-side, he enters it (the water) before them (the venerable ones) and twists and turns his body, or pats, in the fashion of rustics. When he goes to another's house he enters abruptly, either by the back or by the front door; sits down and gets up in a disorderly manner; or he enters screened places and jokes with women and young girls and strokes their necks. Such misconduct is called 'misbehaviour' of body.[2]

What is 'verbal misbehaviour'? A certain bhikkhu has no reverence in his mind. Without finding out the wishes of the venerable ones he preaches on the Law or he preaches on the *Pātimokkha;* or he speaks to others patting them on the shoulder; or he enters another's house and asks of a woman bluntly thus: "Madam so and so of such and such a family, is there or is there not anything to eat? If there is, let me have it. I want to get food". Such words are 'verbal misbehaviour'.[3]

What is 'good behaviour'? It is the opposite of 'misbehaviour'. A certain bhikkhu has reverence in his mind, is obedient, is possessed of modesty and decorum and is thoroughly skilled in the postures. He has enough always, guards his senses and is abstemious as regards food and drink. He

---

1. *Kāyika anācāra.* Cp. Vbh. 246: *Idh'ekacco veḷudānena vā pattadānena vā pupphadānena vā phaladānena vā sināнadānena vā dantakaṭṭhadānena vā cāṭukamyatāya vā muggasūpatāya vā pāribhaṭṭhatāya vā janghapesanikena vā aññataraññatarena buddhapaṭikuṭṭhena micchā ājīvena jīvitaṁ kappeti: ayaṁ vuccati anācāro.*

   Cp. also Th. 937, 938: *Mattikaṁ telaṁ cuṇṇañ ca udakāsanabhojanaṁ gihīnaṁ upanāmenti ākaṅkhantā bahuttaraṁ danta-poṇaṁ kapiṭṭhañ ca pupphakhādaniyāni ca piṇḍapāte ca sampanne ambe āmalakāni ca.*

2. *Kāyika anācāra.* Cp. Nd[1] 228-9.
3. *Vācasika anācāra.* Cp. Nd[1] 230.

never sleeps in the first and last watches of the night. He is endowed with wisdom and is aware of the paucity of his wishes. He is not troubled with worldly cares, is of energetic mind and deeply honours his companions. This is called 'good behaviour'.

'Lawful resort' means lawful resort and unlawful resort. What is 'unlawful resort'? "A certain bhikkhu goes to a harlot's abode, a widow's abode, a virgin's abode, a eunuch's abode, a bhikkunī's abode, to liquor shops; he associates with kings, ministers, heretical monks, evil monks and with such fellows as have no heart of faith, never benefit the four classes and who are disliked by them (the four classes). This is called 'unlawful resort'".[1] The Buddha has declared: "A bhikkhu transgresses (the precept against) impure unlawful resort. What is 'impure unlawful resort'? It is to go to a harlot's abode". 'Lawful resort' is obvious.

And again, there are three kinds of 'lawful resort': lawful resort as close reliance,[2] lawful resort as protection,[3] lawful resort as a bond.[4]

[403] What is 'lawful resort as close reliance'? It is a good friend endowed with the ten meritorious qualities.[5] Owing to these qualities a man hears what he has not heard before and what has been heard is further expounded to him, he destroys doubt, attains to right views and clarity (of mind); and training himself well in the Law, believes strongly and deeply, and increases in virtue, learning, liberality and wisdom.[6] This is called 'lawful resort as close reliance'.

What is 'lawful resort as protection'? When a certain bhikkhu goes to others' houses or to the village, he walks looking groundwards and not further than a fathom's distance; his bearing is dignified, calm and orderly; he is reverenced by the people; he does not look at elephant-chariots or horse-chariots, or at men and women making merry, or at the balcony of the palace, or at street-stalls. Thus he does not look up and down in the four directions. This is called 'lawful resort as protection'.

What is 'lawful resort as a bond'? It is as the Buddha has said: "A bhikkhu dwells within the precincts of his home and land"[7] — this is called 'lawful resort as a bond'. These are called 'lawful resort'. Thus 'lawful resort' is fulfilled. Therefore, it is said, 'endowed with lawful resort'.

---

1. *Gocara* and *agocara*. Cp. Vbh. 247: *Idh'ekacco vesiyāgocaro vā hoti, vidhavāgocaro vā thullakumārīgocaro vā paṇḍakagocaro vā bhikkhunīgocaro vā pānāgāragocaro vā, saṁsaṭṭho viharati rājūhi rājamahāmattehi titthiyehi titthiyasāvakehi ananulomikena gihisaṁsaggena, yāni vā pana tāni kulāni assaddhāni appasannāni anopānabhūtāni akkosakaparibhāsakāni anatthakāmāni ahitakāmāni aphāsukāmāni ayogakkhemakāmāni bhikkhūnaṁ bhikkhunīnaṁ upāsakānaṁ upāsikānaṁ, tathārūpāni kulāni sevati bhajati payirupāsati: ayaṁ vuccati agocaro.*
2. *Upanissayagocara.* 3. *Ārakkhagocara.* 4. *Upanibandhagocara.*
5. *Dasakathāvatthuguṇasamannāgatakalyāṇamitta.* Cp. A. IV, 357: *Puna ca paraṁ Meghiya bhikkhu yāyaṁ kathā abhisallekhikā cetovivaraṇasappāyā, seyyathidaṁ appicchakathā santuṭṭhikathā pavivekakathā asaṁsaggakathā viriyārambhakathā sīlakathā samādhikathā paññākathā vimuttikathā vimuttiñāṇadassanakathā.*
6. Cp. Vis. Mag. 19.
7. Cp. S. V, 148: *Ko ca bhikkhave bhikkhuno gocaro sako pettiko visayo yad idaṁ cattāro satipaṭṭhānā.*

'Fears even a small fault' means fears the small faults committed in the course of training — this is called 'fears even a small fault'.

And again, there is another teaching: One arouses unskilful states of consciousness — this is called slight error. One wishes to dwell far from this 'slight error' seeing and fearing the retribution thereof. This is called seeing danger in 'slight error'.

'Trains himself in the precepts in which he should be trained' — What is the meaning of 'should be trained'? It means the seven groups of restraint.[1] 'Trains himself' means follows all (as taught above). This is called 'trains himself (in the precepts) in which he should be trained'. This is called 'virtue of the rules-of-the-order-restraint'.

Q. What is 'virtue of purity (of livelihood)'? *A.* It is to be not guilty of wrong livelihood. What is wrong livelihood? It is trickery,[2] talkativeness,[3] insinuation,[4] detraction,[5] and giving in order to get more.[6]

What is 'trickery'? There are three bases of 'trickery': —

One schemes, and wants to have the four requisites, coarse and different (from the fine requisites offered to one): a certain bhikkhu corrects his behaviour, temporarily, advertises himself widely, or harbours evil desires; coveting property, he hands over excellent robes and food (to others), and for himself wants what is coarse; or, he pretends as if he did not want to get (any); or, he accepts the four requisites simulating compassion for others—this is called the 'trickery' of scheming for requisites.[7]

A certain bhikkhu having evil desires and coveting property, simulates dignified demeanour, and says: 'I have attained to meditation (*jhāna*)' and recites the Discourses wishing to receive offerings — this is called the 'trickery' of the postures.[8]

A certain bhikkhu who is covetous and talkative, declares to others: "I possess the Ariyan Truth and dwell in solitude;" or, "I practise meditation," "My preaching is deep and subtle," "I possess the signs of a superman."[9] Thus, desiring gain, he extols himself. This is called the 'trickery' (of round-about talk).[10]

Talkativeness means one is not genuine, flatters, jests and poses, hoping for gain. One causes amusement longing to attract gain to oneself. This is called talkativeness.

What is 'insinuation'? A bhikkhu preaches the Law to a rich man whose support he desires. He longs for benefits and does not endeavour for mastery over his own heart. This is called 'insinuation'.

---

1. *Sattāpattikkhandha: pārājika, sanghādisesa, thullaccaya, pācittiya, pāṭidesanīya, dukkaṭa, dubbhāsita.* 2. Should read *kuhanā*. The ideograph means *kosajja*. 3. *Lapanā*. The ideograph also means *vaṅkatā*. 4. *Nemittikatā*. 5. *Nippesikatā*. 6. *Lābhena lābhaṁ nijigiṁsanatā*. For 2-6 Cp. Vbh. 352-3. 7. Nd[1] 224: *Paccayapaṭisevanasaṁkhātaṁ kuhanavatthu*. 8. Ibid: *Iriyāpathasaṁkhātaṁ kuhanavatthu*.
9. These are quite different from the details given at pp. 25-6 in the Vis. Mag. on the same subject. 10. Nd[1] 226: *Sāmantajappanasaṁkhātaṁ kuhanavatthu*.

'Detraction' means that a man wishing to gain benefits, causes people to fear him, because he abuses them, or because he creates dissensions among them; or terrifies people with harmful actions.

What is 'giving in order to get more'? He makes small offerings and expects great returns. This is called 'giving in order to get more'. These many evil actions constitute wrong livelihood.

And again, there is another (teaching concerning) wrong livelihood: (It is) giving bamboo staves, or flowers, leaves and fruits, or tooth-sticks and bath-powder; or, it is to divine, or to interpret dreams, or to make astrological predictions, or to interpret the language of birds, or to conjecture concerning the auspiciousness or inauspiciousness of modes of walking; it is to worship fire[1] and to offer flowers to it; or it is to drive a prosperous trade; or it is to lead armies; or it is to deal in sharp weapons. These, and such other activities constitute wrong livelihood. The not doing of these is called 'virtue of the purity (of livelihood)'.

Q. What is 'virtue of the restraint of the faculties'?

A. On seeing a form, hearing a sound, smelling an odour, tasting a flavour or contacting a tangible, a man resolves to be not entranced by the defiling aspects thereof, and he does not transgress.[2] This is called 'virtue of the restraint of the faculties'. This 'virtue of the restraint of the faculties' is fulfilled through nine activities[3]:—

Through cutting down the signs of evil which arise in the faculties; through overcoming non-mindfulness; through not letting (evil states of consciousness) to continue, as (in the simile of) the man who saves his burning head;[4] through restraint comparable to that of the Venerable Elder Nanda;[5] through conquering evil states of consciousness; through attaining to concentration of mind with ease; through living apart from men who do not guard the faculties; and through living in the company of those who guard the faculties.

Q. What is 'virtue connected with the requisites'?

A. Through eight ways one wisely reflects in accepting alms thus:

The first: one does not take (food and drink) for the sake of violent sport or intoxication; the second: one does not take (food and drink) for the sake of personal charm or beautification; the third; one takes (food and drink) in order to sustain the body and to preserve it; the fourth: one takes (food and drink) in order to stay hunger and thirst; the fifth: one takes (food and drink) in order to observe the holy life; the sixth: one always thinks that food and drink are intended to remove old ills and not to allow new ills

---

1. D. I. 9: *Aggi-homa.*
2. Cp. D. I, 70.
3. Only eight are treated in the explanation which follows.
4. Cp. S. III, 143: *Evaṁ khandhe avekkheyya bhikkhu āraddhaviriyo*
   divā vā yadi vā rattiṁ sampajāno patissato.
   Jaheyya sabbasaññogaṁ kareyya saraṇattamo
   Careyyādittasiso va patthayaṁ accutaṁ padaṁ.
5. Cp. A. I, 25: *Etad aggaṁ....indriyesu-gutta-dvārānaṁ yadidaṁ Nando.*

to arise; the seventh: one takes (food and drink) finding satisfaction with little; the eighth: one takes (food and drink) faultlessly and dwells in comfort.[1]

Q. What is 'one does not take (food and drink) for the sake of violent sport or intoxication'?

A. "I take food greedily. I am strong. Therefore, I like violent sport, rough play, competing with others and running." These constitute 'violent sport'. 'Intoxication' means self-arrogance and dissatisfaction. It is likened to the state of an angry man who beats another. 'Not for the sake of personal charm and beautification': (Not like) those who wish to be loved for the fullness of their body and limbs and good looks, and do not know contentment, being full of desires. 'One takes (food and drink) in order to sustain the body and to preserve it': As a hub needs oil, so one yearns for the peaceful preservation of the body. 'One takes (food and drink) in order to stay hunger and thirst': One, always, takes little food. As a man uses medicine for a disease of the skin, so one takes. 'One takes (food and drink) in order to observe the holy life': One wishes to reach the Noble Path through the advantages of abstemiousness. Feeling as a man who eats the flesh of his child, one takes.[2] 'Intended to remove old ills and not to allow new ills to arise': One takes not too little and not too much. As a man taking a mixture, so one takes. 'One takes (food and drink) finding satisfaction in little': One keeps one's body safe accepting little, always treating one's body as a nurse (treats a patient). 'Faultlessly' means one sets one's body at ease with little. Using in this way, one makes the body faultless and escapes the reproof of the wise. Thus 'one takes (food and drink) faultlessly and dwells in comfort'.

If one's food is suitable, one never feels tired and one does not sleep in the first, middle and last watches of the night. In this way one fulfils tranquillity. Thus 'through eight ways one wisely reflects in accepting alms'. Thus one should accept.

And again, these eight ways are shortened to four considerations: the consideration of what ought to be cut down, the consideration of reality, the consideration of being satisfied with little, the consideration of accepting little.

Q. What is 'the consideration of what ought to be cut down'?

A. The state of not being addicted to 'violent sport', not being in a state of 'intoxication' and the state of not being concerned with 'personal charm and beautification' — these are called 'the consideration of what ought to be cut down'.

Using 'in order to sustain the body and to preserve it', 'in order to stay hunger and thirst', and 'in order to observe the holy life' — these are called 'the consideration of reality'.

---

1. A. II, 40: *Idha bhikkhave bhikkhu paṭisaṅkhā yoniso āhāraṁ āhāreti, n'eva davāya na madāya na maṇḍanāya na vibhūsanāya yāvad eva imassa kāyassa ṭhitiyā yāpanāya vihiṁsūparatiyā brahmacariyānuggahāya: iti purāṇañ ca vedanaṁ paṭihaṅkhāmi navañ ca vedanaṁ na uppādessāmi, yātrā ca me bhavissati anavajjatā ca phāsu-vihāro cāti.*
2. S. II, 98. Also Th. 445: *Uppajje ce rase taṇhā puttamaṁsūpamaṁ sara.*

"I shall subdue the old ills and I shall cause no new ills to arise" — this is called 'the consideration of being satisfied with little'.

"I shall satisfy myself with little and, being faultless, I shall dwell in comfort" — this is called 'the consideration of accepting little'. These are the four considerations.

These four considerations are further shortened to three thus: consideration of cutting down, consideration of mean (lit. taking the middle between two ends), consideration of completion.

A man cuts down the attachment to sense-pleasures through the 'consideration of cutting down' i.e., removes hunger and thirst, destroys the old ills and does not cause new ills to arise. And again, by this 'consideration' a man destroys karmic weariness of the body. The others should be practised in the 'consideration of mean' and the 'consideration of completion'.

And when one reflects on robes he understands that robes are for protection against wind, cold, heat, mosquitoes, gadflies and ants and for covering one's unsightly shame-producing parts. Thus one practises 'consideration of completion'.[1]

And again, one reflects on medicines for ailments.[2]

If that is so, when should one make consideration?

As regards food and the taking of medicine one should make consideration whenever one takes (food and medicine). As regards robes and bedding one should make consideration at the time one accepts. And every day and every hour should one think thus: My life depends on others; therefore, I ought always to reflect'.[3] Thus one should consider everything.

There are four kinds of use taught by predecessors thus: use as theft, use as debt, use as inheritance and use like a master.[4]

What is 'use as theft'? Use (of requisites) by the transgressor of the precepts.

What is 'use as debt'? Use (of requisites) by individuals guilty of immodesty, indecorum and wrong livelihood.

What is 'use as inheritance'? Use (of requisites) by individuals who are strenuous.

What is 'use like a master'? Use (of requisites) by the consummate ones.

And again, there are two kinds of use. Namely, unclean use and clean use.

What is 'unclean'? (Use of requisites by an) individual having modesty and decorum but who is not capable of wise reflection — this is called 'unclean'.

---

1. M. I, 10: *Paṭisaṅkhā yoniso cīvaraṁ paṭisevati yāvad eva sītassa paṭighātāya uṇhassa paṭighātāya ḍaṁsamakasavātātapasiriṁsapa samphassānaṁ paṭighātāya yāvad eva hirikopīnapaṭicchādanatthaṁ.*
2. Ibid.
3. A.V, 87—8: *Parapaṭibaddhā me jīvikā ti pabbajitena abhiṇhaṁ paccavekkhitabbaṁ.*
4. J. V, 253: *Theyyaparibhoga, iṇaparibhoga, dāyajjaparibhoga, sāmiparibhoga.* Vis. Mag. does not attribute these four to the 'ancients' (*porāṇā*) as it is done here.

(Use of requisites by an) individual having modesty and decorum, who reflects wisely, knows, is self-moderated and is possessed of aversion — this is called 'clean'. In this cleanliness one ought to train oneself always. Thus one should understand the four requisites. This is called 'virtue connected with the requisites'.

FIFTH GROUP OF FOUR IN VIRTUE SUMMARIZED

Thus 'virtue of the rules-of-the-order-restraint' should be fulfilled through higher faith; 'virtue of purity of livelihood' should be fulfilled through higher energy; [404] 'virtue of the restraint of faculties' should be fulfilled through higher faith and 'virtue connected with the requisites' should be fulfilled through higher wisdom.

Thus 'virtue of the purity of livelihood' goes together with the rules of the order, *Pātimokkha*. Why? Because, through separation from worldly affairs owing to non-attachment, one becomes quiet of behaviour and acquires restraint of bodily and verbal actions. These two kinds of virtue belong to the 'virtue of the restraint of faculties'. What is the reason? If a man guards his mind in goodness, he can well protect his bodily and verbal actions. '(Virtue) connected with the requisites' is 'restraint of faculties'. What is the reason? One knows the aggregations and their dependence and is disgusted with them, and dwells in Right Mindfulness and Right Concentration. It is as taught by the Blessed One thus: "A bhikkhu understands material food and the five-fold lust".

'Rules-of-the-order-restraint' and 'purity of livelihood' belong to the 'group of virtue'; 'virtue of the restraint of faculties' belongs to the 'group of concentration' and 'virtue connected with the requisites' belongs to the 'group of wisdom'.

WHAT PURIFIES VIRTUE

'What purifies virtue'? If a bhikkhu who has accepted the teaching of meditation[1] and is mindful of the seven groups of offences, sees another committing a Defeat-offence[2] he falls from the state of a bhikkhu and lives in incomplete virtue. If he lives in complete virtue, he will acquire the excellent virtue. If he lives in complete virtue, he will acquire the excellent truth. This is the teaching of the predecessors.

If a bhikkhu sees another committing a Suspension-offence[3] he confesses fully. If he sees another committing any other offence, then he confesses concerning that transgression to one person.[4]

If a bhikkhu sees another[5] committing wrong livelihood, he makes a proper confession concerning that transgression. After he confesses, he resolves: "I will not do it again." Thus having seen, he resolves.

---

1. *Jhāna dhamma*. 2. *Pārājika*. 3. *Sanghādisesa*. 4. *Āpattidesanā*.
5. Probably should read "himself".

When he transgresses '(virtue of) the restraint of faculties' or '(virtue) connected with the requisites' he says: "I will not do it again". If he resolves he will acquire excellent restraint in the future.

When a bhikkhu practises the purity of virtue, he does bodily and verbal actions that ought to be done. He reflects on his actions. He does well and removes ill. Reflecting thus he dwells in the purity of virtue, day and night. Thus doing he is able to purify his virtue.

What is the salient characteristic of the purity of virtue?[1] One can control the passions,[2] destroy rigidity[3] and fulfil concentration.[4] This is the salient characteristic of the purity of virtue.

CAUSES THROUGH WHICH ONE DWELLS IN VIRTUE

'Owing to how many causes does one dwell in virtue?' Through two, one dwells in virtue. The first: one considers the tribulation of the transgression of virtue; the second: one considers the merits of virtue.

What is to consider 'tribulation'? If a man transgresses virtue, he makes demerit and prepares evil places (for himself) and fears the four classes[5] and doubting, blames the wise. Those who are virtuous avoid him. He is not taught meditation. Heavenly beings despise him. He is hated and slighted by all. When he hears others praising the merit of those who are virtuous, he feels sorrowful but does not believe it (the merit of those who are virtuous). He is always angry when he is amongst those of the four classes. He dislikes and hates (good) companions. He opposes those who are virtuous and takes the side of evil companions.

And again, he has not the patience to enter into the way of excellent concentration. If he adorns himself, he looks, especially, ugly. He is disliked even as excrement and urine are disliked by men. (He does not endure) even as a makeshift article does not last long. (He is worthless) even as mud is of no value in the present or the future. He is anxious and dejected always. He is ashamed and remorseful of the evil he has done and he has no peace of mind, like a thief in prison. He has no desire for the Noble (Law), as an outcast has no desire for a king's throne.[6] Though he is learned in the doctrine of wisdom, yet none honour him, even as a dung-fire (is honoured by none). He cannot find a good place in this life and after death he will go to an evil state.

If a man wishes to forsake evil and fulfil the merits of virtue, he should consider thus: The mind of the transgressor of virtue is distracted and dejected. The virtuous man, through strenuous endeavour, grows in belief and becomes an energetic individual endowed with faith.

---

1. *Sīlavisuddhi.* 2. *Kilesa.* 3. *Thīna.* 4. *Samādhi.*
5. Cp. D. II, 85: *Puna ca paraṁ gahapatayo dussīlo sīla-vipanno yaṁ yad eva parisaṁ upasaṁkamati yadi khattiya-parisaṁ yadi brāmaṇa-parisaṁ yadi gahapati-parisaṁ yadi samaṇa-parisaṁ, avisārado upasaṁkamati maṅku-bhūto.*
6. Vis. Mag. 54: *Nirāso saddhamme caṇḍālakumārako viya rajje.*

A man should protect his virtue, with all his strength, as an ant protects her egg, as a yak loves his tail, as one protects an only son or one's sole eye,[1] as a diviner protects himself, as a poor man protects his treasure and as a fisherman protects his boat. More (strenuously) than these should he honour and protect the virtue he has undertaken to observe. If he thus observes, his mind will be guarded, he will dwell in the peace of concentration and his virtue will acquire protection.

---

1. (a) J. III, 375: *Satthā attano sāvake rattiyā tayo vāre divasassa tayo vāre ti rattiṁdivaṁ cha vāre olokento kikī vā aṇḍaṁ viya camarī va vāladhiṁ viya mātā piyaputtaṁ viya ekacakkhuko puriso cakkhuṁ viya rakkhati, tasmiṁ tasmiṁ yeva khaṇe uppannakilesaṁ niggaṇhati.*

   (b) Vis Mag. 36, and Sddh.v. 621:

   Kiki va aṇḍaṁ camarīva vāladhiṁ
   Piyaṁ va puttaṁ nayanaṁ va ekakaṁ,
   Tath' eva sīlaṁ anurakhamānakā,
   Supesalā hotha sadā sagāravā.

   (c) Ap. 61, v.16: *Kikī va aṇḍaṁ rakkheyya camarī-r-iva vāladhiṁ*
   nipako sīlasampanno mamaṁ rakkhi mahāmuni.

   In the Pali passages, (a), (b) and (c) above instead of *ant* the bird, *blue jay*, (*kikī*) occurs.

THE PATH OF FREEDOM

FASCICLE THE SECOND

WRITTEN

BY

THE ARAHANT UPATISSA

WHO WAS CALLED

GREAT LIGHT IN RYO

TRANSLATED IN RYO

BY

TIPIṬAKA SANGHAPĀLA OF FUNAN

ON AUSTERITIES[1]

CHAPTER THE THIRD

Q. Now, if a yogin who dwells in pure virtue aspires to accomplish excellent good merits and wishes to acquire the benefits of the austerities, he should consider thus: "Why should one acquire the benefits of the austerities"?

A. Because of the varying disposition of the yogin. For paucity of wishes, for contentment with little, for freedom from doubt, for the destruction of craving, for the increase of energy, for the sake of using little and not accepting the offerings made to others, for solitude, for the cutting down of clinging and for the protection of moral virtue. These (the merits of the austerities) are the equipment of concentration. These are (practices of) the ancient lineage of the Ariyas.[2] These are the excellent considerations.

THE THIRTEEN AUSTERITIES

What are the austerities? There are thirteen teachings:[3] two teachings connected with robes, namely, dirt-rags*[4] and three robes;†[5] five teachings connected with alms, namely, begged food,†[6] regular alms-round,*[7] one eating,*[8] measured food,*[9] no food after time;*[10] five teachings connected with residence: the first: dwelling in a peaceful place,*[11] the second: dwelling under a tree,*[12] the third: dwelling in a dewy place,*[13] the fourth: dwelling among the graves,*[14] the fifth: any chanced upon place;*[15] and there is a kind of sitting connected with energy, namely, always sitting and not lying down.*[16]

---

1. *Dhuta* (transliteration).
2. Cp.Vis.Mag. 59.
3. Ibid.
4. *Paṁsukūlika-anga.*
5. *Tecīvarika-°.*

† A. I, 38.

6. *Piṇḍapātika-°.*
7. *Sapadānacārika-*
8. *Ekāsanika-'*
9. *Pattapiṇḍika-* .
10. *Khalupacchābhattika-*

* A. III, 219-20

11. *Āraññika-* .
12. *Rukkhamūlika-*
13. *Abbhokāsika-°.*
14. *Sosānika-°.*
15. *Yathāsanthatika-*
16. *Nesajjika-°.*

BRIEF EXPLANATION OF THE THIRTEEN AUSTERITIES

What is the quality of 'dirt-rags'? *A*. The quality of enabling to observe — this is the quality of dirt-rags'. Others are similar.

What is the meaning of the observance of dirt-rags'? The non-acceptance of gifts of householders.

What is the meaning of the observance of 'three robes'? The rejection of extra robes.

What is the meaning of the observance of 'begged food'? The non-acceptance of the invitations of others.

What is the meaning of the observance of 'regular alms-round'? The abandoning of skipped begging.

What is the meaning of the observance of 'one-eating'? The not sitting again.

What is the meaning of the observance of 'measured food'? The abandoning of greed.

What is the meaning of the observance of 'refusing food after time'? The abandoning of the desire to eat afterwards.

What is the meaning of the observance of 'dwelling in a peaceful place'? The abandoning of dwelling in a village.

What is the meaning of the observance of 'dwelling under a tree'? The abandoning of dwelling in a house.

What is the meaning of the observance of 'dwelling in a dewy place'? The abandoning of dwelling in sheltered places.

What is the meaning of the observance of 'dwelling among the graves'? The abandoning of dwelling in other and in good places.

What is the meaning of the observance of 'any chanced upon place'? The abandoning of desire for pleasant places.

What is the meaning of the observance of 'always sitting and not lying down'? The abandoning of beds.

'DIRT-RAGS'

How does one undertake to observe (the austerity of) 'dirt-rags'? One sees the fault of asking householders for robes and the merit of 'dirt-rags' (and undertakes thus:) "I refuse the offerings of householders and observe (the austerity of) 'dirt-rags' ".

What are the benefits of the observance of 'dirt-rags'? ('Dirt-rags') are just as useful as householders' robes[1] and are enough. One does not depend on others. There is no fear of losing, and one is not attached. Thieves do not want 'dirt-rags'. ('Dirt-rags') are always sufficient for one's purpose.

1. *Gahapaticivara*, robes offered by householders.

In getting ('dirt-rags') one is not troubled and (this observance) will be an example to good folk. This observance is proper to those who are doubt-free and virtuous. One lives happily in this life. (This observance) will cause one to be liked by the people, and cause them to practise rightly. These are the benefits of the observance of 'dirt-rags' praised by the Buddha.[1]

Q. How many kinds of 'dirt-rags' are there? Who observes?[2] How does one fail?

A. There are two kinds of 'dirt-rags'. The first: 'dirt-rags' which are ownerless, the second: 'dirt-rags' which are thrown away by people.

Those which one picks up in a cemetery, from a dirt-heap, in the street, or from the road-side and cuts, dyes, pieces together, sews to completion and uses, are called " 'dirt-rags' which are ownerless". Remnants of cut-cloth, torn pieces of cattle-bitten, mouse-gnawed or burnt cloth and cloth thrown away, cloth on corpses, and cast-off cloth of ascetics are called " 'dirt-rags' which are thrown away by people".

What is the observance of 'dirt-rags'? When a bhikkhu refuses the offerings of householders, it is called the observance of 'dirt-rags'.

How does one fail? When a bhikkhu accepts the offerings of householders, it is called failing.

'THREE ROBES'

How does one undertake to observe (the austerity of) 'three robes'? One immediately gives up one's extra robes. Knowing the fault of keeping (extra robes) and seeing the benefits of the observance of 'three robes', (one undertakes thus:) "I refuse extra robes from today and observe (the austerity of) 'three robes'".

What are the benefits of the observance of 'three robes'? It is an observance of good men. A bhikkhu gives up the hoarding of unnecessaries, lessens troubles and becomes modest. As a bird on wing that does not yearn for what it leaves behind is filled with content, so is he. [405] One gets a following of good men. This observance is doubt-free.

Q. What are 'three robes'? What is the observance? How does one fail?

A. Shoulder cloak,[3] upper garment[4] and waist-cloth.[5] These are called 'three robes'.

What is the observance of 'three robes'? When a bhikkhu does not hoard extra robes, it is called the observance of 'three robes'. When a bhikkhu accepts a fourth robe, it is called failing.

---

1. A. III, 219: '*Vaṇṇitaṁ buddhehi buddhasāvakehi*'.
2. According to the explanation which follows, this should be "what is the observance of 'dirt-rags'?"
3. *Saṅghāṭi*. 4. *Uttarāsaṅga*. 5. *Antaravāsaka*.

'BEGGED FOOD'

How does one undertake to observe (the austerity of) 'begged food'? If a bhikkhu accepts an invitation, he interrupts his activities and is not at ease. One sees these draw-backs and the merits of the observance of 'begged food' (and undertakes thus:) "I refuse invitations from today and observe (the austerity of 'begged food')".

What are the benefits of the observance of 'begged food'? One is free to go or stay according to one's wishes. One does not need food to be prepared. One destroys rigidity and pride. One is not greedy of delicacies. One permits others to be benefitted and is never attached to any quarter. One gets a following of good men. This observance is doubt-free.

Q. How many kinds of invitations are there? What is the observance? How does one fail?

A. There are three kinds of invitations.

The first: (general) invitation, the second: invitation to visit, the third: repeated invitation.[1]

The non-acceptance of these three kinds of invitations is the observance of 'begged food'. If a bhikkhu accepts these three kinds of invitations, he fails in the observance of 'begged food'.

'REGULAR ALMS-ROUND'

How does one undertake to observe (the austerity of) 'regular alms-round'? When a bhikkhu is able to obtain tasty food from any house by making a 'regular alms-round', he does not go again (in that direction). If he goes again, it is an ordinary alms-round. If there is a doubtful place he avoids it. One sees these faults (of going again etc.) and the benefits of the observance of 'regular alms-round' (and undertakes thus:) "I abandon the irregular alms-round from today and observe (the austerity of) 'regular alms-round'".

What are the benefits of the observance of 'regular alms-round'? One thinks of benefitting all beings equally, and destroys the fault of enjoyment. One is not pleased when invited, is not pleased with many words, and does not call on householders. One does not walk hurriedly. Rare as the moon at full, one appears and is appreciated and honoured. One gets a following of good men. This observance is doubt-free.

Q. What is a 'regular alms-round'? What is the observance? How does one fail?

A. When a bhikkhu enters a village for alms, he begs in regular order from the last house backwards. This is called 'regular alms-round'.

How does one fail? Skipped begging — this is called failing.

---

1. Cp. Vis. Mag. 66. The Chinese is unclear.

'ONE-EATING'

How does one undertake to observe (the austerity of) 'one-eating'? Eating in two places, eating frequently, taking food frequently, washing the bowl frequently — the opposite of these is 'one-eating'. This is an observance of good men. This observance is doubt-free. One sees the faults (of eating at two places etc.) and the merits of the observance of 'one-eating' (and undertakes thus:) "I abandon eating at two places from today and observe (the austerity of) 'one-eating'".

What are the benefits of the observance of 'one-eating'? One takes neither more nor less. One is not greedy of improper offerings, is not troubled with many ills, is untroubled as regards livelihood, and is happy. This is an observance of good men. This observance is doubt-free.

Q. What is the observance of 'one-eating'? What are the limits?[1] How does one fail?

A. There are three limits: sitting-limit, water-limit, food-limit.

What is 'sitting-limit'? After one ends eating one (cannot) sit again.

After a bhikkhu fetches water and washes his bowl, he cannot eat again. This is called 'water-limit'. What is 'food-limit'? After one thinks: "This lump of food is the last," he should not drink or eat any more. This is called 'food-limit'.

If a bhikkhu sits twice, except in taking liquid-medicine and such other things, he fails in the observance of 'one-eating'. This has been disapproved by the Buddhas. This is called 'food-limit'.

'MEASURED FOOD'

How does one undertake to observe (the austerity of) 'measured food'? If a bhikkhu drinks and eats too much, he increases sleepiness, always hankers for much food, and sets no limit to his appetite. One sees these faults and the merits of the observance of 'measured food' (and undertakes thus:) "From today, I take food without greed, and observe (the austerity of) 'measured food'". This is called undertaking to observe (the austerity of) 'measured food'.

What are the benefits of the observance of 'measured food'? One measures one's meal. One does not eat for belly's sake. One knows that too much eating induces fatigue and therefore one does not desire much, and causes diseases to perish, and abandons rigidity. This is an observance of good men. This observance is doubt-free.

Q. What is the observance of 'measured food'? How does one fail?

---

1. Cp. Vis. Mag. 69.

A. When a bhikkhu receives drink and food, he considers the measure of his wants. He does not take too much food and knows well the (proper) quantity and does not exceed the limit. (This is) called the observance of 'measured food'. If he does otherwise, he fails.

'NO FOOD AFTER TIME'

How does one undertake to observe (the austerity of) 'no food after time'? One abandons expectation and avoids extra food. One knows these faults (expectation etc.) and sees the benefits of the observance of 'no food after time' (and undertakes thus:) "I abandon extra food from today and observe (the austerity of) 'no food after time'".

What are the benefits of the observance of 'no food after time'? One abandons greed, and experiences the joy of self-restraint. One protects the body, and avoids taking food in advance, does not hanker, does not ask others for things, does not follow his inclinations. This is an observance of good men. This observance is doubt-free.

Q. How many kinds of '(no food) after time' are there? What is the observance? How does one fail?

A. There are two kinds of '(no food) after time': immoderate limit, accepting limit.

What is 'immoderate limit'? If a bhikkhu accepts extra food, his offence is (equal to) that of one who accepts food offered to a particular person or persons.[1] He should not eat again. What is 'accepting limit'? A bhikkhu should not accept after he has eaten twenty-one handfuls. If he observes 'no food after time', he abandons extra food. If he accepts extra food he fails in the observance of 'no food after time'.

'DWELLING IN A PEACEFUL PLACE'

How does one undertake (the austerity of) 'dwelling in a peaceful place'? When the village is crowded, one's mind is touched by the five objects of sense and saturated with the desire for pleasure. When one dwells in a crowded place, one is disturbed by people going and coming. One sees these faults and the merits of the observance of 'dwelling in a peaceful place' (and undertakes thus:) "I abandon dwelling in the village from today and observe (the austerity of) 'dwelling in a peaceful place'".

What are the merits of 'peaceful place'? Even when the village is crowded, one's mind is not touched by the five objects of sense and is kept away from attachment. If one dwells in a crowded place, one is disturbed by the going and coming of many: One knows the excellence of the ten kinds of words

1. *Uddesabhatta.*

praised by gods and men. One does not wish to become worldly, and wishes to gain tranquillity. One dwells in solitude, speaks little and meditates, according to one's bent of mind. This is an observance of good men. This observance is doubt-free.

Q. What is the nearest distance of 'dwelling in a peaceful place'? What is the observance? How does one fail?

A. One dwells outside (the village) keeping some distance from the walls and avoiding the far end of the suburb. The nearest distance of 'dwelling in a peaceful place' is five-hundred bow-lengths.[1] One bow-length is four cubits of an average man. Avoidance of dwelling in a village is called 'dwelling in a peaceful place'. If bhikkhu dwells in a village, he fails in the observance of 'dwelling in a peaceful place'.

'DWELLING UNDER A TREE'

How does one undertake to observe (the austerity of) 'dwelling under a tree'? One avoids roofed places. One does not keep animals. One does not build or long for (roofed places). One does not search (for roofed places). One sees the faults (of dwelling in roofed places) and the merits of the observance of '(dwelling) under a tree' (and undertakes thus:) "I abandon roofed places from today and observe (the austerity of) 'dwelling under a tree'. Thus one undertakes to observe.

What are the benefits of '(dwelling) under a tree'? One relies on the place one likes, one does not hold intercourse with the world, one is pleased because one is free from all work, one dwells with the gods, cuts down resentment due to residence, and is free from attachment. This is an observance of good men. This observance is doubt-free.

Q. Under what trees should a bhikkhu dwell? What trees should he avoid? What is the observance? How does one fail?

A. The place on which shadows of trees fall during the day and the place where leaves of trees fall when there is no wind are the places to dwell in. One avoids dangerous decayed trees, rotten trees with hollows and trees haunted by evil spirits. One avoids roofed places. This is the observance of 'dwelling under a tree'. If a bhikkhu goes to (live in) a roofed place, he fails in the observance of 'dwelling under a tree'.

'DWELLING IN A DEWY PLACE'

How does one undertake to observe (the austerity of) 'dwelling in a dewy place'? One does not desire to dwell in roofed places, under trees, and in places where animals and goods are kept. One sees the faults of these, and

---

1. Vin. IV, 183: *Āraññakaṁ senāsanaṁ pañca-dhanusatikaṁ pacchimaṁ.*

the benefits of 'dwelling in a dewy place' (and undertakes thus:) "I avoid unpleasant places from today and observe (the austerity of) 'dwelling in a dewy place'.

What are the benefits of 'dwelling in a dewy place'? One does not go to unpleasant places and abandons negligence and torpor. One goes whithersoever one wills, like a forest-deer and is not attached to any particular place.[1] This is an observance of good men. This observance is doubt-free.

What is the observance? How does one fail? One avoids roofed places and the shelter of trees. This is the observance of 'dwelling in a dewy place'. If one dwells in roofed places and under the shelter of trees, one fails in the observance of 'dwelling in a dewy place'.

'DWELLING AMONG THE GRAVES'

How does one undertake to observe (the austerity of) 'dwelling among the graves'? One who dwells in other places becomes careless and does not fear wrongdoing. One sees these faults and the merits of 'dwelling among the graves' (and undertakes thus:) "I avoid other places from today and observe (the austerity of) 'dwelling among the graves' ". This is the undertaking to observe.

What are the merits of the observance of '(dwelling) among the graves'? One understands the feeling of the time of death. One perceives that all is impure. One acquires the homage of non-humans. One does not cause heedlessness to arise, overcomes passion and is much detached. One does not fear what common folk dread. One contemplates on the emptiness of the body and is able to reject the thought of permanence. This is an observance of good men. This observance is doubt-free.

Q. (What are the merits of 'dwelling among the graves'?). Where should one dwell? What is the observance? How does one fail?

A. If in a place of graves there is always weeping and wailing and smoke and fire, one should consider, find out a calm place, and go to dwell there.

If a bhikkhu dwells 'among the graves', he should not build a hut or make a comfortable bed. He should sit with his back to the wind. He should not sit facing the wind. He should not fall into deep sleep. He should not eat fish. He should not drink milk or buttermilk or eat sesamum or flesh of animals [406]. He should not dwell in a house or use a platter. When a person taking his mat and robes leaves (the monastery) and goes to dwell 'among the graves', he, as it were, flings all his belongings afar. At dawn, he takes mat and robes and returns to the monastery[2] and avoids other dwelling-places. If he dwells in any other place, he breaks or fails in the observance of 'dwelling among the graves'.

---

1. Sn. 39: *Migo araññamhi yathā abandho*
yen' icchakaṁ gacchati gocarāya.
2. *Saṅghārāma* (transliteration).

'ANY CHANCED UPON PLACE'

How does one undertake to observe (the austerity of) 'any chanced upon place'? One does not like the place which men want greedily. One is not troubled when others wish him to leave any place. One sees these faults (greed for place etc.) and the merits of the observance of 'any chanced upon place', (and undertakes thus:) "I abandon the greed for residence and observe (the austerity of) 'any chanced upon place' ". This is the undertaking to observe.

What are the benefits of 'any chanced upon place'? One dwells satisfied with any place, longs for tranquillity, abandons various comforts, is honoured by others, dwells with heart of compassion. This is an observance of good men. This observance is doubt-free.

What is the observance? How does one fail?

To abandon the longing which is dependent on dwelling—this is called dependence on 'any chanced upon place'. If a bhikkhu goes to dwell in a pleasant place, it is called failing.

'ALWAYS SITTING AND NOT LYING DOWN'

How does one undertake to observe (the austerity of) 'always sitting and not lying down'? One sees the faults of sleeping and idling in the dwelling-place and the benefits of 'always sitting and not lying down' (and undertakes thus:). "I abandon sleeping and lying down from today and observe (the austerity of) 'always sitting and not lying down' ". This is the undertaking to observe.

What are the benefits of 'always sitting and not lying down'? One avoids the place where idleness arises. One removes resentment produced on account of one's body, and is freed from the pleasures which taint the organ of touch. One diminishes the enshrouding torpor. One is always tranquil and becomes fit for the practice of excellent concentration. This is an observance of good men. This observance is doubt-free.

What is the observance? How does one fail?

(Its observance is in) the abandoning of sleep and not lying down. If one lies down, it is called failing.

EXPEDIENCE IN THE OBSERVANCE OF THE AUSTERITIES

What are not 'dirt-rags'? They are hemp, cotton, silk and woollen robes[1] and others[2] offered by house-holders. If a bhikkhu accepts these for expedience' sake, he does not fail in the observance of 'dirt-rags'.

---

1. *Khoma, kappāsa, koseyya, kambala*—all transliterations.
2. According to the Chinese "*Samantapāsādikā*" these are *sāṇa* and *bhanga*, two varieties of hemp.

What are (not) 'three-robes'? Extra robes stored for more than ten days; *kaṭhina* robes and those other extra robes used as bedding-holders, bed-spreads,[1] cloth for skin-ailments and the like,[2] napkins,[3] rain-bath cloth, should not be kept if they are not spotless gifts. If a bhikkhu uses these for expedience' sake, he does not fail in the observance of 'three robes'.

What is the teaching as regards expedience in the observance of 'begged-food'? To partake of food given to the Order as a whole,[5] of assured food,[6] of ticket food,[7] of food offered on lunar fortnights,[8] of food offered on a sacred day,[9] of food offered to the many[10] and of food given in honour of a monastery,[11] for expedience' sake is not to fail in the observance of 'begged food'. If one sees faults, one should reject such food.

What is the teaching as regards expedience in the observance of 'regular alms-round'? If a bhikkhu on seeing elephants or horses fighting or in rut, at the gate, avoids them, or on seeing an outcast[12] covers his bowl, or goes behind his preceptor, teacher or a visiting bhikkhu, and thus commits certain faults for expedience' sake, he does not fail in 'regular alms-round'.

What is the teaching as regards expedience in the observance of 'one-eating'? If in the course of taking a meal at the proper time, one sees elephants, horses, cattle or snakes, or if it rains, or if one sees one's preceptor[13] or teacher,[14] or a visiting bhikkhu, and stands up for expedience' sake, and after that resumes one's meal, one does not fail in the observance of 'one-eating'.

In 'measured food' and 'no food after time', there is nothing by way of expedience.

What is the teaching as regards expedience in the observance of 'dwelling in a peaceful place'? If one goes to the village for causing people to undertake the precepts, confession of faults, hearing the Law, the service of the sacred day,[15] the service of the termination of the rainy season residence,[16] sickness, nursing the sick, inquiries regarding doubts on the discourses, and the like, it is not failing in the observance of 'dwelling in a peaceful place'.

What is the teaching as regards expedience in the observance of 'dwelling under a tree'? If a bhikkhu, because of rain, goes to a roofed place and returns when it is bright, he does not fail in the observance of 'dwelling under a tree'.

Expedience in the observance of 'dwelling in a dewy place', 'dwelling amongst the graves', and 'any chanced upon place' is also like this. A bhikkhu may dwell elsewhere.

There is nothing by way of expedience regarding 'always sitting and not lying down'. Yet there is a tradition as regards the expediency of pouring (medicine) into the nose. By this one does not fail in 'always sitting and not lying down'.

1. *Paccattharaṇa.*
2. *Kaṇḍupaṭiccādi.*
3. *Mukhapuñchana.*
4. *Vassikasāṭika.*
5. *Sanghabhatta.*
6. *Niccabhatta.*
7. *Salākabhatta.*
8. *Pakkhikabhatta.*
9. *Uposathabhatta.*
10. *Gaṇabhatta.*
11. *Vihārabhatta.*
12. *Caṇḍāla* (transliteration).
13. *Upajjhāya* (probably transliteration).
14. *Ācarlya* (transliteration).
15. *Uposatha.*
16. *Pavāraṇā.*

MISCELLANEOUS TEACHINGS

And again one fulfils eight teachings through these thirteen austerities. In the *Abhidhamma* these eight are taught: " 'Measured food' and 'one-eating' are involved in 'no food after time'. 'Dwelling under a tree', 'dwelling in a dewy place', 'dwelling among the graves' are involved in 'dwelling in a peaceful place', because, if one gathers funds for building a house, or if one likes to (do remunerative) work, keeps animals or is attached to 'dwelling in a peaceful place', one's mind is not at ease. Thus thinking one dwells in peace 'under a tree', 'among the graves' or 'in a dewy place' ". Thus the eight are fulfilled.

By these eight austerities three teachings are fulfilled: the first: 'dwelling in a peaceful place', the second: 'dirt-rags', the third: 'begged food'. If these three are pure, the austerities are fulfilled. Therefore the Buddha taught the Venerable Elder Nanda thus: "Always you should observe 'dwelling in a peaceful place', 'dirt-rags' and 'begged food'. You should not nurse your body and life. You should not see the objects of lust."[1]

Q. Who is called observer of the austerity-factors?[2] How many kinds of teachings are there regarding austerities? Which of three persons observe the austerities? How many seasons are there for the observance of austerities? Who is an observer and teacher of the austerities?

A. There are thirteen austerities taught by the Buddha. These are precepts of the Buddha. These are called austerity-factors. Here the skilful, unskilful and the non-characterizable[3] should not be taught, because the unskilful man is full of lust. He does not remove lust. He lives in wickedness. He is greedy of worldly advantages. Therefore, unskill is (not) austerity.

How many kinds of teachings are there? There are two teachings of austerities: non-greed and non-delusion. The Buddha has said, "If a bhikkhu who observes (the austerity of) 'dirt-rags' is endowed with paucity of wishes, is contented with little, enjoys tranquillity, is doubt-free and relies on freedom, then he is called one who observes (the austerity of) 'dirt-rags' ".[4] The other austerities are all greedless and delusion-free. By means of this greedlessness, a bhikkhu removes ignorance in thirteen places. And again by this greedlessness which the Buddha made possible (a bhikkhu) arouses in his mind aversion, and being free from doubt, reasonably removes the stain of lust and crookedness. By this freedom from delusion, he removes weariness of the flesh and crookedness. These are the two teachings of austerities. These are greedlessness and freedom from delusion.

---

1. S.II, 281: *Evaṁ kho te Nanda......yaṁ tvaṁ āraññako ca assasi piṇḍapātiko ca paṁsukūliko ca kāmesu ca anapekkho vihareyyāsi.*
2. *Dhutanga.*
3. *Kusala, akusala, avyākata.*
4. Cp. A.III, 219: *Imesaṁ kho bhikkhave pañcannaṁ āraññakānaṁ yvāyaṁ āraññako appicchataṁ yeva nissāya santuṭṭhiṁ yeva nissāya sallekhaṁ yeva nissāya pavivekaṁ yeva nissāya idaṁ aṭṭhitaṁ yeva nissāya āraññako hoti, ayaṁ imesaṁ pañcannaṁ āraññakānaṁ aggo ca seṭṭho ca mokkho ca uttamo ca pavaro ca.*

'Which of the three persons observe the austerities'? The man of greed and the man of delusion observe the austerities. The man of hate cannot observe the austerities. The man of greed and the man of delusion can observe the austerities. The man of greed accomplishes heedfulness through attachment. If he becomes heedless, he overcomes greed. Delusion is non-doubting. By means of the austerities a bhikkhu can fulfil heedfulness. If he is heedful, he can overcome delusion well. That is why the man of greed and the man of delusion observe the austerities.

Heedless men suffer and do evil. A heedless man should not observe (because if he does, he will increase his sufferings), just as a person afflicted with a disease of phlegm worsens on taking hot drinks.

And again there is a tradition. A heedless man should dwell 'in a peaceful place' or 'under a tree'. Why should he dwell 'in a peaceful place'? Because there are no worldly troubles there.

How many seasons are there for the observance of austerities? Eight months are the period for three austerities, namely, 'dwelling under a tree', 'dwelling in a dewy place' and 'dwelling among the graves'. The Buddha has permitted dwelling in roofed places in the rainy season.[1]

Q. 'Who is an observer and teacher of the austerities'?

A. There is one who is an observer and teacher of the austerities. There is one who is an observer but not a teacher of austerities. There is one who is not an observer but only a teacher of austerities, and there is one who is neither an observer nor a teacher of austerities.

Who is 'an observer and teacher of austerities'? The Consummate One who has fulfilled the observance of the austerities.

Who is 'an observer but not a teacher of austerities'? The Consummate One who has not fulfilled the observance of the austerities.

Who is 'not an observer but only a teacher of austerities'? The learner or the commoner who has fulfilled the observance of the austerities.

Who is 'neither an observer nor a teacher of austerities'? The learner or the commoner who has not fulfilled the observance of the austerities.

Q. What is the salient characteristic, function and manifestation of the austerities?

A. Paucity of wishes is the salient characteristic. Contentment is the function. Non-doubting is the manifestation.

And again non-attachment is the salient characteristic. Moderation is the function. Non-retrogression is the manifestation.

What are the initial, medial and final stages of the austerities? The undertaking to observe is the initial stage. Practice is the medial stage and rejoicing is the final stage.

---

1. *Vassāna*.

ON DISTINGUISHING CONCENTRATION

CHAPTER THE FOURTH

Q. Now, what should the yogin who dwells in pure virtue do, when he has already observed the austerities and has reached an excellent station?

A. Let him bring out concentration.

Q. What is concentration? What is its salient characteristic? What is its function? What is its manifestation? What is its near cause? Who observes it? What differences are there between meditation, freedom, concentration and right observance? How many are the causes which produce concentration? How many states are obstacles to progress in concentration? How many benefits of concentration are there? What are the requisites of concentration? How many kinds of concentration are there? What is the bringing out of concentration?

MEANING OF CONCENTRATION

A. Concentration means that one has purity of mind, endeavours steadfastly, dwells with the truth having the benefit of tranquillity and is not distracted. This is called concentration.

And again, it means not allowing one's mind to be bent by the strong wind of passion. It is comparable to the unflickering flame of the lamp behind the palace.

It is said in the *Abhidhamma* thus: "What fixes the mind aright, causes it to be not dependent on any, causes it to be unmoved, undisturbed, tranquillized and non-attached, and rightens the faculty of concentration and the power of concentration [407] is called concentration."[1]

SALIENT CHARACTERISTIC ETC.

What are its salient characteristic, function, manifestation and near cause? Dwelling of mind is its salient characteristic; overcoming of hatred is its function; tranquillity is its manifestation; non-association with defilement and the mind obtaining freedom are its near cause.

Who observes concentration? Namely, he who maintains the mind and the mental properties in a state of equilibrium. It is like the hand which holds a pair of scales evenly.

The even practice of mindfulness and energy is concentration. It is comparable to the evenness of oil in an oiled bowl. Equilibrated thought,

---

1. In his Vimuttimagga and Visuddhimagga, p. 26, Prof. Dr. P. V. Bapat has traced this passage to Vbh. 217: *Yā cittassa ṭhiti saṇṭhiti avaṭṭhiti avisāhāro avikkhepo avisāhaṭa-mānasatā samatho samādhindriyaṁ samādhibalaṁ sammāsamādhi: ayaṁ vuccati samādhi.*

like the equalized energy of four horses of a chariot, is concentration. It is like the attentiveness of a fletcher scrutinizing the straightness of a shaft. It is like a drug which counteracts poison, because it removes resentment. It is said in the *Abhidhamma* thus: "*........is the meaning of concentration." This explanation of concentration is comprehensive.

'Meditation' means the four meditations, namely, the first meditation and others.

'Freedom' means the eight kinds of freedom, namely, one having internal perception of form reflects on external form and so on.[1]

'Concentration' means the three kinds of concentration, namely, initial and sustained application of thought and others.

'Right observance' means the right observance of the nine gradually ascending states.[2]

'What is 'meditation'? It is to contemplate on reality, to remove resentment, to make the mind happy, to discard the hindrances, to gain freedom, to equalize, to arouse concentration skilfully, to acquire liberation, to dwell in right observance, to wish to arouse concentration and to aspire to possess freedom.

BENEFITS PRODUCED BY CONCENTRATION

How many benefits can concentration produce? There are four benefits which concentration can produce. What are the four? Pleasant dwelling in the happiness of truth in the present life; enjoyment of all objects through investigation; acquisition of worldly knowledge; the attainment of perfection.

What is 'pleasant dwelling in the happiness of truth in the present life'? Namely, one acquires concentration and is freed from corruption. One's mind arouses joy, partakes of the joy of the supramundane and dwells pleasantly in the happiness of truth in the present life. Therefore, has the Blessed One said: "He produces joy from quietude, acquires coolness and becomes perfect gradually."[3] And again, the Buddha declared to the bhikkhus: "At

---

* Unintelligible.

1. *Aṭṭha Vimokkha*. Cp. D.II, 70, 71. A. IV, 306. *Rūpī rūpāni passati* etc. In the Abhidharma Saṅgīti Paryāya Padaśāstra, the following account of the eight deliverances or kinds of freedom is given:- "Having (or with) form one reflects on form; not having internal perception of form, one reflects on external form; attaining to and realizing the emancipation of purity through one's body, one dwells; transcending all perceptions of form, destroying all perceptions of sense-reactions, becoming heedless of perceptions of diversity, one enters limitless space, and, attaining to the sphere of the infinity of space, dwells; entirely transcending the sphere of the infinity of space, one enters limitless consciousness, and, attaining to the sphere of the infinity of consciousness, dwells; entirely transcending, the sphere of the infinity of consciousness, one enters nothingness and, attaining to the sphere of nothingness, dwells; entirely transcending the sphere of nothingness, one enters the sphere of neither perception nor non-perception and, attaining to it, dwells; and entirely transcending the sphere of neither perception nor non-perception, one enters the state of the dissolution of perception and sensation and, attaining to and realizing it through the body, dwells".

2. A. IV, 410: *Nava anupubbavihārā*.

3. Not traced.

first I was a naked ascetic; I did not move my body or open my mouth for seven days and seven nights; I sat in silence enwrapped in bliss."[1] This is the meaning, in the Noble Teaching, of 'pleasant dwelling in the happiness of truth in the present life'.

'Enjoyment of all objects through investigation' means that a yogin acquires concentration and is not hindered by objects. Being pliant of mind, he is able to concentrate. He investigates the aggregations, the sense-spheres, the elements and others. He is well-disposed. Therefore, the Blessed One taught the bhikkhus thus: "Thus should you train yourselves. Everything depends on mind. Know this as it is."[2]

'Acquisition of worldly knowledge' means that one having acquired concentration, develops the five faculties of knowledge, namely, psychic power, divine ear, knowledge of others' thoughts, recollection of past existences, and the divine eye. Therefore, the Blessed One has declared: "With concentrated mind one is able to change one's body at will. Thus one produces psychic power in the various modes."[3]

'The attainment of perfection' means that one having a concentrated mind, although one has yet to reach the stage of the learning-ender, may not fall back at all. One gains (a good) reward through concentration. One attains to 'the form', 'the formless' and to perfection. The Buddha has declared: "Those who practise a little of the first meditation are able to join the retinue of Brahmā. All such are born in such a world."[4] These four benefits can be produced by concentration. Each of them causes to arouse.

OBSTACLES TO CONCENTRATION

How many states are obstacles to progress in concentration? Namely, eight states: lust, hatred, indolence, rigidity, agitation, uncertainty, delusion, absence of joy and bliss. All other evil demeritorious states are obstacles.

CAUSES OF CONCENTRATION

How many causes of concentration are there? Namely, eight states are causes: renunciation, non-hatred, brightness, non-disturbedness, all skilful states, sustained application of thought, gladness, and those states that arouse knowledge of the truth. These are causes of concentration.

---

1. Cp. Ud. 3.
2. Cp. Dh. 1: *Manopubbaṇgamā dhammā.*
3. M. II, 18.
4. A. II, 126: *Idha bhikkhave ekacco puggalo vivic'eva kāmehi vivicca akusalehi dhammehi .... paṭhamajjhānaṁ upasampajja viharati. So tad assādeti taṁ nikāmeti tena ca vittiṁ āpajjati, tattha ṭhito tad-adhimutto tabbahulavihārī aparihīno kālaṁ kurumāno Brahma-kāyikānaṁ devānaṁ sahavyataṁ uppajjati.*

REQUISITES OF CONCENTRATION

What are the requisites of concentration? There are seven, namely: virtue, contentment, shielding of the faculties, moderation in drink and food, not sleeping in the first, middle and last watches of the night, the being intent on wisdom and a calm and quiet dwelling-place.

TWO KINDS OF CONCENTRATION

How many kinds of concentration are there?

There are two kinds of concentration. The first is mundane concentration; the second is supramundane concentration. The acquisition of the Noble Fruit is called 'supramundane concentration'; the others are named 'mundane'. Mundane concentration is accompanied by corruption, is connected with the fetters and is bound. This is the flood. This is the bond. This is hindrance. This is the corruption of virtue and views. This is clinging. This is defilement. Such are the qualities of 'mundane concentration'. The opposite of this is named 'supramundane concentration'.

And again, there are two kinds in concentration: wrong concentration[1] and Right Concentration. What is wrong concentration? Unskilful unification of mind is called 'wrong concentration'. Skilful unification of mind is called 'Right Concentration'. Wrong concentration should be abandoned. Right concentration should be practised.

And again, there are two kinds of concentration: access concentration and fixed concentration. The antecedent portion — this is called 'access concentration'. Suppression of the hindrances — this is called 'fixed concentration'.

THREE KINDS OF CONCENTRATION

And again, there are three kinds: concentration with initial and sustained application of thought; without initial and only with sustained application of thought; with neither initial nor sustained application of thought.[2]

What is 'with initial and sustained application of thought'? The first meditation is 'with initial and sustained application of thought'. In the second meditation there is no initial application of thought, but there is sustained application of thought. In the other meditations there is 'neither initial nor sustained application of thought'.

And again, there are three kinds of concentration. Namely, the concentration that is produced together with joy; the concentration that is produced

---

1. *Micchāsamādhi.*
2. D.III, 219: *Tayo samādhi. Savitakko savicāro samādhi, avitakko vicāramatto samādhi, avitakko avicāro samādhi.*

together with bliss; the concentration that is produced together with indifference. The first and the second meditations (*jhānas*) are 'produced together with joy', the third is 'produced together with bliss' and the fourth meditation (*jhāna*) is 'produced together with equanimity'.

And again, there are three kinds of concentration: skilful concentration; skilful result (producing) concentration; real concentration.

What is 'skilful concentration'? The concentration pertaining to the form and the formless practised by the learner of the Noble Path and the commoner is called 'skilful concentration'. The concentration of the learner who is established in the Noble Fruit (in the spheres of form and the formless) and of the commoner who is reborn in the spheres of the form and the formless is called 'result producing concentration'. The concentration of the form and the formless practised by the learning-ender is called 'real concentration'.

FOUR KINDS OF CONCENTRATION

And again, there are four kinds of concentration: the sense plane concentration;[1] the form plane concentration;[2] the formless plane concentration;[3] unincluded concentration.[4]

The putting away of each of the five hindrances by its opposite and the maintaining of it is called 'the sense plane concentration'; the four meditations are called 'the form plane concentration'; the four formless plane meditations and the result of good action (?) are called 'the formless plane concentration'. The concentration of the four Paths and the four Fruits is called 'unincluded concentration'.

And again, there are four practices in concentration: painful practice (of a man of) slow wit; painful practice (of a man of) quick wit; pleasant practice (of a man of) quick wit; pleasant practice (of a man of) slow wit.[5] (Here) the first of these four kinds of men has dense passion, and the second, rare passion; the third has keen faculties, and the fourth, dull faculties.

To a man of dense passion and dull faculties practice is 'painful'; he gains concentration with 'slow wit'.

To a man of dense passion and keen faculties practice is 'painful', though he gains concentration with 'quick wit'.

To a man of rare passion and dull faculties practice is 'pleasant', though he gains concentration with 'slow wit'.

To a man of rare passion and keen faculties practice is 'pleasant'; he gains concentration with 'quick wit'.

---

1. ***Kāmāvacara samādhi.*** Lit., 'That that' practice and 'true keeping'. The rendering is tentative.
2. ***Rūpāvacara samādhi.*** 3. *Arūpāvacara samādhi.* 4. *Apariyāpanna samādhi.*
5. A.II, 149: *Dukkhāpaṭipadā dandhābhiññā, dukkhāpaṭipadā khippābhiññā, sukhāpaṭipadā dandhābhiññā, sukhāpaṭipadā khippābhiññā.*

Because of the density of passion, a densely passionate man overcomes passion with difficulty. Therefore, his practice is painful.

Because of the dullness of faculties, a man of dull faculties has to practise meditation assiduously for a long time and wake up his sluggish wit. Therefore, he is called (a man of) dull faculties.

In this way the others also should be understood.

And again, there are four kinds in concentration, namely, restricted concentration with restricted object; restricted concentration with immeasurable object; immeasurable concentration with restricted object; immeasurable concentration with immeasurable object.[1] What is 'restricted concentration with restricted object'? The concentration that is not able to keep pace with the mind and an object[2] that is weak — these are called 'restricted concentration with restricted object'. What is 'restricted concentration with immeasurable object'? The concentration that is not able to keep pace with the mind and an object that is powerful — these are called 'restricted concentration with immeasurable object'. What is 'immeasurable concentration with restricted object'? The concentration capable of keeping pace with the mind and an object that is weak — these are called 'immeasurable concentration with restricted object'. What is 'immeasurable concentration with immeasurable object'? The concentration that is capable of keeping pace with the mind and an object that is powerful — these are called 'immeasurable concentration with immeasurable object'.

And again, there are four kinds in concentration: will-concentration; effort-concentration; mind-concentration; scrutiny-concentration.[3]

'Will-concentration' is attained by means of the will; 'effort-concentration' is attained by means of effort; what is attained by means of the mind is 'mind-concentration'; what is attained by means of scrutiny is 'scrutiny-concentration'.

And again, there are four kinds in concentration: the concentration to which the Enlightened One attains but not the hearer; the concentration to which the hearer attains but not the Enlightened One; the concentration to which both the Enlightened One and the hearer attain; the concentration to which neither the Enlightened One nor the hearer attains.

The concentration of great commiseration[4] and the concentration of the twin-miracle[5] are attainments of the Enlightened One and not of the hearer. The fruition concentration of the learner[6] is an attainment of the hearer and not of the Enlightened One. The concentration of the nine gradually ascending states and the fruition concentration of the learning-ender are attainments of

1. *Paritta-samādhi, paritta-ārammaṇa; paritta-samādhi, appamāṇa-ārammaṇa; appamāṇa-samādhi, paritta-ārammaṇa; appamāṇa-samādhi, appamāṇa-ārammaṇa.*
2. Lit. *samādhi.* Possibly an error.
3. A.I, 39, 297—*Chanda*, *viriya*, *citta* and *vīmaṁsa.*
4. *Mahā karuṇā samāpatti.*
5. *Yamakapāṭihāriya.*
6. *Sek hiya-phala-samādhi.*

both the Enlightened One and the hearer. And the concentration of inconscience[1] is an attainment neither of the Enlightened One nor the hearer.

And again, there are four kinds in concentration: the concentration that is a cause of origination and not of cessation; of cessation and not of origination; of both origination and cessation; of neither origination nor cessation.

Q. What are causes of 'origination and not of cessation'? Skilful and unskilful concentration of the sense plane are causes of 'origination and not of cessation'. The concentration of the fourfold Noble Path causes cessation and not origination. Skilful concentration of the learner and the commoner pertaining to the form plane and the formless plane cause 'origination and cessation'. [408] The concentration of the Noble Fruit and object concentration cause 'neither origination nor cessation'.

And again, there are four kinds in concentration: the first meditation; the second meditation; the third meditation; the fourth meditation.

Freedom from the five hindrances, the fulfilment of initial and sustained application of thought, joy, ease and unification of mind are called 'the first meditation'.

Freedom from initial and sustained application of thought and the fulfilment of the other three (are called 'the second meditation').

Freedom from joy and the fulfilment of the other two (are called 'the third meditation').

Freedom from ease and the fulfilment of equanimity and unification of mind are called the fourth meditation.

FIVE KINDS OF CONCENTRATION

And again, there are five kinds in concentration, namely the first meditation; the second meditation; the third meditation; the fourth meditation; the fifth meditation. This fivefold (classification of) meditation is based on the five factors of meditation, namely, initial application of thought, sustained application of thought, joy, bliss, unification of mind.

The separation from the five hindrances and the fulfilment of the five factors are called 'the first meditation'.

The separation from initial application of thought and the fulfilment of the other four factors are called 'the second meditation'.

The separation from initial and sustained application of thought and the fulfilment of the other three factors are called 'the third meditation'.

The separation from (initial and sustained application of thought, joy) and the fulfilment of the other two factors are called 'the fourth meditation'.

---

1. The concentration that causes rebirth among the unconscious gods (*asañña samāpatti*).

The separation from (initial and sustained application of thought, joy,) bliss and the fulfilment of two factors are called 'the fifth meditation. (The two factors are) equanimity and unification of mind.

WHY FOUR AND FIVE MEDITATIONS ARE TAUGHT

Q. Why are four and five meditations taught?

A. Because the result depends on two sorts of men. In the second meditation there are two divisions: without initial and sustained application of thought, and without initial and only with sustained application of thought.

Q. How does a yogin induce the second meditation from the first?

A. He considers the coarseness of initial and sustained application of thought, knows the disadvantages of initial and sustained application of thought, and induces the second meditation which is free from initial and sustained application of thought. This is the way of progress in the four meditations.

And again, there is another man. He is able to induce freely the second meditation out of the first meditation. He considers the coarseness of initial application of thought and knows the disadvantages of initial application of thought. He discerns the state of being free from initial application of thought. Possessing restricted sustained application of thought, he induces the second meditation. This is the way of progress in the five meditations. Therefore, the five meditations are taught.

And again, there are five kinds in concentration, namely, complete fixed meditation in the five factors: joyfulness, blissfulness, mindfulness, luminousness and the perception of steadily moving thought. Here 'joyfulness' is in the first and the second meditations. 'Blissfulness' is in the third meditation. 'Mindfulness' is in the knowledge of others' thoughts. 'Luminousness' is in the knowledge of the divine eye. The knowledge of steadily moving thought is born of reflection[1] concentration. This is called 'the perception of steadily moving thought'.

And again there are five kinds in concentration, namely, Right Concentration connected with the fivefold knowledge. These are consequences of present bliss and the bliss to be. These arise depending on the knowledge of the body.

(1) This concentration is practised by the Noble Ones and is passion-free.

(2) This concentration is practised by wise men.

(3) This is the excellent bliss of solitude and the attainment of tranquillity. Although this accomplishes the unique, yet it does not overcome birth and death.

---

1. Lit. "That that knowledge".

(4) This concentration is most pleasant and peaceful. This becomes one endowed with tranquillity. This does not overcome the (belief in) self (which is the cause) of birth and death.

(5) This concentration moves in mindfulness and is a cause of mindfulness. These arise owing to knowledge of the body.

And now, (the acceptance of) objects of meditation, what is connected with the requisites, and the inferior, the middling and the superior have been distinguished. Thus there are many divisions of concentration.

(Further), it should be known that all concentration may be classified under the four meditations.[1]

---

1. D. II, 313: *Katamo ca bhikkhave sammā-samādhi? Idha bhikkhave bhikkhu vivic 'eva kāmehi vivicca akusalehi dhammehi savitakkaṁ savicāraṁ vivekajaṁ pīti-sukhaṁ paṭhamajjhānaṁ upasampajja viharati. Vitakkavicārānaṁ vūpasamā ajjhattaṁ sampasādanaṁ cetaso ekodi-bhāvaṁ avitakkaṁ avicāraṁ samādhijaṁ pīti-sukhaṁ dutiyajjhānaṁ upasampajja viharati. Pītiyā ca virāgā upekhako viharati sato ca sampajāno, sukhaṁ ca kāyena paṭisaṁvedeti yan taṁ ariyā ācikkhanti: 'upekhako satimā sukha-vihārī ti' tatiyajjhānaṁ upasampajja viharati. Sukhassa ca pahānā dukkhassa ca pahānā pubb' eva somanassa-domanassānaṁ atthagamā adukkhaṁ asukhaṁ upekhā-sati-pārisuddhiṁ catutthajjhānaṁ upasampajja viharati. Ayaṁ vuccati bhikkhave sammā-samādhi.*

ON APPROACHING A GOOD FRIEND

CHAPTER THE FIFTH

Q. Then how is concentration brought out?

A. If a man wishes to bring out concentration, he, at first, should approach a pre-eminent friend. Why? If, at first, when a yogin wishes to accomplish excellent concentration, he dwells apart from a good friend, he will not acquire steadfastness. In a Discourse it is said: "Meghiya bhikkhu partakes of deterioration."[1] It is comparable to a man who sets out alone on a distant journey. None guides him. When a man sets out alone, he is like an elephant that is not guided by the goad. If, when a yogin practises, he listens to the discourses and instructions of a good friend, he is able to remove his many difficulties and get into the right method and practice. If he strenuously endeavours and strictly trains himself, then he is able to acquire excellent concentration.

QUALITIES OF A GOOD FRIEND

A good friend who may be likened to a wealthy chief of merchants honoured by all, to a kind good-hearted person, to a dearly loved parent, steadies one, as the chain the elephant.

A good friend on whom one relies and accomplishes all meritorious activities is like a mahout who causes (the elephant) to go backwards and forwards, is like a good road on which a man can take a yoke of oxen, like a physician who cures diseases and removes pain, like the rain from heaven which moistens everything, like a mother who nurses her child, like a father who guides his son, like parents who ward their children from perils and like a teacher who instructs (his pupils). Therefore, the Blessed One declared

---

1. *Hānabhāgiya*. Cp. A. IV, 357: *Idha Meghiya bhikkhu kalyāṇamitto hoti kalyāṇasahāyo kalyāṇsampavaṅko. Aparipakkāya Meghiya cetovimuttiyā ayaṁ paṭhamo dhammo paripakkāya saṁvattati.* The following is a more or less free rendering of the relative passage from the Chinese Chu Agon (Madhyama Āgama) No. 5, Fascicle X, Sūtra No. 56: "Thus have I heard. At one time, when the Enlightened One was wandering in the land of Magadha, he arrived at Jantugāma, and his sole attendant was the Venerable Elder Meghiya.

   And in the morning, the Venerable Elder Meghiya taking bowl and robe went to the village of Jantugāma for alms. And after completing his alms-round, he wended his way to the bank of the river Kimilāla. The land there was level meadow, and it was known as the Grove of Sweet Mango. Beside it ran the excellent waters of Kimilāla, sparklingly clear. Seeing the pleasant place, the Venerable Elder Meghiya was delighted and thought: 'The land here is level meadow and is known as the Grove of Sweet Mango. Beside it runs the excellent waters of Kimilāla, sparklingly clear. Meet is this spot for a clansman for the exercise of energy'.

   And having finished his meal, put aside his bowl and robe, washed his hands and feet, he, with one shoulder bared, went to the presence of the Enlightened One, bowed at the Enlightened One's feet, and sat on one side. And being seated he spoke thus: "Venerable Sir, in the morning, having taken bowl and robe, I went to the village of Jantugāma for alms............and I thought: 'The land here is level meadow and is known as the Grove of Sweet Mango. Beside it runs the excellent waters of Kimilāla,

to (Ā)nanda: "Good companionship is the whole of the holy life."[1] Therefore, one should search for the pre-eminently good man and make him the good friend.

What is meant by pre-eminent good friend? (Here), the fulfilment of acquisition is the meaning (of 'pre-eminent'). The understanding of the *Sutta*, *Abhidhamma* and *Vinaya* is called 'fulfilment of acquisition'.

One understands the seed (?) of *kamma* and is endowed with beneficient worldly knowledge. One knows the Four Noble Truths.

These two kinds of men are merit-fulfillers. They should be searched for.

If these two kinds of merit-fulfillers cannot be found, the fulfiller of seven qualities should be considered as a good friend. Such (a man) should also be searched for.

What are the seven qualities?[2] Loveableness, esteemableness, venerableness, the ability to counsel well, patience (in listening), the ability to deliver deep discourses and the not applying oneself to useless ends.

What is 'lovableness'? Led by two kinds of practice, a man preaches well: dwelling together happily, having come to a mutual understanding and not abusing one another.

sparklingly clear. Meet is this spot for a clansman for the exercise of energy'. How Venerable Sir, if I should go to that calm place in the Grove of Sweet Mango and exercise energy?"

Then the Blessed One said: 'Meghiya, there is no one except you here. Stay awhile until another bhikkhu comes to wait on me. Then you may go to that calm place in the Grove of Sweet Mango to exercise energy'.

A second and a third time the Venerable Elder Meghiya requested permission and for a second and third time did the Blessed One refuse it.

Then the Venerable Elder Meghiya said: 'Venerable Sir, the Blessed One has nothing more to do. The Blessed One need not exert energy any longer. But I, Venerable Sir, have much to do yet. Therefore, Venerable Sir, I wish to enter that calm place in the Grove of Sweet Mango and exercise energy'.

Then the Blessed One said: 'Meghiya, if you wish to exert yourself, I do not stop you. Go Meghiya and do as you please'.

The Venerable Elder Meghiya hearing the words of the Enlightened One and accepting them, bowed at the Enlightened One's feet, walked round Him three times and departed. Arriving at the Grove of Sweet Mango, he went to the foot of a tree prepared a seat and sat down.

And when he was thus seated in the forest, three demeritorious states of mind arose in him, namely, discursive thoughts connected with lust, discursive thoughts connected with hate and discursive thoughts connected with harming. Then the Venerable Elder Meghiya thought of the Blessed One, arose from his seat and forthwith returned to the presence of the Blessed One (and told the Blessed One everything) and the Blessed One said: 'Your mind is not yet ripe for deliverance. If you wish to cause it to ripen, you should train yourself in the five trainings. What are the five? Meghiya, a bhikkhu is a good friend and he should be in the company of a good friend, he should closely associate with a good friend.

'Meghiya, if your mind is not ripe for deliverance, and if you wish to cause it to ripen, this is the first training..

1. S. I, 87-8: *Sakalam eva h-idaṁ Ānanda brahmacariyaṁ yad idaṁ kalyāṇa-mittatā kalyāṇa-sahāyatā kalyāṇa-sampavaṅkatā.*

2. A. IV, 32: *Sattahi bhikkhave dhammehi samannāgato bhikkhu mitto sevitabbo bhajitabbo payirupāsitabbo api panujjamānena pi. Katamehi sattahi? Piyo hoti manāpo ca, garu ca, bhāvaniyo ca, vattā ca, vacanakkhamo ca, gambhirañ ca kathaṁ kattā hoti, no ca aṭṭhāne niyojeti.* Cp. Vis. Mag. 98; *Netti* 164.

'Esteemableness' means that one is tranquillized through the action of virtue, fulfils the protection of mindfulness, is not over-desirous and does not speak much. This is called 'esteemableness'.

'Venerableness' means that one is endowed with the merit of much learning and appreciates well the value of meditation. This is 'venerableness'.

'The ability to counsel well' means that one considers thus: "Let my speech be lovable, esteemable, venerable and fruitful", and benefits others and esteems the truth. Therefore, one restrains oneself from things that ought not to be done. Thus one observes to the end and does not forsake. This is called 'the ability to counsel well'.

'Patience (in listening)' means that one is like a saint, understands well, never hesitates in one's speech and does not flatter*.............This is called 'patience (in listening)'.

'(The ability to deliver) deep discourses' means that one well understands *...............This is called '(the ability to deliver) deep discourses'.

'The not applying oneself to useless ends' means that he understands well the place of *kamma*. This is 'the not applying oneself to useless ends'.

Thus the seven qualities are completed. These (are qualities of) a good friend who should be searched for.

THE SEARCH FOR A GOOD FRIEND

Q. How should one search?

A. If in such and such a place there is one who knows the accomplishment of these merits and is a teacher of meditation, one should go to that teacher. Though one may not know, yet if a fellow-student knows, one should go and serve him.

At the proper time in a befitting way (one approaches a fellow-student) and without expressing one's wishes, one worships him and exchanges the customary greetings and consults him as to what one should do, thus: "In which country and in which place is it safe for a bhikkhu to dwell? Which is the suitable place of meditation for a bhikkhu? What is the name of the teacher who dwells there? For what practices and for what merits is he honoured by all"? Thus one should inquire.

The fellow-student will answer: "In such and such a country, in such and such a monastery, in such and such a place of meditation set apart for the Order, such and such a teacher of meditation is honoured by all".

On hearing this, one should think on this and be happy, and going thither serve that teacher and practise under him.

* Unintelligible.

Adjusting one's robes one should go to the presence of one's preceptor[1] and open to him one's happy heart: "O preceptor, hear me. I wish to go and serve such and such a teacher of meditation".

Hearing this the preceptor will reply: "Sādhu! I too am glad. Your action is praiseworthy. It is called co-residence with a good man and is the action of a good man. It is the practice that accompanies the truth. Great is the merit of learning it and greater that of co-residence. You should go to him. After you go there, you should not be negligent".

A BEGINNER'S DUTIES

If one is good, one studies earnestly, honours (one's teacher) wholeheartedly, not for a while but always. If one uses gentle speech and guards the body and the mouth, then, one may understand and fulfil the practice.

One relies completely on the teacher in all things, does not slight him and obeys him just as a newly-wed bride her mother-in-law. If one sees other bhikkhus lacking robes or liquid-medicine, one prepares (what is lacking) in the customary way.

When on going there one is instructed (through) exposition, precept and posture — in the Good Law — one should adjust one's robes, bow at the feet of the teacher and circumambulate him.

At the water-side which may be by the road or outside the village, he goes to a certain spot, keeps his bowl, robe, sandals, washing-vessel and the meditation mat on a high place. He does not use the water which is near by, and without noise he bathes. After bathing he wears the upper-garment,[2] arranges his robes and, carrying bowl[3] and robe and the meditation mat on his right shoulder, rolls the shoulder-cloak[4] or throws it across the shoulder.

On entering a monastery, he lowers his umbrella and circumambulates the relic mound. If he sees any bhikkhu, he goes to him and asks: "Is there a yogin living here? Is there a 'dirt-rags' man living here? Is there a 'begged-food' man living here? Is there a teacher of discipline living here? Where does he dwell? Which is the way to his dwelling? [409] If there is one, I wish to see him. If there are no such persons and if there is a (sub-) teacher of discipline, I wish to see him. If there is no teacher of discipline, who is the elder here? I wish to see him".

If that bhikkhu is a senior or a venerable one, one should not hand one's bowl and robe. But if he is junior, one should. If there is none, one places one's bowl and robe on the ground. When one sees the elder, one bows at his feet and sits at one side.

A bhikkhu who lives there will give one a seat and water, show the washing-

1. *Upajjhāya.*
2. *Uttarāsanga* (transliteration).
3. *Patta* (transliteration).
4. *Sanghāṭi* (transliteration).

place, serve, give information, take care of bowl and robe and point out the place for easing.

According to the rules for visiting bhikkhus, one should go round, within the precincts of the monastery, before sundown.

If one sees a teacher of discipline, one should talk with him and ask him concerning any faults with regard to which one is in doubt, and which one has not yet committed. Or, if one sees a teacher of *Abhidhamma*, one should inquire concerning the method of acquiring wisdom and about the aggregates, sense-spheres, elements and *kamma*. If one sees an observer of austerities, one should inquire concerning the benefits of the austerities connected with wisdom. If one dwells there, one should go to many and daily make inquiries. If one wishes to leave, one folds one's bedding and bows at the seniors' feet and informs them and leaves. These are the rules for visiting bhikkhus.

How does a yogin dwell in a monastery? When the teacher of meditation comes, one should take his bowl and robe, even if he be a junior. According to the rule of the teacher of meditation, one should practise that which ought to be practised or not practise the ought-not-to-be-practised, and one should not abandon the practising (of that which ought to be practised and of that which ought not to be practised). This is the practice that should be observed at first. Thus should one practise.

If the yogin wishes to let others learn the Law at first, he watches the dwelling-place and keeps the bowls and robes. After sometime has passed, he, at the proper time, approaches the teacher of meditation, salutes him respectfully, and remaining silent a while, sits

Should the teacher of meditation question the yogin, he expresses his desire. If the teacher of meditation does not question, the yogin should not speak. Thereupon he should ask for tooth-sticks and water for washing, and should use them in the proper way.

When the time for the alms-round comes, he should ask permission of the teacher and follow the usual way.

When the meal-time arrives, one should wash the teacher's feet, arrange his seat, give him the bowl and inquire of the teacher what he wants from one's own bowl. Having partaken of the remainder, one gives what is left over to the juniors. Thus one observes and abstains from quarrelling.

After finishing one's meal, one washes the teacher's bowl and puts it in the proper place.

Seeing a suitable time, one approaches the teacher, respectfully salutes him, and remaining silent a while, sits. Should the teacher question, one should express one's desires. Should the teacher not question, one worships and says: "I will now say what I wanted to say from the first. If I am permitted, I wish to ask what I want". Should the teacher permit, one expresses everything. Should the teacher not question, one should worship him.

Finding a suitable opportunity, one should inform him (the teacher) concerning the reason for one's coming there thus: "O teacher, kindly listen to me". If the teacher listens, one should tell him regarding all one's wants. The teacher will say, "Sādhu, I will instruct you in the regular manner. You should observe well. Therefore, the Blessed One uttered these stanzas:-[1]

'One goes, when 'tis the right and proper time,
with lowly heart devoid of thoughts of pride,
to him who guards the Law with holiness.
As when no wayward winds assail a tree,
in pleasant practice of the Law he dwells,
feeding on the joyous calm of truth.
Thus dwelling in the Law he knows the Law
and so expounds that others too may know
The Sublime Law, just as it truly is.
He never speaks in dispraise of the Law,
jests not, flatters not, speaks no fearful words.
He has done with ill will and slothfulness.
He dwells not in anger, revenge, greed or pride,
is not deluded, craves not, is not attached.
Thus does he practise, conquer, and reject.
Conceit of righteous life he does not nurse.
Sincere are his words and always true.
For meditation's sake he knows and learns.
The self-indulgent, heedless, feckless man,
unsuited ever is to know the truth,
and is not one who grows in wisdom's light.
If there's a man conversant with the Law,
a winner of the homage of gods and men,
whose lustrous splendour adds to his faith,
who by much learning ably guards the Law,
who is a happy hearer of tidings glad,
possessor of an ample stock of virtues good,
a follower of truth and a practiser-well,
who causes the arising of excellent wit,
and who has himself reached high wisdom's peak —
if there is such a teacher — under him,
should one with zeal unremitting practise well'".

1. Not traced.

THE PATH OF FREEDOM

FASCICLE THE THIRD

WRITTEN

BY

THE ARAHANT UPATISSA

WHO WAS CALLED

GREAT LIGHT IN RYO

TRANSLATED IN RYO

BY

TIPIṬAKA SANGHAPĀLA OF FUNAN

THE DISTINGUISHING OF BEHAVIOUR[1]

CHAPTER THE SIXTH

KINDS OF BEHAVIOUR

Now, when the teacher[2] on whom one depends has observed one's behaviour for several months and has fixed upon a suitable subject of meditation,[3] he will instruct.

Here, 'behaviour' means the fourteen kinds[4] of behaviour: passion-behaviour, hate-behaviour, infatuation-behaviour, faith-behaviour, intelligence-behaviour, excogitation-behaviour, passion-hate-behaviour, passion-infatuation-behaviour, hate-infatuation-behaviour, passion-hate-infatuation-behaviour, faith-intelligence-behaviour, faith excogitation-behaviour, intelligence-excogitation-behaviour, faith-intelligence-excogitation-behaviour.

And again, there are other kinds of behaviour such as craving-behaviour, opinion-behaviour, pride-behaviour.[5]

Here, in the case of greed and the rest, the meaning does not defer from the above.[6]

FOURTEEN KINDS OF PERSONS

There are fourteen kinds of persons corresponding to the fourteen kinds of behaviour thus:

The person walking in passion,
The person walking in hate,
The person walking in infatuation,

---

1. *Cariyā.* 2. *Ācariya.* 3. *Kammaṭṭhāna.* 4. *Rāga-°, dosa-°, moha-°, saddhā-°, buddhi-°, vitakka-°, rāga-dosa-°, rāga-moha-°, dosa-moha-°, rāga-dosa-moha-*, saddhā-buddhi-*, saddhā-vitakka-*, buddhi-vitakka-°, saddhā-buddhi-vitakka-cariyā*.* (*Lit. qualities of equal measure).
5. *Taṇhā-, diṭṭhi-°, māna-cariyā.* 6. The Chinese is unintelligible.

The person walking in faith,
The person walking in intelligence,
The person walking in excogitation,
The person walking in passion-hate,
The person walking in passion-infatuation,
The person walking in hate-infatuation,
The person walking in passion-hate-infatuation,[1]
The person walking in faith-intelligence,
The person walking in faith-excogitation,
The person walking in intelligence-excogitation,
The person walking in faith-intelligence-excogitation.[2]

Thus 'the person walking in passion', 'the person walking in passion-infatuation' and 'the person walking in passion-hate-infatuation' are called 'persons walking in passion'.[3]

One always behaves passionately and increases passion. This is called 'passion-behaviour'. The others should be distinguished in the same way.

FOURTEEN KINDS REDUCED TO SEVEN

These fourteen kinds of men may be reduced to seven kinds: through the walker in passion and the walker in faith becoming one, the walker in hate and the walker in intelligence becoming one, the walker in infatuation and the walker in excogitation becoming one, the walker in passion-hate and the walker in faith-intelligence becoming one, the walker in passion-infatuation and the walker in faith-excogitation becoming one, the walker in hate-infatuation and the walker in intelligence-excogitation becoming one, the walker in passion-hate-infatuation and the walker in faith-intelligence-excogitation becoming one.[4]

Q. Why does a walker in passion become one with a walker in faith?

A. In a passionate person, when he does good, faith is strong, because this quality approaches passion.

And again, passion and faith are alike owing to three traits: clinging, searching for the good, non-repulsion.

Here 'passion' means the being intent on passion. 'Faith' means the being intent on good. 'Passion' means the search for what is passionally good. 'Faith' means the search for what is morally good. The nature of 'passion' is not to forsake what is bad. The nature of 'faith' is not to forsake what is good. Therefore, a walker in 'passion' becomes one with a walker in 'faith'.

---

1. & 2. Qualities of equal measure. 3. Tentative rendering.
4. *Rāga = saddhā; dosa = buddhi; moha = vitakka; rāga-dosa = saddhā-buddhi; rāga-moha = saddhā-vitakka; dosa-moha = buddhi-vitakka;* the last literally means: Through the two who walk in qualities of equal measure becoming one.

Q. Why does a walker in hate become one with walker in intelligence?

A. In a hating person, when he does good, intelligence is strong, because this quality approaches hate.

And again, hate and intelligence are alike owing to three traits: non-clinging, searching for faults, repulsion.

As a hating person does not cleave (to what is good), so an intelligent person does not cleave (to what is bad). As a hating person is given to fault-finding, so an intelligent person is given to the search for the faults[1] of wrongful conduct. As a hating person repulses others, so an intelligent person repulses the conformations. Therefore, the walker in hate becomes one with the walker in intelligence. They are alike.

Q. Why does a walker in infatuation become one with a walker in excogitation?

A. In an infatuated person who endeavours to arouse virtuous states, incertitude increases, because this quality approaches infatuation and because of separation from faith and wisdom.

And again, infatuation and excogitation are alike owing to two traits: instability and movement. As infatuation is not peaceful because it is disturbed, so excogitation is not peaceful because of various trends of discursive thought. As infatuation moves, not knowing where to go, so excogitation moves because of levity. Therefore, a walker in infatuation becomes one with a walker in excogitation. They are equal.

The others should be distinguished in the same way. Thus they are reduced to seven persons.

MODES OF PRACTICE

Among the seven which persons are of quick practice and which are of slow practice?

The walker in passion is of quick practice, because he is easily led, is strong in faith and because of the rarity of infatuation and excogitation in him.

The walker in hate is of quick practice, because he is easily led, is strong in intelligence and because of the rarity of infatuation and excogitation in him.

The walker in infatuation is of slow practice, because he is led with difficulty owing to infatuation and excogitation and because of the rarity of faith and intelligence in him.

The walker in passion-hate is of quick practice, because he is easily led, strong in faith and intelligence and because of the rarity of infatuation and excogitation in him.

---

1. *Ādīnava*.

The walker in passion-infatuation is of slow practice, because he is led with difficulty, is not believing and because infatuation and excogitation are strong in him.

The walker in hate-infatuation is of slow practice, because he is led with difficulty, lacks intelligence and because infatuation and excogitation are strong in him.

The walker in qualities of equal measure (passion-hate-infatuation or faith-intelligence-excogitation) is of slow practice, because he is led with difficulty, does not dwell in intelligence and because infatuation and excogitation are strong in him.

SEVEN REDUCED TO THREE

Now, these seven persons may be reduced to three according to their basic defilement. They are: the walker in passion, the walker in hate and the walker in infatuation.

CAUSES OF BEHAVIOUR

Q. What are the causes of these three kinds of behaviour? How may it be known that this man is a walker in passion, that man is a walker in hate and yet another is a walker in infatuation?[1] How may they be distinguished through robes, food, bedding, resort and postures?

A. Deeds done in the past are causes of behaviour. The elements are causes of behaviour. The cardinal humours[2] are causes of behaviour.

How do deeds done in the past become causes of behaviour?

One who had accumulated good actions, in past existences, through lovable means, becomes a walker in passion, and also one who passing away from a heavenly mansion is reborn here.

One who (in past existences) had perpetrated inimical deeds of killing, maiming and capturing, becomes a walker in hate, and also one who passing away from a hell or a serpent-state, is reborn here.

One who (in past existences) had partaken freely of intoxicating drink and was devoid (of learning and conversation) becomes a walker in infatuation, and also one who passing away from a bestial state is reborn here. Thus deeds done in the past become causes of behaviour.[3]

---

1. Cp. Vis. Mag. 102: *Tā pan' etā cariyā kiṁ nidānā?* etc.
2. *Dosa* (Sk. doṣa).
3. Cp. Vis. Mag. 102-3: *Tatra purimā tāva tisso cariyā pubbāciṇṇanidānā dhātudosanidānā cā ti ekacce vadanti. Pubbe kira iṭṭhappayogasubhakammabahulo rāgacarito hoti; saggā vā cavitvā idhupapanno. Pubbe chedanavadhabandhanaverakammabahulo dosacarito hoti; nirayanāgayonihi vā cavitvā idhūpapanno. Pubbe majjapānabahulo sutaparipucchāvihīno ca mohacarito hoti, tiracchānayoniyā vā cavitvā idhūpapanno ti. Ekacce* above is commented thus by the Venerable Dhammapāla Thera: *Ekacce ti upatissattheraṁ sandhāyāha. Tena hi Vimuttimagge tathā vuttaṁ* — Pm. 103 (Morontuḍuvē Dhammānanda Thera's Sinhalese ed.).

ELEMENTS AS CAUSES OF BEHAVIOUR

How do elements become causes of behaviour?

Because of the heightening of two elements one becomes a walker in infatuation. They are the element of extension and the element of cohesion.

Because of the heightening of two elements, one becomes a walker in hate. They are the element of mobility and the element of heat.

Because of the equalizing of all elements, one becomes a walker in passion. Thus the different elements become causes of behaviour.

THE HUMOURS AS CAUSES OF BEHAVIOUR

How do the cardinal humours become causes of behaviour? One who has an excess of phlegm becomes a walker in passion. One who has an excess of choler becomes a walker in hate, and one who has an excess of wind becomes a walker in infatuation.

And again, there is another teaching: One who has an excess of phlegm becomes a walker in infatuation, and one who has an excess of wind becomes a walker in passion. Thus the cardinal humours become causes of behaviour.[1]

How may it be known that this man is a walker in passion, that man is a walker in hate and yet another is a walker in infatuation?

SEVEN ASPECTS OF BEHAVIOUR

A. It may be known through the seven aspects of behaviour, namely, through (the manner of seeing) objects, through the defilements, through (the manner of) walking, through (the manner of) robing, through (the manner of) eating, through work and through (the manner of) sleeping.[2]

How may it be known 'through (the manner of seeing) objects'?

One who walks in passion looks at an object as if he had not seen it before. He does not see its faults, and does not consider them. He does not make light of even a little merit (of the object). He cannot free himself of the desire for it. Even after he reflects he cannot mend his ways. Towards the other objects of sense also he behaves in the same way. Thus it may be known that one is a walker in passion.

One who walks in hate looks at an object thus: he does not look long at an object, as though he were tired. When he is affected by the humours,

---

1. Cp. Vis. Mag. 103: *Dvinnaṁ pana dhātūnaṁ ussannattā puggalo mohacarito hoti: paṭhavīdhātuyā ca āpodhātuyā ca. Itarāsaṁ dvinnaṁ ussanattā dosacarito. Sabbāsaṁ samattā pana rāgacarito ti. Dosesu ca semhādhiko rāgacarito hoti, vātādhiko mohacarito, semhādhiko vā mohacarito, vātādhiko vā rāgacarito ti evaṁ dhātudosanidānā ti vadanti.*
2. Cp. Vis. Mag. 104 ff: *Iriyāpatho kiccā bhojanā dassanādito*
   dhammappavattito c'eva cariyāyo vibhāvaye ti.

he quarrels with others often. Even with very good things he is not pleased. Thus he rejects all things. His way of life is determined by the humours. Towards other objects of sense also he behaves in the same way. Thus it may be known that one is a walker in hate.

One who walks in infatuation looks at an object thus: he believes others as regards merits and demerits (of anything). He considers worthless what others consider worthless. He praises what others praise, because he does not know. Towards the other objects of sense also he behaves in the same way. Thus it may be known that one is a walker in infatuation. Thus it may be known 'through (the manner of seeing) objects'.

Q. How may it be known 'through the defilements'?

A. Five are the defilements of one who walks in passion. They are jealousy, pride, wiliness, deceitfulness, sensuality. These are the five.

Five are the defilements of one who walks in hate. They are anger, vindictiveness, hypocrisy, niggardliness, hatred. These are the five.

Five are the defilements of one who walks in infatuation. They are rigidity, negligence, uncertainty, anxiety, infatuation. These are the five. Thus it may be known, 'through the defilements'.

Q. How may it be known 'through (the manner of) walking'?

A. The natural gait of him who walks in passion is thus: Lifting up his feet, he walks swiftly, with even pace. He raises his feet evenly and does not bring them down flat. In walking, he lifts his feet gracefully. Thus is one who walks in passion known 'through (the manner of) walking'.

The natural gait of him who walks in hate is thus: He lifts up his feet jerkily and jerkily puts them down. His feet rub against each other as he puts them down half-way, as if digging the ground. Thus is one who walks in hate known, 'through (the manner of) walking'.

The natural gait of him who walks in infatuation is thus: Shufflingly he lifts his feet up and shufflingly he puts them down. His feet graze against each other. Thus is one who walks in infatuation known, 'through (the manner of) walking'. Thus it may be known 'through (the manner of) walking'.

Q. How may it be known 'through (the manner of) robing'?

A. The natural manner of robing of him who walks in passion is thus: He robes neither shabbily nor tardily. His robes do not sit too low and are well-rounded, elegantly worn and, in many ways, pleasing to see.

The natural manner of robing of him who walks in hate is thus: He robes hurriedly. The robes sit too high, are not well-rounded, are inelegantly worn and, in many ways, are not pleasing to see.

The natural manner of him who walks in infatuation is thus: He dresses tardily. His robes are not well-rounded, are inelegantly worn, and in many ways are not pleasing to see. Thus it may be known, 'through (the manner of) robing'.

Q. How may it be known 'through (the manner of) eating'?

A. A walker in passion relishes tasty, succulent, sweet food.

A walker in hate relishes acid food.

A walker in infatuation relishes anything at all.

And again, when a walker in passion eats, he serves himself a moderate quantity of food, takes it (to the mouth) in well-rounded, moderate lumps. and slowly enjoys its taste. Even if it is of little taste, he enjoys it very much.

When a walker in hate eats, he takes in big mouthfuls of immoderate lumps of food, not well-rounded. If the food is of little taste, he is displeased.

When a walker in infatuation eats, he takes in small, not well-rounded lumps of food. He smears his mouth with food. A part of the food enters his mouth and a part falls back into the vessel. In the act of eating, he is not mindful. Thus it may be known, 'through (the manner of) eating'.

Q. How may it be known, 'through work'?

A walker in passion takes hold of the broom evenly,[1] and unhuriedly sweeps. Without scattering the sand, he cleans well.

A walker in hate hurriedly takes the broom and sweeps, quickly, one end to the other, scattering the sand on both sides and making a harsh noise. He sweeps clean, but not evenly.

A walker in infatuation takes hold of the broom tardily. Though he goes over the ground, certain parts are not swept well and not evenly.

One who washes, dyes, sews and does everything evenly without letting his mind go astray, is a walker in passion.

A walker in hate does all things unevenly, but does not let his mind go astray.

A walker in infatuation is disturbed in mind. He does many things, but nothing successfully. Thus it may be known 'through work'.

Q. How may it be known, 'through (the manner of) sleeping'?

A. A walker in passion prepares his bed unhurriedly and in proper order. He lies down gently and sleeps drawing in his limbs. On being awakened at night, he gets up immediately and answers hesitatingly.

A walker in hate hurries and lies down in any place he gets. He frowns in his sleep. On being awakened at night, he gets up immediately and answers angrily.

---

1. Lit. With even body.

A walker in infatuation does not prepare his bed in an orderly manner. In sleep, his limbs are out, and only his body is covered. On being awakened at night, he murmurs and answers long after. Thus it may be known 'through (the manner of) sleeping'.

ON ROBING, BEGGING, SITTING, SLEEPING, AND RESORT

Q. In what manner and with what thought should one wear the robes, beg, sit, and sleep and what should be one's resort?

A. A walker in passion should robe himself humbly, and his robes should not sit too low. He should not wear bright robes. Thus should he robe himself.

A walker in hate should robe himself with minute care, cleanly and with robes of bright colour. His robes should sit low and be elegant. Thus should he robe himself.

A walker in infatuation should wear whatever robes he gets.

A walker in passion[1] should beg humbly, should not look for clean and tasty food. He should beg little.

A walker in hate may look for succulent, pure and tasty food, and for as much as he likes.

A walker in infatuation should be satisfied with what he gets.

A walker in passion should sleep and sit under shade of trees, by the water's edge, in small secluded woodland glades, or in some half-built shrine, or in a place where there are no beds. Thus should he sleep and sit.

A walker in hate should sleep and sit under shade of trees, by the water's edge, in a level place, in a completed shrine, or in a place provided with beds and sheets.

A walker in infatuation should dwell near his teacher, relying on him.

The resort of a walker in passion should be a place of humble drink and food. When he enters the village for alms, he should, facing the sun, go to the meanest quarter. To such a place he should go.

The resort of a walker in hate is the place where rice, water, meat and drink are complete. When he enters the village for alms, he should not face the sun, and should go where there are many men of faith. To such a place he should go.

The walker in infatuation should take what he gets.

The walker in passion should adopt the posture of standing or walking to and fro; the walker in hate should adopt the posture of sitting or lying down;[2] the walker in infatuation [411] should adopt the posture of walking.

---

1. Text, *Mohacarita.* Obviously an error.

2. Cp.Vis. Mag. 108-9.

MISCELLANEOUS TEACHINGS

Here, there are miscellaneous teachings. A passionate man gains faith through lovable objects. A hating man gains faith through being bound up with unlovely things. An infatuated man gains (faith) through non-investigation.

A passionate mau is like a servant. A hating man is like a master. An infatuated man is like venom.

A passionate man is little affected by the humours. He does not remove the defilements.

A hating man is much affected by the humours, and does not allow himself to be stained by the defilements.

An infatuated man is much affected by the humours. He does not remove the defilements.

A man walking in passion is sensuous.

A man walking in hate is quarrelsome.

A man walking in infatuation is negligent.

THE DISTINGUISHING OF THE SUBJECTS OF MEDITATION[1]

CHAPTER THE SEVENTH

THIRTY-EIGHT SUBJECTS OF MEDITATION

Now, the teacher on whom one depends, having observed one's behaviour, teaches one the thirty-eight subjects of meditation. And again, he teaches one the two associated subjects of meditation.

Q. What are the thirty-eight subjects of meditation?

A. Namely, the ten *kasiṇas*, — earth, water, fire, air, blue-green, yellow, red, white, space, consciousness;[2] the ten perceptions of putrescence, namely, the perception of bloatedness, the perception of discolouration, the perception of festering, the perception of the dismembered, the perception of the gnawed, the perception of the cut and the dismembered, the perception of the fissured, the perception of the blood-stained, the perception of worminess and the perception of the bony;[3] the ten recollections, namely, Recollection of the Buddha, Recollection of the Law, Recollection of the Community of Bhikkhus, recollection of virtue, recollection of liberality, recollection of deities, mindfulness of death, mindfulness of body, mindfulness of respiration, recollection of peace;[4] the four immeasurable thoughts: loving-kindness compassion, appreciative joy, equanimity;[5] the Determining of the elements;[6] the Perception of the foulness of food;[7] the sphere of nothingness, the sphere of neither perception nor non-perception.[8]

METHOD OF DISCERNING THE QUALITIES

These are the thirty-eight subjects of meditation. The distinctive qualities of these thirty-eight subjects of meditation may be known (1) by way of meditation, (2) by way of transcending, (3) by way of increasing, (4) by way of cause, (5) by way of object, (6) by way of speciality, (7) by way of plane, (8) by way of seizing, (9) by way of person.[9]

BY WAY OF MEDITATION

Q. How, 'by way of meditation'?

A. Namely, ten subjects of meditation fulfil access-meditation; eleven

---

1. Cp. Vis. Mag. 110 ff. 2. A.I, 41: *Paṭhavi, āpo, tejo, vāyo, nila, pitā, lohita, odāta, ākāsa, viññāṇa.* For the last two *kasiṇas* Vis. Mag. substitutes *āloka-*° and *paricchinn-ākāsa-kasiṇas.*
3. Pts. I, 49: *Uddhumātaka, vinilaka, vipubbaka, vikkhittaka, vikkhāyitaka, hatavikkhittaka, vicchiddaka, lohitaka, puḷuvaka, aṭṭhika.* The order here is altered to suit the passage above.
4. *Buddhānussati, Dhammānussati. Sanghānussati. sīlānussati, cāgānussati, devatānussati, maraṇānussati, kāyagatā-,*° *ānāpāna-sati, upasamānussati.*
5. Lit. *appamāṇa citta.* Cp. D.III, 223-4: *catasso appamaññāyo.—Mettā, karuṇā, muditā, upekkhā.*
6. *Catudhātuvavatthāna.* 7. *Ahāre paṭikkūla-saññā.* 8. *Akiñcaññāyatana, nevasaññānā-saññāyatana.* 9. Cp. Vis. Mag. 111 ff.

subjects of meditation fulfil the first meditation; three subjects of meditation fulfil the three-fold meditation.

And again, one subject of meditation fulfils the four-fold meditation; nine subjects of meditation fulfil the four-fold and five-fold meditation. And again, four subjects of meditation fulfil the four-fold formless meditation.

Q. Which ten subjects of meditation fulfil access-meditation?

A. Excepting mindfulness of respiration and mindfulness of body, the remaining eight recollections, the determining of the four elements and the perception of the foulness of food are called the ten (objects of) access-meditation.

Q. Which of the eleven subjects of meditation produce the first meditation?

A. The ten perceptions of putrescence and mindfulness of body produce the first meditation.

Q. Which three subjects of meditation produce the three-fold meditation?

A. Namely, loving-kindness compassion and appreciative joy.

Q. Which subject of meditation produces the four-fold meditation?

A. Namely, equanimity.

Q. Which nine subjects of meditation comprise the four-fold and five-fold meditations?

A. Excepting space-*kasiṇa* and consciousness-*kasiṇa*, the remaining eight *kasiṇas* and Mindfulness of respiration.

Q. Which four subjects of meditation comprise the four-fold formless meditation?

A. Space-*kasiṇa*, consciousness-*kasiṇa*, the sphere of nothingness, the sphere of neither perception nor non-perception — these are called the four subjects of meditation.

Thus these should be known 'by way of meditation'.

BY WAY OF TRANSCENDING

Q. How 'by way of transcending'?

A. The sphere-subjects of meditation transcend form. Excepting the formless-*kasiṇas*, the remaining eight *kasiṇas* and what remain of the thirty subjects of meditation, do not transcend form.

Three subjects of meditation transcend the object: the two formless-*kasiṇas* and the sphere of nothingness. The other thirty-five subjects of meditation do not transcend the object.

And again, one subject of meditation transcends perception and sensation, namely, the sphere of neither perception nor non-perception. The other thirty-seven subjects of meditation do not transcend perception and sensation. Thus these should be known 'by way of transcending'.

BY WAY OF INCREASING

Q. How, 'by way of increasing'?

A. Fourteen subjects of meditation should be increased, namely, the ten *kasiṇas* and the four immeasurables. The other twenty-four should not be increased.

Thus these should be known 'by way of increasing'.

BY WAY OF CAUSE

Q How, 'by way of cause'?

A. Nine subjects of meditation are causes of supernormal power, namely, excepting the formless *kasiṇas*, the remaining eight *kasiṇas* and limited-space *kasiṇa*. What remain of the other thirty subjects of meditation do not become causes of supernormal power. Thirty-seven subjects of meditation become insight-causes, namely, (all) except the sphere of neither perception nor non-perception.[1] And again, one subject of meditation does not become insight-cause, namely, the sphere of neither perception nor non-perception. Thus these should be known 'by way of cause'.

BY WAY OF OBJECT

Q. How, 'by way of object'?

A. Twenty-one subjects of meditation have the sign as object. Twelve subjects of meditation have their intrinsic nature as object.

Q. Which twenty-one subjects of meditation have the sign as object?

A. Excepting the consciousness *kasiṇa*, the remaining nine *kasiṇas*, the ten perceptions of putrescence, mindfulness of respiratic n and mindfulness of body.

Q. Which twelve (subjects of meditation) have their intrinsic nature as object?

A. Consciousness *kasiṇa*, the sphere of neither perception nor non-perception and the ten objects of access-meditation.

Q. Which five have neither the sign nor their intrinsic nature as object?

A. Namely, the four immeasurables and the sphere of nothingness.

1. A. IV, 426: *Iti kho bhikkhave yavatā saññāsamāpatti, tavatā aññāpaṭivedho.*

And again, two subjects of meditation have: internally developed object; internal object.

And again, two subjects of meditation: internally developed object; external object.

And again, one subject of meditation: externally developed object and internal object.

And again, twenty-one subjects of meditation: externally developed object; external object.

And again, four subjects of meditation: internally developed object; internal object; prepared external object.

And again, four subjects of meditation: prepared internal object; prepared developed external object; external object.

And again, two subjects of meditation: prepared internally developed object; prepared externally developed external object; prepared internal object; prepared external object.

And again, one subject of meditation: internal-external developed object; internal object.

And again, one subject of meditation: developed internal object; indescribable internal object; external object.

Two subjects of meditation: developed internal object; internal object, namely, consciousness *kasiṇa* and sphere of neither perception nor non-perception.

And again, two subjects of meditation: internally developed object; external object, namely: mindfulness of respiration and mindfulness of body.

And again, one subject of meditation: externally developed object; internal object, namely: recollection of death.

And again, twenty-one subjects of meditation: externally developed object; external object, namely, the ten perceptions of putrescence, the four immeasurable thoughts, the four colour *kasiṇas*, (limited-) space *kasiṇa*, recollection of the Buddha and recollection of the Community of Bhikkhus.

And again, four subjects of meditation: internally developed object; internal object; prepared (object); prepared external object, namely, recollection of virtue, recollection of liberality, the determining of the four elements and the perception of the foulness of food.

And again, four subjects of meditation: prepared internally developed object; prepared externally developed object; prepared external object, namely, the four colour *kasiṇas*.

And again, two subjects of meditation: prepared internally developed object; prepared externally developed object; prepared internal object;

prepared external object, namely, recollection of the Law and recollection of peace.

And again, one subject of meditation: internal-external prepared object; internal object, namely, recollection of deities.

And again, one subject of meditation: inner developed object; inner object; outer object; sphere object; namely, the sphere of nothingness.

And again, two subjects of meditation belonging to the past, namely, consciousness *kasiṇa* and the sphere of neither perception nor non-perception.

And again, one subject of meditation is of the future, namely, recollection of death.

And again, one subject of meditation is of the present, namely, recollection of deities.

And again, six subjects of meditation: prepared past object; prepared future object; namely recollection of the Buddha, recollection of the Community of Bhikkhus, recollection of virtue, recollection of liberality, the determining of the four elements and the perception of the foulness of food.

And again, two subjects of meditation: prepared past object; prepared present object; prepared non-characterizable past-future; namely, nine *kasiṇas*, the ten perceptions of putrescence, the four immeasurable thoughts, mindfulness of respiration, mindfulness of body and the sphere of nothingness.

And again, four subjects of meditation, namely, fire *kasiṇa*, air *kasiṇa*, the perception of worminess and mindfulness of respiration, have unsteady objects. Movement is their medium, but their after-image is steady. All the other thirty-four have steady objects.

Thus these should be known 'by way of object'.

BY WAY OF SPECIALITY

Q. How, 'by way of speciality'?

A. Eight *kasiṇas* and the four formless (objects of) concentration are named special. The eight *kasiṇas*, being true objects, are called (objects of) speciality in concentration. And because in the fourth meditation, *jhāna*, one reaches a special plane, the four formless (objects of) concentration become special.

The ten perceptions of putrescence and the perception of the foulness of food are called special perception, because of colour, form, space, direction, distinctiveness, combination and coherence, and because of the impurity-perception-object.

The ten recollections are called special recollections, because of their subtility and because of attentiveness.

[412] The four immeasurable thoughts are called special, because they cannot be surpassed.

The determining of the four elements is called the speciality of wisdom, because of its connection with the void.

Thus these should be known 'by way of speciality'.

BY WAY OF PLANE

Q. How, 'by way of plane'?

A. Twelve subjects of meditation do not arise in the higher heavens. Namely, the ten perceptions of putrescence, mindfulness of body and the perception of the foulness of food.

And again, thirteen subjects of meditation do not arise in the form existence.[1] Namely, the first twelve and mindfulness of respiration do not arise in the form existence.

No subject of meditation except the four formless (ones) arise in the formless existence.[2]

Thus these should be understood 'by way of plane'.

BY WAY OF SEIZING

Q. How, 'by way of seizing'?

A. Seventeen subjects of meditation seize the sign through sight, i.e., excepting air *kasiṇa* and the formless *kasiṇas*, the remaining seven *kasiṇas* and ten perceptions of putrescence.

And again, one subject of meditation seizes the sign through contact. Namely, mindfulness of respiration.

And again, one subject of meditation seizes the sign through sight or contact. Namely, air *kasiṇa*.

The remaining nineteen subjects of meditation seize the sign through audition.

And again, five subjects of meditation should not be practised by the beginner. Namely, the formless and equanimity. The remaining thirty-five may be practised by the beginner.

Thus these should be known 'by way of seizing'.

BY WAY OF PERSON

Q. How 'by way of person'?

A. A walker in passion should not practise the four immeasurables,

1. *Rūpabhava*. According to Vis. Mag. 113, *Brahmaloka*. 2. *Arūpabhava*.

because of their auspicious sign. Why? A walker in passion is not good at appreciating the auspicious sign. It (the practice of the four immeasurables by a walker in passion) is comparable to a man affected of a disorder of phlegm partaking of very rich food that is harmful to him.

A walker in hate should not practise the ten perceptions of putrescence, because of the arising of resentment-perception. A walker in hate is not good at appreciating it and is comparable to a man with a bilious ailment partaking of hot drinks and food which are harmful to him.

A walker in infatuation, who has not gathered wisdom, should not work at any subject of meditation, because of his lack of skill. Owing to lack of skill, his efforts will be fruitless. It (the practice of meditation by a walker in infatuation) is comparable to a man who rides an elephant without a goad.

A walker in passion should practise the perception of impurity and mindfulness of body, because these help overcome lust.

A walker in hate should practise the four immeasurables, because these help overcome hatred. Or he should practise colour *kasiṇa*, because his mind attends to such.

A walker in faith should practise the six recollections beginning with recollection of the Buddha. Then his faith will gain fixity.

A walker in intelligence should practise the determining of the four elements, the perception of the foulness of food, recollection of death and recollection of peace because he is profound.

And again, a walker in intelligence is not debarred from working at any subject of meditation.

A walker in excogitation should practise mindfulness of respiration, because it eradicates discursive thought.[1]

A walker in infatuation should make inquiries regarding the Law, should hear expositions of the Law in due season, with reverential mind, and should honour the Law. He should live with his teacher. He should heap up wisdom and should practise what pleases him of the thirty-eight subjects of meditation. Recollection of death and the determining of the four elements are specially suited to him.

And again, there is another teaching: "When I investigate the subjects of meditation, I see their distinctive qualities. The six persons may, through discernment, be reduced to three".

Q. If that be so, will there be difficulties at the beginning?

A. There are two kinds of men who walk in passion, namely, (the man) of dull faculties and (the man) of keen faculties. A walker in passion who has dull faculties should practise the investigation of impurity in order to overcome lust. Thus he should practise and overcome lust.

---

1. A. I, 449: *Cetaso vikkhepassa pahānaya ānāpānasati bhāvetabbā.*

The walker in passion who has keen faculties should, at first, increase faith. He should practise the recollections. Thus he should practise and overcome lust.

There are two kinds of men who walk in hate, namely, (the man) of dull faculties and (the man) of keen faculties. A walker in hate who has dull faculties should practise the four immeasurables. By this he will be able to overcome hatred.

The walker in hate who has keen faculties, being one endowed with wisdom, should practise the (meditation of the) special sphere. Thus should one practise and dispel hatred.

There are two kinds of men who walk in infatuation, namely, (the man) of no faculties and (the man) of dull faculties. The walker in infatuation who has no faculties should not work at any subject of meditation. The walker in infatuation who has dull faculties should practise mindfulness of respiration in order to dispel discursive thinking.

Thus (the six persons) can be reduced to three. Therefore, there should be no difficulty. According to this teaching, the *kasiṇas* and mindfulness of respiration are developed (further) through space. All the activities can be fulfilled without difficulty. If a man is endowed with merit, he will have no difficulty in fulfilling all the excellent subjects of meditation.

THE PATH OF FREEDOM

FASCICLE THE FOURTH

WRITTEN

BY

THE ARAHANT UPATISSA

WHO WAS CALLED

GREAT LIGHT IN RYO

TRANSLATED IN RYO

BY

TIPIṬAKA SANGHAPĀLA OF FUNAN

ENTRANCE INTO THE SUBJECT OF MEDITATION

CHAPTER THE EIGHTH

Section One

Q. What is the earth *kasiṇa*?[1] What is the practice of it? What is its salient characteristic? What is its function? What is its near cause? What are its benefits? What is the meaning of *kasiṇa*? How many kinds of earth are there? What is the earth sign? How is a *maṇḍala* made? What is the method of meditating on the earth *kasiṇa*?

EARTH KASINA, ITS PRACTICE, SALIENT CHARACTERISTIC, FUNCTION AND NEAR CAUSE

A. The thought that is produced relying on the earth sign — this is called earth *kasiṇa*. The undisturbed dwelling of the mind — this is called practice. Delight in being linked to the earth sign is its salient characteristic. Non-abandonment is its function. Non-differentiated thought is its near cause.

BENEFITS

What are its benefits?[2] Twelve are its benefits, namely, the sign is easy of acquisition through meditation on the earth *kasiṇa*; at all times and in all actions, mental activity is unimpeded; acquiring supernormal power, a man is able to walk on water just as on earth and to move freely in space; he gains the supernormal power of manifoldness, the knowledge of past lives, the heavenly ear and worldly higher knowledge; he fares well and draws near to the verge of the ambrosial.

1. In this text the ideograph for *paṭhavīkasiṇa* = *pṛthvīkṛtsnāyatana* (Sk.)
2. Cp. Vis. Mag. 175.

MEANING OF KASINA

Q. What is the meaning of *kasiṇa*?

A. Pervasiveness — this is called *kasiṇa*. It is even as the Enlightened One taught in the stanza:-[1]

> "*When a man remembers*
> *the worth of the 'wakened ones,*
> *the joy that wells within him*
> *floods his body through.*
> *So, when with spreading earth-thought*
> *Rose-apple Isle's suffused,*
> *the earth-wrought state is likened*
> *to the body with bliss perfused*".

Meditating thus one causes this *maṇḍala* to prevail everywhere.

KINDS OF EARTH

Q. How many kinds of earth are there? Taking which earth as sign should one practise?

A. There are two kinds of earth.[2] 1. Natural earth. 2. Prepared earth. Solidity is the property of natural earth. This is called natural earth. What is made of earth dug out by a man himself or by another is called prepared earth. Earth is of four colours, namely, white, black,[3] red and the colour of dawn. Here a yogin should not add anything to natural earth. He should exclude white, black and red. Why? When he meditates on earth of these colours, he does not get the after-image. By dwelling on white, black or red, he practises colour *kasiṇa*. Why? If a yogin meditates on natural earth or prepared earth, he will get the (after-) image. If it (i.e., earth) is of dawn-colour, he should take that sign.

NON-PREPARED EARTH

Q. What is non-prepared earth sign?

A. Level ground which is free from thickets, free from roots of trees or tufts of grass, within the range of vision and which arouses steady mental activity — this is earth perception. This is called non-prepared earth.

A practised yogin gains the after-image of earth following either the difficult or the easy way, and dwells without falling. A beginner in the first

---

1. Not traced. Cp. Th. 381: *Buddham appameyyaṁ anussara pasanno pītiyā phuṭasarīro hohisi satatam udaggo.*
2. Cp. Vis. Mag. 123 ff.
3. *Nīla* — also sometimes rendered dark-blue, blue-black, black.

meditation, *jhāna*, takes prepared earth and makes a *maṇḍala*. He should not meditate on non-prepared earth.

ON MAKING A MANDALA

Q. How is a *maṇḍala* made?

A. If a yogin desires to make a *maṇḍala* on the ground, let him at first select a calm place in the monastery, or a cave, or a place under a tree, or a deserted, covered place unlit by the sun, or a place on an unused road. In all such places, let him keep a distance of one fathom, sweep the place clean and make it smooth. In such places let him, with clay of the colour of dawn, prepare the ground in order to cause the arising of the sign. Taking a moderate quantity in a vessel, let him carefully mix it with water and remove grass, roots and dirt from it. With the edge of a cloth let him remove any dirt that may be on the swept place. Let him screen the sitting place and exclude the light, and make a couch of meditation. Let him make a circle according to rule, neither too near nor too far. Let the circle be flat and full and without markings. After that let watery clay unmixed with any other colour or unmixed with special colour be applied. It should be covered and protected until it is dry. When it is dry, [413] it should be edged with another colour. It may be of the size of a round rice-sifter, a metal gong and may be circular, rectangular, triangular or square. Thus it should be understood.

According to the principal teacher's instructions, a circle is the best. The *maṇḍala* may be made on cloth, on a board or on a wall. But it is best on the ground. This is the teaching of predecessor teachers.

METHOD OF EARTH KASINA MEDITATION

Q. How should one meditate upon the earth *kasiṇa*?

A. A yogin who wishes to meditate upon the earth *kasiṇa* should at first consider the tribulations of sense-desires, and again he should consider the benefits of renunciation.

TRIBULATIONS OF SENSE-DESIRES ILLUSTRATED IN TWENTY SIMILES

Q. How should he consider the tribulations of sense-desires?

A. Because they produce little pleasure and severe pain, they are full of tribulations.[1] (1) Sense-desires are likened to a bone because of scanty

1. The first ten similes are at A. III, 97: *Aṭṭhisaṅkhalūpamā kāmā vuttā Bhagavatā, bahudukkhā bahūpāyāsā, ādīnavo ettha bhiyo. Maṁsapesūpamā kāmā vuttā Bhagavatā......... Tiṇukkūpamā kāmā........Aṅgārakāsūpamā kāmā........Supinakūpamā kāmā...... Yācitakūpamā kāmā.........Rukkhaphalūpamā kāmā........Asisūnūpamā kāmā......... Sattisūlūpamā kāmā.......Sappasirūpamā kāmā vuttā Bhagavatā, bahudukkhā bahūpāyāsā ādīnavo ettha bhiyo.*

yield of pleasure; (2) sense-desires are likened to a piece of flesh because they are followed by many (sufferings); (3) sense-desires are likened to a (flaming) torch carried against the wind because they burn; (4) sense-desires are likened to a pit of glowing embers because of the great and the small (?); (5) sense-desires are likened to a dream because they vanish quickly; (6) sense-desires are likened to borrowed goods because they cannot be enjoyed long; (7) sense-desires are likened to a fruit tree because they are chopped down by others; (8) sense-desires are likened to a sword because they cut; (9) sense-desires are likened to a pointed stake because they impale; (10) sense-desires are likened to the head of a venomous snake because they are fearful;[1] (11) sense-desires are likened to a flock of cotton blown about by the wind because they are unresisting by nature; (12) sense-desires are likened to a mirage because they bewilder the fool; (13) sense-desires are likened to darkness because they are blinding; (14) sense-desires are likened to hindrances because they obstruct the way of good; (15) sense-desires are likened to infatuation because they cause the loss of Right Mindfulness; (16) sense-desires are likened to ripening because they are subject to decay; (17) sense-desires are likened to fetters because they bind one to another; (18) sense-desires are likened (to thieves) because they rob the value of merit; (19) sense-desires are likened to a house of hate because they provoke quarrels; (20) and sense-desires are pain-laden because they cause trials innumerable. Having considered the tribulations of sense-desires, in this manner, he should consider the benefits of renunciation.

RENUNCIATION AND ITS BENEFITS

Renunciation. Namely, good practices, like the first meditation, *jhāna*, from the time one retires from the world — these are named renunciation.

Simile No. 14 — A. III, 63: *Kāmacchando bhikkhave āvaraṇo nīvaraṇo.*
Simile No. 17 — D. I, 245: *Kāma-guṇā ariyassa vinaye andūti pi vuccanti, bandhanan ti pi vuccanti.*

1. In the Chinese 'Potaliya' (transliteration) Sutta, the simile of the snake is also found, and the eight doctrines taught in this sutta are illustrated with as many examples, though it is difficult to say exactly which illustration refers to which doctrine. In the Pali there are only seven illustrations. The following is taken from the Chū Agon (*Madhyama Āgama*) No. 203: "Householder, it is as if, not far from a village, there were a huge venomous snake, very vicious, poisonous, black and terrible of aspect, and a man not foolish, not deluded, not insane, in full possession of his senses, desirous of weal and shunning woe, disliking sorrow very much, wishing to live, not wishing to die and disliking death very much, were to come. What do you think, householder, would that man stretch out his hand or any other member of his body to the snake, saying, 'Bite me, bite me'?" Then the householder answered: "No, venerable Gotama, because on seeing the venomous snake he would think: 'If I were to stretch forth my hand or other member of my body and let the snake bite it, I should die or suffer severely'. And so, on seeing that venomous snake, he wishes to flee from it". Householder, the learned, noble disciple also thinks in the same way: 'Sense-desires are like a venomous snake. It was taught by the Blessed One that sense-desires are like a venomous snake. They yield little pleasure, produce much suffering and are pain-laden'. And he abandons sense-desires, becomes freed from evil states of mind and causes to perish all worldly enjoyment and clings to nothing".

Q. What are the benefits of renunciation? *A*. Separation from the hindrances;[1] the dwelling in freedom; the joy of solitude; the dwelling in happiness and mindfulness and the ability to endure suffering; accomplishment of much good and attainment of the ground of great fruition; the benefitting of two places[2] through acceptance of gifts. This (renunciation) is profound wisdom. This is the best of all stations. This is called 'beyond the three worlds'.

And again, what is called renunciation is the renunciation of sense-desires. This is solitude. This is freedom from all hindrances. This is happiness. This is the absence of defilement. This is the super-excellent path. This washes away the dirt of the mind. Through this practice is merit gathered. Through this practice inward calm is won.

Sense-desires are coarse; renunciation is fine. Sense-desires are defiling; renunciation is non-defiling. Sense-desires are inferior; renunciation is superior. Sense-desires are connected with hate; renunciation is unconnected with hate. Sense-desires are not friendly towards fruition; renunciation is the friend of fruition. Sense-desires are bound up with fear; renunciation is fearless.

METHOD OF PRACTICE OF EARTH KASINA

Having, in this manner, considered the tribulations of sense-desires and the benefits of renunciation, one accomplishes happiness through renunciation. One arouses the heart of faith and reverence, and meditates either on the non-prepared or the prepared. Taking food in moderation, one observes the rules regarding the bowl and robes, well. Bodily or mentally one is not heedless, and accepts little.

Having taken a moderate meal, one washes the hands and feet, and sits down and meditates on the Buddha's Enlightenment,[3] the Law and the Order. Through the doing of good actions and through these recollections one becomes happy and thinks: "Now it is possible for me to acquire perfection. Had I not renounced, long would it have been before I reached peace. Therefore, I should endeavour earnestly". And taking the mat of meditation to a place neither too far from nor too near the *maṇḍala*, i.e., about the length of a plough-pole or a fathom (from the *maṇḍala*), one sits down with legs crossed under him, faces the *maṇḍala*, holds the body erect and arouses mindfulness from the very depths of his being, with closed eyes.

After sometime, one is able to exclude all disturbances of body and mind, collect his thoughts and unify his mind. Then opening the eyes neither too wide nor too narrowly, one should fix one's gaze on the *maṇḍala*.

---

1. *Pañca nivaraṇāni.*
2. Cp. A. II, 80: *Atthi bhikkhave dakkhiṇā dāyakato c'eva visujjhati paṭiggāhakato ca.*
3. *Bodhi* — transliteration.

THREE WAYS OF SIGN-TAKING

The yogin should meditate on the form of the *maṇḍala* and take the sign through three ways: through even gazing, skilfulness and neutralizing disturbance.

Q. How, through even gazing?

A. When the yogin dwells on the *maṇḍala*, he should not open his eyes too wide nor shut them entirely. Thus should he view it. If he opens his eyes too wide, they will grow weary, he will not be able to know the true nature of the *maṇḍala*, and the after-image will not arise. If he faces the *maṇḍala* closing the eyes fast, he will not see the sign because of darkness, and he will arouse negligence. Therefore, he should refrain from opening his eyes too wide and closing them fast. He should dwell with earnestness on the *maṇḍala*. Thus should the yogin dwell (on the *maṇḍala*) in order to gain fixity of mind. As a man looking at his own face in a mirror sees his face because of the mirror, i.e., because the face is reflected by the mirror, so the yogin dwelling on the *maṇḍala* sees the sign of concentration which arises, because of the *maṇḍala*. Thus should he take the sign by fixing the mind through even gazing. Thus one takes the sign through even gazing.

Q. How, through skilfulness?

A. Namely, through four ways. The first is to put away any internal lack; the second is to view the *maṇḍala* squarely; third is to supply the deficiency should a partial sign or half the *maṇḍala* appear; (fourth:) at this time if his mind is distracted and becomes negligent, he should endeavour like a potter at the wheel[1] and, when his mind acquires fixity, he should gaze on the *maṇḍala*, and letting it pervade (his mind) fully and without faults consider calmness (?). Thus should skilfulness be known.

Q. How, through neutralizing disturbance?

A. There are four kinds of disturbance: the first is endeavour that is too quick; the second is endeavour that is too slow; the third is elation; the fourth is depression.

Q. What is endeavour that is too quick?

A. It is hurried practice. The yogin is impatient. He sits (to meditate) in the morning. By evening he ceases (to endeavour), because of weariness of body. This is called hurried doing.

Q. What is endeavour that is too slow?

A. It is to stray away from the way of meditation. Though the yogin sees the *maṇḍala* he does not dwell on it with reverence. Often he gets up. Often he lies down.

---

1. Cp. M. II, 18: *Seyyathāpi Udāyi, dakkho kumbhakāro vā kumbhakārantevāsī vā suparikammakatāya mattikāya yaṁ yad eva bhājanavikatiṁ ākaṅkheyya, taṁ tad eva kareyya abhinipphādeyya.*

When a yogin endeavours too vigorously, his body becomes weary and his mind flags. Or, the mind wanders and loses itself in frivolous thoughts. When he endeavours too slowly, his body and mind become dull and lazy and sleep overtakes him.[1]

Elation: If the yogin's mind becomes lax through losing itself in frivolous thoughts, he becomes discontented with the subject of meditation. If he, at first, does not delight in frivolous thoughts, his mind becomes elated through willing. Or again, it becomes elated, if he does many deeds through the will for happiness and bliss.

Depression: The yogin fails owing to agitation and thereby partakes of uneasiness, and dislikes the subject of meditation. If he dislikes the subject of meditation from the start he resents activity and, accordingly through resentment, his mind becomes depressed. And again, his mind becomes weary of initial and sustained application of thought, falls from distinction and, owing to craving, becomes depressed.

When this yogin's mind falls into a state of agitation, quickly, he overcomes and abandons agitation, with the faculty of mindfulness and the faculty of concentration. When his mind falls into a state of negligence, he should overcome and abandon that state of mind-negligence with the faculty of mindfulness and the faculty of energy. When the man of elated mind falls into a lustful state, he should abandon lust forthwith. When the man of depressed mind falls into an angry state, he should abandon anger forthwith. In these four places a man accomplishes and makes his mind move in one direction. If his mind moves in one direction, the sign can be made to arise.

GRASPING SIGN

There are two kinds of signs, namely, the grasping sign and the after-image. What is the grasping sign? When a yogin, with undisturbed mind dwells on the *maṇḍala*, he gains the perception of the *maṇḍala* and sees it as it were in space, sometimes far, sometimes near, sometimes to the left, sometimes to the right, sometimes big, sometimes small, sometimes ugly, sometimes lovely. Occasionally (he sees it multiplied) many (times) and occasionally few (times). He, without scanning the *maṇḍala*, causes the grasping sign to arise through skilful contemplation. This is named grasping sign.

THE AFTER-IMAGE

Through the following of that (the grasping sign) again and again the after-image arises. The after-image means this: what when a man contem-

---

1. A. III, 375: *Accāraddhaviriyaṁ uddhaccāya saṁvattati atilīnaviriyaṁ kosajjāya saṁvattati. Tasṁa ti ha tvaṁ Soṇa viriyasamataṁ adhiṭṭhaha indriyānañ ca samataṁ paṭivijjha tattha ca nimittaṁ gaṇhāhī 'ti.*

plates appears together with mind. Here the mind does not gain collectedness through viewing the *maṇḍala*, but it (the after-image) can be seen with closed eyes as before (while looking at the *maṇḍala*) only in thought. If he wills to see it far, he sees it afar. As regards seeing it near, to the left, to the right, before, behind, within, without, above and below, it is the same. It appears together with mind. This is called the after-image.

THE SIGN

What is the meaning of sign?

The meaning of (conditioning) cause is the meaning of sign. It is even as the Buddha taught the bhikkhus: [414] "All evil demeritorious states occur depending on a sign".[1] This is the meaning of conditioning cause. And again, it is said that the meaning of wisdom is the meaning of the sign. The Buddha has declared: "With trained perception one should forsake".[2] This is called wisdom. And again, it is said that the meaning of image is the meaning of the sign. It is like the thought a man has on seeing the reflection of his own face and image. The after-image is obvious.

PROTECTING THE SIGN

After acquiring the sign the yogin should, with heart of reverence towards his teacher, protect that excellent sign. If he does not protect, he will, surely, lose it.

Q. How should he protect it?

A. He should protect it through three kinds of actions: through refraining from evil, practice of good and through constant endeavour.

How does one refrain from evil? One should refrain from pleasure of work, of various kinds of trivial talk, of sleeping, of frequenting assemblies, immoral habits; (one should refrain from) the non-protection of the faculties,[3] intemperance as regards food, non-practice of the meditations, *jhānas*, and non-watchfulness in the first and last watches of the night, non-reverence for that which he has learned (the rule), the company of bad friends and seeing improper objects of sense. To partake of food, to sit and to lie down, at the improper time, are not wholesome. To conquer these states is (to do) good. Thus he should always practise.

Q. What is the meaning of constant endeavour?

---

1. Cp. D.I, 70: *Idha mahā-raja bhikkhu cakkhunā rūpaṁ disvā na nimittaggāhī hoti nānuvyañjanaggāhī. Yatvādhikaraṇam enaṁ cakkhundriyaṁ asaṁvutaṁ viharantaṁ abhijjhā-domanassā pāpakā akusalā dhammā anvāssaveyyuṁ tassa saṁvarāya pāṭipaijati, rakkhati cakkhundriyaṁ, cakkhundriye saṁvaraṁ āpajjati.*
2. Cp. D.I, 181: *Sikkhā ekā saññā uppajjanti, sikkhā ekā saññā nirujjhanti.*
3. A. III, 116: *Pañc' ime bhikkhave dhammā sekhassa* (= *sekhassāti sikkhakassa sakaranīyassa* —Mp. III, 274) *bhikkhuno parihānāya saṁvattanti. Katame pañca? Kammārāmatā, bhassārāmatā niddārāmatā, saṅgaṇikārāmatā, yathāvimuttaṁ cittaṁ na paccavekkhati.*

A. That yogin having taken the sign always contemplates on its merit as if it were a precious jewel. He is always glad and practises. He practises constantly and much. He practises by day and by night. He is glad when he is seated. He is at ease when he lies down. Keeping his mind from straying hither and thither, he upholds the sign. Upholding the sign, he arouses attention. Arousing attention, he meditates. Thus meditating, he practises. In his practice, he contemplates on the *maṇḍala*. Through this constant endeavour, he sees the sign and protecting the sign in this way, he acquires facility. And if the (after-) image appears in his mind, he gains access-meditation. And if access-meditation appears in his mind, he, by means of this, accomplishes fixed meditation.[1]

ACCESS-MEDITATION

Q. What is access-meditation?

A. It means that the man follows the object unimpeded by his inclinations. Thus he overcomes the hindrances. But he does not practise initial and sustained application of thought, joy, bliss, unification of mind and the five faculties of faith and so forth. Though he gains meditation-strength, diverse trends of thought occur yet. This is called access-meditation.

FIXED MEDITATION, JHANA

Fixed meditation, *jhāna*, follows access. This state acquires the power of mental progress. This is the power of application of thought, faith and the others. This state does not move in the object. This is called fixed meditation, *jhāna*.

Q. What is the difference between access and fixed meditation, *jhāna*?

A. The overcoming of the five hindrances is access. One overcomes these five and thereby fulfils fixed meditation, *jhāna*. Through access one approaches distinction in meditation, *jhāna*. When distinction in meditation is accomplished, it is fixed meditation, *jhāna*. In access-meditation mind and body, not having attained to tranquillity, are unsteady like a ship on waves. In fixed meditation, *jhāna*, mind and body having attained to tranquillity are steady like a ship on unruffled water. Because the factors[2] are not powerful the mind does not dwell long on the object, in access-meditation, like a child.[3] All factors[4] being powerful (in fixed meditation, *jhāna*) one dwells on the object peacefully and long, like a powerful man.[5] In access-

1. *Appanā jhāna*.
2. and 4. Text has *aṅga*. 3. and 5. Cp. Vis. Mag., 126: *Yathā nāma daharo kumārako ukkhipitvā ṭhapiyamāno punappunaṁ bhūmiyaṁ patati, evam eva upacāre uppanne cittaṁ kālena nimittaṁ ārammaṇaṁ karoti, kālena bhavaṅgaṁ otarati. Appanāya pana aṅgāni thāmajātāni honti, tesaṁ thāmajātattā. Yathā nāma balavā puriso āsanā vuṭṭhāya divasam pi tiṭṭheyya, evam eva appanāsamādhimhi uppanne cittaṁ, sakiṁ bhavaṅgavāraṁ chinditvā, kevalam pi rattiṁ kevakam pi divasaṁ tiṭṭhati, kusalajavanapaṭipāṭivasen'eva pavattatī ti.*

meditation one does not practise with facility. Therefore yoga is not accomplished. It is like the forgetfulness of a discourse-reciter who has stopped (reciting) for a long time.[1] In fixed meditation, *jhāna*, practice being facile, yoga is accomplished. It is like a discourse-reciter who keeps himself in training, always, and who does not forget when he recites.

If a man does not overcome the (five) hindrances, he is blind as regards access-meditation.[2] These are the teachings regarding impurity. If a man overcomes the hindrances well, he gains sight (lit. becomes not-blind).

Concerning the accomplishment of fixed meditation, *jhāna*, these are the teachings of purity:—From the state of facility in the sign to (the state of) repelling is called access. Continued repelling of the hindrances is called fixed meditation, *jhāna*.

Q. What is the meaning of access?

A. Because it is near meditation, *jhāna*, it is called access, as a road near a village is called a village road. The meaning is the same, though the names differ.

What is the meaning of fixed meditation, *jhāna*? Fixed meditation, *jhāna*, means yoga. Fixed meditation, *jhāna*, is like the mind entering the *maṇḍala*. There is no difference in meaning between renunciation, meditation (*jhāna*) and fixed meditation, (*jhāna*). Here the yogin, dwelling in access, fixed meditation (*jhāna*) or the first meditation (*jhāna*) should increase the *kasiṇa*.

INCREASING OF THE KASINA

Q. How should he increase?

A. Namely, the *kasiṇa* which is a span and four fingers, at the start, should be gradually increased. Thus should he contemplate; and he will be able gradually to increase with facility. Let him progressively increase it to the size of a wheel, a canopy, the shadow of a tree, a cultivated field, a small neighbourhood, a village, a walled village and a city. Thus should he progress gradually until he fills the great earth. He should not contemplate on such things as rivers, mountains, heights, depths, trees and protuberances, all of which are uneven; he should contemplate on earth as if it were the great ocean. Increasing it in this way, he attains to distinction in meditation.

SKILFULNESS IN FIXED MEDITATION, JHANA

If the yogin attains to access-meditation but is unable to obtain fixed meditation, *jhāna*, he should effect the arising of skilfulness in fixed meditation, *jhāna*, in two ways: the first, through causes; the second, through "good standing".

---

1. A. IV, 195: *Asajjhāyamalā bhikkhave mantā.*
2. Cp. S. V, 97: *Pañcime bhikkhave nīvaraṇā andhakaraṇā ackkhukaraṇā.*

TEN WAYS

By means of ten ways he effects the arising of skilfulness in fixed meditation, *jhāna*, through causes: (1) By the consideration of cleansing the physical basis. (2) By the consideration of equalizing (the work of) the faculties. (3) By skilfulness in taking the sign. (4) By restraining and regulating the mind. (5) By repressing negligence. (6) By (overcoming) mental inactivity. (7) By gladdening the mind. (8) By steadying the mind and fulfilling equanimity. (9) By separation from him who does not practise concentration and by associating with a concentration-practiser. (10) By intentness on fixed meditation concentration.[1]

(1). *Q.* What is the consideration of cleansing the physical basis?

A. Through three kinds of action one accomplishes the cleansing of the physical basis. Namely, through the partaking of suitable food, the enjoyment of the ease of agreeable weather and the practice of a posture that is pleasant.

SIMILE OF THE HORSE-CHARIOT

(2). By the consideration of equalizing (the work) of the faculties, i.e., faith or any of the other four faculties should not be allowed to fall back, through negligence. It is comparable to a swift horse-chariot.[2]

SIMILE OF THE INKED-STRING

(3). Skilfulness in taking the sign: The mind-faculty takes (the sign) well, i.e., neither too hastily nor too slowly. It is like a skilful carpenter, who, having determined well, pulls the inked-string, lets it go at the right moment and thereby marks an even, uncurved line.

(4). By restraining and regulating the mind: There are two ways. By these two, the mind is regulated: the first, through intense effort; the second, through profound investigation of the spheres or the mind becomes discursive, wandering to distant and unsuitable spheres and is thus disturbed.

Through two ways one restrains the mind: One arouses energy. One takes (food) temperately every day. If the mind wanders to unsuitable spheres and objects, one restrains the mind having considered the evil results (of such

---

1. Cp. Vbh.-a. 283: *Api ca ekādasa dhammā samādhi-sambojjhangassa uppādāya saṁvattanti: vatthuvisadakiriyatā, indriyasamattapaṭipādanatā, nimittakusalatā, samaye cittassa paggahaṇatā, samaye cittassa niggahaṇatā, samaye sampahaṁsanatā, samaye ajjhupekkhanatā, asamāhitapuggalaparivajjanatā, samāhitapuggalasevanatā, jhānavimokkhapaccavekkhanatā, tad-adhimuttatā ti.*
2. S.IV, 176; M.III, 97; A.III, 28; *Seyyathāpi bhikkhave subhūmiyaṁ cātummahāpathe ājaññaratho yutto assa ṭhito odhastapatodo tam enaṁ dakkho yoggācariyo assadammasārathi abhirūhitvā vāmena hatthena rasmiyo gahetvā dakkhiṇena hatthena patodaṁ gahetvā yen'icchakaṁ yad icchakaṁ sāreyya pi paccāsāreyya pi.*

actions). Thus one overcomes in two ways: through investigation of various sufferings and through the search for the reward of evil deeds.

(5) (6) and (7). By repressing negligence: Through two ways negligence of mind is fulfilled: through lack of distinction in concentration and through mental inactivity. When there is much negligence, the mind becomes sluggish and torpid. This means that, if the yogin does not gain distinction in concentration, his mind is steeped in negligence because of mental inactivity. Through two ways one should repress. Namely, through the consideration of merit and through the arousing of energy. He should repress negligence of torpor and idleness of mind in four ways:— If he is a voracious person he considers (the faults of) negligence and practises the four restraints. Fixing his mind on the sign of brightness, he dwells in a dewy place, makes his mind rejoice and gets rid of attachment. Through three ways mental inactivity takes place: through insufficiency of skill, dullness of wit, non-obtainment of the ease of solitude. If a yogin's mind is inactive he makes it active in these two ways: through fear and through gladness.

If he considers birth, decay, death and the four states of woe, owing to fear, anxiety and mental agony arise in his mind.[1] If he practises the recollections of the Buddha, the Law, the Community of Bhikkhus, virtue, liberality and deities, he sees the merits of these objects and is gladdened.

(8). By the mind becoming steady and fulfilling equanimity: Through two actions (the mind) fulfils access-meditation: by destroying the hindrances the mind fulfils fixity. Or, arousing the meditation (*jhāna*) factors on already acquired earth (*kasiṇa*), the mind attains to fixity.

After a yogin attains to calmness, there are two states to be abandoned: that which causes inattention, and that which causes middling skill.

(9). Separation from those who do not practise concentration means that a man who has not attained to fixed meditation, access-meditation or restraint meditation, and he who does not train himself in these or practise these should not be served. Association with a meditation practiser means that if a man has attained to fixed meditation, *jhāna*, he should be followed. Under him one should learn. Him should one serve.

(10). By intentness on fixed meditation, *jhāna*, means that the yogin always reverences, enjoys (meditation) and practises much (regarding it) as the deepest depth, as a fountain and as a tender plant.

Through the practice of these ten, fixed meditation, *jhāna*, is obtained.

Q. How (does the yogin) produce skilfulness in fixed meditation, *jhāna*, well, through good standing?

A. That yogin, having well understood the causes (which induce concentration), enters into solitude. With the sign of concentration which he has practised, he induces, in mind, desirous ease, with facility. Through this

---

1. Cp. Nd[1]. 371: *Jātibhayaṁ jarābhayaṁ byādhibhayaṁ maraṇabhayaṁ....duggatibhayaṁ.*

state, the mind acquires good standing. Through the arising of joy, the mind acquires good standing. [415] Through the arising of body-bliss, the mind acquires good standing. Through the arising of brightness, the mind acquires good standing. Through the arising of harmlessness, the mind attains to calmness. Through this calmness, the mind acquires good standing. Thus observing well, the mind attains to equanimity and acquires good standing. Liberating itself from limitless passions, the mind acquires good standing. By reason of freedom, the mind accomplishes the one-function-of-the-Law[1] and practises. Therefore, owing to this excellence, the mind gains increase. Thus established in good standing, the yogin causes the arising of skilfulness in fixed meditation, *jhāna*. Understanding causes and good standing well, in this way, he, in no long time, brings out concentration.

THE FIRST MEDITATION, JHANA

That yogin, having separated himself from lust, having separated himself from demeritorious states, attains to the first meditation, *jhāna*, which is accompanied by initial and sustained application of thought, born of solitude, and full of joy and bliss.[2] This is the merit of earth *kasiṇa*.

THREE KINDS OF SEPARATION FROM LUST AND DEMERITORIOUS STATES

Now, there are three kinds of separation from lust, viz., of the body, of the mind and of the defilements.[3]

Q. What is separation from (lust of) the body?

A. (A man) separates himself from desires, goes to a hill or moor and dwells there. What is separation from (lust of) the mind. With pure heart a man reaches a station of distinction. What is separation from (lust of) the defilements? A man is cut off from kindred, birth and death.

And again, there are five kinds of separation, namely, suppression-separation, part-separation, eradication-separation, tranquillity-separation, emancipation-separation. What is suppression-separation? Namely, practise of the first meditation *jhāna*, and the suppression of the five hindrances. What is part-separation? Namely, practice of penetration-concentration and the suppression of views. What is eradication-separation? Namely, the practice

1. A.IV, 203: *Seyyathāpi Pahārāda mahāsamuddho ekaraso loṇaraso, evam eva kho Pahārāda ayaṁ dhammavinayo ekaraso vimuttiraso.*
2. A.III, 25: *Idha bhikkhave bhikkhu vivicc'eva kāmehi vivicca akusalehi dhammehi savitakkaṁ savicāraṁ vivekajaṁ pīti-sukhaṁ paṭhamajjhānaṁ upasampajja viharati.*
3. (*a*) Nd[1]. 26: *Vivekā ti tayo vivekā, kāyaviveko, cittaviveko, upadhiviveko.*
(*b*) Ibid. 27: *Kāyaviveko ca vūpakaṭṭhakāyānaṁ nekkhammābhiratānaṁ; cittaviveko ca. parisuddhacittānaṁ paramavodānappattānaṁ; upadhiviveko ca nirupadhīnaṁ puggalānaṁ visaṁkhāragatānaṁ.*

of the supramundane Path and the cutting down of many defilements. What is tranquillity-separation? It is the joy of the time when one acquites the (Noble) Fruit. What is emancipation-separation? Namely, *Nibbāna.*[1]

TWO KINDS OF LUST

There are two kinds of lust: the first is lust for things; the second is lust for pleasure. The lust for heavenly mansions and forms, odours, flavours and tangibles which men love is called lust for things. A man clings to this lust for things and attends to it.[2] The separation from these lusts through mind and through suppression — this is solitude, this is renunciation, this is freedom, this is the unassociated, this is called separation from lust.

ROOTS OF DEMERIT

Q. What is separation from demeritorious states?

A. Namely, there are three kinds of roots of demerit: the first is lust, the second is hatred and the third is ignorance.[3] The sensations, perceptions, formations and consciousness connected with these and the actions of body, speech and mind (connected with these) are called demeritorious states.

According to another tradition, there are three kinds of demerit: the first is natural; the second is associated; the third is causally produced. The three roots of demerit are named natural. Sensations, perceptions, formations and consciousness which are connected with these are named associated. The actions of body, speech and mind which are produced are called causally produced. The separation from these three demeritorious states is called renunciation, freedom, the unassociated. This is called separation from demeritorious states. And again, separation from lust means the separation from the hindrance of lust. Separation from demeritorious states is separation from the other hindrances.[4]

---

1. Pts. II, 220: *Sammādiṭṭhiyā katame pañca vivekā? Vikkhambhanaviveko tadaṅgaviveko samucchedaviveko paṭippassaddhiviveko nissaraṇaviveko. Vikkhambhanaviveko ca nīvaraṇānaṁ paṭhamajjhānaṁ bhāvayato, tadaṅgaviveko ca diṭṭhigatānaṁ nibbedhabhāgiyaṁ samādhiṁ bhāvayato, samucchedaviveko ca lokuttaraṁ khayagāmimaggaṁ bhāvayato, paṭippassaddhiviveko ca phalakkhaṇe, nissaraṇaviveko ca nirodho nibbānaṁ.*
2. Nd[1] 1—2: *Dve kāmā, vatthukāmā ca kilesakāmā ca. Katame vatthukāmā? Manāpikā rūpā, manāpikā saddā, manāpikā gandhā, manāpikā rasā, manāpikā phoṭṭhabbā;...... dibba kāmā;......ime vuccanti vatthukāmā. Katame kilesakāmā? Chando kāmo, rāgo kāmo, chandarāgo kāmo,......saṁkapparāgo kāmo; yo kāmesukāmacchando kāmarāgo kāmanandi kāmataṇhā kāmasneho kāmapariḷāho kāmamucchā kāmajjhosānaṁ kāmogho kāmayogo kāmupādānaṁ kāmacchandanīvaraṇaṁ......ime vuccanti kilesakāmā.*
3. D. III, 214: *Tiṇi akusala-mūlāni. Lobho akusala-mūlaṁ, doso akusala-mūlaṁ, moho akusala-mūlaṁ.*
4. Vbh. 256: *Vivicc'eva kāmehi vivicca akusalehi dhammehīti: tattha katame kāmā? Chando kāmo, rāgo kāmo, chandarāgo kāmo; saṁkappo kāmo, rāgo kāmo, saṁkapparāgo kāmo: ime vuccanti kāmā.*
   Tattha katame akusalā dhammā?
   Kāmacchando vyāpādo thīnamiddhaṁ uddhaccakukkuccaṁ vicikicchā: ime vuccanti akusalā dhammā.—Here see Vis. Mag. 141: *Vivicca akusalehi dhammehī ti iminā pañcannaṁ pi nīvaraṇānaṁ, agahitaggahaṇena pana paṭhamena kāmacchandassa, dutiyena sesanīvaraṇānaṁ.*

REASONS FOR TREATING LUST AND DEMERIT SEPARATELY

Q. Since separation from demeritorious states is preached and lust as a demeritorious state is already within it, why should separation from lust be separately preached?

A. Lust is conquered through emancipation. Every Buddha's teaching can remove the defilements well. "The separation from lust is renunciation".[1] This is the teaching of the Buddha. It is like the attainment of the first meditation, *jhāna*. The thought connected with the perception of lust partakes of the state of deterioration.

Thereby lust is connected with the defilements. With the dispersion of lust all defilements disperse. Therefore, separately, the separation from lust is preached.

And again, thus is separation from lust: After gaining emancipation, a man accomplishes the separation from lust.

SEPARATION FROM DEMERITORIOUS STATES

Separation from demeritorious states is thus: Through the acquisition of non-hatred, a man fulfils separation from hatred; through the acquisition of the perception of brightness, he fulfils separation from torpor; through the acquisition of non-distraction, he fulfils separation from agitation and anxiety; through the acquisition of non-rigidity, he fulfils separation from rigidity; through the acquisition of fixed meditation, *jhāna*, he fulfils separation from uncertainty; through the acquisition of wisdom, he fulfils separation from ignorance; through the acquisition of right thought, he fulfils separation from wrong mindfulness; through the acquisition of bliss, he fulfils separation from non-bliss; through the acquisition of the twin bliss of the mind, he fulfils separation from suffering; through the acquisition of all meritorious states, he separates from all demerit. This is just as it is taught in the *Tipiṭaka* thus: "He is full of dispassion, therefore he fulfils separation from lust. He is full of non-hatred and non-delusion, therefore he fulfils separation from demeritorious states".[2]

DIFFERENCE BETWEEN LUST AND DEMERIT

And again, separation from lust is taught as the emancipation of the body, and separation from demeritorious states is taught as the emancipation of the mind.

---

1. It. 61: *Kāmānam-etaṁ nissaraṇaṁ yad-idaṁ nekkhammaṁ.*
2. Prof. Bapat in his Vimuttimagga and Visuddhimagga, p.46 traces this passage to Peṭakopadesa. He quotes from the printed Burmese edition=P.T.S. Ed. 141: *Tattha alobhassa pāripūriyā, vivitto hoti kāmehi. Tattha adosassa pāripūriyā amohassa pāripūriyā ca vivitto hoti pāpakehi akusalehi dhammehi.*

And again, separation from lust is taught as the abandoning of discursive sensuous thought, and the separation from demeritorious states is taught as the abandoning of discursive thoughts of hate and harm.

And again, separation from lust is taught as eschewing of sense-pleasures, and separation from demeritorious states is taught as the eschewing of negligence through indulgence of the body.

And again, separation from lust is taught as the abandoning of the sixfold pleasures of sense and of delight therein. Separation from demeritorious states is taught as the abandoning of discursive thoughts of hate and harm, anxiety and suffering. Also it is taught as (1) the mowing down of pleasure, (2) as indifference.

And again, separation from lust is present bliss of relief from sense-pleasures, and separation from demeritorious states is present bliss of relief from non-subjection to tribulation.

And again, separation from lust is to get beyond the sense-flood entirely. Separation from demeritorious states is the surpassing of all other defilements which cause rebirth in the sense and form (planes).

INITIAL AND SUSTAINED APPLICATION OF THOUGHT

Accompanied by initial application and sustained application of thought: What is initial application of thought? To perceive, to think, to be composed, to excogitate and to aspire rightly, though without understanding, constitute initial application of thought. Such are the qualities of initial application of thought. Owing to the fulfilment of initial application of thought there is initial application of thought in the first meditation, *jhāna*. And again, one dwells on the earth *kasiṇa* and considers the earth sign without end. These constitute initial application of thought. It is comparable to the reciting of discourses by heart.

Q. What are the salient characteristic, function, manifestation and near cause of initial application of thought?

A.[1] ....

What is sustained application of thought? When one practises sustained application of thought, the mind dwells in non-indifference following that which sustained application of thought investigates. This state is called sustained application of thought. In association with this one accomplishes the first meditation, *jhāna*. The first meditation, *jhāna*, is (conjoined) with sustained application of thought. And again, the meditator who dwells on the earth *kasiṇa* considers many aspects which his mind discerns when working on the earth sign. This is sustained application of thought.

---

1. This passage is unintelligible.

Q. What are the salient characteristic, function, manifestation and near cause of sustained application of thought?

A. Reflection following investigation is its salient characteristic. The brightening of the mind — this is its function. The seeing that follows initial application of thought — this is its near cause.

INITIAL APPLICATION AND SUSTAINED APPLICATION OF THOUGHT DISCRIMINATED

Q. What is the difference between initial application and sustained application of thought?

SIMILES OF THE BELL ETC.

A. It is comparable to the striking of a bell. The first sound is initial application of thought. The reverberations that follow constitute sustained application of thought. And again, it is comparable to the relation of the mind to its object. The beginning is initial application of thought; the rest is sustained application of thought. And again, to wish for meditation, *jhāna*, is initial application of thought; to maintain is sustained application of thought. And again, to recall is initial application of thought; to dwell on the recollection is sustained application of thought. And again, the state of the coarse mind is initial application of thought and the state of the fine mind is sustained application of thought. Where there is initial application of thought there is sustained application of thought, but where there is sustained application of thought, there may or may not be initial application of thought. It is taught in the *Tipiṭaka* thus: "The mind beginning to dwell on anything is initial application of thought. If, having acquired initial application of thought, the mind is still unfixed, it is sustained application of thought".[1] To see a person coming in the distance, without knowing whether one is a man or woman and to distinguish the form as male or female is initial application of thought. Thereafter to consider whether he or she is virtuous or not, is rich or poor, noble or humble, is sustained application of thought. Initial application of thought wants (a thing), draws it and brings it near.[2] Sustained application of thought keeps it, holds it, follows and goes after it.

SIMILES OF THE BIRD ETC.

Like a bird taking off from a hill flapping its wings, is initial application

---

1. Dhs. 10, paras 7, 8; 20, paras 84, 85; *Yo tasmiṁ samaye takko vitakko saṅkappo appanā-vyappanā cetaso abhiniropanā sammāsaṅkappo—ayaṁ tasmiṁ samaye vitakko hoti.*
Yo tasmiṁ samaye cāro vicāro anuvicāro upavicāro cittassa anusandhanatā anupekkhanatā —ayaṁ tasmiṁ samaye vicāro hoti.
2. Peṭaka. 142: *Yathā puriso dūrato purisaṁ passati āgacchantaṁ na ca tāva jānāti—eso itthī ti vā puriso ti vā. Yadā tu paṭilabhati: itthī ti vā puriso ti vā evaṁvaṇṇo ti vā evaṁsaṇṭhāno ti vā, ime vitakkayanto uttari upaparikkhanti: kiṁ nu kho ayaṁ sīlavā udādu dussīlo aḍḍho vā duggato ti vā? Evaṁ vicāro vitakke apeti vicāro cariyati, ca, anuvattati ca.* — Traced by Prof. Bapat.

of thought and the planing movement (of a bird in the sky) is sustained application of thought. The first spreading (of the wings) is initial application of thought. The spreading (of the wings) when it is continued long is sustained application of thought.[1] With initial application of thought one protects; with sustained application of thought one searches. With initial application of thought one considers; with sustained application of thought one continues to consider. The walker in initial application of thought does not think of wrong states; the walker in sustained application of thought induces meditation.

Sustained application of thought is like a man who is able, while reciting the discourses in mind, to gather the meaning. Initial application of thought is like a man who sees what he wants to see and after seeing understands it well. Expertness in etymology and dialectic is initial application of thought; expertness in theory and practice is sustained application of thought.[2] To appreciate distinction is initial application of thought; to understand the distinction of things is sustained application of thought. These are the differences between initial application and sustained application of thought.

SOLITUDE

Born of solitude. It is called solitude because of separation from the five hindrances. This is named solitude. And again, it is the merit-faculty of the form plane. And again, it is taught as the access of the first meditation, *jhāna*. And again, it is taught as the meditation-thought. What is produced from this is called born of solitude, as the flower which grows on earth is called earth-flower and the flower which grows in water, water-flower.

JOY AND BLISS

Joy and bliss. The mind at this time is greatly glad and at ease. The mind is filled with coolness. This is called joy.

Q. What are the salient characteristic, function, manifestation and near cause of joy and how many kinds of joy are there?

A. Joy: the being filled with joy is its salient characteristic; to gladden is its function; the overcoming of mental disturbance is its manifestation; buoyancy is its near cause.

How many kinds of joy are there? There are six kinds of joy: one

1. Vis. Mag. 142: *Dukanipātaṭṭhakathāyaṁ pana ākāse gacchato mahāsakuṇassa ubhohi pakkhehi vātaṁ gahetvā pakkhe sannisīdāpetvā gamanaṁ viya ārammaṇe cetaso abhiniropanabhāvena pavatto vitakko; (so hi ekaggo hutvā appeti;) vātagahaṇatthaṁ pakkhe phandāpayamānassa gamanaṁ viya anumajjanasabhāvena pavatto vicāro ti vuttaṁ.*—This simile is not in the Cy., i.e., Manorathapūraṇī.
2. Here again Prof. Bapat has traced this passage to the Peṭaka, 142; *Yathā paliko tuṇhiko sajjhāyaṁ karoti evaṁ vitakko, yathā taṁ yeva anupassati evaṁ vicāro. Yathā apariññā evaṁ vitakko, yathā pariññā evaṁ vicāro. Niruttipaṭisambhidāyañ ca paṭibhānapaṭisambhidāyañ ca vitakko, dhammapaṭisambhidāyañ ca atthapaṭisambhidāyañ ca vicāro.*

proceeds from lust; one, from faith; one, from non-rigidity; one from solitude; one, from concentration and one, from enlightenment factors.

Which, from lust? The joy of passion and the joy that is bound up with the defilements are called joy that proceeds from lust.[1]

Which, from faith? The joy of a man of great faith and the joy produced on seeing a potter.[2]

Which, from non-rigidity? [416] The great joy of the pure-hearted and the virtuous.

Which, from solitude? The joy of the individual who enters the first meditation, *jhāna*.[3]

Which, from concentration? The joy of the individual who enters the second meditation, *jhāna*.[4]

Which, from the enlightenment factors? The joy that follows the treading of the supramundane path in the second meditation, *jhāna*.

FIVE KINDS OF JOY

And again, it is taught that there are five kinds of joy, namely, the lesser thrill, momentary joy, streaming joy, swiftly going joy, all-pervading joy.[5]

The lesser thrill is like the raising of the hairs of the body caused by being wet with fine rain. Momentary joy suddenly arises and suddenly passes away. It is comparable to showers at night. Streaming joy is like oil that streaks down the body without spreading. Swiftly going joy is joy that spreads through the mind and vanishes not long after. It is comparable to the store of a poor man. All-pervading joy permeating the body, continues. It is like a thunder-cloud that is full of rain. Thus the lesser thrill and momentary joy cause the arising of the access through faith. Streaming joy becoming powerful causes the arising of the access. Swiftly going joy dwelling on the *maṇḍala* causes the arising of both the good and the bad, and depends on skill. All-pervading joy is produced in the state of fixed meditation.

BLISS

Q. What is bliss? *A*. Contact with the lovable and the ease-giving is bliss.

---

1. S.IV, 235: *Katamā ca bhikkhave sāmisā pīti. Pañcime bhikkhave kāmaguṇā. Katame pañca. Cakkhuviññeyyā rūpā iṭṭhā kantā manāpā piyarūpā kāmūpasaṁhitā rajanīyā.... pe....kāyaviññeyyā phoṭṭhabbā iṭṭhā kantā....rajanīyā. Ime kho bhikkhave pañca-kāmaguṇā. Yā kho bhikkhave ime pañcakāmaguṇe paṭicca uppajjati pīti, ayaṁ vuccati bhikkhave sāmisā pīti.*
2. What is meant by potter is not clear.
3. A.II, 126: *Idha ekacco puggalo vivicc'eva kāmehi vivicca akusalehi dhammehi savitakkaṁ savicāraṁ vivekajaṁ pītisukhaṁ paṭhamajjhānaṁ upasampajja viharati.*
4. Ibid. 127: *Vitakkavicārānaṁ vūpasamā ajjhattaṁ sampasādo cetaso ekodibhāvaṁ avitakkaṁ avicāraṁ samādhijaṁ pītisukkaṁ dutiyajjhānaṁ upasampajja viharati.*
5. Dhs.-a. 115. *Khuddakā pīti, khaṇikā pīti, okkantikā pīti, pharaṇā pīti, ubbegā pīti ti pañcavidhā hoti.*

Q. What are the salient characteristic, function, manifestation and near cause of bliss? How many kinds of bliss are there? What are the differences between joy and bliss? *A*. Its function is its salient characteristic. Dependence on an agreeable object — this is its agreeable function. Peaceful persuasion is its manifestation. Tranquillity is its near cause.

FIVE KINDS OF BLISS

How many kinds of bliss are there? There are five kinds of bliss, namely, caused bliss, fundamental bliss, the bliss of solitude, the bliss of non-defilement, the bliss of feeling.

What is called caused bliss? Thus it is according to the Buddha's teaching: "The bliss of virtue lasts long". This is called caused bliss. This is a merit of bliss. Thus is fundamental bliss according to the Buddha's teaching: "The Enlightened One produces worldly bliss".[1] The bliss of solitude is the development of concentration-indifference and the destruction of meditation, *jhāna*. The bliss of non-defilement is according to the Buddha's teaching "highest *Nibbāna*".[2] The bliss of dwelling is generally called the bliss of dwelling. According to this treatise, the bliss of dwelling should be enjoyed.[3]

DIFFERENCES BETWEEN JOY AND BLISS

What are the differences between joy and bliss? Buoyancy is joy, ease of mind is bliss. Tranquillity of mind is bliss. Concentration of mind is joy. Joy is coarse; bliss is fine. Joy belongs to the formations-group; bliss belongs to the sensation-group. Where there is joy there is bliss, but where there is bliss there may or may not be joy.

FIRST MEDITATION (JHANA)

The first is the basis for producing the second. After accomplishing the access one enters the first meditation, *jhāna*. The meditation-factors are initial application of thought and sustained applieation of thought, joy, bliss and unification of mind.

What is meditation, *jhāna*? It is equalized meditation on an object. It is the plucking out of the five hindrances. It is to meditate and to overcome.

Enters the first meditation, *jhāna*, and acquires good standing: Having already acquired, having already touched, having already proved, one dwells.

And again, thus is separation from lust and demeritorious states: The first meditation, *jhāna*, is called the special characteristic of separation from the world of sense. The second meditation, *jhāna*, has the special characteristic of

1. Dh. 194: *Sukho Buddhānaṁ uppādo.* 2. Dh. 204: *Nibbānaṁ paramaṁ sukhaṁ.*
3. Cp. I, 75: *Puna ca paraṁ mahā-rāja bhikkhu pītiyā ca virāgā ca upekhako ca viharati sato ca sampajāno, sukhañ ca kāyena paṭisaṁvedeti yan taṁ ariyā āckkihanti: "upekhako satimā sukka-vihārī" ti tatiyajjhānaṁ upasampajja viharati.*

separation from initial application and sustained application of thought. In solitude are joy and bliss; therefore joy and bliss are called the special characteristics of solitude.[1]

And again, thus is separation from lust and demeritorious states: It is to remove well, and to overcome well.

With initial application and sustained application of thought: This is said to be the characteristic of (the first) meditation, *jhāna.*

Joy and bliss born of solitude: This state resembles meditation.

Acquires good standing enters and dwells: One acquires the first meditation, *jhāna*, separates from five factors, fulfils five factors, three kinds of goodness, ten characteristics,[2] and accomplishes the twenty-five merits. With these merits one can obtain rebirth in the Brahma or the deva world.[3]

FIVE HINDRANCES

Separation from five factors: This is separation from the five hindrances. What are the five? Sense-desire, ill will, rigidity and torpor, agitation and anxiety, uncertainty.[4]

Sense-desire: (This refers to) a mind defiled by the dust of passion. Ill will: This is the practice of the ten defilements. Rigidity: This is negligence of the mind. Torpor: This is the desire for sleep owing to heaviness of the body. There are three kinds of torpor: the first, proceeds from food; the second, from time; the third, from the mind. If it proceeds from the mind, one removes it with meditation. If it proceeds from food and time as in the case of the Arahant, because it does not proceed from the mind, it is not a hindrance. If it proceeds from food and time, one cuts it with energy as the Venerable Elder Anuruddha taught: "Since first I destroyed the cankers for fifty-five years, have I not slept the sleep that proceeds from the mind. And during this period for twenty-five years, have I removed the sleep that proceeds from food and time".[5]

---

1. *Petaka.* 147-8: *Tattha katame jhānavisesā? Vivicc'eva kāmehi vivicca pāpakehi akusalehi dhammehi cittacetasikasahagatā kāmadhātusamatikkamanatā pi, ayaṁ jhānaviseso. Avitakkā c'eva avicārā ca sappītikāya satisahagatāya pītisahagatā saññāmanasikārā samudācaranti; ayaṁ jhānaviseso.*
2. (a) M.I, 294-5: *Pāṭhamaṁ kho āvuso jhānaṁ pañcaṅgavippahīnaṁ pañcaṅgasamannāgataṁ: Idh'āvuso paṭhamaṁ jhānaṁ samāpannassa bhikkhuno kāmacchando pahīno hoti byāpādo pahīno hoti, thīnamiddhaṁ pahīnaṁ hoti, uddhaccakukkuccaṁ pahīnaṁ hoti, vicikicchā pahīnā hoti.*
   (b) Vis. Mag. 139: *Pañcangavippahīnaṁ pañcangasamannāgataṁ tividhakalyāṇaṁ dasalakkhaṇasampannaṁ paṭhamajjhānaṁ.*
   (c) Peṭaka 136: *Tattha katamaṁ paṭhamaṁ jhānaṁ? Pañcangavippayuttaṁ pañcangasamannāgataṁ.*
3. From "The first is the basis for producing the second" (p. 90, above) to "the Brahma or the deva world", refers to the first meditation, *jhāna*, formula (p. 83 above): Vivicc' *eva kāmehi vivicca akusalehi dhammehi savitakkaṁ savicāraṁ vivevakajaṁ pītisukkaṁ paṭhamaṁ jhānaṁ upasampajja viharati*", Vis. Mag. 139.
4. *Kāmacchanda, vyāpāda, thīna-middha, uddhaccakukkucca, vicikicchā.*
5. Th. 904 *Pañcapaññāsa vassāni yato nesajjiko ahaṁ*
   pañcavīsati vassāni yato middhaṁ samūhataṁ.

Q. If torpor is a bodily state, how can it be a mental defilement? *A.* The body is produced only by mental defilement. It is like a man drinking wine and taking food. Thus should it be known.

Q. If torpor is a bodily state and rigidity is a mental property, how do these two states unite and become one hindrance? *A.* These two states have one object and one function. What are called torpor and rigidity become one. Agitation is non-tranquillity of mind; anxiety is unsteadiness of mind; the characteristics of these are equal. Therefore they become one hindrance. Uncertainty is the clinging of the mind to diverse objects. There are four kinds of uncertainty: the first is a hindrance to serenity,[1] the second, to insight,[2] the third, to both and the fourth, to things non-doctrinal.

Here, is serenity won through the ending of these uncertainties, or is it possible or not to win tranquillity while having these uncertainties or the uncertainty concerning the self? If one has that uncertainty, it is called a hindrance to serenity; uncertainty concerning the Four Noble Truths and the three worlds is called a hindrance to insight; uncertainty concerning the Buddha, the Law and the Community of Bhikkhus is called a hindrance to both. Uncertainty concerning things like country, town, road, name of man or woman is called hindrance to things non-doctrinal. Uncertainty concerning the Discourses is a hindrance to solitude. Thus should these be understood. What is the meaning of hindrance? Hindrance to vehicle;[3] superposing, defilement, fetter. These are obvious.

Q. There are many fetters such as those which cover the defilements, and others. They are fetters. Then, why are only five hindrances taught?

A. Because these five include all. And again, the attachment to sense-desires includes all attachment to passion; all demeritorious states (of hatred) are included in the attachment to anger; and all demeritorious states of infatuation are included in the attachment to rigidity and torpor, agitation and anxiety and uncertainty. Thus all defilements are included in the attachment to the five hindrances. Because of this the five hindrances are taught.

FIVE FACTORS

Five factors: These are fulfilled (through the fulfilment of) initial and sustained application of thought, joy, bliss, and unification of mind.

Q. It is said that the five factors together constitute the first meditation, *jhāna*. Therefore, it cannot be said that there is a meditation (*jhāna*) outside the five factors. If there is a meditation, *jhāna*, outside the five factors, how can it be said that the first meditation, *jhāna*, consists of the five factors?

---

1. *Samatha* (transliteration).
2. *Vipassanā* (transliteration).
3. *Yāna*.

SIMILES OF CHARIOT AND ARMY

A. By means of the meditation, *jhāna*, factors, meditation (*jhāna*) is fulfilled. There is no meditation, *jhāna*, separate from meditation (*jhāna*) factors. Such meditation, *jhāna*, there is not. One can speak of a chariot because of all the parts of a chariot.[1] There is no chariot outside the parts. Owing to all the parts of an army, one can speak of an army. There is no army separate from the parts. Thus owing to meditation (*jhāna*) factors, it is called meditation, *jhāna*. There is no meditation, *jhāna*, separate from the meditation (*jhāna*) factors.[2] The factors combined are named meditation, *jhāna*. Separately, they are named factors. It is taught that the object is called meditation, *jhāna*, and the attributes, factors. By way of clan they are meditation, *jhāna*. By way of caste they are factors.

Q. In spite of there being mindfulness, energy and others, why are only five factors taught?

A. Because these five through combination accomplish meditation, *jhāna*.

Q. What are the characteristics of combination?

A. Initial application of thought follows the object of mind and acquires fixed meditation. Sustained application of thought goes together with the observing mind. When initial and sustained application of thought are unmixed, they cause the arising of skilfulness. If one is skilful, one produces joy and bliss. If one is skilful, one can produce the heart of joy, and after increasing that, produce the heart of bliss. With these four qualities the mind becomes peaceful. If the mind becomes peaceful, it acquires concentration. These are called the characteristics of combination. Thus, these five, through combination, accomplish (meditation, *jhāna*).

And again, the hindrances are overcome by the perfection of the five. The overcoming of the first hindrance is the first meditation, *jhāna*. Thus the overcoming of the five hindrances results in five meditations, *jhānas*. In the first meditation, *jhāna*, initial application of thought is the special factor; through initial application of thought lust is abandoned. If initial application of thought enters into right concentration, the other factors are also awakened. Among the five factors, sustained application of thought is the beginning of the second meditation; joy, of the third meditation; bliss, of the fourth; and unification of mind, of the fifth. These are the special factors of the meditations, *jhānas*.

And again, with the overcoming of the five hindrances, the five are fulfilled, as it is taught in the *Tipiṭaka:* "Unification of mind is the overcoming of sensuous desire, joy is the overcoming of anger, initial application of thought

---

1. S. I, 135: *Yathā hi angasambhārā hoti saddo ratho iti.*
2. Sp. I, 146: *Yathā pana sarathā sapattisenā ti vutte senaṅgesu eva senā eva senā samutti—evam idha pañcasu aṅgesu yeva jhānasammuti veditabbā.*

is the overcoming of rigidity and torpor, bliss is the overcoming of agitation and anxiety, sustained application of thought is the overcoming of uncertainty".[1] Thus, through the overcoming of the hindrances, the five are fulfilled.

Q. Meditating on the earth *kasiṇa* sign, [417] how does the yogin cause the arising of joy and bliss?

A. The earth *kasiṇa* does not bring joy and bliss. They (joy and bliss) naturally follow the separation from the five hindrances. Thus the son of truth[2] causes the arising of joy and bliss.

Q. If that be so, why does the son of truth not arouse joy and bliss in the fourth meditation, *jhāna*?

A. Because it is not a suitable state, and because he removes joy and bliss in the fourth meditation, *jhāna*. And again because of his having skilfully rooted out the joy and bliss which he caused to arise at first, and because, he, seeing the tribulation of bliss, forsakes it, and attaches himself to deep tranquillity. For these reasons, he does not cause the arising of joy and bliss.

THREE KINDS OF GOODNESS

The three kinds of goodness: These are the initial, medial and final stages of goodness. Purity of practice is the initial stage; the increase of equanimity is the medial stage; rejoicing is the final stage.[3] What is purity of practice? It is the foundation of all goodness. What is the increase of equanimity? It is fixed meditation. What is rejoicing? It is reflection.[4] Thus there are three kinds of goodness in the first meditation, *jhāna*.

TEN CHARACTERISTICS

Fulfilment of the ten characteristics: These comprise the three characteristics of the purity of practice, the three characteristics of the increase of equanimity and the four characteristics of rejoicing.[5] What are the three characteristics of the purity of practice? *A.* The mind purifies itself of that hindrance to the meditation, *jhāna*. Because of purity, the mind acquires the middle sign of serenity, and from that the mind leaps forward. These are called the three characteristics of the purity of practice.

Q. What are the three characteristics of the increase of equanimity?

---

1. Vis. Mag. 141: *Tathā hi samādhi kāmacchandassa paṭipakkho, pīti vyāpādassa, vitakko thīnamiddhassa, sukkhaṁ uddhacca-kukkuccassa, vicāro vicikicchāyā ti Peṭake vuttaṁ.* —But it is not in the Peṭaka.
2. *Dhammaputta*,
3. Cp. Vis. Mag. 147: *Paṭhamassa jhānassa paṭipadā-visuddhi ādi, upekkhānubrūhaṇā majjhe, sampahaṁsanā pariyosānaṁ.*
4. Cp. Vis. Mag. 148: *Paṭipadā-visuddhi nāma sasambhāriko upacāro, upekkhānubrūhaṇā nāma appanā, samapahaṁsanā nāma paccavekkhaṇā ti evam eke vaṇṇayanti.* The comment (in Pm. Sinh. Ed. I, 144:) *eketi Abhayagirivāsino,* is quoted by Prof. Bapat in his Vim. Mag. and Vis. Mag. p. 49.
5. Cp.Ibid. 147. ff.

A. If the mind is pure, it fulfils equanimity; if it attains to solitude, it fulfils equanimity; if it dwells on one object, it fulfils equanimity. These are called the three characteristics. *Q.* What are the four characteristics of rejoicing? *A.* Among these ten characteristics, there is rejoicing by reason of the gradual arising of the states produced; there is rejoicing by reason of the functions of the faculties becoming one; there is rejoicing by reason of the possession of energy; and there is rejoicing by reason of devotion (to these states). These are called the four characteristics. Thus, in the first meditation, *jhāna,* the ten characteristics are fulfilled.

TWENTY-FIVE BENEFITS

Twenty-five benefits: In the first meditation, initial and sustained application of thought, joy, bliss and unification of mind are accomplished. Faith, energy, mindfulness, concentration and wisdom are accomplished. The initial, medial and final stages (of goodness) are accomplished...........[1] is accomplished. Practice is accomplished. Solitude is accomplished. Dependence is accomplished.......[2] is accomplished.........[3] is accomplished. Reflection is accomplished...........[4] is accomplished. Power is accomplished. Freedom is accomplished. Purity is accomplished, and the super-excellent purity is accomplished. Thus a man dwells together with the twenty-five benefits. These are the excellent stations of the deities. They are produced from tranquillity and are called the abodes of joy and bliss. In such excellent abodes surpassing the human do the deities dwell. Hence the Blessed One, the Buddha, declared to the bhikkhus:

SIMILE OF THE BATH-ATTENDANT

"Just as a skilful bath-attendant or his apprentice heaps up bath-powder in a lovely copper vessel, adds water to it, kneads it, and makes it round, saturating it so that it adheres and does not scatter, just so a bhikkhu, having calmed his body and mind, produces joy and bliss and lets it evenly moisten and saturate (him) in such a way that there is no part of him that is not saturated with it. There is no place in his body or mind that is not saturated with joy and bliss born of solitude".[5] Like the skilful bath-attendant or his apprentice is the yogin. The copper vessel is the *kasiṇa* sign. Thus it should be known.

Q. What is the *kasiṇa* sign? *A.* As the copper vessel contains the hard

---

1—4. These terms are not clear, Prof. Bapat has rendered them as: *sankhepa-sangahá, sangaha, anunaya and sevanā* respectively at p. 49, Vim. Mag. and Vis. Mag.

5. D.I, 74 and A. III, 25: *Seyyathāpi bhikkhave dakkho nahāpako vā nahāpakantevāsī vā kaṁsathāle nahāniyacuṇṇāni ākiritvā udakena paripphosakaṁ paripphosakaṁ sanneyya, sā'ssa nahāniyapiṇḍi snehānugatā snehaparetā santarabāhirā phuṭā snehena na ca paggharati, evam eva kho bhikkhave bhikkhu imam eva kāyaṁ vivekajena pītisukhena abhisandeti parisandeti paripūreti parippharati, nāssa kiñci sabbāvato kāyassa vivekajena pīti-sukhena apphuṭaṁ hoti.*

bath-powder which is made fine and bright, so the *kasiṇa* sign contains the hard (earth) out of which one produces joy which is soft and pure and therefore bright. Because the mind and the mental properties fill the object, the copper vessel is said to be like the *kasiṇa* sign. Mind and the mental properties are like the bath-powder. Thus it should be understood.

Q. Why is the bath-powder likened to the mind and the mental properties?

A. As bath-powder, owing to coarseness, does not adhere and is scattered by the wind, so the mind and mental properties when they are separated from joy and bliss, become coarse. And if they are separated from concentration they do not adhere and are scattered by the winds of the five hindrances. Therefore it is said that the bath-powder is like the mind and mental properties. What is comparable to water? Namely, joy and bliss and concentration. As water moistens, renders malleable, makes it round, so joy and bliss moisten and render malleable the mind and mental properties, and produce concentration. Therefore water is like joy and bliss. Like the stirring of the bath-powder with water are initial and sustained application of thought. Thus they should be understood.

Q. What is likened to the rounded thing?

A. Namely, initial and sustained application of thought. As a skilful bath-attendant puts the bath-powder into the copper vessel, mixes it with water, makes it round with his hand, and having made it round, he rounds it further with more wet powder and puts it into the vessel without scattering, so does the yogin place his mind and mental properties in the object and produce tranquillity well. In the first meditation, *jhāna*, joy and bliss should be regarded as water, initial and sustained application of thought as the hand that stirs and makes it (the powder) round. Thus one is able to produce tranquillity well. The mind and mental properties become rounded with joy and bliss and are not scattered because of the mind being kept on the object of meditation. Thus the rounded bath-powder is like initial and sustained application of thought. Just as the bath-powder is moistened thoroughly and just as it, through adhering, does not scatter, so the yogin in the first meditation, *jhāna*, is filled with joy from head to foot and from foot to skull, skin and hair, and dwells without falling. Thus one dwells in the realm of Brahma.

Q. Joy and bliss are called formless states. How then can they fill the body?

A. Name depends on form. Form depends on name. Therefore, if name is full of joy, form also is full of joy. If name is full of bliss, form also is full of bliss. And again, form that is bliss-produced, causes calm of body, and owing to the bliss of form the entire body is tranquillized. Thus there is no contradiction.

THREE KINDS OF REBIRTH

The merit which can produce rebirth in the world of Brahma is thus: In the first meditation, *jhāna*, there are three kinds: lower, middling and upper. When a man considers the special means, but does not remove the five hindrances well and does not reach the state of freedom, it is called lower meditation, *jhāna*. When a man considers the special means and removes the five hindrances, but does not reach the state of freedom, it is called middling meditation, *jhāna*. When a man considers the special means, removes the hindrances well and reaches the state of freedom, it is called higher meditation, *jhāna*. If a yogin attains to the lower first meditation, *jhāna*, after his death he will join the retinue of Brahma, and his life-span will be a third of an aeon; if he practises the middling first meditation, *jhāna*, he will, after his death, be reborn as a chief Brahma, and his life-span will be half an aeon; if he practises the higher first meditation, *jhāna*, he will be reborn as a Great Brahma, and his life-span will be one aeon.[1]

MEDITATION WHICH PARTAKES OF DETERIORATION, STABILITY, DISTINCTION AND PENETRATION

There are four kinds of men who acquire the merit of rebirth in the world of Brahma. A man partakes of deterioration, a man partakes of stability, a man partakes of distinction and a man partakes of penetration.[2]

A man of dull faculties causes the arising of meditation, *jhāna*, but is heedless. And again, through two kinds of conduct in meditation, *jhāna*, a man partakes of deterioration:— (1) Owing to the denseness of the encompassing impurities[3], a man has not sufficient energy to destroy the evil discursive thinking which he caused to arise in the past. Thus, owing to the denseness of the encompassing impurities, he deteriorates. (2) Or, a man who is desirous of meditation, *jhāna*, is given to talk, addicted to sleep, and does not endeavour. Hence he deteriorates.

Q. Who falls back and how?

A. There is an opinion that if a man becomes impure of mind, he will fall back. And again, there is an opinion: Through slow pollution of the mind, one falls back. And again, there is another opinion: If a man loses serenity, he falls back. And there is yet another opinion: If a man does not practise for a long time on the sign he caused to arise in the past, he becomes incapable of making it to arise as he likes and does not attain to concentration. So, he falls back. If a man of dull faculties dwells heedfully, he acquires the recollectedness of that state and partakes of stability in meditation, *jhāna*.

1. *Brahma-pārisajja, Brahma-purohita, Mahā-Brahmā.*
2. Cp. Pts. I, 35 — 6: *Paṭhamajjhānassa lābhiṁ kāmasahagatā saññāmanasikārā samudācaranti, hānabhāgiyo dhammo; tadanudhammatā sati santiṭṭhati, ṭhitibhāgiyo dhammo; avitakkasahagatā saññā manasikārā samudācaranti, visesabhāgiyo dhammo; nibbidāsahagatā saññā manasikārā samudācaranti virāgūpasaṁhitā, nibbdehabhāgiyo dhammo.*
3. *Pariyuṭṭhāna kilesa*:— Cp. Thi. vv. 77—8: *Ayonisomanasikārā kāmarāgena additā,*
ahosiṁ uddhaṭā pubbe citte avasavattini.
Pariyuṭṭhitā kilesehi sukhasaññānuvattinī,
samaṁ cittassa nā!abhiṁ rāgacittavasānugā.

If a man of keen faculties dwells heedfully, he can acquire facility in the second meditation, *jhāna*, which has no initial application of thought. If he develops further, he partakes of distinction in meditation, *jhāna*. If a man of keen faculties dwells heedfully, he can attain to insight with ease. Dispelling the thoughts of agitation and anxiety, and developing further, he, through absence of passion, partakes of penetration in meditation, *jhāna*.

[418] THE PATH OF FREEDOM

FASCICLE THE FIFTH

WRITTEN

BY

THE ARAHANT UPATISSA

WHO WAS CALLED

GREAT LIGHT IN RYO

TRANSLATED IN RYO

BY

TIPIṬAKA SANGHAPĀLA OF FUNAN

CHAPTER THE EIGHTH

Section Two

Here I show how to get the second meditation, jhāna. I consider the tribulation of the first meditation, jhāna, and the benefits of the second meditation, jhāna.[1]

THE SIMILE OF THE YOUNG COW

Now, the yogin who practises the first meditation, *jhāna*, with facility wishes to cause the arising of the second meditation, *jhāna*. Why? If the yogin is not able to practise the first meditation, *jhāna*, with facility, though he wishes to remove initial and sustained application of thought and attain to the second meditation, *jhāna*, he falls back and is not able to enter the second meditation, *jhāna*. Further, he cannot re-enter the first meditation, *jhāna*. Hence the Blessed One taught the simile of the young mountain cow which, being foolish, knows not good pasturage, and which, though inexperienced, wanders to a far off precipitous place. She thinks: "How, if I were to enter the place I never entered before, eat the grass I never ate before and drink the water I never drank before"? Without planting her fore leg firmly, she raises her hind leg, becomes restless and is not able to go forward. And not being able to enter the place she never entered before, eat the grass she never ate before, drink the water she never drank before, she thinks thus: "I cannot go forward. I must return to the old pasturage".[2]

---

1. The passage in italics does not occur in the Sung Dynasty edition in the library of the Japanese Imperial household. This applies to all passages in italics in Section Two of Chapter Eight.
2. This passage does not occur in the Chinese *Ekottara Āgama*. A. IV, 418: *Seyyathā pi bhikkhave gāvī pabbateyyā bālā avyattā akhettaññū akusalā visame pabbate carituṁ, tassā evam assa 'yan nūnāhaṁ agatapubbañ c'eva disaṁ gaccheyyaṁ, akhāditapubbāni*

There is a bhikkhu. He has not yet attained (meditation, *jhāna*). He does not know a subject of meditation.[1] He has not yet separated himself from lust and does not know how to enter the first meditation, *jhāna*. He does not practise this teaching nor study it, but thinks thus: "How, if I were to enter the second meditation, *jhāna*, and rid myself of initial and sustained application of thought"? Being not at ease, he again thinks: "I cannot enter the second meditation, *jhāna*, and I cannot rid myself of initial and sustained application of thought. I must retire, (from this), enter the first meditation, *jhāna*, and separate myself from lust". This foolish bhikkhu is as ignorant and inexperienced as the young mountain cow. Therefore, he should practise the first meditation, *jhāna*. He should make the mind free (from lust).

ENTRANCE INTO THE SECOND MEDITATION, JHANA

Before and after his meal, in the first and in the last watches of the night, according to his wish, a bhikkhu practises adverting, entering, establishing, rising and reflecting.[2] If he enters (the meditation, *jhāna*,) often and goes out of it often and acquires facility in the practice of the first meditation, *jhāna*, he can acquire the bliss of facility, cause the arising of the second meditation, *jhāna*, and surpass the first meditation, *jhāna*. And again he thinks thus: "This first meditation, *jhāna*, is coarse; the second meditation, *jhāna*, is fine". And he sees the tribulations of the first and the merits of the second meditation, *jhāna*.

Q. What are the tribulations of the first meditation, *jhāna*?

A. The hindrances as the near enemy (of this meditation, *jhāna*,) stir up initial and sustained application of thought and cause negligence of body and disturbance of mind. Thereby the concentration becomes coarse and incapable of producing higher knowledge. Therefore, one does not relish the first meditation, *jhāna*, or partake of distinction in it. These are the tribulations of the first meditation, *jhāna*.[3] The merits of the second meditation, *jhāna*, consist in the overcoming of these. Thus we have seen the tribulations of the first meditation, *jhāna*, and the merits of the second.

Here the mind separates itself from the first meditation, *jhāna*, and taking the *kasiṇa* sign as the object of the second meditation, *jhāna*, dwells on it. The mind, dissociated from initial and sustained application of thought, at

---

ca tiṇāni khādeyyaṁ, apītapubbāni ca pānīyāni piveyyan' ti; sā purinaṁ pādam na suppatiṭṭhitaṁ patiṭṭhāpetvā pacchimaṁ pādaṁ uddhareyya, sā na c'eva agatapubbaṁ disaṁ gaccheyya, na ca akhāditapubbāni tiṇāni khādeyya, na ca apītapubbāni pānīyāni piveyya; yasmiṁ c'assā pāde ṭhitāya evam assa 'yan nūnāhaṁ agatapubbañ c'eva disaṁ gaccheyyaṁ, akhāditapubbāni ca tiṇāni khādeyyaṁ, apītapubbāni ca pānīyāni piveyyan' ti, tañ ca padesaṁ na sotthinā pacchāgaccheyya. Taṁ kissa hetu? Tattha hi sā bhikkhave gāvī pabbateyyā bālā avyattā akhettaññū akusalā visame pabbate carituṁ.

1. *Kammaṭṭhāna.*

2. Pts. I, 99—100: *Pañca vasiyo — āvajjanāvasī samāpajjanāvasī adhiṭṭhānavasī vuṭṭhānavasī paccavekkhaṇāvasī.*

3. A. IV, 440: *So kho ahaṁ Ānanda aparena samayena vivicc' eva kāmehi.......paṭhamaṁ jhānaṁ upasampajja viharāmi. Tassa mayhaṁ Ānanda iminā vihārena viharato kāmasahagatā saññāmanasikārā samudācaranti, svāssa me hoti ābādho.*

ease in joy and bliss born of concentration, attains (to the second meditation, *jhāna*). If the yogin strives, he accomplishes the destruction of initial and sustained application of thought quickly. He is at ease in joy and bliss born of concentration and cause the mind to abide tranquilly.

Here I show the four factors of the second meditation, jhāna.

That yogin "attains to and dwells in the second meditation, *jhāna*, which, through the stilling of initial and sustained application of thought, develops internal tranquillity and the state of mind-predominance, is without initial and sustained application of thought, born of concentration, full of joy and bliss".[1] This is the merit of the earth *kasiṇa*. The stilling of initial and sustained application of thought is the stilling of initial and sustained application of thought through clear understanding. And also it is named ending.

Q. What is "the stilling of initial and sustained application of thought"?

A. It is the destruction of the tribulations of initial and sustained application of thought pertaining to the first meditation, *jhāna*. It is the destruction of the roots of all initial and sustained application of thought. It is the co-destruction of the tribulations of initial and sustained application of thought, roots of initial and sustained application of thought, and initial and sustained application of thought themselves. This is "the stilling of initial and sustained application of thought".

And again, after separating himself from the lower coarse meditation, *jhāna*, the yogin attains to the upper fine meditation, *jhāna*, and causes it (the lower) to perish.

"Internal": what is one's own is named "internal". There are three kinds in what is internal: the first is internal in the sense of personal; the second is internal concentration; the third is internal object.

What is "internal in the sense of personal"? The six internal sense spheres. "Internal concentration": The contemplation on one's own bodily state is called "internal concentration". The thought which is inward (subjective), does not go outwards, and the nature of which is to understand is called "internal object". In this treatise "internal in the sense of personal" means "to be in a state of blissfulness".

Faith,[2] right faith and the faith which develops meditation, *jhāna*, are called "tranquillity". In internal concentration this is internal tranquillity.

What are the salient characteristic, function, manifestation and near cause of internal tranquillity? Non-disburbance is the salient characteristic of internal tranquillity. Repose is its function. Non-defilement is its manifestation. Initial and sustained application of thought are its near cause.

---

1. A. I, 53: *Vitakka-vicārānaṁ vūpasamā ajjhattaṁ sampasādanaṁ cetaso ekodibhāvaṁ avitakkaṁ avicāraṁ samādhijaṁ pītisukkaṁ dutiyajjhānaṁ upasampajja viharati.*
2. *Saddhā.*

"Develops the state of mind-predominance": the dwelling of the mind in right concentration is called the development of the state of mind-predominance. What is the meaning of "development of the state of mind-predominance"? "Mind" means mentality. "Predominance" is a name for mindfulness. "State" has the same meaning as that of "natural state" which is taught in the science of sound. "State" means nature. The stilling of initial and sustained application of thought and the arousing of the state of mind-predominance through unification of mind is called "the development of the state of mind-predominance".

What are the salient characteristic, function, manifestation and near cause of 'the state of mind-predominance'?

Pure righteousness is its salient characteristic; repose is its function; unruffledness is its manifestation; and the stilling of initial and sustained application of thought is its near cause.

Q. (It is said that the yogin) "develops internal tranquillity and the state of mind-predominance". If that be so, why are these not included in the first meditation, *jhāna*?

A. In the first meditation, *jhāna*, owing to the waves of initial and sustained application of thought, the mind is muddied.

"Internal tranquillity and the state of mind-predominance": just as, owing to waves, water becoming turbid, does not clearly reflect any image, cast on it, just so in the first meditation, *jhāna*, because of turbidity due to the movement of the waves of initial and sustained application of thought, internal tranquillity and the state of mind-predominance are not clear. Therefore, they are not included in the first meditation, *jhāna*.

'Without initial and sustained application of thought": After the stilling of initial application of thought, there is no initial application of thought. After the stilling of sustained application of thought, there is no sustained application of thought.

Q. The stilling of initial and sustained application of thought is the state that is without initial and sustained application of thought. Are there two kinds of ending of initial and sustained application of thought? Why are two kinds taught?

A. The stilling of initial and sustained application of thought develops internal tranquillity. The state of mind-predominance becomes the cause of the state that is without initial and sustained application of thought, owing to the appearance of the excellent characteristic of joy and bliss which is born of solitude.

And again, the stilling of initial and sustained application of thought is thus: Seeing through initial and sustained application of thought, the tribulation of initial and sustained application of thought, he abandons them. The state that is without initial and sustained application of thought is the stilling of initial and sustained application of thought of the form element.

And again, in what is without initial and sustained application of thought there are two divisions: the first is "without initial and sustained application of thought" that is not due to the stilling of initial and sustained application of thought; (the second) is "without initial and sustained application of thought" that is due to the stilling of initial and sustained application of thought. Thus, without the stilling of initial and sustained application of thought, the five branches of higher knowledge and the third meditation, *jhāna*, are without initial and sustained application of thought. The second meditation, *jhāna*, is without initial and sustained application of thought through skilful seclusion and the stilling of initial and sustained application of thought. These are the two divisions.

"Born of concentration": This refers to concentration. The first meditation, *jhāna*, comes from that consciousness and the second meditation, *jhāna*, comes from the first meditation, *jhāna*. And again, "concentration" means that the second meditation, *jhāna*, comes together with unification of mind.

"Joy and bliss born of concentration": Joy and bliss have already been expounded.

"The second meditation, *jhāna*": It is called so because it follows the first.

"Attains to the second meditation, *jhāna*", means that he enters the second meditation, *jhāna*.

"Meditation, *jhāna*": Internal tranquillity, joy and bliss and unification of mind are called "meditation, *jhāna*".

"Attains to and dwells in the second meditation, *jhāna*": He acquires the second meditation, *jhāna*, which is free from two factors, endowed with two factors, three kinds of goodness and ten characteristics and is associated with twenty-three merits. This is the heavenly abode. This is merit. This is birth in the Abode of Resplendence.[1] This has been expounded at length before.

SIMILE OF THE POOL OF WATER

"Heavenly abode" means that he dwells in a plane surpassing the human because of joy and bliss that proceed from concentration. Therefore it is called "heavenly abode". Hence the Blessed One taught the bhikkhus thus:

---

1. A.II, 127: *Puna ca paraṁ bhikkhave idh' ekacco puggalo vitakkavicārānaṁ vūpasamā ajjhattaṁ sampasādo cetsao ekodibhāvaṁ avitakkaṁ avicāraṁ samādhijaṁ pītisukhaṁ dutiyajjhānaṁ upasampaịja viharati. So tad assādeti....tabbahulavihārī apirihīno kālaṁ kurumāno Ābhassarānaṁ devānaṁ sahavyataṁ uppajjati.*

"As in a pool of water with a spring and into which no water flows from the four directions, nor rain descends, the water wells up cool and pure from within, saturates the entire pool and over-flowing spreads afar, even so [419] joy and bliss, cool and pure, welling up from concentration saturates every part of the body of a bhikkhu. Thus joy which is produceed from concentration saturates the body and the mind".[1]

A yogin entering the second meditation, *jhāna*, should consider his body in the light of this simile of the pool with water welling up from within. The absence of any stream flowing from any of the four directions is to be understood as the stilling of initial and sustained application of thought. As the water welling up from within fills the pool without causing waves to arise in it, [419] so joy and bliss springing from concentration fills the mental and bodily factors and there is no disturbance of mind. As water that is cold cools the body, so joy and bliss born of concentration causes all the mental and bodily factors to be at ease.

Thus is the reward of the practice of concentration: One is reborn in the Abode of Resplendence. There are three kinds of rewards pertaining to the three divisions of the second meditaton, *jhāna:* lower, middling and higher. The yogin who practises the lower meditation, *jhāna*, will, after his death, be reborn in the Abode of Lesser Light. His life-span will be two aeons.[2] If he practises the middling meditation, *jhāna*, he will, after his death, be reborn in the Abode of Measureless Light. His life-span will be four aeons.[3] If he practises the higher meditation, *jhāna*, he will, after his death, be reborn in the Abode of Resplendence and his life-span will be eight acons.[4]

THE THIRD MEDITATION, JHANA

I consider the tribulations of the second meditation, jhāna.

Now a yogin having practised the second meditation, *jhāna*, and acquired facility therein thinks: "The second meditation, *jhāna*, is coarse; the third meditation, *jhāna*, is fine". Knowing the tribulations of the second medita-

1. Chu Agon No. 98: M.I, 276—7; D.I, 74; A.III, 25—6: *Seyyathā pi bhikkave udakarahado ubbhidodako tassa nev' assa puratthimāya disāya udakassa āyumukhaṁ na pacchimāya disāya udakassa āyamukhaṁ na uttarāya disāya udakassa āyamukhaṁ na dakkhiṇāya disāya udakassa āyamukhaṁ, devoca na kālena kālaṁ sammādhāraṁ anuppaveccheyya atha kho tamhā ca udakarahadā sītā vāridhārā ubbhijjitvā tam eva udakarahadaṁ sītena vārinā abhisandeyya parisandeyya paripūreyya parippharеyya, nāssa kiñci sabbāvato udakarahadassa sītena vārinā apphuṭaṁ assa, evam eva kho bhikkhave bhikkhu imam eva kayaṁ samādhijena pītisukhena abhisandeti parisandeti paripūreti, parippharati, nāssa kiñci sabbāvato kāyassa samādhijena pītisukhena apphuṭaṁ hoti.*
2. Vbh. 424: *Dutiyaṁ jhānaṁ parittaṁ bhāvetvā parittābhānaṁ devānaṁ sahavyataṁ uppajjanti. Tesaṁ kittakaṁ āyuppamāṇaṁ ? Dve kappā.*
3. Ibid: *Dutiyaṁ jhānaṁ majjhimaṁ bhāvetvā appamāṇābhānaṁ devānaṁ sahavyataṁ uppajjanti. Tesaṁ kittakaṁ āyuppamāṇaṁ? Cattāro kappā.*
4. Ibid: *Dutiyaṁ jhānaṁ paṇītaṁ bhāvetvā ābhassarānaṁ devānaṁ sahavyataṁ uppajjanti. Tesaṁ kittakaṁ āyuppamāṇaṁ? Aṭṭha kappā.*

tion, *jhāna*, and seeing the merits of the third meditation, *jhāna*, he causes the third meditation, *jhāna*, to arise.

What are the tribulations of the second meditation, *jhāna*? This concentration has initial and sustained application of thought as its near enemy. This meditation, *jhāna*, being accompanied by joy, is coarse. The mind exults in the possession of joy and is not able to arouse other (higher) meditation (*jhāna*) factors. To be attached to joy is a fault. If he understands these faults, he becomes fault-free. One is not able to acquire supernormal power; or one gains the second meditation, *jhāna*, and is not able to partake of distinction. Thus should one understand the tribulations of the second meditation, *jhāna*. The merits of the third meditation, *jhāna*, lie in the overcoming of these (tribulations). If one considers the tribulations of the second meditation, *jhāna*, and the merits of the third, he can remove joy through meditation, *jhāna*, on the *kasiṇa* sign and be at ease because of freedom from joy. Considering thus he can in no long time attain to fixed meditation, *jhāna*, through bliss free from joy.

I will elucidate the factors of the third meditation, jhāna.

That yogin "through the absence of the desire for joy, abides in equanimity, mindful and completely conscious, experiencing in the body that bliss of which the Noble Ones say: "Endowed with equanimity and mindfulness, and completely conscious, he abides in bliss. So he abides in the attainment of the third meditation, *jhāna*".[1]

"Through absence of desire for joy": Joy has already been explained. "Absence of desire": Removing joy one dwells in equanimity. What is "equanimity"? Equipoise, protection, non-retreating, non-advancing, serenity and evenness of mind are called "equanimity". There are eight kinds of equanimity: equanimity of feeling, of effort, of insight, of the enlightenment factors, of the immeasurable states, of the six members (senses), of the meditation (*jhāna*) factors and of purity[2]. The equanimity of feeling is the equanimity of the five faculties. Reflection on the sign of equanimity from time to time—this is the equanimity of effort. If, saying, "I will remove the cause of suffering", one attains to equanimity, it is called the equanimity of insight. The practising of the enlightenment factors is the equanimity of the enlightenment factors. Kindness, compassion, appreciative joy and equipoise — these are called the equanimity of the immeasurable states.

If, on seeing a form, one, being indifferent, is neither glad nor sad, it is called the equanimity of the six members. The dwelling in the attainment of

---

1. A.I, 53: *Pītiyā ca virāgā upekkhako ca viharati sato ca sampajāno sukhañ ca kāyena paṭisaṁvedeti yan taṁ ariyā ācikkhanti upekkhako satimā sukha-vhārī ti tatiyajjhānaṁ upasampajja viharati.*
2. *Vedanupekkhā, viriyupekkhā, vipassanupekkhā, bojjhangupekkhā, appamāṇupekkhā, chaḷangupekkhā, jhānupekkhā, pārisuddhupekkhā*, Cp. Vis. Mag. 160 where *brahmavihārupekkhā* is substituted for *appamāṇupekkhā.*

equanimity because of dispassion is called the equanimity of the meditation (*jhāna*) factors. Equanimity-mindfulness purity is the equanimity of purity.

And again, there are three kinds of equanimity: equanimity regarded as a vehicle of concentration; regarded as the state of little activity; and regarded as non-action. The equalized skilfulness that is present in all meditations, *jhānas*, and is neither hasty nor slow is "equanimity considered as a vehicle of concentration". This inferior equanimity is near the second meditation, *jhāna*, and removes exultation of mind. If the mind is not active, it is called "equanimity regarded as a state of little activity". This equanimity is near the third meditation, *jhāna*, and removes all exultation of mind. If one's mind is not actively concerned with objects, through imperturbability of thought and body, it is called "equanimity regarded as non-action". This equanimity is near the fourth meditation, *jhāna*.

What are the salient characteristic, function, manifestation and near cause of equanimity? Equipoise is its salient characteristic. Non-attachment is its function. Non-action is its manifestation. Dispassion is its near cause.

Q. Why is it taught that equanimity is in this meditation, *jhāna*, and not in the second and the first meditations, *jhānas*?

A. In the second and the first meditations, *jhānas*, the mind, being full of joy, does not become detached. Because of joy and bliss, exultation of mind is not removed. Therefore, this equanimity is not taught as being present in the second and the first meditations, *jhānas*. Owing to absence of joy and bliss, owing to dispassion and owing to the removal of the process of combination in the third meditation, *jhāna*, this meditation (*jhāna*) factor arises. Because of the mastering of the meditation (*jhāna*) factors, it is said "abides in equanimity, mindful and completely conscious".

Q. What are the salient characteristic, function, manifestation and near cause of "mindfulness"?

A. Recollectedness is its salient characteristic; non-forgetting is its function; protection is its manifestation; and the four foundations of mindfulness are it near cause.

What is it to be "completely conscious"? To be conscious is to be aware. It is to be completely conscious rightly. There are four kinds in being completely conscious rightly.[1] They are the being completely conscious of oneself; the being completely conscious of one's distinctive mark; the being completely conscious undeludedly; the being completely conscious basically. Here, to be completely conscious of the four postures, is to be completely conscious of oneself. Entering solitude is to be completely conscious of one's distinctive mark. To know the eight worldly conditions[2] is to be completely conscious

1. Cp. D.- a. I, 184: *Sātthaka-sampajaññaṁ sappāya-sampajaññaṁ gocara-sampajaññaṁ asammoha-sampajaññan ti catubbidhaṁ sampajaññaṁ.*
2. *Aṭṭha loka-dhammā.*

undeludedly. To dwell on the object of concentration is to be completely conscious basically. In this treatise ("completely conscious" in the sense of) "being completely conscious basically" has been taken.

What are the salient characteristic, function, manifestation and near cause of the being "completely conscious"? Non-bewilderment is its salient characteristic; decision is its function; investigation of states is its manifestation; to consider rightly is its near cause.

Q. Should one be mindful and completely conscious in all places?

A. If a man is not mindful and is not completely conscious he is not even able to cause the arising of the access stage of meditation, *jhāna*.

Q. Why is it taught in the third meditation, *jhāna* and not in the second and the first meditations, *jhānas*?

A. Here, joy and all other coarse meditation (*jhāna*) factors are stilled. Concentration becomes fine, enters a place of fineness, and through the state of being completely conscious remains firm in the third meditation, *jhāna*. Thus he gains facility in the exercise of the meditation (*jhāna*) factors.

Again, the foolish mind longs for happiness and easily turns to the bliss of this meditation, *jhāna*, for its exceedingly sweet and named "alluring". Thus (through mindfulness and through the state of being completely conscious) one is able to remove joy and acquires facility in this meditation, *jhāna*.

SIMILE OF THE CALF

Again, joy and bliss are intimate. So, understanding mindfulness and the state of being completely conscious one dwells on the object in bliss separate from joy. It is like a calf following its mother. Unless someone holds it back by the ears, it will follow its mother with its head against her side. One understands bliss that is separate from joy, conjoined with mindfulness, and the state of being completely conscious, and dwells on the object of concentration.[1] On the contrary, if one does not understand, one re-enters joy and partakes of deterioration in concentration. For the acquiring of mastery over the meditation (*jhāna*) factors, mindfulness and the state of being completely conscious are taught. Thus equanimity, mindfulness and the state of being completely conscious are accomplished. Therefore, it is said "abides in equanimity, mindful and completely conscious, experiencing in the body that bliss".

Q. What is mental bliss?

A. Bliss experienced in mind is mental bliss. It comes from mental contact. This is the meaning of mental bliss. This is called "bliss".

Q. What is "body"? The perception-group, formations-group and consciousness-group — these are called "body".

---

1. Cp. Vis. Mag. 163: *Yathā dhenupago vaccho dhenuto apanīto arakkhiyamāno punad-eva dhenuṁ upagacchati.* This simile, common to both the Vis. Mag and the Vim. Mag., has not been traced to its source.

"Experiencing in the body that bliss" means to acquire ease of body.

Q. Then, why is it said that there is no joy in this bliss and that it is not experienced in the body?

A. In the third meditation, *jhāna*, the faculty of bliss is removed. This is according to the teaching of the Blessed One which says, that in the third meditation, *jhāna*, the faculty of bliss is removed.

"That bliss of which the Noble Ones say": "Noble Ones" means the Buddha and his disciples. "Say" means to reveal, establish, explain, point out. Thus is "that bliss of which the Noble Ones say" to be known.

Q. Why do the Noble Ones praise this state of body and not any other?

A. In the third meditation, *jhāna*, although the yogin can easily dwell in pleasing bliss, he does not hold to bliss. The Noble Ones dwell looking beyond bliss. This is an accomplishment of the Noble Ones. Therefore, the Noble Ones praise this excellent meditation, *jhāna*.

"Endowed with equanimity and mindfulness, he abides in bliss": Equanimity, mindfulness and bliss have already been explained.

"Abides in the attainment of the third meditation, *jhāna*": It is called "third" because of the second. The third meditation, *jhāna*, comprises equanimity, mindfulness, the state of being completely conscious, bliss and unification of mind. The accomplishment of these is called (the third) meditation, *jhāna*. "Abides in the attainment" means that one who acquires the third meditation, *jhāna*, separates from one factor, fulfils five factors, three kinds of goodness, ten characteristics and is associated with twenty-two merits.

To dwell in the heaven world means to be born in the Abode of All Lustre.[1] It is to be understood in the same way as it was taught in the first meditation, *jhāna*. "To dwell in the heaven world" is to dwell in that pleasant dwelling which is free from joy. "To dwell in the heaven world" is to dwell in a manner surpassing humans.

SIMILE OF THE LOTUS POND

Hence, the Buddha taught the bhikkhu thus: "Just as in a pond of blue and white lotuses, the blue, red and white lotuses are born, grow and stand in the water and are immersed in the cold water from root to neck, so this body is filled and saturated with bliss that is free from joy".[2] As the blue, red and white lotuses stand in the water, so he abides in the third meditation,

---

1. *Subhakiṇṇa*.
2. Chu Agon No. 98; M.II, 16; A.III, 26: *Seyyathā pi bhikkhave uppaliniyaṁ vā paduminiyaṁ vā puṇḍarīkiniyaṁ vā app' ekacce uppalāni vā padumāni vā puṇḍarīkāni vā udake jātāni udake saṁvaḍḍhāni udakānuggatāni antonimuggaposīni tāni yāva c'aggā yāva ca mūlā sītena vārinā abhisannāni parisannāni paripūrāni paripphuṭāni, nāssa kiñci sabbāvataṁ uppalānaṁ vā padumānaṁ vā puṇḍarīkānaṁ vā sītena vārinā apphuṭaṁ assa, evam eva kho bhikkhave bhikkhu imam eva kāyaṁ nippītikena sukhena abhisandeti parisandeti paripūreti parippharati, nāssa kiñci sabbāvato kāyassa nippītikena sukhena apphuṭam hoti.*

jhāna. His body should be known thus: as the lotuses born in the water [420] are immersed in the water from root to neck, so he abides in the third meditation, *jhāna*, with body and mind filled and saturated with bliss that is free from joy.

Thus is the reward of the practice of concentration: One is reborn in the Abode of the All Lustrous. There are three kinds of rewards pertaining to the three divisions of the third meditation, *jhāna*, namely: higher, middling and lower. If a yogin practises the lower meditation, *jhāna*, he will, after his death, be reborn in the Abode of Lesser Lustre. His life-span will be sixteen aeons. If he practises the middling meditation, *jhāna*, he will, after his death, be reborn in the Abode of Measureless Lustre. His life-span will be thirty-two aeons. If he practises the higher meditation, he will be reborn in the Abode of All Lustre. His life-span will be sixty-four aeons[1].

THE FOURTH MEDITATION, JHANA

I consider the tribulations of the third meditation, jhāna.

Now, a yogin, having practised the third meditation, *jhāna*, and acquired facility therein, wishes to cause the arising of the fourth meditation, *jhāna*, and to transcend the third meditation, *jhāna*. (He thinks), "The third is coarse. The fourth is fine". He sees the tribulations of the third meditation, *jhāna*, and the merits of the fourth meditation, *jhāna*. What are the tribulations of the third meditation, *jhāna*? Joy is the near enemy. Right concentration with bliss is coarse. So he is not able to acquire supernormal power. The third meditation, *jhāna*, does not partake of distinction. Thus he sees the tribulations of the third meditation, *jhāna*. The merits of the fourth meditation, *jhāna*, consist in the over-coming of these (tribulations).

Thus the yogin, on seeing the tribulations of the third meditation, *jhāna*, and the merits of the fourth meditation, *jhāna*, meditates on the *kasiṇa* sign and removes bliss at once. After removing it he can dwell with the mind of equanimity. Thus meditating his mind quickly attains to fixed meditation, *jhāna*, owing to equanimity.

I will elucidate the factors of the fourth meditation, jhāna.

That yogin, "having abandoned pleasure and pain, leaving behind former joy and grief, painless, pleasureless, in the purity of equanimity-mindfulness,

---

1. Vbh. 424—5: *Tatiyaṁ jhānaṁ parittaṁ bhāvetvā parittasubhānaṁ devānaṁ sahavyataṁ uppajjanti. Tesaṁ kittakaṁ āyuppamānaṁ? Soḷasa kappā........Tatiyaṁ jhānaṁ majjhimaṁ bhāvetvā appamāṇasubhānaṁ devānaṁ sahavyataṁ uppajjanti. Tesaṁ kittakaṁ āyuppamānaṁ? Dvattiṁsa kappā......Tatiyaṁ jhānaṁ paṇītaṁ bhāvetvā subhakiṇhānaṁ devānaṁ sahavyataṁ uppajjanti. Tesaṁ kittakaṁ āyuppamānaṁ? Catusaṭṭhi kappā.*

accomplishes the fourth meditation, *jhāna*, and dwells".[1] This is a merit of the earth *kasiṇa.*

"Having abandoned pleasure": This is the abandoning of bodily pleasure. Having abandoned "pain": This is the abandoning of bodily pain. "Leaving behind former joy and grief": Joy is the bliss of the mental properties.[2] This is the leaving behind of these.

Q. It is said, "having abandoned pleasure and pain, leaving behind grief". Where were these abandoned and left behind? *A.* They were abandoned and left behind at the access moments of the meditation, *jhāna.* The Buddha taught the removal of pain in this fourth meditation, *jhāna. Q.* Where does the faculty of pain that has arisen cease entirely? *A.* The Buddha taught the bhikkhus thus: "In the first meditation, *jhāna*, separation from sense-desires is fulfilled. There the faculty of pain which has arisen ceases entirely".[3] *Q.* Why does the faculty of pain cease entirely in the first meditation, *jhāna*? *A.* Because of the fullness of joy, there is bodily ease.[4] Because of bodily ease, the faculty of pain is ended, i.e., through transcending, it is abandoned. Therefore, in the first meditation, *jhāna*, the faculty of pain is removed. In the second meditation, *jhāna*, the faculty of grief is removed. According to the teaching of the Buddha, the removal of the faculty of grief is thus: "Where does the faculty of grief that has arisen cease entirely? Here, bhikkhus, initial and sustained application of thought are stilled, and he abides in the attainment of the second meditation, *jhana.* Here. the faculty of grief which has arisen ceases entirely" [5] Why does the faculty of grief, cease in the second meditation, *jhana*? If a man has initial and sustained application of thought for long, his body and mind become negligent. If his mind becomes negligent, the faculty of grief arises immediately. In the second meditation, *jhāna*, initial and sustained application of thought are stilled. In the third meditation, *jhāna*, the faculty of bliss is removed. The Buddha taught thus: "Where does the faculty of bliss which has arisen cease entirely? Here, bhikkhus, owing to the distaste for joy, one abides in the attainment of the third meditation, *jhāna.* Here the faculty of bliss which

---

1. A. III, 26—7; M. II, 16: *Puna ca paraṁ, Udāyi, bhikkhu sukhassa ca pahānā dukkhassa ca pahānā pubbe va somanassadomanassānaṁ atthagamā adukkhaṁ asukhaṁ upekhāsati-pārisuddhiṁ catutthajjhānaṁ upasampajja viharati.*
2. *Cetasika.*
3. S. V, 213: *Idha bhikkhave bhikkhuno appamattassa ātāpino pahitattassa viharato uppajjati dukkhindriyaṁ......Kattha cuppannaṁ dukkhindriyaṁ aparisesaṁ nirujjhati? Idha bhikkhave bhikkhu vivicc' eva kāmehi vivicca akusalehi dhammehi savitakkaṁ savicāraṁ vivekajaṁ pītisukhaṁ paṭhamaṁ jhānaṁ upasampajja viharati. Ettha cuppannaṁ dukkhindriyaṁ aparisesaṁ nirujjhati.*
4. A. III, 285: *Pītimanassa kāyo passambhati, passaddhakāyo sukhaṁ vediyati.*
5. S. V, 213—4: *Idha pana bhikkhave bhikkhuno appamattassa ātāpino pahitattassa viharato uppajjati domanassindriyaṁ......Kattha cuppannaṁ domanassindriyaṁ aparisesaṁ nirujjhati? Idha bhikkhave bhikkhu vitakkavicārānaṁ vūpasamā ajjhattaṁ sampasādanaṁ cetaso ekodibhāvaṁ avitakkaṁ avicāraṁ samādhijaṁ pītisukhaṁ dutiyaṁ jhānaṁ upasampajja viharati. Ettha cuppannaṁ domanassindriyaṁ aparisesaṁ nirujjhati.*

has arisen ceases entirely".[1] *Q*. Why does the faculty of bliss cease in the third meditation, *jhāna*? *A*. Joy perishes, and so, bliss that arises depending on joy also perishes. Therefore, in the third meditation, *jhāna*, the faculty of bliss perishes.

Q. If the faculties of pain, bliss and grief were removed in the third meditation, *jhāna*, why is their ending taught in the fourth meditation, *jhāna*?

A. These faculties were removed in the third meditation, *jhāna*. The third meditation, *jhāna*, is an approach to the fourth meditation, *jhāna*. In the third meditation, *jhāna*, these having arisen, passed away. Therefore, their removal is taught in the fourth meditation, *jhāna*.

And again, "accomplishes" the "painless" and "pleasureless" means the overcoming of pain and pleasure.[2] Therefore, the overcoming of pain and pleasure is taught as the accomplishment of the painless and pleasureless. And again, it is because in the fourth meditation, *jhāna*, attainment and overcoming occur together. And again, equanimity removes the defilements immediately and entirely. The attaining to the "painless" and "pleasureless" means that the mind does not receive and thought does not reject. This is called the attaining to the "painless" and "pleasureless".

What are the salient characteristic, function, manifestation and near cause of the accomplishing of the "painless" and "pleasureless" ?

Middleness is the salient characteristic. Dwelling in a middle position is the function. Abandoning is the manifestation. Removal of joy is the near cause.

What is the purity of equanimity-mindfulness? Neutrality is called equanimity. That is called equanimity. "Mindfulness" is called attentiveness, recollectedness and Right Mindfulness. These are called "mindfulness". The mindfulness that is clarified and purified by equipoise is called "purity of equanimity-mindfulness".

Q. How is mindfulness clarified and purified by equipoise? *A*. Here imperturbability and non-action are fulfilled, owing to the abandoning of all defilements and owing to resemblance and closeness to that attainment. This non-action is associated with equipoise. Therefore, mindfulness reaches imperturbability and fulfils impassivity. Therefore, this mindfulness is equanimity and acquires clarity and purity.

"Fourth": This means that because of the third, the fourth is fulfilled. "Accomplishes the meditation": This refers to the equanimity-mindfulness

1. S.V, 214: *Idha bhikkhave bhikkhuno appamattassa ātāpino pahitattassa viharato uppajjati sukhindriyaṁ......Kattha cuppannaṁ sukhindriyaṁ aparisesaṁ nirujjhati? Idha bhikkhave bhikkhu pītiya ca virāgā upekhako ca viharati sato sampajāno sukhaṁ ca kāyena paṭisaṁvedeti ......tatiyaṁ jhānaṁ upasampajja viharati. Ettha cuppannaṁ sukhindriyaṁ aparisesaṁ nirujjhati.*
2. S.V., 215: *Idha pana bhikkhave bhikkhuno appamattassa ātāpino pahitattassa viharato uppajjati somanassindriyaṁ......Kattha cuppannaṁ somanassindriyaṁ aparisesaṁ nirujjhati. Idha bhikkhave bhikkhu sukhassa ca pahānā dukkhassa ca pahānā pubbeva somanassadomanassānaṁ atthagamā adukkhamasukhaṁ upekhāsatipārisuddhiṁ catutthaṁ jhānaṁ upasampajja viharati. Ettha cuppannaṁ somanassindriyaṁ aparisesaṁ nirujjhati.*

and unification of mind of the fourth meditation, *jhāna*. This is the meaning of "accomplishes the meditation". "Accomplishes" and "dwells": One separates from one factor, fulfils three factors, three kinds of goodness and ten characteristics, and is associated with twenty-two merits. Thus one abides in the attainment of the fourth meditation, *jhāna*. The reward of this (meditation) is rebirth in the heaven world. The merit of this causes rebirth in the Abode of Great Fruition.[1] This was taught fully before. "To dwell in the heaven world": This is to dwell in a manner surpassing humans. This is to dwell in the bliss of equanimity. This is called dwelling in the heaven world.

SIMILE OF THE WHITE CLOTH

Therefore the Blessed One taught the bhikkhus thus: "As a man might sit down and cover his body with a white cloth from head to foot, in such a way that no part of his body is left uncovered, so a bhikkhu covers his body and limbs with purified mindfulness, in such a way that no part of him is not covered with purified mindfulness".[2] The yogin is like a man who has covered himself with a white cloth. Freed from all subtle defilements, he dwells in the fourth meditation, *jhāna*. Thus should it be known. As the man who covers his body from head to foot with a white cloth is protected from extremes of heat and cold, experiences an even temperature and is undisturbed in body and mind, so that yogin who enters the fourth meditation, *jhāna*, experiences neither pain nor pleasure. This is the bliss of equanimity. With it he fills his body.

Thus is the merit of concentration: One is reborn in the Abode of Great Fruition. A commoner who practises the fourth meditation, *jhāna*, will, after his death, be reborn in the Abode of Great Fruition. If his mind dislikes effort, he will be reborn in the Abode of the Unconscious. His life-span will be fifty aeons.[3] If the yogin is a recluse, he will be reborn in the Abode of Great Fruition, or in one of the five Pure Abodes.[4] Such are the retributory fruits of this meditation, *jhāna*.

Q. Why are the lower, middling and upper (meditation, *jhānas*) and the partaking of distinction of the fruition-ground taught in the third and not in the fourth meditation, *jhāna*?

---

1. *Vehapphala.*
2. Chu Agon No. 98. M. II, 16, 17; A. III, 27: *Seyyathā pi bhikkhave puriso odātena vatthena sasīsaṁ pārupitvā nisinno assa, nāssa kiñci sabbāvato kāyassa odātena vatthena apphuṭaṁ assa, evam eva kho bhikkhave bhikkhu imam eva kāyaṁ parisuddhena cetasā pariyodātena pharitvā nisinno hoti, nāssa kiñci sabbāvato kāyassa parisuddhena cetasā pariyodātena apphuṭaṁ hoti.*
3. Vbh. 425: *Catutthaṁ jhānaṁ bhāvetā......appekacce asaññasattānaṁ devānaṁ sahavyataṁ uppajjanti......Asāññasattānañ ca vehapphalānañ ca devānaṁ kittakaṁ āyuppamāṇaṁ? Pañca kappasatāni* 'Fifty aeons' is obviously an error and it should read 'five hundred'.
4. (*a*) D.III, 237: *Pañca Suddhāvāsa: Avihā, Atappā, Sudassā, Sudassī, Akaniṭṭhā.*
   (*b*) Vbh. 425: *Catunnaṁ jhānaṁ bhāvetvā......appekacce avihānaṁ devānaṁ sahavyataṁ uppajjanti......appekacce atappānaṁ devānaṁ......,appekacce sudassānaṁ devānaṁ......, appekacce sudassīnaṁ devānaṁ ......,appekacce akaniṭṭhānaṁ devānaṁ sahavyataṁ uppajjanti.*

A. There are differences of "coarse" and "fine", according to result, in the third meditation, *jhāna*. Therefore, the excellence of the fruition-ground is taught through the partaking of distinction. In the fourth meditation, *jhāna*, the yogin reaches the limit of the partaking of distinction. Outside this there is no other partaking of distinction. Therefore, there is no partaking of distinction of the fruition-ground.

THE SPHERE OF THE INFINITY OF SPACE

I consider the tribulations of the fourth meditation, jhāna.

Now, the yogin who has acquired boundless happiness in the fourth meditation, *jhāna*, wishes to enjoy the space-concentration and to transcend the realm of form. He considers thus: "Concentration of form is coarse; space-concentration is fine". That yogin sees the tribulations of form and the merits of space-concentration. What are the tribulantions of form? There are many (tribulations) such as the taking up of sticks and weapons, beating, quarrelling, slander, lying, maiming and the like. There are many sufferings such as pain of the eye and other bodily ills, cold and heat, hunger and thirst. These are the severe trials of the sensuous form.

What are the tribulations of the fourth meditation, *jhāna*? The depending on form objects has satisfaction for near enemy. It is called coarse. One who is attached to form and delights in it cannot partake of distinction. But depending on space, one liberates oneself peacefully. In this concentration one fulfils the gross. Thus the yogin sees the tribulations of the fourth meditation, *jhāna*, in form. The merits of space-concentration consist of the overcoming of these.

I have considered the troubles of the fourth meditation, jhāna. And now I show how to enter the concentration of the sphere of the infinity of space.

That yogin having seen form and the great tribulations thereof and the merits of space-concentration, rises from that (form) concentration, abandons the earth *kasiṇa*, the earth sign and practises space-concentration.

He should dwell on space regarding it as an infinite object. If he meditates thus, he quickly completes the destruction of the earth sign and his mind rises out of the earth sign and goes beyond the earth sign to space. Through the acquisition of facility in the perception of the sphere of the infinity of space he attains to fixed meditation, *jhāna*.

That yogin "by passing entiiely beyond perception of form, by the disappearance of the perception of impact, by being freed from attention to perceptions of diversity, thinking, 'Infinite is space', enters into and abides in the sphere of infinite space.[1]

"Entirely" means without remainder. "By passing beyond perception of form": What is perception of form? The perception, the perceiving, the state of having perceived pertaining to one who dwells in the concentration of the form-element — these are called perception of form. "Passing beyond" means the surpassing of this. [421] "By the disappearance of the perception of impact": What is the perception of impact? The perception of visible objects, of sounds, of odours, of flavours, and of tangibles — these are called the perception of impact. "Disappearance" means the ending of these various kinds of (impact-) perception. "By being freed from attention to perceptions of diversity": What are perceptions of diversity? The perception, the perceiving, the state of having perceived pertaining to one who has not attained to concentration and who is endowed with the mind element and the consciousness element — these are called perceptions of diversity. "Freed from attention to perceptions of diversity" means that one is freed from attending to these perceptions of diversity.

Q. Why is it that only the surpassing of perception is taught and not the surpassing of feeling, formations and consciousness?

A. If a man passes beyond perception of form, he passes beyond all the others; and if a man is not freed from perception of form, his mind is not capable of passing beyond the others. Hence the Blessed One taught the surpassing of perception of form with the intention of setting forth the surpassing of all form-objects, because all (form) objects of concentration are dependent on perception.

Q. If that does not happen (i.e., if he does not transcend the perception of form) is there or is there not perception of impact and diversity?

A. There is the perception of impact and diversity in form concentration, because these are removed (later).

Q. Why does he not proceed further in that concentration?

A. He dislikes form, therefore, he does not remove (these perceptions) in that (concentration). This is according to the teaching of the Buddha which says that, owing to the non-removal of these (perceptions of impact) in that (form concentration), sound is a thorn to one entering the first meditation, *jhāna*.[2] Thus disliking form, he goes further. He destroys them here. Therefore, he attains to the imperturbability of the formless attainment and the peacefulness of liberation. Aḷāra Kālāma and Uddaka Rāmaputta when they entered the formless attainment, did not see nor hear those five hundred

1. D. I, 183: *Puna ca paraṁ Poṭṭhapāda bhikkhu sabbaso rūpasaññānaṁ samatikkamā paṭigha-saññānaṁ atthagamā nānatta-saññānaṁ amanasi-kārā "ananto ākāso ti" ākāsānañcāyatanaṁ upasampajja viharati.*
2. A. V, 134—5: *Paṭhamassa jhānassa saddo kaṇṭako.*

carts passing and repassing.[1] Therefore, it is taught as the destruction of the (sense) spheres; and thus, surpassing of all form perception is taught as the destruction of the form states and the perception of impact. "By being freed from attention to perceptions of diversity" means the destruction of the sense states. Again, the surpassing of all form perception is taught as the attainment of the realm of the formless. The disappearance of the perception of impact is taught as the destruction of the outer disturbance to that concentration (of the formless) and the purification of imperturbability. "Freed from attention to perceptions of diversity" is taught as destruction of the inner disturbance to that concentration and the purification of the peacefulness of liberation.

Q. "The sphere of infinite space": What is space?

A. It is the sphere of space, the element of space and vacuity.[2] That which is untouched by the four primaries — this is called vacuity. When a man tranquillizes the mind by means of the perception of limitless space, it is said that he thinks, "Infinite is space". Infinite space means the entering into limitless space. The mind and the mental properties which enter space are called "sphere of space". What is "sphere of space"? Boundlessness is the nature of space. This boundless nature is the "sphere of space". This is taught as the meaning of space. As dwelling in heaven is called heaven, so (dwelling in) the concentration of the sphere of space is called "sphere of space". "Enters into and abides in the sphere of infinite space" means that he acquires the concentration of the sphere of infinite space, passes beyond all form objects, fulfils three factors, three kinds of goodness and ten characteristics, is associated with twenty-two merits and dwells peacefully in the enjoyment of the reward of concentration practice. By reason of these good qualities, he will be reborn in the sphere of infinite space, as it was fully taught before. "By these good qualities he will be reborn in (the sphere of infinite) space" means that he who practises the concentration of the sphere of space will,

---

1. D. II, 130—31: *Bhūta-pubbaṁ bhante Āḷāro Kālāmo addhānamaggapaṭipanno maggā okkamma avidūre aññatarasmiṁ-rukkha-mūle divā-vihāre nisīdi. Atha kho bhante pañcamattāni sakaṭa-satāni Āḷāraṁ Kālāmaṁ nissāya nissāya atikkamiṁsu. Atha kho bhante aññataro puriso tassa sakaṭa-satthassa piṭṭhito āgacchanto yena Āḷāro Kālāmo ten'upasaṁkami, upasaṁkamitvā Āḷāraṁ Kālāmaṁ etad avoca:*
   "Api bhante pañcamattāni sakaṭa-satāni atikkamantāni addasāti?"
   "No kho ahaṁ āvuso addasan" ti.
   "Kim pana bhante saddaṁ assosīti?"
   "Na kho ahaṁ āvuso saddaṁ assosin" ti.
   "Kim pana bhante sutto ahosīti?"
   "Na kho ahaṁ āvuso sutto ahosin" ti.
   "Kim pana bhante saññī ahosīti?"
   "Evam āvuso" ti.
   'So tvaṁ bhante saññī samāno jāgaro pañcamattāni sakaṭa-satāni nissāya nissāya atikkamantāni n'eva addasa na pana saddaṁ assosi, api hi te bhante saṁghāṭi rajena okiṇṇā' ti.
   'Evam āvuso' ti.
   'Atha kho bhante tassa purisassa etad ahosi: "Acchariyaṁ vata bho, abbhutaṁ vata bho! Santena vata bho pabbajitā vihārena viharanti yatra hi nāma saññī samāno jāgaro pañcamattāni sakaṭa-satāni......na pana saddaṁ sossatīti". Āḷāre Kālāme uḷāraṁ pasādaṁ pavedetvā pakkāmīti'.
2. Lit. Empty hole.

after his death, be reborn in the sphere of infinite space. His life-span will be two thousand aeons.[1]

THE CONCENTRATION OF THE SPHERE OF INFINITE CONSCIOUSNESS

I consider the tribulations of the concentration of the sphere of infinite space.

Now, that yogin having acquired mastery in the practice of (the concentration of) the sphere of infinite space wishes to cause the arising of the concentration of the infinite consciousness *kasiṇa* and to transcend the infinite space *kasiṇa*. Considering the concentration of (the sphere of) space as coarse, he sees the fineness (of the concentration) of the sphere of infinite consciousness.

And again, he sees the tribulations of the sphere of infinite space and the merits of the sphere of infinite consciousness. What are the tribulations of the sphere of infinite space? This concentration has form for near enemy. The object of the concentration of the sphere of infinite space is gross, and the perception of impact and the perceptions of diversity have not yet broken away from each other. Here, owing to attachment, the yogin is not able to partake of distinction. Thus he sees the tribulations of the concentration of the sphere of infinite space. The merits of the consciousness *kasiṇa* lie in the overcoming of these.

I show infinite consciousness.

That yogin, having seen the severe troubles of the concentration of the sphere of infinite space and the merits of the sphere of infinite consciousness, should consider the sphere (of infinite consciousness) as calm, and steadily attend to the arising of the consciousness which proceeds spreading through space with the thought, "Infinite is consciousness". Thus his mind is held in the perception of the sphere of infinite consciousness. Thus he meditates and in no long time the mind rises out of the perception of the sphere of infinite space, and passes into the sphere of infinite consciousness. In this perception of the sphere of infinite consciousness, the mind attains to fixed meditation, *jhāna*. Thus "passing entirely beyond the sphere of infinite space, that yogin, thinking, 'Infinite is consciousness', enters into, and abides in the sphere of infinite consciousness". "Entirely" means without remainder. "Passing beyond the sphere of infinite space" means the passing beyond the sphere of infinite space. "Passing beyond" means to go rightly beyond. This is called "passing entirely beyond the sphere of infinite space". "Infinite space": "He attends to that consciousness as infinite with which space is filled".

---

1. Here 'two thousand' is obviously an error. Should read 'twenty thousand'. Cp. Vbh. 425; A. I, 267: *Ākāsānañcāyatanūpagānaṁ bhikkhave devānaṁ vīsatiṁ kappasahassāni āyuppamāṇaṁ.*

Q. Among the form and formless states, which are infinite?

A. Only formless states are infinite, because there are no bounds to the formless, and because they cannot be held. And again, space is limitless. Therefore, it is called infinite. The word "infinite" (*ananta*) means infinite (*ananta*). Thus, the word "infinite" is used. So is the word consciousness.

"Abides in the sphere" means abides in the sphere of infinite consciousness. The mind and the mental properties are called the sphere of infinite consciousness. What is the "sphere of infinite consciousness"? It is boundless consciousness. This is called "the sphere of infinite consciousness". As dwelling in heaven is called heaven, so (dwelling in) the concentration of infinite consciousness is called the sphere of infinite consciousness. When this consciousness is held in concentration, it is called "the sphere of infinite consciousness". "Enters into and abides in the sphere of infinite consciousness" means that he surpasses the spatial object in that concentration of the sphere of infinite consciousness. He fulfils three factors, three kinds of goodness, ten characteristics and is associated with twenty-two merits, and dwells peacefully in the enjoyment of the reward of concentration-practice. By reason of these good qualities, he will be reborn in the sphere of infinite consciousness. This was fully taught before.

Thus is the merit of the practice (of the concentration) of the sphere of infinite consciousness. A man who practises the concentration of infinite consciousness will, after his death, be reborn in the sphere of infinite consciousness. His life-span will be four thousand aeons.[1]

(The exposition of) *the sphere of infinite consciousness has ended.*

THE SPHERE OF NOTHINGNESS

I consider the tribulations of the sphere of infinite consciousness.

Now, that yogin, having acquired mastery in the practice of the concentration of the sphere of infinite consciousness, wishes to cause the arising of the concentration of the sphere of nothingness, and to transcend the sphere of infinite consciousness.

Again, he considers thus: "The concentration of the sphere of infinite consciousness is coarse; the concentration of the sphere of nothingness is fine". And he sees the tribulations of the sphere of infinite consciousness and the merits of the concentration of the sphere of nothingness. What are the tribulations of the concentration of the sphere of infinite consciousness? This concentration has space for near enemy. The consciousness object is coarse. Here, the yogin, owing to attachment, is not able to partake of

---

1. Again an error; should read 'forty thousand'. Cp. Vbh. 425; A. I, 267: *Viññāṇañcāyatanūpagānaṁ bhikkhave devānaṁ cattārīsaṁ kappasahassāni āyuppamāṇaṁ.*

distinction through the considering of infinite perception. The merits of the sphere of nothingness lie in the overcoming of these. That yogin, having seen the tribulations of the sphere of infinite consciousness and the merits of the sphere of nothingness, rises out of the sphere of infinite consciousness peacefully, does not proceed along that consciousness again, does not reflect on it again and puts away that consciousness. Seeing the freedom of the sphere of nothingness, he wishes to attain to it, and considering thus he quickly rises out of consciousness perception. Owing to the perception of the sphere of nothingness, he attains to fixed meditation, *jhāna*. Passing entirely beyond the sphere of infinite consciousness, that yogin, thinking, "There is nothing whatsoever", enters into and abides in the sphere of nothingness.

"Entirely" means without remainder. "Passing beyond the sphere of infinite consciousness" means to go rightly beyond consciousness. This is called "passing entirely beyond the sphere of infinite consciousness". "Nothingness" means that he does not practise (consciousness concentration) again; does not discern again; goes out of that consciousness (sphere), and sees only nothingness. Thus should nothingness be known. "Sphere (of nothingness)": The mind and the mental properties which enter the sphere of nothingness, are called "sphere of nothingness". What is the sphere of nothingness? That which is without the nature of consciousness and empty. The sphere of nothingness is taught as "holding to nothing". "Enters into the sphere" means "attains to the concentration of the sphere of nothingness". "Enters into and dwells": He attains to the concentration of (the sphere of) nothingness, passes beyond the consciousness object, fulfils three factors, three kinds of goodness, ten characteristics and is associated with twenty-two merits, and dwells peacefully in the enjoyment of the reward of concentration. By reason of these good qualities, he is reborn in the sphere of nothingness. This was fully taught before. The merit by which a man is reborn in the sphere of nothingness is thus: He who practises the concentration of the sphere of nothingness will be reborn, after his death, in the sphere of nothingness. His life-span will be six thousand aeons.[1]

(The exposition of) *the concentration of the sphere of nothingness has ended.*

THE SPHERE OF NEITHER PERCEPTION NOR NON-PERCEPTION

I consider the tribulations of the sphere of nothingness.

Now, the yogin having acquired mastery in the practice of concentration of the sphere of nothingness wishes to cause the arising of the concentration of neither perception nor non-perception, and to transcend the sphere of

1. Again an error; should read 'sixty thousand'. Cp. Vbh. 426; A. I, 268; *Ākiñcaññāyatanūpagānaṁ bhikkhave devānaṁ saṭṭhiṁ kappasahassāni āyuppamāṇaṁ.*

nothingness. He considers thus: "The sphere of nothingness is coarse; the sphere of neither perception nor non-perception is fine". And again, he sees the tribulations of the sphere of nothingness and the merits of the sphere of neither perception nor non-perception. [422] What are the tribulations of the sphere of nothingness? It has consciousness for near enemy. It is accompanied by coarse perception. Therefore it is gross. Owing to attachment to it one does not partake of distinction. Thus he sees the tribulations of the sphere of nothingness. The merits of the sphere of neither perception nor non-perception lie in the overcoming of these. And again, this perception is a disease, a boil, a thorn. Non-perception — this is right, tranquil and lofty. Thus he sees the sphere of neither perception nor non-perception. And having seen the sphere of nothingness, having entered it and having reflected upon it, that yogin practises the other concentration by causing calmness to arise out of the solitude of the sphere of nothingness. Meditating thus he passes out of the perception of the sphere of nothingness in no long time, and attains to fixed meditation, *jhāna,* in the sphere of neither perception nor non-perception.

I will show the sphere of neither perception nor non-perception.

"Passing entirely beyond the sphere of nothingness, that yogin enters into and dwells in the sphere of neither perception nor non-perception". "Entirely" means without remainder. "Passing beyond the sphere of nothingness" means the surpassing of the sphere of nothingness and the going beyond it, rightly. This is called "passing entirely beyond the sphere of nothingness". "Neither perception nor non-perception": He, practises the other concentration by causing calmness to arise out of the solitude of the sphere of nothingness. This is called the sphere of neither perception nor non-perception. "Sphere of neither perception nor non-perception": The mind and the mental properties which enter the sphere of neither perception nor non-perception are called the sphere of neither perception nor non-perception. What is the meaning of "sphere of neither perception nor non-perception"? Through the removal of coarse perception, he is endowed with non-perception. Through there being a remainder of fine perception, he enters the sphere of neither perception nor non-perception. Thus should "sphere" and "neither perception nor non-perception" be understood. "Enters into and abides": He attains to the concentration of the sphere of neither perception nor non-perception, passes beyond the sphere of nothingness, fulfils three factors, three kinds of goodness and ten characteristics, is associated with twenty-two merits and dwells in the enjoyment of the reward of concentration practice. By reason of these good qualities, he will be reborn in the sphere of neither perception nor non-perception. This was fully taught before. "By reason of these good qualities he will be reborn in the sphere of neither perception nor non-perception" means that he who practises the concentration of neither perception nor non-perception will be reborn, after his death, in the sphere of neither perception nor non-perception. His life-span will be eighty-four thousand aeons.[1]

Q. Why is this called "sphere of neither perception nor non-perception", and not "sphere of the infinity of consciousness"?

A. He separates from the attachment to infinitude and causes the arising of subtle perception. Therefore, he does not attain to the sphere of the infinity of consciousness.

Q. Why are the cankers not destroyed through this concentration?

A. If a man separates himself from gross perception, he will not be able to see the Path. And again this concentration is exceedingly fine. So he cannot discern the nature of neither perception nor non-perception. Therefore he is not able to destroy the cankers.

(The exposition of the) *sphere of neither perception nor non-perception has ended.*

MISCELLANEOUS TEACHINGS

I further elucidate the meaning of the above.

Q. What are the miscellaneous teachings in the field of concentration?

A. Stoppage of sounds; overturning; rising; transcending; access; initial application of thought; feeling; uncertainty. "Stoppage of sounds": In the first meditation, *jhāna*, speech is stopped. On entering the fourth meditation, *jhāna*, the yogin stops breathing.[2] Gradual stoppage of sounds: When the yogin enters into concentration, he hears sounds, but he is not able to speak because the faculty of hearing and that of speech are not united. To a man who enters form concentration, sound is disturbing. Hence the Buddha taught: "To a man who enters meditation, *jhāna*, sound is a thorn".[3] "Overturning":[4] A man, concentrating on the earth *kasiṇa* develops earth perception through non-earth perception.

Q. If that be so, does he not fulfil "overturning"?

A. This earth perception should be known as that perception. It differs from the four kinds of overturning of perception. Therefore, it does not fulfil "overturning".[5] "Rising":[6] The rising from concentration is conditioned

1. Vbh. 426: *Neva-saññā-nāsaññāyatanūpagānaṁ devānaṁ kittakaṁ āyuppamāṇaṁ? Caturāsīti kappasahassāni.*
2. D. III, 266: *Catutthajjhānaṁ samāpannassa assāsa-passāsā niruddhā honti.*
3. A. V, 134—5: *Saddakaṇṭakā hi bhikkhave jhānā vuttā mayā......Paṭhamassa jhānassa saddo kaṇṭako.*
4. *Vipallāsa.*
5. This is after Prof. Higata. But the text is as follows: "It does not differ from the four kinds of overturning of perception. Therefore it does not fulfil overturning".
6. *Vuṭṭhāna.*

by five causes, namely, painfulness of posture; many bonds; arising of hindrances; unequal skill; and inclination.

When a man enters formless concentration, he does not "rise" owing to "many bonds", because he dwells in imperturbability. If he enters the attainment of dissolution and the attainment of fruition,[1] he can "rise" through previous action[2] and not through any other cause. "Transcending": In transcending there are two kinds, namely, transcending the factor[3] and transcending the object.[4] To pass from form meditation, *jhāna*, to form meditation, *jhāna*, is called "transcending the factor". To pass from form meditation, *jhāna*, to formless concentration, and from formless concentration to formless concentration is called "transcending the object". "Access" is the access of all meditation, *jhāna*. It consists of five factors. "Initial application of thought": In the second meditation, *jhāna*, and the others through continued suppression, the state that is without initial and sustained application of thought is fulfilled. "Feeling": In the fourth meditation, *jhāna*, and the others, through continued suppression, the state that is with equanimity arises without extremes. "Uncertainty": Owing to this, one does not remove the hindrances of sense-desires and the others, and abides in the sphere of neither perception nor non-perception. This is called "with remainder". It is as if, fearing a poisonous snake, a man were to climb up a tree.

There are four kinds of men who cannot enter into concentration. They, surely, will be reborn in states of woe. Without cause they commit the five immediately effective deeds.[5] They are of perverted vision.

(The exposition of) ***Miscellaneous teachings has ended.***

(The exposition of) ***the earth kasiṇa has been concluded.***

* * * *

THE WATER KASINA

Q. What is the water *kasiṇa*? What is the practising of it? What are its salient characteristic, function and manifestation? What are its benefits? How is the sign grasped?

A. The thought that is produced relying on the water sign — this is called the water *kasiṇa*. The undisturbed dwelling of the mind — this is called

---

1. *Nirodha-* and *phala-samāpatti.*
2. Cp. Vis. Mag. 705: *Tathā ākiñcaññāyatanaṁ samāpajjitvā vuṭṭhāya catubbidhaṁ pubbakiccaṁ karoti: nānābaddha-avikopanaṁ, sanghapaṭimānanaṁ, satthu pakkosanaṁ addhānaparicchedan ti.*
3. *Aṅga samatikkama.*
4. *Ārammaṇa samatikkama.*
5. Vbh. 378: *Tattha katamāni pañca kammāni ānantarikāni? Mātā jīvitā voropetā hoti, pitā jīvitā voropetā hoti, arahā jīvitā voropetā hoti, duṭṭhena cittena tathāgatassa lohitaṁ uppāditaṁ hoti, saṁgho bhinno hoti: imāni pañca kammāni ānantarikāni.*

practising. Absorption in the water *kasiṇa* is its salient characteristic. Non-abandonment of water perception is its function. Undivided thought is its near cause.[1]

There are five distinctive kinds of benefits belonging to (the practice of) the water *kasiṇa*: a man is able to dive into the earth and come out of it easily; to shake palaces, mountains or the earth; to bring down rain; cause water to gush from his body and make that (water) appear as it were the ocean. The (other) benefits of the water *kasiṇa* are the same as those of the earth *kasiṇa*. One who practises the water *kasiṇa* well, sees water in all places.

"How is the sign grasped"?: The man who accepts the water *kasiṇa* grasps the sign in water, i.e., natural or prepared water. Here, a practised yogin grasps the water sign in a place where there is no water or on seeing water in various places, i.e., in a well, pot, pond, swamp, river, lake or lagoon. Thus he can see (the sign) wherever he likes, and can arouse the after-image of water. He is unlike a new yogin. A new yogin has to grasp the sign in a prepared place. He is not able to practise the water *kasiṇa* with skill in an unprepared place. Thus that yogin, at first, should find out a calm place, in the monastery or in a rock cave or under a tree, which is not too dark and where the sun does not scorch. It should be a place where there is no dust or wind and where there are no mosquitoes, gadflies or other impediments. In such a place, he buries a bowl or a water pot in clean earth, and makes the rim level with the ground. The circumference should be one fathom. It should be filled with rain-water and unmixed with any colour. The bowl or pot should be full to the brim. Here, he should dwell on the perception of water, and take the sign through three ways: through even gazing, skilfulness and the elimination of disturbance. The rest is as fully taught before under the earth *kasiṇa* and the sphere of neither perception nor non-perception.

The water kasiṇa has ended.

THE FIRE KASINA

Q. What is the fire *kasiṇa*? What is the practising of it? What are its salient characteristic, function and near cause? What are its benefits? How is the sign grasped?

A. The thought that is produced relying on fire — this is called the fire *kasiṇa*. The undisturbed dwelling of the mind — this is called practising. The skilfulness of sending the mind forth into the fire sign is its salient characteristic. Non-abandonment of fire perception is its function. Undivided thought is its near cause.

"What are its benefits"? There are five distinctive benefits. These are displayed in the fire *kasiṇa*. A man is able to produce smoke and flame, is able to reveal things through producing brightness, is able to destroy the

1. In the question it is "manifestation".

light of other forms, is able to burn whatever he likes,[1] is able to know fire through the arising of brightness. The other benefits are equal to those of the earth *kasiṇa*. Owing to the practice of the fire *kasiṇa*, a man is able to see fire everywhere.

"How is the sign grasped"?: The man who takes up the fire sign grasps the sign in fire, i.e., in a natural or a prepared place. Here, a practised yogin grasps the natural sign. (He grasps the sign) on seeing any fire, i.e., a grass-fire, a wood-fire, a forest-fire or a house that is on fire. He develops the natural or the prepared as he pleases and sees the appropriate sign. Thus the after-image of fire occurs to him. The new yogin is different. He is able to grasp the sign only in a prepared place and not in an unprepared place. He follows what is expedient in the practice of the fire *kasiṇa*. The new yogin should at first gather fuel, heap it up in a clean place and burn it. He burns it from below, at about the time the sun rises or sets. He does not think of the smoke or the flames that rise up. He sends his mind towards the fire sign by directing it to the middle of the thick flames and grasps the sign through three ways: through even gazing, skilfulness [423] and the elimination of disturbance. (The rest) is as was fully taught before.

The fire kasiṇa has ended.

THE AIR KASINA

Q. What is the air *kasiṇa*? What is the practising of it? What are its salient characteristic, function and near cause? What are its benefits? How is the sign grasped?

A. The thought that is produced relying on the air sign — this is called the air *kasiṇa*. The training and the undisturbed dwelling of the mind are called the practising of the air *kasiṇa*. Sending forth the mind into the air sign is its salient characteristic. The non-abandoning of air perception is its function. Undivided thought is its near cause.

"What are its benefits?": There are three distinctive benefits in air *kasiṇa*: a man is able to go about with the speed of air, to cause wind to rise and coolness to prevail. The other benefits are the same as those taught in the earth *kasiṇa*. One follows what is expedient in the practice of the air *kasiṇa*.

"How is the sign grasped?": A new yogin grasps the air *kasiṇa* through two ways: through sight and touch. How does he grasp the sign through sight? That yogin, seeing a field of sweet potatoes, a bamboo grove or a grass-land moved by the wind, reflects on air perception. He grasps the sign through three ways: through even gazing, skilfulness and the elimination

1. The first four are similar to those of Vis. Mag. : 175—6.

of disturbance. Thus he grasps the sign through sight. How does he grasp the sign through touch? In a calm abode, a new yogin makes an opening in the wall, inserts a pipe of bamboo or reed into it and sits near it, letting the wind that comes through it touch his body. Thus he grasps the air sign through touch.

A practised yogin is able to grasp the sign whenever the wind touches his body whether he is sitting, walking, standing or lying down. Thus the after-image of air occurs to him. He is unlike the new yogin.

The air kasiṇa has ended.

THE BLUE-GREEN KASINA

Q. What is the blue-green *kasiṇa*? What is the practising of it? What are its salient characteristic, function and near cause? What are its benefits? How is the sign grasped?

A. The thought that is produced relying on the blue-green *kasiṇa* — this is called the blue-green *kasiṇa*. The training and undisturbed dwelling of the mind are called practising. Sending forth the mind into the blue-green sign is its salient characteristic. Non-abandoning of the blue-green perception is its function. Undivided thought is its near cause.

"What are its benefits?": There are five benefits. In the blue-green *kasiṇa*, a man attains to the emancipation of the beautiful. He acquires the position of mastery of the blue[1] that is like a blue flower. He can change all things to blue. He sees the colour of blue anywhere through the practice of the blue *kasiṇa*.[2]

"How is the sign grasped?": The yogin grasps the sign in a prepared place or in a natural place. That yogin sees (the sign) in blue flowers, blue clothes or in blue-coloured things everywhere. He sees it always before him, in pleasure or in pain, and thus the after-image of the blue-green sign occurs to him. A new yogin is different. He grasps the sign in a prepared place. He is not able to grasp it in an unprepared place. He follows what is expedient

---

1. Lit. *Nīla abhibhāyatana*. D. III, 260: *Aṭṭha abhibhāyatanāni*, the eight positions of mastery.
   The following is from the *Abhidharma Sangīti Paryāya Pada Śāstra:-* One having no internal perception of form sees external forms, blue, indigo-coloured, indigo in appearance, indigo in brightness. As cloth of Benares dyed the colour of the *Ummaka* flower, deeply blue, is blue, indigo-coloured, indigo in appearance.......so it is when one having no internal perception of form sees external forms......Seeing such forms, he thinks: "I know, I see". Thus he perceives. This is the fifth position of mastery.
   D. II, 110: *Ajjhattaṁ arūpa-saññi eko bahiddhā-rūpāni passati nīlāni nīla-vaṇṇāni nīla-nidassanāni nīla-nibhāsāni—seyyathā pi nāma ummā-pupphaṁ nīlaṁ nīla-vaṇṇaṁ nīla-nidassanaṁ nīla-nibhāsaṁ—seyhathā vā pana taṁ vatthaṁ Bārāṇaseyyakaṁ ubhato-bhāgo-vimaṭṭhaṁ nīlaṁ nīla-vaṇṇaṁ nīla-nidassanaṁ nīla-nibhāsaṁ—evam eva ajjhattaṁ arūpa-saññī eko bahiddhā-rūpāni passati nīlāni nīla-vaṇṇāni nīla-nidassanāni nīla-nibhāsāni,* "*Tāni abhibhuyya jānāmi passāmīti*" *evaṁ-saññī hoti, idaṁ pañcamaṁ abhibhāyatanaṁ.*
2. Only three are treated in Vis. Mag. 176.

in the practice of the blue-green *kasiṇa.* This yogin makes a *maṇḍala* on a cloth, plank or wall with blue of the colour of the *Asita*[1] flower, in the form of a triangle or a square. He edges it round with another colour. Thus he prepares the blue-green sign. He grasps the sign through three ways: even gazing, skilfulness and the elimination of disturbance. The rest is as was fully taught before.

The blue-green kasiṇa has ended.

THE YELLOW KASINA

Q. What is the yellow *kasiṇa*? What is the practising of it? What are its salient characteristic, function and near cause? What are its benefits? How is the sign grasped?

A. The thought that is produced relying on the yellow sign—this is called the yellow *kasiṇa.* The training and the undisturbed dwelling of the mind—these are called the practising of it. Sending forth the mind into the yellow sign is its salient characteristic. Non-abandoning of the perception of yellow is its function. Undivided thought is the near cause.

"What are its benefits?": There are five distinctive benefits. A man is able to attain to the emancipation of the beautiful. He acquires the position of mastery of the yellow. He considers various yellow colours similar to that of the *Kaṇikāra* flower.[2] Practising the yellow *kasiṇa,* he sees yellow everywhere.

"How is the sign grasped?": The man who takes up the yellow *kasiṇa* grasps the yellow sign either in a prepared place or in a natural place. (The practised yogin) grasps the sign in a non-prepared place. That yogin sees the yellow colour of yellow flowers or yellow clothes anywhere. He sees it always, in pleasure or in pain. Thus the after-image of yellow occurs to him. The new yogin is different. The new yogin grasps the sign in a prepared

---

1. Indigo plant. Black colour (of ashes) black-blue, black — P.T.S. Dict.
2. According to the *Śāstra* quoted in note 1 on page 124, the sixth *abhibhāyatana* differs from the fifth in colour and flower. For *Ummaka, Karṇikāra* is substituted. D. II, 111, confirms this.— *Seyyathā pi nāma kaṇikāra-pupphaṁ pītaṁ pīta-vaṇṇaṁ pīta-nidassanaṁ pīta-nibhāsaṁ.*
The late Venerable Soma Mahā Thera, one of the co-translators of the Vimuttimagga, seeing the *karṇikāra* (*Sinhala, kiṇihiri;* Pterospermum acerifolium) tree at the Island Hermitage in Dodanduwa, in bloom in the early forties, and, recalling this passage of the Vimuttimagga, wrote the following verses:—

In our little island home
Where free the winged and reptile roam,
The spirit weaves on silent loom:
The Karṇikāra is in bloom.

There may frolic elf and gnome,
Ay, hearts grow happy in the loam
Of quiet! 'tis the fecund womb
Of thought serene, the grave of gloom.

place, and is not able to grasp it in a non-prepared place. He follows what is expedient in the practice of the yellow *kasiṇa.* This yogin makes a *maṇḍala* with yellow of the colour of the *Kaṇikāra* flower, on cloth, plank or wall, in the shape of a triangle or square. He edges it with another colour. Thus he prepares the yellow sign. He grasps the sign through three ways: even gazing, skilfulness and the elimination of disturbance. The rest is as was fully taught before.

The yellow kasiṇa has ended.

THE RED KASINA

Q. What is the red *kasiṇa*? What is the practising of it? What are its salient characteristic, function and near cause? What are its benefits? How is the sign grasped?

A. The thought that is produced relying on the red sign — this is called the red *kasiṇa.* The training and the undisturbed dwelling of the mind — these are called the practising of it. Sending forth the mind into the red sign is its salient characteristic. The non-abandoning of the perception of red is its function. Undivided thought is its near cause.

"What are its benefits?": There are four distinctive benefits. A man is able to attain to the emancipation of the beautiful in the red *kasiṇa.* He acquires the position of mastery of the red.[1] He is able to change things into the colour of red. The other benefits are equal to those taught under the earth *kasiṇa.* He who practises the red *kasiṇa* sees the colour of red prevailing everywhere.

"How is the sign grasped?": A man who takes up the red *kasiṇa,* grasps the red sign either in a prepared place or in a natural place. The practised yogin grasps the sign in a natural place, i.e., on seeing red flowers or red clothes anywhere. He sees always, in pleasure or in pain. Thus the after-image of the red sign occurs to him. The new yogin is different. The new

Lean grey tree with outstretched hands,
Your golden flow'r, a symbol, stands
For inward vision yoga-wrought,
For lustrous power nobly bought.

Upward flows life's current strong,
Should it for cool, calm, clean bliss long,
Should it, to sense the silence, throng,
To sense the golden flower's song.

Stem will you the outward flow
Of mind caught fast in maya-glow?
Illusion's lure will you lay low?
Then, let the golden flower blow.

1. In the seventh *abhibhāyatana,* according to the *śāstra* quoted above, the flower associated with the red *abhibhāyatana* is the *Bandhujīvaka.* D. II, 111 confirms: *Seyyathā pi nāma bandhujīvaka-pupphaṁ lohitakaṁ lohitaka-vaṇṇaṁ lohitaka-nidassanaṁ lohitaka-nibhāsaṁ.*

yogin grasps the sign in a prepared place, and is not able to do so in a non-prepared place. He follows what is expedient in the practice of the red *kasiṇa*. This yogin applies a red colour resembling that of the *Bandhujīvaka* flower on cloth, plank or wall, in the shape of a triangle or a square. Or, he makes a *maṇḍala* of red flowers. He edges it with another colour. Thus he prepares the red sign. He grasps the sign through three ways: through even gazing, skilfulness and the elimination of disturbance. The rest is as was fully taught before.

The red kasiṇa has ended.

THE WHITE KASINA

Q. What is the white *kasiṇa*? What is the practising of it? What are its salient characteristic, function and near cause? How is the sign grasped?

A. The thought that is produced relying on the white sign—this is called the white *kasiṇa*. The training and the undisturbed dwelling of the mind—these are called the practising of it. Sending forth the mind into the white sign is its salient characteristic. The non-abandoning of the perception of white is its function. Undivided thought is its near cause.

"What are its benefits?": There are eight distinctive benefits. A man is able to attain to the emancipation of the beautiful, and the positions of mastery of the white.[1] He overcomes rigidity and torpor, dispels darkness, produces brightness and arouses the divine eye through the white *kasiṇa*. The other benefits are the same as those taught in the earth *kasiṇa*. He who practises the white *kasiṇa* sees the colour of white prevailing everywhere.

"How is the sign grasped?": A man who takes up the white *kasiṇa* grasps the white sign either in a prepared or natural place. The practised yogin grasps the sign in a natural place. He sees the sign in various places—in white flowers, moonlight, sunlight, starlight or a round mirror. Beginning with these, he sees the sign always before him, through pleasure and through pain. Thus the after-image of the white sign occurs to him. The new yogin is different. The new yogin grasps the sign in a prepared place. He is not able to grasp it in a non-prepared place. He follows what is expedient in the practice of the white *kasiṇa*. This yogin makes a *maṇḍala* on cloth, plank or wall in the shape of a triangle or a square, with colour resembling that of the morning star. He edges it with another colour. Thus he prepares the white sign. He grasps the sign through three ways: even gazing, skilfulness and the elimination of disturbance. (The rest) is as was fully taught before.

The white kasiṇa has ended.

---

1. *Odāta abhibhāyatana*. In the *śāstra* mentioned above, this, the seventh *abhibhāyatana*, is associated with *Uśanastārakā* (Sk.), *Osadhitārakā* (Pali), the morning star. D. II, page 111 confirms: *Seyyathā pi nāma osadhi-tārakā odātā odāta-vaṇṇā odāta-nidassanā odāta-nibhāsā*.

THE LIGHT KASINA

[424] *Q*. What is the light *kasiṇa*? What is the practising of it? What are its salient characteristic, function and near cause? How is the sign grasped?

A. The thought that is produced relying on the light sign — this is called the light *kasiṇa*. The training and the undisturbed dwelling of the mind — these are called the practising of it. Sending forth the mind into the white sign is its salient characteristic. The non-abandoning of the perception of light is its function. Undivided thought is its near cause.

"What are its benefits?": They are equal to those of the white *kasiṇa*. He who practises the light *kasiṇa* sees light everywhere.

"How is the sign grasped?": A man who takes up the light *kasiṇa*, grasps the light sign in a prepared or in a natural place. The practised yogin grasps the sign in a natural place. He sees the sign in various places — in moonlight, sunlight, lamplight or in the light of gems. Beginning with these he sees (the sign) always through pleasure or through pain. Thus the after-image of the light sign occurs to him. The new yogin is different. The new yogin grasps the sign in a prepared place, and is not able to do so in a non-prepared place. He follows what is expedient in the practice of the light *kasiṇa*. This yogin chooses a wall facing east or west. He fills a bowl with water and keeps it in a sunny place nearby. This water causes a *maṇḍala* of light. From this *maṇḍala*, light rises and is reflected on the wall. Here he sees the light sign. He grasps it in three ways: through even gazing, skilfulness and the elimination of disturbance. (The rest) is as was fully taught before.

The light kasiṇa has ended.

THE PATH OF FREEDOM

FASCICLE THE SIXTH

WRITTEN

BY

THE ARAHANT UPATISSA

WHO WAS CALLED

GREAT LIGHT IN RYO

TRANSLATED IN RYO

BY

TIPIṬAKA SANGHAPĀLA OF FUNAN

CHAPTER THE EIGHTH

Section Three

THE (SEPARATED) SPACE KASINA

What is the (separated) space *kasiṇa*? What is the practising of it? What are its salient characteristic, function and near cause? What are its benefits? How is the sign grasped?

A. In the space *kasiṇa*, there are two kinds: The first is space that is separate from form; the second is space that is not separate from form. The sign of the space *kasiṇa* is space that is separate from form; the space sign that is grasped in an opening is space that is not separate from form. The training and the undisturbed dwelling of the mind — these are called the practising of it. Sending forth the mind into space perception is its function. Undivided thought is its near cause.

"What are its benefits?": There are two distinctive benefits, thus: A man is able to pass through obstructions such as walls, mountains and the like. His bodily activities are not impeded, and he becomes fearless.

"How is the sign grasped?": The man who takes up the space *kasiṇa*, grasps the sign in space that is natural or prepared. The practised yogin grasps the sign in a natural place. He sees the sign in various places — in some opening (in a wall), in the space of an open window, in the space which is between the branches of trees. Beginning with these, he sees it always, in pleasure and in pain. Thus the after-image of the space sign occurs to him. The new yogin is different. The new yogin grasps the sign in a prepared place; and not in a non-prepared place. This yogin goes to a calm abode on the outside of which are no obstructions. He makes a circular opening (in the wall) and grasps the space sign, through three ways: through even gazing, skilfulness and the elimination of disturbance. In this space *kasiṇa*, the fourth and the fifth meditations, *jhānas*, are produced. The rest is as was fully taught before.

The (separated) space kasiṇa has ended.

THE CONSCIOUSNESS KASINA

Q. What is the consciousness *kasiṇa*?

A. It is the concentration of the sphere of infinite consciousness. This is called the consciousness *kasiṇa*. The rest is as was fully taught before.

The ten kasiṇas have ended.[1]

MISCELLANEOUS TEACHINGS

Q. What are the miscellaneous teachings regarding these *kasiṇas*?

A. If one acquires facility in one sign, all other signs follow. If one acquires facility in the first meditation, *jhāna*, through one *kasiṇa*, one is able to acquire facility through the other *kasiṇas* also and is able to cause the arising of the second meditation, *jhāna*. In the same way, if one acquires facility in the second meditation, *jhāna*, one is able to cause the arising of the third meditation, *jhāna*. If one acquires facility in the third meditation, *jhāna*, one is able to cause the arising of the fourth meditation, *jhāna*.

Q. Which are the most excellent of all *kasiṇas*?

A. The four colour *kasiṇas* are the most excellent, because through them one attains to the emancipations[2] and the positions of mastery. The white *kasiṇa* is excellent, because it illumines and because through it an unobstructed state of mind is attained.

Here (the yogin) produces the eight attainments on eight *kasiṇas*, in sixteen ways, peacefully. (1) He dwells wherever he likes and (2) practises the concentration that he likes, (3) whenever he likes, (4) without hindrance, (5) in the direct order[3] and (6) in the reverse order,[4] (7) in the direct and in the reverse order,[5] (8) by developing separately[6] (9) by developing together, (10) by skipping over the middle,[7] (11) by limiting[8] the factor, (12) by limiting the object, (13) by limiting the factor and the object, (14) by fixing[9] the factor, (15) by fixing the object, (16) by fixing the factor and the object.

---

1. This and the subsequent passages in italics in this section do not occur in the Sung edition in the library of the Japanese Imperial household.
2. *Vimokkha.*
3. Lit. Ascending gradually.
4. Lit. Descending gradually.
5. Lit. Ascending and descending gradually.
6. Lit. Increasing each one.
7. Lit. Making little or restricting the middle.
8. Lit. Making little or restricting the factor.
9. Lit. Together with the factor.

(1) "He stays wherever he likes": He dwells in the village or forest — whichever he likes — and enters into concentration. (2) "Practises the concentration that he likes": He produces the concentration which he desires. (3) "Whenever": He enters into concentration at the time he likes. (4) ("Without hindrance"): He is able to remain firm in (concentration) at all times. (5) "In the direct order": He enters the first meditation, *jhāna*, and by degrees rises up to the sphere of neither perception nor non-perception. (6) "In the reverse order": Starting from the sphere of neither perception nor non-perception, he comes down by degrees to the first meditation, *jhāna*. (7) "In the direct and in the reverse order": He excels in ascending and in descending. He enters the third meditation, *jhāna*, from the first meditation, *jhāna*. From the third meditation, *jhāna*, he enters the second, and from the second he enters the fourth.[1] Thus he enters the concentration of the sphere of neither perception nor non-perception. (8) "By developing separately": Having gradually entered the fourth meditation, *jhāna*, he ascends or descends. (9) "By developing together": He enters the fourth meditation, *jhāna*. From that he enters space, and then enters the third meditation, *jhāna*. Thus he enters into concentration in these two ways. (10) "Skipping over the middle": He enters the first meditation, *jhāna*. From this he enters the sphere of neither perception nor non-perception. From this he enters the second meditation, *jhāna*, and therefrom attains to the sphere of nothingness. Thus he abides in that attainment, and understands the sphere of the infinity of space. (11) "Limiting the factor": He enters into the concentration of one meditation, *jhāna*, on eight *kasiṇas*. (12) "Limiting the object": He enters into eight kinds of concentration on three *kasiṇas*. (13) "Limiting the factor and the object": Two meditations, *jhānas*, and one *kasiṇa*. (14) "Fixing the factor": On three *kasiṇas*, he enters (Lit. two, two meditation, *jhānas*). (15) "Fixing the object": He enters two meditations, *jhānas*, on (Lit. two, two *kasiṇas*). (16) "Fixing the factor and the object": This consists of the two (preceding) sentences.

Miscellaneous teachings have ended.

---

1. Cp. (*a*) D. II, 156: '*Handa dāni bhikkhave āmantayāmi vo: "Vayadhammā saṁkhārā, appamādena sampādethāti"*.

Ayaṁ Tathāgatassa pacchimā vācā.

Atha kho Bhagavā paṭhamajjhānaṁ samāpajji. Paṭhamajjhānā vuṭṭhahitvā dutiyajjhānaṁ samāpajji. Dutiyajjhānā vuṭṭhahitvā tatiyajjhānaṁ samāpajji. Tatiyajjhānā vuṭṭhahitvā catutthajjhānaṁ samāpajji. Catutthajjhānā vuṭṭhahitvā ākāsānañcāyatanaṁ samāpajji. Ākāsānañcāyatana-samāpattiyā vuṭṭhahitvā viññāṇañcāyatanaṁ samāpajji. Viññāṇañcāyatana-samāpattiyā vuṭṭhahitvā ākiñcaññāyatanaṁ samāpajji. Ākiñcaññāyatana-samāpattiyā vuṭṭhahitvā nevasaññā-nāsaññāyatanaṁ samāpajji. Nevasaññā-nāsaññāyatana-samāpattiyā vuṭṭhahitvā saññā-vedayita-nirodhaṁ samāpajji.

Atha kho āyasmā Ānando āyasamantaṁ Anuruddhaṁ etad avoca:

'*Parinibbuto bhante Anuruddha Bhagavā'ti.*

'*Na āvuso Ānanda Bhagavā parinibbuto, saññā-vedayita-nirodhaṁ samāpanno'ti.*

Atha kho Bhagavā saññā-vedayita-nirodha-samāpattiyā vuṭṭhahitvā nevasaññā-nāsaññāyatanaṁ samāpajji. Nevasaññā-nāsaññāyatana-samāpattiyā vuṭṭhahitvā ākiñcaññāyatanaṁ samāpajji. Ākiñcaññāyatana-samāpattiyā vuṭṭhahitvā viññāṇañcāyatanaṁ

THE TEN PERCEPTIONS OF PUTRESCENCE

(1) THE PERCEPTION OF BLOATEDNESS

Q. What is the perception of bloatedness? What is the practising of it? What are its salient characteristic, function and near cause? What are its benefits? How is the sign grasped?

A. "The perception of bloatedness": The state of being swollen throughout like a cast off smelly corpse which distends its bag of skin — this is called "bloatedness".[1] The viewing of bloatedness with right knowledge — this is called "perception". The training and the undisturbed dwelling of the mind in that perception — these are called the practising of it. The sending forth of the mind into the perception of bloatedness is its salient characteristic. The disgust connected with the perception of bloatedness is its function. Reflection on malodour and impurity are its near cause.

"What are its benefits?": Nine are the benefits of the perception of bloatedness, thus: A man is able to gain mindfulness as regards the interior of his body, is able to gain the perception of impermanence and the perception of death. He increases disgust and overcomes sense-desires. He removes the clinging to form and well-being. He fares well and approaches the ambrosial.

"How is the sign grasped?": The new yogin who grasps the sign of the putrescence of bloatedness goes alone, without a companion, established in mindfulness, undeluded, with his faculties drawn in and his mind not going to things outside, reflecting on the path of going and coming. Thus he goes to the place of putrescent corpses. Avoiding contrary winds, he remains there, standing or sitting, with the putrescent sign before him, and not too far from nor too near it. And that yogin makes a rock, an ant-hill, tree, bush or a creeper, near the place where the putrescent thing lies, one with the sign, one with the object, and considers thus: "This rock is impure, this is the impure sign, this is the rock". And so also with the ant-hill and the others.

---

samāpajji. Viññāṇañcāyatana-samāpattiyā vuṭṭhahitvā ākāsānañcāyatanaṁ samāpajji. Ākāsānañcāyatana-samāpattiyā vuṭṭhahitvā catutthajjhānaṁ samāpajji. Catutthajjhānā vuṭṭhahitvā tatiyajjhānaṁ samāpajji. Tatiyajjhānā vuṭṭhahitvā dutiyajjhānaṁ samāpajji. Dutiyajjhānā vuṭṭhahitvā paṭhamajjhānaṁ samāpajji. Paṭhamajjhānā vuṭṭhahitvā dutiyajjhānaṁ samāpajji. Dutiyajjhānā vuṭṭhahitvā tatiyajjhānaṁ samāpajji. Tatiyajjhānā vuṭṭhahitvā catutthajjhānaṁ samāpajji. Catutthajjhānā vuṭṭhahitvā samanantarā Bhagavā parinibbāyi.

(*b*) Vis. Mag. 374: *Paṭhamajjhānato pana paṭṭhāya paṭipātiyā yāva nevasaññā-nāsaññāyatanaṁ, tāva punappunaṁ samāpajjanaṁ jhānānulomaṁ nāma. Nevasaññā-nāsaññāyatanato paṭṭhāya yāva paṭhamajjhānaṁ, tāva punappunaṁ samāpajjanaṁ jhānapaṭilomaṁ nāma. Paṭhamajjhānato paṭṭhāya yāva nevasaññā-nāsaññāyatanaṁ, nevasaññā-nāsaññāyatanato paṭṭhāya yāva paṭhamajjhānan ti evaṁ anulomapaṭilomavasena punappunaṁ samāpajjanaṁ jhānānulomapaṭilomaṁ nāma.*

1. Cp. (*a*) A. III, 323-4; M. I, 58; D. II, 295: *Puna ca paraṁ bhikkhave bhikkhu seyyathā pi passeyya sarīraṁ sivatikāya chaḍḍitaṁ......uddhumātakaṁ......so imam eva kāyaṁ upasaṁharati: 'Ayam pi kho kāyo evaṁ-dhammo evaṁ-bhāvī etaṁ anatīto ti'.*

(*b*) S. V. 131: *Uddhumātakasaññā bhikkhave bhāvitā bahulīkatā mahato phāsuvihārāya saṁvattati.*

[425] After making the sign and making the object, he practises, considering the putrescent sign from its intrinsic nature in ten ways: From colour, sex, region, locality, limitation, joints, cavities, low parts, high parts and all sides. He considers all sides of it. "From colour" means: "He determines black as black, the neither black nor white as neither black nor white. He determines white as white and malodorous skin as malodorous". "From sex" means: "He determines whether it is the body of a male or a female, and whether it is that of a young, an adult or an old person". To determine is to determine the long as long, the short as short, the fat as fat, the small as small. "From region" means: "He determines that in this direction is the head; in this, a hand; in this, a leg; in this, the back; in this, the abdomen; in this, the sitting place; in this, the putrescent sign". Thus he understands. "From locality" means: "He determines that on this place[1] is the hand; on this, a leg; on this, the head; on this, the sitting-place; on this, the putrescent sign". "From limitation" means: "He determines (the limit of the body) from head to foot, from below up to the head and the edge of the scalp, understanding the whole body as an assemblage of dung". "From the joints" means: "He determines that there are six joints in the two hands, six joints in the two legs, and that there is one joint of the neck and one at the waist". These are known as the fourteen great joints. "From the cavities" means: "He determines whether the mouth is open or closed, and whether the eyes are open or closed. He determines the hollows of the hands and the feet". "From low parts and from high parts" means: "He determines whether the putrescent sign is in a low place or in a high place; and again, he determines thus: 'I am in a low place, the putrescent sign is in a high place', or, 'The putrescent sign is in a low place, I am in a high place' ". "He considers from all sides" means: "He determines a distance of two or three fathoms from the sign, because he does not grasp the sign by being too near it or too far from it, and considering all things, he grasps the sign (saying), "*Sādhu! sādhu!*". Thus observing he is contented.

That yogin having grasped the sign, noted it well and determined it well, goes alone, without a companion, established in mindfulness, undeluded, with his faculties drawn in and his mind not going to things outside, reflecting on the path of going and coming. To and fro he walks on the path or he sits absorbed in the putrescent sign.

Why does he go without a companion? It is for the sake of acquiring calmness of body. "Established in mindfulness" means: "Owing to non-delusion the faculties are drawn in and the mind does not go to things outside".

Why does he reflect on the path of going and coming? It is for the sake of acquiring calmness of body. Why does he avoid contrary winds? It is for the sake of avoiding malodour. Why does he sit neither far nor near the sign? If he sits far, he cannot grasp the sign. If he sits near, he cannot

---

1. Lit. Bright place — a double translation of *avakāsa*.

get a dislike for it, or see its nature. If he does not know its nature, he is not able to grasp that sign. Therefore, he sits neither too far from nor too near it. Why does he consider the sign on all sides? It is for the sake of non-delusion. Non-delusion is thus: When a yogin goes to a still place and sees the putrescent sign, fear arises in him; at such a time, if the corpse appears to stand up before him, he does not stand up, but reflects. In this way he knows, recollects, rightly understands, regards well and fully investigates the sign. In the same way he considers all signs. This is (the indication of) non-delusion.

Q. Why does he grasp the sign in ten ways? *A*. It is for the sake of binding the mind.

Why does one reflect on the path of going and coming? It is for the sake of progress in the course. "Progress in the course" means: "Though a yogin enters a still place, his mind is sometimes disturbed. If he does not always investigate it, the putrescent sign does not arise. Therefore, a yogin investigates the sign with all his heart by reflecting on the path of going and coming. He investigates the place of meditation. He investigates all signs. Thus should he investigate the sign to be grasped, in the ten ways.

That yogin thus investigates again and again, and sees the sign as if it were with his eyes. This is (the indication of) progress in the course. A new yogin, meditating on a corpse, perceiving (it as) a jewel, rejoices, bears it in mind, resorts to it always, causes the hindrances to perish and arouses the factors of meditation, *jhāna*. Remote form sense-desires and demeritorious states, he abides in the attainment of the first meditation, *jhāna*, which is with initial and sustained application of thought, born of solitude and full of joy and bliss, through the perception of putrescence.

Q. Why is the first meditation, *jhāna*, only developed through the perception of putrescence and not any other meditation, *jhāna*?

A. This perception always follows initial and sustained application of thought because (they go together) and because it is tied down to a place. When initial and sustained application of thought are present, this sign becomes manifest. Without initial and sustained application of thought, the yogin is not able, here, to gain the calming of the mind. Therefore, the first meditation, *jhāna*, is developed and not any other.

And again, it is said that colour, sex and the others of this putrescent sign are considered in many ways. "Are considered in many ways": These (colour, etc.) are objects of initial and sustained application of thought. Separate from initial and sustained application of thought, these cannot be considered. Therefore, only the first meditation, *jhāna*, is developed and not any other.

And again, it is said that this putrescent sign is an unenduring object. On an unenduring object the mind does not go higher. In an impure place joy and bliss can only arise by the rejection of initial and sustained application of thought, which, in a place such as this, depend on malodour. Therefore, only the first meditation, *jhāna*, is developed and not any other.

Q. On an unenduring object how do joy and bliss occur?

A. The unenduring object is not the cause of joy and bliss. And again, joy and bliss arise owing to the removal of the heat of the hindrances and the training of the mind. The rest is as was fully taught above.

The perception of bloatedness has ended.

(2) THE PERCEPTION OF DISCOLOURATION

Q. What is discolouration? What is the practising of it? What are its salient characteristic, function and near cause? What are its benefits? How is the sign grasped?

A. One, two or three nights after death, the body becomes discoloured, and appears as if it were stained blue. This is the discolouration sign. This discolouration is called the blue sign. The understanding of this through right knowledge is called the perception of discolouration.[1] The undisturbed dwelling of the mind (on the sign) is the practising of it. The reflection on the blue sign is its salient characteristic. (The perception of) disagreeableness is its function. The thought of non-durability is its near cause. Its benefits are equal to those of bloatedness. The way of grasping the sign is as was fully taught above.

(The perception of) discolouration has ended.

(3) THE PERCEPTION OF FESTERING

Q. What is perception of festering? What is the practising of it? What are its salient characteristic, function and near cause? What are its benefits? How is the sign grasped?

A. "Festering": Two or three nights after death, the body festers and matter exudes from it like ghee that is poured out. This is the festering of the body. The understanding of this through right knowledge is called the perception of festering.[2] The undisturbed dwelling of the mind (on the sign) is the practising of it. The reflection on the festering sign is its salient characteristic.

1. Cp. A. III, 323-4; M.I, 58, D. II, 295: *Puna ca paraṁ bhikkhave bhikkhu seyyathā pi passeyya sarīraṁ sivathikāya chaḍḍitaṁ ekāhamataṁ vā dvīhamataṁ vā tīhamataṁ vā...... vinīlakaṁ......so imam eva kāyaṁ upasaṁharati: 'Ayam pi kho kāyo evaṁ-dhammo evaṁ-bhāvī etaṁ anatīto ti'.*

2. Cp. M. III, 91: *Puna ca paraṁ, bhikkhave, bhikkhu seyyathā pi passeyya sarīraṁ sivathikāya chaḍḍitaṁ ekāhamataṁ vā dvīhamataṁ vā tīhamataṁ vā uddhumātakaṁ vinīlakaṁ vipubbakajātaṁ; so imam eva kāyaṁ upasaṁharati: Ayaṁ pi kho kāyo evaṁdhammo evaṁbhāvī evaṁanatīto ti. Tassa evam appamattassa ātāpino pahitattassa viharato ye te gehasitā sarasaṁkappā te pahīyanti, tesam pahānā ajjhattaṁ eva cittaṁ santiṭṭhati sannisīdati ekodihoti samādhiyati. Evam pi, bhikkhave, bhikkhu kāyagataṁ satiṁ bhāveti.*

(The perception of) disagreeableness is its function. The thought of non-durability is its near cause. Its benefits are equal to those of bloatedness. The way of grasping the sign is as was fully taught above.

(The perception of) the festering has ended.

(4) THE PERCEPTION OF THE FISSURED

Q. What is the meaning of the fissured? What is the practising of it? What are its salient characteristic, function and near cause?

A. "The fissured" means: "What resembles the scattered parts of a body that has been hacked with a sword". Again, a corpse that is thrown away is also called the fissured. The understanding of this through right knowledge is called the perception of the fissured.[1] The undisturbed dwelling of the mind, (on the sign), is the practising of it. The reflection on the sign of the fissured is its salient characteristic. (The perception of) disagreeableness is its function. The thought of putrescence is its near cause. Its merits are equal to those of bloatedness.

Q. "How is the sign grasped?"

A. The sight of two ears or two fingers that are separated (from a body) causes the arising of the fissured sign. The sign thus grasped appears with one or two inches[2] of space intervening. The rest is as was fully taught above.

(The perception of) the fissured has ended.

(5) THE PERCEPTION OF THE GNAWED

Q. What is the meaning of the gnawed? What is the practising of it? What are its salient characteristic, function and near cause? What are its benefits? How is the sign grasped?

A. "The gnawed": (leavings of a) corpse on which crows, magpies, brown kites, owls, eagles, vultures, wild pigs, dogs, jackals, wolves, tigers or leopards have fared — this is called the gnawed.[3] The understanding of the gnawed sign through right knowledge — this is (the perception of) the gnawed. The undisturbed dwelling of the mind (on the sign) — this is called the practising of it. The reflection on the gnawed is its salient characteristic. (The perception of) disagreeableness is its function. The consideration of putrescence is

1. Cp. S. V, 131: *Vicchiddakasaññā bhikkhave bhāvitā bahulīkatā mahato phāsuvihārāya saṁvattati.*
2. This refers to the Chinese Sun = 1.193 inches.
3. Cp. A. III, 324; M.I, 58; D.II, 295: *Puna ca paraṁ....kākehi vā khajjamānaṁ kulalehi vā khajjamānaṁ gijjhehi vā khajjamānaṁ supāṇehi vā khajjamānaṁ sigālehi vā khajjamānaṁ vividhehi vā pāṇaka-jātehi khajjamānaṁ, so imam eva kāyaṁ upasaṁharati: 'Ayam pi kho kāyo evaṁ-dhammo evaṁ-bhāvī etaṁ anatīto ti'.*

its near cause. Its merits are equal to those of bloatedness. The rest is as was fully taught above.

(The perception of) the gnawed has ended.

(6) THE PERCEPTION OF THE DISMEMBERED

Q. What is the meaning of the dismembered? What is the practising of it? What are its salient characteristic, function and near cause? What are its benefits? [426] How is the sign grasped?

A. The state of (severed) limbs scattered hither and thither is called "the dismembered".[1] The understanding of this through right knowledge — this is called the perception of the dismembered. The undisturbed dwelling of the mind (on the sign) is called the practising of it. The reflection on the dismembered sign is its salient characteristic. (The perception of) disagreeableness is its function. The thought of putrescence is its near cause. Its benefits are equal to those of bloatedness.

"How is the sign grasped?": All the (scattered) limbs are gathered and placed together so that they are about two inches apart from each other. Having arranged them thus, one grasps the sign of the dismembered. This is how the sign is grasped. The rest is as was fully taught above.

(The perception of) the dismembered has ended.

(7) THE PERCEPTION OF THE CUT AND THE DISMEMBERED

Q. What is the meaning of the cut and the dismembered? What is the practising of it? What are its salient characteristic, function and near cause? What are its benefits? How is the sign grasped?

A. "The cut and the dismembered": Corpses, lying in various places, of those done to death with stick, sword or arrow — these are called, the cut and the dismembered.[2] To know the cut and the dismembered through right knowledge is called the perception of the cut and the dismembered. The undisturbed dwelling of the mind (on the sign) is the practising of it. The reflection on the sign of the cut and the dismembered is its salient characteristic. (The perception of) disagreeableness is its function. The thought of putrescence is its near cause. Its benefits are equal to those of bloatedness.

---

1 Cp. A.III, 324; M. I, 58; D. II, 296-7: *Puna ca paraṁ. . . .aṭṭhikāni apagata-sambandhāni disā-vidisāsu vikkhittāni aññena hatthaṭṭhikaṁ aññena pādaṭṭhikaṁ aññena jaṅghaṭṭhikaṁ aññena ūraṭṭhikaṁ aññena kaṭaṭṭhikaṁ aññena piṭṭhi-kaṇṭakaṁ aññena sīsa-kaṭāhaṁ, so imam eva kāyaṁ upasaṁharati: 'Ayam pi kho kāyo evaṁ-dhammo evaṁ-bhāvī etaṁ anatīto ti'.*

2. Cp. Vis. Mag. 179: *Hatañ ca taṁ purimanayen' eva vikkhittakañ cā ti hatavikkhittakaṁ. Kākapādākārena angapaccangesu satthena hanitvā vuttanayena vikkhittassa chavasarīrass' etam adhivacanaṁ.*

"How is the sign grasped"?: This is as was fully taught above.

(The perception of the) cut and the dismembered has ended.

(8) THE PERCEPTION OF THE BLOOD-STAINED

Q. What is the meaning of the blood-stained? What is practising of it? What are its salient characteristic, function and near cause? What are its benefits? How is the sign grasped?

A. The blood-besmeared state of the body and the severed limbs is known as "the blood-stained".[1] The undisturbed dwelling of the mind (on the sign) is called the practising of it. The reflection on the blood-stained sign is its salient characteristic. (The perception of) disagreeableness is its function. The thought of putrescence is its near cause. Its benefits are equal to those of bloatedness.

"How is the sign grasped?": This was fully taught above.

(The percepion of) the blood-stained has ended.

(9) THE PERCEPTION OF WORMINESS

Q. What is worminess? What is the practising of it? What are its salient characteristic, function and near cause? What are its benefits? How is the sign grasped?

A. "Worminess": The state of a body covered with worms as with a heap of white pearls is called worminess. The understanding of this through right knowledge is called the perception of worminess.[2] The undisturbed dwelling of the mind (on the sign) is the practising of it. The reflection on the sign of worminess is its salient characteristic. (The perception of) disagreeableness is its function. The thought of putrescence is its near cause. Its benefits are equal to those of bloatedness. "How is the sign grasped?": This is as was fully taught above.

(The perception of) worminess has ended.

(10) THE PERCEPTION OF THE BONY

Q. What is the bony? What is the practising of it? What are its salient characteristic, function and near cause? What are its benefits? How is the sign grasped?

1. Cp. A. III, 324; M. I, 58; D. II, 296: *Puna ca paraṁ bhikkhave bhikkhu seyyathā pi passeyya sarīraṁ sīvathikāya chaḍḍitaṁ aṭṭhi-saṁkhalikaṁ sa-maṁsa-lohitaṁ nahāru-sambandhaṁ....pe...., so imam eva kāyaṁ upasaṁharati: 'Ayam pi kho kāyo evaṁ-dhammo evaṁ-bhāvī etaṁ anatīto ti'.*
2. A. II, 17; A. V, 106, 310: *Puḷuvakasaññā.* Also S. V, 131: *Puḷavakasaññā bhikkhave bhāvitā bahulīkatā mahato phāsuvihārāya saṁvattati.*

A. "What is the bony"? The state of bones linked chain-like by means of flesh, blood and sinews or by sinews without flesh and blood, or without flesh and blood is called "the bony".[1] The understanding of this through right knowledge is called the perception of the bony. The undisturbed dwelling of the mind (on the sign) is called the practising of it. The reflection on the sign of the bony is its salient characteristic. (The perception of) disagreeableness is its function. The thought of putrescence is its near cause. Its benefits are equal to those of bloatedness.

"How is the sign grasped"? This is as was fully taught above.

(The perception of) the bony has ended.

MISCELLANEOUS TEACHINGS

Q. What are the miscellaneous teachings regarding putrescence?

A. The beginner, being one who is affected by severe passion, should not grasp the sign in that which is not of the same kind. That which is "not of the same kind" means: "Like the body of a man to a woman".

If one is of a calling associated with the perception of putrescence, he should not grasp the putrescent sign, because he, owing to the close connection with these objects, does not develop the idea of their disagreeableness. One does not cause the arising of pure perception on the bodies of beasts (?). One causes the arising of the sign in one bone and grasps the sign in the bone with facility.

And again, if a man grasps the sign of putrescence through colour, he should meditate on the *kasiṇa*. If a man grasps the sign of putrescence through space, he should meditate on that element. If a man grasps the sign of putrescence through putrescence, he should meditate on putrescence.

Q. Why are there ten putrescences and neither more nor less?

A. Because the faults of the body are of ten kinds and because there are ten kinds of perception owing to ten kinds of persons. A passionate person should meditate on the perception of bloatedness. A sensual person should meditate on discolouration. A passionate lover of the beautiful should always meditate on the festering. The others should be understood in the same way.

And again, the sign of putrescence is grasped with difficulty. All signs of putrescence are means of overcoming passion. Therefore, whenever the walker in passion sees the putrescent sign, he should grasp it. Because of these reasons, it is said that among the putrescences there are ten kinds of putrescence perception.

---

1. Cp. A. III, 324; M. I, 58; D. II, 296: *Aṭṭhi-saṁkhalikaṁ apagata-maṁsa-lohitaṁ nahāru-sambandhaṁ....pe....,so imaṁ eva kāyaṁ upasaṁharati: 'Ayam pi kho kāyo evaṁ-dhammo evaṁ-bhāvī etaṁ anatīto ti'.*

Q. Why are these (putrescence signs) not increased?

A. When a man wishes to separate from passion, he causes the arising of the perception regarding the nature of his body. Because, if he has the perception of the nature of his body, he can quickly acquire the perception of its disagreeableness and cause the arising of the after-image. If the perception of putrescence is increased, the sign which he has grasped in his body will disappear. If he loses the perception of his own body, he will not be able to acquire the thought of disagreeableness quickly. Therefore, he should not increase.

And again, it is taught that if a man is without passion, he may increase it for the sake of developing the great thought. This is in accordance with the teaching of the *Abhidhamma:* "One dwells without passion and the rest, practises the first meditation, *jhāna*, rightly, dwells on the perception of bloatedness and causes the arising of the boundless object".[1] The great Elder Siṅgālapitā uttered this stanza:

The heir of the Buddha, he,
the almsman, in the fearful wood,
has with "bony-precept" filled
this earth, entirely.
I think this almsman will,
in no long time, abandon lust.[2]

THE RECOLLECTION OF THE BUDDHA

Q. What is the recollection of the Buddha? What is the practising of it? What are its salient characteristic, function and near cause? What are its benefits? What is the procedure?

A. The Enlightened One is the Blessed One who by his own efforts, without a teacher, understands the Noble Truths which were never heard before. He knows all. He possesses power.[3] He is free. Because of these qualities, he is called the Enlightened One. The yogin remembers the Enlightened One, the Blessed One, the Supremely Enlightened One and the worth of the Enlightenment. He recollects, repeatedly recollects, recollects again and again, does not forget to recollect on these. He remembers (the Enlightened One's) faculties and powers. He practises right recollectedness. Thus is the recollection of the Buddha. The undisturbed dwelling of the mind (in the recollection of the Buddha) — this is called the practising of it. The

1. Not traced.
2. Th. 18: *Ahū buddhassa dāyādo bhikkhu Bhesakaḷāvane,*
kevalaṁ aṭṭhisaññāya aphari paṭhaviṁ imaṁ.
Maññe 'haṁ kāmarāgaṁ so khippam eva pahīyatīti.
—Siṅgālapitā Thera.
3. Nidd. I, 457: *Buddho ti yo so Bhagavā sayambhū anācariyako pubbe ananussutesu dhammesu sāmaṁ saccāni abhisambujjhi, tattha ca sabbaññutaṁ patto, balesu ca vasībhāvaṁ patto.* Also Pts. I, 174 where '*pubbe*' is substituted by '*Buddhe*'.

remembering of the Buddha's worth is its function. The growth in confidence is its near cause.

He who practises the recollection of the Buddha acquires the following eighteen benefits: increase of confidence, mindfulness, wisdom, reverence, merit, great joy, ability to endure hardship, fearlessness, shamefastness in the presence of evil, the state of living near the Teacher, enjoyment of activity belonging to the ground of the Buddhas, (the happiness of) faring well and approaching the ambrosial.[1]

According to the *Netti Sutta*,[2] if a man wishes to meditate on the Buddha, he should worship Buddha images and such other objects. "What is the procedure?": The new yogin goes to a place of solitude and keeps his mind undisturbed. With this undisturbed mind, he remembers him who comes and goes in the same way, the Blessed One, consummate, supremely enlightened, endowed with true knowledge and conduct, sublime, knower of the world, matchless guide of men to be tamed, teacher of divine and human beings, enlightened, blessed.[3] Thus he reaches the further shore of merit.

"Blessed One": Because he gets the praise of the world, he is called the Blessed One. Because he has attained to excellent truth, he is called the Blessed One. Because he is worthy of offerings, he is called the Blessed One. Because he has acquired the highest merits, he is called the Blessed One and because he is the Lord of the Way-Truth, he is called the Blessed One. For these reasons is he called the Blessed One.

"Consummate": Because he is the recipient of gifts, he is consummate. Because he has killed the defilement-foes, he is consummate. Because he breaks the spokes of the wheel of birth and death, he is consummate.[4]

"Supremely enlightened": Because he knows rightly all things, in all his activities, he is called the supremely enlightened. Because he has killed ignorance, he is called the supremely englightened and because he has attained to the enlightenment that is unrivalled, by himself, he is called the supremely enlightened.[5]

"Endowed with true knowledge and conduct": Knowledge means the three kinds of knowledge, i.e., the knowledge of past existences, the knowledge of the passing away and the arising of beings and the knowledge of the extinction of the cankers. The Blessed One has removed the ignorance of the past with the knowledge of past existences, the ignorance of the future with the know-

1. Only thirteen benefits are mentioned.
2. Lit. Netri Sutara.
3. Cp. D. III, 76; A. I, 168; Sn. 132 (*Selasutta*): *Iti pi so Bhagavā arahaṁ Sammāsambuddho vijjācaraṇasampanno sugato lokavidū anuttaro purisadammasārathi satthā devamanussānaṁ buddho Bhagavā.*
4. Cp. Vis. Mag. 198; Sn.-a. 441: *Ārakā hi so sabbakilesehi maggena savāsanānaṁ kilesānaṁ viddhaṁsitattā ti ārakattā arahaṁ; te ca nena kilesārayo maggena hatā ti arīnaṁ hatattā pi arahaṁ.*
5. Cp. Vis. Mag. 201-2.

ledge of the passing away and the arising of beings, and the ignorance of the present with the knowledge of the extinction of the cankers.[1] Having removed the ignorance of the past, the Blessed One sees, when he recollects, all past states in the course of all activities. Having removed the ignorance of the future, the Blessed One sees, when he recollects, all future states in the course of his activities. Having removed all present ignorance, the Blessed One sees, when he recollects, all present states in the course of his activities.

"Conduct" means: "The being endowed with virtue and concentration".

"Virtue" means: "Endowed with all good states". He is called "perfect in knowledge and conduct".

"Perfect" means: "Endowed with supernormal powers". Hence he is called "perfect in knowledge and conduct". (Again) "endowed" means: "possessed of all concentration".

Thus the Blessed One has great compassion and appreciative joy because of omniscience, the three kinds of knowledge and conduct. He acquired knowledge with facility, because he had benefitted the world [427]. He opened the path of science, because he knew all spheres. He is perfect in knowledge because none can surpass him, because he has destroyed all defilements and because of pure right action. He is perfect in conduct, because he has become the eye of the world and because he has blessed those who were unblessed. He is perfectly enlightened through knowledge, because he has become the mainstay of the world and because he has rescued the fear-stricken. He saves through conduct, because he has acquired the supernormal power of the highest truth. He, without a teacher, has acquired that excellent equipose of behaviour towards all things, because he has promoted the weal of the world. Thus, through being perfect in knowledge and conduct, he is called the Blessed One. Thus is "perfect in knowledge and conduct" to be understood.[2]

---

1. M. I, 22-4: *So evaṁ samāhite citte parisuddhe pariyodāte anaṅgaṇe vigatūpakkilese mudubhūte kammaniye ṭhite ānejjappatte pubbenivāsānussatiñāṇāya cittaṁ abhininnāmesiṁ. So anekavihitaṁ pubbenivāsaṁ anussarāmi, seyyathīdaṁ: ekampi jātiṁ dve pi jātiyo...... So evaṁ samāhite citte....ānejjappatte sattānaṁ cutūpapātañāṇāya cittaṁ abhininnāmesiṁ. So dibbena cakkhunā visuddhena atikkantamānusakena satte passāmi cavamāne upapajjamāne ....So evaṁ samāhite citte....ānejjappatte āsavānaṁ khayañāṇāya cittaṁ abhininnāmesiṁ. So idaṁ dukkhanti yathābhūtaṁ abbhaññāsiṁ....*
2. Cp. (a) D. I, 100: *'Katamaṁ pana taṁ bho Gotama caraṇaṁ, katamā sā vijjā ti?' 'Idha Ambaṭṭha Tathāgato loke uppajjati arahaṁ sammāsambuddho....pe....evaṁ kho Ambaṭṭha bhikkhu sīlasampanno hoti.'*

   '....paṭhamajjhānaṁ upasampajja viharati. Idam pi 'ssa hoti caraṇasmiṁ' ....pe ....catutthajjānaṁ upasampajja viharati. Idam pi 'ssa hoti caraṇasmiṁ. Idaṁ kho taṁ Ambaṭṭha caraṇaṁ.

   '....pe....ñāṇa-dassanāya cittaṁ abhinīharati abhininnāmeti....pe....Idam pi 'ssa hoti vijjāya....pe....nāparaṁ itthattāyāti pajānāti. Idam pi 'ssa hoti vijjāya. Ayaṁ kho sā Ambaṭṭha vijjā.

   'Ayaṁ vuccati Ambaṭṭha bhikkhu vijjā-sampanno iti pi caraṇa-sampanno iti pi vijjā-caraṇa-sampanno iti pi. Imāya ca Ambaṭṭha vijjā-caraṇa-sampadāya aññā vijjā-sampadā caraṇa-sampadā uttaritarā vā paṇītatarā vā n'atthi.

   (b) Sn.-a. II, 441: *Sammā sāmañ ca saccānaṁ buddhattā sammāsambuddho.*

"Sublime": Because he has reached the good road, he is named "sublime". Because he will not return again, and because he has attained to the extinction, *Nibbāna*, that is without residue of the substratum of being,[1] he is named "sublime". Again, because his teaching cannot be overturned he is called "sublime". And again, because his teachings are not untrue, he is called "sublime". And again, because his teachings are without disadvantages, he is called "sublime". And again, because his teachings are neither too many nor too few, he is called "sublime".

"Knower of the world": World is of two kinds, i.e., the world of beings and the world of formations.[2] The Blessed One knows the world of being in the course of all his actions. Through the varying desires of beings, through the difference of faculties, through past lives, through the knowledge of the divine eye, through the knowledge of the passing away and arising of beings, through combination, through fulfilment, through various modes of differentiation, through various states of durability and non-durability, through various births, through various states of birth, through various planes, through various actions, through various defilements, through various results, through various kinds of good and evil and through various kinds of binding and unbinding, the Blessed One knows the world of beings.

And again it is said "the world of formations": The Blessed One knows all action and he knows the many formations. Through concentration perception, through causes and conditions, through moral, immoral and the amoral, through various aggregations, through various worlds, through various spheres, through perfect understanding, through impermanence, sorrow and not-self and through the born and the unborn, the Blessed One knows the world of formations. Thus is "knower of the world" to be understood.

"Matchless": Because he is unsurpassable, in the world, he is called "matchless". And again, because he is without an equal, because he is most excellent, because he is incomparable and because others cannot excel him, he is named "matchless".[3]

"Guide of men to be tamed": There are three kinds of persons: a man hears the Law and quickly is able to expound it; another man elucidates the principles of causes and conditions; and yet another makes clear the knowledge of past existences. But the Blessed One, having mastered the eightfold way of

---

1. Cp. It. 38: *Anupādisesa nibbānadhātu.*
2. *Satta-loka, saṁkhāra-loka.*—Cp. Sn.-a. II, 442: *Sabbathā pi viditalokattā lokavidū, so hi sabhāvato samudayato nirodhato nirodhūpāyato ti sabbathā khandhāyatanādibhedaṁ saṁkhāralokaṁ avedi, 'eko loko sabbe sattā āhāraṭṭhitikā, dve lokā nāmañ ca rupañ ca, tayo lokā tisso vedanā, cattāro lokā cattāro āhārā, pañca lokā pañc' upādānakkhandhā, cha lokā cha ajjhattikāni āyatanāni, satta lokā satta viññāṇaṭṭhitiyo, aṭṭha lokā aṭṭha lokadhammā, nava lokā nava sattāvāsā, dasa lokā dasa āyatanāni, dvādasa lokā dvādasāyatanāni, aṭṭhārasa lokā aṭṭhārasa dhātuyo' ti evam pi sabbathā saṁkhāralokaṁ avedi; sattānaṁ āsayaṁ jānāti anusayaṁ jānāti caritaṁ jānāti adhimuttiṁ jānāti, apparajakkhe mahārajakkhe tikkhindriye svākāre dvākāre suviññāpaye duviññāpaye bhabbe abhabbe satte jānātī ti sabbathā sattalokaṁ avedi.*
3. Cp. Sn.-a. II, 443: *Attano pana guṇehi visiṭṭhatarassa kassaci abhāvā anuttaro.*

emancipation, has tamed beings. Therefore, he is named "guide of men to be tamed".[1]

"Teacher of divine and human beings": The Blessed One has rescued divine and human beings from the fearful forest of birth, decay and death. Therefore, he is called "teacher of divine and human beings". And again, he has taught the way of insight and the way of meditation, *jhāna*. Therefore, he is called "teacher of divine and human beings". Thus, in these ways should a man recall (the qualities) of him who comes and goes in the same way.

Further, there is the teaching of the principal teacher: In four ways should the Blessed One be remembered. He came to the world for the last time by his own efforts in the past. He was endowed with excellent virtue. He benefitted the world. During twenty incalculable[2] aeons from his first aspiration to his last birth, he had seen the faculties and the bases of faculties of countless[3] number of commoners. Therefore, he pities the world thus: "I have attained to liberation; now, I should liberate these. I have tamed myself; now, I should tame these. I have gained knowledge; now, I should cause knowledge to arise in these. I have reached *Nibbāna*; now, I should cause these also to reach it".[4]

He has reached completion and contentment in the fulfilling of charity, virtue, renunciation, fortitude, truth, resolution, loving-kindness, equanimity, energy and wisdom. He revealed the birth stories of the time when he was a Bodhisatta, in order to encourage others to gain the light. He was born as a hare and practised charity.[5] One should recollect on virtue through the Saṁkhapāla birth-story;[6] on renunciation, through the Mahā-Govinda birth-story;[7] on fortitude, through the Khanti birth-story;[8] on truth, through the Mahā Sutasoma birth-story;[9] on resolution, through the Dumb-Cripple's birth-story;[10] on loving-kindness, through the Sakka birth-story;[11] on equanimity, through the Lomahaṁsa birth-story;[12] on energy, through the Chief of Merchants' birth-story;[13] (on wisdom), through the Deer birth-story.[14] One should also recollect on the word of the father in the Dīghiti-Kosala birth-story[15] and one should recollect on the reverence of the White Six-tusked Elephant-sage.[16]

---

1. Cp. Sn.-a. II, 443: *Vicitrehi vinayanūpāyehi purisadamme sāreti ti purisadammasārathi.*
2. *Asankheyya.*
3. *Lit.* 10,000,000,000,000.
4. Cp. (*a*) It. 123: *Danto damayataṁ seṭṭho*
santo samayataṁ isi,
mutto mocayataṁ aggo
tiṇṇo tārayataṁ varo.
(*b*) D. III, 54-5: *Buddho so Bhagavā bodhāya dhammaṁ deseti, danto so Bhagavā damathāya dhammaṁ deseti, santo so Bhagavā samathāya dhammaṁ deseti, tiṇṇo so Bhagavā taraṇāya dhammaṁ deseti, parinibbuto so Bhagavā parinibbānāya dhammaṁ desetiti.*
5. J. No. 316, C. Piṭ. 82-3.
6. J. No. 524, C. Piṭ. 91.
7. D. II, 230-251, C. Piṭ. 76.
8. J. No. 313.
9. J. No. 537, C. Piṭ. 101-1.
10. Temiya J. No. 538, C. Piṭ. 96.
11. J. No. 31.
12. Nidāna-kathā, p. 10, C. Pit. p. 102.
13. Kuhaka J. No. 89, Seri Vānija J. No. 3.
14. J. No. 206 (?)
15. J. No. 371.
16. J. No. 514.

Through the White-Horse birth-story[1] one should recollect the visit of the Bodhisatta to help all beings. One should recollect that the Bodhisatta forsook his own life and saved another's life in the Deer birth-story.[2] One should recollect that the Bodhisatta, in the (Great) Monkey birth-story,[3] saved a being from great suffering; and further one should remember that seeing a man who had fallen into a pit, he rescued him with heart of compassion and offered him roots, and fruits of trees and when that man, wishing to eat flesh, hurt the Bodhisatta's head, he taught that man the truth and pointed out the right road to him, in the Great Monkey birth-story.[4] Thus, one should concentrate on the merits of the birth-stories of the Blessed One in many ways.

How should one recollect on the merits of the sacrifices of the Blessed One? The Blessed One fulfilled all things in his previous births. When he was young he removed the longing for all abodes. He removed the longing for child, wife, parents and friends. He forsook that which was hard to forsake. He lived alone in empty places. He aspired after *Nibbāna*. He crossed the Nerañjarā in Magadha. He sat under the Bodhi tree, conquered the king of death and the demon armies. In the first watch of the night, he remembered his past lives; in the middle watch of the night, he gained the divine eye; and in the last watch of the night, he understood sorrow and its cause and saw the excellent.[5] Through the practice of the Noble Eightfold Path, he was able to destroy the cankers and attain to Enlighenment. He removed his body from the world and entered the highest and purest place of the extinction of the cankers. Thus one should recollect the sacrifices of the Blessed One in many ways.

How should one recollect the virtues with which the Blessed One was endowed? The Blessed One acquired emancipation and the state of mind that is together with it, thus: through being endowed with the ten powers of him who comes and goes in the same way, the fourteen kinds of Buddha-knowledge[6] and the eighteen Buddha-virtues;[7] through fulfilment of many meditations, *jhānas*, and through reaching the further shore of freedom. Thus should the yogin recollect.

---

1. J. No. 196.
2. J. No. 12.
3. J. No. 407.
4. J. No. 516.
5. M. I, 248-9: *Iti sākāraṁ sauddesaṁ anekavihitaṁ pubbenivāsaṁ anussarāmi. Ayaṁ kho me Aggivessana rattiyā paṭhame yāme paṭhamā vijjā adhigatā, avijja vihatā vijjā uppannā, tamo vihato āloko uppanno......*
   Iti dibbena cakkhunā visuddhena atikkantamānusakena satte passāmi cavamāne upapajjamāne hīne paṇīte suvaṇṇe dubbaṇṇe sugate duggate yathākammūpage satte pajānāmi. Ayaṁ kho me Aggivessana rattiyā majjhime yāme dutiyā vijjā adhigatā, avijjā vihatā vijjā uppannā, tamo vihato āloko upanno......
   So idaṁ dukkhanti yathābhūtaṁ abbhaññāsiṁ, ayaṁ dukkhasamudayoti yathābhūtaṁ abbhaññāsiṁ, ayaṁ dukkhanirodhoti yathābhūtaṁ abbhaññāsiṁ, ayaṁ dukkhanirodhagāminī paṭipadāti yathābhūtaṁ abbhaññāsiṁ.......; khīṇā jāti......nāparaṁ itthattāyāti abbhaññāsiṁ. Ayaṁ kho me Aggivessana rattiyā pacchime yāme tatiyā vijjā adhigatā, avijjā vihatā vijjā uppannā, tamo vihato āloko uppanno, yathā taṁ appamattassa ātāpino pahitattassa viharato.
6. Lit. *Buddhapaññā*.
7. Lit. *Buddhadhammā*.

What are the ten powers of the Blessed One? He knows the proper from the improper, according to reality; knows the causes and consequences of good actions of the past, future and present, according to reality; knows the various intentions of beings, according to reality; knows the various kinds of behaviour, according to reality; knows the causes and consequences leading to the world of deities, humans and others, according to reality; knows the differences in the faculties of beings, according to reality; knows the pure and that which is with defilement in meditation (*jhāna*), emancipation, concentration and attainment, according to reality; knows his past existences, according to reality; knows the passing away and the arising of beings, according to reality; knows the extinction of the cankers, according to reality.[1] The Blessed One is endowed with these ten powers.

What are the fourteen kinds of Buddha-knowledge? They are, namely, knowledge of sorrow, knowledge of sorrow's cause, knowledge of sorrow's cessation, knowledge of the way, knowledge of the analysis of meaning, knowledge of the analysis of the law, knowledge of the analysis of derivation, knowledge of the analysis of argument, knowledge of the causes and consequences leading to the world of deities, humans and others, knowledge of the differences in the faculties of beings, knowledge of the twin miracle, knowledge of the great thought of compassion, omniscience, and knowledge that is without the hindrances. These are the fourteen kinds of Buddha-knowledge. Thus is the Blessed One endowed with these fourteen kinds of knowledge.[2]

What are the eighteen virtues fulfilled by the Blessed One?[3] Unobstructed Buddha-knowledge of the past; unobstructed Buddha-knowledge of the future; unobstructed Buddha-knowledge of the present; all bodily actions are led by knowledge and appear in accord with it; all verbal actions are led by knowledge and appear in accord with it; all mental actions are led by knowledge and appear in accord with it — these six virtues has the Blessed One fulfilled. Non-impairment of the will; non-impairment of energy; non-impairment of mindfulness; non-impairment of concentration; non-impairment of wisdom; non-impairment of freedom — these twelve virtues has the Blessed One fulfilled. Absence of uncertainty; absence of deception; absence of that which is not clear; absence of hurry; absence of state that is not known; absence of equanimity that is removed from reflection.

---

1. Cp. Pts. II, 175-6; S. V, 304-6: *Ṭhānāṭhāna-, kammavipāka-, nānādhimutti-, nānādhātu-, sabbatthagāmini-paṭipadā-, indriyaparopariyatti-, jhānavimokkhasamādhi-samāpattisaṁkilesavodānavuṭṭhāna-, pubbenivāsānussati-, cutūpapāta-, āsavakkhaya- ñāṇa.*
2. Cp. Pts. I, 3, 133: *Dukkhe-, dukkha-samudaye-, dukkha-nirodhe-, dukkhanirodhagāminiyā paṭipadāya-, atthapaṭisambhide-, dhammapaṭisambhide-, niruttipaṭisambhide-, paṭibhānapaṭisambhide-, indriyaparopariyatte-, sattānaṁ āsayānusaye-, yamakapāṭihīre-, mahākaruṇāsamāpattiyā-, sabbaññuta-, anāvaraṇa- ñāṇaṁ.*
3. (*a*) Lal. V. 183, 343: *Atītaṁse, anāgaṁse, paccuppannaṁse, buddhassa bhagavato appaṭihataṁ ñāṇaṁ. Sabbaṁ kāya kammaṁ, sabbaṁ vacī kammaṁ, sabbaṁ mano kammaṁ ñāṇapubbaṅgamaṁ ñāṇānuparivattaṁ. Natthi chandassa hāni, natthi dhammadesanāya hāni, natthi viriyassa hāni, natthi samādhissa hāni, natthi paññāya hāni, natthi vimuttiyā hāni, natthi davā, natthi ravā, natthi apphuṭaṁ, natthi vegayittataṁ, natthi abyāvaṭamano, natthi appatisankhānupekkhā* — (*Aṭṭhārasa- asādhāraṇa-āveṇika Buddhaguṇā*). See Mil. 105, 285.

"Absence of uncertainty" means: "His bearing is dignified; there is nothing unseemly in his action".

"Absence of deception" means: "He has no craftiness".

"Absence of that which is not clear" means: "That there is nothing that his knowledge cannot sense".

"Absence of hurry" means: "His behaviour is free from hurry".

"Absence of state that is not known" means: "He is completely aware of his mental processes".

"Absence of equanimity that is removed from reflection" means: "There is no state of equanimity in him of which he is not aware".

These eighteen virtues has the Blessed One fulfilled.[1]

And again, the Blessed One has reached the other shore with facility having fulfilled all good through the skilfulness belonging to him who comes and goes in the same way,[2] through the four foundations of mindfulness, through the four right efforts, through the four bases of supernormal power, through the five faculties, the five powers, the six kinds of supernormal knowledge, the seven factors of enlightenment, through the Noble Eightfold Path, through the eight positions of mastery, through the eight kinds of emancipation, through the nine gradually ascending states, through the ten Ariyan abodes and through the way of analytical science. Thus one should recall to mind that Blessed One who has acquired the merits of the Excellent Law through these ways.

How should one remember the benefits with which the Blessed One has blessed the world? The Blessed One has fulfilled all merits and has reached the further shore. No other being could have turned the Wheel, of the Law which the Blessed One set a-rolling out of compassion for all beings. Without making an esoteric and an exoteric division of doctrine, he has opened wide the gate of the immortal.[3] He has caused an incalculable number of deities and humans to acquire the fruit of holiness. He has caused an incalculable

---

(*b*) Sv. III, 994: *Aṭṭhārasa Buddhadhammā nāma: N'atthi Tathāgatassa kāya-duccaritaṁ, n'atthi vacī-duccaritaṁ, n'atthi mano-duccaritaṁ: atīte Buddhassa appaṭihataṁ ñāṇaṁ, anāgate......, paccuppanne Buddhassa appaṭihataṁ ñāṇaṁ: sabbaṁ kāya-kammaṁ Buddhassa Bhagavato ñāṇānuparivatti, sabbaṁ vacī-kammaṁ......, sabbaṁ mano-kammaṁ Buddhassa Bhagavato ñāṇānuparivatti: n'atthi chandassa hāni, n'atthi viriyassa hāni, n'atthi satiyā hāni: n'atthi davā, n'atthi ravā, n'atthi balitaṁ, n'atthi sahasā, n'atthi avyāvaṭo mano, n'atthi akusala-cittan ti.*

(*c*) M. Vyut: *Atīte 'dhvany asaṅgaṁ apratihataṁ jñānadharśanaṁ pravartate. Anāgate-. Pratyutpanne-. Sarvakāyakarmajñānapūrvaṁgamaṁ jñānānuparivarti. Sarvavākkarma-. Sarvamanaskarma-. Nāsti chandasya hāniḥ: nāsti viriyasya hāniḥ; nāsti smṛter hāniḥ; nāsti samādher hāniḥ; nāsti prajñāya hāniḥ; nāsti vimukter hāniḥ; nāsti skalitaṁ; nāsti nānātva saṁjñā; nāsty-asamāhitacittaṁ; nāsti ravitaṁ; nāsti muṣitasmṛtita; nāsty-apratisamkhiyā-yopekṣā.*

1. The last six are not exactly according to the Pali or the Sanskrit. Here the text is not quite clear.
2. M. I, 71: *Cattārimāni Sāriputta Tathāgatassa vesārajjāni.* Cp. Vis. Mag. 524.
3. D. II, 39: *Apārutā tesaṁ amatassa dvārā.*

number of beings to acquire merit with the three miracles, namely, the miracle of supernormal power, the miracle of mind reading and the miracle of instruction.[1] He has aroused confidence in the hearts of men. He has overthrown all soothsaying and all false views. He has obliterated the bad road and opened the good road and made men to acquire the fruit of liberation or birth in the heaven world. He has caused his hearers to obtain peace and dwell in the law of the hearer.[2] He has set down many precepts, preached the *Pātimokkha*, established beings in excellent merit, given them the perfect teaching of the Enlightened One and filled the world full (with the Truth). All beings worship and honour him, and all deities and humans hear him.

Thus the Blessed One, who dwells unperturbed, has compassionated and benefitted the world, has done what should be done.

That yogin recollects him who comes and goes in the same way, thus: Through these ways and these virtues, he arouses confidence in his mind. Being full of confidence and being easy in the recollection, his mind is always undisturbed. Because of his mind being undisturbed, he attains to access-meditation.

Q. How is it that one who meditates on the Buddha attains to access and not to fixed meditation, *jhāna*?

A. In the highest sense, the virtue of the Buddha is a subject of profound wisdom. In this sense the yogin cannot attain to fixed meditation, *jhāna*, owing to abstruseness. And again, he has to recollect not merely one virtue. When he thinks on many virtues he cannot attain to fixed meditation, *jhāna*. This is a subject of meditation of all access-concentration.

Q. Access is attained through concentration on a single object. If he thinks on many virtues, his mind is not concentrated. How then does he gain access?

A. If he recollects the virtues of him who comes and goes in the same way and of the Enlightened One, the yogin's mind becomes concentrated. Therefore, he is untroubled.

Again it is taught that from the recollection of the Buddha, the four meditations, *jhānas*, arise.[3]

The recollection of the Buddha has ended.

---

1. D. I, 212 ff.; III, 220: *Tīṇi pāṭihāriyāni. Iddhi-pāṭihāriyaṁ, ādesanā-pāṭihāriyaṁ, anusāsani-pāṭihāriyaṁ. Ime kho āvuso tena Bhagavatā jānatā passatā....tayo dhammā sammad-akkhātā. Tattha sabbeh 'eva saṁgāyitabbaṁ na vivaditabbaṁ....pe....atthāya hitāya sukhāya deva-manussānaṁ.*
2. *Sāvaka-dhamma.*
3. A. III, 285: *Yasmiṁ Mahānāma samaye ariyasāvako Tathāgataṁ anussarati, nev' assa tasmiṁ samaye rāgapariyuṭṭhitaṁ cittaṁ hoti, na dosapariyuṭṭhitaṁ cittaṁ hoti, na moha-pariyuṭṭhitaṁ cittaṁ hoti, ujugatam ev' assa tasmiṁ samaye cittaṁ hoti Tathāgataṁ ārabbha. Ujugatacitto kho pana Mahānāma ariyasāvako labhati atthavedaṁ, labhati dhammavedaṁ, labhati dhammūpasaṁhitaṁ pāmujjaṁ, pamuditassa pīti jāyati, pītimanassa kāyo passam-*

THE RECOLLECTION OF THE LAW

Q. What is the recollection of the Law? What is the practising of it? What are its salient characteristic, function and near cause? What is the procedure?

A. The Law means extinction, *Nibbāna*, or the practice by means of which extinction, *Nibbāna*, is reached. The destruction of all activity, the abandoning of all defilements, the eradication of craving, the becoming stainless and tranquillized—these are called extinction, *Nibbāna*. What are the practices leading to extinction, *Nibbāna*? Namely, the four foundations of mindfulness, the four right efforts, the five powers, the seven factors of enlightenment, the Noble Eightfold Path—these are called the practices leading to *Nibbāna*. The recollection of the Law is the virtue of renunciation and the virtue of the Way. This recollection is recollectedness and right recollectedness. Thus is recollection of the Law to be understood. The undisturbed dwelling of the mind (in this recollection) is the practising of it. The awareness of the virtues of the Law is its salient characteristic. Analysis of the Law is its function. The understanding of the meaning is its near cause. Its benefits are equal to those of the recollection of the Buddha.

"What is the procedure?": The new yogin goes to a place of solitude and keeps his mind undisturbed. With undisturbed mind, he recollects thus: The Law is well-taught by the Blessed One, is visible, not subject to time, inviting, conducive to perfection, to be attained by the wise, each one for himself.[1]

"The Law is well-taught by the Blessed One": It is free from extremes,[2] therefore it is called "well-taught". There are no inconsistencies in it, therefore it is called "well-taught". There are no contradictions in it and it is endowed with the three kinds of goodness, therefore it is called "well-taught". It is completely spotless, therefore it is called "well-taught". It leads beings to extinction, *Nibbāna*, wherefore it is called "well-taught".

"Visible": Because one gains the Paths and the Fruits in succession, it is called "visible". Because one sees extinction, *Nibbāna*, and the (other) Fruits of the Path, it is called "visible".

"Not subject to time": Without lapse of time fruition occurs. Therefore, it is called "not subject to time".

---

bhati, passaddhakāyo sukhaṁ vediyati, sukhino cittaṁ samādhiyati. (=*Pamuditassā ti duvidhena pītipāmujjena pamuditassa; pīti jāyatī ti pañcavidhā pīti nibbattati; kāyo passambhatī ti nāmakāyo ca karajakāyo ca darathapaṭippassadhiyā paṭippassambhati; sukhan ti kāyikacetasikaṁ sukhaṁ; samādhiyatī ti ārammaṇe sammā ṭhapitaṁ hoti.* — Comy. (Mp.) III, 337.).

1. S. II, 69; A. I, 207; D. III, 5: *Savākkhāto Bhagavatā Dhammo sandiṭṭhiko akāliko ehi-passiko opanayiko paccattaṁ veditabbo viññūhīti.*
2. Vin. I, 10; S. V, 421: *Dve me bhikkhave antā pabbajitena na sevitabbā. Katame dve? Yo cāyaṁ kāmesu kāmasukhallikānuyogo hīno gammo pothujjaniko anariyo anatthasaṁhito. Yo cāyaṁ attakilamathānuyogo dukkho anariyo anatthasaṁhito. Ete te bhikkhave ubho ante anupagamma majjhimā paṭipadā Tathāgatena abhisambuddhā....*

"Inviting": It says: "Come and see my worth!". In the same way, those who have the ability to teach are called men who say "Come and see!".

"Conducive to perfection": If a man acknowledges it, he will reach the immortal. Such is that which is "conducive to perfection". What leads to the fruition of holiness is called that which is "conducive to perfection".

"To be attained by the wise, each one for himself": If a man acknowledges it and does not accept other teachings, he causes the arising of the knowledge of cessation, the knowledge of the unborn and the knowledge of freedom. Therefore, it is called that which is "to be attained by the wise, each one for himself".

Further, the yogin should recollect the Law in other ways thus: It is the eye; it is knowledge; it is peace; it is the way leading to the immortal; it is renunciation; it is the expedience whereby cessation is won; it is the way to the ambrosial; it is non-retrogression; it is the best; it is non-action, solitude, exquisiteness. It is not soothsaying. It is the most excellent object for the wise man's mind. It is to cross over to the other shore; it is the place of refuge. That yogin in these ways and through these virtues recollects the Law, and his mind is filled with confidence. On account of this confidence, his mind is undisturbed. Because of the undisturbed state of the mind, he destroys the hindrances, arouses the meditation, (*jhāna*) factors and dwells in access-concentration. The rest is as was fully taught above.

The recollection of the Law has ended.

THE RECOLLECTION OF THE COMMUNITY OF BHIKKHUS

Q. What is the recollection of the Community of Bhikkhus? (What is the practising of it?) What are its salient characteristic, function and near cause? What is the procedure?

A. The congregation of the saints is the Community of Bhikkhus. This is called the Community of Bhikkhus. The yogin recollects the virtue of the observances of the Community of Bhikkhus. This recollection is recollectedness and right recollectedness. Such is the recollection of the Community of Bhikkhus to be understood. The undisturbed dwelling of the mind in this recollection is the practising of it. Awareness of the virtues of the Community of Bhikkhus is its salient characteristic; reverence is its function; appreciation of the virtues of the Community of Bhikkhus is its near cause. Its benefits are equal to those of the recollection of the Buddha.

"What is the procedure?": The new yogin goes to a place of solitude and keeps his mind undisturbed. With undisturbed mind, he recollects thus: The Community of Hearers of the Blessed One is of good conduct, the Community of Hearers of the Blessed One is of upright conduct, the Community of Hearers of the Blessed One is of righteous conduct, the Community of

Hearers of the Blessed One is of dutiful conduct. This Community of Hearers of the Blessed One, namely, the four pairs of men and the eight kinds of individuals, is worthy of offerings, worthy of hospitality, worthy of gifts, worthy of reverential salutation, is the incomparable field of merit of the world.[1]

"The Community of Hearers of the Blessed One is of good conduct": The Community of Hearers of the Blessed One is of "good conduct", because it follows the good word. It is of "good conduct" and "upright conduct", because it benefits itself and others. It is of "good conduct" and "upright conduct" because it has no enemy. It is of "good conduct" and "upright conduct" because it avoids the two extremes and takes the mean. It is of "good conduct" and "upright conduct", because it is free from hypocrisy. It is "good conduct", because it is free from wickedness and crookedness and free from unclean action of body and speech.

"Is of righteous conduct": It is of "righteous conduct" because it follows the Noble Eightfold Path. And again, "righteous" is an appellation of extinction, *Nibbāna.* It is of "righteous", "good conduct", because it follows the Noble Eightfold Path and reaches extinction, *Nibbāna.* It is of "righteous", "good conduct", because it follows the Four Noble Truths taught by the Buddha.

"Is of dutiful conduct": It is of "dutiful conduct" because it is perfect in the practice of unity in the Community of Bhikkhus. It is of "dutiful conduct", because, seeing the great fruit of virtue and the increase of virtue which follow the practice of unity, it observes this (unity).

"The four pairs of men and the eight kinds of individuals": The Path and the Fruit of Stream-entrance are regarded as the attainments of a pair of men. The Path and the Fruit of Once-returning are regarded as the attainment of a pair of men. The Path and Fruit of Non-returning are regarded as the attainments of a pair of men. The Path and Fruit of the Consummate One are regarded as the attainments of a pair of men. These are called "the four pairs of men".

"The eight kinds of individuals" are they who gain the four Paths and the four Fruits. These are called the eight kinds of individuals. Because the Community of Bhikkhus dwells in these Paths and Fruits, it is said to consist of the four pairs of men. Those who dwell in the four Paths and the four Fruits are called the eight kinds of individuals.

"Hearers": It (the Community of hearers) accomplishes after having heard. Therefore it is called (the Community of) hearers.

"Community": The congregation of saints. It is worthy of hospitality,

---

1. S. II, 69; A. I, 208; D. III, 5: *Supaṭipanno Bhagavato sāvaka-saṁgho uju-paṭipanno Bhagavato sāvaka-saṁgho, ñāya-paṭipanno Bhagavato sāvaka-saṁgho, sāmici-paṭipanno Bhagavato sāvaka-saṁgho, yadidaṁ cattāri purisayugāni aṭṭha-purisa-puggalā, esa Bhagavato sāvaka-saṁgho āhuṇeyyo pāhuṇeyyo dakkhiṇeyyo añjali-karaṇiyo anuttaraṁ puññakkhettaṁ lokassāti.*

worthy of offerings, worthy of gifts, worthy of reverential salutation, and is the imcomparable field of merit of the world.

"Worthy of hospitality": Worthy of hospitality means worthy of receiving invitations.

"Worthy of offerings": Great is the fruit that could be obtained through offerings made to it. And again, it is worthy of receiving offerings.

"Worthy of gifts: One acquires great fruit by gifting various things to it.

"Worthy of reverential salutation": It is fit to receive worship. Therefore it is called worthy of reverential salutation.

"Incomparable": It is possessed of many virtues. Therefore it is called incomparable.

"Field of merit of the world": This is the place where all beings acquire merit. Therefore it is called the field of merit of the world.

And again, the yogin should recollect through other ways thus: This Community of Bhikkhus is the congregation that is most excellent and good. It is called the best. It is endowed with virtue, concentration, wisdom, freedom and the knowledge of freedom. That yogin recollects these various virtues in different ways. Through this recollection of the various virtues, he becomes confident. Owing to the recollection of confidence, his mind is undisturbed. With undisturbed mind he is able to destroy the hindrances, arouse the meditation (*jhāna*) factors and attain to access. The rest is as was fully taught above.

The recollection of the Community of Bhikkhus has ended.

THE RECOLLECTION OF VIRTUE

Q. What is the recollection of virtue? What is the practising of it. What are its salient characteristic, function and near cause? What is the procedure?

A. Through virtue one recollects pure morals. This recollectedness is recollection and right recollectedness. Thus should the recollection of virtue be understood. The undisturbed dwelling of the mind in the recollection of virtue is the practising of it. Awareness of the merit of virtue is its salient characteristic. To see the fearfulness of tribulation is its function. Appreciation of the unsurpassable happiness (of virtue) is its near cause. Twelve are the benefits of the recollection of virtue thus: One honours the Teacher, esteems the Law, and the Community of Bhikkhus, respects the precepts of virtue, esteems offerings, becomes heedful, sees danger in and fears the smallest fault,[1] guards oneself, protects others, has no fear of this world, has no fear of the other world and enjoys the many benefits accruing from the observance of all precepts. These are the benefits of the recollection of virtue.

1. D. I, 63: *Aṇumattesu vajjesu bhaya-dassāvī.*

"What is the procedure?": The new yogin goes to a place of solitude and keeps his mind undisturbed. With this undisturbed mind, he recollects thus: "My virtue is unbroken, indefective, unspotted, unblemished, liberating, praised by the wise, untainted, conducive to concentration".[1]

If unbroken, they are indefective. If indefective, they are unspotted. The others should be known in the same way.

Again, because when virtue is pure, they become the resorting-ground of all good states, they come to be called "unbroken and indefective". As they constitute the honour of caste, they are called unspotted and unblemished. As they constitute the joy of the Consummate One, and bear no tribulation, they are called "praised by the wise". As they are untouched by views, they are called "untainted". As they lead to sure stations, they are called "conducive to concentration".

Further, the yogin should practise recollection of virtue in other ways thinking thus: "Virtue is the bliss of separation from tribulation. This caste is worthy of honour. The treasure of virtue is secure. Its benefits have already been taught". Thus should virtue be understood. That yogin practises recollection of virtue considering its merits through these ways. Owing to his recollectedness and confidence, his mind is not disturbed. With this undisturbed mind he destroys the hindrances, arouses the meditation (*jhāna*) factors and attains to access-meditation. The rest is as was fully taught above.

The recollection of virtue has ended.

THE RECOLLECTION OF LIBERALITY

Q. What is the Recollection of liberality? What is the practising of it? What are its salient characteristic, function and near cause? What is the procedure?

A. Liberality means that one gives one's wealth to others wishing to benefit them, and in order to derive the happiness of benefitting others. Thus is liberality to be understood. One dwells indifferent in the recollection of the virtue of liberality. This recollectedness is recollection and right recollectedness. This is called reçollection of liberality. The undisturbed dwelling of the mind in this recollection is the practising of it. Awareness of the merit of liberality is its salient characteristic. Non-miserliness is its function. Non-covetousness is its near cause.

A man who practises the recollection of liberality gains ten benefits thus: He gains bliss through liberality; he becomes non-covetous through liberality;

---

1. A. III, 286: *Puna ca paraṁ Mahānāma ariyasāvako attano sīlāni anussarati akhaṇḍāni acchiddāni asabalāni akammāsāni bhujissāni viññūpasatthāni aparāmaṭṭhāni samādhisaṁvattanikāni.*

he is not miserly, thinks of others, becomes dear to others, does not fear in others' company, has much joy, acquires the compassionate mind, fares well and approaches the ambrosial.

"What is the procedure?": The new yogin goes to a place of solitude and keeps his mind undisturbed. With undisturbed mind he practises recollection of liberality thus: "Through abandoning things I have benefitted others; therefrom I have gained much merit. The vulgar, by reason of the dirt of covetousness, are drawn to things. I live with mind non-coveting and not unclean. Always I give and enjoy giving to others. Always I give and distribute".[1]

That yogin in these ways practises the recollection of liberality. Through the recollection of liberality his mind is endowed with confidence. Because of this recollection and confidence, his mind is always undisturbed. With undisturbed mind he destroys the hindrances, arouses the meditation (*jhāna*) factors and attains to access-concentration. The rest is as was fully taught above.

The recollection of liberality has ended.

THE RECOLLECTION OF DEITIES

Q. What is the recollection of deities? What is the practising of it? What are its salient characteristic, function and near cause? What is the procedure?

A. Considering the benefit of birth in a heaven, one recollects one's own merits. This recollectedness is recollection and right recollectedness. This is called recollection of deities. The undisturbed dwelling of the mind in this recollection is the practising of it. Awareness of one's own merits and the merits of the deities is its salient characteristic. To admire merit is its function. Confidence in the fruit of merit is its near cause.

A man who practises the recollection of deities gains eight benefits: he increases five qualities, namely, confidence, virtue, learning, liberality and wisdom; he can gain that which heavenly beings desire and to which they are devoted; he is happy in the anticipation of the reward of merit; he honours his body; he is reverenced by heavenly beings. Through this, he is able to practise virtue and recollection of liberality also. He fares well and approaches the ambrosial.

"What is the procedure?": The new yogin goes to a place of solitude and keeps his mind undisturbed. With undisturbed mind he practises the recollection of deities thinking thus: "There are the Four Regents. There are the deities

1. A. III, 287; *Puna ca paraṁ Mahānāma ariyasāvako attano cāgaṁ anussarati 'lābhā vata me suladdhaṁ vata me, yo' haṁ maccheramalapariyuṭṭhitāya pajāya vigatamalamaccherena cetasā agāraṁ ajjhāvasāmi muttacāgo payatapāṇi vossaggarato yācayogo dānasaṁvibhāgarato' ti.*

of *Tāvatiṁsa*, *Yāma*, *Tusita*, *Nimmānarati*, *Paranimmitavasavatti* heavens. There are the Brahma-group deities and other deities. Those deities, being endowed with such confidence, on dying here, were born there. I too have such confidence. Endowed with such virtue, such learning, such liberality and such wisdom, those deities were born there. I too have such wisdom".[1] Thus he recollects his own and the deities' confidence, virtue, learning, liberality and wisdom.

That yogin in these ways and through these virtues practises the recollection of deities, and is thereby endowed with confidence. Owing to confidence and recollectedness, his mind is undisturbed. With undisturbed mind he destroys the hindrances, arouses the meditation (*jhāna*) factors and attains to access-meditation.

Q. Why does one recollect the merit of deities and not of humans?

A. The merit of the deities is the most excellent. They are born in excellent realms and are endowed with excellent minds. Having entered a good realm, they are endowed with good. Therefore one should recollect the merit of the deities and not the merits of men. The rest is as was fully taught above.

The recollection of deities has ended.

The sixth fascicle has ended.

1. A. III, 287; *Puna ca paraṁ Mahānāma ariyasāvako devatānussatiṁ bhāveti 'santi devā Cātummahārājikā, santi devā Tāvatiṁsā, santi devā Yāmā, santi devā Tusitā, santi devā Nimmānaratino, santi devā Paranimmitavasavattino, santi devā Brahmakāyikā, santi devā Taduttari; yathārūpāya saddhāya samannāgatā tā devatā ito cutā tattha uppannā, mayham pi tathārūpā saddhā saṁvijjati; yathārūpena sīlena samannāgatā tā devatā ito cutā tattha uppannā, mayham pi tathārūpaṁ sīlaṁ saṁvijjati; yathārūpena sutena samannāgatā tā devatā tato cutā tattha uppannā, mayham pi tathārūpaṁ sutaṁ saṁvijjati; yathārūpena cāgena samannāgatā tā devatā ito cutā tattha uppannā, mayham pi tathārūpo cāgo saṁvijjati; yathārūpāya paññāya samannāgatā tā devatā ito cutā tattha uppannā, mayham pi tathārūpā paññā saṁvijjati' ti.*

[418] THE PATH OF FREEDOM

FASCICLE THE SEVENTH

WRITTEN

BY

THE ARAHANT UPATISSA

WHO WAS CALLED

GREAT LIGHT IN RYO

TRANSLATED IN RYO

BY

TIPIṬAKA SANGHAPĀLA OF FUNAN

CHAPTER THE EIGHTH

Section Four

MINDFULNESS OF RESPIRATION

Q. What is mindfulness of respiration?[1] What is the practising of it? What are its salient characteristic, function and near cause? What are its benefits? What is the procedure?

A. Inhalation[2] is the incoming breath. Exhalation[3] is the outgoing breath. The perceiving of the incoming breath and the outgoing breath—this is being mindful, mindfulness and right mindfulness. The undisturbed dwelling of the mind (in this mindfulness) is the practising of it. To cause the arising of perception as regards respiration is its salient characteristic. Attending to contact[4] is its function. Removal of discursive thought[5] is its near cause.

BENEFITS

"What are its benefits?": If a man practises mindfulness of respiration, he attains to the peaceful, the exquisite, the lovely, and the blissful life. He causes evil and demeritorious states to disappear and to perish as soon as they arise.[6] He is not negligent as regards his body or his organ of sight. His body and mind do not waver or tremble.[7] He fulfils the four foundations of mindfulness, the seven enlightenment factors and freedom. This has been praised by the

---

1. *Ānāpānasati.* 2. *Āna.* 3. *Apāna.* 4. *Phassa.* 5. *Vitakka.*
6. S. V, 321-22: *Ānāpānasati samādhi bhāvito bahulīkato santo ceva paṇito ca asecanako ca sukho ca vihāro uppannupanne ca pāpake akusale dhamme ṭhānaso antaradhāpeti vūpasameti.*
7. S. V, 316: *Ānāpānasatisamādhissa bhikkhave bhāvitattā bahulīkatattā neva kāyassa iñjitattaṁ vā hoti phanditattaṁ vā na cittassa iñjitattaṁ vā hoti phanditattaṁ vā.*

Blessed One. This is the abode of the Noble Ones, of Brahma and of the Tathāgata.[1]

PROCEDURE

"What is the procedure?": The new yogin having gone to a forest, to the foot of a tree or to a wide open space, sits down, with legs crossed under him, with the body held erect, with mindfulness established in front. He is mindful in respiration. Mindful of the outgoing breath, that yogin knows, when he breathes out a long breath: "I breathe out a long breath"; [430] when he breathes in a long breath, he knows: "I breathe in a long breath"; when he breathes in a short breath, he knows: "I breathe in a short breath"; when he breathes out a short breath, he knows: "I breathe out a short breath". Thus he knows. "I am breathing in, in such and such a way", thus he trains himself. "I am breathing out, in such and such a way", thus he trains himself. (Experiencing the whole body; calming the bodily formations), experiencing joy, experiencing bliss, experiencing the mental formations, calming the mental formations, (experiencing the mind), gladdening the mind, concentrating the mind, freeing the mind, discerning impermanence, discerning dispassion, discerning cessation, discerning renunciation, thus he trains himself. "Discerning renunciation, I breathe out in such and such a way", thus he trains himself; "discerning renunciation, I breathe in, in such and such a way", thus he trains himself.[2]

Here, he trains himself in "breathing in" means: "mindfulness is fixed at the nose-tip or on the lip".[3] These are the places connected with breathing

---

1. S. V, 326: *Ānāpānasatisamādhiṁ sammāvadamāno vadeyya ariyavihāro iti pi brahmavihāro iti pi tathāgatavihāro iti pī ti.*
2. S. V, 311-12: *Idha bhikkhave bhikkhu araññagato vā rukkhamūlagato vā suññāgāragato vā nisīdati pallaṅkaṁ ābhujitvā ujuṁ kāyaṁ paṇidhāya parimukhaṁ satiṁ upaṭṭhapetvā so sato va assasati sato passasati.*

   Dīghaṁ vā assasanto dīghaṁ assasāmīti pajānāti, dīghaṁ vā passasanto dīghaṁ passasāmīti pajānāti. Rassaṁ vā assasanto rassaṁ assasāmīti pajānāti, rassaṁ vā passasanto rassaṁ passasāmīti pajānāti.

   Sabbakāyapaṭisaṁvedī assasissāmīti sikkhati, sabbakāyapaṭisaṁvedī passasissāmīti sikkhati. Passambhayaṁ kāyasaṅkhāraṁ assasissāmīti sikkhati, passambhayaṁ kāyasaṅkhāraṁ passasissāmīti sikkhati.

   Pītipaṭisaṁvedī assasissāmīti sikkhati, pītipaṭisaṁvedī passasissāmīti sikkhati. Sukhapaṭisaṁvedī assasissāmīti sikkhati, sukhapaṭisaṁvedī passasissāmīti sikkhati.

   Cittasaṅkhārapaṭisaṁvedī assasissāmīti sikkhati, cittasaṅkhārapaṭisaṁvedī passasissāmīti sikkhati. Passambhayaṁ cittasaṅkhāraṁ assasissāmīti sikkhati, passambhayaṁ cittasaṅkhāraṁ passasissāmīti sikkhati. Cittapaṭisaṁvedī assasissāmīti sikkhati, cittapaṭisaṁvedī passasissāmīti sikkhati.

   Abhippamodayaṁ cittaṁ assasissāmīti sikkhati, abhippamodayaṁ cittaṁ passasissāmīti sikkhati. Samādahaṁ cittaṁ assasissāmīti sikkhati, samādahaṁ cittaṁ passasissāmīti sikkhati. Vimocayaṁ cittaṁ assasissāmīti sikkhati, vimocayaṁ cittaṁ passasissāmīti sikkhati.

   Aniccānupassī assasissāmīti sikkhati, aniccānupassī passasissāmīti sikkhati. Virāgānupassī assasissāmīti sikkhati, virāgānupassī passasissāmīti sikkhati. Nirodhānupassī assasissāmīti sikkhati, nirodhānupassī passasissāmīti sikkhati. Paṭinissaggānupassī assasissāmīti sikkhati, paṭinissaggānupassī passasissāmīti sikkhati.
3. Mp. III, 202; Spk. I, 238: *Parimukhaṁ satiṁ upaṭṭhapetvā ti, kammaṭṭhān' ābhimukhaṁ satiṁ ṭhapayitvā, mukha-samīpe vā katvā ti attho. Ten' eva Vibhange, "ayaṁ sati upaṭṭhitā hoti supaṭṭhitā nāsik' agge vā mukha-nimitte vā. Tena vuccati parimukhaṁ satiṁ upaṭṭhapetvā"* (Vbh. 252) *ti.*

in and breathing out. That yogin attends to the incoming breath here. He considers the contact of the incoming and the outgoing breath, through mindfulness that is fixed at the nose-tip or on the lip. Mindfully, he breathes in; mindfully, he breathes out. He does not consider (the breath) when it has gone in and also when it has gone out.[1] He considers the contact of the incoming breath and the outgoing breath, at the nose-tip or on the lip, with mindfulness. He breathes in and breathes out with mindfulness. It is as if a man were sawing wood. That man does not attend to the going back and forth of the saw. In the same way the yogin does not attend to the perception of the incoming and the outgoing breath in mindfulness of respiration. He is aware of the contact at the nose-tip or on the lip, and he breathes in and out, with mindfulness.[2] If, when the breath comes in or goes out, the yogin considers the inner or the outer, his mind will be distracted. If his mind is distracted, his body and mind will waver and tremble. These are the disadvantages. He should not purposely breathe very long or very short breaths. If he purposely breathes very long or very short breaths, his mind will be distracted and his body and mind will waver and tremble. These are the disadvantages.

He should not attach himself to diverse perceptions connected with breathing in and breathing out. If he does so, his other mental factors will be disturbed. If his mind is disturbed, his body and mind will waver and tremble. Thus countless impediments arise because the points of contact of the incoming breath and the outgoing breath are countless. He should be mindful and should not let the mind be distracted. He should not essay too strenuously nor too laxly. If he essays too laxly, he will fall into rigidity and torpor. If he essays too strenuously, he will become restless. If the yogin falls into rigidity and torpor or becomes restless, his body and mind will waver and tremble.[3] These are the disadvantages.

To the yogin who attends to the incoming breath with mind that is cleansed of the nine lesser defilements the image[4] arises with a pleasant feeling similar to that which is produced in the action of spinning cotton or silk cotton. Also,

---

1. Cp. Pts. 165: *Assāsādimajjhapariyosānaṁ satiyā anugacchato ajjhattaṁ vikkhepagatena cittena kāyo pi cittaṁ pi sāraddhā ca honti iñjitā ca phanditā ca, passāsādimajjhapariyosānaṁ satiyā anugacchato bahiddhā vikkhepagatena cittena kāyo pi....pe....phanditā ca.*
2. Cp. Pts. I, 171: *Seyyathāpī rukkho same bhūmibhāge nikkhitto, tamenaṁ puriso kakacena chindeyya, rukkhe phuṭṭhakakakacadantānaṁ vasena purisassa sati upaṭṭhitā hoti, na āgate vā gate vā kakacadante manasikaroti, na āgatā vā gatā vā kakacadantā aviditā honti, padhānañ ca paññāyati, payogañ ca sādheti, visesaṁ adhigacchati: Yathā rukkho same bhūmibhāge nikkhitto, evaṁ upanibandhanā nimittaṁ, yathā kakacadantā evaṁ assāsa-passāsā, yathā rukkhe phuṭṭhakakakacadantānaṁ vasena purisassa sati upaṭṭhitā hoti, na āgate vā gate vā kakacadante manasikaroti, na āgatā vā gatā vā kakacadantā aviditā honti, padhānañ ca paññāyati, payogañ ca sādheti, visesaṁ adhigacchati—evamevaṁ bhikkhū nāsikagge vā mukhanimitte vā satiṁ upaṭṭhapetvā nisinno hoti, na āgate vā gate vā assāsapassāse manasikaroti na āgatā vā gatā vā assāsapassāsā aviditā honti, padhānañ ca paññāyati, payogañ ca sādheti, visesaṁ adhigacchati.*
3. Pts. I, 166: *Linena cittena kosajjānupatitena kāyo pi cittaṁ pi sāraddhā ca honti iñjitā ca phanditā ca, atipaggahitena cittena uddhaccānupatitena kāyo pi....pe....phanditā ca.*
4. *Nimitta.*

it is likened to the pleasant feeling produced by a breeze.[1] Thus in breathing in and out, air touches the nose or the lip and causes the setting-up of air perception mindfulness. This does not depend on colour or form.[2] This is called the image. If the yogin develops the image and increases it at the nose-tip, between the eye-brows, on the forehead or establishes it in several places,[3] he feels as if his head were filled with air. Through increasing in this way his whole body is charged with bliss. This is called perfection.

And again, there is a yogin: he sees several images from the beginning. He sees various forms such as smoke, mist, dust, sand of gold, or he experiences something similar to the pricking of a needle or to an ant's bite. If his mind does not become clear regarding these different images, he will be confused. Thus he fulfils overturning and does not gain the perception of respiration. If his mind becomes clear, the yogin does not experience confusion. He attends to respiration and he does not cause the arising of other perceptions. Meditating thus he is able to end confusion and acquire the subtle image. And he attends to respiration with mind that is free. That image is free. Because that image is free, desire arises. Desire being free, that yogin attends to respiration and becomes joyful. Desire and joy being free, he attends to respiration with equipoise. Equipoise, desire and joy being free, he attends to respiration, and his mind is not disturbed. If his mind is not disturbed, he will destroy the hindrances, and arouse the meditation (*jhāna*) factors. Thus this yogin will reach the calm and sublime fourth meditation, *jhāna*. This is as was fully taught above.

COUNTING, CONNECTION, CONTACTING AND FIXING

And again, certain predecessors[4] taught four ways of practising mindfulness of respiration. They are counting, connection, contacting and fixing.[5] *Q.* What is counting? *A.* A new yogin counts the breaths from one to ten, beginning with the outgoing breath and ending with the incoming breath. He does not count beyond ten. Again, it is taught that he counts from one to five but does not count beyond five. He does not miss. At that time (i.e., when he misses) he should count (the next) or stop that count. Thus he dwells in mindfulness of respiration, attending to the object. Thus should counting be understood.

"Connection": Having counted, he follows respiration with mindfulness, continuously. This is called connection.

---

1. Vis. Mag. 285: *Api ca kho kassaci sukhasamphassaṁ uppādayamāno, tūlapicu viya, kappāsapicu viya, vātadhārā viya ca upaṭṭhātī ti ekacce āhu. Ayaṁ pana aṭṭhakathāsu vinicchayo:-....*
2. Cp. Vis. Mag. 286: *Athā'nena taṁ nimittaṁ neva vaṇṇato manasikātabbaṁ, na lakkhaṇato paccavekkhitabbaṁ.*
3. Cp. Manual of a Mystic (P.T.S. translation) of Yogāvacara's Manual 8 ff.
4. Possibly *Porāṇā.*
5. Vis. Mag. 278: *Tatrāyaṁ manasikāravidhi:- gaṇanā, anubandhanā, phusanā, ṭhapanā.* Here it is interesting to note that the Venerable Buddhaghosa Thera does not ascribe this teaching to '*ekacce*' as he usually does; nor does he go to the *Aṭṭhakathā* for authority.

"Contacting": Having caused the arising of air perception, he dwells, attending to the contact of respiration at the nose-tip or on the lip. This is called contacting.

"Fixing": Having acquired facility in contacting, he should establish the image, and he should establish joy and bliss and other states which arise here. Thus should fixing be known.

That counting suppresses uncertainty. It causes the abandoning of uncertainty. Connection removes gross discursive thinking and causes unbroken mindfulness of respiration. Contacting removes distraction and makes for steady perception. One attains to distinction through bliss.

SIXTEEN WAYS OF TRAINING IN MINDFULNESS OF RESPIRATION

(1) and (2) "Breathing in a long breath, breathing out a short breath, breathing in a short breath, thus he trains himself"[1]...................

....

Knowledge causes the arising of non-confusion and the object. *Q*. What is non-confusion and what is the object? *A*. The new yogin gains tranquillity of body and mind and abides in mindfulness of respiration. The respirations become subtle. Because of subtility they are hard to lay hold of. If at that time, the yogin's breathing is long, he, through fixing, knows it is long. If the image arises he considers it through its own nature. Thus should non-confusion be known. And again he should consider the breaths, whether long or short (as the case may be). Thus should he practise. And again, the yogin causes the arising of the clear image through the object. Thus should one practise.

(3) "Experiencing the whole body, I breathe in', thus he trains himself": In two ways he knows the whole body, through non-confusion and through the object. *Q*. What is the knowledge of the whole body through non-confusion? *A*. A yogin practises mindfulness of respiration and develops concentration through contact accompanied by joy and bliss. Owing to the experiencing of contact accompanied by joy and bliss the whole body becomes non-confused. *Q*. What is the knowledge of the whole body through the object? *A*. The incoming breath and the outgoing breath comprise the bodily factors dwelling in one sphere. The object of respiration and the mind and the mental properties are called "body". These bodily factors are called "body".[2] Thus should the whole body be known. That yogin knows the whole body thus: "Though there is the body, there is no being or soul".[3]

---

1. This paragraph is not clear. Unintelligibility is not an uncommon feature of this Chinese text. The quotations (1) and (2) are not in full. The rest, (3) to (16), are from S. V, 311-12 quoted earlier.
2. Cp. S. V, 329-30: *Kāyaññatarāhaṁ Ānanda etaṁ vadāmi yad idaṁ assāsapassāsaṁ.*
3. As. 38, Sec. 93: *Tasmiṁ kho pana samaye dhammā honti dhammesu dhammānupassi viharatī ti ādisu nissattanijjīvatāyaṁ. Svāyam idhāpi nissattanijjīvatāyam eva vattati.*

THE THREE TRAININGS

"Thus he trains himself" refers to the three trainings. The first is the training of the higher virtue, the second is the training of the higher thought, the third is the training of the higher wisdom.[1] True virtue is called the training of the higher virtue; true concentration is called the training of the higher thought; and true wisdom is called the training of the higher wisdom. That yogin by these three kinds of training meditates on the object, recollects the object and trains himself. He practises repeatedly. This is the meaning of "thus he trains himself".

(4) " 'Calming the bodily formation, I breathe', thus he trains himself": Which are the bodily formations? He breathes in and out with such bodily formations as bending down; stooping, bending all over, bending forward, moving, quivering, trembling and shaking.[2] And again, he calms the gross bodily formations and practises the first meditation, *jhāna*, through the subtle bodily formations. From there, he progresses to the second meditation, *jhāna*, through the more subtle bodily formations. From there, he progresses to the third meditation, *jhāna*, through the still more subtle bodily formations. From there, he progresses to the fourth meditation, *jhāna*, having ended (the bodily formations) without remainder. *A*. If he causes the ending of respiration without remainder,[3] how is he able to practise mindfulness of respiration? *A*. Because he has grasped well the general characteristics, the image arises even when the respirations lapse. And because of these many characteristics, he is able to develop the image and enter into meditation, *jhāna*.

(5) " 'Experiencing joy through the object, I breathe in', thus he trains himself". [431] He attends to respiration. He arouses joy in two meditations, *jhānas*. This joy can be known through two ways: through non-confusion and through the object.[4] Here the yogin enters into concentration and experiences joy through non-confusion, through investigation, through overcoming and through the object.

(6) " 'Experiencing bliss, I breathe in', thus he trains himself": He attends to respiration. He arouses bliss in three meditations, *jhānas*. This

---

1. Cp. Pts. I, 184: *Sabbakāyapaṭisamvedī assāsapassāsānaṁ saṁvaraṭṭhena sīlavisuddhi, avikkhepaṭṭhena cittavisuddhi, dassanaṭṭhena diṭṭhivisuddhi; yo tattha saṁvaraṭṭho ayaṁ adhisīlasikkhā, yo tattha avikkhepaṭṭho ayaṁ adhicittasikkhā, yo tattha dassanaṭṭho ayaṁ adhipaññāsikkhā.*
2. Cp. Pts. I, 184-5: *Yathārūpehi kāyasaṇkhārehi yā kāyassa ānamanā, vinamanā, sannamanā, paṇamanā, iñjanā, phandanā, calanā, kampanā 'passambhayaṁ kāyasaṅkhāraṁ assasissāmīti' sikkhati, 'passambhayaṁ kāyasaṅkhāraṁ passasissāmīti' sikkhati.*
3. See note 2 on page 120.
4. Cp. Vis. Mag. 287: *Tattha dvīhākārehi pīti paṭisaṁviditā hoti; ārammaṇato ca asammohato ca. Kathaṁ ārammaṇato pīti paṭisaṁviditā hoti? Sappītike dve jhāne samāpajjati: tassa samāpattikkhaṇe jhānapaṭilābhena ārammaṇato pīti paṭisaṁviditā hoti, ārammaṇassa paṭisaṁviditattā. Kathaṁ asammohato? Sappītike dve jhāne samāpajjitvā vuṭṭhāya jhānasampayuttaṁ pītiṁ khayato vayato sammasati, tassa vipassanākkhaṇe lakkhaṇapaṭivedhena asammohato pīti paṭisamviditā hoti.*

bliss can be known through two ways: through non-confusion and through the object. The rest is as was fully taught above.

(7) " 'Experiencing the mental formations, I breathe in', thus he trains himself": "Mental formations" means: "Perception and feeling". He arouses these mental formations in four meditations, *jhānas*. He knows through two ways: through non-confusion and through the object. The rest is as was fully taught above.

(8) " 'Calming the mental formations, I breathe in', thus he trains himself": The mental formations are called perception and feeling. He calms the gross mental formations and trains himself. The rest is as was fully taught above.

(9) " 'Experiencing the mind, I breathe in', thus he trains himself": He attends to the incoming breath and the outgoing breath. The mind is aware of entering into and going out of the object, through two ways: through non-confusion and through the object. The rest is as was fully taught above.

(10) " 'Gladdening the mind, I breathe in', thus he trains himself": Joy means rejoicing. In two meditations, *jhānas*, he causes the mind to exult. Thus he trains himself. The rest is as was fully taught above.

(11) " 'Concentrating the mind, I breathe in', thus he trains himself": That yogin attends to the incoming breath and the outgoing breath. Through mindfulness and through meditation, *jhāna*, he causes the mind to be intent on the object. Placing the mind well he establishes it.[1] Thus he trains himself.

(12) " 'Freeing the mind, I breathe in', thus he trains himself": That yogin attends to the incoming breath and the outgoing breath. If his mind is slow and slack, he frees it from rigidity; if it is too active, he frees it from restlessness. Thus he trains himself. If his mind is elated, he frees it from lust. Thus he trains himself. If it is depressed, he frees it from hatred. Thus he trains himself. If his mind is sullied, he frees it from the lesser defilements. Thus he trains himself. And again, if his mind is not inclined towards the object and is not pleased with it, he causes his mind to be inclined towards it. Thus he trains himself.

(13) " 'Discerning impermanence, I breathe in', thus he trains himself": He attends to the incoming breath and the outgoing breath. Discerning the incoming and the outgoing breath, the object of the incoming and the outgoing breath, the mind and the mental properties and their arising and passing away, he trains himself.

(14) " 'Discerning dispassion, I breathe in', thus he trains himself": He attends to the incoming breath and the outgoing breath (thinking) thus: "This is impermanence; this is dispassion; this is extinction, this is *Nibbāna*". Thus he breathes in and trains himself.

1. Cp. Pts. I, 191: *Dīghaṁ assāsavasena cittassa ekaggatā avikkhepo samādhi, dīghaṁ passāsavasena...., yā cittassa ṭhiti saṇṭhiti avaṭṭhiti avisāhāro avikkhepo....*

(15) " 'Discerning cessation, I breathe in', thus he trains himself": Discerning many hindrances, according to reality, (he thinks), "These are impermanent, the destruction of these is extinction, *Nibbāna*". Thus with tranquillized vision he trains himself.

(16) " 'Discerning renunciation, I breathe in', thus he trains himself": Discerning tribulation according to reality, (he thinks), "These are impermanent", and freeing himself from tribulation, he abides in the peace of extinction, *Nibbāna*. Thus he trains himself and attains to bliss. The tranquil and the sublime are to be understood thus: All activities are brought to rest. All defilements are forsaken. Craving is destroyed. Passion is absent. It is the peace of blowing out.[1]

Of these sixteen, the first twelve fulfil serenity and insight, and are discerned as impermanence. The last four fulfil only insight. Thus should serenity and insight be understood.[2]

And again, all these are of four kinds. The first is that practice which leads to the completion of discernment. There is a time when one discerns (impermanence) through attending to the incoming breath and the outgoing breath. This is called the knowledge of the long and the short through practising. Calming the bodily formations and the mental formations, gladdening the mind, concentrating the mind and freeing the mind — this is called the arising of the knowledge of the whole body, bliss and the mental formations. "Experiencing the mind" means: "The completion of discernment". "There is a time when one discerns" and so forth refers to the four activities which always begin with the discernment of impermanence.

And again, practice means attaining to a state (of meditation, *jhāna*) through mindfulness of respiration. This is practice. Through this mindfulness of respiration, one attains to the state which is with (-out, even) initial application of thought. That is the state which is with initial and sustained application of thought, and the state of sustained application of thought.[3] The experiencing of joy is the state of the second meditation, *jhāna*. The experiencing of bliss is the state of the third meditation, *jhāna*. The experiencing of the mind is the state of the fourth meditation, *jhāna*.

And again, all these are of two kinds. They are practice and fulfilment. Such practice as is included within fulfilment does not cause decrease of the sixteen bases. Practice is like a seed; it is the cause of merit. Fulfilment is like a flower or a fruit, because it proceeds from a similar thing.

If mindfulness of respiration is practised, the four foundations of mindfulness are fulfilled. If the four foundations of mindfulness are practised,

---

1. S. I, 136; A. V, 8: *Etaṁ santaṁ, etaṁ paṇitaṁ, yad idaṁ sabbasaṅkhārasamatho sabbūpadhipaṭinissaggo taṇhakkhayo virāgo nirodho nibbānan ti.*
2. Vis. Mag. 291: *Idaṁ catutthacatukkaṁ suddhavipassanā vasen'eva vuttaṁ. Purimāni pana tiṇi samathavipassanā vasena. Evaṁ catunnaṁ catukkānaṁ vasena soḷasavatthukāya ānāpānasatiyā bhāvanā veditabbā.*
3. D. III, 219: *Tayo samādhi. Savitakko savicāro samādhi, avitakko vicāra-matto samādhi, avitakko avicāro samādhi.*

the seven enlightenment factors are fulfilled. If the seven enlightenment factors are practised, freedom and wisdom are fulfilled.[1]

THE FOUR FOUNDATIONS OF MINDFULNESS

Q. How is such a state attained?

A. The foundation of mindfulness which begins with the long incoming breath and the long outgoing breath is the reviewing of the body. That which begins with the experiencing of joy is the reviewing of feeling. That which begins with the experiencing of the mind is the reviewing of thought. That which begins with the discernment of impermanence is the reviewing of states. Thus one who practises mindfulness of respiration fulfils the four foundations of mindfulness.[2]

THE SEVEN ENLIGHTENMENT FACTORS

How are the seven enlightenment factors fulfilled through the practice of the four foundations of mindfulness? If the yogin practises the (four) foundations of mindfulness, he is able to abide non-confused in mindfulness; this is called the enlightenment factor of mindfulness. That yogin, abiding in mindfulness, investigates subjection to ill, impermanence and phenomena; this is called the enlightenment factor of inquiry into states. Inquiring into states (*dhammā*) thus, he strives earnestly without slackening; this is called the enlightenment factor of exertion. Developing exertion, he arouses joy that is clean; this is called the enlightenment factor of joy. Through the mind being full of joy, his body and mind are endowed with calm; this is called the enlightenment factor of calm. Through calmness his body attains to ease and his mind is possessed of concentration; this is called the enlightenment factor of concentration. Owing to concentration, the mind acquires equanimity; this is called the enlightenment factor of equanimity. Thus because of the

---

1. S. V, 329: *Ānāpānasatisamādhi kho Ānanda eko dhammo bhāvito bahulīkato cattāro satipaṭṭhāne paripūreti. Cattāro satipaṭṭhānā bhāvitā bahuīkatā satta bojjhaṅge paripūrenti. Satta bojjhaṅgā bhāvitā bahulīkatā vijjāvimuttiṁ paripūrenti.*
2. S. V, 323-4: *Yasmiṁ samaye Ānanda bhikkhu dīghaṁ vā assasanto dīghaṁ assasāmīti pajānāti, dīghaṁ vā passasanto dīghaṁ passasāmīti pajānāti, rassaṁ vā assasanto...., rassaṁ vā passasanto...., sabbakāyapaṭisaṁvedī assasissāmīti sikkhati,.... passasissāmīti sikkhatī, passambhayaṁ kāyasaṅkhāraṁ assasissāmīti sikkhati,.... passasissāmīti sikkhati, kāye kāyānupassī Ānanda bhikkhu tasmiṁ samaye viharati....*
   Yasmiṁ samaye Ānanda bhikkhu pītipaṭisaṁvedī assasissāmīti sikkhati...., sukhapaṭisaṁvedī...., cittasaṅkhārapaṭisaṁvedī...., passambhayaṁ cittasaṅkhāraṁ...., vedanāsu vedanānupassī Ānanda bhikkhu tasmiṁ samaye viharati....
   Yasmiṁ samaye Ānanda bhikkhu cittapaṭisaṁvedī assasissāmīti sikkhati...., abhippamodayaṁ cittaṁ...., samādahaṁ cittaṁ...., vimocayaṁ cittaṁ...., citte cittānupassī Ānanda bhikkhu tasmiṁ samaye viharati....
   Yasmiṁ samaye Ānanda bhikkhu aniccānupassī assasissāmīti sikkhati...., virāgānupassī...., nirodhānupassī...., paṭinissaggānupassī...., dhammesu dhammānupassī Ānanda bhikkhu tasmiṁ samaye viharati.... (For full text of abbreviated portions see note 2 on page 157).

practice of the four foundations of mindfulness, the seven enlightenment factors are fulfilled.[1]

How are freedom and wisdom fulfilled through the practice of the seven enlightenment factors? The yogin who has practised the seven enlightenment factors much, gains in a moment[2] the wisdom of the Path and the Fruit of freedom. Thus because of the practice of the seven enlightenment factors, wisdom and freedom are fulfilled.[3]

A. All formations[4] are endowed with initial and sustained application of thought according to planes.[5] That being so, why is only initial application

---

1. S. V, 331-33: *Yasmiṁ samaye Ānanda bhikkhu kāye kāyānupassī viharati upaṭṭhitasati, tasmiṁ Ānanda bhikkhuno sati hoti asammuṭṭhā; yasmiṁ samaye Ānanda bhikkhuno upaṭṭhitasati asammuṭṭhā, satisambojjhaṅgo tasmiṁ samaye bhikkhuno āraddho hoti; satisambojjhaṅgaṁ tasmiṁ samaye Ānanda bhikkhu bhāveti; satisambojjhaṅgo tasmiṁ samaye bhikkhuno bhāvanā pāripūriṁ gacchati; so tathā sato viharanto taṁ dhammaṁ paññāya pavicinati pavicarati parivīmaṁsaṁ āpajjati.*

Yasmiṁ samaye Ānanda bhikkhu tathā sato viharanto taṁ dhammaṁ paññāya pavicinati pavicarati parivīmaṁsaṁ āpajjati; dhammavicayasambojjhaṅgo tasmiṁ samaye bhikkhuno āraddho hoti; dhammavicayasambojjhaṅgaṁ tasmiṁ samaye bhikkhu bhāveti. Dhammavicayasambojjhaṅgo tasmiṁ samaye bhikkhuno bhāvanāpāripūriṁ gacchati; tassa taṁ dhammaṁ paññāya pavicinato pavicarato parivīmaṁsaṁ āpajjato āraddhaṁ hoti viriyaṁ asallīnaṁ.

Yasmiṁ samaye Ānanda bhikkhuno taṁ dhammaṁ paññāya pavicinato pavicarato parivīmaṁsaṁ āpajjato āraddhaṁ hoti viriyaṁ asallīnaṁ, viriyasambojjhaṅgo tasmiṁ samaye bhikkhuno āraddho hoti; viriyasambojjhangaṁ tasmiṁ samaye bhikkhu bhāveti; viriyasambojjhaṅgo tasmiṁ samaye bhikkhuno bhāvanā pāripūriṁ gacchati; āraddhaviriyassa uppajjati pīti nirāmisā.

Yasmiṁ samaye Ānanda bhikkhuno āraddhaviriyassa uppajjati pīti nirāmisā pītisambojjhaṅgo tasmiṁ samaye Ānanda bhikkhuno āraddho hoti, pītisambojjhaṅgaṁ tasmiṁ samaye bhikkhu bhāveti; pītisambojjhaṅgo tasmiṁ samaye bhikkhuno bhāvanā pāripūriṁ gacchati; pītimanassa kāyo pi passambhati cittaṁ pi passambhati.

Yasmiṁ samaye Ānanda bhikkhuno pītimanassa kāyo pi passambhati cittam pi passambhati, passaddhisambojjhaṅgo tasmiṁ samaye bhikkhuno āraddho hoti; passaddhisambojjhaṅgaṁ tasmiṁ samaye bhikkhu bhāveti; passaddhisambojjhaṅgo tasmiṁ samaye bhikkhuno bhāvanā pāripūriṁ gacchati; passaddhakāyassa sukhino cittaṁ samādhiyati.

Yasmiṁ samaye Ānanda bhikkhuno passaddhakāyassa sukhino cittaṁ samādhiyati, samādhisambhojjhaṅgo tasmiṁ samaye bhikkhuno āraddho hoti; samādhisambojjhaṅgaṁ tasmiṁ samaye bhikkhu bhāveti; samādhisambojjhaṅgo tasmiṁ samaye bhikkhuno bhāvanā pāripūriṁ gacchati. So tathā samāhitaṁ cittaṁ sādhukaṁ ajjhupekkhitā hoti.

Yasmiṁ samaye Ānanda bhikkhu tathā samāhitaṁ cittaṁ sādhukaṁ ajjhupekkhitā hoti, upekhāsambojjhaṅgo tasmiṁ samaye bhikkhuno āraddho hoti; upekhāsambojjhaṅgaṁ tasmiṁ samaye bhikkhu bhāveti; upekhāsambojjhaṅgo tasmiṁ samaye bhikkhuno bhāvanā pāripūriṁ gacchati.

Yasmiṁ samaye Ānanda bhikkhu vedanāsu, citte, dhammesu dhammānupassī viharati upaṭṭhitasati tasmiṁ samaye Ānanda bhikkhuno sati hoti asammuṭṭhā.

Yasmiṁ samaye Ānanda bhikkhuno upaṭṭhitasati hoti asammuṭṭhā, satisambojjhaṅgo tasmiṁ samaye bhikkhuno āraddho hoti, satisambojjhaṅgaṁ tasmiṁ samaye bhikkhu bhāveti; satisambojjhaṅgo tasmiṁ samaye bhikkhuno bhāvanā pāripūriṁ gacchati. Yathā paṭhamaṁ satipaṭṭhānaṁ evaṁ vitthāretabbaṁ. So tathā samāhitaṁ cittaṁ sādhukaṁ ajjhupekkhitā hoti.

Yasmiṁ samaye Ānanda bhikkhu tathā samāhitaṁ cittaṁ sādhukaṁ ajjhupekkhitā hoti, upekhāsambojjhaṅgo tasmiṁ samaye bhikkhuno āraddho hoti; upekhāsambojjhaṅgaṁ tasmiṁ samaye bhikkhu bhāveti, upekhāsambojjhaṅgo tasmiṁ samaye bhikkhuno bhāvanā pāripūriṁ gacchati.

Evaṁ bhāvitā kho Ānanda cattāro satipaṭṭhānā evaṁ bahulīkathā sattabojjhaṅge paripūrenti.

2. *Kshaṇa* (transliteration).

3. Cp. S. V, 333; *Kathaṁ bhāvitā ca sattabojjhaṅgā kathaṁ bahulīkathā vijjāvimuttiṁ paripūrenti?*
Idhānanda bhikkhu satisambojjhaṅgaṁ bhāveti vivekanissitaṁ....pe....uphekhāsambojjhaṅgaṁ bhāveti vivekanissitaṁ virāganissitaṁ nirodhanissitaṁ vossaggapariṇāmiṁ.
'Evam bhāvitā kho Ānanda sattabojjhaṅgā evaṁ bahulīkatā vijjāvimuttiṁ paripūrentiti.

4. *Saṅkhārā.*

5. *Bhūmi.*

of thought suppressed in mindfulness of respiration, and not the other?

A. It[1] is used here in a different sense. Discursiveness is a hindrance to meditation, *jhāna*. In this sense, it[2] is suppressed.

Why is air contact pleasant? Because it calms the mind. It is comparable to the soothing of a heavenly musician's (gandhabba's) mind with sweet sounds. By this discursive thinking is suppressed. And again, it is like a person walking along the bank of a river. His mind is collected, is directed towards one object and does not wander. Therefore in mindfulness of respiration, the suppression of discursive thinking is taught.[3]

Mindfulness of respiration has ended.[4]

MINDFULNESS OF DEATH

Q. What is mindfulness of death? What is the practising of it? What are its salient characteristic, function and near cause? What are its benefits? What is the procedure?

A. The cutting off of the life-faculty — this is called death. The undisturbed mindfulness of this — this is called the practising of it. The cutting off of one's life is its salient characteristic. Disagreeableness is its function. Well-being is its near cause.

What are its benefits? He who practises mindfulness of death is possessed of diligence as regards the higher meritorious states, and of dislike as regards the demeritorious. He does not hoard clothes and ornaments. He is not stingy. He is able to live long, does not cling to things, is endowed with the perception of impermanence, the perception of subjection to ill and the perception of not-self. He fares well and approaches the ambrosial. When he comes to die, he does not suffer bewilderment.

What is the procedure? The new yogin enters a place of solitude and guards his thoughts. He considers the death of beings with mind undistracted thus: "I shall die; I shall enter the realm of death; I shall not escape death". Thus it is taught in the Nettipada Sutta:[5] "If a man wishes to meditate on death, he should contemplate a person who is on the point of being killed and he should know the causes of death".

Here there are four kinds in mindfulness of death: (1) Associated with anxiety. (2) Associated with fear. (3) Associated with indifference. (4) Associated with wisdom.

The mindfulness associated with the loss of one's own beloved child is associated with anxiety. The mindfulness connected with the sudden death

1. and 2. indicate *vitakka*.
3. (*a*) Vis. Mag. 291 quotes A. IV, 353: *Ānāpānasati bhāvetabbā vitakkūpacchedāya.*
   (*b*) A. III, 449: *Cetaso vikkhepassa pahānāya ānāpānasati bhāvetabbā.*
4. This and the subsequent passages in italics in this section do not occur in the Sung Dynasty edition mentioned earlier.
5. Transliteration, *Netri-pada-sūtra;* probably refers to *Netri-pada-śāstra* of *Upagupta* referred to in *Abhidharmakośa śāstra.*

of one's own child is associated with fear. The mindfulness of death by a burner (of corpses) is associated with indifference. Remembering (the nature of) the world, one develops aversion — this is called associated with wisdom. Here the yogin should not practise the mindfulness associated with anxiety, fear or indifference, because [432] through them he is not able to remove tribulation. Tribulation can only be removed through the mindfulness associated with wisdom.

There are three kinds of death thus: death according to general opinion, death as a complete cutting off, momentary death. What is "death according to general opinion"? Death as it is understood in common parlance. This is called "death according to general opinion". "Death as a complete cutting off" means: "The Consummate One has cut off the defilements". "Momentary death" means: "The momentary perishing of all formations".[1]

And again, there are two kinds in death: untimely death and timely death. Death through suicide, murder or disease, or through being cut off in the prime of life without (assignable) cause is called untimely death. Death through the exhaustion of the life-span or through old age is called timely death.[2] One should recall to mind these two kinds of death.

And again, predecessor-teachers[3] have taught the practice of mindfulness of death in these eight ways:[4] through the presence of a murderer; through the absence of an efficient cause;* through inference; through the body being common to the many; through the weakness of the life-principle; through the distinguishing of time; through the absence of the sign; through the shortness of the moment. How should one practise mindfulness of death "through the presence of a murderer"? *A.* Like a man who is being taken to a place to be killed. When that man sees the murderer drawing out a sword and following him, he thinks thus: "This man intends to kill me; I shall be killed at any moment; I shall be killed at any step. I shall surely be killed if I turn back. I shall surely be killed if I sit down; I shall surely be killed if I sleep". Thus should the yogin practise mindfulness of death "through the presence of a murderer". *Q.* How should one practise mindfulness of death "through the absence of an efficient cause"? There is no cause or skill that can make life immortal. When the sun and the moon rise, no cause or skill can make them turn back. Thus the yogin practises mindfulness of death. *Q.* How does one practise mindfulness of death "through inference"? *A.* Many kings who possessed great treasures, great vehicle-kings, Mahā Sudassana of great supernormal power, Mandhātu and all other kings entered the state of death. And again, many sages of old, Vessamitta and Yamataggi, who possessed

---

1. Cp. Vis. Mag. 229: *Yaṁ pan'etaṁ arahantānaṁ vaṭṭadukkhasamucchedasankhātaṁ samucchedamaraṇaṁ, sankhārānaṁ khaṇabhangasankhātaṁ khaṇikamaraṇaṁ, rukkho mato, lohaṁ mataṁ ti ādisu sammutimaraṇañ ca, na tam idha adhippetaṁ.*
2. Cp. Ibid: *Kālamaraṇa* and *akālamaraṇa.*
3. *Porāṇakācariyā.*
4. *Vadhakapaccupaṭṭhānato, sampattivipattito* (?), *upasaṁharaṇato, kāyabahusādhāraṇato, āyudubbalato, addhānaparicchedato, animittato, khaṇaparittato.* Cp. Vis. Mag. 230.

* This is different from Vis. Mag.

great supernormal power and who caused fire and water to issue forth from their bodies, also entered the state of death. Great hearers of old like the Venerable Elders Sāriputta, Moggallāna and others, who were possessed of immense wisdom and power also entered the state of death. Many Pacceka-buddhas who attained enlightenment without owning a teacher, and who were endowed with all virtue, also entered the state of death. And again, they who come and go in the same way, the Consummate, Supremely Enlightened, Matchless Ones, endowed with knowledge and conduct, who have won the further shore of merit — many such also entered the state of death. How shall I with my brief life-span escape entry into the state of death? Thus the yogin practises mindfulness of death "through inference". *Q*. How does one practise mindfulness of death" through the body being common to the many"? *A*. Through the disorder of wind and phlegm, the state of death is fulfilled. Through the disturbance of many worms or through lack of drink and food, the state of death is fulfilled. Or through being bitten by poisonous snakes, centipedes, millepedes, or rats, death is fulfilled. Or through being mauled by a lion, a tiger or a leopard, or through being attacked by a demon (nāga), or through being gored by a cow, death is fulfilled. Or through being killed by humans or non-humans, death is fulfilled. Thus one practises mindfulness of death "through the body being common to the many". *Q*. How does one practise mindfulness of death "through the weakness of the life-principle"? *A*. In two ways one practises mindfulness of death through the weakness of the life-principle. Through the state of being placed in powerlessness and through dependence on the powerless, the weakness of the life-principle is fulfilled.

SIMILES OF THE FOAM, PLANTAIN TRUNK AND BUBBLE

Q. How is the life-principle weak through its being placed in powerlessness? *A*. There is no substantiality in this body as it is taught in the simile of the foam, in the simile of the plantain trunk and in the simile of the bubble,[1] because it is devoid of reality and it is separate from reality. Thus through the state of being placed in powerlessness, the life-principle is weak. *Q*. How is the life-principle weak through dependence on the powerless? *A*. This is kept together by the incoming breath and the outgoing breath, by the four great primaries, by drink and food, by four postures and by warmth. Thus it depends on the powerless. Therefore the life-principle is weak. Thus one practises mindfulness of death "through the weakness of the life-principle" in two ways. *Q*. How does one practise mindfulness of death "through the distinguishing of time"? *A*. All beings were born is the past (and suffered death). At present, (nearly) all enter the state of death without

1. S. III, 142: *Pheṇapiṇḍūpamaṁ rūpaṁ, vedanā bubbulupamā;*
Marīcikūpamā saññā, saṅkhārā kadalūpamā;
Māyūpamañca viññāṇaṁ dīpitādiccabandhunā.
For details of the similes see the earlier portion of the sutta.

reaching a hundred years. Thus one practises mindfulness of death "through the distinguishing of time". And again one practises thus: "I wonder whether it is possible for me to live a day and a night. I wonder whether during that time I could think on the teaching of the Blessed One—could I have that opportunity! I wonder whether I could live even for a day. Or could I live for half a day, or for a short while. Could I live long enough to partake of a single meal, half a meal, or even long enough to gather and partake of four or five morsels of food! Could I live long enough to breathe out having breathed in, or could I live long enough to breathe in having breathed out".[1] (Thus) one practises mindfulness of death "through the distinguishing of time".

Q. How does one practise mindfulness of death "through the absence of the sign"? *A.* There is no sign. Therefore there is no fixed time for death. Thus one practises mindfulness of death "through the absence of the sign". *Q.* How does one practise mindfulness of death "through the shortness of the moment"?[2] *A.* If one reckons the causes of the present and not those of the past or the future, beings exist but a single conscious moment. Nothing exists for two moments. Thus all beings sink in the conscious moment.[3] It is taught in the *Abhidhamma* thus: "In the past

---

1. A. III, 305-6: *Yvāyaṁ bhikkhave bhikkhu evaṁ maraṇasatiṁ bhāveti 'aho vatāhaṁ rattindivaṁ jīveyyaṁ, Bhagavato sāsanaṁ manasikareyyaṁ, bahu vata me kataṁ assā' ti, yo cāyaṁ bhikkhave bhikkhu evaṁ maraṇasatiṁ bhāveti 'aho vatāhaṁ divasaṁ jīveyyaṁ Bhagavato sāsanaṁ manasikareyyaṁ bahu vata me kataṁ assā' ti, yo cāyaṁ bhikkhave bhikkhu evaṁ maraṇasatiṁ bhāveti 'aho vatāhaṁ tadantaraṁ jīveyyaṁ yadantaraṁ ekaṁ piṇḍapātaṁ bhuñjāmi, Bhagavato sāsanaṁ manasikareyyaṁ, bahu vata me kataṁ assā' ti, yo cāyaṁ bhikkhave bhikkhu evaṁ maraṇasatiṁ bhāveti 'aho vatāhaṁ tadantaraṁ jīveyyaṁ yadantaraṁ cattāro pañca ālope saṁkhāditvā ajjhoharāmi, Bhagavato sāsanaṁ manasikareyyaṁ, bahu vata me kataṁ assā' ti; ime vuccanti bhikkhave bhikkhū: pamattā viharanti, dandhaṁ maraṇasatiṁ bhāventi āsavānaṁ khayāya.*
   Yo ca khvāyaṁ bhikkhave bhikkhu evaṁ maraṇasatiṁ bhāveti 'aho vatāhaṁ tadantaraṁ jīveyyaṁ yadantaraṁ ekam ālopaṁ saṁkhāditvā ajjhoharāmi, Bhagavato sāsanaṁ manasikareyyam, bahu vata me kataṁ assā' ti, yo cāyaṁ bhikkhave bhikkhu evaṁ maraṇasatim bhāveti 'aho vatāhaṁ tadantaraṁ jīveyyaṁ yadantaraṁ assasitvā vā passasāmi passasitvā vā assasāmi, Bhagavato sāsanaṁ manasikareyyaṁ bahu vata me kataṁ assā' ti; ime vuccanti bhikkhave bhikkhū: appamattā viharanti, tikkhaṁ maraṇasatiṁ bhāventi āsavānaṁ khayāya. Tasmā ti ha bhikkhave evaṁ sikkhitabbaṁ:—
   Appamattā viharissāma, tikkhaṁ maraṇasatiṁ bhāvessāma āsavānaṁ khayāyā ti.
   Evaṁ hi vo bhikkhave sikkhitabban ti.
2. Transliteration of *kṣaṇa*. 120 *kṣaṇas* = 1 *tatkṣaṇa*; 60 *tatkṣaṇas* = 1 *lava*; 30 *lavas* = 1 *muhūrta*; 30 *muhūrtas* = 1 day and 1 night. (*Abhidharmakośa*, Fascicle 12). Therefore

   $$1\ kṣaṇa = \frac{24 \times 60 \times 60}{30 \times 30 \times 60 \times 120} = \frac{1}{75} = 0.0133\ldots\ldots \text{of a second.}$$

   The following is given in the *Dīrgha Āgama*, No. 22, Taisho Edition, p. 146:— 60 *khaṇas* = 1 *laya*; 30 *layas* = 1 *muhutta*; 100 *muhuttas* = 1 *upamā*. Below are two other tables:—
   (*a*) 60 *kṣaṇas* = 1 *lava*; 30 *lavas* = 1 hour; 30 hours = 1 day;

   $$1\ kṣaṇa = \frac{24 \times 60 \times 60}{30 \times 30 \times 60} = 1.6 \text{ seconds.}$$

   (*b*) 120 *kṣaṇas* = 1 *tatkṣaṇa*; 60 *tatkṣaṇas* = 1 *lava*; 30 *lavas* = 1 *muhūrta*; 50 *muhūrtas* = 1 hour; 6 hours = 1 day;

   $$1\ kṣaṇa = \frac{24 \times 60 \times 60}{6 \times 50 \times 30 \times 60 \times 120} = \frac{1}{750} = 0.0013\ldots \text{of a second.}$$

3. *Cittakkhaṇa.*

conscious moment, one did not live, one is not living, one will not live. In the future conscious moment, one did not live, one is not living, one will not live. In the present conscious moment, one did not live, one will not live, only one is living".[1]

And again, it is taught in this stanza:

"*Life and personality, sorrow, happiness and all*
are joined to one thought; quickly the moment passes.
By the yet-not-become, nothing is born; by the present one lives.
When mind's shattered, the world dies;[2] *so the world's end was taught*".

Thus one practises mindfulness of death through the shortness of the moment. That yogin through these ways practises mindfulness of death and develops (the perception of) disagreeableness. Owing to facility in (the perception of) disagreeableness and owing to facility in mindfulness, his mind is not disturbed. When his mind is undisturbed, he is able to destroy the hindrances and cause the arising of the meditation (*jhāna*) factors and attain to access-concentration.

Q. What is the difference between the perception of impermanence and mindfulness of death?

A. The perception of the passing away of the aggregations is called the perception of impermanence. The mindfulness of the destruction of the faculties is called mindfulness of death. The practice of the perception of impermanence and the perception of not-self is called the rejection of pride. He who practises mindfulness of death can dwell in the perception of impermanence and the perception of subjection to ill through the thought of the cutting off of life and the destruction of the mind. These are the differences between them.

Mindfulness of death has ended.

MINDFULNESS OF BODY

Q. What is mindfulness of body? What is the practising of it? What are its salient characteristic and function? What are its benefits? What is the procedure?

---

1. Looked at from the point of view of the changing *khandhas*, there is no important divergence to be noted here. For instance, in Vis. Mag. 301 this occurs:
Khaṇikattā ca dhammānaṁ, yehi khandhehi te kataṁ
amanāpaṁ niruddhā te kassa dāni 'dha kujjhasi?
The so-called being of the present did not exist in the past and will not exist in the future.
2. Nd[1]. 42, 117-18: *Jīvitaṁ attabhāvo ca sukhadukkhā ca kevalā*
ekacittasamāyuttā lahuso vattati-kkhaṇo.
....
Anibbattena na jāto, paccuppannena jīvati,
cittabhaṅgamato loko.......................

A. Mindfulness as regards the nature of the body is the practising of it. That mindfulness is mindfulness and right mindfulness. Thus is mindfulness of body to be understood. The undisturbed dwelling of the mind in this mindfulness is the practising of it. The becoming manifest of the nature of the body is its salient characteristic. The perception of disagreeableness is its function. The indication of the unreal is its manifestation.[1]

What are its benefits? A man who practises mindfulness of body can endure. He can bear to see the fearful and he can bear heat, cold and the like. He is endowed with the perception of impermanence, the perception of not-self, the perception of impurity and the perception of tribulation. He attains to the four meditations, *jhānas*, with ease, gains a clear view of things, is pleased with his practice, fares well and approaches the ambrosial.

What is the procedure? The new yogin enters a place of solitude, sits down and guards his thoughts. With mind undisturbed, he meditates on the nature of his body. How does he practise mindfulness of body?

THIRTY-TWO PARTS OF THE BODY

This body consists of head-hair, body-hair, nails, teeth, skin, flesh, sinews, bones, marrow, kidneys, liver, heart, spleen, lungs, bile, gorge, grease, fat, brain,[2] midriff, intestines, mesentery, excrement, urine, pus, blood, phlegm, sweat, synovial fluid, tears, nasal mucus, saliva, and is impure. The new yogin at first should recite vocally these thirty-two parts of the body in the direct and in the reverse order. He should always vocally recite well and investigate these (thirty-two parts). Vocally reciting well he should investigate always. Thereafter he should reflect on them only mentally in these four ways: through colour, through the formations, the form, the basis. He may, with discrimination, take one or two [433] or more and grasp the crude sign. Thus the yogin is able to cause the manifestation of three trends of thought, namely, of colour, of disliking and of space. When the yogin causes the arising of the sign through colour, he is able to meditate with facility through the colour *kasiṇa*. When he causes the arising of the sign through disliking he is able to meditate with facility on impurity. When the yogin causes the arising of the sign through space, he is able to meditate with facility on the elements. If the yogin practises on the *kasiṇas*, he will get to the fourth meditation, *jhāna*. If the yogin practises on impurity, he will get to the first meditation, *jhāna*. If he practises on the elements, he will get to access-concentration.

Here a walker in hate causes the manifestation of the sign through colour; a walker in passion, through disliking; and a walker in wisdom, through the elements. And again, a walker in hate should meditate through colour; a

---

1. This is not among the questions.
2. M. I, 57; III, 90; D. II, 293-94; Vbh. 193: (*matthalunga* does not occur in these references:—) *Atthi imasmiṁ kāye kesā lomā nakhā dantā taco maṁsaṁ nahārū aṭṭhī aṭṭhimiñjā vakkaṁ hadayaṁ yakanaṁ kilomakaṁ pihakaṁ papphāsaṁ antaṁ antaguṇaṁ udariyaṁ karīsaṁ pittaṁ semhaṁ pubbo lohitaṁ sedo medo assu vasā kheḷo siṅghānikā lasikā muttan ti.*

walker in passion, through disliking and a walker in wisdom, through the elements.

MINDFULNESS IN THIRTEEN WAYS

And again, one should recall to mind the nature of the body through thirteen ways: through seed, place, condition, oozing, gradual formation, worms, connection,[1] assemblage, loathsomeness, impurity, dependence, non-awareness of obligation, finitude.

Q. How should a man reflect on the nature of the body through "seed"?

A. As elaeagnus pungens, *kosātakī**,[2] and the like burn, so this body produced from the impure seed of parents also burns. This is impure. Thus one should recall to mind the nature of the body through "seed".

Q. How should one reflect on the nature of the body through "place"? *A.* This body does not come out of *uppala*,*[3] *kumuda**[4] or *puṇḍarīka*.*[5] This comes out of the place where impurity, malodour and uncleanness are pressed together. This body lies across the womb from left to right. It leans against the back-bone of the mother, wrapped in the caul. This place is impure. Therefore the body is also impure. Thus should one recall the nature of the body through "place".[6]

Q. How should one reflect on the nature of the body through "condition"? *A.* This body is not fed with gold, silver or gems. It does not grow up through being fed with *candana**,[7] *tagara**,[8] aloe-wood and the like. This body grows in the womb of the mother and is mixed with nasal mucus, saliva, slobber and the tears which the mother swallows. This body is nourished with foul-smelling food and drink produced in the mother's womb. Rice, milk,[9] beans, nasal mucus, saliva, slobber and phlegm which are swallowed by the mother form part of this body. On malodorous, filthy fluid is this brought up. Thus should one recall to mind the nature of the body through "condition".

Q. How should one reflect on the nature of the body through "oozing"? *A.* This body is like a bag of skin with many holes exuding filth and urine. This body is filled with filth and urine. This body is a conglomeration of drink and food taken in, of nasal mucus, saliva, filth and urine. These various

---

1. Lit. "dwelling peacefully". Cp Vis. Mag. 355, under *Aṭṭhīsu*, where "*ukkipitvā ṭhitaṁ*" "*patiṭṭhitaṁ*" are used in a similar description.
* Transliteration.
2. Trichosanthes dioeca, or luffa acutangula or luffa petandra.
3. Blue lotus (Nymphaea Coerulea). 4. Edible white water-lily (Nymphaea esculenta).
5. White lotus (Nymphaea Alba).
6. Vbh.-a. 96: *Ayaṁ hi satto mātuhucchimhi nibbattamāno na uppala-paduma-puṇḍarīkādisu nibbattati; attha kho heṭṭhā āmāsayassa upari pakkāsayassa, udarapaṭala-piṭṭhikaṇṭakā-naṁ vemajjhe, paramasambādhe, tibbandhakāre, nānākuṇapagandha-paribhāvite, asuci-paramaduggandha-pavana-vicarite, adhimattajegucche kucchippadese pūtimaccha-pūtikum-māsa-candanikādisu kimi viya nibbattati.*
7. Sandal wood. 8. The fragrant powder of the shrub Tabernaemontana coronaria.
9. Unintelligible.

impurities ooze from the nine openings.[1] Thus should one recall to mind the nature of the body through "oozing".

Q. How should one reflect on the nature of the body through "gradual formation"? *A.* This body gradually forms itself according to its previous *kamma*. In the first week the *kalala** is formed.

In the second week the *abbuda** is formed.
In the third week the *pesi** is formed.
In the fourth week the *ghana** is formed.
In the fifth week five parts[2] are formed.
In the sixth week four parts are formed.
In the seventh week again four parts are formed.
In the eighth week again twenty-eight parts are formed.
In the ninth and tenth weeks the backbone is formed.
In the eleventh week three hundred bones are formed.
In the twelfth week eight hundred parts are formed.
In the thirteenth week nine hundred parts are formed,
In the fourteenth week one hundred lumps of flesh are formed.
In the fifteenth week blood is formed.
In the sixteenth week the midriff is formed.
In the seventeenth week the skin is formed.
In the eighteenth week the colour of the skin is formed.
In the nineteenth week the wind according to *kamma* fills the body.
In the twentieth week the nine orifices are formed.
In the twenty-fifth week the seventeen thousand textures of the skin are formed.
In the twenty-sixth week the body is endowed with hardness.
In the twenty-seventh week the body is endowed with the powers.
In the twenty-eighth week the ninety-nine thousand pores are produced.

In the twenty-ninth week the whole is completed. And again it is taught that in the seventh week the child's body is complete, that it leans back with hanging head in a crouching position. In the forty-second week, by the aid of the *kamma*-produced wind, it reverses its position, turns its feet upwards and its head down and goes to the gate of birth. At this time it is born. In the world it is commonly known as a being. Thus one should reflect on the nature of the body through "gradual formation".[3]

---

1. Cp. (*a*) Sn. 197: *Ath' assa navahi sotehi asucī savati sabbadā.*
(*b*) Th. 1134: *Na jātu bhastaṁ dubhato mukhaṁ chupe;*
dhiratthu pūraṁ navasotasandani.
(*c*) Th. 394: *Āturaṁ asuciṁ pūtiṁ passa Kulla samussayaṁ*
uggharantaṁ paggharantaṁ bālānaṁ abhinanditaṁ.

* Transliterations. These are stages of the embryo.

2. *Pasākhā.*

3. Cp. S. I, 206: *Paṭhamaṁ kalalaṁ hoti, kalalā hoti abbudaṁ,*
abbudā jāyate pesī, pesī nibbattati ghano,
ghanā pasākhā jāyanti, kesā lomā nakhāni ca.
Yañ cassa bhuñjate mātā, annaṁ pānañ ca bhojanaṁ,
tena so tattha yāpeti, mātukucchigato naro ti.
(—*Tattha paṭhaman ti, paṭhamena paṭisandhi-viññāṇena saddhiṁ Tisso ti vā Phusso ti vā nāmaṁ n' atthi. Atha kho tīhi jāti-uṇṇ' aṁsūhi kata-sutt' agge saṇṭhita-tela-binduppamāṇaṁ*

THE WORMS THAT RELY ON THE BODY

Q. How should one reflect on the nature of the body through "worms"?

A. This body is gnawn by eighty thousand worms. The worm that relies on the hair is called "hair-iron". The worm that relies on the skull is called "swollen ear". The worm that relies on the brain is called "maddener". In this class there are four kinds. The first is called *ukurimba.** The second is called *shibara.** The third is called *daraka.** The fourth is called *dakashira.** The worm that relies on the eye is called "eye-licker". The worm that relies on the ear is called "ear-licker". The worm that relies on the nose is called "nose-licker". There are three kinds here. The first is called *rukamuka.** The second is called *aruka.**[1] The third is called *manarumuka.** The worm that relies on the tongue is called *muka.** The worm that relies on the root of the tongue is called *motanta.** The worm that relies on the teeth is called *kuba.** The worm that relies on the roots of the teeth is called *ubakuba.** The worm that relies on the throat is called *abasaka.** The worms that rely on the neck are of two kinds. The first is called *rokara.** The second is called *virokara.** The worm that relies on the hair of the body

---

kalalṁ hotī ti. Yaṁ sandhāya vuttaṁ:—
Tila-telassa yathā bindu, sappi-maṇḍo anāvilo,
evaṁ vaṇṇa-paṭibhāgaṁ kalalaṁ sampavuccatī ti.

Kalalā hoti abbudan ti, tasmā kalalā sattāh' accayena maṁsa-dhovana-udaka-vaṇṇaṁ abbudaṁ nāma hoti. Kalalan ti nāmaṁ antaradhāyati. Vuttam hi c' etaṁ:—
Sattāhaṁ kalalaṁ hoti paripakkaṁ samūhataṁ,
vivaṭṭamānaṁ taṁ bhāvaṁ abbudaṁ nāma jāyatī ti.

Abbudā jāyate pesī ti, tasmā pi abbudā sattāh' accayena vilīna-tipu-sadisā pesī nāma sañjāyati. Sā marica-phāṇitena dīpetabbā. Gāma-dārakā hi supakkāni maricāni gahetvā, sāṭak' ante bhaṇḍikaṁ katvā, pīḷetvā maṇḍaṁ ādāya, kapāle pakkhipitvā, ātape ṭhapenti. Taṁ sukkamānaṁ sabba-bhāgehi muccati. Evarūpā pesī hoti. Abbudan ti nāmaṁ antaradhāyati. Vuttam pi c'etaṁ:—

Sattāhaṁ abbudaṁ hoti paripakkaṁ samūhataṁ,
vivaṭṭamānaṁ taṁ bhāvaṁ pesī nāma ca jāyatī ti.

Pesī nibattati ghano ti, tato pesito sattāh' accayena kukkuṭ' aṇḍasaṇṭhāno ghano nāma maṁsa-piṇḍo nibbattati. Pesī ti nāmaṁ antaradhāyati. Vuttam pi c'etaṁ:—
Sattāhaṁ pesī bhavati paripakkaṁ samūhataṁ,
vivaṭṭamānaṁ taṁ bhāvaṁ ghano ti nāma jāyatī ti.

Yathā kukkuṭiyā aṇḍaṁ samantā parimaṇḍalaṁ,
evaṁ ghanassa saṇṭhānaṁ nibbattaṁ kamma-paccayā ti.

Ghanā pasākhā jāyantī ti, pañcame sattāhe dvinnaṁ hattha-pādānaṁ sīsassa c' atthāya pañca piḷakā jāyanti. Yaṁ sandhāy' etaṁ vuttaṁ: "Pañcame, bhikkhave, sattāhe pañca piḷakā saṇṭhahanti kammato" (?) ti. Ito paraṁ chaṭṭha-sattamādīni sattāhāni atikkamma desanaṁ sankhipitvā dvācattāḷise sattāhe pariṇata-kālaṁ gahetvā dassento kesā ti ādim āha.

Tattha kesā lomā nakhāni cā ti, dvā-cattāḷise sattāhe etāni jāyanti. Tena so tattha yāpetī ti, tassa hi nābhito uṭṭhahitanālo mātu-udara-paṭalena ekābaddho hoti. So uppaḷa-daṇḍako viya chiddo. Tena āhāra-raso saṁsaritvā āhārāsamuṭṭhāna-rūpaṁ samuṭṭhāpeti. Evan so dasamāse yāpeti. Mātu-kucchigato naro ti, mātuyā tiro-kucchi-gato, kucchiyā abbhantara-gato ti attho. Iti Bhagavā 'evaṁ kho, yakkha, ayaṁ satto anupubbena mātu-kucchiyaṁ vaḍḍhati, na ekappahāren' eva nibbattatī' ti dasseti.—Spk. I, 300-1).

* Transliterations.

1. Cp. (*a*) S. IV, 198: *Seyyathāpi bhikkhave puriso arugatto pakkagatto saravanaṁ paviseyya; tassa kusakaṇṭakā ceva pāde vijjheyyuṁ arupakkāni gattāni vilikkheyyuṁ.*
   (*b*) M. I., 506: *Seyyathāpi Māgandiya kuṭṭhī puriso arugatto pakkagatto kimīhi khajjamāno nakhehi vaṇamukhāni vippatacchamāno.....*
   (c) Mil 357: *Arugatta-pakkagatto puḷuvākiṇṇa-sabbakāyo.*

is called "body-hair licker". The worm that relies on the nails is called "nail-licker". The worms that rely on the skin are of two kinds. The first is called *tuna.** The second is called *tunanda.** The worms that rely on the midriff are of two kinds. The first is called *viramba.** The second is called *mavirambà.** The worms that rely on the flesh are of two kinds. The first is called *araba.** The second is called *raba.** The worms that rely on the blood are of two kinds. The first is called *bara.** The second is called *badara.** The worms that rely on the tendons are of four kinds. The first is called *rotara.** The second is called *kitaba.** The third is called *baravatara.** The fourth is called *ranavarana.** The worm that relies on the veins is called *karikuna.** The worms that rely on the roots of the veins are of two kinds. The first is called *sivara.** The second is called *ubasisira.** The worms that rely on the bones are of four kinds. The first is called *kachibida.** The second is called *anabida.** The third is called *chiridabida.** The fourth is called *kachigokara.** The worms that rely on the marrow are of two kinds. The first is called *bisha.** The second is called *bishashira.** The worms that rely on the spleen are of two kinds. The first is called *nira.** The second is called *bita.** The worms that rely on the heart are of two kinds. The first is called *sibita.** The second is called *ubadabita.** The worms that rely on the root of the heart are of two kinds. The first is called *manka.** The second is called *sira.** The worms that rely on the fat are of two kinds. The first is called *kara.** The second is called *karasira.** The worms that rely on the bladder are of two kinds. The first is called *bikara.** The second is called *mahakara.** The worms that rely on the root of the bladder are of two kinds. The first is called *kara.** The second is called *karasira.** The worms that rely on the belly are of two kinds. The first is called *rata.** The second is called *maharata.** The worms that rely on the mesentery are of two kinds. The first is called *sorata** The second is called *maharata.** The worms that rely on the root of the mesentery are of two kinds. The first is called (*si-*) *ba.** The second is called *mahasiba.** The worms that rely on the intestines are of two kinds. The first is called *anabaka.** The second is called *kababaka.** The worms that rely on the stomach are of four kinds. The first is called *ujuka.** The second is called *ushaba.** The third is called *chishaba.** The fourth is called *senshiba.** The worms that rely on the ripened womb are of four kinds. The first is called *vakana.** The second is called *mahavakana.** The third is called *unaban.** The fourth is called *punamaka.** The worm that relies on the bile is called *hitasoka.** The worm that relies on saliva is called *senka.** The worm that relies on sweat is called *sudasaka.** The worm that relies on oil is called *jidasaka.** The worms that rely on vitality are of two kinds. The first is called *subakama.** The second is called *samakita.** The worms that rely on the root of vitality are of three kinds. The first is called *sukamuka.** The second is called *darukamuka.** The third is called *sanamuka.** There are five[1] kinds of

* Transliterations.

1. Only four are explained below.

worms: those that rely on the front of the body and gnaw the front of the body; those that rely on the back of the body and gnaw the back of the body; those that rely on the left side of the body and gnaw the left side of the body; those that rely on the right side of the body and gnaw the right side of the body. These worms are called *candasira,** *sinkasira,** *hucura** and so forth. There are three kinds of worms that rely on the two lower orifices. The first is called *kurukulayuyu.** The second is called *sarayu** The third is called *kandupada.** Thus one should recall to mind the nature of the body through "worms".

Q. How should one reflect on the nature of the body through "connection"? *A*. The shin-bone is connected with the foot-bone; the shin-bone is connected with the thigh-bone; the thigh-bone is connected with the hip-bone; the hip-bone is connected with the backbone; the backbone is connected with the shoulder-blade; the shoulder-blade is connected with the humerus; the humerus is connected with the neck-bone; the neck-bone is connected with the skull; the skull is connected with the cheek-bones. The cheek-bones are connected with the teeth. Thus by the connection of the bones and the covering of the skin, this unclean body is kept in position and is complete. This body is born of *kamma.* Nobody makes this. Thus should one recall the nature of the body through "connection".

BONES OF THE BODY

How should one reflect on the nature of the body through "assemblage"? There are nine bones of the head, two cheek bones, thirty-two teeth, seven neck-bones, fourteen ribs, twenty-four side-bones, eighteen joints of the spine, two hip-bones, sixty-four hand-bones, sixty-four foot-bones, and sixty-four soft-bones which depend on the flesh. These three hundred bones and eight or nine hundered tendons are connected with each other. There are nine hundred muscles, seventeen thousand textures of the skin, eight million hairs of the head, ninety-nine thousand hairs of the body, sixty interstices, eighty thousand worms. Bile, saliva and brain are each a *palata** in weight — in Ryo this is equal to four *ryo* — and blood is one *attha** in weight — in Ryo this is equal to three *sho.* All these many and varied forms are only a heap of filth, a collection of urine and are called body. Thus should one recollect on the nature of the body through "assemblage".

How should one reflect on the nature of the body through "loathsomeness"? A man esteems purification most. The things which a man holds dear are such means of adorning himself as sweet perfume, unguents and pastes and beautiful clothes, and bedspreads, pillows, mats and cushions used for sleeping and sitting, bolsters, blankets, canopies, bedding, and various kinds of food and drink, dwelling-places and gifts. A man manifests much attachment to

---

* Transliterations.

these (at first) and afterwards dislikes them. Thus one should reflect on the nature of the body through "loathsomeness".

IMPURITY OF THE BODY

How should one reflect on the nature of the body through "impurity"? When clothes and adornments become dirty they can be made clean again. Their purity can be renewed because their nature is pure. But the body is impure. Thus should one reflect on the nature of the body through "impurity".

SOME DISEASES

How should one reflect on the nature of the body through "dependence"? Depending on a pond, flowers are produced. Depending on a garden, fruits are produced. In the same way, depending on this body, various defilements and diseases are produced. Thus ache of eye, ear, nose tongue, body, head, mouth and teeth, throat-ailments, shortness of the breath, heat and cold, abdominal ache, heart-disease, epilepsy, flatulence, diarrhoea and vomiting, leprosy, goitre, vomiting of blood, itch, smallpox, skin-disease, ague, contagious diseases, gonorrhoea, chills and others give endless trouble to this body. Thus one should reflect on the nature of the body through "dependence".

How should one reflect on the nature of the body through the "non-awareness of obligation"? Now, a man prepares tasty food and drink and takes them for his body's sake. He bathes and perfumes his body and clothes it with garments for sleeping and sitting. Thus he tends his body. But on the contrary, ungratefully, this body which is like a poisonous tree goes to decay, to disease and to death. The body is like an intimate friend who does not know his obligations. Thus one should reflect on the nature of the body through the "non-awareness of obligation".

How should one reflect on the nature of the body through "finitude"? This body will be consumed by fire or devoured (by animals) or go to waste. This body is finite. Thus should one reflect on the nature of the body through "finitude".

This yogin, through these ways, practises mindfulness of body. Through the acquisition of facility in mindfulness and wisdom, his mind becomes undisturbed. When his mind is undisturbed, he is able to destroy the hindrances, cause the arising of the meditation (*jhāna*) factors and attain to the distinction for which he yearns.

Mindfulness of body has ended.

THE RECOLLECTION OF PEACE

Q. What is the recollection of peace? What is the practising of it? What are its salient characteristic, function and near cause? What are its benefits? What is the procedure? *A.* Peace is the stilling of the movements of the mind and body. Complete stilling is called peace. One recalls peace to mind, well. This is recollectedness, recollection and right recollectedness. This is called the recollection of peace. The undisturbed dwelling of the mind in this recollection is called the practising of it. The manifestation of lasting merit is its salient characteristic. Non-restlessness is its function. Sublime freedom is its near cause.

What are its benefits? When a man practises the recollection of peace, happily he sleeps, happily he awakes, is endowed with calm. His faculties are tranquil and he is able to fulfil his aspirations. He is pleasant of mein, modest of demeanour and is esteemed by others. He fares well and approaches the ambrosial.

What is the procedure? The new yogin enters into a place of solitude and sits down with mind intent (on the recollection of peace) and undisturbed. If this bhikkhu calms his faculties, his mind will be quietened and he will enjoy tranquillity immediately. This bhikkhu sees and hears, through bodily, verbal and mental action, through the recollection of peace and through the merits of peace. It was taught by the Blessed One thus: "That bhikkhu is endowed with virtue, endowed with concentration, endowed with wisdom, endowed with freedom and is endowed with the knowledge of freedom. Great, I declare, is the gain, great is the advantage of one[1] who sees that bhikkhu. Great, I declare, is the advantage of one who hears that bhikkhu. Great, I declare, is the advantage of one who goes near to that bhikkhu. Great, I declare, is the advantage of one who pays homage to that bhikkhu. Great, I declare, is the advantage of one who reflects on that bhikkhu or lives the holy life under him.

"How is that so? Bhikkhus who listen to the words of that bhikkhu will be able to gain the twofold seclusion, namely, that of the body and that of the mind".[2]

In the recollection of peace, one recollects (that bhikkhu) thus: When that bhikkhu entered the first meditation, *jhāna*, he destroyed the hindrances. One recollects: When he entered the second meditation, *jhāna*, he destroyed initial and sustained application of thought. One recollects: When he entered the third meditation, *jhāna*, he destroyed joy. One recollects: When he entered the fourth meditation, *jhāna*, he destroyed bliss. One recollects: When he entered the sphere of the infinity of space, he destroyed perception of form, perception of sense reaction and perception of diversity. One

---

1. Bhikkhu (lit).
2. S. V, 67: *Ye te bhikkhave bhikkhu sīlasampannā samādhisampannā paññāsampannā vimuttisampannā vimuttiñāṇadassanasampannā dassanaṁ pāhaṁ bhikkhave tesaṁ bhikkhūnaṁ bahukāraṁ vadāmi. Savanaṁ...... Upasaṅkamanaṁ...... Payirūpāsanaṁ...... Anussatiṁ.... Anupabbajjaṁ pāhaṁ bhikkhave tesaṁ bhikkhūnaṁ bahukāraṁ vadāmi. Taṁ kissa hetu. Tathārūpānaṁ bhikkhave bhikkhūnaṁ dhammaṁ sutvā dvayena vūpakāsena vūpakaṭṭho viharati kāyavūpakāsena ca cittavūpakāsena ca.*

recollects: When he entered the sphere of the infinity of consciousness, he destroyed space. One recollects: When he entered the sphere of nothingness, he destroyed the perception of the sphere of the infinity of consciousness. One recollects: When he entered the sphere of neither perception nor non-perception, he destroyed the perception of the sphere of nothingness. One recollects: When he entered the state of the dissolution of perception and sensation, he destroyed perception and sensation. One recollects: When he attained to the Fruit of Stream-entrance, he destroyed the defilements which are together with views (Lit. as that of views)[1]. One recollects: When he attained to the Fruit of Once-returning, he destroyed coarse passion, coarse hatred and coarse defilements.[2] One recollects: When he attained to the Fruit of Non-returning, he destroyed fine defilements, fine passion and fine hate.[3] One recollects: When he attained to the Fruit of the Consummate One, he destroyed all defilements.[4] And one recollects: When he attains to extinction, *Nibbāna*, he destroys everything. Thus in the recollection of peace (one recalls that bhikkhu to mind.)

That yogin, in these ways and through these merits recalls peace to mind, and is endowed with confidence. Through being unrestricted in faith, he recollects with ease, is in mind undisturbed. When his mind is undisturbed, he destroys the hindrances, causes the arising of meditation (*jhāna*) factors and attains to access-meditation.

The recollection of peace has ended.

MISCELLANEOUS TEACHINGS

The following are the miscellaneous teachings concerning these ten recollections. One recalls to mind the merits of the Buddhas of the past and the future—this is called the practice of the recollection of the Buddha. In the same way one recollects on the Pacceka-buddhas. If a man recalls to mind one of the doctrines that has been taught, it is called the practice of the recollection of the Law. If a man recalls to mind the merits of the life of one hearer, it is called the recollection of the Community of Bhikkhus. If a man recalls virtue to mind, it is called the practice of the recollection of virtue. If a man recollects liberality, it is called the recollection of liberality. If a man rejoices in the recollection of liberality, he gives to men who are

---

1. D. I, 156: *Idha Mahāli bhikkhu tiṇṇaṁ saṁyojanānaṁ (sakkāyadiṭṭhi, vicikicchā, sīlabbata-parāmāsa) parikkhayā sotāpanno hoti.*
2. Ibid.: *Tiṇṇaṁ saṁyojanānaṁ parikkhayā rāga-dosa-mohānaṁ tanuttā sakadāgāmi hoti.*
3. Ibid.: *Pañcannaṁ orambhāgiyānaṁ saṁyojanānaṁ parikkhayā opapātiko hoti.*
4. Ibid.: *Āsavānaṁ khayā anāsavaṁ ceto-vimuttiṁ paññā-vimuttiṁ diṭṭhe va dhamme sayaṁ abhiññā sacchikatvā upasampajja viharati.*

worthy, and resolves to make that (giving) his object. [435] If he is offered food that is not (proper to be) offered, he should not partake of even a handful of it. The recollection of deities endows one with confidence. There are five doctrines. One should practise the recollection of deities.

The seventh fascicle has ended.

THE PATH OF FREEDOM

FASCICLE THE EIGHTH

WRITTEN

BY

THE ARAHANT UPATISSA

WHO WAS CALLED

GREAT LIGHT IN RYO

TRANSLATED IN RYO

BY

TIPIṬAKA SANGHAPĀLA OF FUNAN

CHAPTER THE EIGHTH

Section Five

THE IMMEASURABLE THOUGHT OF LOVING-KINDNESS

Q. What is loving-kindness?[1] What is the practising of it? What are its salient characteristic, function and manifestation? What are its benefits? What is the procedure?

A. As parents, on seeing their dear and only child, arouse thoughts of loving-kindness and benevolence towards that child, so one arouses thoughts of loving-kindness and benevolence towards all beings. Thus is loving-kindness to be known. The undisturbed dwelling of the mind in this practice is called the practising of it. To cause the arising of benevolence is its salient characteristic. The thought of loving-kindness is its function. Non-hatred is its manifestation. If a man practises loving-kindness, he is benefitted in eleven ways thus: Happily he sleeps; happily he awakes; he does not see bad dreams; he is dear to humans; he is dear to non-humans; deities protect him; fire, poison, sword and stick come not near him; he concentrates his mind quickly; the colour of his face is pleasingly bright; at the time of death he is not bewildered; if he attains not the sublime state, he is reborn in the world of Brahma.[2]

---

1. *Mettā.*
2. A. V, 342; Pts. II, 130: *Mettāya bhikkhave cetovimuttiyā āsevitāya bhāvitāya bahulīkatāya yānīkatāya vatthukatāya anuṭṭhitāya paricitāya susamāraddhāya ekādasānisaṁsā pāṭikaṅkhā. Katame ekādasa? Sukhaṁ supati, sukhaṁ paṭibujjhati, na pāpakaṁ supinaṁ passati, manussānaṁ piyo hoti, amanussānaṁ piyo hoti, devatā rakkhanti nāssa aggi vā visaṁ vā satthaṁ vā kamati, tuvaṭaṁ cittaṁ samādhiyati, mukhavaṇṇo vippasīdati, asammūḷho kālaṁ karoti, uttariṁ appaṭivijjhanto brahmalokūpago hoti.*

DISADVANTAGES OF ANGER AND RESENTMENT

What is the procedure? The new yogin who aspires to practise loving-kindness, should at first reflect on the disadvantages of anger and resentment and on the advantages of patience and bear patience in mind. What is meant by "should at first reflect on the disadvantages of anger and resentment"? If a man arouses anger and resentment, his thoughts of loving-kindness will be consumed and his mind will become impure. Thereafter he will frown; thereafter he will utter harsh words; thereafter he will stare in the four directions; thereafter he will lay hold of stick and sword; thereafter he will convulse with rage and spit blood; thereafter he will hurl valuables hither and thither; thereafter he will break many things; thereafter he will kill others or kill himself. And again, if a man is angry and resentful always, he, owing to his wicked mind, is liable to kill his parents, or kill a Consummate One or cause a schism in the Community of Bhikkhus, or draw blood from the body of an Enlightened One. Such fearful acts is he liable to do. Thus should one reflect.

SIMILE OF THE SAW

And again, one should reflect thus: I am called a hearer; I shall be put to shame, if I do not remove anger and resentment. I remember the simile of the Saw.[1] I like to enjoy good states (of mind); if now I arouse anger and resentment, I shall be like a man desirous of taking a bath, entering into a cesspool. I am one who has heard much;[2] if I do not overcome anger and resentment, I shall be forsaken like a physician who is afflicted with vomiting and diarrhoea. I am esteemed by the world; if I do not remove anger and resentment, I shall be cast away by the world like a painted vase containing filth, and uncovered. (Further, one reflects thus:) When a wise man grows angry and resentful, he inflicts severe sufferings. So he will be poisoned out of the fear of terrible punishment. If a man who is bitten by a snake has the antidote and refrains from taking it, he is like one who seems to relish suffering and not happiness. In the same way, a bhikkhu who arouses anger and resentment and does not suppress these, quickly, is said to be one who relishes suffering and not happiness, because he accumulates more fearful *kamma* than this anger and this resentment. And again, one should reflect on anger and resentment thus: He who arouses anger and resentment will be laughed at by his enemies, and cause his friends to be ashamed of him. Though he may have deep virtue, he will be slighted by others. If he was honoured before, he will be despised hereafter. Aspiring after happiness, he will acquire misery. Outwardly calm, he will be inwardly perturbed. Having eyes, he

---

1. (*a*) Th. 445: *Uppajjate sace kodho āvajja kakacūpamaṁ.*
(*b*) M. I, 129, 186, 189: *Ubhatodaṇḍakena ce pi bhikkhave kakacena corā ocarakā aṅgamaṅgāni okanteyyuṁ, tatra pi yo mano padoseyya na me so tena sāsanakaro ti.*
2. *Bahussuta.*

will not see. Being intelligent, he will be ignorant. Thus one should reflect on the disadvantages of anger and resentment.

Q. What is meant by "one should reflect on the advantages of patience"?

A. Patience is power.[1] This is armour. This protects the body well and removes anger and resentment. This is honour. This is praised by the wise. This causes the happiness of not falling away. This is a guardian. This guards all. This helps one to understand the meaning of things well. This is called "putting others to shame". And further, one should reflect thus: I have shorn off the hair of the head; now I must cultivate patience.[2] I have received the alms of the country; I will cause great merit to accrue to the givers, through having a mind of patience. I bear the form and the apparel of the Consummate Ones;[3] this patience is a practise of the Noble Ones; therefore I will not allow anger to remain in my mind. I am called a hearer. I will cause others to call me a hearer in truth. The givers of alms give me many things; through this patience I will cause great merit to accrue to them. I have confidence; this patience is the place of confidence in me. I have knowledge; this patience is the sphere of knowledge in me. If there is the poison of anger and resentment in me, this patience is the antidote which will counteract the poison in me. Thus one should reflect on the disadvantages of anger and resentment and on the advantages of patience, and resolve: "I will reach patience. When people blame me, I will be patient. I will be meek and not haughty".[4] Thus the yogin proceeds towards the bliss of patience and benefits himself. He enters into a place of solitude, and with mind undisturbed begins to fill his body (with the thought) thus: "I am happy. My mind admits no suffering". What is meant by "I have no enemy; I have no anger; I am happily free from all defilements and perform all good".? That yogin controls his mind and makes it pliant. He makes his mind capable of attainment. If his mind is pliant, and is able to bear the object, he should practise loving-kindness. He should regard all beings as (he regards) himself. In practising loving-kindness towards all beings, the yogin cannot at the start develop loving-kindness for enemies, wicked men, beings without merit and dead men. That yogin develops loving-kindness for one towards whom he behaves with respectful reserve, whom he honours, whom he does not slight, towards whom he is not indifferent, and by whom he has been benefitted and, therefore, in regard to whom he is not jealous or ill-disposed. He should develop loving-kindness for such a one, thus: "I esteem a man who is of such and such a nature, namely, a man endowed with honour, learning, virtue, concentration and wisdom. I am benefitted through alms, sweet speech, liberality and intentness on that. These are of advantage to me". Thus he recalls to mind the virtues he esteems

---

1. (*a*) Dh. 399: *Khantibalaṁ balāṇikaṁ.* (*b*) Pts. II, 171: '*Byāpādassa pahīnattā abyāpādo khantīti' khantibalaṁ.* 2. Cp. Ps. I, 79: *Āvuso, pabbajito nāma adhivāsana...*
3. Th. 961 *S[illegible]rattaṁ arahaddhajaṁ.*
4. Cp. Ud. 45: *Sutvāna vākyaṁ pharusaṁ udīritaṁ adhivāsaye bhikkhu aduṭṭhacitto 'ti.*

and the benefits he has acquired (in and through that one), and develops loving-kindness towards that one. One should develop the benevolent mind and always reflect and investigate. One should have a mind that is without anger and resentment. One should wish to be endowed with tranquillity, to be free from hatred, to be endowed with all merits and to gain good advantages. One should wish to gain a good reward, a good name, to gain confidence, to gain happiness, to be endowed with virtue, knowledge, liberality and wisdom. One should wish for happy sleep and happy awaking. One should wish to have no evil dreams. One should wish to become dear to humans and to be honoured by them. One should wish to become dear to non-humans and to be honoured by them. One should wish to be protected by the gods; to be untouched by fire, poison, sword or stick and the like; to concentrate the mind quickly; to have a pleasant complexion; to be born in the Middle Country;[1] to meet good men; to perfect oneself; to end craving; to be long-lived; and to attain to the peace and happiness of the Immortal.

And again, one should recollect thus: If one has not yet produced demerit, one should wish not to produce it; and if one has already produced it, one should wish to destroy it. If one has not yet produced merit, one should wish to produce it; and if one has already produced it, one should wish to increase it.[2] And again, one should not wish to produce undesirable states, and if one has produced them, one should wish to destroy them. (One should wish to produce) desirable states of mind, (and if one has) produced them, one should wish to increase them)

That yogin is able to gain confidence by means of the heart of kindness. Through confidence that is free, he can establish his mind. Through establishing that is free, he can dwell in mindfulness. Through mindfulness that is free, through establishing that is free and through confidence that is free, he is endowed with the unshakable mind, and he understands the state of the unshakable (mind). That yogin by these means and through these activities develops the thought[3] of loving-kindness for himself, repeats it and understands unshakability. [436] Having by these means and through these activities developed the thought of loving-kindness and repeated it, he makes his mind pliant and gradually develops the thought of loving-kindness for a person whom he holds dear. After he has developed the thought of loving-kindness for a person whom he holds dear, he gradually develops the thought of loving-kindness for an indifferent person. After he has developed the thought of loving-kindness for an indifferent person, he gradually develops the thought of

---

1. *Majjhimadesa.*
2. A. II, 15; IV, 462: *Imesaṁ kho bhikkhave pañcannaṁ sikkhādubbalyānaṁ pahānāya cattāro sammappadhānā bhāvetabbā. Katame cattāro? Idha bhikkhave bhikkhu anuppannānaṁ akusalānaṁ dhammānaṁ anuppādāya chandaṁ janeti vāyamati viriyaṁ ārabhati cittaṁ paggaṇhāti padahati, uppannānaṁ pāpakānaṁ akusalānaṁ dhammānaṁ pahānāya . . . , anuppannānaṁ kusalānaṁ dhammānaṁ uppādāya. . ., uppannānaṁ kusalānaṁ dhammānaṁ ṭhitiyā asammosāya bhiyyobhāvāya vepullāya bhāvanāya pāripūriyā candaṁ janeti vāyamati viriyaṁ ārabhati cittaṁ paggaṇhāti padahati.*
3. *Saññā.*

loving-kindness for an enemy. Thus he encompasses all beings (with loving-kindness) and identifies himself with them. If he does not develop loving-kindness for an indifferent person or is unable to do so and develops dislike, he should reflect thus: "In me are states of demerit. I have dislike. Wishing to acquire merit, I stirred up confidence and was ordained. And again, I said, 'I will develop great loving-kindness and compassion for the weal of all beings, through the merit of the Great Teacher'. If I cannot develop loving-kindness towards one indifferent person, how shall I develop loving-kindness towards enemies?". If that yogin is still unable to destroy dislike and hate, that yogin should not endeavour to develop loving-kindness, but should adopt another way to remove the hatred he has for that person.

TWELVE MEANS OF REMOVING HATRED

Q. What are the means of success in removing hatred?

A. (1) One should share in order to benefit the other (whom one hates). One should consider: (2) merit, (3) goodwill, (4) one's own *kamma*, (5) debt-cancellation, (6) kinship, (7) one's own faults. (8) One should not consider the suffering inflicted on oneself. One should investigate: (9) the nature of the faculties, (10) the momentary destruction of states, (11) and aggregation. (12) One should investigate emptiness. One should bear these in mind.

(1) Even if one is angry, one should give the other what he asks, accept willingly what he gives. And in speaking with him, one should always use good words. One should do what the other does. By such action, the destruction of the anger of the one and the other takes place. (2) Merit—if one sees the merits of the other, one ought to think: "This is merit. This is not demerit".

SIMILE OF THE POND

It is like this: There is a pond covered with duckweed, and one, having removed the duckweed, draws out water.[1] If the other has no merit, one should develop loving-kindness for him thus: "This man has no merit; surely, he will fare ill".[2] (3) Goodwill—one should think thus (of

---

1. A. III, 187-8: *Seyyathā pi āvuso pokkharaṇī sevālapaṇakapariyonaddhā, atha puriso āgaccheyya ghammābhitatto ghammapareto kilanto tasito pipāsito, so taṁ pokkharaṇiṁ ogāhetvā ubhohi hatthehi iti c'iti ca sevālapaṇakaṁ apaviyūhitvā añjalinā pivitvā pakkameyya, evam eva kho āvuso yvāyaṁ puggalo aparisudhavacīsamācāro parisuddhakāyasamācāro, yassa aparisuddhavacīsamācāratā, na sāssa tasmiṁ samaye manasikātabbā, yā ca khvāssa parisuddhakāyasamācāratā, sāssa tasmiṁ samaye manasikātabbā. Evaṁ tasmiṁ puggale āghāto paṭivinetabbo.*
2. Ibid. 189: *Seyyathā pi āvuso puriso ābādhiko dukkhito bāḷhagilāno addhānamaggapaṭipanno, tassa purato pi 'ssa dūre gāmo pacchato pi 'ssa dūre gāmo, so na labheyya sappāyāni bhojanāni, na labheyya sappāyāni bhesajjāni na labheyya paṭirūpaṁ upaṭṭhākaṁ na labheyya gāmantanāyakaṁ, tam enaṁ aññataro puriso passeyya addhānamaggapaṭipanno, so tasmiṁ purise kāruññaṁ yeva upaṭṭhāpeyya, anudayaṁ yeva upaṭṭhāpeyya anukampaṁ yeva*

gaining) the other's goodwill: If a man does not revere (the other) let him arouse the thought of goodwill. If he is not revered, he should make merit. And again, the destruction of demerit is well-faring. Thus should the changing of hatred to goodwill be known. (4) One's own *kamma*—one should consider one's own evil *kamma*[1] thus: "The evil that I do will cause anger to arise in others". (5) Debt-cancellation—(thus one thinks:) "Owing to my past *kamma*, others blame me. Now I am free from debt. Reflecting on this evidence (of debt-cancellation), I am glad". (6) Kinship—he remembers that beings succeed one another in (the cycle of) birth and death, thus: "This is my kinsman", and arouses the thought of kinship.[2] (7) One's own faults—one arouses self-perception thus: "That man's anger is produced on account of me. I acquire demerit on account of him". Thus arousing self-perception[3] one sees one's own faults. (8) One should not consider—one should not consider the perception (of one's own suffering) which is unrelated to hatred. Suffering—(one thinks thus:) "Owing to folly, I see my own suffering as a hindrance". Thus one should see. One suffers by oneself, because one does not think on loving-kindness. It appears so (i.e., as a hindrance) because of mental suffering. Avoiding the place where the enemy lives, one should dwell where one does not hear (his voice) or see him. (9) Nature of the faculties—one should investigate thus: "To be tied to the lovely and the unlovely is the nature of the faculties. Therefore I hate. Because of this I am unmindful". (10) The momentary destruction of states—one should investigate thus: "That man suffers because of birth. All these states perish in one thought-moment. With which state in him am I angry?". (11) Aggregation—one should investigate thus: "The inner and the outer aggregates produce suffering. It is not possible for me to be angry with any part or place". (12) Emptiness—one should investigate thus: In the absolute sense it cannot be said, "This man causes suffering" or "This man suffers".

---

upaṭṭhāpeyya 'aho vatāyaṁ puriso labheyya sappāyāni bhojanāni labheyya sappāyāni bhesajjāni labheyya paṭirūpaṁ upaṭṭhākaṁ labheyya gāmantanāyakaṁ. Taṁ kissa hetu? Māyaṁ puriso idh' eva anayavyasanaṁ āpajjatī' ti. Evam eva kho āvuso yvāyaṁ puggalo aparisuddhakāyasamācāro aparisuddhavacīsamācāro na ca labhati kālena kālaṁ cetaso vivaraṁ cetaso pasādaṁ, evarūpe āvuso puggale kāruññaṁ yeva upaṭṭhāpetabbaṁ anudayā yeva upaṭṭhāpetabbā anukampā yeva upaṭṭhāpetabbā 'aho vata ayam āyasma kāyaduccaritaṁ pahāya kāyasucaritaṁ bhāveyya, vacīduccaritaṁ pahāya vacīsucaritaṁ bhāveyya, manoduccaritaṁ pahāya manosucaritaṁ bhāveyya. Taṁ kissa hetu? Māyam āyasmā kāyassa bhedā parammaraṇā apāyaṁ duggatiṁ vinipātaṁ nirayaṁ uppajjatī' ti. Evaṁ tasmiṁ puggale āghāto paṭivinetabbo.

1. A. V, 88: *Kammassako 'mhi kammadāyādo;* M. I, 390: *Evaṁ pahaṁ Puṇṇa: kammadāyādā sattā ti vadāmi.*
2. S. II, 189-90: *Na so bhikkhave satto sulabharūpo, yo na mātābhūtapubbo iminā dīghena addhunā. Taṁ kissa hetu? Anamataggāyaṁ bhikkhave saṁsāro pubbākoṭi na paññāyati avijjānīvaraṇānaṁ sattānaṁ taṇhāsaṁyojanānaṁ sandhāvataṁ saṁsarataṁ.*

   Evaṁ dīgharattaṁ kho bhikkhave dukkhaṁ paccanubhūtaṁ tibbaṁ paccanubhūtaṁ vyasanaṁ paccanubhūtaṁ kaṭasi vaḍḍhitā, yāvañcidaṁ bhikkhave alam eva sabbasaṅkhāresu nibbindituṁ alaṁ virajjituṁ alaṁ vimuccituṁ ti.

   Na so bhikkhave satto sulabharūpo yo na pitābhūtapubbo...
   Na so bhikkhave satto sulabharūpo yo na bhātābhūtapubbo...
   Na so bhikkhave satto sulabharūpo yo na bhaginībhūtapubbo...
   Na so bhikkhave satto sulabharūpo yo na puttobhūtapubbo...
3. *Atta saññā.*

This body is the result of causes and conditions. There is no soul-entity in the aggregates.

Therefore the Blessed One uttered this stanza:-

He who dwells amidst the village grove,
experiencing pleasure and pain,
is not burned because of self or other
but because his mind is passionate.
If one's mind were cleansed of passion's stain,
who could touch that one immaculate?[1]

Thus after that yogin has clearly understood the way of destroying hatred, has identified friends, indifferent ones and enemies with himself, and acquired facility in the practice, he should gradually arouse the thought of loving-kindness and develop it for various bhikkhus in (his) dwelling-place. After that he should develop loving-kindness for the Community of Bhikkhus in (his) dwelling-place. After that he should develop loving-kindness for the deities in his dwelling-place. After that he should develop loving-kindness for beings in the village outside his dwelling-place. Thus (he develops loving-kindness for beings) from village to village, from country to country. After that he should develop (loving-kindness for beings) in one direction. That yogin "pervades one quarter with thoughts of loving-kindness; and after that, the second; and after that, the third; and after that, the fourth. Thus he spreads loving-kindness towards all beings of the four directions, above, below and pervades the whole world with thoughts of loving-kindness immense immeasurable, without enmity, without ill will.[2] Thus that yogin develops loving-kindness and attains to fixed meditation in three ways: through comprehending all beings, through comprehending all village-domains[3] and through comprehending all directions. He attains to fixed meditation, *jhāna*, through developing loving-kindness for one being, and in the same way, for two, three and for all beings. He attains to fixed meditation, *jhāna*, through developing loving-kindness for beings of one village-domain, and in the same way for (beings of) many villages. He attains to fixed meditation, *jhāna*, through developing loving-kindness for one being in one direction, and in the same way (for beings) in the four directions. Here when one develops loving-kindness for one being, if that being is dead, that object is lost. If he loses the object, he cannot arouse loving-kindness. Therefore he should develop the thought of loving-kindness widely. Thus practising he can fulfil great fruition and merit.

---

1. Ud. 12: *Gāme araññe sukhadukkhaputṭho*
nev' attato no parato dahetha,
phusanti phassā upadhiṁ paṭicca,
nirupadhiṁ kena phuseyyuṁ phassā 'ti.
2. D. II, 186; D. III, 223-4: *Idh' āvuso bhikkhu mettā-sahagatena cetasā ekaṁ disaṁ pharitvā viharati, tathā dutiyaṁ, tathā tatiyaṁ, tathā catutthaṁ. Iti uddham adho tiriyaṁ sabbadhi sabbattatāya sabbāvantaṁ lokaṁ mettā-sahagatena cetasā vipulena mahaggatena appamāṇena averena avyāpajjhena pharitvā viharati.*
3. *Gāmakkhetta.*

Q. What are the roots, manifestation, fulfilment, non-fulfilment and object of loving-kindness?

A. Absence of greed is a root; absence of hatred is a root; absence of delusion is a root. Willing is a root. Right consideration[1] is a root. What is its "manifestation"? The making visible of these roots is its manifestation. What is its "fulfilment"? When one is endowed with loving-kindness he destroys hatred, removes impure affection and purifies his bodily, verbal and mental actions. This is called "fulfilment". What is its "non-fulfilment"? Through two causes one fails in the practice of loving-kindness: through regarding friends as enemies and through impure affection. "Non-fulfilment" is produced when one arouses the feeling of enmity and rivalry. Thus should "non-fulfilment" be known. What is its "object"? Beings are its "object".[2]

TEN PERFECTIONS

Q. That is wrong. In the absolute sense there is no being. Why then is it said that beings are its object? *A*. Owing to differences in faculties, in common parlance, it is said that there are beings. Now, the Bodhisatta* and the Mahāsatta* develop loving-kindness for all beings and fulfil the ten perfections.[3]

Q. How is it so? *A*. The Bodhisatta and the Mahāsatta develop loving-kindness for all beings and resolve to benefit all beings and give them fearlessness.[4] Thus they fulfil the perfection of giving.[5]

The Bodhisatta and the Mahāsatta develop loving-kindness for all beings. For the sake of benefitting all beings, they cause separation from suffering and do not lose the faculty of truth. It is like the relation of a father to his children. Thus they fulfil the perfection of virtue.[6]

---

1. *Sammā manasikāra.*
2. *Sattārammaṇa.*— Cp. Mp. II, 41: *Ime pana cattāro brahmavihārā vaṭṭā honti, vaṭṭapādā honti, vipassanāpādā honti, diṭṭhadhammasukhavihārā honti, abhiññāpādā vā nirodhapādā vā, lokuttarā pana na honti. Kasmā? Sattārammaṇattā ti.*

* Transliteration. Cp. Sv. II, 428: *Atha Mahāsatto . . . pañca-mahā-vilokanaṁ nāma vilokesi.*

3. Ud.-a. 128: *Yathā vā te Bhagavanto dāna-pāramiṁ pūretvā, sīla-nekkhamma-paññā-viriya-khanti-sacca-adhiṭṭhāna-mettā-upekkhā-pāramī ti imā dasa pāramiyo dasa-upapāramiyo, dasa paramattha-pāramiyo ti samatiṁsa pāramiyo pūretvā, pañca mahā-pariccāge pariccajitvā, pubba-yoga-pubba-cariya-dhamm' akkhāna-ñāt' attha-cariyādayo pūretvā, buddhi-cariyāya koṭim patvā āgatā, tathā ayam pi Bhagavā āgato.*
4. Abhaya.— Cp. A. IV, 246: *Idha bhikkhave ariyasāvako pāṇātipātaṁ pahāya pāṇātipatā paṭivirato hoti. Pāṇātipātā paṭivirato bhikkhave ariyasāvako aparimāṇānaṁ sattānaṁ abhayaṁ deti averaṁ deti avyāpajjhaṁ deti; aparimāṇānaṁ sattānaṁ abhayaṁ datvā averaṁ datvā avyāpajjhaṁ datvā aparimāṇassa abhayassa averassa avyāpajjhassa bhāgī hoti. Idaṁ bhikkhave paṭhamaṁ dānaṁ mahādānaṁ aggaññaṁ rattaññaṁ vaṁsaññaṁ porāṇaṁ asaṁkiṇṇaṁ asaṁkiṇṇapubbaṁ na saṁkīyati na saṁkīyissati appaṭikuṭṭhaṁ samaṇehi brāhmaṇehi viññūhi . . .*

   Puna ca paraṁ bhikkhave ariyasāvako adinnādānaṁ pahāya adinnādānā paṭivirato hoti . . . pe . . . kāmesu micchācāraṁ pahāya kāmesu micchācārā paṭivirato hoti . . . pe . . . musāvādaṁ pahāya musāvādā paṭivirato hoti . . . pe . . . surāmerayamajjapamādaṭṭhānā paṭivirato hoti. Surāmerayamajjapamādaṭṭhānā paṭivirato bhikkhave ariyasāvako aparimāṇānaṁ sattānaṁ abhayaṁ deti . . . pe . . . avyāpajjhassa bhāgī hoti. Idaṁ bhikkhave pañcamaṁ dānaṁ mahādānaṁ aggaññaṁ . . . pe . . .
5. *Dāna-pārami* (*pāramī* is transliterated in this section).
6. *Sīla.*

The Bodhisatta and the Mahāsatta develop loving-kindness for all beings. For the sake of benefitting all beings, they acquire non-greed, and in order to remove the non-merit of beings, they attain to meditation, *jhāna*,[1] and enter into homelessness. Thus they fulfil the perfection of renunciation.[2]

The Bodhisatta and the Mahāsatta develop loving-kindness for all beings. For the sake of benefitting all beings, they consider merit and non-merit. Understanding in accordance with truth, devising clean expedients, they reject the bad and take the good. Thus they fulfil the perfection of wisdom.[3]

The Bodhisatta and the Mahāsatta develop loving-kindness for all beings. For the sake of benefitting all beings, they, without abandoning energy, exert themselves at all times. Thus they fulfil the perfection of energy.[4]

The Bodhisatta and the Mahāsatta develop loving-kindness for all beings. For the sake of benefitting all beings, they practise patience and do not grow angry when others blame or hate them. Thus they fulfil the perfection of patience.[5]

The Bodhisatta and the Mahāsatta [743] develop loving-kindness for all beings. For the sake of benefitting all beings, they speak the truth, dwell in the truth and keep the truth. Thus they fulfil the perfection of truth.[6]

The Bodhisatta and the Mahāsatta develop loving-kindness for all beings. For the sake of benefitting all beings, they do not break their promises but keep them faithfully unto life's end. Thus they fulfil the perfection of resolution.[7]

The Bodhisatta and Mahāsatta develop loving-kindness for all beings. For the sake of benefitting all beings, they identify themselves with all beings and fulfil the perfection of loving-kindness.[8]

The Bodhisatta and the Mahāsatta develop loving-kindness for all beings. For the sake of benefitting all beings, they regard friends, indifferent ones and enemies, equally, without hatred and without attachment. Thus they fulfil the perfection of equanimity.[9]

In these ways do the Bodhisatta and the Mahāsatta practise loving-kindness and fulfil the ten perfections.

I elucidate (further) loving-kindness and the four resolves.†

---

1. Nearly always this is partially transliterated. Cp. M. I, 246: *Na kho panāhaṁ imāya kaṭukāya dukkarakārikāya adhigacchāmi uttariṁ manussadhammā alamariyañāṇadassana-visesaṁ, siyā nu kho añño maggo bodhāyāti. Tassa mayhaṁ Aggivessana etadahosi: Abhijānāmi kho panāhaṁ pitu Sakkassa kammante sītāya jambucchāyāya nisinno vivicc' eva kāmehi vivicca akusalehi dhammehi savitakkaṁ savicāraṁ vivekajaṁ pītisukhaṁ paṭhamaṁ jhānaṁ upasampajja viharitā, siyā nu kho eso maggo bodhāyāti. Tassa mayhaṁ Aggivessana satānusāri viññāṇaṁ ahosi: eso va maggo bodhāyāti.*
2. *Nekkhamma.*
3. *Paññā* (transliteration).
4. *Viriya.*
5. *Khanti.*
6. *Sacca.*
7. *Adhiṭṭhāna.*
8. *Mettā.*
9. *Upekkhā.*

† This and all subsequent passages in italics and marked † are omitted in the Sung edition mentioned before.

THE FOUR RESOLVES

Now, the Bodhisatta and the Mahāsatta having practised loving-kindness, having fulfilled the ten perfections, fulfil the four resolves. They are the resolve of truth, the resolve of liberality, the resolve of peace and the resolve of wisdom.[1]

Here, the perfection of truth, the perfection of resolution and the perfection of energy, fulfil the resolve of truth.

The perfection of giving, the perfection of virtue and the perfection of renunciation, fulfil the resolve of liberality.

The perfection of patience, the perfection of loving-kindness and the perfection of equanimity, fulfil the resolve of peace.

The perfection of wisdom fulfil the resolve of wisdom.

Thus the Bodhisatta and the Mahāsatta having practised loving-kindness and fulfilled the ten perfections, fulfil the four resolves and attain to two states, namely, serenity and insight.[2]

Here, the resolve of truth, the resolve of liberality and the resolve of peace fulfil serenity. The resolve of wisdom fulfils insight. Through the fulfilment of serenity, they attain to all meditations, *jhānas*, and hold to emancipation and concentration firmly. They cause the arising of the concentration of the twin-miracle[3] and the concentration of the attainment of great compassion.[4] With the attainment of insight, they are endowed with all supernormal knowledge,[5] analytical knowledge,[6] the powers,[7] the confidences.[8] Thereafter they cause the arising of natural knowledge[9] (?) and omniscience.[10] Thus the Bodhisatta and the Mahāsatta practise loving-kindness, and gradually attain to Buddhahood.

Loving-kindness has ended.†

THE IMMEASURABLE THOUGHT OF COMPASSION

Q. What is compassion? What is the practising of it? What are its salient characteristic, function and manifestation? What are its benefits? What is the procedure?

A. As parents who on seeing the suffering of their dear and only child, compassionate it, saying, "O, how it suffers!", so one compassionates all beings. This is compassion. One dwells undisturbed in compassion — this

---

1. The order is different from D. III. 229: *Cattāri adiṭṭhānāni. Paññā-addiṭṭhānaṁ saccādiṭṭhānaṁ, cāgādiṭṭhānaṁ, upasamādhiṭṭhānaṁ.*
2. *Samatha, vipassanā* (transliteration).
3. *Yamakapāṭihāriya.*
4. *Mahākaruṇāsamāpatti.*
5. *Abhiññā.*
6. *Paṭisambhidā.*
7. *Bala.*
8. *Vesārajja.*
9. *Pakati-ñāṇa.*
10. *Sabbaññutā-ñāṇa.*

is called the practising of it. The non-manifestation of non-advantage is its salient characteristic. Happiness is its function. Harmlessness[1] is its manifestation. Its benefits are equal to those of loving-kindness.

What is the procedure? The new yogin enters into a place of solitude and sits down with mind collected and undisturbed. If he sees or hears of a person stricken with disease, or a person affected by decay, or a person who is full of greed, he considers thus: "That person is stricken with suffering. How will he escape suffering?".[2] And again, if he sees or hears of a person of perverted mind and bound with the defilements, or a person entering into ignorance, or one, who, having done merit in the past does not now train himself, he considers thus: "That person is stricken with suffering; he will fare ill. How will he escape suffering?".[3] And again, if he sees or hears of a person who follows demeritorious doctrines and does not follow meritorious doctrines, or of a person who follows undesirable doctrines and does not follow desirable doctrines, he considers thus: "That person is stricken with suffering; he will fare ill. How will he escape suffering?".[4]

That yogin by these means and through these activities develops the thought of compassion for these persons and repeats it. Having by these means and through these activities developed the thought of compassion and repeated it, he makes his mind pliant, and capable of bearing the object. Thereafter he gradually develops (compassion) for an indifferent person and an enemy. The rest is as was fully taught above. Thus he fills the four directions.

Q. What is the fulfilment of compassion and what, non-fulfilment? *A.* When a man fulfils compassion, he separates from harming and from killing. He is not afflicted. He separates from impure affection. Through two causes compassion is not fulfilled: through resentment produced within himself and through affliction.

Q. All do not suffer. Suffering does not prevail always. Then how is it possible to compassionate all beings? *A.* As all beings have at some previous time experienced suffering, they can grasp the sign well and practise compassion

---

1. *Ahimsā, avihiṁsā.* (*a*) A. I, 151: *Sabbhi dānaṁ upaññattaṁ ahiṁsāsaññamo damo* (=*Ahiṁsā ti karuṇā c'eva karuṇā-pubbabhāgo ca*—Mp. II, 250).
(*b*) Sv. III, 982: *Avihiṁsā ti karuṇā karuṇā-pubba-bhāgopi. Vuttam pi c'etaṁ: tattha katamā avihiṁā? Yā sattesu karuṇā karuṇāyanā karuṇāyitattaṁ karuṇā-cetovimutti, ayaṁ vuccati avihiṁsā ti.*
(c) Dh. 300: *Yesaṁ divā ca ratto ca ahiṁsāya rato mano* (=*Ahiṁsāya rato ti 'so karuṇāsahagatena cetasā ekaṁ disaṁ pharitvā viharatī' ti evaṁ vuttāya karuṇābhāvanāya rato*—Dh.-a. III, 459).
2. Cp. (a) Pts. I, 128: *'Jarāya anusahagato lokasannivāso'ti passantānaṁ Buddhānaṁ Bhagavantānaṁ sattesu mahākaruṇā okkamati... 'Byādīhi abhibhūto lokasannivāso'ti ... 'Taṇhāya uḍḍito lokasannivāso'ti...*
(*b*) S. I, 40: *Taṇhāya uḍḍito loko, jarāya parivārito.*
3. Pts. I, 128-9: *'Mahābandhanabandho lokasannivāso... mohabandhanena... kilesbandhanena... tassa natth' añño koci bandhaṁ mocetā aññatra mayā'ti;... 'tīhi duccaritehi vippaṭipanno lokasannivāso' ti passantānaṁ...*
4. Ibid. 129-30: *'Pañcahi kāmaguṇehi rajjati lokasannivāso' ti... 'aṭṭhahi micchattehi niyato lokasannivāso' ti...*

in all places. Again, sorrow of birth and death is the common property of all beings. Therefore all beings can in all places practise compassion.

Compassion has ended.†

THE IMMEASURABLE THOUGHT OF APPRECIATIVE JOY

Q. What is appreciative joy? What is the practising of it? What are its salient characteristic, function and manifestation? What are its benefits? What is the procedure?

A. As parents, who, on seeing the happiness of their dear and only child are glad, and say, "*Sādhu!*" so, one develops appreciative joy for all beings. Thus should appreciative joy be known. The undisturbed dwelling of the mind in appreciative joy — this is called the practising of it. Gladness is its salient characteristic. Non-fear is its function. Destruction of dislike is its manifestation. Its benefits are equal to those of loving-kindness.

What is the procedure? The new yogin enters a place of solitude and sits down with mind collected and undisturbed. When one sees or hears that some person's qualities are esteemed by others, and that he is at peace and is joyful, one thinks thus: "*Sādhu! sādhu!* may he continue joyful for a long time!". And again, when one sees or hears that a certain person does not follow demeritorious doctrines, or that he does not follow undesirable doctrines and that he follows desirable doctrines, one thinks thus: "*Sādhu! sādhu!* may he continue joyful for a long time!". That yogin by these means and through these activities develops the thought of appreciative joy and repeats it. Having by these means and through these activities developed the thought of appreciative joy and repeated it, he makes his mind pliant, and capable of bearing the object. Thereafter he gradually develops appreciative joy for an indifferent person and an enemy. The rest is as was fully taught above. Thus with appreciative joy he fills the four directions.

Q. What is the fulfilment of appreciative joy? What is its non-fulfilment? *A*. When one fulfils appreciative joy, he removes unhappiness, does not arouse impure affection and does not speak untruth. Through two causes appreciative joy is not fulfilled: through resentment produced within himself and derisive action. The rest is as was fully taught above.

Appreciative joy has ended.

THE IMMEASURABLE THOUGHT OF EQUANIMITY

Q. What is equanimity? What is the practising of it? What are its salient characteristic, function and manifestation? What are its benefits? What is the procedure?

A. As parents are neither too attentive nor yet inattentive towards any one of their children, but regard them equally and maintain an even mind towards them, so through equanimity one maintains an even mind towards all beings. Thus should equanimity be known. The dwelling undisturbed in equanimity—this is called the practising of it. Non-attachment is its salient characteristic. Equality is its function. The suppression of disliking and liking is its manifestation. Its benefits are equal to those of loving-kindness.

Q. What is the procedure? That yogin at first attends to the third meditation, *jhāna*, with loving-kindness, with compassion and with appreciative joy. Having attained to the third meditation, *jhāna*, and acquired facility therein, he sees the severe trials of loving-kindness, compassion and appreciative joy. Liking and disliking are near. These (loving-kindness etc.) are connected with fawning, elation and gladness. The merits of equanimity lie in the overcoming of these severe trials. That yogin, having seen the severe trials of loving-kindness, compassion and appreciative joy and the merits of equanimity, develops equanimity towards a neutral person[1] and makes the mind calm. Having developed and repeated it, he makes his mind pliant and capable of bearing the object. Thereafter, he gradually develops (it) towards an enemy and then towards a friend. The rest is as was fully taught above. Thus he fills the four directions. That yogin practising thus attains to the fourth meditation, *jhāna*, through equanimity. In three ways he attains to fixed meditation, *jhāna*, through comprehending beings, through comprehending village-domains and through comprehending all directions.

Q. When the yogin practises equanimity, how does he consider beings?

A. The yogin considers thus: "In loving-kindness, compassion and appreciative joy, one is overjoyed with beings", and removing joy, he induces equanimity. As a man might leap for joy on meeting a long-lost friend [438] and later, calm down, having been with him for sometime, so having lived long with loving-kindness, compassion and appreciative joy, the yogin attains to equanimity. And again, there is a man. He speaks concerning beings, "Beings consider thus: What is the fulfilment of equanimity? What is its non-fulfilment?". When equanimity is fulfilled, one destroys disliking and liking and does not cause the arising of ignorance. Through two causes equanimity is not fulfilled: through resentment produced within oneself and through the arising of ignorance.[2]

MISCELLANEOUS TEACHINGS

Again I elucidate the meaning of the four immeasurables.†

What are the miscellaneous teachings concerning the four immeasurables?[3]

1. Lit. neither likable nor not likable.
2. What follows is unintelligible.
3. The miscellaneous teachings are in many places unintelligible as it is here. This portion is not in the three editions of the Sung, Yuan and Ming dynasties, i.e., roughly about 1239 A.C., 1290 A.C., and 1601 A.C., respectively. Also it is not found in the old Sung edition, 1104-1148 A.C., belonging to the library of the Japanese Imperial Household.

One attains to distinction in the four immeasurables through practising (them) towards animals, immoral persons, moral persons, those who dislike passion, hearers, Silent Buddhas and Supreme Buddhas regarding them as a mother regards her children according to their stage in life[1] (lit. seasons).

Q. Why is the third and not the fourth meditation, *jhāna*, attained in loving-kindness, compassion and appreciative joy?

A. Through constant dwelling on the sorrows (of others) one develops loving-kindness, compassion and appreciative joy. (And so no equanimity is present). Therefore the third meditation, *jhāna*, is attained and not the fourth.

Again the plane of equanimity belongs to the fourth meditation, *jhāna*, because it is endowed with two kinds of equanimity, namely, neutral feeling[2] and neutrality as regards states.[3] Dwelling in the plane of equanimity and regarding all beings with equal favour, one accomplishes equanimity. Owing to the nature of the planes of the three immeasurables, the third meditation, *jhāna*, and not the fourth, is produced. And again, it is said that the four meditations, *jhānas*, are produced with the four immeasurables. The Blessed One has declared: "Further, O bhikkhu, you should develop the concentration which is with initial and sustained application of thought; you should develop that which is without initial, and only with, sustained application of thought; you should develop that which is without initial and without sustained application of thought; you should develop that which is with joy; (you should develop that which is without joy); you should develop that which is accompanied by equanimity.[4]

Q. Why are these four immeasurables and not five or three taught? *A.* Were that so, uncertainty might arise concerning all. And again, in order to overcome hatred, cruelty, dislike and lust, one accomplishes the four immeasurables. And again, it is said that these four are (overcome with) only loving-kindness. If one arouses (in oneself) hatred, cruelty, unhappiness, one, through suppressing them in the four ways, attains to distinction.

Equanimity is the purification of loving-kindness, compassion and appreciative joy, because through it hatred and lust are destroyed.

Further, it should be understood that the four immeasurables are of one nature though their signs are different. Thus owing to the suppression of tribulation, owing to the object which comprises beings, owing to the wish to benefit, they fulfil one characteristic.

---

1. Cp. Sv. III, 1008: *Appamaññā ti pamāṇaṁ agahetvā anavasesa-pharaṇa-vasena appamaññā.*
2. *Vedanupekkhā.* 3. *Dhammassa majjhattatā.*
4. Lit. without sustained application of thought (*vicāra*) with only initial application of thought (*vitakka*) which is evidently an error.
   Cp. (*a*) S. IV, 360: *Katamo ca bhikkhave asaṅkhatagāmi maggo. Savitakko savicāro samādhi avitakko vicāramatto samādhi avitakko avicāro samādhi. Ayaṁ vuccati bhikkhave asaṅkhatagāmi maggo.*
   (*b*)D. III, 219: *Tayo samādhi. Savitakko savicāro samādhi, avitakko vicāra-matto samādhi, avitakko avicāro samādhi (—Samādhisu paṭhama-jjhāna-samādhi savitakka-*

And again, it is said that owing to the distinction in states, owing to the appropriation of object (?) and advantage, they are different, as the Blessed One taught in the Haliddavasana Sutta[1]: "In the sphere of the beautiful, loving-kindness is first;* in the sphere of (infinite) space, compassion is first;** in the sphere of (infinite) consciousness, appreciative joy is first;† in the sphere of nothingness, equanimity is first".‡

Q. Why are they to be understood thus? *A*. They should be understood thus because of their being the sufficing condition.

Q. How? *A*. If one develops the mind of loving-kindness, all beings are dear to him. Because they are always dear to him, he causes his mind

---

savicāro. Pañcaka-nayena dutiya-jjhāna-samādhi avitakka-vicāramatto. Seso avitakko-avicāro—Sv. III, 1003).

(c) A. IV, 300: *Mettā me cetovimutti bhāvitā bhavissati bahulīkatā yānikatā vatthukatā anuṭṭhitā paricitā susamāraddhā ti. Evaṁ hi te bhikkhu sikkhitabbaṁ.*

Yato kho te bhikkhu ayaṁ samādhi evaṁ bhāvito hoti bahulīkato, tato tvaṁ bhikkhu imaṁ samādhiṁ savitakkam pi savicāraṁ bhāveyyāsi, avitakkam pi vicāramattaṁ bhāveyyāsi, avitakkam pi avicāraṁ bhāveyyāsi, sappītikam pi bhāveyyāsi, nippītikam pi bhāveyyāsi sātasahagataṁ pi bhāveyyāsi, upekkhāsahagatam pi bhāveyyāsi. Yato kho te bhikkhu ayaṁ samādhi evaṁ bhāvito hoti subhāvito, tato te bhikkhu evaṁ sikkhitabbaṁ:—

Karuṇā me cetovimutti....muditā me cetovimutti....upekhā me cetovimutti bhāvitā....anuṭṭhitā paricitā susamāraddhā ti.

1. S. V. 119-21: *Kathaṁ bhāvitā ca bhikkhave mettācetovimutti kiṁgatikā hoti kimparamā kimphalā kimpariyosānā?*

Idha bhikkhave bhikkhu mettāsahagataṁ satisambojjhaṅgaṁ bhāveti....mettāsahagataṁ upekhāsambojjhaṅgaṁ bhāveti viveka° virāga° nirodhanissitaṁ vossaggapariṇāmiṁ. So sace ākaṅkhati appaṭikkūle paṭikkūlasaññī vihareyyanti, paṭikkūlasaññī tattha viharati. Sace ākaṅkhati paṭikkūle appaṭikkūlasaññī vihareyyanti, appaṭikkūlasaññī tattha viharati. Sace ākaṅkhati appaṭikkūle ca paṭikkūle ca paṭikkūlasaññī vihareyyanti, paṭikkūlasaññī tattha viharati. Sace ākaṅkhati paṭikkūle ca appaṭikkūle ca appaṭikkūlasaññī vihareyyanti, appaṭikūlasaññī tattha viharati. Sace ākaṅkhati appaṭikkūlañca paṭikkūlañca tad ubhayaṁ abhinivajjetvā upekhako vihareyyaṁ sato sampajāno ti, upekhako tattha viharati sato sampajāno. Subhaṁ vā kho pana vimokkhaṁ upasampajja viharati, subhaparamāhaṁ (= Kasmā pan' etāsaṁ mettādīnaṁ subha-paramāditā vuttā Bhagavatā ti? Sabhāgavasena tassa tassa upanissayatā. Mettāvihārissa hi sattā appaṭikkūlā honti. Ath'assa appaṭikkūlā-paricayā appaṭikkūlesu parisuddha-vaṇṇesu nīlādīsu cittañ upasaṁharato appakasiren'eva tattha cittaṁ pakkhandati. Iti mettā subha-vimokhassa upanissayo hoti, na tato paraṁ. Tasmā subha-paramā ti vuttā*—Spk. III, 172-3), *bhikkhave mettācetovimuttiṁ vadāmi. Idha paññassa bhikkhuno uttariṁ vimuttiṁ appaṭivijjhato.*

Kathaṁ bhāvitā ca bhikkhave karuṇācetovimutti kiṁgatikā hoti kimparamā kimphalā kimpariyosānā?

*Idha bhikkhave bhikkhu karuṇāsahagataṁ satisambojjhaṅgaṁ bhāveti... pe ..., karuṇāsahagataṁ upekhāsambojjhaṅgaṁ bhāveti....vossaggapariṇāmiṁ. So sace ākaṅkhati appaṭikkūle paṭikkūlasaññī vihareyyanti, paṭikkūlasaññī tattha viharati....Sace ākaṅkhati appaṭikkūlañca paṭikkūlañca tad ubhayaṁ abhinivajjetvā upekhako vihareyyaṁ sato sampajāno ti, upekhako tattha viharati sato sampajāno. Sabbaso vā pana rūpasaññānaṁ samatikkamā paṭighasaññānaṁ atthagamā nānattasaññānaṁ amanasikārā ananto ākāso ti ākāsānañcāyatanaṁ upasampajja viharati, ākāsānañcāyatanaparamāhaṁ** bhikkhave karuṇācetovimuttiṁ vadāmi. Idha paññassa bhikkhuno uttariṁ vimuttiṁ appaṭivijjhato.*

Kathaṁ bhāvitā ca bhikkhave muditācetovimutti kiṁgatikā hoti kimparamā kimphala kimpariyosānā?

Idha bhikkhave bhikkhu muditāsahagataṁ satisambojjhaṅgaṁ bhāveti....muditāsahagataṁ upekhāsambojjhaṅgaṁ bhāveti....Sabbaso vā pana ākāsānañcāyatanaṁ samatikkamma anantaṁ viññāṇan ti viññāṇañcāyatanaṁ upasampajja viharati. Viññāṇañcāyatanaparamāhaṁ† bhikkhave muditācetovimuttiṁ vadāmi. Idha paññassa bhikkhuno uttariṁ vimuttiṁ appaṭivijjhato.

Kathaṁ bhāvitā ca bhikkhave upekhācetovimutti... kimpariyosānā?

Idha bhikkhave bhikkhu upekhāsahagataṁ satisambojjhaṅgaṁ bhāveti... Sabbaso vā pana viññāṇañcāyatanaṁ samatikkamma natthi kiñciti ākiñcaññāyatanaṁ upasampajja viharati. Ākiñcaññāyatanaparamāhaṁ‡ bhikkhave upekhācetovimuttiṁ vadāmi. Idha paññassa bhikkhuno uttariṁ vimuttiṁ appaṭivijjhato ti.

to consider the blue-green, yellow (or other) colour *kasiṇa*, and attains to fixed meditation, *jhāna*, without difficulty. At this time the yogin accomplishes the fourth meditation, *jhāna*, of the element of form. Therefore loving-kindness is first in (the sphere of) the beautiful.[1] At that time the yogin, depending on loving-kindness which he has developed in the fourth meditation, *jhāna*, of the element of form, surpasses that (element).

Q. How is that shallow? *A*. He practises loving-kindness; therefore he knows the tribulations of the element of form. How? Seeing the sufferings of beings he develops loving-kindness through a material cause. After that he understands the tribulations of the element of form. He causes the mind to consider the abandoning of forms and of space, and attains to fixed meditation, *jhāna*, without difficulty in the sphere of the infinity of space, because he depends on it. Therefore it is said that compassion is first in the sphere of the infinity of space.[2] That yogin surpasses the sphere of the infinity of space through appreciative joy.

Q. What is the meaning? *A*. That yogin, when he practises appreciative joy, contemplates on limitless consciousness, and is not attached to anything. How? (Through) this appreciative joy (the yogin) attains to fixed meditation, *jhāna*, through contemplation on beings in the un-attached sphere of the infinity of consciousness. After that, being not attached, he grasps the object of limitless consciousness. Freed from form and attached to space, he considers limitless consciousness and through contemplating many objects, he attains to fixed meditation without difficulty. Therefore, in the sphere of the infinity of consciousness, appreciative joy is first.[3]

Q. That yogin transcends the sphere of the infinity of consciousness through equanimity. What is the meaning of it?

A. That yogin, practising equanimity fulfils freedom from attachment. How? If one does not practise equanimity, he will be attached (to things) and (think), "This being gets happiness", (or this being) "gets suffering". Or he depends on joy or bliss. Thereafter he turns away from all attachment. He turns away from the sphere of the infinity of consciousness[4] and is happy. He attains to fixed meditation, *jhāna*, without difficulty. His mind is not

---

1. See Comy. (Spk. III, 172-3) passage marked * included in note 1 under *mettā*, page 195.
2. *Karuṇā-vihārissa daṇḍābhighātādi-rūpa-nimittaṁ sattadukkhaṁ samanupassantassa karuṇāya pavatti-sambhavato rūpe ādīnavo suparividito hoti. Ath' assa suparividitarūpādīnavattā paṭhavī kasiṇādisu aññataraṁ ugghāṭetvā rūpa-nissaraṇe ākāse cittaṁ upasaṁharato appakasiren' eva tattha cittaṁ pakkhandati. Iti karuṇā ākāsānañcāyatanassa upanissayo hoti, na tato paraṁ. Tasmā 'ākāsānañcāyatanaparamā' ti vuttā.*—Spk. III, 173, being comment on sutta passage marked ** in note 1, page 195.
3. *Muditā-vihārissa pana tena tena pāmojja-kāraṇena uppanna-pāmojja-sattānaṁ viññāṇaṁ samanupassantassa muditāya pavatti-sambhavato viññāṇa-ggahana-paricitaṁ cittaṁ hoti. Ath'assa anukkamādhigataṁ ākāsānañcāyatanaṁ atikkamma ākāsa-nimitta-gocare viññāṇe cittaṁ upasaṁharato appakasiren' eva tattha cittaṁ pakkhandati. Iti muditā viññāṇañcāyatanassa upanissayo hoti, na tato paraṁ. Tasmā' 'viññāṇañcāyatana-paramā' ti vuttā.*—Spk. III, 173—comment on passage marked †, page 195.
4. Lit. *ākiñcaññāyatana*.

attached to any object. Why? Because in the sphere of nothingness he cannot be attached either to consciousness or to infinity. Therefore, in the sphere of nothingness, equanimity is first.[1]

Miscellaneous teachings have ended.†

THE DETERMINING OF THE FOUR ELEMENTS

Q. What is the determining of the four elements? What is the practising of it? What are its salient characteristic, function and manifestation? What are its benefits? What is the procedure?

A. To discern the four elements within one's form — this is called distinguishing the four elements. The undisturbed dwelling of the mind (in determining) — this is called the practising of it. Close investigation of the four elements is its salient characteristic. The understanding of emptiness is its function. The removing of the thought of being[2] is its manifestation.

What are its benefits? There are eight benefits: One who practises the determining of the four elements overcomes fear, worldly pleasure and discontent, is even-minded towards desirable and undesirable (objects), destroys the idea of male and female, is endowed with great wisdom, fares well and approaches the ambrosial. His states of mind are clear. He is able to perfect all his actions.

What is the procedure? The new yogin grasps the elements in two ways: briefly and in detail. *Q.* What is the grasping of the elements briefly? *A.* That yogin enters a place of solitude, and with mind collected considers thus: "This body should be known by the four elements. There is in this body the nature of solidity – that is the earthy element;[3] (there is) the nature of humidity — that is the watery element;[4] (there is) the nature of heat — that is the fiery element;[5] (there is) the nature of motion — that is the element of air.[6] Thus in this body there are only elements. There is no being.[7] There is no soul".[8] In this way one grasps the elements briefly. Again it is said that the yogin grasps the elements briefly. He understands the body through understanding the midriff, its colour, its form, its place. Thus that yogin grasps the elements briefly. He understands the nature of the whole body through understanding the midriff, its colour, its form, its place. He understands this body through understanding flesh, its colour, its form, its place. That yogin, having under-

---

1. *Upekkhā-vihārissa pana 'sattā sukhitā vā hontu, dukkhato vā vimuccantu, sampatta-sukhato vā mā vigacchantū' ti abhogābhāvato sukha-dukkhādīhi paramattha-ggāha-vimukha-sambhavato avijjamāna-ggahaṇa-dukkhaṁ cittaṁ hoti. Ath' assa paramattha-ggāhato vimukha-bhāva-paricita-cittassa paramatthato avijjamāna-ggahaṇa-dukkha-cittassa ca anukkamādhigataṁ viññāṇānañcāyatanaṁ samatikkama-sabhāvato avijjamāne paramattha-bhūtassa viññāṇassa abhāve cittaṁ upasaṁharato appakasiren' eva tattha cittaṁ pakkhandati. Iti upekkhā ākiñcaññāyatanassa upanissayo hoti, na tato paraṁ. Tasmā 'ākiñcaññāyatana-paramā' ti vuttā ti.*— Spk. III, 173-4—comment on sutta passage marked ‡ in note 1, page 195).
2. *Satta.* 3. *Paṭhavī-dhātu.* 4. *Āpo-dhātu.* 5. *Tejo-dhātu.* 6. *Vāyo-dhātu.*
7 and 8. *Nissatta nijjīva.* See note 2, p. 229.

stood the whole body through understanding flesh, its colour, its form, its place, understands this whole body through understanding the veins, their colour, their form, their place. That yogin, having understood the whole body through understanding the veins, their colour, their form, their place, understands the whole body through understanding the bones, their colour, their form, their place. That yogin in these four ways dominates his mind. After dominating his mind, he makes his mind pliant and capable of bearing the object. That yogin, having in these four ways dominated his mind and having made his mind pliant and capable of bearing the object, in these four (other) ways knows that which has the nature of solidity as the element of earth; that which has the nature of humidity as the element of water; that which has the nature of heat as the element of fire; that which has the nature of motion as the element of air. Thus that yogin, in these four ways, knows that there are only elements and that there is no being and no soul. Here the other ways also are fulfilled. Thus one grasps the elements briefly.

TWENTY WAYS OF GRASPING THE ELEMENT OF EARTH

How does one grasp the elements in detail? One grasps the element of earth in detail through twenty ways, namely, (through) hair of the head and of the body, nails, teeth, skin, flesh, sinews, veins, bones, marrow, kidneys, heart, liver, lungs, spleen, gorge, intestines, mesentery, midriff, excrement, brain (that are) in this body.

TWELVE WAYS OF GRASPING THE ELEMENT OF WATER

One grasps the element of water in detail through twelve ways, namely, (through) bile, saliva, pus, blood, sweat, fat, tears, grease, slobber, nasal mucus, synovial fluid, [439] urine (that are) in the body.

FOUR WAYS OF GRASPING THE ELEMENT OF FIRE

One grasps the element of fire in detail through four ways, namely, (through) fever heat and normal heat of the body, weather, equality of cold and heat and (the heat) by means of which one digests the fluid or solid nutriment which one takes. These are called the element of fire.

SIX WAYS OF GRASPING THE ELEMENT OF AIR

One grasps the element of air in detail through six ways, namely, (through) the air discharged upwards, the air discharged downwards, the air which depends on the abdomen, the air which depends on the back,[1] the air which depends on the limbs, the air inhaled and exhaled.[2]

---

1. Vbh.-a. 5: *Vātā ti kucchivāta-piṭṭhivātādi-vasena veditabbā.*
2. Netti 74: *Katamehi chahi ākārehi vāyodātuṁ vitthārena pariganhāti? Uddhaṁgamā vātā adhogamā vātā kucchisayā vātā koṭṭhāsayā vātā aṅgamaṅgānusārino vātā assāso passāso.*

Thus when one sees this body in forty-two ways, only the elements manifest themselves. There is no being. There is no soul. Thus the elements are grasped in detail.

And again, predecessor-teachers[1] have said that one should determine the four elements through ten ways, namely, through the meaning of terms,[2] through object, aggregation, powder,[3] non-separation, condition,[4] characteristic,[5] similarity and dissimilarity,[6] sameness and difference,[7] puppet.

First, the chapter which refers to the meaning of terms is as follows:—

Q. How should one determine the elements through terms?

A. Two terms, viz., the common and the special terms. Here the four primaries are common (terms). Earth-element, water-element, fire-element, air-element are special terms.

Q. What is the meaning of "four primaries"?

A. Great manifestation is called primary. They are great; they are illusory; but they appear real. Therefore they are called "primaries" "Great": By way of *yakkha* and others" the term great is applied.

Q. Why is the "great manifestation" called great?

The elements are "great manifestation" as the Blessed One has declared in the following stanza:

> "*I declare the size of earth to be*
> *two hundred thousand nahutas and four.*
> *Four hundred thousand nahutas and eight*
> *is of water the bulk; air's in space*
> *which reckoned is at nahutas six*
> *and nine times a hundred thousand; in that*
> *this world of ours lies. There is in the world*
> *consuming fire that will in mighty flames*
> *rise up to Brahma's world for seven days*".[8]

"Great manifestation" is thus. Therefore they are called the primaries.

Q. How do the primaries that are unreal appear as real?

A. What are called primaries are neither male nor female. They are seen through the form of a man or a woman. And element is neither long nor short. It is seen through the form of the long and the short. An element is neither a tree nor a mountain, but it is seen through the form of a tree or a mountain. Thus the primaries are not real, but appear real and are called primaries.

What is the meaning of "by way of *yakkha* and others"? It is as if a *yakkha* were to enter into a man and take possession of him. Through the possession of the *yakkha* that man's body would manifest four qualities:

---

1. *Porāṇā*. 2. *Vacanatthato*. 3. *Cuṇṇato*. 4. *Paccayato*. 5. *Lakkhaṇādito*. 6. *Sabhāgavisabhāgato*. 7. *Nānattekattato*. 8. Not traced.

hardness, (excess of) water, heat and lightness of movement. In the same way the four elements in union with the body fulfil four qualities. Through the union of the earthy element hardness is fulfilled. Through the union of the watery element fluidity is fulfilled. Through the union of the fiery element heat is fulfilled. And through the union of the airy element lightness of movement is fulfilled. Therefore the primaries are to be known "by way of *yakkha* and others". Primary is the meaning of the word.

THE FOUR ELEMENTS

Q. What is the meaning of earth-element, water-element, fire-element and air-element?

A. Extensiveness and immensity are called the meaning of earth. Drinkability and preservation—these constitute the meaning of water. Lighting up is the meaning of fire. Movement back and forth is the meaning of air.

What is the meaning of element? It means the retention of own form, and next the essence of earth is the earthy element. The essence of water is the watery element. The essence of fire is the fiery element. The essence of air is the airy element.

What is the essence of earth? The nature of hardness; the nature of strength; the nature of thickness; the nature of immobility; the nature of security; and the nature of supporting. These are called the essence of earth.

What is the essence of water? The nature of oozing; the nature of humidity; the nature of fluidity; the nature of trickling; the nature of permeation; the nature of increasing; the nature of leaping; and the nature of cohesion. These are called the essence of water.

What is called the essence of fire? The nature of heating; the nature of warmth; the nature of evaporation; the nature of maturing; the nature of consuming; and the nature of grasping. These are called the essence of fire.

What is the essence of air? The nature of supporting; the nature of coldness; the nature of ingress and egress; the nature of easy movement; the nature of reaching low; and the nature of grasping. These are called the essence of air.

These are the meanings of the elements. Thus one should determine the elements through the meaning of words.

Q. How should one determine the elements through "objects"?

A. In the element of earth, stability is the object. In the element of water, cohesion is the object. In the element of fire, maturing is the object. In the element of air interception is the object.

And again, in the element of earth, upstanding is the object; in the element of water, flowing down is the object; in the element of fire, causing to go upwards is the object; in the element of air, rolling on is the object. And again, owing to the proximity of two elements, one, at first, (in stepping forward) raises up one foot; and afterwards, owing to the proximity of two elements, one lifts up the (other) foot. Owing to the proximity of two elements, one at first sits or sleeps. And owing to the proximity of two elements, one afterwards gets up and walks. Owing to the proximity of two elements, at first, rigidity and torpor are induced. Owing to the proximity of two elements, one becomes energetic afterwards. Owing to the proximity of two elements, there is heaviness in one at first. Owing to the proximity of two elements, there is lightness afterwards. Thus one should determine the four primaries through "object"[1].

How should one determine the four primaries through "aggregation"? Aggregation consists of the earth-element, the water-element, the fire-element and the air-element. By means of these elements form, smell, taste and touch take place. These eight are produced generally together; they co-exist and do not go apart. This combination is named aggregation. And again, there are four kinds, namely, aggregation of earth, aggregation of water, aggregation of fire and aggregation of air. In the aggregation of earth, the earth-element predominates; and the water-element, the fire-element and the air-element gradually, in order, become less. In the aggregation of water, the water-element predominates; and the earth-element, the air-element and the fire-element gradually, in order, become less. In the aggregation of fire, the fire-element predominates; and the earth-element, the air-element and the water-element gradually, in order, become less. In the aggregation of air, the air-element predominates; and the fire-element, the water-element and the earth-element gradually, in order, become less.[2] Thus one should determine the elements through "aggregation".

Q. How should one determine the four primaries through "powder"?

A. One determines the element of earth that is next the finest particle of space.[3] This earth is mixed with water; therefore it does not scatter. Being matured by fire, it is odourless; being supported by air, it rolls. Thus one should determine. Again, predecessors have said: "If pulverized into dust, the earth-element in the body of an average person will amount to one *koku*

---

1. Cp. Ps. I, 260-61: *Tass' evaṁ abhikkamato ekekapāduddharaṇe paṭhavīdhātu āpodhātū ti dve dhātuyo omattā honti mandā, itarā dve adhimattā honti balavatiyo. Tathā atiharaṇa-vītiharaṇesu. Vossajjane tejodhātu-vāyodhātuyo omattā honti mandā, itarā dve adhimattā balavatiyo. Tathā sannikkhepana-sannirumbhanesu. Tattha uddharaṇe pavattā rūpā-rūpadhammā atiharaṇaṁ na pāpuṇanti. Tathā atiharaṇe pavattā vītiharaṇaṁ, vītiharaṇe pavattā vossajjanaṁ, vossajjane pavattā sannikkhepanaṁ, sannikkhepane pavattā sannirumbhanaṁ na pāpuṇanti. Tattha tatth' eva pabbapabbaṁ sandhisandhiṁ odhi-odhiṁ hutvā tattakapāle pakkhitta-tilā viya taṭataṭāyantā bhijjanti.*
2. Cp. A. III, 340-41: *Atha kho āyasmā Sāriputto....aññatarasmiṁ padese mahantaṁ dārukkhandhaṁ disvā bhikkhū āmantesi:— Passatha no tumhe āvuso amuṁ mahantaṁ dārukkhandhan ti? Evam āvuso ti.*

   Ākaṅkhamāno āvuso bhikkhu iddhimā cetovasippatto amuṁ dārukkhandhaṁ paṭhavī tveva adhimucceyya. Taṁ kissa hetu? Atthi āvuso amusmiṁ dārukkhandhe paṭhavidhātu, yaṁ nissāya bhikkhu iddhimā... pe... paṭhavī tveva adhimucceyya. Ākaṅkhamāno āvuso bhikkhu iddhimā cetovasippatto amuṁ dārukkhandhaṁ āpo tveva adhimucceyya ... pe... tejo tveva adhimucceyya... vāyo tveva adhimucceyya...
3. *Ākāsaparamāṇu.*

and two *sho*.[1] Then, if mixed with water, it will become six *sho* and five *go*.[2] Matured by fire, it is caused to roll by the wind". Thus one should determine the body through "powder".

Q. How should one determine the body through "non-separation"? *A*. The earth-element is held together by water; is matured by fire; is supported by air. Thus the three elements are united. The element of water rests on earth; is matured by fire; is supported by air. Thus the three elements are held together. The element of fire rests on the earth; is held together by water; is supported by air. Thus the three elements are matured. The element of air rests on earth; is held together by water; is matured by fire. Thus the three elements are supported. The three elements rest on earth. Held together by water, the three elements do not disperse. Matured by fire, the three elements are odourless. Supported by air, the three elements roll on, and dwelling together, they do not scatter. Thus the four elements in mutual dependence dwell and do not separate. Thus one determines the elements through non-separation.

Q. How should one determine the elements through "condition"? *A*. Four causes and four conditions produce the elements. What are the four? They are *kamma*, consciousness, season and nutriment. What is *kamma*? The four elements that are produced from *kamma* fulfil two conditions, namely, the producing-condition[3] and *kamma*-condition.[4] The other elements fulfil the decisive-support-condition.[5] Consciousness:- The four elements that are produced from consciousness fulfil six conditions, namely, producing-condition, co-nascence-condition,[6] support-condition,[7] nutriment-condition,[8] faculty-condition,[9] presence-condition.[10] The other elements fulfil condition,[11] support-condition and presence-condition.

In the consciousness at the moment of entry into the womb, corporeality fulfils seven conditions, namely, co-nascence-condition, mutuality-condition,[12] support-condition, nutriment-condition, faculty-condition, result-condition,[13] presence-condition.

The consciousness of the birth-to-be fulfils three conditions in regard to the pre-born body, namely, post-nascence-condition,[14] support-condition and presence-condition. The four primaries that are produced from season fulfil two conditions, namely, producing-condition and presence-condition. The other elements fulfil two conditions, namely, support-condition and presence-condition. Nutriment:- The four primaries that are produced from food fulfil three conditions, namely, producing-condition, nutriment-condition and presence-condition. The other elements fulfil two conditions,

1. 1 koku = 10 sho.
2. 10 go = 1 sho = 1.588 quart, 0.48 standard gallon, 1.804 litres.
3. *Janaka-paccayā*.
4. *Kamma-paccayā*.
5. *Upanissaya-paccayā*.
6. *Saha-jāta-paccayā*.
7. *Nissaya-paccayā*.
8. *Āhāra-paccayā*.
9. *Indriya-paccayā*.
10. *Atthi-paccayā*.
11. *Paccayā*.
12. *Añña-mañña-paccayā*.
13. *Vipāka-paccayā*.
14. *Pacchā-jāta-paccayā*.

namely, support-condition and presence-condition. Here the four elements that are produced by *kamma* are co-nascent elements. (Elements that are mutually dependent) fulfil four conditions, namely, co-nascence-condition, mutuality-condition, support-condition, presence-condition. Other elements fulfil two conditions, namely, support-condition and presence-condition. Thus one should know (the elements) produced from consciousness, produced from season and produced from food. The earth-element becomes a condition of the other elements by way of resting-place. The water-element becomes a condition of the other elements by way of binding. The fire-element becomes a condition of the other elements by way of maturing. The air-element becomes a condition of the other elements by way of supporting. Thus one determines the elements through "condition".

[440] How should one determine the elements through "characteristic"? *A.* The characteristic of the earth-element is hardness. The characteristic of the water-element is oozing. The characteristic of the fire-element is heating. The characteristic of the air-element is coldness. Thus one determines the elements according to "characteristic".

Q. How should one determine the elements through "similarity and dissimilarity"? *A.* The earthy element and the watery element are similar because of ponderability. The fire-element and the air-element are similar because of lightness. The water-element and the fire-element are dissimilar. The water-element can destroy the dryness of the fire-element; therefore they are dissimilar. Owing to mutuality, the earth-element and the air-element are dissimilar. The earth-element hinders the passage of the air-element; the air-element is able to destroy the earth-element. Therefore they are dissimilar. And again, the four elements are similar owing to mutuality or they are dissimilar owing to their natural characteristics. Thus one determines the elements according to "similarity and dissimilarity".

Q. How should one determine the elements through "sameness and difference"? *A.* The four elements that are produced from *kamma* are of one nature, because they are produced from *kamma;* from the point of characteristics they are different. In the same way one should know those that are produced from consciousness, from season and from nutriment.

The (portions of the) earth-element of the four causes and conditions are of one nature owing to characteristics; from the point of cause they are different. In the same way one should know the air-element, the fire-element and the water-element of the four causes and conditions. The four elements are of one nature owing to their being elements, owing to their being great primaries; are of one nature owing to their being things; are of one nature owing to their impermanence; are of one nature owing to their suffering; are of one nature owing to their being not-self. They are different owing to characteristics; are different owing to object; are different owing to *kamma*; are different owing to differing nature of consciousness; are different owing to the differing nature of the season; are different owing to the different nature of nutriment; are different owing to differences of nature; are different owing to differences of arising; are different owing to the differences in birth; are different owing to differences in faring. Thus one determines the elements through "sameness and difference".

SIMILE OF THE PUPPET

Q. How should one determine the elements through "puppet"? *A*. It is comparable to a skilful master of puppets who makes of wood (effigies) of humans, complete in every part, in the form of man or woman, and makes these walk, dance, sit or squat through the pulling of strings. Thus these puppets are called bodies; the master of puppets is the past defilement by which this body is made complete; the strings are the tendons; the clay is flesh; the paint is the skin; the interstices are space. (By) jewels, raiment and ornaments (they) are called men and women. Thoughts (of men and women) are to be known as the tugging by the element of air. Thus they walk, dwell, go out, or come in, stretch out, draw in, converse or speak.[1]

These puppet-men, born together with the element of consciousness, are subject to anxiety, grief and suffering through the causes and conditions of anxiety and torment. They laugh or frolic or shoulder. Food sustains these puppets; and the faculty of life[2] keeps these puppets going. The ending of life results in the dismembering of the puppet. If there happens to be defiling *kamma*, again a new puppet will arise. The first beginning of such a puppet cannot be seen; also, the end of such a puppet cannot be seen.[3] Thus one determines the elements through "puppet". And that yogin by these ways and through these activities discerns this body through "puppet" thus: "There is no being; there is no soul".

When that yogin has investigated through the object of the elements and through the arising of feeling, perception, the formations and consciousness, he discerns name and form. Thenceforward he sees that name-and-form is suffering, is craving, is the source of suffering; and he discerns that in the destruction of craving lies the destruction of suffering, and that the Noble

---

1. (*a*) Sn. 193-94: *Caraṁ vā yadi vā tiṭṭhaṁ, nisinno uda vā sayaṁ,*
sammiñjeti pasāreti,—esā kāyassa iñjanā.
Aṭṭhinahārusaṁyutto tacamaṁsāvalepano
Chaviyā kāyo paṭicchanno yathābhūtaṁ na dissati.

(*b*) Ps. I, 252: "*Nāvā māluta vegena jiyāvegena tejanaṁ*
Yathā yāti tathā kāyo yāti vātāhato ayaṁ.
Yantasuttavesen' eva cittasuttavasen' idaṁ
payuttaṁ kāyayantam pi yāti ṭhāti nisīdati.
Ko nāma ettha so satto yo vinā hetupaccaye
attano ānubhāvena tiṭṭhe vā yadi vā vaje' ti.

(*c*) Ps. I, 265; Sv. I, 197: *Abbhantare attā nāma koci sammiñjento va pasārento vā n'atthi. Vutta-ppakāra-citta-kiriya-vāyodhātu-vipphārena pana suttākaḍḍhana-vasena dāru-yantassa hattha-pāda-lāḷanaṁ viya sammiñjana-pasāraṇaṁ hotīti evaṁ pajānanaṁ pan' ettha asammoha-sampajaññan ti veditabbaṁ.*

2. *Jīvitindriya.*

3. S. II, 178; III, 149, 151: *Anamataggāyaṁ bhikkhave saṁsāro pubbākoṭi na paññāyati avijjānivaraṇānaṁ sattānaṁ taṇhāsaṁyojanānaṁ sandhāvataṁ saṁsarataṁ.*

Eightfold Path leads to the complete destruction of suffering. Thus that yogin discerns the Four Noble Truths fully. At that time he sees the tribulation of suffering through impermanence, sorrow and not-self. Always attending to these, his mind is undisturbed. He sees the merit of the destruction of suffering through wisdom, tranquillity and dispassion. In this way that yogin, seeing the tribulation of suffering and the merits of cessation, dwells peacefully endowed with the faculties, the powers and the factors of enlightenment.[1] He makes manifest the consciousness that proceeds from perception of the formations and attains to the element of the most excellent.[2]

The determining of the four elements has ended.

THE LOATHSOMENESS OF FOOD

Q. What is the perception of the loathsomeness of food?[3] What is the practising of it? What are its salient characteristic, function, near cause[4] and manifestation? What are its benefits? What is the procedure?

A. The yogin, attending to the loathsomeness of what in the form of nourishment is chewed, licked, drunk or eaten,[5] knows and knows well this perception. This is called the perception of the loathsomeness of food. The undisturbed dwelling of the mind in this perception is the practising of it. The understanding of the disadvantages of food is its salient characteristic. Disagreeableness is its function. The overcoming of desire is its manifestation.

What are its benefits? The yogin can acquire eight benefits: He who develops the perception of the loathsomeness of food knows the nature of morsels of food; he understands fully the five-fold lust; he knows the material aggregate; he knows the perception of impurity; he develops fully the mindfulness as to the interior of his body; his mind shrinks from desiring what is tasty;[6] he fares well; he approaches the ambrosial.

What is the procedure? The new yogin enters into a place of solitude, sits down with mind composed and undisturbed, and considers the loathsomeness of what in the form of nourishment is chewed, licked, drunk or eaten as follows: "Such and such are the several hundred sorts of tasty food cooked clean. They are relished of the people. Their colour and smell are perfect. They are fit for great nobles. But after these foods enter into the body, they become impure, loathsome, rotten, abominable".

One develops the perception of the loathsomeness of food in five ways: through (the task of) searching for it; through (the thought of) grinding it; through receptacle; through oozing; and through aggregation.

---

1. *Indriya, bala, bojjhaṅga.*
2. *Sappi-maṇḍa dhātu.*
3. *Āhāre paṭikkūla saññā.*
4. Not answered in comment.
5. *Khajja, leyya, peyya, bhojja.*
6. Cp. Th. 580: *Rasesu anugiddhassa jhāne na ramatī mano.*

Q. How should the yogin develop the perception of the loathsomeness of food through (the task of) "searching for it"?

A. This yogin sees that many beings encounter trouble in searching for drink and food; they commit many evil deeds such as killing and thieving (for the sake of food). Further, he sees that these beings are the recipients of various forms of suffering and are killed or deprived of liberty. And again, he sees that such beings commit diverse evil actions such as eagerly searching for things, deceiving and pretending to be energetic. Thus these beings perform evil. Seeing food thus, he develops dislike through the thought: "Impure urine and excrement are due to drink and food".[1]

THE DWELLING OF THE HOMELESS

And again, he sees the dwelling of the homeless man in the clean forest-retreat where fragrant flowers bloom, where birds sing and the cry of the wild is heard. In that prosperous field which the good man cultivates, are shadows of trees, groves and water which captivate the mind of others. The ground is flat and exceedingly clean; so there is nothing uneven.[2] Seeing this, men admire them with awe. Here are no quarrels and noises. This place where the homeless man trains for enlightenment is like the dwelling of Brahma.[3] In such a place the mind is unfettered; and he, reciting (the Law) and developing concentration always, enjoys the practice of good deeds. (Leaving such a place) the homeless man goes in search of food in cold and heat, wind and dust, mud and rain. He traverses steep paths. With bowl in hand, he begs for food, and in begging enters others' houses.[4] Seeing that, the yogin stirs up the thought of tribulation in his mind as follows: "Drink and food are impure. They come out in the form of excrement and urine. For that one goes in search of food". Thus abandoning, he should look for the highest bliss.

And again, the yogin sees the practice of the homeless man. When he (the homeless man) begs, he has to pass the places where fierce horses, elephants and other animals gather and the places where dogs and pigs live. He has to go to the places where evil-doers live. He has to tread on mud or excreta

---

1. In the text this precedes the previous sentence.
2. Cp. Th. 540: *Supupphite Sītavane sītale girikandare*
gattāni parisiñcitvā caṅkamissāmi ekako.
1103: *Kadā mayūrassa sikhaṇḍino vane dijassa sutvā girigabbhare rutaṁ*
paccuṭṭhahitvā amatassa pattiyā saṁciñtaye taṁ nu kadā bhavissati.
1135: *Varāhaeṇeyyavigāḷhasevite pabbhārakūṭe pakaṭe 'va sundare*
navambunā pāvusasittakānane tahiṁ guhāgehagato ramissasi.
1136: *Sunīlagīvā susikhā supekhuṇā sucittapattacchadanā vihaṁgamā*
sumañjughosatthanitābhigajjino te taṁ ramissanti vanamhi jhāyinaṁ.
1137: *Vuṭṭhamhi deve caturaṅgule tiṇe sampupphite meghanibhamhi kānane*
nagantare viṭapisamo sayissaṁ taṁ me mudu hohiti tūlasannibhaṁ.
3. Cp. Th. 245: *Yathā Brahmā tathā eko yathā devo tathā duve,*
yathā gāmo tathā tayo kolāhalaṁ tatuttarin ti.
4. Cp. Th. 1118: *Muṇḍo virūpo abhisāpam āgato kapālahattho 'va kulesu bhikkhasu,*
yuñjassu satthu vacane mahesino, itissu maṁ citta pure niyuñjasi.

in unclean places. He has to stand at the gates of other's houses, silently, for sometime. He has to conceal his body with a cloth. Further, he doubts as regards obtaining alms.[1] This yogin thinks: "This man's food is like dog's food", and he arouses disagreeableness as regards food thus: "This searching for food is most hateful. How could I take this food? I will simply beg from others". Thus one develops the perception of the loathsomeness of food through "searching for it".

Q. How should the yogin develop the perception of the loathsomeness of food through "grinding"?

A. That yogin sees a man who, having searched for and obtained drink and food, sits down in front of these. He makes the (solid food) soft, by mixing it with fish sauce. He kneads it with his hand, grinds it in his mouth, gathers it with his lips, pounds it with his teeth, turns it with his tongue, unites it with his saliva and serum.[2] These are most repulsive and unsightly as the vomit of a dog. Thus one develops the perception of the loathsomeness of food through "grinding".

Q. How should one develop the perception of the loathsomeness of food through "receptacle"?

A. Thus these foods are swallowed and go into the stomach mixed with impurities and remain there. After that they go to the intestines. They are eaten by hundreds of kinds of worms. Being heated, they are digested. Thus they become most repugnant. It is like one's vomit thrown into an unclean vessel. Thus one develops the perception of the loathsomeness of food through "receptacle".

Q. How should one develop the perception of the loathsomeness of food through "oozing"?

A. These foods are digested by heat and mixed with new and old impurities. Like fermented liquor escaping from a broken vat, they flood the body. By flowing, they enter into the veins, the textures of the skin, face and eyes. They ooze out of nine openings and ninety-nine thousand pores. Thus through flowing, [441] these foods separate into five parts: one part is eaten by worms; one part is changed to heat; one part sustains the body; one part becomes urine; and one part is assimilated with the body. Thus one develops the perception of the loathsomeness of food through "oozing".

Q. How should one develop the perception of the loathsomeness of food through "aggregation"?

A. This drink and food which flow become hair of the head and the body, nails and the rest. They cause to set up one hundred and one parts

---

1. Cp. Sn. 711-12: *Na muni gāmam āgamma kulesu sahasā care,*
ghāsesanaṁ chinnakatho na vācam payutaṁ bhaṇe.
'Alatthaṁ yad, idaṁ sādhu; nālatthaṁ kusalām iti';
ubhayen' eva so tādī rukkhaṁ va upanivattati.

2. Lit. Thin blood.

of the body. If they do not trickle out, they cause one hundred and one diseases. Thus one develops the perception of the loathsomeness of food through "aggregation".

That yogin by these ways and through these activities develops the perception of the loathsomeness of food. Through disliking, his mind becomes free and is not distracted. His mind being undistracted he destroys the hindrances, arouses the meditation (*jhāna*) factors and dwells in access-concentration.

The perception of the loathsomeness of food has ended.†

The sphere of nothingness and the sphere of neither perception nor non-perception are as was taught under the earth *kasiṇa* before.

Here the stanza says:—

The subjects of meditation are here
indicated to the yogin in brief
as if a man were pointing out the way
to Pāṭaliputta.[1]
What's told concisely he can know in full.
He sees what lies before and what behind
and with discernment viewing understands
truth from untruth.
From what have been here in detail set forth,
namely, the marks and the merits complete,
one ought to know, just as it is, the scope
of Freedom's Path.

The chapter of the thirty-eight subjects of meditation has ended.

The eighth chapter of the subjects of meditation has ended.

THE EIGHTH FASCICLE OF THE PATH OF FREEDOM.

---

1. *Pāliputta*(transliteration).

THE PATH OF FREEDOM

FASCICLE THE NINTH

WRITTEN

BY

THE ARAHANT UPATISSA

WHO WAS CALLED

GREAT LIGHT IN RYO

TRANSLATED IN RYO

BY

TIPIṬAKA SANGHAPĀLA OF FUNAN

THE FIVE FORMS OF HIGHER KNOWLEDGE

CHAPTER THE NINTH

Now, when that yogin, having practised concentration, dwells easy in the fourth meditation, *jhāna,* he is able to cause the arising of the five forms of higher knowledge, namely, supernormal power,[1] divine hearing,[2] knowledge of others' thoughts,[3] recollection of former lives,[4] divine sight.[5]

"Supernormal power" means "transformation". "Divine hearing" means "beyond the reach of human audition". "Knowledge of others' thoughts" means "the understanding of others' thoughts". "Recollection of former lives" means "the remembrance of past lives". "Divine sight" means "beyond the reach of human vision".

Q. How many kinds of supernormal power are there? Who develops it? What is the procedure?

THREE KINDS OF SUPERNORMAL POWER

A. There are three kinds of supernormal power, namely, the supernormal power of resolve, the supernormal power of transformation, the supernormal power caused by mind. What is the supernormal power of resolve? That yogin being one becomes many; and being many becomes one. Developing the body, he reaches the world of Brahma. This is called the supernormal power of resolve.[6] What is the supernormal power of transformation? That yogin discards his natural body and appears in the form of a boy or a snake

1. *Iddhividhā.* 2. *Dibbasotañāṇa* 3. *Cetopariyañāṇa.* 4. *Pubbenivāsānussatiñāṇa.*
5. *Dibbacakkhuñāṇa.*
6. Cp. Pts. II, 207-10: *Katamā adiṭṭhānā iddhi? Idha bhikkhu anekaviditaṁ iddhividhaṁ paccanubhoti: eko pi hutvā bahudhā hoti, bahudhā pi hutvā eko hoti....yāva Brahmalokā pi kāyena vasaṁ vatteti... Ayaṁ adiṭṭhānā iddhi.*

or a king of Brahmas. These constitute the supernormal power of transformation.[1] What is the supernormal power caused by mind? That yogin calls up from this body another body, readily, and endows it with all members and faculties, according to his will. This is called the supernormal power caused by mind.[2]

SEVEN KINDS OF SUPERNORMAL POWER

And again, there are seven kinds of supernormal power, namely, the supernormal power diffused by knowledge, the supernormal power diffused by concentration, the supernormal power of the Ariyas, the supernormal power born of *kamma*-result, the supernormal power of the meritorious, the supernormal power accomplished by magic, the supernormal power accomplished by the application of the means of success.

Q. What is the supernormal power diffused by knowledge? *A*. By the view of impermanence, one rejects the perception of permanence and accomplishes the supernormal power diffused by knowledge. By the Path of Sanctity, one rejects all defilements and accomplishes the supernormal power diffused by knowledge. Thus should supernormal power diffused by knowledge be understood. It is as in the case of Venerable Elder Bakkula, of the Venerable Elder Saṅkicca and of the Venerable Elder Bhūtapāla. Thus is supernormal power diffused by knowledge.[3]

Q. What is the supernormal power diffused by concentration? *A*. By the first meditation, *jhāna*, one rejects the hindrances and accomplishes the supernormal power diffused by concentration. By the attainment of the sphere of neither perception nor non-perception, one rejects the perception of nothingness and accomplishes the supernormal power diffused by concentration. It is as in the case of the Venerable Elder Sāriputta, of the Venerable Elder Khāṇukoṇḍañña, of the lay-sister Uttarā and of the lay-sister Sāmāvatī. Thus is the supernormal power diffused by concentration.[4]

---

1. Pts. II, 210: *Katamā vikubbanā iddhi?....So pakativaṇṇaṁ vijahitvā kumārakavaṇṇaṁ vā dasseti, nāgavaṇṇaṁ vā dasseti, supaṇṇavaṇṇaṁ vā dasseti, yakkhavaṇṇaṁ vā dasseti, indavaṇṇaṁ vā dasseti, devavaṇṇaṁ vā dasseti, Brahmavaṇṇaṁ vā dasseti....Ayaṁ vikubbanā iddhi.*
2. Ibid. 210-11: *Katamā manomayā iddhi? Idha bhikkhu imamhā kāyā aññaṁ kāyaṁ abhinimmināti rūpiṁ manomayaṁ sabbaṅgapaccaṅgaṁ ahīnindriyaṁ......Ayaṁ manomayā iddhi.*
3. Ibid. 211: *Katamā ñāṇavipphārā iddhi? 'Aniccānupassanāya niccasaññāya pahānaṭṭho ijjhatīti' ñāṇavipphārā iddhi, 'dukkhānupassanāya sukhasaññāya, anattānupassanāya attasaññāya....paṭinissaggānupassanāya ādānassa pahānaṭṭho ijjhatīti' ñāṇavipphārā iddhi. Āyasmato Bakkulassa ñāṇavipphārā iddhi, āyasmato Saṅkiccassa ñāṇavipphārā iddhi, āyasmato Bhūtapālassa ñāṇavipphārā iddhi. Ayaṁ ñāṇavipphārā iddhi.*
4. (a) Ibid., 211-12: *Katamā samādhivipphārā iddhi? 'Paṭhamajjhānena nīvaraṇānaṁ pahānaṭṭho ijjhatīti' samādhivipphārā iddhi,... pe... 'nevasaññānāsaññāyatanasamāpattiyā ākiñcaññāyatanasaññāya pahānaṭṭho ijjhatīti' samādhivipphārā iddhi. Āyasmato Sāriputtassa samādhivipphārā iddhi, āyasmato Sañjīvassa samādhivipphārā iddhi, āyasmato Khāṇukoṇḍaññassa samādhivipphārā iddhi; Uttarāya upāsikāya samādhivipphārā iddhi, Sāmāvatiyā upāsikāya samādhivipphārā iddhi. Ayaṁ samādhivipphārā iddhi.*

   (b) A. I, 26: *Etad aggaṁ bhikkhave mama sāvikānaṁ upāsikānaṁ paṭhamaṁ jhāyīnaṁ yadidaṁ Uttarā Nandamātā.*

Q. What is the supernormal power of the Noble Ones? *A.* Here if a bhikkhu wishes to dwell perceiving non-repugnance in the repugnant, he could dwell perceiving non-repugnance. Here if a bhikkhu wishes to dwell perceiving repugnance in the non-repugnant, he could dwell perceiving repugnance. Here if a bhikkhu wishes to dwell perceiving non-repugnance in the non-repugnant and in the repugnant, he could dwell perceiving non-repugnance. Here if a bhikkhu wishes to dwell perceiving repugnance in the repugnant and in the non-repugnant, he could dwell perceiving repugnance. *Q.* How does one dwell perceiving repugnance in the non-repugnant? *A.* One fills the non-repugnant with the thought that is impure or regards it as impermanent. *Q.* How does one dwell perceiving non-repugnance in the repugnant and in the non-repugnant? *A.* One diffuses the repugnant and the non-repugnant with thoughts of loving-kindness and regards them as elements: *Q.* How does one dwell perceiving repugnance in the non-repugnant and in the repugnant? *A.* One fills the non-repugnant and the repugnant with the thought that they are impure or regards them as impermanent. *Q.* How does one dwell indifferent, conscious and knowing separate from the non-repugnant and the repugnant? *A.* Here a bhikkhu, seeing a form with the eye is not delighted, is not anxious, dwells indifferent, aware, knowing. It is the same as to the (objects appearing at) the other doors. This is called the supernormal power of the Noble Ones.[1] *Q.* What is the supernormal power born of *kamma*-result? *A.* All deities, all birds, some men, some born in states of suffering, perform the supernormal power of traversing the sky. This is called the supernormal power born of *kamma*-result.[2] *Q.* What is the supernormal power of the meritorious? *A.* It is as in the case of a wheel-king; of Jotika, the rich householder; of Jaṭila, the

---

1. Pts. II, 212-13: *Katamā ariyā iddhi? Idha bhikkhu sace ākaṅkhati 'Paṭikkūle apaṭikkūlasaññī vihareyyan' ti, apaṭikkūlasaññī tattha viharati; sacce ākaṅkhati 'Apaṭikkūle paṭikkūlasaññī vihareyyan' ti, paṭikkūlasaññī tattha viharati; sace ākaṅkhati 'Paṭikkūle ca apaṭikkūle ca apaṭikkūlasaññī vihareyyan' ti, apaṭikkūlasaññī tattha viharati; sace ākaṅkhati 'Apaṭikkūle ca paṭikkūle ca paṭikkūlasaññī vihareyyan' ti, paṭikkūlasaññī tattha viharati; sace ākaṅkhati 'Paṭikkūle ca apaṭikkūle ca tadubhayaṁ abhinivajjetvā upekkhako vihareyyaṁ sato sampajāno' ti, upekkhako tattha viharati sato sampajāno.*

   Kathaṁ paṭikkūle apaṭikkūlasaññī viharati? Aniṭṭhasmiṁ vatthusmiṁ mettāya vā pharati, dhātuto vā upasaṁharati. Evaṁ paṭikkūle apaṭikkūlasaññī viharati.

   Kathaṁ apaṭikkūle paṭikkūlasaññī viharati? Iṭṭhasmiṁ vatthusmiṁ asubhāya vā pharati, aniccato vā upasaṁharati. Evaṁ apaṭikkūle paṭikkūlasaññī viharati.

   Kathaṁ paṭikkūle ca apaṭikkūle ca apaṭikkūlasaññī viharati? Aniṭṭhasmiṁ ca iṭṭhasmiṁ ca vatthusmiṁ mettāya vā pharati, dhātuto vā upasaṁharati. Evaṁ paṭikkūle ca apaṭikkūle ca apaṭikkūlasaññī viharati.

   Kathaṁ apaṭikkūle ca paṭikkūle ca paṭikkūlasaññī viharati? Iṭṭhasmiṁ ca aniṭṭhasmiṁ ca vatthusmiṁ asubhāya vā pharati, aniccato vā upasaṁharati. Evaṁ apaṭikkūle ca paṭikkūle ca paṭikkūlasaññī viharati.

   Kathaṁ paṭikkūle ca apaṭikkūle ca tadubhayaṁ abhinivajjetvā upekkhako viharati sato sampajāno? Idha bhikkhu cakkhunā rūpaṁ disvā n' eva sumano hoti na dummano, upekkhako viharati sato sampajāno; sotena saddaṁ sutvā, ghānena gandhaṁ ghāyitvā, jivhāya rasaṁ sāyitvā, kāyena phoṭṭhabbaṁ phusitvā, manasā dhammaṁ viññāya n'eva sumano hoti na dummano, upekkhako viharati sato sampajāno. Evaṁ paṭikkūle ca apaṭikkūle ca tadubhayaṁ abhinivajjetvā upekkhako viharati sato sampajāno. Ayaṁ ariyā iddhi.

2. Ibid 213: *Katamā kammavipākajā iddhi? Sabbesaṁ pakkhīnaṁ, sabbesaṁ devānaṁ, ekaccānaṁ manussānaṁ, ekaccānaṁ vinipātikānaṁ. Ayaṁ kammavipākajā iddhi.*

rich householder; of Ghosita, the rich householder. And again, it is said that it is as in the case of the five persons of great merit. This is called the supernormal power of the meritorious.[1] *Q.* What is the supernormal power accomplished by magic? *A.* A magician recites spells and goes through the sky. There he causes to appear elephants, horses, chariots, infantry or various other groups of an army. This is called the supernormal power accomplished by magic.[2] *Q.* What is the supernormal power accomplished by the application of the means of success. *A.* By renunciation, one accomplishes the rejection of lustful desire; by the Path of Sanctity, one accomplishes the rejection of all defilements. It is like a potter finishing his work. Thus through the application of the means of success, all things are accomplished. This is called the supernormal power accomplished by the application of the means of success.[3]

PROCEDURE OF DEVELOPING SUPERNORMAL POWER

Q. Who practises supernormal power? How is supernormal power developed? *A.* It is said that there are nine connected with space. Again it is said that there are five in space. All men who attain to the fourth meditation, *jhāna*, with facility, develop supernormal power. Again it is said that the fourth meditation, *jhāna*, of the realm of form, makes for distinction. Therefore one develops supernormal power. Again it is said that two of the four meditations, *jhāna*, are ease-giving. Thus is supernormal power practised. *Q.* How is supernormal power developed? *A.* Here a bhikkhu develops the basis of supernormal power which is endowed with the activities of endeavour and the concentration of will. It is the same with the concentration of energy, the concentration of thought and the concentration of scrutiny.[4] "Will" is the wish to do. "Concentration" is non-distraction of the mind. That yogin wishes for supernormal power and the bases of supernormal power, and practises concentration and resolves upon the four kinds of endeavour. He endeavours to preclude the arising of evil demeritorious states that have not yet arisen; he endeavours to reject the evil demerit-

---

1. Pts. II, 213: *Katamā puññavato iddhi? Rājā Cakkavatti vehāsaṁ gacchati saddhiṁ caturaṅginiyā senāya antamaso assabandhagopake purise upādāya; Jotikassa gahapatissa puññavato iddhi, Jaṭilassa gahapatissa puññavato iddhi, Meṇḍakassa gahapatissa puññavato iddhi, Ghositassa gahapatissa puññavato iddhi, pañcannaṁ mahāpuññānaṁ puññavato iddhi. Ayaṁ puññavato iddhi.*
2. Ibid.: *Katamā vijjāmayā iddhi? Vijjādharā vijjaṁ parijapetvā vehāsaṁ gacchanti: ākāse antalikkhe hatthiṁ pi dassenti, assaṁ pi dassenti, rathaṁ pi dassenti, pattiṁ pi dassenti, vividhaṁ pi senābyūhaṁ dassenti. Ayam vijjāmayā iddhi.*
3. Ibid. 213-14: *Kathaṁ tattha tattha sammāpayogapaccayā ijjhanaṭṭhena iddhi? 'Nekkhammena kāmacchandassa pahānaṭṭho ijjhatīti' tattha tattha sammāpayogapaccayā ijjhanaṭṭhena iddhi,... Arahattamaggena sabbakilesānaṁ pahānaṭṭho ijjhatīti' tattha tattha sammāpayogapaccayā ijjhanaṭṭhena iddhi. Evaṁ tattha tattha sammāpayogapaccayā ijjhanaṭṭhena iddhi.*
4. D. II, 213: *Yāva supaññattā v'ime tena Bhagavatā jānatā passatā arahatā sammāsambuddhena cattāro iddhipādā iddhipahutāya iddhi-visavitāya iddhi-vikubbanatāya. Katame cattaro? Idha bho bhikkhu chanda-samādhi-padhāna-saṁkhāra-samannāgataṁ iddhipādaṁ bhāveti, viriya-samādhi... citta-samādhi... vīmaṁsā-samādhi-padhāna-saṁkhāra-samannāgataṁ iddhipādaṁ bhāveti.*

orious states that have already arisen; he endeavours to cause the arising of meritorious states that have not yet arisen; he endeavours to increase and to consciously reproduce the meritorious states that have already arisen; and to develop them fully. These are called "the activities of endeavour". "Endowed" means that one is endowed with these three qualities. Thus the six parts of the term are completed. "Basis of supernormal power": That by which one attains to supernormal power — the "basis of supernormal power" is only that. Therefore that state is called "basis of supernormal power". And again, the fulfilment of the activities of endeavour and the concentration of will — this is called the "basis of supernormal power". It is the means of attending to supernormal power. This is the principal meaning. "Develops" means: "Practises and repeats it". This is called "the development of the basis of supernormal power endowed with the activities of endeavour and the concentration of will". Thus that yogin practises. This is the means of success:- Sometimes he falls back; sometimes he abides. He causes the arising of energy. He fulfils [442] this basis of supernormal power which is endowed with concentration of energy and the activities of endeavour. (In) this means of success, he sometimes slackens, sometimes falls back, sometimes is perturbed. When the mind slackens, he produces the mental characteristic of alacrity; when the mind falls away, he produces concentration of mind; when the mind is perturbed, he produces the characteristic of equanimity. Thus his mind acquires the basis of supernormal power which is endowed with concentration of mind and the activities of endeavour. If one has a mind that is without defilement, one understands advantage and disadvantage with ease. He practises (saying): "Now is the time to develop", or "now is not the time to develop". Thus he accomplishes "the basis of supernormal power which is endowed with concentration of scrutiny and the activities of endeavour". Thus that yogin develops the four bases of supernormal power. His mind, being wieldy, responds to the body, and his body responds to the mind. Thus that yogin sometimes controls the body with his mind, and sometimes the mind with his body. Depending on the body, the mind changes; depending on the mind, the body changes. Depending on the body, the mind resolves; depending on the mind, the body resolves. The perception of bliss and lightness adheres to the body. In that state he accomplishes and abides. Practising thus, that yogin reaches the acme of lightness, makes his body exceedingly pliant, and attains to the capacity-limit of resolve, even as a ball of iron made red-hot is capable of being fashioned into any shape easily. Thus having through mental culture made his body light, he, owing to the lightness of body, enters the fourth meditation, *jhāna* , and is mindful and tranquil. Rising therefrom, he knows space, and resolves through knowledge. Thus his body is able to rise up in space. Having resolved through knowledge, he can rise up in space. It is comparable to cottonwool blown by the wind.[1] Here the new yogin should not go far quickly, because he might, in the course of his application, arouse fear. If he stirs up fear, his meditation, *jhāna*, will fall away. Therefore the new yogin should not go far quickly. He should go gradually. At first one *shaku*;[2] then he gradually rises and applies himself. And again, he attempts one fathom according to his size. Thus one should reach gradually the point he desires to reach.

Q. Is it possible that the yogin will fall down from the sky, if he loses his meditation, *jhāna*, there? *A.* No. This begins from one's meditation-seat. If, having gone far, the meditation, *jhāna*, is lost, one reaches the sitting place. One sees the body in the first posture (and thinks): "This is the possessor of supernormal power. This is his serenity-practice".

SUPERNORMAL POWER OF RESOLVE

That yogin applies himself gradually, and becomes capable of easy attainment. "He is able to enjoy supernormal power in the various modes. Being one, he becomes many; being many, he becomes one. Or he becomes visible (or invisible) or he goes across a wall; he goes across a barrier; he goes across a hill; he goes unimpeded as if he were in space. He can sink into the earth or come out of it, as if in water. He can walk on water as on dry land. He can move in space as a bird on the wing. In the greatness of supernormal power and might, he can handle the sun and the moon. He raises up his body and reaches the world of Brahmā.

"Being one, he becomes many": He, being one, makes himself many. He makes himself appear a hundred or a thousand, or a ten thousand and so on through supernormal power. He enters the fourth meditation, *jhāna*, and rising therefrom peacefully resolves through knowledge: "May I be many!", like Cullapanthaka, the Consummate One (arahant).

---

1. Cp. S. V, 283-85: *Yasmiṁ Ānanda samaye Tathāgato kāyam pi citte samādahati cittam pi ca kāye samādahati sukhasaññañca lahusaññañca kāye okkamitvā viharati, tasmiṁ Ānanda samaye Tathāgatassa kāyo lahutaro ceva hoti mudutaro ca kammaniyataro ca pabhassarataro ca.*

Seyyathāpi Ānanda ayoguḷo divasaṁ santatto lahutaro ceva hoti mudutaro ca kammaniyataro ca pabhassarataro ca, evam eva kho Ānanda yasmiṁ samaye Tathāgato kāyam pi citte samādahati, cittam pi kāye samādahati, sukhasaññañca lahusaññañca kāye okkamitvā viharati, tasmiṁ Ānanda samaye Tathāgatassa kāyo lahutaro ceva hoti mudutaro ca kammaniyataro ca pabhassarataro ca.

Yasmiṁ Ānanda samaye Tathāgato kāyam pi citte samādahati, cittam pi kāye samādahati, sukkhasaññañca lahusaññañca kāye okkamitvā viharati, tasmiṁ Ānanda samaye Tathāgatassa kāyo appakasireneva pathaviyā vehāsaṁ abbhuggacchati, so anekavihitaṁ iddhividhaṁ paccanubhoti, eko pi hutvā bahudhā hoti,... pe ... Yāva Brahmalokā pi kāyena vasaṁ vatteti.

Seyyathāpi Ānanda tūlapicu vā kappāsapicu vā lahuko vātupādāno appakasireneva pathaviyā vehāsaṁ abbhuggacchati, evam eva kho Ānanda yasmiṁ samaye Tathāgato kāyam pi citte samādahati, cittam pi kāye samādahati, sukhasaññañca lahusaññaca kāye okkamitvā viharati, tasmiṁ Ānanda samaye Tathāgatassa kāyo appakasireneva pathaviyā vehāsaṁ abbhuggacchati, so anekavihitaṁ iddhividhaṁ pacchanubhoti, eko pi hutvā bahudhā hoti,... pe ... yāva Brahmalokā pi kāyena vasaṁ vattetīti.

2. Nearly a foot.

"Being many, he becomes one": Desiring to change from many to one, he resloves through knowledge thus: "May I change from many to one!", like Cullapanthaka, the Consummate One.[1]

"He becomes visible or invisible. He goes across a wall; he goes across a barrier; he goes across a hill; he goes unimpeded as if in space": That yogin, having practised on the space *kasiṇa* enters the fourth meditation, *jhāna*, and rising therefrom peacefully, goes across a wall, goes across a barrier, goes across a hill. In going along, he resolves through knowledge thus: "Let there be space!". Having attained to space, that yogin, in space, goes across a wall, goes across a barrier, goes across a hill. He goes unimpeded as if in space.

What is the meaning of "He becomes visible"? It means "opens". What is the meaning of "He becomes invisible"? It means "not open". That yogin causes to open what is not open, and he goes across a wall; he goes across a barrier; he goes across a hill. What is the meaning of "He goes unimpeded"? "He can sink into the earth and come out of it as if in water". That yogin practises on the water *kasiṇa* and enters the fourth meditation, *jhāna*. Rising therefrom peacefully, he marks off a part of the earth, and resolves through knowledge: "Let there be water!". That yogin can sink into the earth and come out of it as if in water.[2]

Without obstruction "he can walk on water as if on earth". That yogin practises on the earth *kasiṇa* and enters the fourth meditation, *jhāna*. Rising therefrom peacefully, he marks off a part of water and resolves through knowledge thus: "Let there be earth!". Having produced earth, that yogin is able to move on water without difficulty as if on land.

---

1. Cp. (a) A. I, 24: *Etad aggaṁ bhikkhave mama sāvakānaṁ bhikkhūnaṁ manomayaṁ kāyaṁ abhinimminantānaṁ yadidaṁ Cullapanthako* (= *So ñāṇaparipākaṁ āgamma tattha khayavayaṁ paṭṭhapetvā cintesi: idaṁ coḷakhaṇḍaṁ pakatiyā paṇḍaraṁ parisuddhaṁ upādiṇṇakasarīraṁ nissāya kiliṭṭhaṁ jātaṁ, cittam pi evaṁgatikaṁ evā ti. Samādhiṁ bhāvetvā cattāri rūpāvacarajjhānāni padakāni katvā saha paṭisambhidāhi arahattaṁ pāpuṇi. So manomayañāṇalābhī hutvā eko hutvā bahudhā, bahudhā hutvā eko bhavituṁ samattho ahosi.*—Mp. I, 216).
   (b) Pts. II, 207: *'Eko pi hutvā bhudhā hotīti'. Pakatiyā eko bahulaṁ āvajjati, sataṁ vā sahassaṁ vā satasahassaṁ vā āvajjati; āvajjitvā ñāṇena adhiṭṭhāti 'bahulo homīti', bahulo hoti. Yathāyasmā Cullapanthako eko pi hutvā bahudhā hoti, evamevaṁ so iddhimā cetovasippatto eko pi hutvā bahudhā hoti.*
   'Bahudhā pi hutvā eko hotīti'. Pakatiyā bahulo ekaṁ āvajjati; āvajjitvā ñāṇena adhiṭṭhāti 'eko homīti', eko hoti. Yathāyasmā Cullapanthako bahudhā pi hutvā eko hoti, evamevaṁ so iddhimā cetovasippatto bahudhā pi hutvā eko hoti.
2. Pts. II, 207-8: *'Āvibhavan' ti. Kenaci anāvaṭaṁ hoti appaṭicchannaṁ vivaṭaṁ pākaṭaṁ. 'Tirobhāvan' ti. Kenaci āvaṭaṁ hoti paṭicchannaṁ pihitaṁ paṭikujjitaṁ.*
   'Tirokuḍḍaṁ tiropākāraṁ tiropabbataṁ asajjamāno gacchati, seyyathāpi ākāse' ti. Pakatiyā ākāsakasiṇasamāpattiyā lābhī hoti, tirokuḍḍaṁ tiropākāraṁ tiropabbataṁ āvajjati; āvajjitvā ñāṇena adhiṭṭhāti 'ākāso hotūti', ākāso hoti. So tirokuḍḍaṁ tiropākāraṁ tiropabbataṁ āvajjamāno gacchati. Yathā manussā pakatiyā aniddhimanto kenaci anāvaṭe aparikkhitte asajjamānā gacchanti, evamevaṁ so iddhimā cetovasippatto tirokuḍḍaṁ tiropākāraṁ tiropabbataṁ asajjamāno gacchati, seyyathāpi ākāse.
   'Paṭhaviyā pi ummujjanimujjaṁ karoti, seyyathāpi udake 'ti. Pakatiyā āpokasiṇasamāpattiyā lābhī hoti, paṭhaviṁ āvajjati; āvajjitvā ñāṇena adhiṭṭhāti 'udakaṁ hotūti', udakaṁ hoti. So paṭhaviyā ummujjanimujjaṁ karoti. Yathā manussā pakatiyā aniddhimanto udake ummujjanimujjaṁ karonti evamevaṁ so iddhimā cetovasippatto paṭhaviyā ummujjanimujjaṁ karoti, seyyathāpi udake.

"He moves like a bird on the wing in space": Here there are three kinds of movement: movement on foot; movement on air; and mind-movement. Here the yogin gets the concentration of the earth *kasiṇa* and resolves through knowledge for a path in space, and moves on foot. Or if he gets the concentration of the air *kasiṇa* he resolves upon air, and goes through air like cotton-wool. Or he fills his body and mind with the movement of the mind. The perception of bliss and lightness adheres to his body. Thus his body becomes buoyant, and he goes by the movement of the mind like a bird on the wing. Thus he goes by the movement of the mind.

"In the (greatness of) supernormal power and might,[1] he can handle the sun and the moon": Having supernormal power, that yogin gets control of the mind. Having trained his mind, he enters the fourth meditation, *jhāna*, and rising from it peacefully, he handles the sun and the moon with the resolve through knowledge thus: "Let my hand reach them!", and he reaches them with his hand. Sitting or lying down, that yogin can handle the sun and the moon.[2]

"He raises up his body and reaches the world of Brahmā": Having supernormal power that yogin gets control of the mind and goes up even to the world of Brahmā, happily. These are the four bases of supernormal power.

By training the mind thus he resolves that the distant should be near, or that the near should become distant. He resolves that many should become few, or that the few should become many. He sees Brahmā's form with divine sight. He hears the voice of Brahmā[3] with divine hearing and he knows Brahmā's mind with the knowledge of others' thoughts. That yogin has three formations.[4] He goes to Brahmā's world through two formations. This is

---

1. Lit. Supernormal power and divine might.
2. Pts. II, 208-9: '*Udake pi abhijjamāne gacchati, seyyathāpi paṭhaviyan' ti. Pakatiyā paṭhavīkasiṇasamāpattiyā lābhī hoti, udakaṁ āvajjati; āvajjitvā ñāṇena adhiṭṭhāti 'paṭhavī hotūti' paṭhavī hoti. So abhijjamāne udake gacchati. Yathā manussā pakatiyā aniddhimanto abhijjamānāya paṭhaviyā gacchanti, evamevaṁ so iddhimā cetovasippatto abhijjamāne udake gacchati, seyyathāpi paṭhaviyaṁ.*

   '*Akase pi pallaṅkena caṅkamati, seyyathāpi pakkhī sakuṇo' ti. Pakatiyā paṭhavīkasiṇasamāpattiyā lābhī hoti, ākāsaṁ āvajjati; āvājjitvā ñāṇena adhiṭṭhāti 'paṭhavī hotūti', paṭhavī hoti. So ākāse antalikkhe caṅkamati pi tiṭṭhati pi nisīdati pi seyyaṁ pi kappeti. Yathā manussā pakatiyā aniddhimanto paṭhaviyā caṅkamanti pi tiṭṭhanti pi nisīdanti pi seyyaṁ pi kappenti, evamevaṁ so iddhimā cetovasippatto ākāse antalikkhe caṅkamati pi tiṭṭhati pi nisīdati pi seyyaṁ pi kappeti, seyyathāpi pakkhī sakuṇo.*

   '*Ime pi candimasuriye evaṁ-mahiddhike evaṁ-mahānubhāve pāṇinā parāmasati parimajjatīti'. Idha so iddhimā cetovasippatto nisinnako vā nipannako vā candimasuriye āvajjati; āvajjitvā ñāṇena adhiṭṭhāti 'hatthapāse hotūti', hatthapāse hoti. So nisinnako vā nipannako vā candimasuriye pāṇinā āmasati parāmasati parimajjati. Yathā manussā pakatiyā aniddhimanto kiñcid eva rūpagataṁ hatthapāse āmasanti parāmasanti parimajjanti, evamevaṁ so iddhimā cetovasippatto nisinnako vā nipannako vā candimasuriye pāṇinā āmasati parāmasati parimajjati.*
3. Lit. *Devā.*
4. *Sankhārā.*

the teaching of the supernormal power of resolve in full.[1]

Supernormal power of resolvé has ended.‡

SUPERNORMAL POWER OF TRANSFORMATION

Now the yogin, wishing to acquire the supernormal power of transformation, practises the four bases of supernormal power. He gets control of the mind. He makes his body easy in his mind; and he makes his mind easy in his body. He makes his mind easy with his body; and he makes his body easy with his mind. He resolves upon his mind with his body; and he resolves upon his body with his mind. The perception of bliss and the perception of lightness adhere to his body. In that he abides. Practising thus that yogin reaches the acme of lightness, making his body exceedingly pliant and reaches the capacity-limit of resolve, even as an iron ball made red-hot is capable of being fashioned into any shape easily. Thus having through mental culture made his mind pliant and capable of resolve, he resolves to fill his body with his mind. If that yogin wishes to take the form of a boy, he, discarding his form, enters the fourth meditation, *jhāna*, and rising from it peacefully changes into the form of a boy, gradually. In changing his body, he resolves through knowledge: "May I fulfil the form of a boy!". Thus resolving, he can fulfil the form of a boy. In the same way in changing into the form of a snake or of a *garuḷa*, a *yakkha*, an *asura*, or into the form of Sakka-Inda or Brahmā, the ocean, a mountain, a forest, a lion, a tiger, a leopard, an elephant, a horse, infantry, groups of an army, he resolves through knowledge thus: "May I fulfil the form of infantry!". Resolving thus, he fulfils the form of infantry (and so on).[2]

---

1. Pts. II, 209-10: '*Yāva Brahmalokā pi kāyena vasaṁ vattetīti. Sace so iddhimā cetovasippatto Brahmalokaṁ gantukāmo hoti, dūre pi santike adhiṭṭhāti 'santike hotūti' santike hoti, santike pi dūre adhiṭṭhāti 'dūre hotūti' dūre hoti; bahukaṁ pi thokaṁ adhiṭṭhāti 'thokaṁ hotūti' thokaṁ hoti, thokaṁ pi bahukaṁ adhiṭṭhāti 'bahukaṁ hotūti' bahukaṁ hoti; dibbena cakkhunā tassa Brahmuno rūpaṁ passati, dibbāya sotadhātuyā tassa Brahmuno saddaṁ suṇāti, cetopariyañāṇena tassa Brahmuno cittaṁ pajānāti. Sace so iddhimā cetovasippatto dissamānena kāyena Brahmalokaṁ gantukāmo hoti, kāyavasena cittaṁ pariṇāmeti, kāyavasena cittaṁ adhiṭṭhāti; kāyavasena cittaṁ pariṇāmetvā kāyavasena cittaṁ adhiṭṭhahitvā sukhasaññañ ca lahusaññañ ca okkamitvā dissamānena kāyena Brahmalokaṁ gacchati. Sace so iddhimā cetovasippatto adissamānena kāyena Brahmalokaṁ gantukāmo hoti, cittavasena kāyaṁ pariṇāmeti, cittavasena kāyaṁ adhiṭṭhāti; cittavasena kāyaṁ pariṇāmetvā cittavasena kayaṁ adhiṭṭhahitvā sukhasaññañ ca lahusaññañ ca okkamitvā adissamānena kāyena Brahmalokaṁ gacchati. So tassa Brahmuno purato rūpaṁ abhinimmināti manomayaṁ sabbaṅgapaccaṅgaṁ ahīnindriyaṁ. Sace so iddhimā caṅkamati, nimmito pi tattha caṅkamati; sace so iddhimā tiṭṭhati, nimmito pi tattha tiṭṭhati; sace so iddhimā nisīdati, nimmito pi tattha nisīdati; sace so iddhimā seyyaṁ kappeti, nimmito pi tattha seyyaṁ kappeti; sace so iddhimā dhūpāyati, nimmito pi tattha dhūpāyati; sace so iddhimā pajjalati, nimmito pi tattha pajjalati; sace so iddhimā dhammaṁ bhāsati, nimmito pi tattha dhammaṁ bhāsati; sace so iddhimā pañhaṁ pucchati, nimmito pi tattha pañhaṁ pucchati; sace so iddhimā pañhaṁ puṭṭho vissajjeti, nimmito pi tattha pañhaṁ puṭṭho vissajjeti; sace so iddhimā tena Brahmunā saddhiṁ santiṭṭhati sallapati sākacchaṁ samāpajjati, nimmito pi ti tattha tena Brahmunā saddhiṁ santiṭṭhati sallapati sākacchaṁ samāpajjati; Yañ ñad eva hi so iddhimā karoti, tan tad eva hi so nimmito karotīti. Ayaṁ adhiṭṭhānā iddhi.*
2. Pts. II, 210: *Katamā vikubbanā iddhi?*
   Sikhissa Bhagavato Arahato Sammāsambuddhassa Abhibhū nāma sāvako Brahmaloke ṭhito sahassīlokadhātuṁ sarena viññāpeti. So dissamānena pi kāyena dhammaṁ deseti,

Q. What is the difference between the supernormal power of resolve and the supernormal power of transformation? *A*. In the supernormal power of resolve, one resolves without discarding the form. In the supernormal power of transformation, one discards the form. This is the difference.

The supernormal power of transformation has ended.‡

SUPERNORMAL POWER CAUSED BY MIND

Now the yogin wishes to acquire the supernormal power caused by the mind. Having got control of mind, he develops the bases of supernormal power and enters into the fourth meditation, *jhāna*. Rising therefrom peacefully, he attends to the interior of his body with the thought: "It is like an empty pot". Further that yogin meditates thus: "Within this hollow body of mine I will cause changes as I like. I will cause it to change". And in changing, he resolves through knowledge thus: "Following it I will accomplish!". Thus considering, he accomplishes the change. By this means, he makes many forms. Thereafter he engages himself in various activities. If the yogin wishes to go to the world of Brahmā with a created body, he creates it in the form of a Brahmā before entering the Brahmā world. The form which is made according to his will is complete with all factors, and there is no faculty wanting in it. If [443] the possessor of supernormal power walks to and fro, that created man also walks to and fro. If the possessor of supernormal power sits, or lies down, or sends forth vapour and flame, or asks questions, or answers, that created man also sits or lies down, sends forth vapour and flame, or asks questions, or answers. Because that made form springs from supernormal power, it does so.[1]

The supernormal power caused by mind has ended.‡

MISCELLANEOUS TEACHINGS

What are the miscellaneous teachings? The form which supernormal

---

adissamānena pi kāyena dhammaṁ deseti, dissamānena pi heṭṭhimena upaḍḍhakāyena adissamānena pi uparimena upaḍḍhakāyena dhammaṁ deseti, dissamānena pi uparimena upaḍḍhakāyena adissamānena pi heṭṭhimena upaḍḍhakāyena dhammaṁ deseti. So pakativaṇṇaṁ vijahitvā kumārakavaṇṇaṁ vā dasseti, nāgavaṇṇaṁ vā dasseti, supaṇṇavaṇṇaṁ vā dasseti, yakkhavaṇṇaṁ vā dasseti, Indavaṇṇaṁ vā dasseti, devavaṇṇam vā dasseti, Brahmavaṇṇaṁ vā dasseti, samuddavaṇṇaṁ vā dasseti, pabbatavaṇṇaṁ vā dasseti, vanavaṇṇaṁ vā dasseti, sīhavaṇṇaṁ vā dasseti, byagghavaṇṇaṁ vā dasseti, dīpivaṇṇaṁ vā dasseti, hatthivaṇṇaṁ vā dasseti, assaṁ pi dasseti, rathaṁ pi dasseti, pattiṁ pi dasseti, vividhaṁ pi senābyūhaṁ dasseti. Ayaṁ vikubbanā iddhi.

1. Pts. II, 210-11: *Katamā manomayā iddhi? Idha bhikkhu imamhā kāyā aññaṁ kāyaṁ abhinimmināti rūpiṁ manomayaṁ sabbaṅgapaccaṅgaṁ ahīnindriyaṁ. Seyyathāpi puriso muñjamhā isikaṁ pavāheyya, tassa evam assa—'Ayaṁ muñjo ayaṁ isikā, añño muñjo aññā isikā, muñjamhā tv eva isikā pavāḷhā'ti; seyyathāpi vā pana puriso asiṁ kosiyā pavāheyya, tassa evam assa—'Ayaṁ asi ayaṁ kosi, añño asi aññā kosi, kosiyā tv eva asi pavāḷho' ti; seyyathāpi vā pana puriso ahiṁ karaṇḍā uddhareyya, tassa evam assa—'Ayaṁ asi ayaṁ karaṇḍo, añño asi añño karaṇḍo, karaṇḍā tv eva ahi ubbhato' ti. Evam evaṁ bhikkhu imamhā kāyā aññaṁ kāyaṁ abhinimmināti rūpiṁ manomayaṁ sabbaṅgapaccaṅgaṁ ahīnindriyaṁ. Ayaṁ manomayā iddhi.*

power creates could be distinguished at any time. At this time he does not appear. He knows when it is not the time. During that time should he wish to speak, he makes himself invisible. He does not appear at any moment. The created form has no life-principle. Drinks, foods, things, and various forms of knowledge created proceed by way of nine objects, namely, limited object, sublime object, limitless object, past object, future object, present object, internal object, external object, internal-external object.

Miscellaneous Teachings have ended.‡

DIVINE HEARING

Q. Who practises divine hearing? How is it developed?

A. One who enters the fourth meditation, *jhāna*, with facility on eight *kasiṇas* and two *kasiṇas* causes the arising of divine hearing relying on the physical organ of hearing.

Q. How is the form element of the fourth meditation, *jhāna*, set free?

A. It occurs then.[1]

Q. How is it developed? *A*. The new yogin practises the four bases of supernormal power and controls his mind. He enters the fourth meditation, *jhāna*. Rising therefrom peacefully and depending on the physical organ of hearing, he attends to the sound sign. Hearing a sound afar off, or hearing a sound nearby, he attends to the sound sign. Hearing a gross sound or hearing a fine sound, he attends to the sound sign. Hearing a sound from the east, he attends to the sound sign. Thus as to all regions. Through the practice of the purity of mind and the purification of the ear element, that yogin strengthens the mental formations. That yogin hears what is beyond the reach of human ears owing to the purified divine hearing. He hears both sounds, namely, divine sounds and human sounds, also sounds afar and sounds near.[2] Here the predecessors have said: "At first the new yogin hears the sound of beings within himself after that he hears the sound of beings outside his body. Thence he hears the sound of beings anywhere. Thus he strengthens attention gradually". Again it is said: "At first the new yogin cannot hear the sound of beings within himself, because he is not able to hear fine sounds. He cannot reach the field of these (sounds) with the physical ear. But the new yogin could hear the sound of conchs, drums and the like, with the physical ear".

---

1. The question and the answer are not clear.
2. D. I, 79: *Seyyathā pi mahā-rāja puriso addhāna-magga-paṭipanno so suṇeyya bheri-saddam pi mutiṅga-saddam pi saṅkha-paṇava-deṇḍima-saddam pi. Tassa evam assa: "Bheri-saddo" iti pi, "mutiṅga-saddo" iti pi, "saṅkha-paṇava-deṇḍima-saddo" iti pi. Evam eva kho mahā-rāja bhikkhu evaṁ samāhite citte parisuddhe pariyodāte anaṅgane vigatūpakkilese mudu-bhūte kammaniye ṭhite āneñjappatte dibbāya sota-dhātuyā cittaṁ abhinīharati abhininnāmeti. So dibbāya sota-dhātuyā visuddhāya atikkanta-mānusikāya ubho sadde suṇāti, dibbe ca mānuse ca, ye dūre santike ca.*

Fine sounds or gross sounds, sounds afar off or sounds nearby could be heard with divine hearing. Here the new yogin should not attend to extremely fearful sounds, because he will (going to the other extreme) become attached to lovable sounds, and because he will stir up fear in his mind.

Knowledge of divine hearing proceeds in three objects, namely, limited object, present object and external object. If one loses physical hearing, one also loses divine hearing. Here, the hearer, who acquires facility (in the practice), is able to listen to the sounds of a thousand world-systems. The Silent Buddhas can hear more. There is no limit to the power of hearing of the Tathāgata.

Divine hearing has ended.‡

KNOWLEDGE OF OTHERS' THOUGHTS

Q. Who develops the knowledge of others' thoughts? How is it developed?

A. One entering the fourth meditation, *jhāna*, on the light *kasiṇa* and acquiring facility therein, gains divine sight and causes the arising of the knowledge of others' thoughts.

How is it developed? The new yogin having acquired the bases of supernormal power and having got control of the mind, enters the light *kasiṇa* which is pure and immovable. Rising from the fourth meditation, *jhāna*, peacefully, he, at first, fills his body with light. He sees the colour of his own heart through divine sight. Through this colour he perceives his own states of consciousness, and knows through the changes in colour the changes in his own mind: "This colour proceeds from the faculty of joy; this colour proceeds from the faculty of fear; this colour proceeds from the faculty of equanimity". If the consciousness which is accompanied by the faculty of joy arises, the heart is of the colour of curds and ghee. If the consciousness which is accompanied by the faculty of melancholy arises, it (the heart) is purple in colour. If the consciousness which is accompanied by the faculty of equanimity arises, it (the heart) is of the colour of honey. If the consciousness which is accompanied by lustful desire arises, it (the heart) is yellow in colour. If the consciousness which is accompanied by anger arises, it (the heart) is black in colour. If the consciousness which is accompanied by ignorance arises, it (the heart) is muddy in colour. If the consciousness which is accompanied by confidence and knowledge arises, it (the heart) is pure in colour. Thus that yogin understands the changes in colour through the changes within himself. At this time he diffuses other bodies with light and sees the colour of others' hearts through divine sight. He understands the changing colours through the changes in their hearts, and the changes in their hearts through the changing colours.[1] Having understood thus, he causes the arising of the knowledge of others' thoughts. Having aroused the knowledge of others' thoughts, he leaves off attending to the changes of colour and holds to the heart only as object. That yogin practises thus. Therefore his mind becomes pure.

If a certain individual has the heart of loving-kindness, he (the yogin) knows that that individual possesses the heart of loving-kindness. If a certain individual has the heart of hate, he knows that that individual has the heart of hate. If a certain individual has not the heart of hate, he knows that that individual has not the heart of hate.[2] Thus he knows all.

The knowledge of others' thoughts proceeds in eight objects, namely, limited object, lofty object, the path object, the immeasurable object, the past object, the future object, the present object and the external object.[3] The knowledge of the thoughts of those who are freed from the cankers is not within the power of the commoner. The thoughts of the beings of the formless realms are knowable only by the Buddhas. If the hearer gains freedom, he knows the thoughts (of beings) of a thousand world-systems. The Silent Buddhas know more. As to the Tathāgata, there is no limit.

The knowledge of others' thoughts has ended.‡

RECOLLECTION OF PAST LIVES

Q. Who practises the knowledge of the recollection of past lives? How many kinds of knowledge of the recollection of past lives are there? How is it developed?

A. He who enters the fourth meditation, *jhāna*, with facility on the eight *kasiṇas* and the two *kasiṇas*, is able to cause the arising of the knowledge of the recollection of past lives.

Again it is asked: What is the form plane meditation?

The fourth meditation, *jhāna*, of the form plane where there is freedom of the mind.

Again it is asked: "In the fourth meditation, *jhāna*, how many kinds

---

1. Cp. Vis. Mag. 409, where only three colours are given and are different from those mentioned here.
2. Cp. A. I, 255; D.I, 79-80; S. II, 121-22; V, 265: *Evaṁ bhāvitesu kho bhikkhu catusu iddhipādesu evaṁ bahulīkatesu parasattānaṁ parapuggalānaṁ cetasā ceto paricca pajānāti. Sarāgam vā cittaṁ sarāgaṁ cittanti pajānāti, vītarāgaṁ vā cittaṁ... pe ..., sadosaṁ vā cittaṁ... pe ..., vītadosaṁ vā cittaṁ... pe ..., samohaṁ vā cittaṁ... pe ..., vītamohaṁ vă cittaṁ... pe ..., saṅkhittaṁ vā cittaṁ... pe ..., vikkhīttaṁ vā cittaṁ... pe ..., mahaggataṁ vā cittaṁ... pe ..., amahagattaṁ vā cittaṁ... pe ..., sauttaraṁ vā cittaṁ... pe ..., anuttaraṁ vā cittaṁ... pe ..., asamāhitaṁ vā cittaṁ... pe ..., samāhitaṁ vā cittaṁ... pe ..., avimuttaṁ va cittaṁ... pe ..., vimuttaṁ vā cittaṁ vimuttaṁ cittan ti pajānāti.*
3. Vis. Mag. 431: *Cetopariyañāṇaṁ paritta-mahaggata-appamāṇa-magga-atītānāgata-paccuppanna-bahiddhārammaṇa-vasena aṭṭhasu ārammaṇesu pavatti.*

of knowledge of the recollection of past lives can be made to arise"? *A*. There are three kinds of knowledge of the recollection of past lives.

Q. With the fourth meditation, *jhāna*, how many kinds of recollection of past lives are possible?

A. There are three kinds of recollection of past lives: many lives, birth made, practice made.

"Many lives" means: recollection of past lives produced through four ways, viz., one develops the sign well, then one grasps the mental sign, one calms one's faculties and one develops that ability. These four ways produce the recollection of past lives. Of these the recollection of seven past lives is the best. Through "birth made" means: deities, *nāgas* (demons) and *garuḷas* (mythical birds) remember their past lives naturally. Of these the best remember fourteen past lives.

"Practice made" means to produce by way of the four bases of supernormal power.

Q. How is the knowledge of the recollection of past lives developed? *A*. The new yogin, having practised the four bases of supernormal power, gains control of the mind through confidence, and becomes immovable and pure. He, having sat down, remembers what he had done in the day or all that he had done bodily, mentally and verbally. Thus also as regards the actions of the night. In the same way he recollects all that he had done during a day, during two days and thus backwards to one month. In the same way he remembers all that he had done during two months, one year, two years, three years, a hundred years up to his last birth. At this time the mind and the mental properties of the preceding birth and the mind and the mental properties of the succeeding birth appear. Owing to the mind and the mental properties of the preceding birth, he gets (the succeeding) birth. Owing to mind-succession, he is able to see the causes and conditions and remember the (backward) rolling of consciousness. The two (the preceding and the succeeding) are not disjoined and are produced in this world, having been produced in that world. Through such practice of the mind that is purified, that yogin remembers his varied lot in the past. Thus (he remembers) one life, two lives, three lives, four lives and so forth. The new yogin remembers all pertaining to this life. If any yogin is not able to remember his past births he should not give up exerting himself. He should develop meditation, *jhāna*, again and again. He, in developing meditation, *jhāna*, well, should purify the mind with action similar to the correct method of burnishing a mirror.[1] Having purified his mind, he remembers his past exactly. If he continues

1. D. I, 80; M. II, 19-20: *Seyyathāpi, Udāyi, itthi vā puriso vā daharo yuvā maṇḍakajātiko ādāse vā parisuddhe pariyodāte acche vā udakapatte sakaṁ mukhanimittaṁ paccavekkhamāno sakaṇikaṁ vā sakanikan ti jāneyya, akaṇikaṁ vā akaṇikan ti jāneyya,—evam eva kho, Udāyi, akkhātā mayā sāvakānaṁ paṭipadā, yathā paṭipannā me sāvakā parasattānaṁ parapuggalānaṁ cetasā ceto paricca pajānanti, sarāgaṁ vā cittaṁ: sarāgaṁ cittan ti pajānāti...*

to remember [444] his past beginning with one life, he is exceedingly glad. Having found out the way he should not recall to mind his states of existence in the animal world and in the formless realm, and, because of inconscience, births in the plane of the unconscious deities. In this the Venerable Elder Sobhita is most excellent.[1]

The knowledge of the recollection of past lives proceeds in seven objects. They are limited, lofty, immeasurable, past, internal, external and internal-external.[2]

His lot in the past, the country and the village should be recalled to mind.[3] To remember the past is knowledge of the recollection of past lives. To remember the continuity of aggregates through knowledge is knowledge of the recollection of past lives. Outsiders remember forty aeons. They cannot remember more than that, because of their feebleness. The noble hearers remember ten thousand aeons; more than this, the chief hearers; more than this, the Silent Buddhas; and more than this, the Tathāgatas, the Supremely Enlightened Ones, who are able to recall to mind their own and others' previous lives, activities, spheres and all else.[4] The rest remember only their own previous lives and a few of the previous lives of others. The Supremely Enlightened Ones recall to mind everything they wish to recall. Others recall gradually. The Supremely Enlightened Ones, either through

---

1. A. I, 25: *Etad aggaṁ bhikkhave mama sāvakānaṁ bhikkhūnaṁ pubbenivāsaṁ annussarantānaṁ yadidaṁ Sobhito.*
2. Cp. Vis. Mag. 433: *Pubbenivāsañāṇaṁ paritta-mahaggata-appamāṇa-magga-atīta-ajjhatta-bahiddhā na vattabbārammaṇavasena aṭṭhasu ārammaṇesu pavattati.*
3. D. I, 81-2; M. II, 20-1: *Seyyathāpi, Udāyi, puriso sakamhā gāmā aññaṁ gāmaṁ gaccheyya, tamha pi gāmā aññaṁ gāmaṁ gaccheyya, so tamhā gāmā sakaṁ yeva gāmaṁ paccāgaccheyya; tassa evam assa:— Ahaṁ kho sakamhā gāmā amuṁ gāmaṁ āgañchiṁ, tatra evaṁ aṭṭhāsiṁ evaṁ nisīdiṁ evaṁ abhāsiṁ evaṁ tuṇhī ahosiṁ, tamhā pi gāmā amuṁ gāmaṁ āgañchiṁ, tatrāpi evaṁ aṭṭhāsiṁ evaṁ nisīdiṁ evaṁ abhāsiṁ evaṁ tuṇhī ahosiṁ, so 'mhi tamhā gāmā sakaṁ yeva gāmaṁ paccāgato ti. Evam eva kho, Udāyi, akkhātā mayā sāvakānaṁ paṭipadā, yathā paṭipannā me sāvakā anekavihitaṁ pubbenivāsaṁ anussaranti, seyyathīdaṁ: ekaṁ pi jātiṁ... pe ... Tatra ca pana me sāvakā bahū abhiññāvosānapāramippattā viharanti.*
4. Cp. S. II, 190-92: *Bhūtapubbaṁ bhikkhave imissa Vepullassa pabbatassa Pācinavaṁso tveva samaññā udapādi. Tena kho pana bhikkhave samayena manussānaṁ Tivarā tveva samaññā udapādi. Tivarānaṁ bhikkhave manussānaṁ cattārisaṁ vassasahassāni āyuppamāṇaṁ ahosi. Tivarā bhikkhave manussā Pācinavaṁsaṁ pabbataṁ catuhena ārohanti catuhena orohanti.*

   Tena kho pana bhikkhave samayena Kakusandho bhagavā arahaṁ sammāsambuddho loke uppanno hoti... pe ...

   Bhūtapubbaṁ bhikkhave imassa Vepullassa pabbatassa Vaṅkako tveva samaññā udapādi. Tena kho pana bhikkave samayena manussānaṁ Rohitassā tveva samaññā udapādi. Rohitassānaṁ bhikkhave manussānaṁ tiṁsavassasahassāni āyuppamāṇaṁ ahosi. Rohitassā bhikkhave manussā Vaṅkakaṁ pabbataṁ tīhena ārohanti tīhena orohanti.

   Tena kho pana bhikkhave samayena Koṇāgamano bhagavā arahaṁ sammāsambuddho uppanno hoti... pe ...

   Bhūtapubbaṁ bhikkhave imassa Vepullassa pabbatassa Supasso tveva samaññā udapādi. Tena kho pana bhikkhave samayena manussānaṁ Suppiyā tveva samaññā udapādi. Suppiyānaṁ bhikkhave manussānaṁ visativassasahassāni āyuppamāṇaṁ ahosi. Suppiyā bhikkhave manussā Supassaṁ pabbataṁ dvīhena ārohanti dvīhena orohanti.

   Tena kho pana bhikkhave samayena Kassapo bhagavā arahaṁ sammāsambuddho loke uppanno hoti... pe ...

   Etarahi kho pana bhikkhave imassa Vepullassa pabbatassa Vepullo tveva samaññā udapādi. Etarahi kho pana bhikkhave imesaṁ manussānaṁ Māgadhakā tveva samaññā udapādi. Māgadhakānaṁ bhikkhave manussānaṁ appakaṁ āyuppamāṇaṁ parittaṁ

entering into concentration[1] or without entering into concentration, are able to recall to mind always. The rest can recall only through entering into concentration.

The knowledge of the recollection of past lives has ended.‡

DIVINE SIGHT

Q. Who practises divine sight? How many kinds of divine sight are there? How is divine sight developed?

A. He who enters the fourth meditation, *jhāna*, on the light *kasiṇa* and acquires facility therein, and by him who is in possession of natural sight.

How many kinds of divine sight are there? *A.* There are two kinds of divine sight, namely, that which is produced by well-wrought kamma[2] and that which is produced by the strength of energetic developing.[3] Here, divine sight which is accumulated kamma is born of (kamma) result. Thereby one can see whether there are jewels or not in a treasury. "That which is produced by the strength of energetic developing" means that which is produced by the practice of the four bases of supernormal power.

How is divine sight developed? Having practised the four bases of supernormal power and gained control of the mind, the new yogin, being pure and immovable, enters the light *kasiṇa*. Attaining to the fourth meditation, *jhāna*, he attends to and resolves upon the perception of light and the perception of day thus: "This day is like night; this night is like day".[4] His mind being free from all obstruction and from all clinging, he is able to strengthen his mind and increase light. To that yogin who strengthens and increases his light, there is nothing obscure. There is nothing covered, and he surpasses the sun in splendour. Practising thus, that yogin diffuses his body with light and attends to colour and form. With the purified divine sight which surpasses human vision, that yogin "sees beings disappearing and reappearing, coarse and fine, beautiful and ugly, faring well or faring ill, according to their deeds.[5] Here, if one wishes to cause the arising of divine sight, he should suppress these defilements: uncertainty, wrong mindfulness, rigidity and torpor, pride, wrong joy, slanderous talk, excessive exercise of energy, too little exercise of energy, frivolous talk, perceptions of diversity, excessive

---

lahukaṁ. Yo ciraṁ jīvati so vassasataṁ appaṁ vā bhiyyo. Māgadhakā bhikkhave manussā Vepullaṁ pabbataṁ muhuttena ārohanti muhuttena orohanti.

Etarahi kho panāhaṁ bhikkhave arahaṁ sammāsambuddho loke uppanno... pe ...

1. *Samādhi* (transliteration).
2. *Sucaritakammanibbatta.*
3. *Viriyabhāvānā balanibbatta.*
4. Cp. D. III, 223: *Idh' avuso bhikkhu ālokasaññaṁ manasi-karoti, divā-saññaṁ adhiṭṭhāti yathā divā tathā rattiṁ, yathā rattiṁ tathā divā, iti vivaṭena cetasā apariyonaddhena sappabhāsaṁ cittaṁ bhāveti.*
5. It. 100; A. IV, 178: *Iti dibbena cakkhunā visuddhena atikkantamānusakena satte passāmi cavamāne upapajjamāne, hīne paṇite suvaṇṇe dubbaṇṇe sugate duggate yathākammūpage satte pajānāmi.*

investigation of forms. If any one of these defilements appears in the course of the practice of divine sight, concentration is lost. If concentration is lost, light is lost, vision of objects is lost. Therefore these defilements should be well suppressed. If he suppresses these defilements, but does not acquire facility in concentration, his power of divine sight is limited, owing to non-acquirement of facility. That yogin sees a limited splendour with limited divine sight. His vision of forms is also limited; therefore the Blessed One taught thus: "At a time when my concentration is limited, my eye is limited; and with a limited eye I know a limited splendour and I see limited forms. At a time when my concentration is immeasurable, my eye is possessed of immeasurable divine sight; and with an immeasurable divine sight, I know immeasurable splendour and I see immeasurable forms".[1]

---

1. M. III, 157-162: *Aham pi sudaṁ, Anuruddhā, pubbe va sambodhā anabhisambuddho Bodhisatto va samāno obhāsañ c' eva sañjānāmi dassanañ ca rūpānaṁ. So kho pana me obhāso na cirass' eva antaradhāyati dassanañ ca rūpānaṁ. Tassa mayhaṁ, Anuruddhā, etad ahosi: Ko nu kho hetu ko paccayo yena me obhāso antaradhāyati dassanañ ca rūpānan ti? Tassa mayhaṁ, Anuruddhā, etad ahosi: Vicikicchā kho me udapādi, vicikicchādhikaraṇañ ca pana me samādhi cavi, samādhimhi cute obhāso antaradhāyati dassanañ ca rūpānaṁ; so 'ham tathā karissāmi yathā me puna na vicikicchā uppajjissatīti. So kho ahaṁ, Anuruddhā, appamatto ātāpī pahitatto viharanto obhāsañ c' eva sañjānāmi dassanañ ca rūpānaṁ. So kho pana me obhāso na cirass' eva antaradhāyati dassanañ ca rūpānaṁ. Tassa mayhaṁ, Anuruddhā, etad ahosi: Ko nu kho hetu ko paccayo yena me obhāso antaradhāyati dassanañ ca rūpānan ti? Tassa mayhaṁ, Anuruddhā, etad ahosi: Amanasikāro kho me udapādi, amanasikārādhikaraṇañ ca pana me samādhi cavi, samādhimhi cute obhāse antaradhāyati dassanañ ca rūpānaṁ. So 'ham tathā karissāmi yathā me puna na vicikicchā uppajjissati na amanasikāro ti. So kho ahaṁ, Anuruddhā,—pe—tassa mayhaṁ, Anuruddhā, etad ahosi; Thīnamiddhaṁ kho me udapādi, thīnamiddhādhikaraṇañ ca pana me samādhi cavi, samādhimhi cute obhāso antaradhāyati dassanañ ca rūpānaṁ. So 'haṁ tathā karissāmi yathā me puna na vicikicchā uppajjissati na amanasikāro na thīnamiddhan ti. So kho ahaṁ, Anuruddhā,—pe—tassa mayhaṁ, Anuruddhā, etad ahosi: Chambhitattaṁ kho me udapādi, chambhitattādhikaraṇañ ca pana me samādhi cavi, samādhimhi cute obhāso antaradhāyati dassanañ ca rūpānaṁ. (Seyyathāpi, Anuruddhā, puriso addhānamaggapaṭipanno, tassa ubhatopasse vadhakā uppateyyuṁ, tassa ubhatonidānaṁ chambhitattaṁ uppajjeyya,—evam eva kho me, Anuruddhā, chambhitattaṁ udapādi, chambhitattādhikaraṇañ ca pana me samādhi cavi, samādhimhi cute obhāso antaradhāyati dassanañ ca rūpānaṁ.) So 'haṁ tathā karissāmi yathā me puna na vicikicchā uppajjissati na amanasikāro na thīnamiddhaṁ na chambhitattan ti. So kho ahaṁ, Anuruddhā,—pe—tassa mayhaṁ, Anuruddhā, etad ahosi: Ubbillaṁ kho me udapādi, ubbillādhikaraṇañ ca pana me samādhi cavi, samādhimhi cute obhāso antaradhāyati dassanañ ca rūpānaṁ. (Seyyathāpi, Anuruddhā, puriso ekaṁ nidhimukhaṁ gavesanto sakideva pañca nidhimukhāni adhigaccheyya, tassa tatonidānaṁ ubbillaṁ uppajjeyya,—evam eva kho, Anuruddhā, ubbillaṁ kho me udapādi, ubbillādhikaraṇañ ca pana me samādhi cavi, samādhimhi cute obhāso antaradhāyati dassanañ ca rūpānaṁ.) So 'ham tathā karissāmi yathā me puna na vicikicchā uppajjissati na amanasikāro na thīnamiddhaṁ na chambhitattaṁ na ubbillan ti. So kho ahaṁ, Anuruddhā—pe—tassu mayhaṁ, Anuruddhā, etad ahosi: Duṭṭhullaṁ kho me udapādi, duṭṭhullādhikaraṇañ ca pana me samādhi cavi, samādhimhi cute obhāso antaradhāyati dassanañ ca rūpānaṁ. So 'ham tathā karissāmi yathā me puna na vicikicchā uppajjissati na amanasikāro na thīnamiddhaṁ na chambhitattaṁ na ubbillaṁ na duṭṭhullan ti. So kho ahaṁ, Anuruddhā—pe—tassa mayhaṁ, Anuruddhā, etad ahosi: Accāraddhaviriyaṁ kho me udapādi, accāraddhaviriyādhikaraṇañ ca pana me samādhi cavi, samādhimhi cute obhāso antaradhāyati dassanañ ca rūpānaṁ. (Seyyathāpi, Anuruddhā, puriso ubhohi hatthehi vaṭṭakaṁ gāḷhaṁ gaṇheyya, so tatth' eva matameyya,—evam eva kho, Anuruddhā, accāraddhaviriyaṁ udapādi accāraddhaviriyādhikaraṇañ ca ... dassanañ ca rūpānaṁ.) So 'haṁ tathā karissāmi yathā me puna na vicikicchā uppajjissati na amanasikāro na thīnamiddhaṁ na chambhitattaṁ na ubbillaṁ na duṭṭhullaṁ na accāraddhaviriyan ti. So kho ahaṁ, Anuruddhā—pe—tassa mayhaṁ, Anuruddhā, etad ahosi: Atilīnaviriyaṁ kho me udapādi atilīnaviriyādhikaranañ ca ... dassanañ ca rūpānaṁ. (Seyyathāpi, Anuruddhā, puriso vaṭṭakaṁ sithilaṁ gaṇheyya, so tassa hatthato uppateyya,—evam eva kho me, Anuruddhā, atilīnaviriyaṁ udapādi ... dassanañ ca rūpānaṁ.) So 'ham tathā karissāmi yathā me puna na vicikicchā upajjissati na amanasikāro ... na accāraddhaviriyaṁ na atilīnaviriyan ti. So kho ahaṁ, Anuruddhā—*

Here, the new yogin should neither cling to forms nor fear forms. These faults are to be understood as in the explanation given before.

Divine sight proceeds in five objects: limited-object, present object

---

pe—tassa mayhaṁ, Anuruddhā, etad ahosi: Abhijappā kho me udapādi abhijappādhikaraṇañ ca pana ... dassanañ ca rūpānaṁ. So 'haṁ tathā karissāmi yathā me puna na vicikicchā uppajjissati ... na atilīnaviriyaṁ na abhijappā ti. So kho ahaṁ, Anuruddhā—pe—tassa mayhaṁ, Anuruddhā, etad ahosi: Nānattasaññā kho me udapādi ... dassanañ ca rūpānaṁ. So 'haṁ tathā karissāmi yathā me puna na vicikicchā uppajjissati ... na abhijappā na nānattasaññā ti.

So kho ahaṁ, Anuruddhā, appamatto ātāpī pahitatto viharanto obhāsañ c' eva sañjānāmi dassanañ ca rūpānaṁ. So kho pana me obhāso na cirass' eva antaradhāyati dassanañ ca rūpānaṁ. Tassa mayhaṁ, Anuruddhā, etad ahosi: Ko nu kho hetu ko paccayo yena me obhāso antaradhāyati dassanañ ca rūpānan ti? Tassa mayhaṁ, Anuruddhā, etad ahosi: Atinijjhāyitattaṁ kho me rūpānaṁ udapādi ... dassanañ ca rūpānaṁ. So 'ham tathā karissāmi yathā me puna na vicikicchā uppajjissati ... na nānattasaññā na atinijjhāyitattaṁ rūpānan ti. So kho ahaṁ, Anuruddhā, Vicikicchā cittassa upakkileso ti iti viditvā vicikicchaṁ cittassa upakkilesaṁ pajahiṁ; Amanasikāro cittassa upakkileso ti iti viditvā amanasikāraṁ cittassa upakkilesaṁ pajahiṁ; Thīnamiddhaṁ cittassa upakkileso ti ... pajahiṁ; Chambhitattaṁ ... pajahiṁ; Ubbillaṁ ... pajahiṁ; Duṭṭhullaṁ ... pajahiṁ; Accāraddhaviriyaṁ ... pajahim; Atilīnaviriyaṁ ... pajahiṁ; Abhijappā ... pajahiṁ; Nānattasaññā ... pajahiṁ; Atinijjhāyitattaṁ rūpānaṁ cittassa upakkileso ti iti viditvā atinijjhāyitattaṁ rūpānaṁ cittassa upakkileso ti iti viditvā atinijjhāyitattaṁ rūpānaṁ cittassa upakkilesaṁ pajahiṁ.

So kho ahaṁ, Anuruddhā, appamatto ātāpī pahitatto viharanto obhāsaṁ hi kho sañjānāmi na ca rūpāni passāmi; rūpāni hi kho passāmi na ca obhāsaṁ sañjānāmi kevalam pi rattiṁ kevalam pi divasaṁ kevalam pi rattindivaṁ. Tassa mayhaṁ, Anuruddhā, etad ahosi: Ko nu kho hetu ko paccayo yo 'haṁ obhāsaṁ hi kho sañjānāmi na ca rūpāni passāmi, rūpāni hi kho passāmi na ca obhāsaṁ sañjānāmi kevalam pi rattiṁ kevalam pi divasaṁ kevalam pi rattindivan ti? Tassa mayhaṁ, Anuruddhā, etad ahosi: Yasmiṁ kho ahaṁ samaye rūpanimittaṁ amanasikaritvā obhāsanimittaṁ manasikaromi, obhāsaṁ hi kho tamhi samaye sañjānāmi na ca rūpāni passāmi. Yasmiṁ panāhaṁ samaye obhāsanimittaṁ amanasikaritvā rūpanimittaṁ manasikaromi, rūpāni hi kho tamhi samaye passāmi na ca obhāsaṁ sañjānāmi kevalam pi rattiṁ kevalam pi divasaṁ kevalam pi rattindivan ti.

So kho ahaṁ, Anuruddhā, appamatto ātāpī pahitatto viharanto parittañ c' eva obhāsaṁ sañjānāmi parittāni ca rūpāni passāmi, appamāṇañ ca obhāsaṁ sañjānāmi appamāṇāni ca rūpāni passāmi, kevalam pi rattiṁ kevalam pi divasaṁ kevalam pi rattindivaṁ. Tassa mayhaṁ, Anuruddhā, etad ahosi: Ko nu kho hetu ko paccayo yo 'haṁ parittañ c' eva obhāsaṁ sañjānāmi parittāni ca rūpāni passāmi appamāṇañ c 'eva obhāsaṁ sañjānāmi appamāṇāni ca rūpāni passāmi kevalam pi rattiṁ kevalam pi divasaṁ kevalam pi rattindivan ti? Tassa mayhaṁ, Anuruddhā, etad ahosi: Yasmiṁ kho samaye paritto samādhi hoti, parittam me tamhi samaye cakkhu hoti; so 'haṁ parittena cakkhunā parittañ c' eva obhāsaṁ sañjānāmi parittāni ca rūpāni passāmi. Yasmiṁ pana samaye apparitto me samādhi hoti, appamāṇaṁ me tamhi samaye cakkhu hoti; so 'haṁ appamāṇena cakkhunā appamāṇañ c' eva obhāsaṁ sañjānāmi appamāṇāni ca rūpāni passāmi kevalam pi rattiṁ kevalam pi divasaṁ kevalam pi rattindivan ti. Yato kho me, Anuruddhā, Vicikicchā cittassa upakkileso ti iti viditvā vicikicchā cittassa upakkileso pahīno ahosi; Amanasikāro citassa upakkileso ti iti viditvā amanasikāro cittassa upakkileso pahīno ahosi; Thīnamiddhaṁ ... pahīno ahosi; Chambhitattaṁ ... pahīno ahosi; Ubbillaṁ ... pahīno ahosi; Duṭṭhullaṁ ... pahīno ahosi; Accāraddhaviriyaṁ ... pahīno ahosi; Atilīnaviriyaṁ ... pahīno ahosi; Abhijappā ... pahīno ahosi; Nānattasaññā ...pahīno ahosi; Atinijjhāyitattaṁ rūpānaṁ cittassa upakkileso ti iti viditvā atinijjhāyitattaṁ rūpānaṁ cittassa upakkileso pahīno ahosi. Tassa mayhaṁ, Anuruddhā, etad ahosi: Ye kho me cittassa upakkilesā, te me pahīnā. Handa dānahaṁ tividhena samādhiṁ bhāvemīti. So kho ahaṁ, Anuruddhā, savitakkam pi savicāraṁ samādhiṁ bhāvesiṁ, avitakkam pi vicaramattaṁ samadhiṁ bhāvesiṁ, avitakkam pi avicāraṁ samādhiṁ bhāvesiṁ, sappītikam pi samādhiṁ bhāvesiṁ, nippītikaṁ pi samādhiṁ bhāvesiṁ, sātasahagatam pi samādhiṁ bhāvesiṁ, upekhāsahagatam pi samādhiṁ bhāvesiṁ. Yato kho me, Anuruddhā, savitakko savicāro samādhi bhāvito ahosi, avitakko vicāramatto samādhi bhāvito ahosi, avitakko avicāro samādhi bhāvito ahosi, sappītiko pi samādhi bhāvito ahosi, nippītiko pi samādhi bhāvito ahosi, upekhāsahagato samādhi bhāvito ahosi, ñāṇañ ca pana me dassanaṁ udapādi: Akuppā me vimutti, ayam antimā jāti, na 'tthi dāni punabbhavo ti.

Idam avoca Bhagavā. Attamano āyasmā Anuruddho Bhagavato bhāsitaṁ abhinanditi.

internal-object, external-object and internal-external-object.[1] From divine sight four kinds of knowledge are produced. The knowledge of the future,[2] the knowledge of the kamma sprung from each self, the knowledge of the passing away of beings according to their deeds and the knowledge of kamma-result. Here, through the knowledge of the future, he knows the arising of the form of the future.[3] Through the knowledge of the kamma sprung from each self, he knows the kamma which others make. By that kamma he knows that such and such a man will go to such and such a world.[4] Through the knowledge of the passing away of beings according to their deeds, he sees the world in which beings will appear, and he knows that such and such a man will be born in such and such a world through such and such a kamma.[5] Through the knowledge of the kamma-result, he knows the time of arrival here; he knows the state he will reach here; he knows the defilement which causes the arrival here; he knows the means of arrival here; he knows that such and such a kamma will mature; he knows that such and such a kamma will not mature; he knows that such and such a kamma will result in much; and he knows that such and such a kamma will result in little.[6]

Here the hearer who acquires freedom sees a thousand world-systems. The Silent Buddha sees more than that, and there is no limit to the vision of the Tathāgata.

Divine sight has ended.‡

---

1. Cp. Vis. Mag: 434: *Dibbacakkhuñāṇaṁ paritta-paccuppanna-ajjhatta-bahiddhārammaṇa-vasena catūsu ārammaṇesu pavattati. The fifth, ajjhattabahiddha-ārammaṇa*, is not in Vis. Mag.
2. *Anāgataṁsañāṇa, Kammasakatañāṇa (Svamayākammañāṇa), Yathākammūpagañāṇa, Kammavipākañāṇa*, Vis. Mag. mentions only the first and the third.
3. D. III, 75-6: *Asīti-vassa-sahassāyukesu bhikkhave manussesu Metteyyo nāma Bhagavā loke uppajjissati arahaṁ Sammā-Sambuddho vijjā-carṇa-sampanno . . . So aneka-sahassaṁ bhikkhu-saṁghaṁ pariharissati, seyyathā pi 'haṁ etarahi aneka-sataṁ bhikkhu-saṁghaṁ pariharāmi.*

   Atha kho bhikkhave Saṁkho nāma rājā yen'assa yūpo raññā Mahā-Panādena kārāpito, taṁ yūpaṁ ussāpetvā ajjhāvasitvā daditvā vissajjetvā samaṇa-brāhmaṇa-kapaṇiddhika-vanibbaka-yācakānaṁ dānaṁ datvā Metteyyassa Bhagavato arahato Sammā-Sambuddhassa santike kesa-massuṁ ohāretvā kāsāyāni vatthāni acchādetvā agārasmā anagāriyaṁ pabbajissati. So evaṁ pabbajito samāno eko vūpakaṭṭho appamatto ātāpī pahitatto viharanto na cirass' eva yass' atthāya kula-puttā sammad eva agārasmā anagāriyaṁ pabbajanti, tad anuttaraṁ brahmacariyaṁ pariyosānaṁ diṭṭhe va dhamme sayaṁ abhiññā sacchikatvā upasampajja viharissati.
4. D. I, 83: *So dibbena cakkhunā visuddhena atikkanta-mānusakena satte passati cavamāne upapajjamāne, hīne paṇīte suvaṇṇe dubbaṇṇe sugate duggate yathā-kammūpage satte pajānāti.*
5. D. III, 111-12: *Idha bhante ekacco Samaṇo va Brāhmaṇo vā ātappam anvāya padhānam anvāya. . . pe . . . tathā-rūpaṁ ceto-samādhiṁ phusati yathā samāhite citte dibbena cakkhunā visuddhena atikkanta-mānusakena satte passati cavamāne upapajjamāne hīne paṇīte suvaṇṇe dubbaṇṇe sugate duggate yathā-kammūpage satte pajānāti: "Ime vata bhonto sattā kāya-duccaritena samannāgatā vacī-duccaritena samannāgatā mano-duccaritena samannāgatā ariyānaṁ upavādakā micchā-diṭṭhikā micchā-diṭṭhi-kamma-samādānā, te kāyassa bhedā param maraṇā apāyaṁ duggatiṁ vinipātaṁ nirayam uppannā. Ime vā pana bhonto sattā kāya-sucaritena samannāgatā vacī. . . pe . . . mano-sucaritena samannāgatā ariyānaṁ anupavādakā sammā-diṭṭhikā sammā-diṭṭhi-kammā-samādānā, te kāyassa bhedā param maraṇā sugatiṁ saggaṁ lokaṁ uppannā ti".*
6. Dh-a, III, 65-6: *Te 'atth' eso upāyo' ti sabbe ekacchandā hutvā 'yaṁ kiñci katvā taṁ māressāmā ti attano upaṭṭhāke samādapetvā kahāpaṇasahassaṁ labhitvā purisaghātakammaṁ katvā carante core pakkosāpetvā, 'Mahāmoggallānatthero nāma Kālasilāyaṁ vasati,*

MISCELLANEOUS TEACHINGS

Here there are the following miscellaneous teachings: If one practises one kind of concentration with the purpose of seeing forms through divine sight, he can only see forms. He cannot hear sounds. If he practises one kind of concentration for the purpose of hearing sounds through divine hearing, he can hear sounds only. He cannot see forms. If he practises concentration for the purpose of seeing and hearing, he can see and hear. If he practises concentration for the purpose of seeing, hearing and knowing others' thoughts, he can see, hear and know others' thoughts. If he practises concentration for the purpose of seeing in one direction, he cannot see in another direction, he cannot hear and he cannot know others' thoughts. If he practises concentration much, he can see in all directions, he can hear and he can know others' thoughts. Five supernormal powers are worldly higher knowledge. These are possessed by the denizens of the form plane who are with the cankers and commoners with the fetters. Meritorious higher knowledge belongs to both the learner and the commoner. To the Consummate One belongs non-characterizable higher knowledge. The five kinds of higher knowledge are not produced in the formless plane.

The section on supernormal power in the Path of Freedom has ended.‡

---

tattha gantvā taṁ mārethā' ti tesaṁ kahāpaṇe adaṁsu. Corā dhanalobhena sampaṭicchitvā 'theraṁ māressamā' ti gantvā tassa vasanaṭṭhānaṁ parivāresuṁ. Thero tehi parikkhittabhāvaṁ ñatvā kuñcikacchiddena nikkamitvā pakkāmi. Te taṁ divasaṁ theraṁ adisvā pun' ekadivasaṁ gantvā parikkhipiṁsu. Thero ñatvā kaṇṇikāmaṇḍalaṁ bhinditvā ākāsaṁ pakkhandi. Evan te paṭhamamāse pi majjhimamāse pi theraṁ gahetuṁ nāsakkhiṁsu. Pacchimamāse pana sampatte thero attanā katakammassa ākaḍḍhanabhāvaṁ ñatvā na apagañchi. Corā gahetvā theraṁ taṇḍulakaṇamattāni 'ssa aṭṭhīni karontā bhindiṁsu. Atha naṁ "mato" ti saññāya ekasmiṁ gumbapiṭṭhe khipitvā pakkamimsu. Thero 'Satthāraṁ passitvā va parinibbāyissāmī' ti attabhāvaṁ jhānaveṭhanena veṭhetvā thiraṁ katvā ākāsena Satthu santikaṁ gantvā Satthāraṁ vanditvā 'bhante parinibbāyissāmī' ti āha. 'Parinibbāyissasi Moggallānā' ti. Āma bhante' ti. 'Kattha gantvā' ti. Kālasilāpadesaṁ bhante' ti. 'Tena hi Moggallāna mayhaṁ dhammaṁ kathetvā yāhi, tādisassa hi me sāvakassa idāni dassanaṁ natthī ti. So 'evaṁ karissāmi bhante' ti Satthāraṁ vanditvā ākāse uppatitvā parinibbānadivase Sāriputtatthero viya nānappakārā iddhiyo katvā dhammaṁ kathetvā Satthāraṁ vanditvā Kālasilāṭaviṁ gantvā parinibbāyi.

ON DISTINGUISHING WISDOM

CHAPTER THE TENTH

Q. What is wisdom? What is its salient characteristic? What is its function? What is its manifestation? What is its near cause? What are its benefits? What is the meaning of wisdom? Through what merits can wisdom be acquired? How many kinds of wisdom are there?

A. The seeing, by the mind, of objects as they are—this is called wisdom.[1] And again, the considering of advantage and non-advantage, and of the sublime, is called wisdom. It is according to the teaching of the Abhidhamma.

WISDOM DEFINED

What is wisdom? This wisdom (*paññā*) is understanding (*paññā*). This

---

1. *Yathābhūtañāṇadassana.*—Cp. (a) S. III, 13: *Samādhim bhikkhave bhāvetha, samāhito bhikkhave bhikkhu yathābhūtam pajānāti.*

(b) S. II, 31-2: *Iti kho bhikkhave avijjūpanisā saṅkhārā,. . . pe . . . bhavūpanisā jāti, jātūpanisaṁ dukkhaṁ, dukkhūpanisā saddhā, saddhūpanisaṁ pāmojjaṁ, pāmojjūpanisā pīti, pītūpanisā passaddhi, passaddhūpanisaṁ sukhaṁ, sukhūpaniso samādhi, samādhūpanisaṁ yathābhūtañāṇdassanaṁ, yathābhūtañāṇadassanūpanisā nibbidā, nibbidūpaniso virāgo, virāgūpanisā vimutti, vimuttūpanisaṁ khaye ñāṇaṁ.* (=*Tassa kammaṭṭhānaṁ nissāya dubbalā pīti uppajjati. Tad assa saddh' upanisaṁ pāmojjaṁ, taṁ balava-pītiyā paccayo hoti. Balavā pīti daratha-paṭippassaddhiyā paccayo: sā appanā-pubbabhāga-sukhassa: taṁ sukhaṁ pādaka-jjhāna-samādhissa: so samādhinā citta-kallataṁ janetvā taruṇavipassanāya kammaṁ karoti. Icc' assa pādaka-jjhāna-samādhi taruṇa-vipassanāya paccayo hoti: taruṇa-vipassanā balava-vipassanāya: balava-vipassanā maggassa: maggo phalavimuttiyā: phala-vimutti paccavekkhaṇa-ñāṇassā ti.*—Spk. II, 55-6).

(c) A. IV, 336: *Satisampajaññe bhikkhave asati satisampajaññavipannassa hatupanisaṁ hoti hirottappaṁ, hirottappe asati hirottappavipannassa hatupaniso hoti indriyasaṁvaro, indriyasaṁvare asati indriyasaṁvaravipannassa hatupanisaṁ hoti sīlaṁ, sīle asati sīlavipannassa hatupaniso hoti sammāsamādhi, sammāsamādhimhi asati sammāsamādhivipannassa hatupanisaṁ hoti yathābhūtañāṇadassanaṁ, yathābhūtañāṇadassane asati yathābhūtañāṇadassanavipannassa hatupaniso hoti nibbidāvirāgo, nibbidāvirāge asati nibbidāvirāgavipannassa hatupanisaṁ hoti vimuttiñāṇadassanaṁ.*

(d) D. II, 313: *Katamo ca bhikkhave sammā-samādhi?*
Idha bhikkhave bhikkhu vivicc' eva kāmehi vivicca akusalehi dhammehi savitakkaṁ savicāraṁ vivekajaṁ pīti-sukhaṁ paṭhamajjhānaṁ upasampajja viharati. Vitakka-vicārānaṁ vūpasamā ajjhattaṁ sampasādanaṁ cetaso ekodi-bhāvaṁ avitakkaṁ avicāraṁ samādhijaṁ pīti-sukhaṁ dutiyajjhānaṁ upasampajja viharati. Pītiyā ca virāgā upekhako viharati sato ca sampajāno, sukhañ ca kāyena paṭisaṁvedeti yan taṁ ariyā ācikkhanti: 'upekhako satimā sukhavihārī ti' tatiya-jjhānaṁ upasampajja viharati. Sukhassa ca pahānā dukkhassa ca pahānā pubb' eva somanassa-domanassānaṁ atthagamā adukkhaṁ asukhaṁ upekhā-sati-pārisuddhiṁ catutthajjhānaṁ upasampajja viharati. Ayaṁ vuccati bhikkhave sammā-samādhi.

(e) Vis Mag. 438: *Kān 'assā lakkhaṇā-rasa-paccupaṭṭhāna-padaṭṭhānānī ti. Ettha pana dhammasabhāvapaṭivedhalakkhaṇā paññā; dhammānaṁ sabhāvapaṭicchādaka-mohandha-kāraviddhaṁsanarasā; asammohapaccupaṭṭhānā; samāhito yathābhūtaṁ jānāti passatī ti vacanato pana samādhi tassā padaṭṭhānaṁ.*

From the foregoing it will be seen that without *samādhi* (=four or any one of the *jhānas*) no development of *paññā* is possible. And it will be noted that this treatise as well as the Vis. Mag., beginning with *sīla* and by way of *samādhi* (*jhāna*), come to *paññā* in keeping with the teaching of the seven purifications (*Satta Visuddhi*—M. I, 149-50) and of the three trainings (of higher virtue, higher thought and higher wisdom,—*adhisīla-sikkhā, adhicitta-sikkhā, adhipaññā-sikkhā*—D. III, 219).

is knowledge. This is investigation of the truth, distinguishing,[1] synecdoche. That investigation is learned, skilful, clever, and in considering, it sees clearly and draws knowledge (?). Wisdom is good; wisdom is faculty; wisdom is power; wisdom is sword; wisdom is a tower; wisdom is light; wisdom is splendour; wisdom is a lamp; and wisdom is a gem. Non-delusion, investigation of the truth, right views—these are called wisdom.[2] The attainment of truth is its salient characteristic. Investigation is its function. Non-delusion is its manifestation. The four truths are its near cause. And again, clear understanding is its salient characteristic; the entering into the true law is its function; the dispelling of the darkness of ignorance is its manifestation; the four kinds of analytical science are its near cause.

BENIFITS OF WISDOM

What are its benefits? Incalculable are the benefits of wisdom. This is the statement in brief:—

Through wisdom are all morals made to shine.
Two kinds of wisdom lead to *jhāna*-heights.
Through wisdom does one tread the Holy Path
and see the fruition great of sanctity.
Supreme is wisdom; 'tis the eye of things.
The loss of wisdom is impurity.
Unrivalled is the growth in wisdom's state.
Through wisdom does one break all heresy.
The vulgar drawn by craving practise ill;
Not so the wise, the highest of all kind,
who rightly live and teach what profits both
this world and that. They being free and strong
see states of woe and welfare multiform,
and know condition, cause, mind, matter, norm.
This wisdom is the doctrine of the Truths.
This wisdom is the pasture of the good.
Through wisdom one attains to excellence.
Through wisdom one roots out the evil brood,
which are called craving, hatred, ignorance,
and birth and death, and all the rest that is,
which naught else ever can exterminate.

---

1. Lit. Excellent characteristic.
2. Cp. Dhs. 11, para. 16: *Yā tasmiṁ samaye paññā pajānanā vicayo pavicayo dhammavicayo sallakkhaṇā upalakkhaṇā paccupalakkhaṇā paṇḍiccaṁ kosallaṁ nepuññaṁ vebhavyā cintā upaparikkhā bhūrī medhā pariṇāyikā vipassanā sampajaññaṁ patodo paññā paññindriyaṁ paññābalaṁ paññāsatthaṁ paññāpāsādo paññā-āloko paññā-obhāso paññāpajjoto paññā-ratanaṁ amoho dhammavicayo sammādiṭṭhi—idaṁ tasmiṁ samaye paññindriyaṁ hoti.*

MEANING OF WISDOM

Q. What is the meaning of wisdom? *A*. It means "knowledge" and it means "removing well". Through what merits can wisdom be acquired? Through these eleven merits, [445] namely, searching the meaning of the scriptures, many good deeds, dwelling in purity, serenity and insight, the Four Truths, work of science (?), calming the mind, dwelling in meditation, *jhāna*, at all times, ridding the mind of the hindrances, separating from the unwise and the habit of associating with the wise.

TWO KINDS OF WISDOM

How many kinds of wisdom are there? *A*. Two kinds, three kinds and four kinds. *Q*. What are the two kinds in wisdom? *A*. Mundane wisdom and supramundane wisdom.[1] Here wisdom which is associated with the Noble Path and Fruit is supramundane wisdom. Others are mundane wisdom. Mundane wisdom is with cankers, with fetters and with tangle. This is flood. This is yoke. This is hindrance. This is contact. This is faring on. This is contamination.[2] Supramundane wisdom is without cankers, is without fetters, is without tangle, the non-flood, the non-yoked, the non-hindered, the non-contacted, the not faring on, the non-contaminated.

FIRST GROUP OF THREE IN WISDOM

The three kinds in wisdom are wisdom sprung from thought, wisdom sprung from study and wisdom sprung from culture.[3] Here wisdom which one acquires without learning from others is the wisdom that *kamma* is property of each one or the wisdom which is conformable to the truth in respect of vocational works or works of science. Thus is wisdom sprung from thought to be known. The wisdom that is got by learning from others is called wisdom sprung from study. Entering into concentration one develops all wisdom—this is wisdom sprung from concentration.

SECOND GROUP OF THREE IN WISDOM

Again there are three kinds in wisdom: skill in profit, skill in loss, skill

---

1. *Lokiya-, lokuttara-paññā.*
2. Cp. Dhs. 125 para. 584: *Lokiyaṁ sāsavaṁ saṁyojaniyaṁ ganthaniyaṁ oghaniyaṁ, yoganiyaṁ, nivaraṇiyaṁ parāmaṭṭhaṁ upādāniyaṁ saṅkilesikaṁ.*
3. D. III, 219: *Cintā-mayā paññā, suta-mayā paññā, bhāvanā-mayā paññā* (=*cintāmay' ādisu ayaṁ vitthāro. Tattha katamā cintāmayā paññā? Yoga-vihitesu vā kamm' āyatanesu yoga-vihitesu vā sipp'āyatanesu yoga-vihitesu vā vijjāyatanesu kamma-ssakataṁ vā saccānulomikaṁ vā rūpaṁ aniccan ti vā ...pe... viññāṇaṁ aniccan ti vā yaṁ evarūpaṁ anulomikaṁ khantiṁ diṭṭhiṁ ruciṁ muniṁ pekkhaṁ dhamma-nijjhāna-khantiṁ parato asutvā paṭilabhati, ayaṁ vuccati cintāmayā paññā. Yoga-vihitesu vā kamm' āyatanesu ... pe... dhamma-nijjhāna-khantiṁ parato sutvā paṭilabhati, ayaṁ vuccati sutamayā paññā. Tattha katamā bhāvanāmayā paññā? Sabbā pi sammāpannassa pāññā bhāvanāmayā paññā.*—Sv. III, 1002).

in means. Here as one attends to these states, demeritorious states are put away; meritorious states are made to increase. This wisdom is called skill in profit. Again, as one attends to these states, demeritorious states arise, and meritorious states are put away. This wisdom is called "skill in loss". Here, the wisdom of all means of success is called "skill in means".[1]

THIRD GROUP OF THREE IN WISDOM

And again, there are three kinds in wisdom, namely, the wisdom that accumulates, the wisdom that does not accumulate and the wisdom that neither accumulates nor does not accumulate. The wisdom of the Four Paths is called the wisdom that does not accumulate. The neither describable nor non-describable wisdom of the Fruit of the four stages and the object of three stages—this is wisdom that neither accumulates nor does not accumulate.[2]

FIRST GROUP OF FOUR IN WISDOM

The four kinds in wisdom are knowledge produced by one's own *kamma*, knowledge that conforms to the truth, knowledge connected with the Four Paths and knowledge connected with the Four Fruits. Here, right view concerning the ten bases is the knowledge produced by one's own *kamma*. "Adaptable patience" in one who regards the aggregates as impermanent, ill, and not-self is called knowledge that conforms to the truth. The wisdom of the Four Paths is called knowledge connected with the Four Paths. The wisdom of the Four Fruits is called knowldege connected with the Four Fruits.[3]

SECOND GROUP OF FOUR IN WISDOM

And again, there are four kinds in wisdom, namely, wisdom of the sensuous element, wisdom of the form element, wisdom of the formless element and

---

1. D. III, 220 *Tīṇi kosallāni-Āya-kosallaṁ, apāya-kosallaṁ, upāya-kosallaṁ* (*—Kosallesu āyo ti vaḍḍhi, apāyo ti avaḍḍhi. Tassa tassa kāraṇaṁ upāyo. Tesaṁ pajānanaṁ kosallaṁ. Vitthāro pana Vibhange* (325-6) *vutto yeva. Vuttaṁ h' etaṁ: Tattha katamaṁ āya-kossallaṁ? Ime dhamme manasikaroto anuppannā c' eva akusalā dhammā na uppajjanti, uppannā ca akusalā dhammā nirujjhanti. Ime vā pana me dhamme manasikaroto anuppannā c' eva kusalā dhammā uppajjanti, uppannā ca kusalā dhammā bhiyyo-bhāvāya vepullāya bhāvanāya pāripūriyā saṁvattanti. Yā tattha paññā pajānanā sammā-diṭṭhi idaṁ vuccati āya-kosallaṁ. Tattha katamaṁ apāya-kosallaṁ? Ime me dhamme manasikaroto anuppannā c' eva akusalā dhammā uppajjanti, uppannā ca kusalā dhammā nirujjhanti. Ime vā pana me dhamme manasikaroto anuppannā c' eva kusalā dhammā n'uppajjanti, uppannā ca akusalā dhammā bhiyyo-bhāvāya vepullāya bhāvanāya pāripūriyā saṁvattanti. Yā tattha paññā pajānanā sammā-diṭṭhi, idaṁ vuccati apāya-kosallaṁ. Sabbā pi tatr' upāyā paññā upāya-kosallan ti. Idaṁ pana accāyika-kicce vā bhaye vā uppanne tassa tassa tikicchan' atthaṁ ṭhān' uppattiyā kāraṇa-jānana-vasen' eva veditabbaṁ.*—Sv.III 1005).
2. Cp. Vbh. 326: *Tīsu bhūmīsu kusale paññā ācayagāmini paññā. Catūsu bhūmīsu paññā apacayagāminī paññā. Tīsu bhūmīsu kiriyāvyākate paññā neva ācayagāminī na apacayagāminī paññā.*
3. Cp. Vbh. 328: *Tattha katamaṁ kammassakataṁ ñāṇaṁ? Atthi dinnaṁ atthi yiṭṭhaṁ, atthi hutaṁ, atthi sukaṭadukkaṭānaṁ kammānaṁ phalavipāko, atthi ayaṁ loko, atthi paraloko, atthi mātā, atthi pitā, atthi sattā opapātikā, atthi loke samaṇabrāhmaṇā sammaggatā sammāpaṭipannā ye imaṁ ca lokaṁ parañ ca lokaṁ sayaṁ abhiññā sacchikatvā pavedentīti: yā evarūpā paññā pajānanā ...pe... amoho dhammavicayo sammādiṭṭhi:*

the wisdom of the unfettered. Here, meritorious wisdom of the sensuous element which is neither characterizable nor non-characterizable is wisdom of the sensuous element. Meritorious wisdom of the form element which is neither characterizable nor non-characterizable is called wisdom of the form element. Meritorious wisdom of the formless element which is neither characterizable nor non-characterizable is called wisdom of the formless element. Wisdom of the Paths and the Fruits is called unfettered wisdom.[1]

THIRD GROUP OF FOUR IN WISDOM

And again, there are four kinds in wisdom, namely, knowledge of the Law, knowledge of succession, knowledge of discrimination, and general knowledge. The wisdom of the Four Paths and the Four Fruits is called knowledge of the Law. That yogin knows the past, the future and the present through knowledge of the Law, and through this also he knows the distant past and the distant future. The knowledge of the (four) truths is knowledge of succession. The knowledge of others' minds is called the knowledge of discrimination. The kinds of knowledge that are other than these three are called general knowledge.[2]

FOURTH GROUP OF FOUR IN WISDOM

And again there are four kinds in wisdom, namely, wisdom which is due to combination and not due to non-combination; wisdom which is due to non-combination and not to combination; wisdom which is due to combination and also to non-combination; wisdom which is due to neither combi-

---

idaṁ vuccati kammassakataṁ ñāṇaṁ. Ṭhapetvā saccānulomikaṁ ñāṇaṁ sabbā pi sāsavā kusalā paññā kammassakataṁ ñāṇaṁ.

Tattha katamaṁ saccānulomikaṁ ñāṇaṁ? Rūpaṁ aniccan ti vā vedanā aniccā ti vā saññā aniccā ti vā saṅkhārā aniccā ti vā viññāṇaṁ aniccan ti vā yā evarūpā anulomikā khanti diṭṭhi ruci muti pekkhā dhammanijjhānakhanti: idaṁ vuccati saccānulomikaṁ ñāṇaṁ.

Catūsu maggesu paññā maggasamaṅgissa ñāṇaṁ.

Catūsu phalesu paññā phalasamaṅgissa ñāṇaṁ.

Maggasamaṅgissa ñāṇaṁ dukkhe p' etaṁ ñāṇaṁ . . . dukkhanirodhagāminiyā paṭipadāya p' etaṁ ñāṇaṁ.

1. Vbh. 329: *Kāmāvacarakusalāvyākate paññā kāmāvacarā pañña. Rūpāvacarakusalāvyākate paññā rūpāvacarā paññā. Arūpāvacarakusalāvyākate paññā arūpāvacarā paññā. Catūsu maggesu ca catūsu phalesu paññā apariyāpannā paññā.*

2. D. III, 226: *Cattāri ñāṇāni. Dhamme ñāṇaṁ, anvaye ñāṇaṁ, paricce ñāṇaṁ sammuti-ñāṇaṁ.* (*=Dhamme-ñāṇaṁ ti eka-paṭivedha-vasena catu-sacca-dhamme ñāṇaṁ. Catu-sacc' abbhantare nirodha-dhamme ñāṇañ ca. Yath' āha: "Tattha katamaṁ dhamme ñāṇaṁ? Catusu maggesu, catusu phalesu ñāṇaṁ". Anvaye-ñāṇan ti cattāri saccāni paccavekkhato disvā yathā idāni, evaṁ atīte pi anāgate pi: Ime va pañcakkhandhā dukkha-saccaṁ, ayam eva taṇhā-samudaya-saccaṁ, ayam eva nirodho nirodha-saccaṁ, ayam eva maggo magga-saccan ti, evaṁ tassa ñāṇassa anugatiyaṁ ñāṇaṁ. Ten' āha: "So iminā dhammena ñāṇena diṭṭhena pattena viditena pariyogāḷhena atītānāgatena yaṁ netī" ti. Paricce-ñāṇan ti paresaṁ citta-paricchede ñāṇaṁ. Yath' āha: "Tattha katamaṁ paricce-ñāṇaṁ? Idha bhikkhu para-sattānaṁ para-puggalānaṁ cetasā ceto-paricca pajānātī" ti vitthāretabbaṁ. Ṭhapetvā pana imāni tīṇi ñāṇāni avasesaṁ sammuti-ñāṇaṁ nāma. Yath-āha: "Tattha katamaṁ sammuti-ñāṇaṁ? Ṭhapetvā dhamme-ñāṇaṁ, ṭhapetvā anvaye' ñāṇaṁ, ṭhapetvā paricce-ñāṇaṁ avasesaṁ sammuti-ñāṇan ti.* —Sv. III, 1019-20).

nation nor to non-combination. Here meritorious wisdom of the sensuous element is due to combination and not to non-combination. The wisdom of the Four Paths is due to non-combination and not to combination. Meritorious wisdom of the form element and the formless element is due to combination and also to non-combination. Characterizable wisdom of the Fruit of the four stages and of the object of the three stages is neither due to combination nor to non-combination.[1]

FIFTH GROUP OF FOUR IN WISDOM

And again, there are four kinds in wisdom. There is wisdom which is due to aversion and not to penetration. There is wisdom which is due to penetration and not to aversion. There is wisdom which is due to aversion and also to penetration. There is wisdom which is due neither to aversion nor to penetration. Here the wisdom which is due to aversion and which is not due to penetration of supernormal knowledge and the knowledge of the Four Truths is called wisdom which is due to aversion and not due to penetration. That which is due to supernormal knowledge is due to penetration and not due to aversion. The wisdom of the Four Paths are due to aversion and also to penetration. The other kinds of wisdom are due neither to aversion nor to penetration.[2]

SIXTH GROUP OF FOUR IN WISDOM

And again, there are four kinds in wisdom, namely, analysis of meaning, of the Law, of interpretation and of argument. Knowledge in regard to meaning is analysis of meaning. Knowledge in regard to doctrine is analysis of the Law. Knowledge in regard to etymological interpretation is analysis of interpretation. Knowledge in regard to knowledge is analysis of argument.[3]

SEVENTH GROUP OF FOUR IN WISDOM

Knowledge in regard to consequence of cause is analysis of meaning. Knowledge in regard to cause is analysis of the Law. Understanding in

---

1. Vbh. 330: *Tattha katamā paññā ācayāya no apacayāya? Kāmāvacarakusale paññā ācayāya no apacayāya. Catūsu maggesu paññā apacayāya no ācayāya. Rūpāvacara-arūpāvacarakusale paññā ācayāya ceva apacayāya ca. Avasesā paññā neva ācayāya no apacayāya.*
2. Ibid. : *Tattha katamā paññā nibbidāya no paṭivedhāya? Yāya paññāya kāmesu vītarāgo hoti, na ca abhiññāyo paṭivijjhati na ca saccāni: ayaṁ vuccati paññā nibbidāya no paṭivedhāya. Sveva paññāya kāmesu vītarāgo samāno abhiññāyo paṭivijjhati, na ca saccāni: ayaṁ vuccati paññā paṭivedhāya no nibbidāya. Catūsu maggesu paññā nibbidāya ceva paṭivedhāya ca. Avasesā paññā neva nibbidāya no paṭivedhāya.*
3. Ibid. 293, 331: *Tattha katamā catasso paṭisambhidā? Atthapaṭisambhidā dhammapaṭisambhidā niruttipaṭisambhidā paṭibhānapaṭisambhidā. Atthe ñāṇaṁ atthapaṭisambhidā. Dhamme ñāṇaṁ dhammapaṭisambhidā. Tatra dhammaniruttābhilāpe ñāṇaṁ niruttipaṭisambhidā. Ñāṇesu ñāṇaṁ paṭibhānapaṭisambhidā. Imā catasso paṭisambhidā.*

regard to the analysis of the Law is analysis of interpretation. Knowledge in regard to knowledge is analysis of argument.[1]

EIGHTH GROUP OF FOUR IN WISDOM

And again, the knowledge of ill and cessation is analysis of meaning. The knowledge of the origin of ill and the Path is called analysis of the Law. Etymological interpretation of the Law is called analysis of interpretation. Knowledge in regard to knowledge is called analysis of argument.[2]

NINTH GROUP OF FOUR IN WISDOM

And again, knowledge of the Law, namely, the discourses, mixed verse and prose, expositions, verse, solemn utterances, sayings, birth-stories, supernormal phenomena, divisions according to matter* is called analysis of the Law. One knows the meaning of what is spoken: "This is the meaning of what is spoken". This is called analysis of meaning. Knowledge of the meaning of what has been preached is called the analysis of interpretation. Knowledge in regard to knowledge is called analysis of argument.[3]

TENTH GROUP OF FOUR IN WISDOM

And again, knowledge in respect of the eye is called analysis of the Law. Eye-knowledge in respect of views is called analysis of meaning. Knowledge in interpreting what has been preached is called analysis of interpretation. Knowledge in regard to knowledge is called analysis of argument.[4]

ELEVENTH GROUP OF FOUR IN WISDOM

And again, there are four kinds of knowledge, namely, knowledge of ill,

---

1. Vbh. 293: *Hetumhi ñāṇaṁ dhammapaṭisambhidā. Hetuphale ñāṇaṁ atthapaṭisambhidā. Tatra dhammaniruttābhilāpe ñāṇaṁ niruttipaṭisambhidā. Ñāṇesu ñāṇaṁ paṭibhāṇapaṭisambhidā.*
2. Ibid: *Dukkhe ñāṇaṁ atthapaṭisambhidā. Dukkhasamudayeñāṇaṁ dhammapaṭisambhidā. Dukkhanirodhe ñāṇaṁ atthapaṭisambhidā. Dukkhanirodhagāminiyā paṭipadāya ñāṇaṁ dhammapaṭisambhidā. Tatra dhammaniruttābhilāpe ñāṇaṁ niruttipaṭsambhidā. Ñāṇesu ñāṇaṁ paṭibhāṇapaṭisambhidā.*

* *Sutta, geyya, veyyākaraṇa, gāthā, udāna, itivuttaka, jātakā, abbhutadhamma vepulla* (*vedalla*) —transliteration.

3. Vbh. 294: *Idha bhikkhu dhammaṁ jānāti suttaṁ geyyaṁ veyyākaraṇaṁ gāthaṁ udānaṁ itivuttakaṁ jātakaṁ abbhutadhammaṁ vedallaṁ: ayaṁ vuccati dhammapaṭisambhidā. So tassa tass' eva bhāsitassa atthaṁ jānāti: ayaṁ imassa bhāsitassa attho, ayaṁ imassa bhāsitassa attho ti: ayaṁ vuccati atthapatisambhidā. Tatra dhammaniruttābhilāpe ñāṇaṁ niruttipaṭisambhidā. Ñāṇesu ñāṇaṁ paṭibhāṇapaṭisambhidā.*
4. Vbh. 296: *Yasmiṁ samaye akusalaṁ cittaṁ uppannaṁ hoti somanassasahagataṁ diṭṭhigatasampayuttaṁ, rūpārammaṇaṁ vā ...pe... dhammārammaṇaṁ vā yaṁ yaṁ vā pan' ārabbha, tasmiṁ samaye phasso hoti ...pe ...avikkhepo hoti: ime dhammā akusalā. Imesu dhammesu ñāṇaṁ dhammapaṭisambhidā. Tesaṁ vipāke ñāṇaṁ atthapaṭisambhidā. Yāya niruttiyā tesaṁ dhammānaṁ paññatti hoti, tatra dhammaniruttābhilāpe ñāṇaṁ niruttipaṭisambhidā. Yena ñāṇena tāni ñāṇāni jānāti: imāni ñāṇāni idam atthajotakāniti, ñāṇesu ñāṇaṁ paṭibhāṇapaṭisambhidā.*

of the origin of ill, of the ceasing of ill and of the Path. Knowledge in regard to ill is knowledge of ill. Knowledge in regard to the origin of ill is knowledge of the origin of ill. Knowledge in regard to the ceasing of ill is knowledge of the ceasing of ill. Knowledge which practises to completion is knowledge of the Path.[1]

The Distinguishing of Wisdom in the Path of Freedom has ended.

The Ninth Fascicle has ended.

1. D. III, 227: *Dukkhe ñāṇaṁ, samudaye ñāṇaṁ, nirodhe ñāṇaṁ, magge ñāṇaṁ.*

THE PATH OF FREEDOM

FASCICLE THE TENTH

WRITTEN

BY

THE ARAHANT UPATISSA

WHO WAS CALLED

GREAT LIGHT IN RYO

TRANSLATED IN RYO

BY

TIPIṬAKA SANGHAPĀLA OF FUNAN

THE FIVE METHODS[1]

CHAPTER THE ELEVENTH

Section One

Here, if the new yogin aspires after release from decay and death, and wishes to remove the cause of arising and passing away, wishes to dispel the darkness of ignorance, to cut the rope of craving and to acquire holy wisdom, he should develop the methods, namely, the aggregate-method,[2] sense-organ-method,[3] element-method,[4] conditioned-arising-method[5] and truth-method.[6]

THE AGGREGATE OF FORM

Q. What is the aggregate-method? *A*. The five aggregates are, the aggregate of form,[7] the aggregate of feeling,[8] the aggregate of perception,[9] the aggregate of formation,[10] and the aggregate of consciousness.[11] *Q*. What is the aggregate of form? *A*. The four primaries and the material qualities derived from the primaries.[12]

FOUR PRIMARIES DEFINED

Q. What are the four primaries? Earth-element,[13] water-element,[14] fire-element,[15] air-element.[16] What is the earth-element? That which has

1. *Upāya* 2. *Khandha-upāya* 3. *Āyatana-upāya* 4. *Dhātu-upāya*
5. *Paṭiccasamuppāda-upāya* 6. *Sacca-upāya* 7. *Rūpa* 8. *Vedanā* 9. *Saññā*
10. *Saṅkhārā* 11. *Viññāṇa* 12. Dhs. 124, para. 584: *Tattha katamaṁ sabbaṁ rūpaṁ? Cattāro ca mahābhūtā catunnañ ca mahābhūtānaṁ upādāya rūpaṁ—idaṁ vuccati sabbaṁ rūpaṁ.*
13. *Paṭhavī-dhātu* 14. *Āpo-dhātu* 15 *Tejo-dhātu* 16. *Vāyo-dhātu*

the nature of hardness and the nature of solidity. This is called the earth-element. What is the water-element? That which has the nature of flowing and the nature of cohesiveness. This is called the water-element. What is the fire-element? That which has the nature of heating and the nature of maturing matter. This is called the fire-element. What is the air-element? That which has the nature of moving and the nature of supporting. This is called the air-element.[1]

The new yogin overcomes difficulties in two ways, namely, through viewing these briefly and through viewing these at length. This should be understood as was fully taught in the determining of the four elements.

DERIVED MATERIAL QUALITIES

What are the derived material qualities? The sense-organs of eye, ear, nose, tongue, body, matter as sense-object, sound as sense-object, odour as sense-object, taste as sense-object, femininity, masculinity, life-principle, body-intimation, speech-intimation, element of space, buoyancy of matter, impressibility of matter, adaptibility of matter, integration of matter, continuity of matter, decay of matter, impermanency of matter, solid food,[2] the basis of the material element and the material quality of torpor.[3]

SENSE-ORGAN OF EYE

What is the sense-organ of eye? By this matter is seen. Visible objects

---

1. Cp. Vis. Mag. 351-2: *Yo imasmiṁ kāye thaddhabhāvo vā, kharabhāvo vā ayaṁ paṭhavīdhātu; yo ābandha nabhāvo vā, dravabhāvo vā ayaṁ āpodhātu; yo paripācanabhāvo vā uṇhabhāvo vā, ayaṁ tejodhātu; yo vitthambhanabhāvo vā samudīraṇabhāvo vā, ayaṁ vāyodhātū ti evaṁ sankhittena dhātuyo pariggahetvā punappunaṁ: paṭhavīdhātu āpodhātū ti dhātumattato nissattato nijjīvato āvajjitabbaṁ manasikātabbaṁ paccavekkhitabbaṁ.*

2. Cp. (a) Vis. Mag. 444: *Cakkhu, sotaṁ, ghānaṁ, jivhā, kāyo, rūpaṁ, saddo, gandho, raso, itthindriyaṁ purisindriyaṁ, jīvitindriyaṁ, hadayavatthu, kāyaviññatti, vacīviññatti, ākāsadhātu, rūpassa lahutā, rūpassa mudutā, rūpassa kammaññatā, rūpassa upacayo, rūpassa santati, rūpassa jaratā rūpassa aniccatā, kabaḷinkāro āhāro;*
(b) *Rūpārūp.* 1: *Cakkhudhātu sotadhātu ... kāyadhātu rūpadhātu saddadhātu ... phoṭṭhabbadhātu, itthindriyaṁ purisindiyaṁ jīvitindriyaṁ, hadayavatthu, ākāsadhātu, kāyaviññatti, vacīviññatti, rūpassa lahutā, rūpassa mudutā, rūpassa kammaññatā: rūpassa upacayo, rūpassa santati, rūpassa jaratā, rūpassa aniccatā; kabaḷinkāro āhāro ceti evaṁ aṭṭhavīsatividhesu rūpesu ādito (paṭṭhāya?) catubbidhaṁ rūpaṁ bhūtarūpaṁ nāma; sesaṁ upādārūpaṁ nāma.*

3. *Middharūpaṁ.* (a) Cp. Vis. Mag. 450: *Aṭṭhakathāyam pana balarūpaṁ ...rogarūpaṁ, ekaccānaṁ matena middharūpan ti evaṁ aññāni pi rūpāni āharitvā: addhā munī 'si sambuddho, natthi nivaraṇā tavā ti ādīni vatvā middharūpaṁ tāva natthi yevā ti paṭikkhittaṁ.* (=*Ekaccānan ti Abhayagirivāsīnaṁ* — Pm., 455, Dhammānanda Thera's Ed.).
(b) Abhmv. 72: *Tattha: "samodhānan" ti sabbam eva idaṁ rūpaṁ samodhānato paṭhavīdhātu āpodhātu tejodhātu vāyodhātu, cakkhāyatanaṁ ...pe... jaratā aniccatā ti aṭṭhavīsatividhaṁ hoti; ito aññaṁ rūpaṁ nāma natthi. Keci pana middhavādino middharūpaṁ nāma atthīti vadanti, te "addhā munī 'si sambuddho, natthi nīvaraṇā tavā" ti ca, "thīna-middha-nīvaraṇaṁ nīvaraṇañ c' eva avijjānīvaraṇena nīvaraṇa-sampayuttan" ti sampayutta-vacanato ca; mahāpakaraṇe Paṭṭhāne: "nīvaraṇaṁ dhammaṁ paṭicca nīvaraṇo dhammo uppajjati na purejāta-paccayā" ti ca; "arūpe pi kāmacchanda-nīvaraṇaṁ paṭicca thina-middha-uddhacca-kukkuccāvijjā-nīvaraṇāni" ti evam ādhīhi virujjhanato arūpam eva middhan ti paṭikkhipitabbā.*
698. *Arūpe pi pan' etassa, middhass' uppatti-pāṭhato*
niṭṭham etth' āvagantabbaṁ, na tam rūpan ti viññunā.

impinging on this, visual consciousness is aroused.[1] This is called the sense-organ of eye. And again, the sensory matter that depends on the three small fleshy discs round the pupil, and the white and black of the eye-ball that is in five layers of flesh, blood, wind, phlegm and serum, is half a poppy-seed in size, is like the head of a louseling, is made by the four primaries according to past *kamma*,[2] and in which the primary of heat is in excess, is called the sense-organ of the eye. [446] It is as has been taught by the Possessor of Great Skill, the Venerable Elder Sāriputta, "The organ of visual sense, by which one sees objects, is small and subtle like (the head of) a louse".[3]

SENSE-ORGAN OF EAR

What is the sense-organ of ear? By this sounds are heard. Sound impinging on this, auditory consciousness is aroused. This is called the sense-organ of ear. And again, the sensory matter that is in the interior of the two ear-holes, is fringed by tawny hair, is dependent on the membrane, is like the stem of a blue-green bean, is produced by the four primaries according to *kamma* and in which the element of space is in excess, is called the sense-organ of ear.[4]

SENSE-ORGAN OF NOSE

What is the sense-organ of nose? By this odours are sensed. Odour impinging on this, olfactory consciousness arises. This is called the sense-organ of nose. And again, the sensory matter that, in the interior of the nose, where the three meet,[5] is dependent on one small opening, is like a *Koviḷāra*[6] (flower in shape), is produced by the four primaries, according to past *kamma*, and in which the primary of air is in excess, is called the sense-organ of nose.

SENSE-ORGAN OF TONGUE

What is the sense-organ of tongue? By this tastes are known. Taste impinging on this, gustatory consciousness is aroused. This is called the

1. M. III, 285: *Cakkhuñ ca, bhikkhave, paṭicca rūpe ca uppajjati cakkhuviññāṇaṁ.*
2. S. IV, 132: *Cakkhuṁ bhikkhave purāṇakammaṁ abhisaṅkhataṁ abhisañcetayiṭaṁ vedaniyaṁ daṭṭhabbaṁ ...pe... givhā purāṇakammaṁ abhisaṅkhatā abhisañcetayitā vedaniyā daṭṭhabbā ...Mano purāṇakammaṁ abhisaṅkhato abhisañcetayito vedaniyo daṭṭhabbo.*
3. Vis. Mag. 446; Abhmv. 66; Dhs. A. 307: *Vuttam pi c' etaṁ Dhammasenāpatinā:*
   Yena cakkhuppasādena rūpāni samanupassati
   parittaṁ sukhumaṁ c' etaṁ ūkāsirasamūpaman ti.

   The common source of this verse has not been traced.
4. Cp. Abhmv. 66: *Suṇātīti sotaṁ; taṁ tanu-tamba-lomācite aṅguliveṭhaka-saṇṭhāne padese vuttappakārāhi dhātūhi kat' ūpakāraṁ utu-citt' āhārehi upatthambhiyamānaṁ āyunā paripāliyamānaṁ; sotaviññāṇādīnaṁ vatthu-dvāra-bhāvaṁ sādhayamānaṁ tiṭṭhati.*
5. Cp. Ibid: *Ghāyatīti ghāṇaṁ, taṁ sasambhāra-ghāṇabilassa anto ajapada-saṇṭhane padese yathāvuttappakāraṁ hutvā tiṭṭhati.*
6. A sort of ebony, *Bauhinia variegata*— P.T.S. Dict.

sense-organ of tongue. And again, the sensory matter that is two-finger breadths in size, is in shape like a blue lotus,[1] is located in the flesh of the tongue, is a product of the four primaries, is wrought according to past *kamma*, and in which the primary of water is in excess, is called the sense-organ of tongue.

SENSE-ORGAN OF BODY

What is the sense-organ of body? By this tangibles are known. By the impact of tangibles on this, tactual consciousness is aroused. This is called sense-organ of body. And again, it is the sensory matter that is in the entire body, excepting the hair of the body and of the head, nails, teeth and other insensitive parts, is produced by the four primaries, according to past *kamma*, and in which the primary of earth is in excess. This is called the sense-organ of body. Material sense-object is the reaction of visible objects, auditory sense-object is the reaction of sound, olfactory sense-object is the reaction of odour, gustatory sense-object is the reaction of flavour. Femininity is the characteristic of female nature; masculinity is the characteristic of male nature; that which preserves the body wrought by *kamma*, is called life-principle; body intimation means bodily activities; speech intimation means verbal activities; what delimits matter is called the element of space. Buoyancy of matter means, the lightness-characteristic of material nature; impressibility of matter means, the plasticity-characteristic of material nature; adaptibility of matter means, the workability-characteristic of material nature; these three are the characteristics of non-sluggishness in material nature; the accumulation of these sense-organs is called the integration of matter. This integration of matter is called the continuity of matter. The arising of material objects is the coming to birth of matter; the maturing of material objects is the decay of matter; matter decays—this is called the impermanency of matter. That, by which beings get nutritive essence, is called solid food. The growth which is dependent on the primaries and the element of consciousness, is called the sense-organ of the material element. All primaries are characterized by the material quality of torpor. These twenty-six material qualities and the four primaries make up thirty kinds of matter.[2]

DIFFERENCE BETWEEN THE FOUR PRIMARIES AND DERIVED MATTER

Q. What is the difference between the four primaries and the matter

---

1. (a) Uppala. Cp. J. V, 37: *Nila-ratta-set-uppala, ratta-seta-paduma, seta-kumuda, kalla-hāra*—The seven kinds of lotuses. See P.T.S. Dict.
   (b) Abhmv. 66: *Sāyatīti jivhā; jīviatm avhāyatīti vā jivhā; sā sasambhāra-jivhāmajjhassa upari uppala-dalagga-saṇṭhāne padese yathāvuttappakārā hutvā tiṭṭhati.*
2. According to Abhmv. 71, there are twenty-eight only — verse 695:—
   Bhūtā rūpāni cattāri, upādā catuvīsati
   aṭṭhavisati rūpāni, sabbān' eva bhavanti hi.

derived from the four primaries? *A.* Depending on one another, the four primaries are produced. Though the four derived material qualities are produced in dependence on the four primaries, the four primaries do not depend on the derived material qualities and the material qualities derived from the four primaries are not interdependent.

SIMILE OF THE THREE STICKS

The four primaries should be known as three sticks which stand supporting one another. The material qualities derived from the four primaries should be known as the shadow cast by the three sticks, which support each other. This is the difference between them. Here the yogin knows that all these thirty material qualities are of five kinds by way of arising, group, birth, diversity, unity.

MATERIAL QUALITIES BY WAY OF ARISING

Q. How, by way of arising? *A.* Nine material qualities arise owing to the cause-condition of *kamma.* They are the sense-organs of eye, ear, nose, tongue and body, femininity, masculinity, life-principle, and the basis of the material element. Two material qualities arise owing to the cause-condition of consciousness. They are body-intimation and speech-intimation. One material quality arises owing to the cause-condition of the caloric order and consciousness. It is the auditory sense-object. Four material qualities arise owing to the cause-condition of caloricity, consciousness and nutriment. They are buoyancy of matter, impressibility of matter, adaptibility of matter and the material quality of torpor. Twelve material qualities arise owing to four cause-conditions. They are material sense-object, olfactory sense-object, gustatory sense-object, space-element, integration of matter, continuity of matter, birth of matter, solid food and the four elements.

Of two material qualities, namely decay of matter and impermanency of matter, there is no arising. And again, decay depends on birth; and depending on decay, there is impermanency. Thus one should know the character of these by way of arising.

MATERIAL QUALITIES BY WAY OF GROUP

Q. How, by way of group?[1] *A.* Nine groups are produced by *kamma.* Nine groups are produced by consciousness. Six groups are produced by caloric order. Three groups are produced by nutriment.

Q. What are the nine groups produced by *kamma*? *A.* They are the eye-decad, ear-decad, nose-decad, tongue-decad, body-decad femininity-decad, masculinity-decad, basis-decad, life-ennead.[2]

---

1. *Kalāpa.*
2. *Cakkhu-dasaka-, sota-dasaka-, ghāna-dasaka-, kāya-dasaka-, itthindriya-dasaka-, puris-indriya-dasaka-, āyatana-dasaka-kalāpa* (possibly for *hadayavatthu*); *jīvita-navaka-kalāpa.*

Q. What is the eye-decad? *A*. The four elements of eye-sentience are its basis. And again, it consists of the four primaries, form, odour, flavour, contact,[1] life-principle and the sentient eye. This decad is produced together and does not separate. This is called "group" and this is called the eye-decad. The arising of this is birth; its maturing is called decay; its destruction is called impermanency; what delimits it is called space-element; these four and the group arise together. When the eye-decad decays, it produces a second decad; these two kinds of decads should be known as "group". Coming after is called succession. These six states arise together. When decay sets in, the second eye-decad produces a third decad. These, the second and the third eye-decads are called "group". Coming after is called succession. The first decad is scattered, the second decad decays, the third decad arises. These occur in one moment. Thus the eye-decad arises. None can discern the interval. So quick it is that by worldly knowledge it cannot be known. There is a yogin. He sees the succession of the eye. It is like a flowing stream. It is like the flame of a lamp.[2] Thus should the eye-decad be known. In the same way one should know the ear-decad, the nose-decad, the tongue-decad, the body-decad, femininity-decad, masculinity-decad, life-principle-ennead at length.

Q. What are the nine consciousness-born groups? *A*. Bare-octad, bare-body-intimation-ennead, bare-speech-intimation-heptad, bare-buoyancy-ennead, buoyancy-body-intimation-decad, buoyancy-speech-intimation-undecad, bare-eye-ennead, eye-body-intimation-decad, eye-speech-intimation-undecad.

Q. What is the consciousness-born-bare-octad? *A*. The four elements and visible object, odour, flavour and contact which depend on the elements. These eight are named the bare-octad.

The arising of these is birth; the maturing of these is decay; destruction of these is impermanency; what delimits these is space-element; these four states arise in them. At the time of their destruction, this bare octad sets going a second bare-octad together with the second consciousness. Destruction of the first bare (-octad) and the arising of the second bare (-octad) occur in a moment.*

In the same way, the bare-buoyancy-nonary and the bare-eye-ennead (should be understood). These six groups[3] are not destroyed in the first and not produced in the second, do not occur in one instant, because no two intimations can take place in one conscious track. The rest should be known in the way it was fully taught before.

---

1. *Ojā* according to abhms.
2. Abhms. Ch. VI, 10: *Catu-samuṭṭhāna-rupā-kalāpa-santati kāmaloke dīpa-jālā viya nadi soto viya.*
* This line is unintelligible.
3. Bare-body-intimation, bare-speech-intimation, buoyancy-body-intimation, buoyancy-speech-intimation, eye-body-intimation, eye-speech-intimation.

Q. What are the six groups produced by the caloric order? *A.* Bare-octad, bare-sound-ennead, bare-buoyancy-ennead, buoyancy-sound-decad, bare-eye-ennead, eye-sound-decad. External groups are of two kinds: bare-octad and sound-ennead.

Q. What are the three groups which are produced in nutriment? *A.* Bare octad, bare-buoyancy-ennead and bare-eye-ennead.

Of groups that are produced by caloric order and nutriment, the continuity, *kamma* and basis should be known as equal. The rest is as was taught above. The divine life-ennead is fulfilled in the sensuous element and in the sphere of action. Eight groups continue because of life: nose, tongue, body, masculinity or femininity, and the three beginning with buoyancy, and torpidity. These are not in the form-element. The divine life-ennead pertains to the unconscious Brahmas. In their body all the sense-organs exist. (Thus one should know), through groups.

MATERIAL QUALITIES BY WAY OF BIRTH

Q. How, through birth? *A.* It should be known by way of a male or female entering a womb. In the first moment thirty material qualities are produced.[1] They are the basis-decad, body-decad, femininity-decad, masculinity-decad. In the case of a person who is neither a male nor a female, twenty material qualities are produced.[2] They are the basis-decad and the body-decad.

Taking birth in the sensuous element, a male or a female possessed of the faculties and the sense-organs arouses seventy material qualities at the time of birth. They are the basis-decad, the body-decad, the eye-decad, the ear-decad, the nose-decad, the tongue-decad, the femininity or masculinity-decad.

When a blind male or female is born in an evil state, that person arouses sixty material qualities, at the moment of birth, namely, (all) except the eye-decad. In the same way a deaf person [447] arouses sixty material qualities, namely, (all) except the ear-decad. A deaf and blind person arouses fifty material qualities namely, (all) except the eye-decad and the ear-decad. When one who is neither a male nor a female is born, at the beginning of an aeon, in an evil state, having faculties and sense-organs, that person arouses sixty material qualities at the moment of birth, namely, (all) except the masculinity or femininity decad. A person, who is neither a male nor a female and is blind,

---

1. Abhms. 77, v. 746: *Gabbhaseyyaka-sattassa, paṭisandikkhaṇe pana*
tiṁsā rūpāni jāyante, sabhāvass' eva dehino.
2. (a) Ibid. v. 747: *Abhāva-gabbhaseyyānaṁ; aṇḍajānañ ca vīsati*
bhavanti paña rūpāni, kāyavatthuvasena tu,
(b) Cp. Vbh-a. 169-70: *Evaṁ pavattamāne c' etasmiṁ nāmarūpe yasmā abhāvaka-gabbhaseyyakānaṁ aṇḍajānañ ca paṭisandhikkhaṇe vatthu-kāyavasena rūpato dve santatisīsāni tayo ca arūpino khandhā pātubhavanti, tasmā tesaṁ vitthārena rūparūpato vīsati-dhammā tayo ca arūpino khandhā ti ete tevīsati-dhammā viññāṇapaccayā nāma-rūpan ti veditabbā.*

produces fifty material qualities, namely, (all) except the eye-faculty-decad and the masculinity or femininity-decad. A person who is neither a male nor a female and who is deaf arouses fifty material qualities, namely, (all) except the ear-decad and masculinity or femininity. A person who is neither a male nor a female, and is blind and deaf, arouses forty material qualities, namely, the basis-decad, the body-decad, the nose-decad and the tongue-decad. Brahmā arouses forty-nine material qualities at the moment of birth. They are the basis-decad, the eye-decad, the ear-decad, the body-decad and the life-principle-ennead. The beings of the divine-plane of inconscience arouse nine material qualities at the moment of birth, namely, the life-principle-ennead. Thus one should know through birth.

MATERIAL QUALITIES BY WAY OF DIVERSITY,— GROUPS OF TWO IN MATERIAL QUALITIES

Q. How, through diversity? *A.* All material qualities are of two kinds. They are gross or subtle. Here, twelve material qualities are gross, because internal and external material sense-objects are seized through impact. The other eighteen material qualities are subtle, because they are not seized through impact. And again, there are two kinds of material qualities. They are internal and external. Here, five material qualities are internal, because the five sense-organs of eye and others are limited. The other thirty-five material qualities are external matter, because they are not limited. And again, there are two kinds. They are faculty and non-faculty.[1] Here eight material qualities are faculty. They are the five internals (possibly, five sentient organs), the faculty of femininity, of masculinity and life; they are so because of dependence. The other twenty-two are non-faculty, because they are non-dependent.[2]

GROUPS OF THREE IN MATERIAL QUALITIES

All material qualities can be divided into three kinds. They are non-material qualities and arrested material qualities.[3] Here nine material qualities are feeling. They are the eight faculties and the material basis, because they are produced owing to *kamma*-result. Nine material qualities are the sense-object of sound, body-intimation, speech-intimation, buoyancy of matter, impressibility of matter, workability of matter, decay of matter, impermanency of matter and torpidity. These are not produced through *kamma*-result. The other twelve material qualities are breakable ones because they have two kinds of significance (?). And again, material qualities are of three kinds: visible and reacting, invisible and reacting and invisible and

1. Lit. Life-faculty and non-life-faculty.
2. Cp. Dhs. 125-27, para. 585.
3. Lit. Having broken material qualities.

non-reacting.[1] Here one material quality is visible and reacting, that is, material sense-object, because it can be seen and touched. Eleven material qualities are invisible and reacting. They are gross matter except material sense-object, because they cannot be seen but can be touched. Eighteen material qualities are invisible and non-reacting. All other subtle matter is invisible and non-reacting.

FOUR KINDS OF MATERIAL QUALITIES

Again, all material qualities are of four kinds, by way of intrinsic nature of matter, material form, material characteristics and delimitation of matter. Here nineteen material qualities are intrinsic. They are the twelve gross material qualities, femininity, masculinity, life-principle, element of water, solid food, material basis and material quality of eye, because they limit (?). Seven material qualities are material form. They are body-intimation, speech-intimation, buoyancy of matter, impressibility of matter, workability of matter, integration of matter, continuity of matter and intrinsic nature of matter, because they change. Three material qualities are material characteristics. They are birth of matter, decay of matter and impermanency of matter, because they are conditioned. One material quality is delimitation of matter. It is space-element, because it defines the groups. Here, through intrinsic nature one discriminates, not through the others. Thus one should understand through diversity.

MATERIAL QUALITIES BY WAY OF UNITY

Q. How, through unity? *A*. All material qualities are one, as being not a condition, as not being non-conditioned, as being dissociated from condition, causally related, put-together, worldly, cankerous, binding, fettering, as being with flood, yoke, hindrance, as being infected, as being with faring-on, passion, as being indeterminate, objectless, non-mental, dissociated from mind, as not arising together with pleasure, as not arising together with pain, as arising together with non-pain and non-pleasure, as neither group nor non-group, as neither learning nor non-learning, as neither broken by views nor broken by concentration. Thus one should know the character of matter through unity. This is called the aggregate of matter.

---

1. D. III, 217: *Tividhena rūpa-saṁgaho. Sanidassana-sappaṭighaṁ rūpaṁ, anidassana-sappaṭighaṁ rūpaṁ, anidassana-appaṭighaṁ rūpaṁ* (=*Sanidassan' ādisu attānaṁ ārabbha pavattena cakkhuviññāṇa-saṅkhātena saha nidassanen āti sanidassanaṁ. Cakkhu-paṭihanana-samatthato saha-paṭighenā ti sappaṭighaṁ. Tam atthato rūp'āyatanam eva. Cakkhu-viññāṇa-saṅkhātaṁ nāssa nidassanan ti anidassanaṁ. Sot' ādi-paṭihananasamatthato saha-paṭighenā ti sappaṭighaṁ. Taṁ atthato cakkhāyatanan' ādini nava āyatanāni. Vuttappakāraṁ nāssa nidassanan ti anidassanaṁ. Nāssa paṭigho ti appaṭighaṁ. Taṁ atthato ṭhapetvā das' āyat-anāni avasesaṁ sukhuma-rūpaṁ*—Sv. III, 997).

AGGREGATE OF FEELING

Q. What is the aggregate of feeling? *A*. From the point of characteristic, feeling is of one kind, as being experienced by the mind only. From the point of sense-organ, it is of two kinds thus: bodily and mental. From the point of intrinsic nature, it is of three kinds: blissful feeling, painful feeling, feeling that is neither blissful nor painful.[1] From the point of the Law, it is of four kinds: meritorious, demeritorious, retributive and objective. From the point of faculties, there are five kinds, namely, pleasure-faculty, pain-faculty, joy-faculty, grief-faculty, indifference-faculty.[2] From the point of black and white, it is of six kinds, namely, cankerous feeling of pleasure, non-cankerous feeling of pleasure, cankerous feeling of pain, non-cankerous feeling of pain, cankerous feeling of neither pain nor pleasure, non-cankerous feeling of neither pain nor pleasure. From the point of method, it is of seven kinds thus: feeling born of eye-contact, of ear-contact, of nose-contact, of tongue-contact, of body-contact, contact of mind-element, contact of mind-consciousness. Fully one hundred and eight kinds of feeling are fulfilled. Six states of feeling are aroused from craving; six from renunciation; six from grief-craving; six from grief-renunciation; six from equanimity-craving; six from equanimity-renunciation. Six times six are thirty-six, and in the three divisions of time, these thirty-six are increased three times. This is called the aggregate of feeling.[3]

AGGREGATE OF PERCEPTION

Q. What is the aggregate of perception? *A*. From the point of characteristic, perception is single, because only the mind apprehends objects. From the point of black and white, it is of two kinds, namely, perception-reversal and perception-non-reversal.[4] From the point of demerit, it is of three kinds, namely, lustful-perception, hating-perception and harming-perception. From the point of merit, it is of three kinds, namely, renunciation-perception, non-hating-perception and non-harming-perception.[5] From the point of not knowing the significant nature of sense-organ, it is of four kinds, namely, the perception of the ugly as beautiful, of ill as well, of impermanence as non-impermanence, of not-self as self. From the point of knowing the significant nature of sense-organ, it is of four kinds, namely, perception of the

---

1. S. IV, 231-32: *Katamā ca bhikkhave dve vedanā. Kāyikā ca cetasikā ca. Imā vuccanti bhikkhave dve vedanā. Katamā ca bhikkhave tisso vedanā. Sukhā vedanā dukkhā vedanā adukkhamasukhā vedanā. Imā vuccanti bhikkhave tisso vedanā.*
2. Ibid. 232: *Katamā ca bhikkhave pañca vedanā. Sukhindriyaṁ dukkhindriyaṁ somanassindriyaṁ domanassindriyaṁ upekkhindriyaṁ. Imā vuccanti bhikkhave pañca vedanā.*
3. S. IV, 232: *Katamā ca bhikkhave chattiṁsa vedanā. Cha gehasitāni somanassāni cha nekkhammasitāni somanassāni cha gehasitāni domanassāni cha nekkhammasitāni domanassāni cha gehasitā upekkhā cha nekkhammasitā upekkhā. Imā vuccanti bhikkhave chattiṁsa vedanā.*
4. *Saññā vipallāsa, saññā avipallāsa.*
5. D. III, 215: *Tisso akusala-saññā. Kāma-saññā, vyāpāda-saññā, vihiṁsā saññā. Tisso kusala-saññā. Nekkhamma-saññā, avyāpāda-saññā, avihiṁsā-saññā.*

ugly, perception of ill, perception of impermanence and perception of not-self.[1] According to the Vinaya, it is of five kinds, thus: the perception of the ugly as beautiful, of the ugly as ugly, of the beautiful as beautiful and the perception of uncertainty. From the point of object, there are six kinds thus: form-perception, sound-perception, perception of odour, perception of taste, perception of contact, perception of ideas.[2] By way of door, there are seven kinds thus: perception that is born of eye-contact, ear-contact, nose-contact, tongue-contact, body-contact, mind-element-contact, consciousness-element-contact. Thus should the several kinds of perception be known. This is called the aggregate of perception.[3]

AGGREGATE OF FORMATIONS

Q. What is the aggregate of formations? *A.* Contact, volition, initial application of thought, sustained application of thought, joy, confidence, energy, mindfulness, concentration, wisdom, life-principle, (removal of) hindrance, non-greed, non-hate, modesty, decorum, repose, wish to do, resolve, equanimity, attention, greed, hatred, delusion, conceit, views, agitation and anxiety, uncertainty, indolence, immodesty, indecorum[4] and all other mental properties, except feeling and perception, belong to the aggregate of formations.

THIRTY-ONE SIMILES

Here contact means mind touches object. It is likened to a sunbeam

---

1. A. II, 52: *Anicce bhikkhave niccan ti saññāvipallāso cittavipallāso diṭṭhivipallāso, adukkhe bhikkhave dukkhan ti saññāvipallāso . . . , anattani bhikkhave attā ti saññāvipallāso . . . , asubhe bhikkhave subhan ti saññāvipallāso cittavipallāso diṭṭhivipallāso . . .*

   Anicce bhikkhave aniccan ti na saññāvipallāso . . . , dukkhe bhikkhave dukkhan ti na saññāvipallāso . . . , anattani bhikkhave anattā ti na saññā vipallāso . . . , asubhe bhikkhave asubhan ti na saññāvipallāso . . .

   Anicce niccasaññino dukkhe ca sakhasaññino
   Anattani ca attā ti asubhe subhasaññino
   Micchadiṭṭhigatā sattā . . .
   . . .
   Aniccan aniccato dakkhuṁ dukkham addakkhu dukkhato
   Anattani anattā ti asubham asubhat' addasuṁ
   Sammadiṭṭhisamādānā sabbadukkham upaccagun ti.

2. Vbh. 102, 104: *Rūpasaññā loke piyarūpaṁ sātarūpaṁ etth'esā taṇhā pahīyamānā pahīyati, ettha nirujjhamānā nirujjhati. Saddasaññā . . .pe. . . gandhasaññā. . . rasasaññā . . . phoṭṭhabbasaññā . . . dhammasaññā loke piyarūpaṁ etth'esā taṇhā pahīyamānā pahīyati, ettha nirujjhamānā nirujjhati.*
3. Cp. Vbh.-a. 19: *Cakkhusamphassajā saññā ti ādīni atītādivasena niddiṭṭha-saññaṁ sabhāvato dassetuṁ vuttāni. Tattha cakkhusamphassato, cakkhusamphassasmiṁ vā jātā chakkhusamphassajā nāma. Sesesu pi es'eva nayo. Ettha ca purimā pañca cakkhuppasādādivatthukā va. Manosamphassajā hadaya-vatthukā pi avatthukā pi. Sabbā catubhūmikā-saññā.*
4. *Phassa, cetanā, vitakka, vicāra, pīti, saddhā, viriya, sati, samādhi, paññā, jīvitindriya, nīrvaraṇe* (*pahīna*,—suggested by Prof. Higata), *alobha, adosa, hiri, ottappa passaddhi, chanda, adhimokkha, upekkhā, manasikāra, lobha, dosa, moha, māna, diṭṭhi, uddhacca-kukkucca* (in the explanation *thīna* is substituted for *kukkucca*), *vicikicchā, kosajja, ahiri, anottappa.*

touching a wall.[1] This is the basis of perception. Volition means the movement of mind. It is like the movement of the foot or like the scaffolding to the builder of a house. This is the near cause of door-object. Initial application of thought is mental action. It is likened to the reciting of discourses by heart. Perception is its near cause. Sustained application of thought is investigation of objects by the mind. It is likened to thought that follows the sense. Initial application of thought is its near cause. Joy is delight of mind. It is likened to a man gaining something. Exulting is its near cause. Confidence is purity of mind. It is likened to a man purifying water through the uttering of spells. The four attributes of stream-entrance[2] are its near cause. Energy is vigour of mind. It is likened to the energy of an ox bearing a burden. The eight bases of agitation[3] are its near cause. Mindfulness is the guarding of the mind. It is likened to the oil which protects the bowl. The four foundations of mindfulness are its near cause. Concentration is unification of mind. It is likened to the flame of the lamp behind the palace. The four meditations, *jhānas*, are its near cause. Wisdom is seeing with the mind. It is likened to a man who has eyes.[4] The Four Noble Truths are its near cause. Life-faculty is formless *dhamma*. This is life. It is like water to lotus.[5] Name and form are its near cause. The rejection of the hindrances is the breaking free from the evils of the mind. It is likened to a man, wishing to enjoy life, avoiding poison.[6] The activity of the four meditations, *jhānas*, is its near cause. Non-greed is the expelling of attachment from the mind. It is likened to a man who gets rid of something that torments

---

1. S. II, 103: *Seyyathāpi bhikkhave kuṭāgāraṁ vā kuṭāgārasālā vā uttarāya vā dakkhiṇāya vā pācīnāya vā vātapānā suriye uggacchante vātapānena rasmi pavisitvā kvāssa patiṭṭhitā ti? Pacchimāya bhante bhittiyan ti. Pacchimā ce bhikkhave bhitti nāssa kvāssa patiṭṭhitā ti? Paṭhaviyaṁ blante ti. Paṭhavī ce bhikkhave nāssa kvāssa patiṭṭhitā tt? Āpasmiṁ bhante ti. Āpo ce bhikkhave nāssa kvāssa patiṭṭhitā ti? Appatiṭṭhitā bhante ti. Evam eva kho bhikkhave kabaḷinkāre ce bhikkhave āhāre natthi rāgo natthi nandi natthi taṇhā . . . pe . . . Phasse ce bhikkhave āhāre. . . pe . . . Manosañcetanāya ce bhikkhave āhāre . . . pe. . . Viññāṇe ce bhikkhave āharc natthi rāgo natthi nandi natthi taṇhā appatiṭṭhitaṁ tattha viññāṇaṁ avirūḷhaṁ.*
2. S. V, 347: *Sappurisasaṁsevo hi bhante sotāpattiaṅgaṁ, saddhamma-savaṇaṁ sotāpattiaṅgaṁ, yonisomanasikāro sotāpattiaṅgaṁ, dhamnānudhammapaṭipatti sotāpattiaṅgan ti.*
3. Pts.-a. III, 547: *Aṭṭhasaṁvegavatthūni nāma: Jāti-jarā-byādhi-maranāṇi cattāri, apāyadukkhaṁ pañcamaṁ, atīte vaṭṭamūlakaṁ dukkhaṁ, anāgate vaṭṭamūlakaṁ dukkhaṁ, paccuppanne āhārapariyeṭṭhimūlakaṁ dukkhan 'ti.*
4. Sn. v, 1142: *Passāmi naṁ manasā cakkhunā va*
   rattindivaṁ, brāhmaṇa, appamatto;
   namassamāno vivasemi rattiṁ;
   —ten' eva maññāmi avippavāsaṁ.
5. D. I, 75: *Seyyathā pi mahā-rāja uppaliniyaṁ paduminiyaṁ puṇḍarīkiniyaṁ app ekaccāni uppalāni vā padumāni vā puṇḍarīkāni vā udake-jātāni ukade-saṁvaḍḍhāni udakā 'nuggatāni anto-nimuggā-posīni, tāni yāva c' aggā yāva ca mūlā sītena vārinā abhisannāni parisannāni paripūrāni paripphuṭṭhāni, nāssa kiñci sabbāvantaṁ uppalānaṁ vā padumānaṁ vā puṇḍarīkānaṁ vā sītena vārinā apphutaṁ assa.*
6. (a) Dh. v. 123: *Visaṁ jīvitukāmo 'va, pāpāni parivajjaye.*
   (b) M. II, 260: *Seyyathāpi, Sunakkhatta, āpānīyakaṁso vaṇṇasampanno gandhasampanno, so ca kho visena saṁsaṭṭho; atha puriso āgaccheyya jīvitukāmo amaritukāmo dukkhapaṭikkūlo. Taṁ kiṁ maññasi, Sunakkhatta? Api nu so puriso amuṁ āpanīyakaṁsaṁ piveyya yaṁ jaññā: Imāhaṁ pitvā maraṇaṁ vā nigacchāmi maraṇamattaṁ vā dukkhan ti? No h' etaṁ bhante,*

him. Renunciation is its near cause. Non-hatred is the state of a mind that is not angry. It is likened to cat-skin.[1] The four immeasurables are its near cause. Modesty is the feeling of shame in a man when he does wrong. It is likened to the loathing one has for excrement and urine.[2] Self-respect is its near cause. Decorum is the fear to do what is wrong. It is like fearing one's superior. Respect for others is its near cause.[3] [448] Calm is the appeasement of mental excitement. It is like taking a cold bath in the heat of summer. Joy is its near cause. The wish to do is the wish to do good. It is like a believing giver of alms. The four supernormal powers are its near cause. Resolve is the inclination of the mind. It is like water flowing deep downwards.[4] Initial and sustained application of thought are its near cause. Equanimity is that state of mind where it does not move back and forth. It is like a man holding a pair of scales.[5] Energy and the others are its near cause. Attention regulates the mind. It is like a helmsman. Both merit and demerit are its near cause. Greed is the clinging of the mind. It

---

1. (a) Th. v. 1138 *Tathā tu kassāmi yathāpi issaro;*
yaṁ labbhatī tena pi hotu me alaṁ;
taṁ taṁ karissāmi yathā atandito
biḷārabhastaṁ va yathā sumadditaṁ.

(b) M. I, 128-29: *Seyyathāpi bhikkhave biḷārabhastā madditā sumadditā suparimadditā mudukā tūlinī chinnasassarā chinnababbharā atha puriso āgaccheyya kaṭṭhaṁ vā kaṭhalaṁ vā ādāya, so evaṁ vadeyya: ahaṁ imaṁ biḷārabhastaṁ madditaṁ sumadditaṁ suparimadditaṁ mudukaṁ tūliniṁ chinnasassaraṁ chinnababbharaṁ kaṭṭhena vā kaṭhalena vā sarasaraṁ karissāmi bharabharaṁ karissāmīti. Taṁ kiṁ maññatha bhikkhave, api nu so puriso amuṁ biḷārabhastaṁ madditaṁ . . . kaṭṭhena vā kaṭhalena vā sarasaraṁ kareyya bharabharaṁ kareyyāti? No h' etaṁ bhante, taṁ kissa hetu: asu hi bhante biḷārabhastā madditā sumadditā suparimadditā mudukā tūlinī chinnasassarā chinnababbharā sā na sukarā kaṭṭhena vā kaṭhalena vā sarasaraṁ kātuṁ bharabharaṁ kātuṁ, yāvadeva ca pana so puriso kilamathassa vighātassa bhāgī assāti. Evam eva kho bhikkhave pañc'ime vacanapathā yehi vo pare vadamānā vadeyyuṁ: kālena vā akālena vā bhūtena vā abhūtena vā saṇhena vā pharusena vā atthasaṁhitena vā anatthasaṁhitena vā mettacittā vā dosantarā vā. Kālena vā bhikkhave pare vadamānā vadeyyuṁ akālena vā; bhūtena vā abhūtena vā, saṇhena vā . . . pharusena vā; atthasaṁhitena vā anathasaṁhitena vā; mettacittā vā bhikkhave pare vadamānā vadeyyuṁ dosantarā vā. Tatrapi kho bhikkhave evaṁ sikkhitabbaṁ: Na c'eva no cittaṁ vipariṇataṁ bhavissati na ca pāpikaṁ vācaṁ nicchāressāma hitānukampī ca viharissāma mettacittā na dosantarā, tañ ca puggalaṁ mettāsahagatena cetesā pharitvā viharissāma, tadārammaṇañ ca sabbāvantaṁ lokaṁ biḷārabhastāsamena cetasā vipulena mahaggatena appamāṇena averena abyāpajjhena pharitvā viharissāmāti. Evaṁ hi vo bhikkhave sikkhitabbaṁ.*

2. Sn. v. 835: *Disvāna Taṇhaṁ Aratiñ ca Rāgaṁ*
nāhosi chando api methunasmiṁ.
Kim ev' idaṁ muttakarisapuṇṇaṁ?
Pādā pi naṁ samphusituṁ na icche.

3. D. III, 212: *Atthi kho āvuso tena Bhagavatā jānatā passatā arahatā Sammā-Sambuddhena dve dhammā sammadakkhātā. Tattha sabbeh'eva saṁgāyitabbaṁ . . . pe . . . atthāya hitāya sukhāya deva-manussānaṁ. Katame dve? Hiri ca ottappan ca.* (= *Hirī ca ottappañ cā ti yaṁ hiriyati hiriyitabbena ottappati ottappitabbenā ti evaṁ vitthāritāni hiri-ottappāni. Api c' ettha ajjhatta-samuṭṭhānā hirī. Bahiddhā samuṭṭhānaṁ ottappaṁ. Attādhipateyyā hirī. Lokādhipateyyaṁ ottappaṁ. Lajjā sabhāva-saṇṭhitā hirī. Bhaya-sabhāva-saṇṭhitaṁ ottappaṁ.*— Sv. III, 978.).

4. A. V, 114: *Seyyathā pi bhikkhave upari pabbate thullaphusitake deve vassante deve galagalāyante taṁ udakaṁ yathāninnaṁ pavattamānaṁ pabbatakandarapadarasākhā paripūreti.*

5. A. IV, 282: *Seyyathā pi Byagghapajja tulādhāro vā tulādhārantevāsī vā tulaṁ paggahetvā jānāti 'ettakena vā onataṁ ettakena vā unnatan' ti.*

is likened to a goose. Lovable and desirable forms are its near cause. Hatred is the excitement of mind. It is like an angered venomous snake.[1] The ten bases of hatred are its near cause. Delusion is mental blindness. It is like a man without eyes.[2] The four reversals are its near cause. Conceit is haughtiness of mind. It is like two men fighting. The three kinds are its near cause. Views are mental obsessions. They are compared to the blind men feeling the elephant.[3] The not giving heed to another's voice is its near cause. Excitement is the non-tranquil state of mind. It is like water that is boiling. Anxiety is its near cause. Sluggishness is the slackening of mind. It is compared to desiring the foul. The falling off of good owing to the performance of evil is its near cause. Uncertainty is the leaping of the mind on to diverse objects. It is like a traveller to a distant land who is bewildered at a junction of two roads.[4] Wrong attention is its near cause. Indolence is negligence of mind. It is compared to a hibernating snake. The eight bases of indolence are its near cause. Immodesty is that state of mind which is not ashamed of doing ill. It is comparable to a *caṇḍāla*. Irreverence is its near cause. Indecorum is the non-fearing of the mind to do evil. It is like a wicked king. The non-esteem of the six is its near cause. These are called the aggregate of formations.

AGGREGATE OF CONSCIOUSNESS

Q. What is the aggregate of consciousness? *A*. It is eye-consciousness, ear-consciousness, nose-consciousness, tongue-consciousness, body-consciousness, mind-element and mind-consciousness-element. Here, eye-consciousness is the cognizing of forms dependent on the eye. This is called eye-consciousness. Ear-consciousness is the cognizing of sounds dependent on the ear. This is called ear-consciousness. Nose-consciousness is the cognizing of odours dependent on the nose. This is called nose-consciousness. Tongue-consciousness is the cognizing of flavours dependent on the tongue. This is called tongue-consciousness. Body-consciousness is the cognizing of tangibles dependent on the body. This is called body-consciousness. Mind-element

---

1. M. II, 261: *Seyyathāpi, Sunakkhatta, āsiviso ghoraviso, atha puriso āgaccheyya jīvitukāmo amaritukāmo sukhakāmo dukkhapaṭikkūlo. Taṁ kiṁ maññasi, Sunakkhatta? Apu nu so puriso amussa āsīvisassa ghoravissa hatthaṁ vā aṅguṭṭhaṁ vā dajjā, yaṁ jaññā: Iminā 'haṁ daṭṭho maraṇaṁ vā nigacchāmi maraṇamattaṁ vā dukkhan ti? No h' etaṁ, bhante.*
2. It. 84: *Mūḷho atthaṁ na jānāti*
   Mūḷho dhammaṁ na passati,
   Andhaṁ tamaṁ tadā hoti
   yaṁ moho sahate naraṁ.
3. Ud. 68: . . . *sannipātitā kho te deva yāvatikā Sāvatthiyaṁ jaccandhā 'ti. Tena hi bhaṇe jaccandhānaṁ hatthiṁ dassehī' ti. Evaṁ devā 'ti kho bhikkhave so puriso tassa rañño paṭissutvā jaccandhānaṁ hatthiṁ dassesi: ediso jaccandhā hatthī 'ti. Ekaccānaṁ jaccandhānaṁ hatthissa sisaṁ dassesi: ediso jaccandhā hatthī 'ti, . . . Yehi bhikkhave jaccandhehi hatthissa sīsaṁ diṭṭhaṁ ahosi, te evam āhaṁsu: ediso deva hatthī seyyathā pi kumbho 'ti . . .*
4. S. III, 108-9: *Dvidhāpatho ti kho Tissa vicikicchāyetaṁ adhivacanaṁ. Vāmamaggo ti kho Tissa aṭṭhaṅgikassetaṁ micchāmaggassa adhivacanaṁ, seyyathīdaṁ micchādiṭṭhiyā . . . micchāsamādhissa. Dakkhiṇamaggo ti kho Tissa ariyassetaṁ aṭṭhangikassa maggassa adhivacanaṁ, seyyathīdaṁ sammādiṭṭhiyā . . . sammāsamādhissa.*

depends on the five-door-adverting and the receiving of the desirable and the non-desirable. The cognizing (of form etc.) immediately after the five kinds of consciousness is called mind-element. Mind-consciousness-element: The mind, excepting these six kinds of consciousness, is called mind-consciousness-element. These seven kinds of consciousness should be known through these three ways: through organ-object, through object, through states.

THROUGH SENSE-ORGAN-OBJECT

Q. How, through sense-organ-object? *A.* Five kinds of consciousness are different as to sense-organ and as to object. Mind-element and mind consciouness-element are one as to sense-organ. Five-fold is the object of mind-element. Six-fold is the object of mind-consciousness-element. Five kinds of consciousness are as to state, internal; as to organ, internal; as to object, external. Mind-element is as to state, internal; as to organ, external; as to object, external. Mind-consciousness-element is as to state, internal; as to organ, external; as to object, internal and external. In respect of the six kinds of consciousness, organ and object proceed from the past. In respect of mind-consciousness-element, organ-production occurs at the moment of conception. There is no object of organ in the formless sphere because organ is produced first. Thus it should be understood through organ-object.

THROUGH OBJECT

Q. How, through object? *A.* Each of the five kinds of consciousness has its limits. These (five) are not produced by one another. They are produced neither before nor after but at once, and are not produced separately. Through the five kinds of consciousness, all states cannot be known; only the first arising can be known. Through the mind-element, all states cannot be known; only those which proceed in the mind can be known. Through the six kinds of consciousness there is no establishing of postures. Through apperception[1] there is the fixing of them. Through the six kinds of consciousness there is no fixing of bodily and verbal activity. (Through apperception these are fixed). Through the six kinds of consciousness, meritorious and demeritorious states are not fixed. Through apperception these are fixed. Through the six kinds of consciousness, one does not enter or emerge out of concentration. Through apperception, one enters into concentration and is pacified through overcoming opposites. Through the six kinds of consciousness, nothing is caused to perish or to be produced. Through overcoming of opposites or through registration, perishing and production are caused. Mind-consciousness-element is born of result. Through the six kinds of consciousness one does not sleep, awake or dream. Through opposites one sleeps. Through

1. *Javana.*

subtle light one awakes. Through apperception one dreams. Thus one should know through object.

THROUGH STATES

Q. How, through states? *A*. Five kinds of consciousness are with initial and sustained application of thought. Mind-element is with initial and sustained application of thought. Mind-consciousness-element is with initial and sustained application of thought, or is without initial and only with sustained application of thought, or is neither with initial nor with sustained application of thought. Five kinds of consciousness act together with equanimity. Body-consciousness acts either together with pleasure or with pain. Mind-consciousness-element acts together with joy or grief or equanimity. Five kinds of consciousness are results. Mind-element is either result or means. Mind-consciousness-element is meritorious or demeritorious or result or means. Six kinds of consciousness do not arise without condition, are worldly states, with cankers, with fetters, with tangle, with flood, with yoke, with hindrance, infected, clinging, defiling, are not removed through seeing or through meditation. They are neither "group" nor "non-group". They are neither training nor non-training. They are the subtle fetters of the sense-plane, are not fixed and are not vehicle. Mind consciousness-element has the nature of breaking up. Thus one should know to distinguish by way of states. This is called the aggregate of consciousness. Thus should the five aggregares be known.

And again, one should know the distinctive qualities of the five aggregates through four ways thus: through word meaning, through characteristic, through discrimination, through comprehension.

THROUGH WORD MEANING

Q. How, through word meaning? *A*. Material object means thing that is visible. Feeling means sensibility. Formations means work. Consciousness means awareness. Aggregate means variety and group. Thus one should know through word meaning.

THROUGH CHARACTERISTIC

Q. How, through characteristic? *A*. Material quality is its own characteristic, like a thorn. The four primaries are its near cause. The characteristic of feeling is sensitiveness. It is like disliking a leper. Contact is near cause. To support is the characteristic of perception. It is compared to an image. Contact is its near cause. The characteristic of formation is unity. It is like the turning of the wheel. Its near cause is contact. The characteristic of consciousness is awareness; it is likened to the perceiving of taste. Name and form are near cause. Thus one should know through characteristic.

THROUGH DISCRIMINATION

Q. How, through discrimination? *A*. The aggregates are discriminated by the threefold discrimination of the five aggregates, the five clinging aggregates and the five aggregates of the Law.[1] Here the five aggregates are all phenomena.[2] The five clinging aggregates are all cankerous states. The five aggregates of the Law are: the aggregate of virtue, the aggregate of concentration, the aggregate of wisdom, the aggregate of freedom and the aggregate of the knowledge and discernment of freedom.[3] Here the five aggregates are to be taken.

THROUGH COMPREHENSION

Q. How, through comprehension? *A*. There are three comprehensions: sense-sphere-comprehension, element-comprehension, truth-comprehension.[4] Here the aggregate of form is comprehended in eleven sense-spheres. Three aggregates are comprehended in the sense-sphere of states. The aggregate of consciousness is comprehended in the sense-sphere of the mind.

The aggregate of matter is comprehended in eleven elements. Three aggregates are comprehended in the element of states. The aggregate of consciousness is comprehended in seven elements. The aggregate of virtue, the aggregate of concentration, the aggregate of wisdom, the aggregate of the knowledge and discernment of freedom are comprehended in the sense-sphere and element of states. The aggregate of freedom is comprehended in the sense-sphere of states, the sense-sphere of mind, the element of states and the mind-consciousness-element. The five aggregates are comprehended in the Truths or not comprehended in the Truths. The five aggregates of clinging are comprehended in the Truth of Ill and in the Truth of Origin. The aggregates of virtue, concentration and wisdom are comprehended in the Path-Truth. The aggregate of freedom is not comprehended in the Truths. The aggregate of knowledge and discernment of freedom is comprehended in the Truth of Ill. Some states are comprehended in the aggregates and not in the Truths. Some states are comprehended in the Truths and not in the aggregates. Some states are comprehended in the aggregates and also in the Truths. Some states are comprehended neither in the Truths nor in the aggregates. Here, the material qualities that are linked with the faculties do not associate with the Path (?). The recluse-fruit is comprehended in the aggregates and not in the Truths. *Nibbāna* is comprehended in the Truths and not in the aggregates.

---

1. *Pañcakkhandhā, pañcupādānakkhandhā, pañcadhammakkhandhā.*
2. *Sankhata-dhammā.*
3. A. III, 134: *Idha bhikkhave bhikkhu asekhena sīlakkhandhena samannāgato hoti, asekhena samādhikkhandhena samannāgato hoti, asekhena paññakkhandhena samannāgato hoti, asekhena vimuttikkhandhena samannāgato hoti, asekhena vimuttiñāṇadassanakkhandhena samannāgato hoti.*
4. *Āyatana, dhātu, sacca.*

Three Truths are comprehended in the aggregates and also in the Truths. Restraint is not comprehended in the aggregates and also not in the Truths. Thus should one discern the method of understanding the aggregates. This is called the aggregate method.

The aggregate method has ended.

TWELVE SENSE-ORGANS AND SENSE-OBJECTS

Q. What is the sense-organ method? *A.* There are twelve sense-organs (and sense-objects): sense-organ of eye, sense-object of matter, sense-organ of ear, sense-object of sound, sense-organ of nose, sense-object of odour, sense-organ of tongue, sense-object of taste, sense-organ of body, sense-object of touch, sense-organ of mind, sense-object of ideas.[1] Here, eye-organ is sentient element. By this one sees material objects. Material object is elemental form. This is the field of eye. The ear-organ is sentient element. By this one hears sounds. Sound-object is elemental expression. This is the field of the ear. Nose-organ is sentient element. By this one smells. Odour-object is elemental scent. It is the field of the nose. Tongue-organ is sentient element. By this one tastes. Taste-object is elemental flavour. This is the field of the tongue. The body-organ is sentient element. By it one feels fineness, smoothness (and so on). Touch-object is hardness, softness, coolness and warmth of the elements of earth, water, fire and air. This is the field of the body. Mind organ is the element of the seven kinds of consciousness. Element of ideas comprises the three formless aggregates, the eighteen subtle material qualities and *Nibbāna*. These are the twelve sense-organs (and sense-objects).

And again, these twelve sense-organs (and sense-objects) should be known by their distinctive qualities in five ways: through word meaning, limits, condition, arising of . . .* distinctive thought and comprehension.

THROUGH WORD MEANING

Q. How, through word meaning? *A.* Eye means, seeing. Material object means appearance. Ear means, hearing. Sound means, noise. Nose means, olfaction. Odour means, smell. Tongue means, tasting. Taste means, flavour. Body means, experiencing. Touch means, contact. Mind means, knowing. Idea means, non-living.[2] Organ means, entrance into the formless, place, resting-place. Thus one should know through word meaning.

---

1. D. III, 102: *Chay imāni bhante ajjhattika-bāhirāni āyatanāni, cakkhuṁ c' eva rūpā ca, sotañ c' eva saddā ca, ghānañ c' eva gandhā ca, jivhā c' eva rasā ca, kāyo c' eva phoṭṭhabbā ca, mano c' eva dhammā ca.*

* Unintelligible.

2. Lit. *Nijjīva.*

THROUGH LIMITS

Q. How, through limits? *A*. Eye and ear do not reach the object. Nose, tongue and body reach the object. Mind is together with object. There is another teaching: Ear reaches the object, because if there is an obstruction nearby one does not hear sounds, as when a spell is wrought. And again, there is another teaching: Eye by itself reaches the object, because one cannot see the reverse side of a wall. Thus should one know through limits.

THROUGH CONDITION

Q. How, through condition? *A*. Depending on eye, material object, light and attention, eye-consciousness arises. Here, to the arising of eye-consciousness, the eye is in the fourfold relation of pre-nascence-condition, support-condition, faculty-condition, presence-condition.[1] (To eye-consciousness) material object is in the threefold relation of post-nascence-condition, object-condition, presence-condition. Light is in the threefold relation of pre-nascence-condition, support-condition and presence-condition. Attention is in the twofold relation of continuity-condition and absence-condition.

Depending on ear, sound, ear-cavity and attention, ear-consciousness arises. Thus should one know through the distinguishing of condition. Depending on nose, smell, air and attention, nose-consciousness arises. Depending on tongue, taste, water and attention, tongue-consciousness arises. Depending on body, touch and attention, bodily consciousness arises. Depending on mind, ideas, life-continuum and attention, mind-consciousness arises.

Here, mind is . . .* ideas are the object of states. There are four kinds in this: Past, present and future of six internal sense-organs comprise the first; past, future and present of five external sense-objects, excepting non-sense-organ faculty, comprise the second. The third is the sense-object of ideas. There are eleven things viz., being, direction, season, . . .* comprise the fourth.** These are called the object of states.

Concentration is intentness of mind on object. It is like light. Attention is mind-door-adverting. Consciousness is apperception. Here, to mind-consciousness, mind is in the relation of support-condition. Ideas are in the relation of object-condition. Life-continuum is in the relation of support-condition. Attention is in the twofold relation of continuity-condition and presence-condition. Thus should it be understood through condition.

Q. How, through the arising of distinctive thought? *A*. Three kinds are fulfilled at the eye-door. They are the objects of very great intensity, great intensity and slight intensity.[2] Of these, those of very great intensity

1. In rendering the *paccayas*, here and elsewhere, in this translation, we have generally followed Venerable Nyāṇatiloka Mahā Thera's "*Paṭiccasamuppāda*".
* Unintelligible
** The meaning is not clear.
2. Cp. Compendium of Philosophy, 127.

fulfil seven stages and are born in *avīci*, the great hell. After the vibration of the life-continuum, adverting, discerning, receiving, examining, determining, apperceiving and registering follow.

SIMILE OF THE THREAD

Here the life-continuum is the consciousness-faculty of becoming. It is likened to the drawing of thread.[1] Adverting is conditioned by the visible object at the eye-door. Through the visible object entering the field (of presentation?), the life-continuum vibrates, and is followed by adverting to the visible object. Adverting which depends on the eye is followed by discerning. This is followed by reception in the sense of experience. Then follows examining in the sense of (investigating) experience. After that comes determining in the sense of understanding. Determining proceeds and is followed by apperception according to action. Apperception proceeding in the sense of full cognition and not in the sense of means is followed by registration of effect. After that consciousness lapses into the life-continuum.

SIMILE OF THE MANGO

Q. What is the illustration? *A*. The king sleeps in his chamber, having closed the door. A slave-girl massages the king's feet. The queen sits near him. Ministers and courtiers are ranged in front of him. A deaf man is guarding the door with his back against it. At that time the king's gardener, bringing mangoes, knocks at the door. Hearing that sound, the king awakes, and says to the slave-girl, "Go and open the door". The slave goes to the door-keeper and speaks to him in gesture. That deaf door-keeper understands her wish and opens the door and sees the mangoes. The king takes his sword. The slave brings the fruits and hands them to a minister. The minister presents them to the queen. The queen washes them and sorts the ripe from the raw, places them in a vessel and gives them to the king. Getting them, the king eats the fruits. After eating them, he talks of the merit or non-merit of them. After that he sleeps again.

The sleeping king is the life-continuum. The king's gardener, bringing mangoes and knocking at the door, is the impact of the visible object on the eye-door. The awakening of the king by the knocking at the door, and his command to open the door, illustrate the vibration of the life-continuum. The slave-girl's gestures, in requesting the door-keeper to open the door, is adverting. The opening of the door by the deaf door-keeper and the sight of the mangoes illustrate eye-consciousness. The taking of the sword by the king and the handing of the fruits by the slave to the minister illustrate reception. The presentation of the fruits by the minister to the queen is examining. The

---

1. Cp. D. I, 54: *Seyyathā pi nāma sutta-guḷe khitte nibbeṭhiyamānam eva phaleti.* Perhaps the simile was drawn from this portion of the sutta.

actions of washing, sorting, placing the fruits in a vessel and offering them to the king illustrate determining. The eating by the king is apperception. His talking as to the merits or demerits of the fruits illustrate registration of effect, and his sleeping again is the lapsing into the life-continuum.[1]

Here, consciousness depending on the impact of objects of middling intensity at the eye-door proceeds up to apperception and immediately lapses into the life-continuum. Through the impact of objects of lower intensity, consciousness lapses into the life-continuum immediately after determining. In the same way the procedure at the other doors should be understood. At the mind-door there is no impact of object. Conditioned by attention, and free from activities is the object grasped at the mind-door. Here, with reference to a very great object three stages are produced (after vibration) of the life-continuum, namely, adverting, apperception and registration. With reference to the objects of great and slight intensity two stages are fulfilled: adverting and apperception.[2] Here, feeling and perception should be known through various conditions.

Through the conditioning of right-attention[3] and non-right-attention, various kinds of merit and demerit should be known. Thus one should know through manifestation of the interlocking of distinctive thought.*

Q. How, through comprehension? *A*. There are three kinds of comprehension, namely, aggregate-comprehension, element-comprehension, truth-comprehension. Here, ten sense-spheres are comprehended in the aggregate of matter. The sense-sphere of mind is comprehended in the aggregate of consciousness. The sense-sphere of states, excepting *Nibbāna*, is comprehended in the four aggregates. Eleven sense-spheres are comprehended in eleven elements. The sense-sphere of mind is comprehended in seven elements. The five internal sense-spheres are comprehended in the Truth of Ill. The five external sense-spheres are either comprehended or not comprehended in the Truth of Ill. The sense-sphere of mind is either comprehended or not comprehended in the Truth of Ill. The sense-sphere of states is either comprehended or not comprehended in the Truth of Ill. Thus should comprehension be known. In this way one develops discernment through the sense-sphere method. This is called sense-sphere method.

Sense-sphere method has ended.

ELEMENT METHOD

Q. What is the element-method? *A*. There are eighteen elements, namely, eye-element, material-element, eye-consciousness-element; ear-

1. Cp. Compendium of Philosophy, 30 for mango simile.
2. Cp. Ibid. 128.
3. *Sammā-manasikāra* (?)
* Not quite clear.

element, sound-element, ear-consciousness-element; nose-element, odour-element, nose-consciousness-element; tongue-element, taste-element, tongue-consciousness-element; body-element, touch-element, body-consciousness-element; mind-element, states-element, mind-consciousness-element.[1] Here, the sensory organ of eye is eye-element. Material form is material element. Eye-consciousness is eye-consciousness-element. In the same way the others should be known. Mind-door-adverting translates the objects. Mind-element decides the result.

[450] The mind-element is just mind-sphere. All kinds of consciousness except the ideas-element and the six consciousness-elements are mind-consciousness-element. The rest is as was taught at length under sense-sphere. Here, ten elements are comprehended in the form-aggregate. The ideas-element, excepting *Nibbāna*, is comprehended in the four aggregates. Seven elements are comprehended in the consciousness-aggregate. Eleven elements are comprehended in eleven sense-organs (and sense-objects). Seven-elements are comprehended in the mind-organ. Eleven elements are comprehended in the Truth of Ill. Five elements are comprehended in the Truth of Ill, or not comprehended in the Truth of Ill. Ideas-element is comprehended in the Four Truths, or not comprehended in the Four Truths. Mind-consciousness-element is comprehended in the Truth of Ill or not comprehended in the Truth of Ill.

Q. What is the limit of manifestation?

A. Just the sphere of ideas-element is the limit. The assemblage of the characteristics of a variety of states is called aggregate. The characteristic of entrance is called sense-organ. The characteristic of intrinsic nature is called element. Again, the Blessed One has taught the Truth of Ill by way of the aggregates for the quick witted man. He taught the Truth of Ill by way of the sense-sphere for the average man, and he taught the Truth of Ill by way of the elements for the slow witted man.

And again, he has expounded form in brief to those who have the characteristic of attachment to name and aggregate, by way of discernment of name. He has expounded name and sense-sphere, in brief, through the determining of form, to those inclined towards attachment to form. He has expounded the elements through determining mind and form to those inclined to be attached to mind and form.

And again, he has expounded the intrinsic nature of the sense-spheres. He has expounded the aggregates. He has expounded the (internal) sense-spheres and objects. And he has expounded the sense-spheres. He has taught the arising of consciousness and element, through (internal) sense-sphere and

---

1. Vbh. 87: *Aṭṭhārasa dhātuyo: cakkhudhātu rūpadhātu cakkhuviññāṇadhātu sotadhātu saddadhātu sotaviññāṇadhātu ghānadhātu gandhadhātu ghānaviññāṇadhātu jivhādhātu rasadhātu jivhāviññāṇadhātu kāyadhātu phoṭṭhabbadhātu kāyaviññāṇadhātu manodhātu dhammadhātu manoviññāṇadhātu.*

object. Thus should the distinctions in the element method be known. This is called element method.

Element method has ended.

CONDITIONED ARISING METHOD

(*a*) DIRECT ORDER

Q. What is the conditioned arising method? *A.* Conditioned by ignorance are the formations; conditioned by the formations, consciousness; conditioned by consciousness, name-form; conditioned by name-form, the six-sphered-sense; conditioned by the six-sphered-sense, contact; conditioned by contact, feeling; conditioned by feeling, craving; conditioned by craving, clinging; conditioned by clinging, becoming, conditioned by becoming, rebirth; conditioned by rebirth, decay, death, sorrow, lamentation, pain, grief and despair spring up. Such is the origin of this entire mass of ill.[1]

(*b*) REVERSE ORDER

By the cessation of ignorance, the cessation of the formations (occurs); by the cessation of the formations, the cessation of consciousness; by the cessation of consciousness, the cessation of name-form; by the cessation of name-form, the cessation of the six-sphered-sense; by the cessation of the six-sphered-sense, the cessation of contact; by the cessation of contact, the cessation of feeling; by the cessation of feeling, the cessation of craving; by the cessation of craving, the cessation of clinging; by the cessation of clinging, the cessation of becoming; by the cessation of becoming, the cessation of rebirth; by the cessation of rebirth, decay, death, sorrow, lamentation, pain, grief and despair cease. Such is the cessation of this entire mass of ill.[2]

IGNORANCE

Here ignorance is ignorance of the Four Truths. Formations are bodily, verbal and mental actions. Consciousness is rebirth consciousness. Name-

---

1. Ud. 1; S. II, 1: *Avijjāpaccayā bhikkhave saṅkhārā; saṅkhārapaccayā viññāṇaṁ; viññāṇapaccayā nāmarūpaṁ; nāmarūpapaccayā saḷāyatanaṁ; saḷāyatanapaccayā phasso; phassapaccayā vedanā; vedanāpaccayā taṇhā; taṇhāpaccayā upādānaṁ; upādānapaccayā bhavo; bhavapaccayā jāti; jātipaccayā jarāmaraṇaṁ soka-parideva-dukkha-domanass-upāyāsā sambhavanti. Evaṁ 'etassa kevalassa dukkhakkhandhassa samudayo hoti.*
2. Ud. 2; S. II, 1-2: *Avijjāya tveva asesavirāganirodhā saṅkhāranirodho; saṅkhāranirodhā viññāṇanirodho; viññāṇanirodhā nāmarūpanirodho; nāmarūpanirodhā saḷāyatananirodho; saḷāyatananirodhā phassanirodho; phassanirodhā vedanānirodho; vedanānirodhā taṇhānirodho; taṇhānirodhā upādānanirodho; upādānanirodhā bhavanirodho; bhavanirodhā jātinirodho; jātinirodhā jarāmaraṇaṁ soka-parideva-dukkha-domanassupāyāsā nirujjhanti. Evaṁ 'etassa kevalassa dukkhakkhandhassa nirodho hotīti.*

form means the mental properties which arise together with the continuity of mind and the embryo (*kalala*). Six-sphered-sense means the six internal sense-spheres. Contact means the six groups of contact. Feeling means the six groups of feeling. Craving means the six groups of craving. Clinging means the four clingings. Becoming means sense-plane becoming, form-plane becoming and formless-plane becoming where *kamma* works. Rebirth means the arising of the aggregates in becoming. Decay means the maturing of the aggregates. Death means the destruction of the aggregates.

FORMATIONS

Q. How do the formations arise, conditioned by ignorance? How do decay and death arise, conditioned by rebirth? *A*. The five clinging groups arise for the uninstructed commoner, because of his ignorance of the Four Truths. In the long night (of ignorance), he clings to self and goods thinking: "These are my goods, this is my self". Thus he enjoys and clings to enjoyment. The thought of becoming brings about reconception. In that thought of becoming there is no knowledge. He clings to becoming because he desires it.[1]

SIMILE OF THE SEEDS

It is like seeds placed in a fertile field. If consciousness is extinguished, becoming is extinguished. This is the meaning of conditioned by ignorance the formations arise. Mental formations, conditioned by ignorance, enter the course of becoming, and integrate. Becoming proceeds; thus it is continued. Consciousness does not separate from mind in becoming. Therefore, conditoned by the formations, consciousness arises.

SIMILE OF THE SUN

As without the sun, there is in the world neither light nor any increase of it, so without consciousness, name-form dees not take shape and there is no growth of it.

SIMILE OF THE TWO BUNDLES OF REEDS

As (in the simile of the bundles of) reeds depending on each other, so conditioned by consciousness, name-form arises. Conditioned by the (internal) sense-spheres, the other mental qualities arise together.[2] The development

1. S. II, 94: *Yañ ca kho etaṁ bhikkhave vuccati cittaṁ iti pi mano iti pi viññāṇaṁ iti pi tatrāssutavā puthujjano nālaṁ nibbindituṁ nālaṁ virajjituṁ nālaṁ vimuccituṁ.*
Taṁ kissa hetu? Dīgharattaṁ hetaṁ bhikkhave assutavato puthujjanassa ajjhositaṁ mamāyitaṁ parāmaṭṭhaṁ etaṁ mama eso hamasmi eso me attā ti.
Tasmā tatrāssutavā puthujjano nālaṁ nibbindituṁ nālaṁ virajjituṁ nālaṁ vimuccituṁ.
2. S. II, 114: *Seyyathāpi āvuso dve naḷakalāpiyo aññamaññaṁ nissāya tiṭṭheyyuṁ, evam eva kho āvuso nāmarūpapaccayā viññāṇaṁ viññāṇapaccayā nāmarūpaṁ, nāmarūpapaccayā saḷāyatanaṁ, saḷāyatanapaccayā phasso...*

of the mind-sphere is due to name. Conditioned by the four primaries, nutriment and caloric order, the other five (internal) sense-spheres develop and increase. The other does not depend on these. Therefore, conditioned by name-form, the six-sphered-sense arises. By the union of the other faculties, objects, elements and consciousness, contact arises. Therefore, conditioned by the six-sphered-sense, contact arises. Through the sense of touch one experiences pain, pleasure and neither pain nor pleasure. Should one not be touched (then there would be no feeling for him). Therefore, conditioned by contact, feeling arises. The uninstructed commoner experiences pleasure and clings to it and craving for more, he experiences pain; and overcoming it (pain), he, desiring ease, develops the feeling of neither pain nor pleasure, or equanimity.[1] Therefore, conditioned by feeling, craving arises. Through craving, one clings to what is lovely. Therefore, conditioned by craving, clinging arises. Through that clinging, one sows the seed of becoming. Therefore, conditioned by clinging, there is becoming. According to one's deeds one is born in various states. Therefore there is rebirth, and through birth, there is decay and death. Thus, conditioned by birth, there is decay and death.

SIMILE OF THE SEED, SHOOT AND PLANT

As paddy-seeds are conditioned by the paddy plant, so conditioned by ignorance the formations arise. Conditioned by the seed is the bud;[2] so is the arising of consciousness, by the formations. Conditioned by the bud is the leaf; so is the arising of name-form, by consciousness. Conditioned by the leaf is the branch; so is the arising of the six-sphered-sense, by name-form. Conditioned by the branch is the plant; so is the arising of contact, by the six-sphered-sense. Conditioned by the plant is the flower; so is the arising of feeling, by contact. Conditioned by the flower is the nectar; so is the arising of craving, by feeling. Conditioned by the nectar is the ear of rice; so is the arising of clinging, by craving. Conditioned by the ear of rice is the seed; so is the arising of becoming, by clinging. Conditioned by the seed is the bud; so is the arising of birth, by becoming. Thus the several successions come to be. Thus one cannot know the past or the future. Thus birth succeeds beginning with the causal condition of ignorance. Of it the past or the future cannot be known.[3]

WHAT CONDITIONS IGNORANCE

Q. By what is ignorance conditioned? *A.* Ignorance is indeed con-

---

1. Cp. Vbh.-a. 180: *Dukkhī sukhaṁ patthayati, sukhī bhiyyo pi icchati,*
upekhā pana santattā sukham icc' eva bhāsitā.
2. Cp. (a) Vbh.-a. 196: *Bīje sati ankuro viya.*
(b) Mhv. XV, 43: *Bījamhā nikkhamma ankuro.*
3. Cp. S. II, 178: *Anamataggāyaṁ bhikkhave saṁsāro pubbākoṭi na paññāyati avijjānīvaraṇānaṁ sattānaṁ taṇhāsaṁyojanānaṁ sandhāvataṁ saṁsarataṁ.*

ditioned by ignorance.[1] The latencies become the condition of the encompassing defilements. The encompassing defilements become the condition of the latencies.[2]

And again, all defilements become the condition of ignorance according to the teaching of the Buddha thus: "From the origin of the cankers, origin of ignorance arises".[3] And again, it is likened to a single thought-state (?). Seeing a form with the eye, the uninstructed commoner develops craving. The bare enjoyment of that time is delusion of mind. This is called ignorance. Through attachment to this ignorance, one conditions the formations. Through attachment to these formations, one conditions consciousness and knows the associated states of mind and the material object produced by the formations. Conditioned by this consciousness, name-form arises. From feeling joy is produced. Conditioned by joy and conditioned by the joy-producing material object, the bare faculties arise. Thus conditioned by name-form the six-sphered-sense arises. Conditioned by pleasurable contact, feeling arises. Conditioned by the craving for feeling, craving arises. Through attachment to bare pleasure and conditioned by craving, clinging arises. Through attachment to and conditioned by clinging, there is becoming. Conditioned by becoming, birth arises, and when living (begins) to end—this is decay. To scatter and to destroy—this is death. Thus in one moment the twelvefold conditioned arising is fulfilled.

Q. Of the factors of the twelvefold conditioned arising, how many are defilements, how many are actions, how many are results, how many are past, how many are future, how many are present, how many are cause-conditions, how many have already developed? What is conditioned arising? What is conditioned arising doctrine? What are the differences between these two? Why is conditioned arising so profound?

---

1. (a) Cp. S. IV, 50: *Avijjā kho bhikkhu eko dhammo yassa pahānā bhikkhuno avijjā pahīyati vijjā uppajjatīti.*
(b) Netti. 79: *Vuttaṁ hi: avijjāpaccayā saṁkhārā, saṁkhārapaccayā viññāṇaṁ. Evaṁ sabbo paṭiccasamuppādo. Iti avijjā avijjāya hetu, ayonisomanasikāro paccayo. Purimikā avijjā pacchimikāya avijjāya hetu. Tattha purimikā avijjā avijjānusayo, pacchimikā avijjā avijjāpariyuṭṭhānam. Purimiko avijjānusayo pacchimikassa avijjāpariyuṭṭhānassa hetubhūto paribrūhanāya bījaṅkuro viya samanantarahetutāya. Yaṁ pana yatthā phalaṁ nibbattati, idaṁ tassa paramparahetutāya hetubhūtaṁ. Duvidho hi hetu: samanantarahetu paraṁparahetu ca. Evaṁ avijjāya pi duvidho hetu: samanantarahetu paraṁparahetu ca.*

2. Cp. (a) Dhs. 79, Sec. 390: *Yaṁ tasmiṁ samaye aññāṇaṁ adassanaṁ anabhisamayo ananubodho asambodho appaṭivedho asaṁgāhanā apariyogāhanā asamapekkhanā apaccavekkhanā apaccakkhakammaṁ dummejjhaṁ balyaṁ asampajaññaṁ moho pamoho sammoho avijjā avijjogho avijjāyogo avijjānusayo avijjāpariyuṭṭhānaṁ avijjālaṅgī moho akusalamūlaṁ—ayaṁ tasmiṁ samaye moho hoti.*
(b) Netti. 14: *Paññāya anusayā pahiyyanti, anusayesu pahīnesu pariyuṭṭhānā pahiyyanti. Kissa anusayassa pahīnattā? Taṁ yathā khandhavantassa rukkhassa anavasesamūluddharaṇe kate pupphaphalapavāḷaṅkurasantati samucchinnā bhavati, evaṁ anusayesu pahīnesu pariyuṭṭhānasantati samucchinnā bhavati pidahitā paṭicchannā. Kena? Paññāya.*
(c) Peṭaka. 105: *Tathā hi purimā koṭi na paññāyati; tattha avijjānusayo avijjāpariuṭṭhānassa hetu purimā hetu pacchā paccayo sā pi avijjā saṅkhārānaṁ paccayo.*

3. Cp. M. I, 54: *Āsavasamudayā avijjāsamudayo, āsavanirodhā avijjānirodho.*

A. Three are the defilements, namely, ignorance, craving and clinging. Two are actions, namely, the formations and becoming. The other seven results.

SIMILE OF THE COLOURS OF A PAINTER

Here, the defilements are a cause of future life, like the colours of a painter. Their objects are not self-produced, as also are the colour-object of the painter. Defilements cause becoming like the different colours of the painter. These two are past, namely, ignorance and the formations. These two are of the future, namely, birth and decay-and-death. The other eight are of the present. Thus it is as to the three divisions of time. Therefore one should know that birth and death proceed from beginningless time. The factors of the twelve-fold conditioned arising should not be taught (separately). Further, no conditioned arising should be taught which does not consist of these twelve. Then, what is conditioned arising? Just these twelve which in turn become condition. Therefore this is called conditioned arising. The twelve factors are states which have already developed. What is the difference between the two? The working of conditioned arising being different (in each case) and being not complete, one cannot speak of it. Be they conditioned or non-conditioned,[1] they cannot be explained. States of conditioned arising that have already developed, have finished their task and are conditioned. This is the difference between the two. Why is this conditioned arising profound? One is able to know the way and characteristic by which ignorance conditions the formations. A delivered one, without the aid of another, is able to discern its working, characteristics and nature. These constitute the profound nature of conditioned arising.[2]

CONDITIONED ARISING TO BE KNOWN IN SEVEN WAYS

[451] And again, this conditioned arising should be known through seven ways thus: through the three links, the four groups, the twenty modes, the wheel, order, discernment and through comprehension.

FIRST. THREE LINKS

Q. How, through the three links? *A*. Here the interval between the formations and consciousness is the first link; the interval between feeling and craving is the second link; the interval between becoming and rebirth is the third link. The conditioning of the present effect by past actions through the defilements

---

1. *Sankhata, asankhata.*
2. S. II, 92; D. II, 55: *'Acchariyaṁ bhante abbhutaṁ bhante yāva gambhīro cāyaṁ bhante paṭicca-samuppādo gambhīrāvabhāso ca. Atha ca pana me uttānakuttānako viya khāyatīti.' Mā h'evaṁ Ānanda avaca, mā h'evaṁ Ānanda avaca. Gambhīro cāyaṁ Ānanda paṭicca-samuppādo gambhīrāvabhāso ca.*

is the first link. The conditioning of the present defilements by present effects is called the second link; the conditioning of future effects by present defilements is called the third link. The first and the third are condition-effect-link[1] and becoming-link.[2] The second link is effect-condition link[3] and non-becoming-link. *Q.* What is becoming-link?

A. Endlessly, the not yet enlightened aggregates, sense-organs and elements, through the conditioning of past actions and defilements, go again and again to various modes of birth. This is becoming-birth-link.[4] *Q.* How is it fulfilled?

DEATH OF THE IGNORANT CRAVING EVIL-DOER

A. Here a man, who performs actions which are associated with ignorance and craving, is an evil-doer. When he comes to die, he suffers. Lying on his death-couch, he does not see this world. He does not see that world. He loses mindfulness and cannot recover it. At this time he suffers the ill of rebirth. Mindfulness draws away from his mind, and strength from his body. He loses his faculties gradually. The body quakes. Vitality ebbs and his body becomes like a dried *tāla* leaf. At this time he is like one asleep and dreaming.

ACTION, ACTION-SIGN, DESTINY, DESTINY-SIGN

Through action, four states arise. They are action, action-sign, destiny, destiny-sign.[5]

What is action? The merit and non-merit one has made. They are heavy or light, many or few. The action-sign that uprises (as result) conforms to the action already done. The action-sign resembles action already done. Destiny: A happy destiny arises through the conditioning of merit. An evil destiny arises through the conditioning of demerit. Destiny-sign: At the time of entry into the womb, three objects unite to produce rebirth. Rebirth

---

1. *Hetu-phala-sandhi.* 2. *bhava-sandhi.* 3. *Phala-hetu-sandhi.*
4. *Bhava-jāti-sandhi.* Cp. Spk. II, 72: *Bhava-jātinam antare eko ti.*
5. Cp. (a) Abhs. V, par. 12: . . . *Tathā ca marantānaṁ pana maraṇakāle yathārahaṁ abhimukhībhūtaṁ bhavantare paṭisandhi-janakaṁ kammaṁ vā taṁ kamma-karaṇa-kāle rūpādikam upaladdha-pubbam upakaraṇa-bhūtañ ca kamma-nimittaṁ vā anantaram uppajjamānabhave upalabhitabbam upabhoga-bhūtañ ca gati-nimittaṁ vā kamma-balena channaṁ dvārānaṁ aññatarasmiṁ paccupaṭṭhāti.*
(b) Spk. II, 218: *Maṁsa-pesi-vatthusmiṁ: goghāṭako ti, go-maṁsapesiyo katvā, sukkhāpetvā, vallūra-vikkayena anekāni vassāni jīvikaṁ kappesi. Ten' assa narakā cavana-kāle maṁsa pesī yeva nimittaṁ ahosi. So maṁsa-pesi-peto jāto.*
(c) Ibid. 372-73: *Ettakesu ṭhānesu Channa-tthero Sāriputta-ttherena pucchita-pucchitaṁ pañhaṁ arahatte pakkhipitvā kathesi. Sāriputta-tthero pana tassa puthujjana-bhāvaṁ ñatvāpi 'tvaṁ puthujjano' ti vā 'anāsavo' ti vā avatvā tuṇhī yeva ahosi. Cunda-tthero pan' assa puthujjana-bhāvaṁ ñapessāmi ti cintetvā ovādaṁ adāsi.*
. . .
Satthaṁ āharesī ti, jīvita-hāraka-satthaṁ āhari, kaṇṭhanāḷaṁ chindi. Ath' assa tasmiṁ khaṇe bhayaṁ okkami, gatinimittaṁ upaṭṭhāsi. So attano puthujjana-bhāvaṁ ñatvā, saṁvigga-citto vipassanaṁ paṭṭhapetvā, sankhāre parigaṇhanto arahattaṁ patvā, samasīsi hutvā, parinibbuto.

depends on the place of birth, namely, a palace, habitation, mountain, tree, or river, according to destiny. The appropriate grasping-sign arises, and the man, leaning or sitting or lying (on his death-couch), grasps that. After the consciousness which apperceives the past action or the action-sign or the destiny or the destiny-sign ends, the last consciousness arises without a break gradually through apperceptional consciousness. Only that action or action-sign or destiny or destiny-sign becomes the object of the basic resultant consciousness. Like the lighting of a lamp by a lamp,[1] or like fire issuing from a flame is re-linking consciousness.[2]

In the womb of the mother, through the impurity of parents, thirty material qualities are fulfilled by action of ten (?) sense-spheres. In the moment of decay, forty-six material qualities are fulfilled,*

Thus consciousness conditions name-form. Name-form conditions consciousness.[3] Thus the link of becoming is fulfilled. Here, the fulfilment of the three links should be understood.

FOUR GROUP DIVISION

Q. How, through the four groups? *A.* Ignorance and the formations are divisions of the groups of action and defilement of the past. Consciousness, name-form, the six-sphered-sense, contact and feeling are divisions of the groups of effect in the present. Craving, clinging and becoming are divisions of action, and defilement of the present. Rebirth, and decay-and-death are divisions of effect of the future. Thus one should know through the four-group division.

TWENTY MODES

Q. How, through twenty modes? *A.* Through the grasping of ignorance and of past craving and clinging and through the defilement-sign being grasped. Through the grasping of the formations of past becoming and through the action-sign being grasped. Through the grasping of consciousness, of name-

---

(d) Vbh.-a. 156: *Gatinimittaṁ nāma nibbattanaka-okāse eko vaṇṇo upaṭṭhāti. Tattha niraye upaṭṭhahante lohakumbhī-sadiso hutvā uppaṭṭhāti. Manussaloke upaṭṭhahante mātukucchi kambalayāna-sadisā hutvā upaṭṭhāti. Devaloke upaṭṭhahante kappa-rukkha-vimāna-sayanādīni upaṭṭhahanti.*

1. Mil. 71: *Rājā āha: Bhante Nāgasena, na ca sankamati paṭisandahati cāti.—Āma mahārāja, na ca sankamati paṭisandahati cāti.—Katham bhante Nāgasena na ca sankamati paṭisandahati ca, opammaṁ karohiti.—Yathā mahārāja kocid eva puriso padīpato padīpaṁ padīpeyya, kin nu kho so mahārāja padīpo padīpamhā sankanto ti.—Na hi bhante ti.—Evam eva kho mahārāja na ca sankamati paṭisandahati cāti.*
2. M. II, 262 ff.: *Saṁvattanikaṁ viññaṇaṁ.*

* The text is very confused here.

3. S. II, 104: *Paccudāvattati kho idaṁ viññāṇam nāmarūpamhā nāparaṁ gacchati, ettāvatā jāyetha vā jīyetha vā mīyetha vā cavetha vā upapajjetha vā yad idaṁ nāmarūpapaccayā viññāṇaṁ, viññāṇapaccayā nāmarūpaṁ, nāmarūpapaccayā saḷāyatanaṁ, ...pe...*

form, of the six-sphered-sense, of contact, of feeling and through birth and decay-and-death of the result-sign of the present being grasped. Through the grasping of craving, clinging and through the defilement-sign of the present being grasped. Through the grasping of becoming the present formations are grasped through the action-sign. Through the grasping of birth, decay and death, future consciousness, name-form, the six-sphered-sense, contact, feeling are grasped. These twenty-four states become twenty.

It is according to the teaching in the Abhidhamma: "In the previous *kamma*-becoming, delusion is ignorance, effort is the formations, desire is craving, grasping is clinging, volition is becoming. Thus these five states of the previous *kamma*-becoming are causes of the present rebirth. From the maturity of the sense-organs, here, delusion is ignorance; effort is the formations; desire is craving; grasping is clinging; volition is becoming. Thus these five states, here in *kamma*-becoming are causes of rebirth in the future. Here, rebirth is consciousness; descent is name-form; sensory organism is sense-organ; the being touched is touch; the being felt is feeling. Thus these five states, here, in rebirth-becoming are cause of *kamma* already done. Thus one should know through twenty ways".[1]

How, through wheel? Ignorance conditions the formations; the formations condition consciousness; thus birth conditions decay and death. Thus the whole aggregate of ill arises. Therefore all constitute the aggregate of ill. Not knowing is called ignorance. Ignorance conditions the formations. Thus should it be known by way of the wheel.

DIRECT AND REVERSE ORDER

How, through order? Order is of two kinds. They are, the one which begins from ignorance and the one which begins from decay and death. Questioned as to that which begins from ignorance, one should answer in the direct order; and questioned as to that which begins from decay and death, the answer should be in the reverse order.

And again, that which begins from ignorance is fixed; one can see the way to the future. That which begins with decay is the end; one can see the way to the past. Thus one should know through order.

---

1. Pts. I, 52: *Purimakammabhavasmiṁ moho avijjā, āyuhanā saṅkhārā, nikanti taṇhā, upagamanaṁ upādānaṁ, cetanā bhavo; ime pañca dhammā purimakammabhavasmiṁ idha paṭisandhiyā paccayā . . . Idha paripakkattā āyatanānaṁ moho avijjā, āyuhanā saṅkhārā, nikanti taṇhā, upagamanaṁ upādānaṁ, cetanā bhavo; ime pañca dhammā idhakamma-bhavasmiṁ āyatiṁ paṭisandhiyā paccayā. Āyatiṁ paṭisandhi viññāṇaṁ, okkanti nāma-rūpaṁ, pasādo āyatanaṁ, phuṭṭho phasso, vedayitaṁ vedanā; ime pañca dhammā āyatiṁ upapattibhavasmiṁ idha katassa kammassa paccayā. Iti ime catusaṅkhepe tayo addhe vīsatiyā ākārehi tisandhiṁ paṭiccasamuppādaṁ jānāti passati aññāti paṭivijjhati. Taṅ ñātaṭṭhena ñāṇaṁ, pajānanaṭṭhena paññā; tena vuccati—'Paccaya pariggahe paññā dhammaṭṭhitiñāṇaṁ'.*

MUNDANE AND SUPRAMUNDANE CONDITIONED ARISING

Q. How, through discernment? *A*. There are two kinds of conditioned arising: mundane conditioned arising and supramundane conditioned arising. Here, that which begins from ignorance is mundane. *Q*. What is supramundane conditioned arising? *A*. Ill depends on ill. Confidence depends on confidence. Joy depends on joy. Rapture depends on rapture. Calm depends on calm. Bliss depends on bliss. Concentration depends on concentration. Right views depend on right Views. Aversion depends on aversion. Dispassion depends on dispassion. Freedom depends on the knowledge of the freedom of extinction. This is called supramundane conditioned arising.[1]

FOUR KINDS OF CONDITIONED ARISING

Again, four kinds of conditioned arising are taught thus: the defilement-action is cause; seed is cause; doing is cause; common action is cause.

Q. What is meant by "defilement-action is cause"? *A*. It is that which begins from ignorance. What is meant by "seed is cause"? It is likened to the succession of seed and bud. What is meant by "doing is cause"? It is likened to the change of material qualities. What is meant by "common action is cause"? It is likened to earth, snow, mountain, sea sun and moon.

There is another teaching. Common action is not a cause. Material qualities, consciousness, states and caloricity are causes. There is no common action, according to the teaching of the Blessed One thus:

With none is kamma shared, none can rob it,
and by itself comes the fruit of merit won.[2]

Thus one should know through discernment.

THROUGH COMPREHENSION

Q. How, through comprehension? *A*. There are four kinds of comprehension: aggregate-comprehension, sense-organ-comprehension, element-comprehension and truth-comprehension. Here, ignorance, the formations,

---

1. There is another classification of conditioned arising at Netti. 67: *Es' ev' anto dukkhassā ti paṭiccasamuppādo. So duvidho: lokiko ca lokuttaro ca. Tattha lokiko: avijjāpaccayā saṁkhārā yāva jarāmaraṇā, lokuttaro: sīlavato avippaṭisāro jāyati yāva nāparaṁ itthattāyā ti pajānāti.* See p. 229, note 1 (c), and last note of appendix.
2. Not traced. Cp. Sv. I, 37: *Kammassakā hi sattā, attano kammānurūpaṁ eva gatiṁ gacchanti, n'eva pitā puttassa kammena gacchati, na putto pitu kammena, na matā puttassa, na putto mātuyā, na bhātā bhaginiyā, na ācariyo antevāsino, na antevāsī ācariyassa kammena gacchati.*

contact, craving, clinging and becoming are comprehended in the aggregate of the formations. Consciousness is comprehended in the consciousness-aggregate. Name-form is comprehended in the four aggregates. The six-sphered-sense is comprehended in the two aggregates. Feeling is comprehended in the feeling-aggregate. Birth and decay and death are comprehended in the aggregate of form and in the aggregate of the formations. Ignorance, the formations, contact, feeling, craving, clinging, becoming, rebirth and decay and death are comprehended in the sense-sphere of ideas. Consciousness is comprehended in the mind-sphere. Name-form is comprehended in the five internal sense-spheres. The six-sphered-sense is comprehended in the six internal sense-spheres. Ignorance, the formations, contact, feeling, craving, clinging, becoming, rebirth and decay and death are comprehended in the element of ideas. Consciousness is comprehended in the mind-consciousness-element. Name-form is comprehended in the five elements. The six-sphered-sense is comprehended in the twelvefold truth. Ignorance, craving and clinging are comprehended in the tenfold truth. The other nine are comprehended in the Truth of Ill. Supramundane conditioned arising way-factor is comprehended in the Path-truth. The extinction of conditioned arising is comprehended in the Truth of Cessation. Thus one should know through comprehension. Through these ways should one understand the method of conditioned arising. This is called conditioned arising method.

Conditioned arising method has ended.

The Tenth Fascicle of the Path of Freedom has ended.

[452] THE PATH OF FREEDOM

FASCICLE THE ELEVENTH

WRITTEN

BY

THE ARAHANT UPATISSA

WHO WAS CALLED

GREAT LIGHT IN RYO

TRANSLATED IN RYO

BY

TIPIṬAKA SANGHAPĀLA OF FUNAN

THE FIVE METHODS

CHAPTER THE ELEVENTH

Section Two

THE FOUR NOBLE TRUTHS

Q. What is the method of understanding the Noble Truths?

A. There are Four Noble Truths: the Noble Truth of Ill, the Noble Truth of the Origin of Ill, the Noble Truth of the Cessation of Ill and the Noble Truth of the Path leading to the Cessation of Ill.

TRUTH OF ILL

Q. What is the Noble Truth of Ill? *A.* "Birth is ill; old age is ill; death is ill; sorrow is ill; lamentation and misery are ill; grief and despair are ill; association with those one does not like is ill; separation from those one likes is ill; the not getting of what is wished for is ill: in short the five aggregates of clinging are ill".[1]

"Birth is ill": This is the arising of the aggregates of various beings. All these are assemblages of ill. "Old age is ill": All the elements, proceeding from birth, come to maturity and lose vigour, colour, faculties, memory and intellect. "Death is ill": Fear of the ending of life. "sorrow is ill": On going to the place of suffering, fear arises. This is the burning within. "Lamentation is ill": Suffering reaches verbal expression. This is to burn within

---

1. D. II, 304 ff; Vbh. 99: *Cattāri ariyasaccāni: dukkhaṁ ariyasaccaṁ dukkhasamudayo ariyasaccaṁ dukkhanirodho ariyasaccaṁ dukkhanirodhagāminī paṭipadā ariyasaccaṁ.*
Tattha katamaṁ dukkhaṁ ariyasaccaṁ?
Jāti pi dukkhā jarā pi dukkhā maraṇaṁ pi dukkhaṁ sokaparidevadukkhadomanassupāyāsā pi dukkhā appiyehi sampayogo dukkho piyehi vippayogo dukkho yam p'icchaṁ na labhati tam pi dukkhaṁ; sankhittena pancupādānakkhandhā pi dukkhā.

and without. "Misery is ill": This is the suffering of the body. By this one suffers bodily pain. This is the meaning. "Grief and despair are ill": These are sufferings of the mind. By these one suffers mental anguish. This is the meaning. "Association with those one does not like is ill": This means that one is united with persons one dislikes. "Separation from those one likes is ill": This means that one is separated from persons one likes. "The not getting of what is wished for": A man loses happiness because he is not able to separate from those whom he dislikes, and because he is not able to unite with those whom he likes. Being unable to secure these he loses happiness. "In short the five aggregates of clinging are ill": One is not able to separate oneself from these five aggregates of clinging. Therefore these five aggregates of clinging are ill.[1]

FIVE GROUPS OF CLINGING

Q. What are the five aggregates of clinging? *A*. The form aggregate of clinging, the feeling aggregate of clinging, the perception aggregate of clinging, the formation aggregate of clinging, the consciousness aggregate of clinging. These should be understood according to the full explanation under the method of (understanding) the aggregates.

TWO KINDS OF ILL

Here ill is of two kinds thus: ill of sense-sphere and innate ill. The ill of birth, the ill of death, the ill of association with those one dislikes, the ill of separation from those one likes, the ill of not getting what is wished for; in short, the ill of the aggregates of clinging, are called ill of sense-sphere. The ill of sorrow, the ill of lamentation and the ill of grief and despair are called innate ill.

---

1. Cp. Vbh. 99: *Tattha katamā jāti? Yā tesaṁ tesaṁ sattānaṁ tamhi tamhi sattanikāye jāti sañjāti okkanti abhinibbatti khandhānaṁ pātubhāvo āyatanānaṁ paṭilābho ayaṁ vuccati jāti.*

   Tattha katamā jarā? Yā tesaṁ tesaṁ sattānaṁ tamhi tamhi sattanikāye jarā jīraṇatā khaṇḍiccaṁ pāliccaṁ valittacatā āyuno saṁhāni indriyānaṁ paripāko: ayaṁ vuccati jarā.

   Tattha katamaṁ maraṇaṁ? Yā tesaṁ tesaṁ . . . cuti cavanatā bhedo antaradhānaṁ maccu maraṇaṁ kālakiriyā khandhānaṁ bhedo kaḷevarassa nikkhepo jīvitindriyassa upacchedo: idaṁ vuccati maraṇaṁ.—The explanation given above is quite different. Cp. Ibid. 367: *Maraṇaṁ paṭicca bhayaṁ bhayānakaṁ chambhitattaṁ lomahaṁso cetaso utrāso: idaṁ vuccati maraṇabhayaṁ.*

   Ibid. 99-100: *Tattha katamo soko? Ñātivyasanena vā phuṭṭhassa bhogavyasanena vā phuṭṭhassa rogavyasanena vā phuṭṭhassa sīlavyasanena vā phuṭṭhassa diṭṭhivyasanena vā phuṭṭhassa aññataraññatarena vyasanena samannāgatassa aññataraññatarena dukkhadhammena phuṭṭhassa soko socanā socitattaṁ antosoko antoparisoko cetaso parijjhāyanā domanassaṁ sokasallaṁ: ayaṁ vuccati soko* (—Cp. Nidd. I, 128 which adds *antoḍāho antopariḍāho* to the list.).

   Tattha katamo paridevo? Ñātivyasanena vā phuṭṭhassa . . . ādevo paridevo ādevanā paridevanā ādevitattaṁ paridevitattaṁ vācā palāpo vippalāpo lālapo lālapanā lālapitattaṁ: Ayaṁ vuccati paridevo.

   Tattha katamaṁ dukkhaṁ? Yaṁ kāyikaṁ asātaṁ kāyikaṁ dukkhaṁ kāyasamphassajaṁ asātaṁ dukkhaṁ vedayitaṁ kāyasamphassajā asātā dukkhā vedanā: idaṁ vuccati dukkhaṁ.

THREE KINDS OF ILL

Ill is of three kinds thus: the ill of misery, change and existence.[1] Here bodily and mental suffering are the ill of misery. Pleasurable feeling connected with the cankers is subject to renewal. Therefore it is called the ill of change. The five aggregates of clinging constitute the ill of existence.

Thus should the Noble Truth of Ill be known.

TRUTH OF THE ORIGIN OF ILL

Q. What is the Noble Truth of the Origin of Ill?

A. "Even this craving, causing new rebirths, accompanied by delight and passion, finding gratification now here and now there, namely, the craving for pleasure, the craving for existence and the craving for annihilation". Here "causing new rebirth" means: "Craving, wherever it is, causes rebirth". "Even this craving" means: "Craving is the origin of ill; it is not a co-arising". "Accompanied by delight and passion" means: "Craving causes the arising of delight. This is called manifestation. It causes to stain. This is called passion. It stirs up delight conjoined with passion". "Finding gratification now here and now there" means "It causes individuality to arise in various places where there are lovable forms and so forth, and to delight and find gratification therein". "Namely, the craving for pleasure, the craving for existence and the craving for annihilation": Everything, except the craving for existence and the craving for annihilation, is comprehended in

---

Tattha katamaṁ domanassaṁ? Yaṁ cetasikaṁ asātaṁ cetasikaṁ dukkhaṁ cetosamphassajaṁ asātaṁ dukkhaṁ vedayitaṁ cetosamphassajā asātā dukkhā vedanā: idaṁ vuccati domanassaṁ.

Tattha katamo upāyāso? ñātivyasanena vā phuṭṭhassa . . . āyāso upāyāso āyāsitattaṁ upāyāsitattaṁ: ayaṁ vuccati upāyāso.

Tattha katamo appiyehi sampayogo dukkho? Idha yassa te honti aniṭṭhā akantā amanāpā rūpā saddā gandhā rasā phoṭṭhabbā ye vā pan' assa te honti anatthakāmā ahitakāmā aphāsukāmā ayogakkhemakāmā, yā tehi saṁgati samāgamo samodhānaṁ missībhāvo: ayaṁ vuccati appiyehi sampayogo dukkho.

Tattha katamo piyehi vippayogo dukkho? Idha yassa te honti iṭṭhā kantā manāpā rūpā saddā . . . , ye vā pan'assa te honti atthakāmā hitakāmā phāsukāmā yogakkhemakāmā, mātā vā pitā vā bhātā vā bhaginī vā mittā vā amaccā vā ñātisālohitā vā, yā tehi asaṁgati asamāgamo asamodhānaṁ amissībhāvo: ayaṁ vuccati piyehi vippayogo dukkho.

Ibid. 101: *Tattha katamaṁ yam p' icchaṁ na labhati tam pi dukkhaṁ? Jātidhammānaṁ sattānaṁ evaṁ icchā uppajjati: aho vata mayaṁ na jātidhammā assāma, na ca vata no jāti āgaccheyyāti, na kho pan' etaṁ icchāya pattabbaṁ: idam pi yam p' icchaṁ na labhati tam pi dukkhaṁ. Jarādhammānaṁ sattānaṁ . . . pe . . . vyādhidhammānaṁ sattānaṁ maraṇadhammānaṁ sattānaṁ sokaparidevadukkhadomanassupāyāsadhammānaṁ sattānaṁ evaṁ icchā uppajjati: aho vata mayaṁ na sokaparidevadukkhadomanassupāyāsadhammā assāma, na ca vata no sokaparidevadukkhadomanassupāyāsā āgaccheyyun ti, na kho pan 'etaṁ icchāya pattabbaṁ: idaṁ pi yam p' icchaṁ na labhati tam pi dukkhaṁ.*

Tattha katame saṁkhittena pañcupādānakkhandhā pi dukkhā? Seyyathīdaṁ: rūpūpādānakkhandho vedanūpādānakkhandho saññūpādānakkhandho saṁkhārūpādānakkhandho viññāṇūpādānakkhandho: ime vuccanti saṁkhittena pañcupādānakkhandhā pi dukkhā.

Idaṁ vuccati dukkhaṁ ariyasaccaṁ.

1. D. III, 216: *Tisso dukkhatā: Dukkha-dukkhatā, saṁkhāra-dukkhatā, viparināma-dukkhatā* The order is difierent here.

the craving for pleasure. The craving for existence arises together the with view of eternalism.[1] The craving for annihilation arises together with the view of nihilism.[2] Thus should the Noble Truth of the Origin of ill be known.[3]

TRUTH OF THE CESSATION OF ILL

Q. What is the Noble Truth of the Cessation of Ill?

A. "The utter fading away and cessation of that very craving, leaving it, giving it up, the being delivered from, the doing away with it".[4] Thus should be known the Noble Truth of the Cessation of Ill. *Q.* No. This is also the ending of the origin, because the Blessed One has said: "The cause of ill is destroyed". *A.* The cause of ill is destroyed. Therefore the state of not coming to birth and of not perishing is accomplished. It corresponds to realization. Therefore the Blessed One taught: "The ending of the origin is the ending of ill".

TRUTH OF THE PATH LEADING TO CESSATION OF ILL

Q. What is the Path leading to the Cessation of Ill? *A.* It is the Noble Eightfold Path of Right View, Right Thought, Right Speech, Right Action, Right Livelihood, Right Exertion, Right Mindfulness, Right Concentration. Right View is the knowledge of the Four Truths. Right Thought means the three meritorious thoughts. Right Speech is the separation from the four wrong (verbal) actions. Right Action is separation from the three wrong actions. Right livelihood is separation from wrong livelihood. Right

1. *Sassataditthi.*
2. *Ucchedadhitthi.*
3. S. V, 421; Vin. I, 10: Vbh. 101-3; D. II, 308-10: *Katamañ ca bhikkhave dukkha-samudayaṁ ariya-saccaṁ? Yāyaṁ taṇhā ponobhavikā nandi-rāga-sahagatā tatra tatrābhi-nandinī, seyyathīdaṁ kāma-taṇhā bhava-taṇhā vibhava-taṇhā.*
   Sā kho pan' esā bhikkhave taṇhā kattha uppajjamānā uppajjati, kattha nivisamānā nivisati? Yaṁ loke piya-rūpaṁ sāta-rūpaṁ, etth' esā taṇhā uppajjamānā uppajjati, ettha nivisamānā nivisati.
   Kiñci loke piya-rūpaṁ sāta-rūpaṁ? Cakkhuṁ loke piya-rūpaṁ sāta-rūpaṁ . . . pe . . . Sotaṁ loke . . . Ghānaṁ loke . . . Jivhā loke . . . Kāyo loke . . . Mano loke . . .
   Rūpā loke . . . pe . . .
   Cakkhu-viññāṇaṁ loke . . . pe . . .
   Cakkhu-samphasso loke . . . pe . . .
   Cakkhu-samphassajā vedanā loke . . . pe . . .
   Rūpa-saññā loke . . . pe . . .
   Rūpa-sañcetanā loke . . . pe . . .
   Rūpa-taṇhā loke . . . pe . . .
   Rūpa-vitakko loke . . . pe . . .
   Rūpa-vicāro loke . . . pe . . .
   Dhamma-vicāro loke piya-rūpaṁ sāta-rūpaṁ etth' esā taṇhā uppajjamānā uppajjati, ettha nivisamānā nivisati. Idaṁ vuccati bhikkhave dukkha-samudayaṁ ariya-saccaṁ.
4. Ibid. 310-11: *Katamañ ca bhikkhave dukkha-nirodhaṁ ariya-saccaṁ? Yo tassā yeva taṇhāya asesa-virāga-nirodho cāgo paṭinissaggo mutti anālayo . . . Idaṁ vuccati bhikkhave dukkha-nirodhaṁ ariya-saccaṁ.*

Exertion is the fourfold right exertion. Right Mindfulness means the four foundations of mindfulness. Right Concentration is the fourfold meditation, *jhāna*.[1]

And again, if a man practises the Noble Path, he sees *Nibbāna*—this is called Right View. He awakes only in *Nibbāna*—this is called Right Thought. He abandons wrong speech—this is Right Speech. He rejects wrong doing—this is Right Action. He gives up wrong livelihood—this is Right Livelihood. He abandons wrong exertion—this is Right Exertion. He recalls *Nibbāna* to mind—this is Right Mindfulness. He concentrates on *Nibbāna*—this is Right Concentration. Here, the faculty of wisdom, the power of wisdom, the basis of supernormal power of scrutiny and the enlightenment factor of the investigation of states accomplish the entry into internal Right View. The faculty of exertion, the power of exertion, the basis of supernormal power of exertion, the basis of supernormal power of will, the enlightenment factor of exertion, and the fourfold right exertion accomplish the entry into internal Right Effort. The faculty of mindfulness, the power of mindfulness, the enlightenment factor of mindfulness and the four foundations of mindfulness accomplish the entry into internal Right Mindfulness. The faculty of concentration, the power of concentration, the basis of supernormal power of thought, the faculty of faith, the power of faith, the enlightenment factor of concentration, the enlightenment factor of joy, the enlightenment factor of calm and the enlightenment factor of equanimity accomplish the entry into internal Right Concentration. These thirty-seven enlightenment accessories accomplish the entry into the Noble Eightfold Path. Thus should the Noble Truth of the Path leading to the Cessation of Ill be known. Thus should the Four Noble Truths be understood.

---

1. D. II, 311-13: *Katamañ ca bhikkhave dukkha-nirodha-gāminī-paṭipadā ariya-saccaṁ? Ayam eva Ariyo Aṭṭhangiko Maggo, seyyathīdaṁ sammādiṭṭhi sammā-saṁkappo sammā-vācā sammā-kammanto sammā-ājīvo sammā-vāyāmo sammā-sati sammā-samādhi.*

Katamā ca bhikkhave sammā-diṭṭhi? Yaṁ kho bhikkhave dukkhe ñāṇaṁ dukkha-samudaye ñāṇaṁ dukkha-nirodhe ñāṇaṁ dukkha-nirodha-gāminiyā paṭipadāya ñāṇaṁ, ayaṁ vuccati bhikkhave sammā-diṭṭhi.

Katamo ca bhikkhave sammā-saṁkappo? Nekkhamma-saṁkappo avyāpāda-saṁkappo avihiṁsā-saṁkappo, ayaṁ vuccati bhikkhave sammā-saṁkappo.

Katamā ca bhikkhave sammā-vācā ? Musā-vādā veramaṇī, pisuṇāya vācāya veramaṇī, pharusāya vācāya veramaṇī, samphappalāpā veramaṇī, ayaṁ vuccati bhikkhave sammā-vācā.

Katamo ca bhikkhave sammā-kammanto? Pāṇātipātā veramaṇī, adinnādānā veramaṇī, kāmesu micchācārā veramaṇī, ayaṁ vuccati bhikkhave sammā-kammanto.

Katamo ca bhikkhave sammā-ājīvo? Idha bhikkhave ariya-sāvako micchā-ājīvaṁ pahāya sammā-ājīvena jīvikaṁ kappeti, ayaṁ vuccati bhikkhave sammā-ājīvo.

Katamo ca bhikkhave sammā-vāyāmo? Idha bhikkhave bhikkhu anuppannānaṁ pāpakānaṁ akusalānaṁ dhammānaṁ anuppādāya chandaṁ janeti vāyamati, viriyaṁ ārabhati, cittaṁ paggaṇhāti padahati. Uppannānaṁ papākānaṁ akusalānaṁ dhammānaṁ pahanāya chandaṁ janeti vāyamati, viriyaṁ ārabhati, cittaṁ paggaṇhāti padahati. Anuppannānaṁ kusalānaṁ dhammānaṁ uppādāya chandaṁ janeti vāyamati, viriyaṁ ārabhati, cittaṁ paggaṇhāti padahati. Upannānaṁ kusalānaṁ dhammānaṁ ṭhitiyā asammosāya bhiyyobhāvāya vepullāya bhāvanāya pāripūriyā chandaṁ janeti vāyamati, viriyaṁ ārabhati, cittaṁ paggaṇhāti padahati. Ayaṁ vuccati bhikkhave sammā-vāyāmo.

Katamā ca bhikkhave sammā-sati? Idha bhikkhave bhikkhu kaye kāyānupassī viharati ātāpī sampajāno satimā vineyya loke abhijjhā-domanassaṁ, vedanāsu . . . pe . . . citte . . . pe . . . dhammesu dhammānupassī viharati ātāpī sampajāno satimā vineyya loke abhijjhā-domanassaṁ. Ayaṁ vuccati bhikkhave sammā-sati.

Q. Why are four Noble Truths taught and not three or five? *A.* (If three or five were taught) all might be doubted. These are the consequences and causes of the mundane and the supramundane. Therefore they are four. *Q.* What is the consequence (and what, the cause) of mundane truth? *A.* ill and origin are the consequence and cause of mundance truth. Cessation is the consequence of supramundane truth. The Path is the cause of supramundane truth. Therefore four and not three or five are taught. And again, because of the four sentences: "One should comprehend, one should abandon, one should realize, one should practise",[1] there are four.

The characteristics of these Four Noble Truths should be known through eleven ways: through the meaning of words,[2] through characteristics,[3] through series in beliefs,[4] through analogy,[5] through discrimination, through enumeration, through sameness, through difference, through one kind and so forth,[6] through inclusion.

THROUGH WORD MEANING

Q. How, through the meaning of words? *A.* The Noble Truths are the teaching of the Holy One. Therefore they are called Noble Truths. Through understanding these well, one fulfils the Four Noble Truths. "Truth" means: "Thus-isness, non-variability, identity". Ill is the consequence. Origin is the cause. Cessation is ending continued. The Path is the highest view. Thus should these be known through the meaning of words.

THROUGH CHARACTERISTICS

Q. How, through characteristics? *A.* Ill is the characteristic of suffering.

Katamo ca bhikkhave sammā-samādhi? Idha bhikkhave bhikkhu vivicc' eva kāmehi vivicca akusalehi dhammehi savitakkaṁ savicāraṁ vivekajaṁ pīti-sukhaṁ paṭhamajjhānaṁ upasampajja viharati. Vitakka-vicārānaṁ vūpasamā ajjhattaṁ sampasādanaṁ cetaso ekodi-bhāvaṁ avitakkaṁ avicāraṁ samādhijaṁ pīti-sukhaṁ dutiyajjhānaṁ upasampajja viharati. Pītiyā ca virāgā upekhako viharati sato ca sampajāno, sukhañ ca kāyena paṭisaṁvedeti yan taṁ ariyā ācikkhanti: 'upekhako satimā-sukha vihārī ti' tatiya-jjhānaṁ upasampajja viharati. Sukhassa ca pahānā dukkhassa ca pahānā pubb' eva somanassa-domanassānaṁ atthagamā adukkhaṁ asukhaṁ upekhā-sati-pārisuddhiṁ catutthajjhānaṁ upasampajja viharati. Ayaṁ vuccati bhikkhave sammā-samādhi.

Idaṁ vuccati bhikkhave dukkha-nirodha-gāmini-paṭipadā ariya-saccaṁ.

1. (a) S. V, 422: *Taṁ kho panidaṁ dukkhaṁ ariyasaccaṁ pariññeyyan ti me bhikkhave pubbe ananussutesu dhammesu cakkhuṁ udapādi ñāṇaṁ udapādi paññā udapādi vijjā udapādi āloko udapādi . . . Taṁ kho panidaṁ . . . pariññātan ti me bhikkhave . . . āloko udāpādi.*

. . . Taṁ kho panidaṁ dukkhasamudayam ariyasaccam pahātabban ti me bhikkhave pubbe . . . pahīnan ti me bhikkhave pubbe . . . āloko udapādi.

. . . Taṁ kho panidaṁ dukkhanirodhaṁ ariyasaccaṁ sacchikātabban ti me bhikkhave pubbe . . . sacchikatan ti me bhikkhave pubbe . . . āloko udapādi.

. . . Taṁ kho panidaṁ dukkhanirodhagāminī paṭipadā ariyasaccam bhāvetabban ti me bhikkhave pubbe . . . bhāvitan ti me bhikkhave pubbe . . . āloko udapādi.

(b) Cp. Abhmv. vv. 1382-83:

Pariññābhisamayena, dukkhaṁ abhisameti so
pahānābhisamen' esa, tathā samudayam pi ca,
bhāvanā-vidhinā yeva, maggaṁ abhisameti taṁ
ārammaṇakriyāy' eva, nirodhaṁ sacchikaroti so.

2. *Padattha.* 3. *Lakkhaṇa.* 4. *Kama.* 5. *Upamā.* 6. *Ekavidhādi.*

Origin is the characteristic of cause. Cessation is the characteristic of non-birth. The Path is the characteristic of the means of success. And again, ill is the characteristic of grief, despair, the put together, the limited. Origin is the characteristic of accumulation, cause, condition, fetters, clinging. Cessation is the characteristic of renunciation, solitude, the non-conditioned and the choice. The Path is the characteristic of vehicle, arriving, seeing, reliance. Thus should these be known through characteristics.

THROUGH SERIES

Q. How, through series? *A.* The Truth of Ill is taught first, becuase it is gross and because it could be easily understood in this world. The Truth of Origin is taught next. The ending of the origin is the ending of ill. After that the Truth of Cessation is taught for the purpose of ending completely. And the Path is taught last. This (method) is like (that of) a clever physician, who at first gets at the root of the disease and later inquires as to the contributory causes. For the ending of the disease, he prescribes according to the nature of the disease. Here, one should know the disease as ill; the cause and condition as origin; the ending of the disease as cessation; and the medicine as the Path. Thus should these be known through series.[1]

IN BRIEF

Q. How, in brief? *A.* Birth is ill; the being born is the origin; the ending of ill is cessation; the path leading to the cessation of ill is the Path. Where there is defilement, there is ill. Defilement is the origin. The removal of defilement is cessation. The means of removal is the Path. (The Truth of Ill removes the illusion of self; (the Truth of) Origin removes the view of nihilism; (the Truth of) Cessation removes the view of eternalism; (the Truth of) the Path removes all wrong views. Thus should these be known in brief.

---

1. Cp. (a) A. III, 238: *Seyyathā pi bho puriso ābādhiko dukkhito bāḷhagilāno, tassa kusalo bhisakko ṭhānaso ābādhaṁ nīhareyya, evam eva kho bho yato yato tassa bhoto Gotamassa dhammam suṇāti yadi suttaso yadi geyyaso yadi veyyākaraṇaso yadi abbhutadhammaso, tato tato sokaparidevadukkhadomanassupāyāsā abbhatthaṁ gacchanti.*

(b) A. IV, 340: *'Bhisakko' ti bhikkhave Tathāgatass' etaṁ adhivacanaṁ arahato sammāsambuddhassa.*

(c) It. 101: *Aham-asmi bhikkhave brāhmaṇo yācayogo sadā payatapāṇi antimadehadhāro anuttaro bhisakko sallakatto* (= *Anuttaro bhisak(k)o sallakatto ti duttikicchassa vaṭṭadukkharogassa tikicchanato uttamo bhisak(k)o, aññehi anuddharaṇīyānaṁ rāgādisallānaṁ kantanato samucchedavasena samuddharaṇato uttamo sallakantanavejjo*—It.-a. II, 143).

(d) Peṭaka. 123-24: *Tattha dve rogā sattānaṁ avijjā ca bhavataṇhā ca. Etesaṁ dvinnaṁ rogānaṁ nighātāya Bhagavatā dve bhesajjāni vuttāni samatho ca vipassanā ca. Imāni dve bhesajjāni paṭisevento dve aroge sacchikaroti: rāga-virāgaṁ cetovimuttiṁ avijjāvirāgañ ca paññāvimuttiṁ.*

Tattha taṇhārogassa samatho bhesajjaṁ, rāgavirāgā cetovimutti arogaṁ. Avijjārogassa vipassanā bhesajjaṁ, avijjāvirāgā paññāvimutti arogaṁ.

Evaṁ hi Bhagavā c'āha: dve dhammā pariññeyyā nāmañ ca rūpañ ca, dve dhammā pahātabbā avijjā ca bhavataṇhā ca, dve dhammā bhāvetabbā samatho ca

SIMILES OF THE POISONOUS TREE, THE SHIP, THE BURDEN

Q. How, through analogy? *A*. Ill should be regarded as a poisonous tree; origin, as a seed; cessation, as the parching of the seed; the Path as fire.

One should regard ill as this shore of fear; origin, as the flood; cessation, as the other shore that is free from suffering and fear; and the Path, as the ship that sails well.[1]

[453] One should regard ill as the carrying of a burden; origin, as the taking on of the burden; cessation, as the laying down of the burden; and the Path, as the method of laying down the burden. Thus should these be known through analogy.[2]

THROUGH DISCRIMINATION

Q. How, through discrimination? *A*. There are four kinds in truth: Speech that is true, knowledge, absolute truth and Ariyan Truth. Here, a man speaks true words and not words that are untrue — this is called speech that is true. Investigation of falsehood — this is knowledge. *Nibbāna* is absolute truth. The truth practised by the Saint is Ariyan Truth. Here, Ariyan Truth should be realized. Thus should these be known through discrimination.

---

vipassanā ca, dve dhammā sacchikātabbā vijjā ca vimutti cā ti.

Tattha samathaṁ bhāvento rūpaṁ parijānāti. Rūpaṁ parijānanto taṇhaṁ pajahati. Taṇhaṁ pajahanto rāgavirāgā cetovimuttiṁ sacchikaroti. Vipassanaṁ bhāvento nāmaṁ parijānāti. Nāmaṁ parijānanto avijjaṁ pajahati. Avijjaṁ pajahanto avijjāvirāgā paññāvimuttiṁ sacchikaroti.

Yadā bhikkhuno dve dhammā pariññātā bhavanti nāmañ ca rūpañ ca, tathā'ssa dukkhadhammā pahīnā bhavanti avijjā ca bhavataṇhā ca. Dve dhammā bhāvitā bhavanti samatho ca vipassanā ca. Dve dhammā sacchikātabbā bhavanti vijjā ca vimutti ca.

1. (a) S. IV, 174-5: *Atha kho so bhikkhave tassa purisassa evam assa. Ayaṁ kho mahā udakaṇṇavo orimantīraṁ sāsaṅkaṁ sappaṭibhayaṁ pārimantīraṁ khemaṁ appaṭibhayaṁ natthi ca nāvā santāraṇī uttarasetu vā aparāpāraṁgamanāya. Yaṁ nūnāhaṁ tiṇakaṭṭha-sākhā-palāsaṁ saṅkaḍḍhitvā kullaṁ bandhitvā taṁ kullaṁ nissāya hatthehi ca pādehi ca vāyamamāno sotthinā pāraṁ gaccheyyanti.*

Mahā udakaṇṇavo ti kho bhikkhave catunnaṁ oghānaṁ adhivacanaṁ, kāmoghassa bhavoghassa diṭṭhoghassa avijjoghassa.

Orimantīraṁ sāsaṅkaṁ sappaṭibhayan ti kho bhikkhave sakkāyassetaṁ adhivacanaṁ.

Pārimantīraṁ khemaṁ appaṭibhayan ti kho bhikkhave nibbānassetaṁ adhivacanaṁ.

Kullan ti kho bhikkhave ariyassetaṁ aṭṭhangikassa maggassa adhivacanaṁ, seyyathidaṁ sammādiṭṭhiyā . . . pe . . . sammāsamādhissa.

Hatthehi ca pādehi ca vāyāmo ti kho bhikkhave viriyārambhassetaṁ adhivacanaṁ.

Tiṇṇo pārangato thale tiṭṭhati brāhmaṇo ti kho bhikkhave arahato etaṁ adhivacanan ti.

(b) Sn. 321:

Yathā pi nāvaṁ daḷhaṁ āruhitvā
phiyen' arittena samangibhūto,
so tāraye tattha bahū pi aññe
tatr' ūpāyaññū kusalo mutīmā.

2. Cp. (a) M. I, 139-40: *Kathañ ca bhikkhave bhikkhu ariyo pannaddhajo pannabhāro visamyutto hoti? Idha bhikkhave bhikkhuno asmimāno pahīno hoti ucchinnamūlo tālavatthukato anabhāvakato āyatiṁ anuppādadhammo. Evaṁ kho bhikkhave bhikkhu ariyo pannaddhajo pannabhāro visaṁyutto hoti.*

THROUGH ENUMERATION

Q. How, through enumeration? *A.* Except craving, all skilful, unskilful and indeterminate states of the three planes compose the Truth of Ill; craving is the Truth of Origin; the removal of craving is the Truth of Cessation; the Noble Eightfold Path is the Truth of the Path. Again, except craving, all other defilements and the skilful, unskilful and indeterminate states of the three planes compose the Truth of Ill; craving and the defilements (associated with it) compose the Truth of Origin; the removal of these is the Truth of Cessation; the path is the Truth of the Path. Again, except craving, all defilements and skilful, unskilful and indeterminate states of the three planes compose the Truth of Ill; craving and the defilements, and all the unskilful states compose the Truth of Origin; the removal of these is the Truth of Cessation; the path is the Truth of the Path. And again, except craving and the defilements and all unskilful states (associated with it) the other unskilful states of the three planes and the indeterminate states of the three planes compose the Truth of Ill; craving, the remaining defilements, unskilful states and skilful states of the three planes compose the (Truth of) Origin; the removal of these is the Truth of Cessation; the path is the Truth of the Path. Here, to wish for the delightful is craving. Origin means "with craving" and "with latent tendencies". Other defilements are origin in the sense of removing and in the sense of manifestation of becoming. All unskilful states are origin in the sense of causing to be. Merit of the three planes is origin. Here, craving and the other defilements are origin.

(b) Th. 604, 656: *Pariciṇṇo mayā satthā, kataṁ buddhassa sāsanaṁ,*
ohito garuko bhāro bhavanetti samūhatā.

(c) Dh. 402; Sn. 626: *Yo dukkhassa pajāṇāti, idh' eva khayam attano,*
pannabhāraṁ visaṁyuttaṁ, tam ahaṁ brūmi 'Brāhmaṇaṁ'.

(d) S. III, 25-6: *Sāvatthiyaṁ Tatra kho . . . pe . . .*

Bhārañ ca vo bhikkhave desissāmi, bhārahārañ ca bhārādānañ ca bhāranikkhepanañ ca. Taṁ suṇātha . . .

Katamo ca bhikkhave bhāro? Pañcupādānakkhandhā tissa vacaniyaṁ. Katame pañca? Seyyathīdaṁ rūpupādānakkhandho . . . viññāṇupādānakkhandho. Ayaṁ vuccati bhikkhave bhāro.

Katamo ca bhikkhave bhārahāro? Puggalo tissa vacaniyaṁ. Yoyaṁ āyasmā evaṁ nāmo evaṁ gotto. Ayaṁ vuccati bhikkhave bhārahāro.

Katamañ ca bhikkhave bhārādānaṁ? Yāyaṁ taṇhā ponobhavikā nandirāgasahagatā tatra tatrābhinandinī, seyyathīdaṁ, kāmataṇhā bhavataṇhā vibhavataṇhā. Idaṁ vuccati bhikkhave bhārādānaṁ.

Katamañ ca bhikkhave bhāranikkhepanaṁ? Yo tassā-yeva taṇhāya asesavirāganirodho cāgo paṭinissaggo mutti anālayo. Idaṁ vuccati bhikkhave bhāranikkhepanan ti.

Idam avoca Bhagavā . . . etad avoca Satthā:

Bhārā have pañcakkhandhā,
bhārahāro ca puggalo,
bhārādānaṁ dukkhaṁ loke,
bhāranikkhepanaṁ sukhaṁ.

Nikkhipitvā garuṁ bhāraṁ,
aññaṁ bhāraṁ anādiya,
samūlaṁ taṇhaṁ abbhuyha,
nicchāto parinibbuto.

All merit of the three planes belong to the Truth of Ill or the Truth of Origin. Because of the characteristics of despair, misery, the put together and the limited, there is the Truth of Ill. Because of the characteristics of accumulation, cause and condition, clinging and combination, the Truth of Origin is fulfilled. Thus should these be understood through enumeration.

THROUGH SAMENESS

Q. How, through sameness? *A*. These Four Truths are one through four ways: through the meaning of truth; the meaning of thus-isness; the meaning of doctrine; and the meaning of the void. Thus these should be known through sameness.[1]

THROUGH DIFFERENCE

Q. How, through difference? *A*. There are two truths: mundane and supramundane truth.[2] Mundane truth is canker, fetter, tangle, flood, yoke, hindrance, contact, clinging, defilement.[3] It is called ill and origin. Supramundane truth is without canker, without fetter, without tangle, without flood, without yoke, without hindrance, without contact, without clinging, without defilement. It is Cessation and the Path. Three Truths are conditioned. The truth of Cessation is unconditioned.[4] Three Truths are without[*] form. The Truth of Ill is with and without form.[5] The Truth of Origin is unskilful. The Truth of the Path is skilful. The Truth of Cessation is indeterminate. The Truth of Ill is skilful, unskilful and indeterminate.[6] The Truth of Ill enables to understand; the Truth of Origin enables to remove; the Truth of Cessation enables to attain; and the Truth of the Path enables to practise.[7] Thus should these be known through difference.

---

1. Cp. (a) D· III, 273: *It' ime dasa dhammā bhūtā tacchā tathā avitathā anaññathā sammā Tathāgatena abhisambuddhā.* (=*Bhūtā ti sabhāvato vijjamānā. Tacchā ti yathāvā. Tathā ti yathā vuttā tathā sabhāvā. Avitathā ti yathā vuttā na tathā na honti. Anaññathā ti vutta-ppakārato na aññathā*—Sv. III, 1057).
   (b) S. V, 430-31: *Cattārimāni bhikkhave tathāni avithatāni anaññathāni. Katamāni cattāri? Idaṁ dukkhan ti bhikkhave tatham etaṁ avitatham etaṁ anaññatatham etam. Ayaṁ dukkhasamudayo ti tatham etaṁ . . . ayaṁ dukkhanirodho ti tatham etaṁ . . . Ayaṁ dukkhanirodhagāminī paṭipadā ti tatham etaṁ avitatham etaṁ anaññatham etaṁ.* (=*Sabhāva-vijahan' aṭṭhena tathaṁ. Dukkhaṁ hi dukkham eva vuttaṁ sabhāvassa amoghatāya avitathaṁ. Na dukkhaṁ adukkhaṁ nāma hoti. Añña-sabhāvānupagamena anaññathaṁ. Na hi dukkhaṁ samudayādi-sabhāvaṁ upagacchati. Samudayādīsu pi es' eva nayo ti*—Spk. III, 298).
2. Vbh. 116: *Dve saccā lokiyā; dve saccā lokuttarā.*
3. Vbh. 12; Dhs. par. 584-85: *Sabbaṁ rūpaṁ . . . lokiyaṁ sāsavaṁ saṁyojaniyaṁ ganthaniyaṁ oghaniyaṁ yoganiyaṁ nīvaraṇiyaṁ parāmaṭṭhaṁ upādāniyaṁ saṅkilesikaṁ.*
4. Vbh. 116: *Tīṇi saccā saṁkhatā; nirodhasaccaṁ asaṁkhataṁ.*

* Should read 'with'. Perhaps an error (see n. 5 below).

5. Vbh. 116: *Tīṇi saccā rūpā; dukkasaccaṁ siyā rūpaṁ siyā arūpaṁ.*
6. Ibid. 112: *Samudayasaccaṁ akusalaṁ; maggasaccaṁ kusalaṁ; nirodhasaccaṁ avyākataṁ dukkhasaccaṁ siyā kusalaṁ siyā akusalaṁ siyā avyākataṁ.*
7. See n. 1 (a) p. 274.

THROUGH ONE KIND ETC.

Q. How, through one kind and so forth? *A.* They are of one kind thus: The body which has consciousness is ill. Origin is pride, and the removal of that is Cessation. Mindfulness of the body is the Path. They are of two kinds thus: Name and form are ill; ignorance and craving are Origin; the removal of these is cessation; serenity[1] and insight[2] are the Path. They are of three kinds thus: (Misery of the suffering of the three planes*) is the Truth of Ill; the three unskilful faculties** are origin; the removal of these is cessation. Virtue, concentration and wisdom[3] are the Path. They are of four kinds thus: (The four kinds of nutriment)[4] are ill. The four kinds of overturning[5] are origin; the removal of overturning is cessation, the four foundations of Mindfulness[6] are the Path. They are of five kinds thus: The five states of birth[7] are ill; the five hindrances[8] are origin; the removal of the hindrances is cessation; the five faculties are the Path.[9] They are of six kinds thus: The six organs of contact are ill;[10] the six groups of craving[11] are origin; the removal of the groups of craving is cessation; the six elements of escape[12] are the Path.

---

1. *Samatha.*　　　2. *Vipassanā.*
*This whole sentence is given as *dukkha-dukkha.*
**Perhaps should read 'roots' —*Tīṇi akusala mūlāni.*
3. *Sīla, samādhi, paññā.*
4. The text is not quite clear.
5. Netti. 85: *Tattha rūpaṁ paṭhamaṁ vipallāsavatthu: asubhe subhan ti, vedanā dutiyaṁ vipallāsavatthu: dukkhe sukhan ti, saññā saṁkhārā ca tatiyaṁ vipallāsavatthu: anattani attā ti, viññāṇaṁ catutthaṁ vipallāsavatthu: anicce niccan ti.*
6. *Cattāro satipaṭṭhānā.*
7. D. III, 234: *Pañca gatiyo. Nirayo, tiracchāna-yoni, pettivisayo, manussā, devā.*
8. Ibid: *Pañca nīvaraṇāni. Kāmacchanda-nīvaraṇaṁ, vyāpāda-nīvaraṇaṁ, thīna-middha-nīvaraṇaṁ, uddhacca-kukkucca-nīvaraṇaṁ, vicikicchā-nīvaraṇaṁ.*
9. A. V, 16: *Pañcaṅgavippahīno bhikkhave bhikkhu pañcaṅgasamannāgato imasmiṁ dhamma-vinaye 'kevalī vusitavā uttamapuriso' ti vuccati.*
　　Kathañ ca bhikkhave bhikkhu pañcaṅgavippahīno hoti? Idha bhikkhave bhikkhuno kāmacchando pahīno hoti, vyāpādo pahīno hoti, thīnamiddhaṁ pahīnaṁ hoti, uddhacca-kukkuccaṁ pahīnaṁ hoti, vicikicchā pahīnā hoti. Evaṁ kho bhikkhave bhikkhu pañcaṅga-vippahīno hoti.
　　Kathañ ca . . . pañcaṅgasamannāgato hoti? Idha bhikkhave bhikkhu asekhena sīlak-khandhena samannāgato hoti, asekhena samādhikkhandhena samannāgato hoti, asekhena paññākkhandhena samannāgato hoti, asekhena vimuttikkhandhena samannāgato hoti, asekhena vimuttiñāṇadassanakkhandhena samannāgato hoti. Evaṁ kho bhikkhave bhikkhu pañcaṅgasamannāgato hoti.
　　Pañcaṅgavippahīno kho bhikkhave bhikkhu pañcaṅgasamannāgato imasmiṁ dhamma-vinaye 'kevalī vusitavā uttamapuriso' ti vuccati ti.
10. S. IV, 70: *Chay ime bhikkhave phassāyatanā adantā aguttā arakkhitā asaṁvutā dukkhā-dhivāhā honti. Katame cha? Cakkhuṁ . . . mano bhikkhave phassāyatanaṁ adantaṁ . . .*
11. S. II, 3: *Katamā ca bhikkhave taṇhā? Cha yime bhikkhave taṇhākāyā. Rūpataṇhā saddataṇhā gandhataṇhā rasataṇhā phoṭṭhabbataṇhā dhammataṇhā. Ayaṁ vuccati bhikkhave taṇhā.*
12. Cp. A. III, 290-92; D. III, 247-50: *Cha nissaraṇiya dhātuyo...*
　　(a) *nissaraṇaṁ h' etaṁ āvuso vyāpādassa, yadidaṁ mettā ceto-vimutti...*
　　(b) *nissaraṇaṁ h' etaṁ āvuso vihesāya, yadidaṁ karuṇā ceto-vimutti...*
　　(c) *nissaraṇaṁ h' etaṁ āvuso aratiyā, yadidaṁ muditā ceto-vimutti...*
　　(d) *nissaraṇaṁ h' etaṁ āvuso rāgassa, yadidaṁ upekhā ceto-vimutti...*
　　(e) *nissaraṇaṁ h' etaṁ āvuso sabba-nimittānaṁ, yadidaṁ animittā ceto-vimutti...*
　　(f) *nissaraṇaṁ h' etaṁ āvuso vicikicchā-kathaṁkathā-sallassa, yadidaṁ 'asmiti' māna-samugghāto.*

They are of seven kinds thus: The seven stations of consciousness[1] are ill; the seven latent tendencies[2] are origin; the removal of the seven latent tendencies is cessation; the seven enlightenment factors[3] are the Path. They are of eight kinds thus: The eight worldly conditions[4] are ill; the eight errors[5] are origin; the removal of the eight errors is cessation; the Noble Eightfold Path is the Path.[6] They are of nine kinds thus: The nine abodes of beings[7] are ill; the nine roots of craving[8] are origin; the removal of these is cessation; the nine basic states of wise attention[9] are the Path. They are of ten kinds thus:

---

1. D. III, 253: *Satta viññāṇa-ṭṭhitiyo* (1) *Sant' āvuso sattā nānatta-kāyā nānatta-saññino, seyyathā pi manussā ekacce ca devā ekacce ca vinipātikā. Ayaṁ paṭhamā viññāṇa-ṭṭhiti.* (2) *Sant' āvuso sattā nānatta-kāyā ekatta-saññino seyyathā pi devā Brahma-kāyikā paṭhamābhinibbattā. Ayaṁ dutiyā viññāṇa-ṭṭhiti.* (3) *Sant' āvuso sattā ekatta-kāyā nānatta-saññino, seyyathā pi devā Ābhassarā. Ayaṁ tatiyā viññāṇa-ṭṭhiti.* (4) *Sant' āvuso sattā ekatta-kāyā ekatta-saññino, seyyathā pi devā Subhakiṇhā. Ayaṁ catutthā viññāṇa-ṭṭhiti.* (5) *Sant' āvuso sattā sabbaso rūpa-saññānaṁ samatikkamā, paṭigha-saññānaṁ atthagamā, nānatta-saññānaṁ amanasikārā, 'Ananto ākāso ti' ākāsānañcāyatanūpagā. Ayaṁ pañcamī viññāṇa-ṭṭhiti.* (6) *Sant' āvuso sattā sabbaso ākāsānañcāyatanaṁ samatikkamma 'Anantaṁ viññāṇan ti' viññāṇañcāyatanūpagā. Ayaṁ chaṭṭhī viññāṇa-ṭṭhiti.* (7) *Sant' āvuso sattā sabbaso viññāṇañcāyatanaṁ samatikkamma 'N'atthi kiñciti' ākiñcaññāyatanūpagā. Ayaṁ sattamī viññāṇa-ṭṭhiti.*
2. D. III, 254: *Satta anusayā. Kāmarāgānusayo, paṭighānusayo, diṭṭhānusayo, vicikicchānusayo, mānānusayo, bhavarāgānusayo, avijjānusayo.*
3. D. III, 251-2: *Satta sambojjhaṅgā. Sati-sambojjhaṅgo, dhamma-vicaya-sambojjhaṅgo, viriya-sambojjhaṅgo, pīti-sambojjhaṅgo, passaddhi-sambojjhaṅgo, samādhi-sambojjhaṅgo, upekhā-sambojjhaṅgo.*
4. Ibid. 260: *Aṭṭha loka-dhammā. Lābho ca alābho ca yaso ca ayaso ca nindā ca pasaṁsā ca sukhañ ca dukkhañ ca.*
5. Ibid. 254: *Aṭṭha micchattā. Micchā-diṭṭhi, micchā-saṁkappo, micchā-vācā, micchā-kammanto, micchā-ājīvo, micchā-vāyāmo, micchā-sati, micchā-samādhi.*
6. Ibid. 255: *Aṭṭha sammattā. Sammā-diṭṭhi . . . pe . . . sammā-samādhi.*
7. Ibid. 263: *Nava sattāvāsā.* The first four—the first four at n. 1 above (*Satta viññāṇa-ṭṭhitiyo*); the fifth—*Sant' āvuso sattā asaññino appaṭisaṁvedino seyyathā pi devā Asañña-sattā. Ayaṁ pañcamo sattāvāso . . .*; the next three—(5), (6), (7) of n. 1 above; and the last—*Sant' āvuso sattā sabbaso ākiñcaññāyatanaṁ samatikamma nevasaññānāsaññāyatanūpagā. Ayaṁ navamo sattāvāso.*
8. Vbh. 390; A. IV, 400-1: *Taṇhaṁ paṭicca pariyesanā, pariyesanaṁ paṭicca lābho, lābhaṁ paṭicca vinicchayo, vinicchayaṁ paṭicca chandarāgo, chandarāgaṁ paṭicca ajjhosānaṁ, ajjhosānaṁ paṭicca pariggaho, pariggahaṁ paṭicca macchariyaṁ, macchariyaṁ paṭicca ārakkhādhikaraṇaṁ, daṇḍādānasatthādānakalahaviggahavivādā tuvaṁtuvaṁpesuññamusāvādā aneke pāpakā akusalā dhammā sambhavanti.*
   Ime kho bhikkhave nava taṇhāmūlakā dhammā ti.
9. Pts. I, 86: *Nava yoniso manasikāramūlakā dhammā:— aniccato yoniso manasikaroto pāmojjaṁ jāyati, pamuditassa pīti jāyati, pītimanassa kāyo passambhati, passaddhakāyo sukhaṁ vedeti, sukhino cittaṁ samādhiyati, samāhitena cittena 'idam dukkhan' ti yathābhūtaṁ pajānāti, 'ayaṁ dukkhasamudayo' ti yathābhūtaṁ pajānāti, 'ayaṁ dukkhanirodho' ti yathābhūtaṁ pajānāti, 'ayaṁ dukkhanirodhagāminī paṭipadā' ti yathābhūtaṁ pajānāti; dukkhato yoniso manasikaroto pāmojjaṁ jāyati, pamuditassa pīti jāyati, . . . pe . . . sukhino cittaṁ samādhiyati, samāhitena cittena 'idaṁ dukkhan' ti yathābhūtaṁ pajānāti, 'ayaṁ dukkhasamudayo' ti yathābhūtaṁ pajānāti, 'ayaṁ dukkhanirodho' ti yathābhūtaṁ pajānāti; ayaṁ dukkhanirodhagāminī paṭipadā' ti yathābhūtaṁ pajānāti; anattato yoniso manasikaroto pāmojjaṁ jāyati . . . pe . . . Rūpaṁ aniccato yoniso manasikaroto pāmojjaṁ jāyati . . . pe . . . rūpaṁ dukkhato yoniso manasikaroto pāmojjaṁ jāyati . . . pe . . . rūpaṁ anattato yoniso manasikaroto pāmojjaṁ jāyati . . . pe . . . vedanaṁ, saññaṁ, saṅkhāre, viññāṇaṁ, cakkhuṁ . . . pe . . . jarāmaraṇaṁ aniccato yoniso manasikaroto pāmojjaṁ jāyati . . . pe . . . jarāmaraṇaṁ dukkhato yoniso manasikaroto pāmojjaṁ jāyati . . . pe . . . vedanaṁ, saññaṁ, saṅkhāre, viññāṇaṁ, cakkhuṁ . . . pe . . . jarāmaraṇaṁ anattato yoniso manasikaroto pāmojjaṁ jāyati . . . pe . . . sukhino cittaṁ samādhiyati, samāhitena cittena 'idam dukkhan' ti yathābhūtaṁ pajānāti, 'ayaṁ dukkhasamudayo' ti yathābhūtaṁ pajānāti, 'ayaṁ dukkhanirodho' ti yathābhūtaṁ pajānāti, 'ayaṁ dukkhanirodhagāminī paṭipadā' ti yathābhūtaṁ pajānāti. Ime nava yoniso manasikāramūlakā dhammā.*

The formations in the ten directions are ill;[1] the ten fetters[2] are origin; the removal of the fetters is cessation;[3] the ten perceptions are the Path.[4] Thus one should know through one kind and so forth.

THROUGH INCLUSION

Q. How, through inclusion? *A.* There are three kinds of inclusion, namely, inclusion of aggregation, of sense-sphere, and of element. Here, the Truth of Ill is included in the five aggregates;[5] The Truth of Origin and the Truth of the Path are included in the aggregate of mental formations; Cessation is not included in any aggregate. The Truth of Ill is included in the twelve-sense-spheres. Three Truths are included in the sense-sphere of ideas. The

---

1. Cp. Nd 410: *Disā sabbā sameritā ti. Ye puratthimāya disāya saṁkhārā, te pi eritā sameritā calitā ghaṭṭitā aniccatāya jātiyā anugatā jarāya anusaṭā byādhinā abhibhūtā maraṇena abbhāhatā dukkhe patiṭṭhitā atāṇā aleṇā asaraṇā asaraṇibhūtā. Ye pacchimāya disāya saṁkhārā, ye uttarāya disāya saṁkhārā, ye dakkhiṇāya disāya saṁkhārā, ye puratthimāya anudisāya saṁkhārā, ye pacchimāya anudisāya saṁkhārā, ye uttarāya anudisāya saṁkhārā, ye dakkhiṇāya anudisāya saṁkhārā, ye heṭṭhimāya disāya saṁkhārā, ye uparimāya disāya saṁkhārā, ye dasadisāsu saṁkhārā, te pi eritā sameritā calitā ghaṭṭitā aniccatāya jātiyā anugatā jarāya anusaṭā byādhinā abhibhūtā maraṇena abbhāhatā dukkhe patiṭṭhitā atāṇā aleṇā asaraṇā asaraṇibhūtā. Bhāsitam pi c'etaṁ:*

   Kiñcā pi cetaṁ jalati vimānaṁ
   obhāsayaṁ uttariyaṁ disāya
   rūpe raṇaṁ disvā sadā pavedhitaṁ,
   tasmā rūpe na ramati sumedho. (S. I, 148).

   Maccun' abbhāhato loko jarāya parivārito
   taṇhāsallena otiṇṇo icchādhumāyiko sadā. (Th. 448; cp. Jat. VI, 26).

   Sabbo ādipito loko, sabbo loko padhūpito,
   sabbo pajjalito loko, sabbo loko pakampito ti; (S. I, 133).

   disā sabbā sameritā.

2. D. III, 234: *Pañc' oram-bhāgiyāni saṁyojanāni. Sakkāya-diṭṭhi, vicikicchā, silabbata-parāmāso, kāmacchando, vyāpādo.*
   Pañc'uddham-bhāgiyāni saṁyojanāni. Rūpa-rāgo, arūpa-rāgo, māno, uddhaccaṁ, avijjā.

3. Cp. (a) It. 18: *Sa sattakkhattuṁ paramaṁ*
   sandhāvitvāna puggalo,
   dukkhassantakaro hoti
   sabbosaṁyojanakkhayā ti.

   (b) Th. 181-2: *Yato ahaṁ pabbajito sammāsambuddhasāsane,*
   vimuccamāno uggacchiṁ, kāmadhātuṁ upaccagaṁ.
   Brahmuno pekkhamānassa tato cittaṁ vimucci me;
   akuppā me vimuttiti sabbasaṁyojanakkhayā' ti.

4. A. V, 105: *Dasa yimā bikkhave saññā bhāvitā bahulīkatā mahapphalā honti mahānisaṁsā amatogadhā amatapariyosānā. Katamā dasa? Asubhasaññā, maraṇasaññā, āhāre paṭikkūlasaññā, sabbaloke anabhiratasaññā, aniccasaññā, anicce dukkhasaññā, dukkhe anattasaññā, pahānasaññā, virāgasaññā, nirodhasaññā.*

5. Cp. (a) S. III, 196: *Dukkhaṁ dukkhan ti bhante vuccati. Katamannu kho bhante dukkhan ti? Rūpaṁ kho Rādha dukkhaṁ, vedanā dukkhā, saññā, dukkhā, sankhārā dukkhā, viññāṇaṁ dukkhaṁ.*
   (b) Vbh-a. 50: *Yad aniccaṁ taṁ dukkhan ti* vacanato pana tad eva khandhapañcakaṁ dukkhaṁ. Kasmā? Abhiṇhasampatipiḷanato. Abhiṇhasampatipīlanākāro dukkhalakkhaṇaṁ.* *S. III, 22 *passim.*
   (c) Netti. 42: *Pañcakkhandhā dukkhaṁ.*
   (d) Dh. 202: *N'atthi rāgasamo aggi, n'atthi dosasamo kali,*
   N'atthi khandhādisā dukkhā, n'atthi santiparaṁ sukhaṁ.

Truth of Ill is included in the eighteen elements. Three Truths are included in the element of ideas. Thus one should know through inclusion. Through these ways knowledge of the Noble Truths should be known. This is called the method of understanding the Noble Truths.

ON DISCERNING TRUTH

CHAPTER THE TWELFTH

Section One

AGGREGATES, ELEMENTS, SENSE-SPHERES

Now the yogin has understood the aggregates, elements, sense-spheres, conditioned arising and the Truths. He has also heard concerning virtue, austerities and meditation, *jhāna*.

SIMILES OF THE THREE HUNDRED HALBERDS AND OF THE BURNING HEAD

The commoner fears ill-faring, because he is not enlightened. If after contemplating on the fearfulness of ill-faring and of beginningless birth and death, he should think of not missing this opportunity, or on the similes of the points of the three hundred halberds,[1] and of the man desirous of saving his burning head,[2] the yogin is yet unable to understand the Four Noble Truths, he should proceed to discern the Noble Truths by way of analogy. He should develop the wish to do, strive earnestly, and accomplish (the knowledge of the Truths) through completing the mindfulness of concentration.

PROCEDURE

Q. What is the procedure? At first the yogin should listen to the Four Noble Truths expounded in brief or in detail or in brief and in detail. Through

---

1. (a) M. III, 165-66; S. II, 100: *Seyyathāpi bhikkhave coraṁ āgucāriṁ gahetvā rañño dasseyyuṁ, Ayante deva coro āgucārī, imissa yaṁ icchitaṁ taṁ daṇḍaṁ paṇehīti, tam enaṁ rājā evaṁ vadeyya: Gacchatha bho imaṁ purisaṁ pubbaṇhasamayaṁ sattisatena hanathāti, tam enaṁ pubbaṇhasamayaṁ sattisatena haneyyuṁ.*

   Atha rājā majjhantikaṁ samayaṁ evaṁ vadeyya: Ambho kathaṁ so purisoti? Tatheva deva jīvatīti, tam enaṁ rājā evaṁ vadeyya. Gacchatha bho taṁ purisaṁ majjhantikaṁ samayaṁ sattisatena hanathāti, tam enaṁ majjhantikaṁ samayaṁ sattisatena haneyyuṁ.

   Atha rājā sāyaṇhasamayaṁ evaṁ vadeyya. Ambho kathaṁ so puriso ti? Tatheva deva jīvatīti, tam enaṁ rājā evaṁ vadeyya: Gacchatha bho taṁ purisaṁ sāyaṇhasamayaṁ sattisatena hanathāti, tam enaṁ sāyaṇhasamayaṁ sattisatena haneyyuṁ.

   Taṁ kiṁ maññatha bhikkhave ? Api nu so puriso divasaṁ tihi sattisatehi haññamāno tato nidānaṁ dukkhaṁ domanassaṁ paṭisaṁvediyethāti?

   Ekissā pi bhante sattiyā haññamāno tato nidānaṁ dukkhaṁ domanassaṁ paṭisaṁvediyetha ko pana vādo tīhi satttsatehi haññāmāno ti?

   Evam eva kvāhaṁ bhikkhave viññāṇāhāro daṭṭhabbo ti vadāmi.

   (b) S. I, 128; Thi. 58, 141: *Sattisūlūpamā kāmā khandhānaṁ adhikuṭṭanā,*
   yaṁ tvaṁ kāmaratiṁ brūsi arati dāni sā mamaṁ.

2. (a) A. II, 93: *Seyyathāpi bhikkhave ādittacelo vā ādittasīso vā, tass' eva celassa vā sīsassa vā nibbāpanāya adhimattaṁ chandañ ca vāyāmañ ca ussāhañ ca ussoḷhiñ ca appaṭivāniñ ca satiñ ca sampajaññañ ca kareyya, evam eva kho bhikkhave tena puggalena tesaṁ yeva kusalānaṁ dhammānaṁ paṭilābhāya adhimatto chando ca...*

   (b) S. V, 440: *Ādittaṁ bhikkhave celaṁ vā sīsaṁ vā anajjhupekkhitvā amanasikaritvā anabhisametānaṁ catunnaṁ ariyasaccānaṁ yathābhūtaṁ abhisamayāya adhimatto chando ca vāyāmo ca ussāho ca ussoḷhī ca appaṭivānī ca sati ca sampajaññañ ca karaṇīyaṁ.*

hearing, seizing the sense and reiteration, he should bear them in mind. At this time the yogin enters into a quiet place, sits down and composes his mind. He does not let it run hither and thither, and recalls to mind the Four Noble Truths. First he should recall to mind the Truth of Ill through aggregation, sense-sphere and element. The idea of aggregation should be recalled to mind through one's own characteristics and through the characteristics of the aggregates, in the way it was taught, under thé method of understanding the aggregates. The (idea of) sense-sphere should be recalled to mind through the characteristic of sense-sphere, in the way it was taught, under the method of understanding the sense-spheres. The (idea of) element should be recalled to mind through the characteristics of element, in the way it was taught, under the method of understanding the elements. Thus having understood aggregate, sense-sphere and element, that yogin knows that there are only aggregates, sense-spheres and elements, and that there is no being or soul. Thus he gains the perception of the formations[1] and gets to know the two divisions, namely, name and form. Here the ten sense-spheres and the ten elements of the aggregate of matter constitute form. Four aggregates, the sense-sphere of mind and the seven elements constitute name. The sense-sphere of ideas and the element of ideas are name and form. Name is one, form is another. Form is void of name and name, of form. Name is not separate from form, and form is not separate from name, like drum-sound.[2] Only through dependence on name, form proceeds; and through dependence on form, name proceeds, like the journeying afar of the blind and the cripple.[3]

DIFFERENCES BETWEEN NAME AND FORM

Q. What are the differences between name and form?

A. Name has no body; form has body. Name is hard to discern; form is easily discerned. Namc proceeds quickly; form proceeds slowly. Name

---

1. *Saṅkhāra-saññā.*
2. Cp. Vis. Mag. 595: *Yathā ca daṇḍābhihataṁ bheriṁ nissāya sadde pavattamāne aññā bherī añño saddo, bherisaddā asammissā, bheri saddena suññā, saddo bheriyā suñño, evam eva vatthudvārārammaṇasankhātaṁ rūpaṁ nissāya nāme pavattamāne aññaṁ rūpaṁ, aññaṁ nāmaṁ, nāmarūpā asammissā, nāmaṁ rūpena suññaṁ; rūpaṁ nāmena suññaṁ; api ca kho bheriṁ paṭicca saddo viya, rūpaṁ paṭicca nāmaṁ pavattati.*
3. Vis. Mag. 596:
   (a) *Yatha jacchandho ca piṭhasappī ca disā pakkamitukāmā assu. Jaccandho piṭhasappiṁ evam āha:- ahaṁ kho bhaṇe sakkomi pādehi pādakaraniyaṁ kātum, n'atthi ca me cakkhūni yehi samavisamaṁ passeyyan ti. Piṭhasappī pi jacchandhaṁ evam āha:- ahaṁ kho bhaṇe sakkomi cakkhunā cakkhukaraṇiyaṁ kātuṁ, n'atthi ca me pādāni yehi abhikkameyyaṁ vā paṭikkameyyaṁ vā ti. So tuṭṭhahaṭṭho jaccandho piṭhasappiṁ aṁsakūṭaṁ āropesi. Piṭhasappī jaccandhassa aṁsakūṭena nisīditvā evam āha:- vāmaṁ muñca! dakkhiṇaṁ gaṇha! dakkhiṇaṁ muñca! vāmain gaṇhā ti.*
   Tattha jaccandho pi nittejo dubbalo na sakena tejena sakena balena gacchati; piṭhasappī pi nittejo dubbalo na sakena tejena sakena balena gacchati; na ca tesaṁ aññamaññaṁ nissāya gamanaṁ nappavattati. Evam eva nāmam pi nittejaṁ, na sakena tejena uppajjati, na tāsu tāsu kiriyāsu pavattati; rūpaṁ pi nittejaṁ na sakena tejena uppajjati, na tāsu tāsu kiriyāsu pavattati, na ca tesaṁ aññamaññaṁ nissāya uppatti vā pavatti vā na hoti.

does not accumulate; form accumulates. Name excogitates, knows, considers, is aware; form does not do these. Form walks, leans, sits, lies down, bends and stretches; name does not do these. Name knows: "I go", "I lean", "I sit", "I lie down", "I bend", "I stretch"; form does not know these. Form drinks, eats, chews, tastes; name does not do these. Name knows: "I drink", "I eat", "I chew", "I taste"; form does not know these. Form claps the hands, frolics, laughs, cries and talks in many ways; name does not do these. Name knows thus: "I clap", "I frolic", "I laugh", "I cry", "I talk in such and such a manner"; form does not know these. These are the differences between name and form; and that yogin knows name [454] and form thus: "Only name and form are here; there is no being, there is no soul". Thus he, making it manifest, gets the perception of the formations.

SUMMARY OF THE TRUTH OF ILL

Now, this is a summary of the whole Truth of Ill: One, causing to arise knowledge of pure views, according to reality, discerns name and form. All these should be known as descriptive of the Truth of Ill. That yogin, having made manifest the Truth of Ill, considers the idea of a being.[1] Thereafter he should attend to the cause and condition of Ill.

CAUSE AND CONDITION OF ILL

Q. What are the cause and condition of ill?

A. That yogin knows thus: This ill has birth for cause and condition; birth has becoming for cause and condition; becoming has clinging for cause and condition; clinging has craving for cause and condition; craving has feeling for cause and condition; feeling has contact for cause and condition; contact has the six sense-spheres for cause and condition; the six sense-spheres have name-form for cause and condition; name-form has consciousness for cause and condition; consciousness has the formations for cause and condition; the formations have ignorance for cause and condition. Thus depending on ignorance there are the formations; depending on the formations there is consciousness; depending on birth there are decay, death, and grief. Thus all the aggregates of ill arise. Thus that yogin introspects the links of conditioned arising at length,

THE PURITY OF TRANSCENDING UNCERTAINTY

Now, this is the summary: Depending on feeling there arises craving.

(b) Abhv. 1220-21: *Nāmaṁ nissāya rūpan tu, rūpaṁ nissāya nāmakaṁ*
pavattati sadā sabbaṁ, pañcavokāra-bhūmiyaṁ;
imassa pana atthassa, āvibhāvattham eva ca
jaccandha-piṭhasappinaṁ, vattabbā upamā idha.

1. Cp. Vis. Mag. 597: *Evaṁ nānānayehi nāmarūpaṁ vavatthāpayato sattasaññaṁ abhibhavitvā asammohabhūmiyaṁ ṭhitaṁ nāmarūpānaṁ yāthāvadassanaṁ Diṭṭhivisuddhī ti veditabbaṁ. Nāmarūpavavatthānan ti pi sankhāraparicchedo ti pi ekass' eva adhivacanaṁ.*

One makes manifest the origin of ill. The knowledge of the Law of conditioned arising, Ariyan understanding of conditioned arising and knowledge of the purity of transcending uncertainty are terms descriptive of the knowledge which makes manifest the Truth of Origin.[1]

TRUTH OF CESSATION

That yogin, after having grasped the Truth of the Origin of Ill and transcended the uncertainty of the three phases of time, considers the cessation of ill. The destruction of what is the destruction of ill? That yogin knows thus: When birth is destroyed, ill is destroyed; when birth is destroyed, becoming is destroyed; when becoming is destroyed, clinging is destroyed; when clinging is destroyed, craving is destroyed. When ignorance is destroyed, the formations are destroyed. Thus, with the destruction of ignorance, the formations are destroyed; with the destruction of the formations, consciousness is destroyed. Decay, death, sorrow, lamentation, misery and grief are destroyed through the destruction of birth. Thus all the aggregates of ill are destroyed. Thus having considered the links of conditioned arising at length, he views them in brief thus: Depending on feeling there is craving. Owing to its destruction, ill is destroyed. Thus he makes manifest the Truth of Cessation.

TRUTH OF THE PATH

Now, that yogin, having grasped the Truth of Cessation considers the Path of the Cessation of Ill thus: What Path and what perfection constitute the destruction of craving? He considers the five clinging aggregates[2] and the tribulation of these. (He thinks), "This is the Path, this is perfection". He eradicates craving, and causes the arising of the Way-Truth. One should know this as has been taught fully under the method of understanding the Truth.

ONE HUNDRED AND EIGHTY WAYS OF KNOWING THE FIVE CLINGING AGGREGATES

Thus that yogin, having serially grasped the Four Truths, knows the five clinging aggregates in one hundred and eighty ways and by way of accumulation. He considers at length all matter of the past, future and the present, internal and external, great and small, gross and subtle, and far and near as impermanent, ill, and not-self. In the same way, he deals with all feeling, perception,

---

1. Cp. Vis. Mag. 604: *Evaṁ nānānayehi nāmarūpapaccayapariggahaṇena tīsu addhāsu kankhaṁ vitaritvā ṭhitaṁ ñāṇaṁ kankhāvitaraṇavisuddhī ti veditabbaṁ dhammaṭṭhitiñāṇan ti pi yathābhūtañāṇan ti pi sammādassanan ti pi etass' ev' ādhivaccanaṁ.*
2. *Pañcupādānakkhandhā.*

formations and consciousness.[1] In each aggregate there are twelve states preceeding at the door. In five aggregates, twelve times five make sixty. Thus the sixty kinds of seeing of impermanence, sixty kinds of seeing of ill, and sixty kinds of seeing of not-self constitute one-hundred and eighty. And again, there are one hundred and eighty states proceeding at the door: six internal sense-spheres; six external sense-spheres; six kinds of consciousness; six kinds of contact; six kinds of feeling; six kinds of perception; six kinds of volition; six kinds of craving; six kinds of initial application of thought; six kinds of sustained application of thought.[2] These ten sixes make up sixty; sixty kinds of seeing of impermanence, sixty kinds of seeing of ill and sixty kinds of seeing of not-self. Three times sixty are one hundred and eighty.

Thus he discerns and investigates the formations through impermanence: The endless years, seasons, months, fortnights, days, nights, hours and thought-instants, roll on producing new states in succession like the flame of a lamp.[3]

---

1. Pts. I, 53-4: *Kathaṁ atītānāgatapaccuppannānaṁ dhammānaṁ saṅkhipitvā vavatthāne paññā sammasane ñānaṁ?*

Yaṁ kiñci rūpaṁ atītānāgatapaccuppannaṁ ajjhattaṁ vā bahiddhā vā oḷārikaṁ vā sukhumaṁ vā hīnaṁ vā paṇītaṁ vā yaṁ dūre santike vā, sabbaṁ rūpaṁ aniccato vavattheti, ekaṁ sammasanaṁ; dukkhato vavattheti, ekaṁ sammasanaṁ; anattato vavattheti, ekaṁ sammasanaṁ. Yā kāci vedanā...pe...yā kāci saññā...pe...ye keci saṅkhāra ...pe...yaṁ kiñci viññāṇaṁ atītānāgatapaccupannaṁ ajjhattaṁ vā bahiddhā vā oḷarikaṁ vā sukhumaṁ vā hīnaṁ vā paṇītaṁ vā yaṁ dūre santike vā, sabbaṁ viññāṇaṁ aniccato vavattheti, ekaṁ sammasanaṁ; dukkhato vavattheti, ekaṁ sammasanaṁ; anattato vavattheti, ekaṁ sammasanaṁ. Cakkhuṁ...pe...jarāmaraṇaṁ atītānāgatapaccuppannaṁ aniccato vavattheti, ekaṁ sammasanaṁ; dukkhato vavattheti, ekaṁ sammasanaṁ; anattato vavattheti, ekaṁ sammasanaṁ.

'Rūpaṁ atītānnāgatapaccuppannaṁ aniccaṁ khayaṭṭhena, dukkhaṁ bhayaṭṭhena, anattā asārakaṭṭhenāti' sankhipitvā vavatthāne paññā sammasane ñāṇaṁ. 'Vedanā... pe...saññā...pe...saṅkhārā...pe...viññāṇaṁ...pe...cakkhuṁ...pe...jarāmaraṇaṁ atītānāgatapaccuppannaṁ aniccaṁ khayaṭṭhena, dukkhaṁ bhayaṭṭhena, anattā asārakaṭṭhenāti' sankhipitvā vavatthāne paññā sammasane ñāṇaṁ.

'Rūpaṁ atītānāgatapaccuppannaṁ aniccaṁ saṅkhataṁ paṭiccasamuppannaṁ khayadhammaṁ vayadhammaṁ virāgadhammaṁ nirodhadhamman' ti saṅkhipitvā vavatthāne paññā sammasane ñāṇaṁ. 'Vedanā...pe...saññā...pe...saṅkhāra...pe...viññāṇaṁ...pe...cakkhuṁ...pe...jarāmaraṇaṁ atītānāgatapaccuppannaṁ aniccaṁ saṅkhataṁ paṭṭccasamuppannaṁ khayadhammaṁ vayadhammaṁ virāgadhammaṁ nirodhdamman' ti saṅkhipitvā vavatthāne paññā sammasane ñāṇaṁ.

'Jātipaccayā jarāmaraṇaṁ, asati jātiyā natthi jarāmaraṇan' ti saṅkhipitva vavatthāne paññā sammasane ñāṇaṁ; 'atītaṁ pi addhānaṁ anāgataṁ pi addhānaṁ jātipaccayā jarāmaraṇaṁ, asati jātiyā natthi jarāmaraṇan' ti saṅkhipitvā vavatthāne paññā sammasane ñāṇaṁ; 'bhavapaccayā jāti, asati...pe...upādānapaccayā bhavo, asati...pe...taṇhāpaccayā upādānaṁ, asati...pe...vedanāpaccayā taṇhā, asati...pe...phassapaccayā vedanā, asati...pe...saḷāyatanapaccayā phasso, asati...pe...nāmarūpaccayā saḷāyatanaṁ, asati...pe...viññāṇapaccayā nāmarūpaṁ, asati...pe...saṅkhārapaccayā viññāṇaṁ, asati..., pe...avijjāpaccayā saṅkhārā, asati avijjāya natthi saṅkhārā' ti sankhipitvā vavatthāne paññā sammasane ñāṇaṁ. 'Atītaṁ pi addhānaṁ anāgataṁ pi adhānaṁ avijjāpaccayā saṅkhārā, asati avijjāya natthi saṅkhārā' ti saṅkhipitvā vavatthāne paññā sammasane ñāṇaṁ. Tañ ñātaṭṭhena ñānaṁ pajānanaṭṭhena paññā; tena vuccati—'Atītānāgata-pacuppannānaṁ dhammānaṁ saṅkhipitvā vavatthāne paññā sammasane ñāṇaṁ.'

2. Cp. Vis. Mag. 608: *Ettha ca: cakkhuṁ...pe...jarāmaraṇan* (quoted at n. 1, above) *ti imina peyyālena dvārārammaṇehi saddhiṁ dvārappavattā dhammā, pañcakkhandhā, cha dvārāni, cha ārammaṇāni, cha viññāṇāni, cha phassā, cha vedanā, cha saññā, cha ceteanā, cha taṇhā, cha vitakkā, cha vicārā.*

3. Cp. Mil. 40: *Opammaṁ karohīti — Yathā mahārāja kocid eva puriso padīpaṁ padīpeyya, kiṁ so sabbarattiṁ dipeyyāti.— Āma bhante sabbarattiṁ padīpeyyāti.— Kin-nu kho mahārāja yā purime yāme acci sā majjhime yāme accīti. — Na hi bhante ti. — Ya majjhime*

Thus he discerns and investigates the formations through suffering: Through ill-faring a man experiences unhappiness, hunger and fear; he is separated from dear ones; he experiences old age, disease, death, sorrow, lamentation, misery and grief. Such are the vicissitudes of the formations.

IMPERMANENCE, ILL, NOT-SELF

Thus he discerns and considers the formations as not-self: What is according to the teaching, concerning cause and condition of the aggregates, of the sense-spheres and of the elements, is the Truth. According to *kamma*-result and conditioned arising, beings are born. There is no abiding being. There is no intrinsic nature in objects.

He considers form as impermanent in the sense of extinction, as ill in the sense of fear, as not-self in the sense of unreality. Thus he considers it in brief and at length. And in the same way he thinks that feeling, perception, the formations, consciousness are impermanent in the sense of extinction, are suffering in the sense of fear, are not-self in the sense of unreality. Thus briefly and at length he discerns. Here, through the discernment of impermanence, he removes the idea of permanence; through the discernment of ill, he removes the idea of bliss; and through the discernment of not-self, he removes the idea of self.

THE SIGNLESS, THE UNHANKERED, AND THE VOID

Q. How does he discern fully through impermanence? *A.* In discerning the formations as they are, he limits the formations as not existing before their arising and as not going beyond their fall; and his mind, springing forth into the signless element, attains to peace. Thus he discerns through impermanence, fully.

Q. How does he discern through ill? *A.* In discerning the formations his mind is agitated with fear as regards hankering and springs forth into the unhankered. Thus he discerns through ill, fully.

Q. How does he discern fully through not-self? *A.* In discerning all states, he regards them as alien, and his mind springs forth to the element of the void and attains to peace. Thus he discerns not-self, fully.[1]

---

yāme acci sā pacchime yāme accīti. — Na hi bhante ti. — Kin-nu kho mahārāja añño so ahosi purime yāme padīpo, añño majjhime yāme padīpo, añño pacchime yāme padīpo ti. — Na hi bhante, taṁ yeva nissāya sabbarattiṁ padīpito ti. Evam eva kho majārāja dhammasantati sandahati, añño uppajjati añño nirujjhati, apubbaṁ acarimaṁ viya sandahati, tena na ca so na ca añño pacchimaviññāṇasangahaṁ gacchatīti.

1. Cp. (a) Pts. II, 58: *Aniccato manasikaroto khayato saṅkhārā upaṭṭhahanti, Dukkhato manasikaroto bhayato saṅkhārā upaṭṭhahanti. Anattato manasikaroto suññato saṅkhārā upaṭṭhahanti.*

   (b) Ibid. 61: *Aniccato manasikaroto animitto vimokkho adhimatto hoti, animittavimokkhassa adhimattattā saddhāvimutto hoti; dukkhato manasikaroto appaṇihito vimokkho adhimatto hoti, appaṇihitavimokkhassa adhimattattā kāyasakkhī hoti; anattato manasikaroto suññato vimokkho adhimatto hoti, suññatavimokkhassa adhimattattā diṭṭhippatto hoti.*

Thus discerning the three states of becoming, the five states of existence, the seven stations of consciousness, the nine abodes of beings, through extinction, fear and unreality, he investigates these.[1]

The discernment of Truth has ended.

THE KNOWLEDGE OF THE RISE AND FALL

That yogin, having discerned the five clinging aggregates, applies the three characteristics to them, wishing for the happiness of being released from phenomena.[2] And when the internal five clinging aggregates are grasped by way of the characteristics, he penetrates rise and fall thus: "All these states, not having been, arise; and having arisen, pass away".[3] Here, in grasping (the aggregates) there are three kinds: defilement-grasp, concentration-grasp, insight-grasp.

DEFILEMENT-GRASP

Here, the infatuated commoner clings to and grasps willingly the sign of the defilements owing to mental reversal, and regards the world of sights, sounds, tangibles and ideas as blissful and permanent. It is likened to moths flying into a flame.[4] This is called defilement-grasp.

---

1. Cp. Vis. Mag. 656: *Tassa evaṁ jānato evaṁ passato tīsu bhavesu, catūsu yonisu, pañcasu gatīsu, sattasu viññāṇaṭṭhitīsu navasu sattāvāsesu cittaṁ paṭilīyati...*
2. *Sankhārā.*
3. Cp, Pts.-a. I, 256: *Tass'evaṁ pākaṭībhūta-sacca-paṭiccasamuppāda-nayalakkhaṇabhedassa, "Evaṁ kira nām'ime dhammā anuppannapubbā uppajjanti, uppannā nirujjhanti" ti niccanavā 'va hutvā saṅkhārā upaṭṭhahanti.*
4. (a) Ud. 72: *Evam me sutaṁ. Ekaṁ samayaṁ Bhagavā Sāvatthiyaṁ viharati Jetavane Anāthapiṇḍikassa ārāme. Tena kho pana samayena Bhagavā rattandhakāratimisāyaṁ abbhokāse nisinno hoti, telappadīpesu jhāyamānesu. Tena kho pana samayena sambahulā adhipātakā tesu telappadīpesu āpātaparipātaṁ anayaṁ āpajjanti, byasanaṁ āpajjanti, anabyasanaṁ āpajjanti. Addasā kho Bhagavā te sambahule adhipātake tesu telappadīpesu āpātaparipātaṁ anayaṁ āpajjante byasanaṁ āpajjante anabyasanaṁ āpajjante. Atha kho Bhagavā etam atthaṁ viditvā ṭāyaṁ velāyaṁ imaṁ udānaṁ udānesi:*

   Upātidhāvanti na sāram enti, navaṁ navaṁ bandhanaṁ brūhayanti,
   patanti pajjotam iv' ādhipātā, diṭṭhe sute iti h' eke niviṭṭhā'ti.

   (=Tena ca samayena bahū paṭanga-pāṇakā patantā patantā tesu tela-ppadipesu nipatanti. Tena vuttaṁ: tena kho pana samayena sambahulā adhipātakā ti ādi.

   Tattha adhipātakā ti paṭanga-pāṇakā: ye salabhā ti pi vuccanti. Tehi dīpa-sikhaṁ adhipatanato adhipātakā ti adhippetā. Āpāta-paripātan ti, āpātaṁ paripātaṁ āpatitvā āpatitvā, paripatitvā paripatitvā abhimukhaṁ pātañ c' eva paribbhamitvā pātañ ca katvā ti attho. Āpāte padīpassa attano āpātha-gamane sati paripatitvā paripatitvā ti attho. Anayan ti, avaḍḍhiṁ, dukkhaṁ. Byasanan ti, vināsaṁ. Purima-padena hi maraṇa-mattaṁ dukkhaṁ, pacchima-padena maraṇaṁ tesaṁ dīpeti. Tattha keci pāṇakā saha patanena mariṁsu, keci maraṇa-mattaṁ dukkhaṁ āpajjiṁsu. Etam atthaṁ viditvā ti, etaṁ adhipātaka-pāṇakānaṁ atta-hitaṁ ajānantānaṁ att' ūpakkama-vasena niratthaka-byasanappattiṁ viditvā tesaṁ viya diṭṭhi-gatikānaṁ diṭṭh' abhinivesena anayabyasana-ppattidīpanaṁ imaṁ udānaṁ udānesi.

   Tattha upātidhāvanti na sāram enti ti, sīla-samādhi-pañña-vimutti-ādibhedaṁ sāraṁ na enti, catusacc' ābhisamaya-vasena na adhigacchanti. Tasmiṁ pana sa-upāya sāre tiṭṭhante yeva vimutt' ābhilāsāya taṁ upentā viya hutvā pi diṭṭhivipallāsena atidhāvanti atikkamitvā gacchanti. Panc' upādāna-kkhandhe niccaṁ subhaṁ sukhaṁ attani abhini-

CONCENTRATION-GRASP

Q. What is concentration-grasp? *A*. Here a yogin wishes to gain concentration and grasps the sign in each of the thirty-eight subjects of meditation, with the mind, beginning with the knowledge of Right Mindfulness, and thereby chains the mind as one chains an elephant to make it quiet.[1] This is called concentration-grasp.

INSIGHT-GRASP

Q. What is insight-grasp? *A*. A man, beginning with the wisdom of steady viewing, discerns the characteristic of intrinsic nature[2] of form, feeling, perception, the formations and consciousness. Wishing for and happy in equanimity, he grasps the characteristics. It is like a man who lays hold of a poisonous snake.[3] This is called insight-grasp. It is well when a man grasps by way of insight.

Q. What is the grasping of the characteristics of feeling, perception, the formations and consciousness? *A*. Characteristics of form: One grasps the form-conciousness by way of the earth-element, water-element, fire-element, air-element, sense-sphere of eye or sense-sphere of body. Characteristic of feeling: One grasps feeling by way of the pleasurable, the painful or the neither pleasurable nor painful. Characteristics of perception: One grasps perception by way of form-perception or perception of states. Characteristics of the formations: One grasps the formations through contact, volition, initial application of thought, sustained application of thought, or deliberation. Characteristics of consciousness: One grasps consciousness through eye-consciousness or mind-consciousness. One grasps one's particular meditation and produces the sign skilfully. Thus one grasps the characteristics of form, feeling, perception, the formations and consciousness.

---

visitvā gaṇhantā ti atttho. Navaṁ navaṁ bhandhnaṁ brūhayantī ti, tathā gaṇhantā ca taṇhā-diṭṭhi-saṅkhātaṁ navaṁ navaṁ bandhanaṁ brūhayanti, vaḍḍhayanti. Patanti pajjotam iv' ādhipātā, diṭṭhe sute iti h' eke niviṭṭhā ti, evaṁ taṇhā-diṭṭhi-bandhanehi baddhattā eke samaṇa-brāhmaṇā diṭṭhe attanā cakkhu-viññāṇena diṭṭhi-dassanena vā diṭṭhe anussav' upalabbhamatten' eva ca sute iti hi ekantato evam etan ti niviṭṭhā, diṭṭh' ābhinívesena sassatan ti ādinā abhiniviṭṭhā, ekanta-hitaṁ vā nissaraṇaṁ ajānantā rāgādīhi ekadasahi aggīhi āditta-bhava-ttaya-saṅkhātaṁ angāra-kāsuṁ yeva ime viya adhipātā imaṁ pajjotaṁ patanti, na tato sīsaṁ ukkhipituṁ sakkontī ti. — Ud.-a. 355-6.).

(*b*) Vbh.-a. 146: *Salabho viya dīpasikhābhinipātaṁ.*

1. Th. 1141: *Ārammaṇe taṁ balasā nibandhisaṁ nāgaṁ va thambhamhi*
daḷhāya rajjuyā,
taṁ me suguttaṁ satiyā subhāvitaṁ anissitaṁ
sabbabhavesu hehisi.

2. *Sabhāva lakkhaṇa.*

3. Asl. 173: *Yathā hi purisassa sāyaṁ geham paviṭṭhaṁ sappam ajapadadaṇḍaṁ gahetvā pariyesamānassa taṁ thusakoṭṭhake nipannaṁ disvā 'sappo nu kho no ti' avalokentassa sovatthikattayaṁ disvā nibbemātikassa 'sappo na sappo ti' vicinane majjhattatā hoti evam-evaṁ yā āraddhavipassakassa vipassanāñāṇena lakkhaṇattaye diṭṭhe saṅkhārānaṁ aniccabhāvādivicinane majjhattatā uppajjati ayaṁ vipassanupekkhā.*

TWO WAYS OF GRASPING OF THOUGHT-CHARACTERISTICS

And again, through two ways one grasps the characteristics of thought: through object and through taking to heart. *Q.* How does one grasp the characteristics of thought through the object? *A.* Thought arises owing to object. One should grasp that. "Through this form-object, feeling-object, perception-object, formation-object, and consciousness-object, thought arises", —thus one grasps. This is the grasping of the characteristics of thought through the object. *Q.* How does one grasp the characteristics of thought through taking to heart? *A.* "Through taking to heart, thought arises", —thus one should consider. "Through taking feeling, perception and the formations to heart, thought arises",—thus should one introspect. Thus through the taking to heart one grasps the characteristics of thought.

Q. What is the grasping well of the characteristics? *A.* Through these activities and these characteristics, one grasps form, feeling, perception, the formations and consciousness.

[455] And again, one is able to grasp the characteristics through these activities and these attributes. This is called the grasping well of the characteristics. "One penetrates rise and fall" means: "One sees clearly, 'There is arising; there is passing away' ". Here the form that has arisen continues. The sign of birth is arising. The characteristic of change is passing away. When these two passages are perceived with the eye of wisdom, there is knowledge of "rise and fall". The feeling that has arisen, continues. The characteristic of the coming to be of feeling, perception, the formations and consciousness is arising; the characteristic of change in them is passing away. When these two passages are perceived with the eye of wisdom, there is knowledge of "rise and fall".

CHARACTERISTICS OF RISE AND FALL IN THREE WAYS

And again, one can be well acquainted with the characteristics of rise and fall through three ways: through cause, condition and own property. *Q.* How can one be well acquainted with the characteristics of arising through "cause"? *A.* The aggregates arise owing to craving, ignorance, and *kamma*. When a man perceives this with the eye of wisdom, he becomes familiar with the characteristics of arising through "cause".[1] How can one be well acquain-

---

Yathā tath' assa purisassa ajapadena daṇḍena gāḷhaṁ sappaṁ gahetvā 'kin n' āham imaṁ sappam aviheṭhento attānañ ca iminā adasāpento muñceyyan ti' muñcanākāram eva pariyesato gahaṇe majjhattatā hoti evamevaṁ yā lakkhaṇattayassa diṭṭhattā āditte viya tayo bhave passato saṅkhāragahaṇe majjhattatā ayaṁ saṅkhārupekkhā. Iti vipassanupekkhāya siddhāya saṅkhārupekkhā pi siddhā va hoti.

1. Cp. Pts. I, 55: *'Avijjāsamudayā rūpasamudayo' ti paccayasamudayaṭṭhena rūpakkhandhassa udayaṁ passati, 'taṇhāsamudayā rūpasamudayo' ti paccayasamudayaṭṭhena rūpakkhandhassa udayaṁ passati, 'kammasamudayā rūpasamudayo' ti paccayasamudayaṭṭhena rūpakkhandhassa udayaṁ passati.*

ted with the characteristics of arising through "condition"? Conditioned by nutriment, the form-aggregate arises. Conditioned by contact, three aggregates arise. Conditioned by name-form, the aggregate of consciousness arises.[1] When a man perceives these with the eye of wisdom, he becomes familiar with the characteristics of arising through "condition". *Q*. How can one be well acquainted with the characteristics through "own property"? *A*. The formations arise, renewing themselves. It is like the succession in the flame of a lamp. When a man perceives this with the eye of wisdom, he becomes familiar with the characteristics of arising through "own property". One can see the characteristics of the Truth of Origin through cause and condition. One can see the Truth of Ill through the arising of thought,[2] through condition and through own property. One can see by means of characteristics of the being observed.* Thus one can be acquainted with the characteristics of arising through three ways.

Q. How can one be well acquainted with falling through three ways? *A*. Through the falling away of cause, the falling away of condition and the falling away of own property. Here through the falling away of craving, ignorance, and *kamma*, the falling away of the aggregates is fulfilled.[3] When one perceives this with the eye of wisdom, one becomes familiar with the characteristics of falling away, through the falling away of condition. Through the falling away of nutriment, the falling away of the form-aggregate is fulfilled;[4] through the falling away of contact, the falling away of three aggregates is fulfilled; through the falling away of name-form, the falling away of the aggregate of consciousness is fulfilled.[5] When a man sees this with the eye of wisdom, he becomes familiar with the falling away by way of the falling away of condition. The falling away of the formations is likened to recession in the flame of a lamp. When a man sees this with the eye of wisdom, he becomes familiar with falling away by way of own property. Here, through the falling away of the cause, one sees the Truth of Cessation. Owing to characteristics, (the first) seeing[6] is fulfilled. Through the grasping of the characteristics of the non-become, through the falling away of condition, through own property, through the destruction of views and through the characteristics of the Truth of Ill, the first seeing is fulfilled.

---

1. Cp. Pts. 57: *Rūpakkhandho āhārasamudayo, vedanā saññā saṅkhārā tayo khandhā phassasamudayā, viññāṇakkhandho nāmarūpasamudayo.*

2. *Vitakka.* *Lit. 'the being seen'.

3. Cp. Pts. I, 55-57: *'Avijjānirodhā rūpanirodho' ti paccayanirodhaṭṭhena rūpakkhandhassa vayaṁ passati, 'taṇhānirodhā rūpanirodho' ti paccayanirodhaṭṭhena rūpakkhandhassa vayaṁ passati, kammanirodhā rūpanirodho,' ti paccayanirodhaṭṭhena rūpakkhandhassa vayaṁ passati...*

4. S. III, 59: *Āhāranirodhā rūpanirodho.*

5. Cp. Pts. I, 57: *'Nāmarūpanirodhā viññāṇanirodho' ti paccayanirodhaṭṭhena viññāṇakkhandhassa vayaṁ passati.*

6. *Dassana.*

ACQUIRING THE HIGHEST KNOWLEDGE

Q. How does one acquire the highest knowledge by seeing the Truth of ill through rise and fall and through the characteristics? *A*. How is the destruction of views the cause? One is able to see what he has not yet seen through the sign of the Truth of Ill. Ill pervades all (things). With the destroying of pernicious *kamma*, one sees things as they are. One causes the arising of the thought which is associated with the characteristics of phenomena, and rescues the mind from pernicious *kamma*. Having seen the tribulation of *kamma* according to reality, one causes the arising of the thought which is associated with the characteristics of phenomena, and rescues the mind from pernicious *kamma*. Here one sees ill everywhere, because one goes to the furthest end (investigates fully).

SIMILE OF THE BIRD SURROUNDED BY FIRE

It is like a winged bird surrounded by a fire. Before it flies away into the open sky, it is not free of subjection to fear. But when it sees the tribulation of the surrounding fire and is affected by the fearfulness thereof, it flies away. Thus it should be known. Here, through cause, through condition and through arising, one becomes familiar with the sign of the arising of conditioned arising. This being, this becomes: Owing to the arising of this (cause) the arising of this (result) is fulfilled.[1] Owing to the destruction of the cause, and of the destruction of condition: Through the seeing of this destruction, one becomes familiar with the characteristics of birth according to conditioned arising. This not being, this does not arise: Owing to the destruction of this, this ceases.[2] One can be familiar with arising, having seen its ceasing through own property and through rise and fall: One can see the arising of conditioned arising and the constructed[3] states. One can see the arising and the cessation of this and also the stability of this.

FOUR STATES

One should, through rise and fall, know the four states: through oneness, diversity, non-effort and inherent nature.[4] Seeing the unbroken sequence of the formations, a man holds the flux[5] to be single and does not cling to the idea of multiple fluxes. He does not hold it to be same throughout, because he sees the destruction of it (momentarily), and because of the succession of the formations. He does not cling to self because by nature the formations

1. Ud. 1: *Imasmiṁ sati idaṁ hoti, imass' uppādā idaṁ uppajjati, yadidaṁ: avijjāpaccayā saṅkhārā.*
2. *Ud.* 2: *Imasmiṁ asati idaṁ na hoti, imassa nirodhā idaṁ nirujjhati yadidaṁ: avijjānirodhā saṅkhāranirodho.*
3. *Saṅkhata.*
4. *Ekatta, nānatta, avyāpāra, dhammatā.* Cp. Vis. Mag. 585; Vbh-a. 198-9.
5. *Santāna.*

are uncertain, and because of the succession of the formations. The uninstructed commoner, through wrongly grasping oneness, falls into eternalism or nihilism. Through wrongly grasping diversity, he falls into eternalism. Through wrongly grasping non-effort, he falls into the self-theory.[1] Thus through wrongly grasping the states, he falls into the theory of non-effort (?). Here, in the sense of entirety (wholeness),[2] in the sense of distinctiveness of oneness and in the sense of the inclusion of different characteristics, the characteristic of oneness is fulfilled (?). In the sense of understanding, it is diversity. In the sense of defilement, it is single. In the sense of means it is multiple. As the fruit of craving, it is one; as the fruit of *kamma*, it is varied. That yogin, seeing oneness thus, does not cling to the view of discrete (series); and seeing diversity, he does not cling to the eternalist theory of oneness.

If he sees oneness, he removes annihilationism. If he sees diversity, he removes eternalism. That yogin, thus, through rise and fall, knows oneness and diversity.

NON-EFFORT IN THE ARISING OF THE FORMATIONS

Q. How does one see non-effort in the arising of the formations? By what reason are all phenomena characterized by non-effort and immovability, and how do they proceed without being caused to arise by others? *A.* Owing to intrinsic nature, cause and effect, union, origin, there is conditioned arising. Thus through inherent nature birth causes one to be born. Here, in the sense of non-life and non-motion, non-effort should be known. In the sense of own nature and condition, inherent nature should be known. Here there is the manifestation of emptiness and non-effort, and also of the *kamma* and the formations. The manifestation of non-effort is called inherent nature. The manifestation of inherent nature is called the formations. Here through the correct seizure of oneness, one becomes familiar with ill; through the correct seizure of diversity, one becomes familiar with impermanence, and through the correct seizure of non-effort and inherent nature, one becomes familiar with not-self.

Q. Does the yogin review the rise and fall of all formations without remainder or only one? *A.* Grasping the characteristics in various subjects, he becomes familiar with rise and fall and causes that knowledge to fill all formations without remainder. It is like a man who, having tasted the water of the sea in one spot, knows all sea-water to be salty.[3] Thus should it be known. He fills all formations in two ways: by way of object and by way of non-delusion. Here, grasping the characteristics, one becomes familiar with arising and falling away of all formations. This knowledge of rise and fall is the discernment of all formations. All formations are discerned at the first moment of arising and in the last moment of falling away. They are

---

1. *Atta-vāda.* 2. *Samanta.*
3. A. IV, 199; *Puṇa ca paraṁ bhante mahāsamuddo ekaraso loṇaraso.*

empty before the first moment of arising, and are empty after the last moment of falling away, because there is no other arising before they arose, and there is no other falling away after their fall. Therefore the knowledge of the rise and fall is the knowledge of the discernment of all formations.

The knowledge of rise and fall has ended.

REVIEWING OF BREAKING UP

Thus that yogin enjoys dwelling upon the characteristics of arising and passing away, discerns the formations as subject to breaking up and develops concentration. Effortlessly he produces intellection and sees the breaking up of mind-states. Through the form-object and through the arising and passing away of the mind, he sees the rise and fall of the mind-states associated with that object. In the same way he sees the rise and fall of the mind-states which are associated with these objects, through the perception-object, the formation-object, the consciousness-object and through the rise and fall of mind.

BREAKING UP THROUGH THREE WAYS—

(a) THROUGH ASSEMBLAGE

And again, he sees breaking up through three ways: through assemblage, duality and through understanding.

Q. How, through assemblage? *A.* Through assemblage, he sees the falling away of the postures in their several spheres and the associated mind and the mental properties with them. And again, he grasps form-impermanence, feeling-impermanence, perception-impermanence, formation-impermanence and consciousness-impermanence. After that he sees the breaking up of the mind and the mental properties which are associated with the object of impermanence, by way of assemblage. In the same way, with the object of ill and the object of not-self.[1] Thus one should discern through assemblage.

(b) THROUGH DUALITY

Q. How, through duality? *A.* Having discerned impermanence of form, he arouses the states of mind that conform to impermanence and he sees the arising and the passing away of the mind. Thus having investigated the impermanence of feeling, perception, the formations and consciousness, he arouses the state of mind that conforms to the object of impermanence and

---

1. Cp. Pts. I, 57-8: *Rūpārammaṇatā cittaṁ uppajjitvā bhijjati, taṁ ārammaṇaṁ paṭisaṅkhā tassa cittassa bhaṅgaṁ anupassati.*

'Anupassatīti'. Kathaṁ anupassati? Aniccato anupassati no niccato dukkhato anupassati no sukhato, anattato anupassati no attato...

Vedanārammaṇatā ... pe ... saññārammaṇatā ... pe ... saṅkhārārammaṇatā ... pe ... viññāṇārammaṇatā: cakkhuṁ ... pe ... jarāmaraṇārammaṇatā cittaṁ uppajjitvā bhijjati, taṁ ārammaṇaṁ paṭisaṅkhā tassa cittassa bhaṅgaṁ anupassati.

sees the arising and the passing away of the mind. In the same way, with the object of suffering and the object of not-self. Thus he should discern through duality.

(c) THROUGH UNDERSTANDING

Q. How, through understanding? *A*. Having discerned the impermanence of form, he arouses the mind together with the object of impermanence [456] and sees the arising and the passing away of the mind. Thus through the understanding of insight, he sees the breaking up of many mind-states. He discerns the impermanence of feeling, perception, the formations and consciousness, and arouses the state of mind that conforms to the object of impermanence, and sees the arising and the falling away of mind-states. Thus he sees again and again the breaking up of mind-states. Thus through understanding he sees the breaking up of many states. Likewise, he discerns ill and not-self. Thus having understood, he grasps breaking up. That object of ill and breaking up makes for intentness. Intent on the formations always, he attains to well-being every moment. Through this understanding, that yogin, independent of another, knows the whole world by itself (and as unenduring) as a poppy seed on the point (of an awl),[1] and that in every concentrated thought-moment there is the change of arising, stability and destruction.[2]

SIMILES OF DRUM-SOUND, TOWN OF GODS, LIGHTNING

At this time the yogin again sees as it is taught in the stanzas thus:

Depending on each other do the two
called name and form, by nature carry on.
When one breaks up the other also breaks;
together do they always start their course.
The five states of form, odour and the rest,
rise not form eye, and also not from forms;
yet are not different from the set of two.
The states conditioned from a cause arise,
like the sound when a drum is struck.
The states of form, odour and the rest,
rise not from ear, and also not from sounds;
yet are not different from the set of two.
The five states of form, odour and the rest,
rise not from nose and also not from smell;

1. Cp. Sn. 625: *Vāri pokkharapatte va, āragge-r-iva sāsapo,*
Yo na lippati kāmesu, tam ahaṁ brūmi brāhmaṇaṁ.
2. Cp. I, 152: *Uppādo paññāyati vayo paññāyati ṭhitassa aññathattaṁ paññāyati. Imāni kho bhikkhave tīṇi saṅkhatassa saṅkhatalakkhaṇānī ti.*

yet are not different from the set of two.
The five states of form, odour and the rest,
rise not from tongue, and also not from taste;
yet are not different from the set of two.
The five states of form, odour and the rest,
rise not from body; also not from touch;
yet are not different from the set of two.
These are not born of form material;
these do not rise out of the sphere of thought;
they rise depending on condition-cause
like the sound when a drum is struck.
The functions are themselves without strength;
weak is the former cause; what has become
is feeble, poor. Infirm is that which is
to others bound. Co-states are also weak.
There is no strength at all in union;
and what rolls on is always impotent,
for what rolls on has no abiding strength.
It has no pith; it cannot cause to rise;
'tis coreless even as a town of gods;[1]
none cause this to be; 'tis not produced,
by self, and does not by its strength remain.
On other states, depending, does it rise,
and what it does produce is called corrupt.
Weak is this body, it is not produced,
by itself and is low. It is not 'cause'
or 'object', by itself. It has no pith
and is not free of states conditioned, but
is truly due to many complex-states.
Short is its life, because it is most weak;
it goes not anywhere; from nowhere comes;
and is not born in some land, distant, far.
The mind is not a person, soul or self;
at every point of thought it is bound up,
with what is pleasing or with what is ill.
It passes over mountain, sea and clime,
sees eighty thousand aeons in a trice,
lives only once and does not come again,
does not to two thought-moments bind itself,
and in it is all past and future lost.
All that remains is merely aggregate
and this is ever falling without end
and so will also fall the state to be.

---

1. *Gandhabba nagara.*

There are no different signs occuring here,
from the non-born there is no coming here,
in the sense that is highest there is none
who goes or comes. And in the future will
no heaping be, but just a going-on.
The world does not with dhamma ever mix.
One cannot see the future or the source.
All dhammas are un-made—they are like space—
and rising like the lightning, perish soon.

Thus seeing endless destruction, that yogin enters into concentration. Just as in rubbing sticks together for fire, sparks flash forth, just so is the class of enlightenment moments. When illuminattion, joy, calm, bliss, resolve, uplift, presentation, equanimity and desire[1] arise, if he is not intelligent, the yogin will arouse thoughts of distraction or conceit in this state.

Q. How can he remove distraction? *A*. That yogin arouses rapture for the doctrine. That rapture pacifies his mind; and sitting again, he calms the mind and makes it conform to the doctrine. If his mind conforms to the doctrine, he rejects the idea of permanence through concentration of the reviewing of breaking up. Being free from the idea of permanence, he becomes familiar with the method and removes (distraction of mind).

Q. How does the yogin remove conceit? *A*. That yogin causes the arising of illumination in the doctrine at first, believes that he has attained to the supramundane state, thinks that he has attained what he has not attained and does not endeavour further. Thus he arouses conceit. The intelligent yogin knows that defilement disturbs meditation, and knows that worldly states have the formations for object, Thus he knows that the supramundane state has *Nibbāna* for object. Having seen thus, he removes distraction and conceit by this knowledge and seeing only breaking up, practises well and practises repeatedly.

The knowledge which is the discernment of falling away has ended.

The Eleventh Fascicle has ended.

1. Cp. Vis. Mag. 633: *Obhāso, ñāṇaṁ, pīti, passaddhi, sukhaṁ, adhimokkho, paggaho, upaṭṭhānaṁ, upekkhā, nikanti*. *Nikanti* is mistranslated into Chinese as renunciation, it being equated with the Sk. *nishkrānta*.

THE PATH OF FREEDOM

FASCICLE THE TWELFTH

WRITTEN

BY

THE ARAHANT UPATISSA

WHO WAS CALLED

GREAT LIGHT IN RYO

TRANSLATED IN RYO

BY

TIPIṬAKA SANGHAPĀLA OF FUNAN

ON DISCERNING TRUTH

CHAPTER THE TWELFTH

Section Two

FEAR KNOWLEDGE

Thus to that yogin who discerns breaking up, owing to breaking-up-discernment, knowledge of fear arises.

SIMILES OF THE MAN WITH THE SWORD, POISONOUS SNAKE, AND HEAP OF FIRE

The cause of the aggregates, the arising of the aggregates, the three planes of becoming,[1] the five kinds of faring-on,[2] the seven stations of consciousness,[3] and the nine abodes of sentience,[4] appear to him as fearful as a wicked man who takes up a sword,[5] a poisonous snake,[6] or a heap of fire.[7] Thus owing to his discernment of breaking-up, fear arises: fear of the cause of aggregation; fear of the arising of aggregation. Thus considering the three planes of becom-

---

1. D. III, 216: *Tayo bhavā. Kāma-bhavo, rūpa-bhavo, arūpa-bhavo.*
2. Ibid. 234: *Pañca gatiyo: Ṇirayo, tiracchāna-yoni, pettivisayo, manussā, devā.*
3. Ibid. 253—See n. 1 p. 280.
4. Ibid. 263—See n. 7 p. 280.
5. S. III, 115: *Vadhakaṁ rūpaṁ Vadhakaṁ rūpan ti yathābhūtaṁ pajānāti. Vadhakaṁ vedanaṁ. Vadhakaṁ saññaṁ. Vadhake saṅkhāre. Vadhakaṁ viññāṇaṁ Vadhakaṁ viññānanti yathābhūtaṁ pajānāti.*
6. S. IV, 174: *Cattāro āsīvisā uggatejā ghoravisā ti kho bhikkhave catunnetaṁ mahābhūtānaṁ adhivacanaṁ, paṭhavīdhātuyā āpodhātuyā tejodhātuyā vāyodhātuyā.*
7. S. II, 84-5: *Seyyathāpi bhikkhave dasannaṁ va kaṭṭhavāhānaṁ vīsāya vā kaṭṭhavāhānaṁ tiṁsāya vā kaṭṭhavāhānaṁ cattārīsāya vā kaṭṭhavāhānaṁ mahā aggikkhandho jāleyya. Tatra puriso kālena kālaṁ sukkhāni ceva tiṇāni pakkhipeyya, sukkhāni ca gomayāni pakkhipeyya, sukkhāni ca kaṭṭhāni pakkhipeyya. Evañhi so bhikkhave mahā aggikkhandho tadāhāro tadupādāno ciraṁ dīghamaddhānaṁ jāleyya.*

ing, the five kinds of faring-on, the seven stations of intelligence, the nine abodes of sentience as impermanent, he grasps the idea of fear and causes the arising of the signless[1] through tranquillity. Attending to ill and fearing birth, he causes the arising of the birthless[2] through tranquillity. Attending to not-self, he fears the sign of birth and causes the arising of the signless and the birthless through tranquillity. He reviews tribulation and repulsion and observes conformable patience.[3] This is the explanation in full.

The cause of the arising of fear-knowledge has ended.

KNOWLEDGE OF THE DESIRE FOR RELEASE

Practising (the knowledge of) fear, that yogin produces the knowledge of the desire for release. When he fears the sign of the aggregates, the knowledge of the desire for release arises. When he fears the arising of the aggregates, the knowledge of the desire for release arises. When he fears the three planes of becoming, the five kinds of faring-on, the seven stations of intelligence, and the nine abodes of sentience, the knowledge of the desire for release arises. It is like a bird hemmed in by a fire desiring to escape it, and like a man surrounded by robbers seeking to get free of them. Thus if that yogin fears the cause of the aggregates, the coming to be of the aggregates, the three planes of becoming, the five kinds of ill-faring, the seven abodes of consciousness and the nine abodes of sentience, the knowledge of the desire for release arises.[4] Attending

---

Evam eva kho bhikkhave upādāniyesu dhammesu assādānupassino viharato taṇhā pavaḍḍhati. Taṇhāpaccayā upādānaṁ ... pe ... Evam etassa kevalassa dukkhakkhandhassa samudayo hoti.

1. *Animitta.* 2. *Ajāta.*

3. Cp. (a) Dh-a II, 207: *So there anumodanaṁ karonte ekaggacitto hutvā dhammaṁ sunanto sotāpattimaggassa orato anulomikaṁ khantiṁ nibbattesi, thero pi anumodanaṁ katvā pakkāmi. Upāsakaṁ theraṁ anugantvā nivattamānaṁ ekā yakkhinī dhenuvesena āgantvā ure paharitvā māresi. So kālaṁ katvā Tusitapure nibbatti. Dhammasabhāyaṁ kathaṁ samuṭṭhāpesuṁ: 'coraghātako pañcapaṇṇāsavassāni kakkhaḷakammaṁ katvā ajj'eva tato mutto ajj'eva therassa bhikkhaṁ datvā ajj'eva kālakato, kahaṁ nu kho nibbatto' ti. Satthā āgantvā 'kāya nu'ttha bhikkhave etarahi kathāya sannisinnā' ti pucchitvā, 'imāya nāmā' ti vutte, 'bhikkhave Tusitapure nibbatto' ti āha. 'Kiṁ bhante vadetha ettakaṁ kālaṁ ettake manusse ghātetvā Tusitavimāne nibbatto' ti. 'Āma bhikkhave mahanto tena kalyāṇamitto laddho, so Sāriputtassa dhammadesanaṁ sutvā anulomañāṇaṁ nibbattetvā ito cuto Tusitavimāne nibbatto' ti vatvā imaṁ gātham āha:*

'Subhāsitaṁ suṇitvāna nagare coraghātako
anulomakhantiṁ laddhāna modati tidivaṁ gato' ti.

(b) Pts. II, 240-41: *Pañcakkhandhe suññato passanto anulomikaṁ khantiṁ paṭilabhati, 'pañcannaṁ khandhānaṁ nirodho paramasuññaṁ nibbānan' ti passanto sammattaniyāmaṁ okkamati.*

. . .

Pañcakkhandhe jātidhammato passanto anulomikaṁ khantiṁ paṭilabhati, 'pañcannaṁ khandhānaṁ nirodho ajātaṁ nibbānan' ti passanto sammattaniyāmaṁ okkamati.

. . .

Pañcakkhandhe upāyāsadhammato passanto anulomikaṁ khantiṁ paṭilabhati; 'pañcannaṁ khandhānaṁ nirodho anupāyāsaṁ nibbānan' ti passanto sammattaniyāmaṁ okkamati.

4. Cp. Pts. I, 61: *'Uppādo bhayan' ti muñcitukamyatā paṭisaṅkhā santiṭṭhanā paññā saṅkhārupekkhāsu ñāṇaṁ, 'pavattaṁ bhayan' ti muñcitukamyatā paṭisaṅkhā santiṭṭhanā*

to impermanence, he fears the cause; attending to ill, he fears birth; attending to not-self, he fears both cause and birth. Then the knowledge of the desire for release arises. Here the commoner and the learner*

[457]

This is the full explanation.

The knowledge of the desire for release has ended.

ADAPTIVE KNOWLEDGE

Practising the knowledge of the desire for release that yogin wishes to free himself from all action and attain to *Nibbāna*. Wishing to arouse only one sign (?), he arouses knowledge conformable to the Way of Escape. Through three ways adaptive knowledge[1] arises. He transcends the formations through three ways: Reviewing the impermanence of the five aggregates, he attains to adaptive knowledge. The extinction of the five aggregates is permanent *Nibbāna*. Reviewing the ill of the five aggregates, he attains to adaptive knowledge. The extinction of the aggregates is blissful *Nibbāna*. Thus he transcends the formations. Reviewing not-selfness of the five aggregates, he attains to adaptive knowledge. The extinction of the aggregates is absolute *Nibbāna*. He transcends the formations considering them as impermanent, ill and not-self. *Q*. Through what knowledge does he transcend the formations, and through what knowledge is transcending of the formations completed? *A*. He transcends the formations through adaptive knowledge. The transcending of the formations is completed through Path-knowledge. *Q*. What is adaptive knowledge? *A*. The knowledge which conforms to the four foundations of mindfulness, the four right efforts, the four bases of supernormal power, the five faculties, the five powers, the seven enlightenment factors and the factors of the Noble Eightfold Path,[2] is called adaptive knowledge. This is the full explanation of adaptive knowledge.

Adaptive knowledge has ended.

KNOWLEDGE OF ADOPTION

Adaptive knowledge arises from dwelling upon the characteristics of the formations immediately after. But when he attends taking *Nibbāna* as object,

---

paññā saṅkhārupekkhāsu ñāṇaṁ ...pe... 'upāyāso bhayan' ti muñcitukamyatā paṭisaṅkhā santiṭṭhanā paññā saṅkhārupekkhāsu ñāṇaṁ.

* The rest of the sentence is unintelligible. Possibly this refers to a passage of Pts. I, 60-4.

1. *Anulomañāṇa.*

2. Cp. Vis. Mag. 678: *Cattāro satipaṭṭhānā, cattāro sammappadhānā cattāro iddhipādā, pañcindriyāni, pañcabalāni, satta bojjhangā, ariyo aṭṭhangiko maggo ti hi ime sattatiṁsa dhammā bojjhangaṭṭhena bodhī ti laddhamānassa ariyamaggassa pakkhe bhavattā bodhipakkhiyā nāma; pakkhe bhavattā ti nāma upakārabhāve ṭhitattā.*

While Vis. Mag. calls these *bodhipakkhiyā*, Vim. Mag. calls them *anulomañāṇa* See Preface to Vbh. XIV-XVI, for a discussion on *bodhipakkhiya-dhammā*.

he arouses the knowledge of adoption.[1] *Q*. What is adoption? *A*. The passing beyond of commoner-states, is called adoptive knowledge. . . .*

And again, the sowing of the seed of *Nibbāna*, is called adoption. It is as has been stated in the *Abhidhamma*: "The overcoming of birth is named adoption.[2] The victory of non-birth is also named adoption".[3] And again, the overcoming of the cause of birth is adoption. To pass over to non-birth and the signless is named adoption. This is the first turning to *Nibbāna*. From without, he produces the wisdom of procedure. This is the full explanation of adoption.

The knowledge of adoption has ended.

By means of the knowledge of adoption, he knows ill, immediately after. He cuts off origin, and makes cessation manifest. He practises the Path, and attains to the Path-knowledge of Stream-entrance and all accessories of enlightenment. At this time the yogin sees the limited, the unconditioned, and the sublime, through seclusion. He understands the Four Noble Truths in one moment, in one comprehension, not before or after (each other).

He understands at once ill, the cutting off of origin, the realization of cessation and the practice of the Path. Thus he understands. It is taught in the simile in verse thus:

By boat one goes with goods leaving this bank,
And cutting the stream, reaches that.

SIMILES OF THE BOAT, LAMP, AND SUN

It is like the crossing in the boat. The four actions occur simultaneously, neither before nor after. The man leaves this bank, cuts the stream, carries the goods and reaches the further bank. Like the leaving of this bank is the knowledge that understands ill; like the cutting of the stream is the cutting off of the origin; like the arrival at the further bank is the realization of cessation; like the carrying of the foods is the practising of the Path.[4]

Or it is like a lamp which in one moment, neither before nor after, fulfils four functions thus: the burning of the wick; the dispelling of darkness; the

---

1. *Gotrabhūñāṇa*. Cp. Vis. Mag. 673.
* This passage is unintelligible.
2. Pts. I, 66: '*Jātim abhibhuyyatīti*' *gotrabhū*.
3. Cp. Ibid. 67: '*Jātiyā vuṭṭhitvā ajātiṁ pakkhandatīti*' *gotrabhū*.
4. Vis. Mag. 690-1: (*a*) *Yathā nāvā apubbaṁ acarimaṁ ekakkhaṇe cattāri kiccāni karoti:— orimatīraṁ pajahati, sotaṁ chindati, bhaṇḍaṁ vahati, pārimaṁ tīraṁ appeti, evam eva maggañāṇaṁ . . . pe . . . nirodhaṁ sacchikiriyā-abhisamayena abhisameti; etthā pi yathā nāvā orimatīraṁ pajahati, evaṁ maggañāṇaṁ dukkhaṁ parijānāti; yathā sotaṁ chindati, evam samudayaṁ pajahati; yathā bhaṇḍaṁ vahati, evaṁ sahajātādi-paccayatāya maggaṁ bhāveti; yathā pārimaṁ tīraṁ appeti, evam pārimatīrabhūtaṁ nirodhaṁ sacchikarotī ti evaṁ upamāsaṁsandanaṁ veditabbaṁ.*

consumption of oil; and the production of light.[1]

And again, it is like the sun which performs four functions simultaneously, neither before nor after, thus: It makes forms visible, dispels darkness, removes cold and produces light. Like the making visible of forms, is the knowledge which understands ill; like the dispelling of darkness, is the destruction of origin; like the removal of cold, is the realization of cessation; like the production of light, is the practising of the Path. Thus is the Ariyan knowledge compared to the sun.[2]

Q. Of the knowledge that understands ill, of the removal of origin, of the realization of cessation and of the practising of the Path, what are the signs? *A*. If the yogin does not understand ill, the four reversals occur. And at that time the yogin sees the limited, the unconditioned and the element of the sublime through solitude. Through the knowledge that occurs in one moment, he realizes the Four Truths at the same time, neither before nor after. *Q*. How should these be understood. *A*. By means of the knowledge of arising and falling away, he cannot comprehend the flood of ill and the tribulation of the formations as they truly are. He practises on a sign which does not belong to the formations. And he passes over to that which is not formation. Thus he sees the tribulation of the formations as they are through causing the mind to practise on a sign belonging to the formations, and passes over to that which is not formations. Here he comprehends the flood of ill and reaches the end. And again, it is said that if that is so, he should be able to discern the Truth through the solitude and the knowledge of adoption. The knowledge of adoption arises from the formations, and passes over that which is non-formation. When the knowledge of adoption which arises from the sign of the formations passes over to that which is non-formation, he can attain to *Nibbāna*. Intentness on the cause is its only object. Through intentness on the object, he can develop concentration of mind. When he gets con-

---

(*b*) Petaka: 134: *Evaṁ diṭṭhanto yathā nāvā jalaṁ gacchanto cattāri kiccāni karoti, pārimaṁ tīraṁ pāpeti, orimaṁ tīraṁ jahati, sāraṁ vahati, sotaṁ chindati, evam eva samathavipassanā yuganandhā vattamānā ekakāle ekakkhaṇe ekacitte cattāri kiccāni karoti, dukkhaṁ pariññābhisamayena abhisameti, yāva maggaṁ bhāvanābhisamayena abhisameti.*

1. (*a*) Vis. Mag. 690: *Yathā padipo apubbaṁ acarimaṁ ekakkhaṇena cattāri kiccāni karoti:— vaṭṭiṁ jhāpeti, andhakāraṁ vidhamati, ālokaṁ parividaṁseti, sinehaṁ pariyādiyati—evam eva maggañāṇaṁ apubbaṁ acarimaṁ ekakkhaṇena cattāri saccāni abhisameti, dukkhaṁ pariññābhisamayena abhisameti, samudayaṁ pahānābhisamayena abhisameti, maggaṁ bhāvanābhisamayena abhisameti, nirodhaṁ sacchikiriyābhisamayena abhisameti.*

(*b*) Petaka. 134-5: *Yathā dīpo jalanto ekakāle apubbaṁ acarimaṁ cattāri kiccāni karoti, andhakāraṁ vidhamati, ālokaṁ pātukaroti, rūpaṁ nidassiyati, upādānaṁ pariyādiyati, evam eva samathavipassanā yuganandhā vattamānā ekakāle . . . pe . . .*

2. (*a*) Vis. Mag. 690: *Yathā suriyo udayanto apubbaṁ acarimaṁ saha pātubhāvā cattāri kiccāni karoti:— rūpagatāni obhāseti, andhakāraṁ vidhamati, ālokaṁ dasseti, sītaṁ paṭippassambheti—evam eva maggañāṇaṁ . . . pe . . . nirodhaṁ sacchikiriyābhisamayena abhisameti. Idhā pi yathā suriyo rūpagatāni obhāseti, evaṁ maggañāṇaṁ dukkhaṁ parijānāti; yathā andhakāraṁ vidhamati, evaṁ samudayaṁ pajahati; yathā ālokaṁ dasseti, evaṁ sahajātāni paccayatāya maggaṁ bhāveti; yathā sītaṁ paṭippassambheti, evaṁ kilesapaṭippassaddhiṁ nirodhaṁ sacchikaroti ti evaṁ upamāsaṁsandanaṁ veditabbaṁ.*
Vis. Mag. attributes these three similes to the ancient teachers—'*Vuttaṁ h' etaṁ Porāṇehi*'.

(*b*) Petaka. 134: *Yathā vā sūriyo udayanto ekakāle apubbaṁ acarimaṁ cattāri kiccāni karoti, andhakāraṁ vidhamati, ālokaṁ pātukaroti, rūpaṁ nidassiyati, sītaṁ pariyādiyati, evaṁ eva samathavipassanā yuganandhā vattamānā ekakāle . . . pe . . .*

centration, he produces serenity and insight, and also can fulfil the enlightenment accessories. Thereby he understands the Truth through the knowledge of adoption. From that knowledge of adoption the knowledge of the Path is produced immediately. At that time he can get the concentration of *Nibbāna*. His mind attains to concentration and develops serenity and insight and the enlightenment accessories. Therefore it is only through the knowledge of the Path that one can discern the Truth.

SIMILE OF THE BURNING CITY

It is like a man stepping across the threshold of the gate of a burning city. When he has placed one foot outside the city, he is not yet entirely outside the city. Thus at that time, the knowledge of adoption arises from that object of the formations and passes over to that which is non-formation. But here it cannot be said that he has done with the defilements, because many states are yet not perfected. Just as when a man places both his feet outside the threshold of the gate of the burning city, it can be said that he is out of the burning city, just so when the knowledge of adoption arouses the knowledge of the Path without end, it could be said that one has gone out of the walled city of the defilements, because the states are complete. Therefore, through the knowledge of adoption, one fulfils the discernment of Truth.[1]

Q. What is meant by discernment? *A*. The Four Noble Truths occur in one moment—this is understanding. Here Path-knowledge and the balance of the faculties mean equilibrium; the powers mean immovability; the enlightenment factors mean vehicle; the factors of the Eightfold Path mean cause; the foundations of mindfulness mean dwelling; the right efforts mean distinction; the bases of supernormal power mean contrivance; truth means Truth; serenity means non-disturbance; insight means vision; the twofold means non-separation; the purity of virtue means shielding; the purity of thought means non-excitement; the purity of views means seeing; skill in wisdom means shedding; illumination of indifference means pervading everywhere; the faculty of the knowledge of extinction means complete sloughing; uniformity of attention means the development of regenerate desire; renunciation means the extinction of contact and feeling; concentration means the setting-up in front;[2] mindfulness means shelter; wisdom means Truth; the sublime means supreme distinction; *Nibbāna* means ultimate rest.

---

1. Cp. Vis. Mag. 672 f.
2. Cp. A. II, 210: *Ujuṁ kāyaṁ panidhāya parimukhaṁ satiṁ upaṭṭhapetvā* (=*Parimukhaṁ satiṁ upaṭṭhapetvā ti kammaṭṭhānābhimukhaṁ satiṁ ṭhapayitvā, mukhasamīpe vā katvā ti attho. Ten'eva Vibhaṅge ayaṁ vuttaṁ: sati upaṭṭhitā hoti supaṭṭhitā nāsikagge vā mukhanimitte vā, tena vuccati parimukhaṁ satiṁ upaṭṭhapetvā ti* (Vbh. 252) — Mp. III, 202).

THREE FETTERS

Thus that yogin knows presently, sees presently and cuts off the three fetters, i.e., self-illusion, uncertainty, addiction to rites and ceremonies, and the defilements standing in that place.[1]

Q. What is self-illusion *A.* Here seeing form, the uninstructed commoner thinks: "This is the self; the self is form; form is the abode of the self; in form there is the self". Thus in the same way he thinks of feeling, perception, the formations or consciousness thus: "consciousness is the self; the self is consciousness; consciousness is the abode of the self; in consciousness is the self". This is called self-illusion.[2] This self is cut off and thereby sixty-two views,[3] beginning with self-illusion, are also cut off.

Q. What is uncertainty? *A.* Uncertainty regarding ill, origin, cessation, the Path, the Buddha, the Law, the Community of Bhikkhus, the beginning, the end, and the beginning and the end, or uncertainty concerning the doctrine of cause and condition, is called uncertainty.[4] This is cut off.

Q. What is addiction to rites and ceremonies. *A.* There are two kinds in addiction to rites and ceremonies. They are, (addiction due to) craving and (addiction due to) delusion. (Here one thinks thus:) "Through this vow, through this conduct, through this painful practice and through this holiness, I shall be reborn in heaven or I shall be reborn in every heaven". This is called addiction to rites and ceremonies due to craving. Here a recluse or a brahmin thinks: "Through this virtue, through this purity and the action of purity of virtue, (I shall be reborn etc.)". This is called addiction to rites and ceremonies due to delusion.[5] This is also cut off.

---

1. Cp. Pts. II, 94: *Sotāpattimaggena sakkāyadiṭṭhi vicikicchā sīlabbataparāmāso, imāni tiṇi saññojanāni pahiyanti; diṭṭhānusayo vicikicchānusayo, ime dve anusayā byantihonti.*
2. Cp. M. I, 8; III, 17; Vbh. 364: *Tattha katamā sakkāyadiṭṭhi? Idha assutavā puthujjano ariyānaṁ adassāvī ariyadhammassa akovido ariyadhamme avinīto, sappurisānaṁ adassāvī sappurisdhammassa akovido sappurisadhamme avinitto, rūpaṁ attato samanupassati, rūpavantaṁ vā attānaṁ, attani vā rūpaṁ, rūpasmiṁ vā attānaṁ; vedanaṁ... saññaṁ ... saṁkhāre... viññāṇaṁ attato samanupassati, viññāṇavantaṁ vā attānaṁ, attani vā viññāṇaṁ, viññāṇasmiṁ vā attānaṁ: yā evarūpā diṭṭhi diṭṭhigataṁ... pe ...vipariyesagāho: ayaṁ vuccati sakkāyadiṭṭhi.*
3. Vbh. 400: *Tattha katamāni dvāsaṭṭhi diṭṭhigatāni Brahmajāle* (D. I, 44-5.) *veyyākaraṇe vuttāni Bhagavatā? Cattāro sassatavādā, cattāro ekaccasassatikā, cattāro antānantikā, cattāro amarāvikkhepikā, dve adhiccasamuppannikā, soḷasa saññīvādā, aṭṭha asaññīvādā, aṭṭha nevasaññī-nāsaññīvādā, satta ucchedavādā, pañca diṭṭha-dhammanibbānavādā. Imāni dvāsaṭṭhi diṭṭhigatāni Brahmajāle veyyākaraṇe vuttāni Bhagavatā.*
4. Cp. Dhs. 198, par. 1118; Vbh. 364-5: *Tattha katamā vicikicchā? Satthari kaṁkhati vicikicchati, dhamme kaṁkhati vicikicchati, saṁghe kaṁkhati vicikicchati, sikkhāya kaṁkhati vicikicchati; pubbante kaṁkhati vicikicchati, aparante kaṁkhati vicikicchati, pubbantāparante kaṁkhati vicikicchati, idappaccayatā-paṭiccasamuppannesu dhammesu kaṁkhati vicikicchati: yā evarūpā kaṁkhā kaṁkhāyanā kaṁkhāyitattaṁ vimati vicikicchā dveḷhakaṁ dvedhāpatho saṁsayo anekaṁsagāho āsappanā parisappanā apariyogāhanā thambhitattaṁ cittassa manovilekho: ayaṁ vuccati vicikicchā.*

   These two references (i.e., Dhs. and Vbh.) are not identical.
5. Cp. Vbh. 365; Dhs. 183, par. 1005: *Tattha katamo sīlabbataparāmāso? Ito bahiddhā samaṇabrahmaṇānaṁ sīlena suddhivatena suddhisīlabbatena suddhīti — evarūpā diṭṭhi diṭṭhigataṁ diṭṭhigahaṇaṁ diṭṭhikantāro diṭṭhivisūkāyikaṁ diṭṭhivipphanditaṁ diṭṭhisaññojanaṁ — gāho paṭiggāho abhiniveso parāmāso kummaggo micchāpatho micchattaṁ titthāyatanaṁ vipariyesagāho — ayaṁ vuccati sīlabbataparāmāso.*

Q. What are the defilements standing in that place? *A*. Sense-desire, hate and infatuation which cause ill-faring are called the defilements standing in that place. [458] These are also cut down. At this time one realizes the Fruit of Stream-entrance. If a man has not yet attained to the stage of a Stream-entrant, he dwells in the Stream-entrant's place of departure, or the eighth place. Or else, in the ground of vision or concentration or in the wisdom procedure which arises from both. This is the full explanation of the knowledge of the Path of Stream-entrance. Immediately after, the Stream-entrant cuts off the three fetters. Therefore his object is unconditioned. The method which is not different from the Path and other states arouses the fruitional knowledge and the fruitional consciousness of the Stream-entrant.

Having seen the Path, Fruit and *Nibbāna*, he cuts off the defilements and sees the remaining defilements. This is Stream-entrance, non-retrogression. This is to be born of the breast of the Blessed One. This is to be born of the mouth of the Blessed One. This is the *dhamma* that is born of *dhamma*.[1] This is the getting of the limbs of *dhamma*. It is separation from all things. It is called the good course endowed with vision. It is called familiarity with the Noble Doctrine. It is the dwelling at the threshold of the Sublime.[2] Here, perfecting his vision, he sees the Good Law. After seeing the Good Law, he fulfils knowledge. If his knowledge is fulfilled, he enters the stream of the Noble Doctrine and becomes familiar with wisdom, and opening the gate of the Sublime, he dwells within it. Therefore it is said in the verse thus:

Royal is that one who wins the stream,
a king of deva-realms is he,
a ruler of all worlds that be,
for Fruit of Stream is verily supreme![3]

ONCE-RETURNER

Dwelling in this stage, that yogin endeavours further wishing to obtain the Fruit of Once-return, and he sees birth, destruction and the rest. As explained above he sees. He develops in the way through which he saw the Path. Depending on the faculties, the powers and enlightenment-intellection,

---

1. (a) S. II, 221; M. III, 29: *Yaṁ kho taṁ, bhikkhave, sammā vadamāno vedeyya: Bhagavato putto oraso mukhato jāto dhammajo dhammanimmito dhammadāyādo no āmisadāyādo ti,—Sāriputtam eva taṁ sammā vadamāno vadeyya: Bhagavato putto oraso mukhato jāto dhammajo dhammanimmito dhammadāyādo no āmisadāyādo ti.*
   (b) S. III, 83: *Pañcakkdandhe pariññāya, sattasaddhammagocarā,*
   pasaṁsiyā sappurisā, puttā buddhassa orasā.
2. S. II, 43: *Yato kho bhikkhave ariyasāvako evaṁ paccayaṁ pajānāti, evaṁ paccayasamudayaṁ pajānāti, evaṁ paccayanirodhaṁ pajānāti, evaṁ paccayanirodhagāminiṁ paṭipadaṁ pajānāti, ayaṁ vuccati bhikkhave ariyasāvako diṭṭhisampanno iti pi, dassanasampanno iti pi, āgato imaṁ saddhammaṁ iti pi, passati imaṁ saddhammaṁ iti pi, sekhena ñaṇena samannāgato iti pi sekhāya vijjāya samannāgato iti pi, dhammasotaṁ samāpanno iti pi, ariyo nibbedhikapañño iti pi, amatadvāraṁ āhacca tiṭṭhati iti pīti.*
3. Cp. Dh. 178: *Pathavyā ekarajjena saggassa gamanena vā*
   Sabbalokādhipaccena sotāpatti phalaṁ varaṁ.

he discerns the Truth. Thus he practises and goes towards cessation. He cuts off coarse passion and hatred and the defilements standing in that place.[1] By this Path he gains the Fruit of Once-return immediately.

NON-RETURNER

Dwelling in this stage, he endeavours further, wishing to obtain the Fruit, of Non-return, and sees birth, destruction and the rest. As explained above he sees: He develops in the way through which he saw the Path. Depending on the faculties, the powers and enlightenment-intellection, he understands the truth and goes towards cessation. He cuts off fine passion and hate and the defilements standing in that place. By this Path he gains the Fruit of Non-return immediately.[2]

SAINTSHIP

Dwelling in this stage, he endeavours further wishing to obtain the Fruit of Stainship and sees birth, destruction and the others. As explained above he sees. He develops in the same way by which he saw the Path. Depending on the faculties, the powers and enlightenment-intellection, he discerns the Truth. Thus he cuts off desire for the form and the formless; and he cuts off conceit, agitation, ignorance and all other defilements without remainder.[3] Thereafter that yogin gains the Fruit of Saintship. He sees the Path; he sees the Fruit of enlightenment, and he sees the extirpation of the defilements. Thus that bhikkhu becomes a Consummate One, eradicates the cankers, does what there is to do, lays down the burden, attains to the goal, removes the fetters, knows liberation,[4] is sepatate from the five and (endowed with) the six factors, and attains to security. He is not fettered by death, removes cessation associated with other (false) truths, believes in and looks for the stainless, attends to the calming of the bodily formations,[5] and gains the highest guerdon. He is called one who has removed hatred, one who has won the further shore,[6] one who has broken free of the defilements, one who is without fetters

---

1. Pts. II, 94: *Sakadāgāmimaggena oḷārikaṁ kāmarāgasaññojanaṁ paṭighasaññojanaṁ, imāni dve sāññojanāni pahīyanti, oḷāriko kāmarāgānusayo paṭighānusayo, ime dve anusayā byantihonti.*
2. Ibid. 94-5: *Anāgāmimaggena aṇusahagataṁ kāmarāgassññojanaṁ paṭighasaññojanaṁ, imāni dve saññojanāni pahīyanti, aṇusahagato kāmarāgānusayo paṭighānusayo, ime dve anusayā byantihonti.*
3. Ibid. 95: *Arahattamaggena rūparāgo arūparāgo māno uddhaccaṁ avijjā — imāni pañca saññojanāni pahīyanti, mānānusayo bhavarāgānusayo avijjānusayo — ime tayo anusayā byantihonti. Evaṁ saññojanāni pahīyanti, anusayā byantihonti.*
4. D. III, 83: *Imesaṁ hi Vāseṭṭha catunnaṁ vaṇṇānaṁ yo hoti bhikkhu arahaṁ khīṇāsavo vusitavā kata-karaṇīyo ohita-bhāro anuppatta-sadattho parikkhīṇa-bhava-saṁyojano sammadaññā vimutto, so tesaṁ aggam akkhāyati dhammen' eva no adhammena.*
5. Cp. Ibid. 269: *Idh' āvuso bhikkhu pañcaṅgavippahīno hoti chaḷaṅga-samannāgato ekārakkho caturāpasseno panunna-pacceka-sacco samavaya-saṭṭhesano anāvila-saṁkappo passàddha-kāya-saṁkhāro suvimutta-citto suvimutta-pañño.*
6. Cp. S. IV, 175: *Pārimaṁ tīraṁ khemaṁ appaṭibhayaṁ ti kho bhikkhave nibbānàssetaṁ adhivacanaṁ.*

and hindrances, possessor of Ariyan wings, remover of the burden, the dissociated one, recluse, *brāhmaṇa*, the purified one, knower of the lore, highest brahmin, Consummate One, one who has attained (knowledge), has sloughed off, conqueror, the man tranquillized who arouses tranquillity. This is the full explanation of Consummate One.

THREE KINDS OF STREAM-ENTRANT

Here, if a Stream-entrant does not endeavour further in this life, he falls into one of three classes. The three classes of Stream-entrants are: *ekabījin* (one-seeder), *sattakkhattuparama* (one who will be born seven times at most), *kolaṅkola* (one who will be born in good families).

Sattakkhattuparama is of weak faculty; *kolaṅkola* is of middling faculty; and *ekabījin* is of keen faculty.

Sattakkhattuparama: After dwelling in divine-realms (for six births), he, in his seventh birth, is born here, and makes an end of ill.

Kolaṅkola: He is born in a good family three or four* times, and makes an end of ill.

Ekabījin: With one more birth as a man, he makes an end of ill.

If a Once-returner does not make further endeavour in this life, he returns to this world once more, and makes an end of ill.[1]

FIVE KINDS OF NON-RETURNER

If a Non-returner makes no further endeavour in this life. he will be reborn in a Pure Abode.[2] According to the difference of faculties, there are five kinds of Non-returners: *Antarā parinibbāyin*, *upahacca parinibbāyin*, *asaṅkhāra parinibbāyin*, *sasaṅkhāra parinibbāyin*, *uddhaṁsota Akaniṭṭhagāmin*. Here, he who makes the Ariyan Path mainfest in order to remove the remaining fetters and latencies and passes away without reaching the middle of his life-span is *antarā parinibbāyin*. He who makes the Ariyan Path manifest, in order to remove the remaining fetters and latencies, and passes away after reaching the middle of his life-span, is *upahacca parinibbāyin*. He who makes the Ariyan Path manifest, in order to remove the remaining fetters and latencies without external stimulus, is *asaṅkhāra parinibbāyin*. He who makes the Ariyan Path manifest, in order to remove the remaining fetters and latencies

---

* Evidently a copyist's error. Should be two or three.

1. A. I, 233: *So tiṇṇaṁ saṁyojanānaṁ parikkhayā sattakkhattuparamo hoti sattakkhattuparamaṁ deve ca mānuse ca sandhāvitvā saṁsaritvā dukkhassa antaṁ karoti. So tiṇṇaṁ saṁyojanānaṁ parikkhayā kolaṅkolo hoti dve vā tiṇi vā kulāni sandhāvitvā saṁsaritvā dukkhassa antaṁ karoti. So tiṇṇaṁ saṁyojanānaṁ parikkhayā ekabījī hoti ekaṁ yeva mānusakaṁ bhavaṁ nibbattevā dukkhassa antaṁ karoti. So tiṇṇaṁ saṁyojanānaṁ parikkhayā rāgadosamohānaṁ tanuttā sakadāgāmī hoti sakid eva imaṁ lokaṁ āgantvā dhukkhassa antaṁ karoti.*
2. D. III, 237: *Pañca suddhāvāsā. Avihā, Atappā, Sudassā, Sudassī, Akaniṭṭhā.*

with external stimulus, is *sasaṅkhāra parinibbāyin*. From *Avihā* he goes to *Atappā*; from *Atappā* he goes to *Sudassā* from *Sudassā* he goes to *Sudassī*; from *Sudassī* he goes to *Akaniṭṭhā*. In *Akaniṭṭhā* he makes the Ariyan Path manifest in order to remove the remaining fetters and latencies, and passes away. This is the *uddhaṁsota Akaniṭṭhagāmin*.[1] The life-span in *Avihā* is ten thousand aeons; in *Atappā*, twenty thousand; in *Sudassā*, forty thousand; in *Sudassi*, eighty thousand; and in *Akaniṭṭhā*, one hundred and sixty thousand.[2] In each of the four spheres there are five persons, and in the *Akaniṭṭhā*, four. There, the up-stream-goer is not. Thus there are twenty-four persons.

The Consummate One has removed all defilements. No more has he. Therefore there is no cause of future birth in him. Because he has no cause, he is free from becoming. He destroys the formations. He cuts off ill. He stirs up no more ill. This verily is the end of ill. Therefore it is taught in the stanza thus:

SIMILE OF THE FIERY SPARKS

As when a smith beats red-hot iron to shape,
sparks fly, fall into water, and then cease;
so is his ending wrought in sequence true,
and of his faring-on there is no trace.

Escaping thus and breaking himself loose
from lust, and tangle and corruptions base,
he gains the blissful state immovable,
and of his faring-on there is no trace.[3]

---

1. D. III, 237: *Pañca anāgāmino. Antarā-parinibbāyī, upahaccaparinibbāyī, asaṁkhāra-parinibbāyī, sasaṁkhāra-parinibbāyī, uddhaṁsoto Akaniṭṭha-gāmī.* (= *Anāgāmisu āyuno majjhaṁ anatikkamitvā antarā va kilesa-parinibbānaṁ arahattaṁ patto antarā-parinibbāyī nāma. Majjhaṁ upahacca atikkamitvā patto upahacca-parinibbāyī nāma. Asaṅkhārena appayogena akilamanto sukhena patto asaṅkhāra-parinibbāyī nāma. Sasaṅkhārena sappayogena kilamanto dukkhena patto sasaṅkhāra-parinibbāyī nāma. Ime cattāro pañcasu pi suddh' āvāsesu labbhanti.*

   Uddhaṁ-soto Akaniṭṭha-gāmī ti ettha pana catukkaṁ veditabbaṁ. Yo hi avihato paṭṭhāya cattāro devaloke sodhetvā Akaniṭṭhaṁ gantvā parinibbāyati, ayaṁ uddhaṁsoto Akaniṭṭha-gāmī nāma. Yo avihato paṭṭhāya dutiyaṁ vā tatiyaṁ vā catutthaṁ vā devalokaṁ gantvā parinibbāyati, ayaṁ uddhaṁ-soto na Akaniṭṭha-gāmī nāma. Yo kāma-bhavato ca Akaniṭṭhesu nibbattetvā parinibbāyati, ayaṁ na uddhaṁ-soto Akaniṭṭha-gāmī nāma. Yo heṭṭhā catusu devalokesu tattha tatth' eva nibbattitvā parinibbāyati, ayaṁ na uddhaṁ-soto na Akaniṭṭha-gāmī ti—Sv. III, 1029-30).
2. Possibly a copyist's error. The life-span in these heavens should be—one thousand, two thousand, four thousand, eight thousand, sixteen thousand respectively. Cp. Vbh. 425: *Avihānaṁ devānaṁ kittakaṁ āyuppamāṇaṁ? Kappasahassaṁ. Atappānaṁ devānaṁ kittakaṁ āyuppamāṇaṁ? Dve kappasahassāni. Sudassānaṁ devānaṁ kittakaṁ āyuppamāṇaṁ? Cattāri kappasahassāni. Sudassinaṁ devānaṁ kittakaṁ āyuppamāṇaṁ? Aṭṭha kappasahassāni. Akaniṭṭhānaṁ devānaṁ kittakaṁ āyuppamāṇaṁ? Soḷasa kappasahassāni.*
3. Ud. 93: *Ayoghanahatass' eva jalato jātavedasso*
   anupubbūpasantassa yathā na ñāyate gati,
   evaṁ sammāvimuttānaṁ kāmabandhoghatārinaṁ
   paññāpetuṁ gati n'atthi pattānaṁ acalaṁ sukhan ti.

MISCELLANEOUS TEACHINGS*

The following are the miscellaneous teachings here: insight, initial application of thought, joy, feeling, plane, faculty, emancipation, defilements, two attainments in concentration.

SERENITY AND INSIGHT

Insight is of two kinds, namely, of the method of serenity and of bare insight. *Q.* What is insight by way of serenity? Having acquired concentration, one overcomes the hindrances by concentration-strength, and one understands form after one penetrates name by way of the factors of meditation, *jhāna*. Here beginning with concentration one proceeds to insight.

Bare insight: One overcomes the hindrances through understanding-strength. One discerns name after form has been penetrated by way of the bodily formations. Beginning with insight, he develops serenity.[1]

INITIAL APPLICATION OF THOUGHT AND BARE INSIGHT

Bare insight is with initial application of thought. In the first meditation, *jhāna*, the Path and the Fruit of insight are with initial application of thought. In the third meditation, *jhāna*, insight and adoption are with initial application of thought, and the Path and the Fruit are without initial application of thought. The Path in the plane of initial application of thought fulfils the eight factors of the Path. In the plane that is without initial application of thought, seven factors remove consideration.

---

* The section preceding this, owing to unintelligibility, is untranslated.

1. (a) A. II, 157; Pts. II, 92-6: *Idh' āvuso bhikkhu samathapubbaṅgamaṁ vipassanaṁ bhāveti, tassa samathapubbaṅgamaṁ vipassanaṁ bhāvayato maggo sañjāyati. So taṁ maggaṁ āsevati bhāveti bahulīkaroti, tassa taṁ maggaṁ āsevato bhāvayato bahulīkaroto saññojanāni pahīyanti, anusayā byantihonti.*

   Puna ca paraṁ āvuso bhikkhu vipassanāpubbaṅgamaṁ samathaṁ bhāveti, tassa vipassanāpubbaṅgamaṁ samathaṁ bhāvayato maggo sañjāyati. So taṁ maggaṁ āsevati . . . ; tassa taṁ maggaṁ āsevato . . . anusayā byantihonti. . .

   ‡ *Kathaṁ samathapubbaṅgamaṁ vipassanaṁ bhāveti? Nekkhamma-vasena cittassa ekaggatā avikkhepo samādhi, tattha jāte dhamme aniccato anupassanaṭṭhena vipassanā, dukkhato anupassanaṭṭhena vipassanā, anattato anupassanaṭṭhena vipassanā. Iti paṭhamaṁ samatho, pacchā vipassanā; tena vuccati—samathapubbaṅgamaṁ vipassanaṁ bhāveti. . .*

   ‡‡ *Kathaṁ vipassanāpubbaṅgamaṁ samathaṁ bhāveti? Aniccato anupassanaṭṭhena vipassanā, dukkhato anupassanaṭṭhena vipassanā, anattato anupassanaṭṭhena vipassanā; tattha jātānaṁ dhammānañ ca vossaggārammaṇatā cittassa ekaggatā avikkhepo samādhi. Iti paṭhamaṁ vipassanā pacchā samatho; tena vuccati—vipassanāpubbaṅgamaṁ samathaṁ bhāveti.*

   (b) *Nekkhamma* is explained as *kāmānaṁ nissaraṇaṁ*—(1) A. III, 245: *Idha bhikkhave bhikkhuno kāmaṁ manasikaroto kāmesu cittaṁ na pakkhandati, na ppasīdati na santiṭṭhati na vimuccati, nekkhammaṁ kho pan' assa manasikaroto nekkhamme cittaṁ pakkhandati pasīdati santiṭṭhati vimuccati. Tassa taṁ cittaṁ sukataṁ subhāvitaṁ suvuṭṭhitaṁ suvimuttaṁ suvisaṁyuttaṁ kāmehi, ye ca kāmapaccayā uppajjanti āsavā vighātapariḷāhā, mutto so tehi, na so taṁ vedanaṁ vediyati. Idam akkhātaṁ kāmānaṁ nissaraṇaṁ.* (2) It. 61: *Kāmānam-etaṁ nissaraṇaṁ yad-idaṁ nekkhammaṁ.*

JOY

At first the bare insight worker experiences the suffering of the formations. Through adaptive knowledge of insight he fulfils non-suffering, and develops adoption. The Path and the Fruit bring about joy together. Then the bare insight worker gains perfection of the ease of the formations. In the second meditation, *jhāna*, insight and Path and Fruit bring about joy. In the third and the fourth meditations, *jhānas*, insight, Path and Fruit bring about joy. In the Path and the Fruit of the plane of joy, the seven enlightenment factors arise. The six kinds of enlightenment in the plane of non-joy remove the enlightenment-initial-application-of-thought that is joy.

FEELING

At first the bare insight worker experiences the suffering of the formations. Insight and adaptive knowledge bring about equanimity. Adoption, the Path and the Fruit bring about joy. Then the bare insight worker gains perfection of the ease of the formations. In the third meditation (*jhāna*), insight, the Path and the Fruit bring about joy. In the fourth meditation (*jhāna*), insight, the Path and the Fruit bring about equanimity.

PLANE

There are two kinds of planes: plane of seeing and plane of volition. Here, the Path of Stream-entrance is the plane of seeing. The other three Paths and the four Fruits of the recluse are the plane of volition. Not having seen before, one sees now. This is the plane of seeing. One sees

---

(c) Pts.-a. III, 586: *Vossaggārammaṇatā 'ti ettha vossaggo nibbānaṁ. Nibbānaṁ hi saṅkhatavossaggato pariccāgato Vossaggo 'ti vutto, vipassanā ca taṁsampayuttadhammā ca nibbānaninnatāya ajjhāsayavasena nibbāne patiṭṭhitattā nibbānapatiṭṭhā nibbānārammaṇā. Patiṭṭhā 'pi, hi ālambīyatī 'ti ārammaṇaṁ nāma hoti. Nibbāne patiṭṭhanaṭṭhen' eva nibbānārammaṇā. Aññattha pāḷiyam 'pi hi "Patiṭṭhā ārammaṇan" 'ti vuccati, yath' āha: "Seyyathā 'pi āvuso nalāgāraṁ vā tiṇāgāraṁ vā sukkhaṁ kolāpaṁ terovassikaṁ puratthimāya ce 'pi disāya puriso ādittāya tiṇukkāya upasaṅkameyya, labhetha aggi otāraṁ, labhetha aggi ārammaṇaṁ?" 'ti ādi. Tasmā tattha jātānaṁ dhammānaṁ vossaggārammaṇatāya nibbāna-patiṭṭhābhāvena hetubhūtena uppādito yo cittassa ekaggatā-saṅkhāto upacārappaṇābhedo avikkhepo, so Samādhī 'ti vipassanāto pacchā uppādito nibbedhabhāgiyo samādhi niddiṭṭho hoti. Tasmā yeva hi, Iti paṭhamaṁ vipassanā pacchā samatho 'ti vuttaṁ.*

In (x) *samathapubbaṅgama vipassanā* (‡ above) the abandonment (*pahāna*) is of the five hindrances (*pañca nīvaraṇā*) beginning with sense-desire (*kāmacchanda*) by means of the first meditation (*paṭhamajjhāna*). In (y) *vipassanāpubbaṅgama samatha* (‡ ‡ above) the abandonment (*pahāna*) is of all stain (*sabbamala*) by means of the concentration partaking of penetration (*so sabbamalavirahito nibbedhabhāgiyo samādhi sesasamādhito adhikattā adhicittan 'ti vuccati*—Pts.-a. I, 228).

Sometimes the *samatha* in (x) is mistakenly equated with that in (y) because the word used in both instances is serenity (*samatha*). But they are different. While in the one *samatha* of the first meditation (*paṭhamajjhāna*) by way of suppression abandonment is meant, in the other *samatha* of substitution abandonment is meant—Pts. I, 27: *Vikkhambanappahānañ ca nīvaraṇānaṁ paṭhamajjhānaṁ bhāvayato, tadaṅgappahānañ ca diṭṭhigatānaṁ nibbedhabhāgiyaṁ samādhiṁ bhāvayato (→ Tadaṅgappahāṇañ ca diṭṭhigatā-*

thus and attends to it. This is called the plane of volition.[1] And again, there are two planes: the plane of the learner and the plane of the learning-ender. Here, the four Paths and the three Fruits of the recluse are of the plane of the learner. Arahatship is learning-ender's plane.

FACULTIES

There are three supramundane faculties, namely, the faculty which assures knowledge of the unknown, the faculty of perfect knowability and the faculty of him who has known. Here, the knowledge of the Stream-winner's Path is called the faculty which assures knowledge of the unknown. The knowledge of the three (other) Paths and of the (first) three Fruits is called the faculty of perfect knowability. The faculty of him who has known belongs to the plane of Fruition of the Saint. One who knows all *dhammas* without remainder is possessed of the faculty of him who has known.[2]

THE THREE EMANCIPATIONS

Here, there are three kinds, namely, the signless emancipation, the unhankered emancipation and the void emancipation.[3] Here, the absence of

---

naṁ nibbedhabhāgiyaṁ samādhiṁ bhāvayato 'ti diṭṭhigatānaṁ yeva pahānaṁ oḷārikavasena vuttan 'ti veditabbaṁ. Diṭṭhigatā hi oḷārikā, niccasaññādayo sukhumā. Tattha: diṭṭhigatan 'ti diṭṭhi yeva diṭṭhigataṁ, 'gūthagataṁ', 'muttagatan' 'ti ādīni viya. Gantabbabhāvato ca diṭṭhiyā gatamattam ev' etan 'ti 'pi diṭṭhigataṁ, dvāsaṭṭhidiṭṭhisu antogadhattā diṭṭhisu gatan 'ti 'pi diṭṭhigataṁ; bahuvacanena tesaṁ diṭṭhigatānaṁ. Nibbedhabhāgiyaṁ samādhin 'ti vipassanāsampayuttaṁ samādhiṁ—Pts.-a. I, 122).

1. Cp. (a) Peṭaka. 130: *Catasso ariyabhūmiyo, cattāri sāmaññaphalāni, tattha yo yathābhūtaṁ pajānāti, esā dassanabhūmi.*

(b) Netti 8: *Imāhi dvihi paññāhi manasikārasampayuttassa yaṁ ñāṇaṁ uppajjati dassanabhūmiyaṁ vā bhāvanābhūmiyaṁ vā, ayaṁ bhāvanāmayī paññā, parato ghosā sutamayī paññā, paccattasamuṭṭhitā yonisomanasikārā cintāmayī paññā, yaṁ parato ca ghosena paccattasamuṭṭhitena ca yonisomanasikārena ñāṇaṁ uppajjati, ayaṁ bhāvanāmayī paññā.*

Ibid. 14: *Tīṇi ca saccāni saṁkhatāni nirodhadhammāni: dukkhaṁ, samudayo, maggo. Nirodho asaṁkhato.*

Tattha samudayo dvisu bhūmisu pahiyyati: dassanabhūmiyā ca bhāvanābhūmiyā ca.

Dassanena tīṇi saṁyojanāni pahiyyanti: sakkāyadiṭṭhi, vicikicchā, sīlabbataparāmāso. Bhāvanāya satta saṁyojanāni pahiyyanti: kāmacchando, byāpādo, rūparāgo, arūparāgo māno, uddhaccaṁ, avijjā ca niravasesā.

Ibid. 50: *Dassanabhūmi niyāmāvakkantiyā padaṭṭhānaṁ. Bhāvanābhūmi uttarikānaṁ phalānaṁ pattiyā padaṭṭhānaṁ.*

2. (a) Ibid 15: *Yaṁ pana evaṁ jānāti: khīṇā me jāti ti idaṁ khaye-ñāṇaṁ, nāparaṁ itthattāyā ti pajānāti idaṁ anuppāde-ñāṇaṁ.*

Imāni dve ñāṇāni aññātāvindriyaṁ.

Tattha yañ ca aññātaññassāmītindriyaṁ yañ ca aññindriyaṁ, imāni aggaphalaṁ arahattaṁ pāpuṇantassa nirujjhanti.

(b) D. III, 219: *Tīn' indriyāni. Anaññātaṁ-ñassāmītindriyaṁ, aññindriyaṁ, aññātāv-indriyaṁ.* (=*Anaññāta-ñassāmī t' indriyan ti: Ito pubbe na aññātaṁ aviditaṁ dhammaṁ jānissāmī ti, paṭipannassa uppannaṁ indriyaṁ sot' āpatti-magga-ñāṇass' etaṁ adhivacanaṁ.*

Aññ'indriyan ti aññābhūtaṁ jānanabhūtaṁ indriyaṁ. Sot'āpatti phalato paṭṭhāya chasu ṭhānesu ñāṇass' etaṁ adhivacanaṁ.

Aññātāv' indriyan ti aññātavīsu jānana-kicca-pariyosāna-pattesu dhammesu indriyaṁ. Arahatta-phalass' etaṁ adhivacanaṁ—Sv. III, 1002).

3. Pts. II, 35: *Tayo' me bhikkhave vimokkhā. Katame tayo? Suññato vimokkho, animitto vimokkho, appaṇihito vimokkho.* (=*Āgamanaṁ pana duvidhaṁ: vipassanāgamanaṁ maggāgamanañ ca. Tattha magge vipassanāgamanaṁ labbhati, phale maggāgamanaṁ.*

the sign in the adoption knowledge of the Path, is the singless emancipation. The absence of hankering is unhankered emancipation. The absence of attachment is void emancipation. And again, these three emancipations fulfil different Paths through penetration; and they fulfil one Path through attainment.

Q. How do these fulfil different Paths through penetration? *A.* Through impermanence-penetration, the signless emancipation is fulfilled. Through ill-penetration, the unhankered emancipation is fulfilled. Through not-self-penetration, void emancipation is fulfilled.

Q. How is the signless emancipation fulfilled through impermanence-penetration? *A.* Attention to impermanence destroys the formations, and emancipates the mind in many ways. Thus faith and the other four faculties are got. And the knowledge of the thus-isness of the sign makes manifest the impermanence of all compounded things, arouses fear of the sign of the formations and, through proceeding in the signless, surpasses the sign through the emancipation that is without sign: and the release from the aggregates takes place. Thus the signless emancipation is fulfilled through impermanence-penetration.

Q. How is the unhankered emancipation fulfilled through ill-penetration? *A.* Attention to ill develops fear towards the formations and emancipates the mind in many ways. Thus concentration and the four other faculties are got. And the knowledge of the thus-isness of birth makes manifest the ill of all compounded things, arouses fear towards birth, gains the knowledge of birth and, proceeding in the birthless, surpasses birth through the emancipation that is without hankering; and the release from the aggregates takes place. Thus the unhankered emancipation is fulfilled through ill-penetration.

Q. How is the void emancipation fulfilled through not-self-penetration? *A.* Attention to Not-self makes manifest the voidness of the formations and stirs up aversion for them. Thus wisdom and the four other faculties are got. And the knowledge of the thus-isness of the faculties and of birth make manifest the not-self of all compounded things. Liberating itself from the sign and birth, the mind, proceeding along the signless, the birthless, goes beyond to breaking-up and *Nibbāna*, through the emancipation that is void; and the release from the aggregates takes place. Thus through not-self-penetration, the void emancipation is fulfilled. Thus do these three emancipations fulfil different Paths through penetration.

Anattānupassanā hi suññatā nāma, suññatavipassanāya maggo suññato, suññatamaggassa phalaṁ suññataṁ. Aniccānupassanā animittā nāma, animittānupassanāya maggo animitto. Idaṁ pana nāmaṁ Abhidhammapariyāyena labbhati; Suttantapariyāyena na labbhati. Tatha hi "Gotrabhūñāṇaṁ animittaṁ nibbāṇaṁ ārammaṇaṁ katvā animitta-nāmakaṁ hutvā sayaṁ āgamaniyaṭṭhāne ṭhatvā maggassa nāmaṁ deti" 'ti vadanti. Tena maggo animitto 'ti vutto. Maggāgamanena phalaṁ animittan 'ti yujjati yeva. Dukkhānupassanā saṅkhāresu paṇidhiṁ sukkhāpetvā āgatattā appaṇihitā nāma. Appaṇihitavipassanāya maggo appaṇihito,. appaṇihitamaggassa phalaṁ appaṇihitan 'ti evam vipassanā attano nāmaṁ maggassa deti, maggo phalassā 'ti idaṁ āgamanato nāmaṁ nāma. Evaṁ saṅkhārupekkhā vimokkhavisesaṁ niyameti 'ti—Pts.-a. III, 551).

Q. How do these three emancipations fulfil one Path through penetration? *A*. With the signless emancipation, three emancipations are gained. Owing to the signless, there is emancipation of the mind. Although emancipation is gained, there is hankering left, yet; therefore unhankered emancipation is won. Thus the three emancipations are fulfilled. Through attention (to impermanence etc.) emancipation of the mind is gained. Through emancipation from the sign and attachment, void emancipation is won and the three emancipations are fulfilled; because if emancipation from attachment is fulfilled, it also is emancipation due to attention to the sign. Thus after attaining to the three emancipations the one Path is fulfilled.

EMANCIPATION AND THE ENTRANCE INTO IT

Q. What is the difference between emancipation and the entrance into emancipation? *A*. The freedom from the defilements that cloud Path-knowledge is emancipation. The entry into the sublime way [460] is entrance into emancipation. Again emancipation is only Path-knowledge; its object which is *Nibbāna* is called the entering into emancipation.

ONE HUNDRED AND THIRTY-FOUR DEFILEMENTS

There are one hundred and thirty-four defilements. They are the three immoral roots, the three kinds of seeking, the four cankers, the four knots, the four floods, the four yokes, the four clingings, the four wrong courses of action, the five kinds of meanness, the five hindrances, the six roots of contention, the seven latencies, the eight worldly conditions, the nine conceits, the ten defilements, the ten courses of immoral action, the ten fetters, the ten errors, the twelve reversals, the twelve risings of immoral consciousness.

THREE IMMORAL ROOTS

Here, the three immoral roots are lust, hatred and delusion.[1] (Of these three), hatred is thinned in two Paths. It perishes without remainder in the Path of Non-return. Lust and delusion are thinned in three Paths. They perish without remainder in the Path of Saintship.

THE THREE KINDS OF SEEKING

The three kinds of seeking are the seeking for pleasure, for existence and for holiness.[2] Of these three, the seeking for holiness is destroyed without remainder in the Path of Stream-entrance. The seeking for pleasure is destroyed in the Path of Non-return. And the seeking for existence is destroyed in the Path of Saintship.

---

1. D. III, 214: *Tiṇi akusala mūlāni. Lobho akusala-mūlaṁ, doso akusala-mūlaṁ, moho akusala-mūlaṁ.*
2. Ibid. 216: *Tisso esanā. Kāmesanā, bhavesanā, brahmacariyesanā.*

THE FOUR CORRUPTIONS

The four cankers are the canker of lust, of becoming, of views and of ignorance.[1] Here, the canker of views is destroyed through the Path of Stream-entrance; the canker of lust is destroyed through the Path of Non-return; the cankers of becoming and ignorance are destroyed through the Path of Saintship.

THE FOUR KNOTS

The four knots are the knot of the group of covetousness, the knot of the group of ill will, the knot of the group of addiction to rites and ceremonies and the knot of the group of the obsession that "this is the truth".[2]

Here, the knots of the group of addiction to rites and ceremonies and the knot of the group of the obsession that "this is the truth" are cut through the Path of Stream-entrance. The knot of the group of ill will is cut through the Path of Non-return. The knot of the group of covetousness is cut through the Path of Saintship.

THE FOUR FLOODS

The four floods are the flood of lust, the flood of becoming, the flood of views and the flood of ignorance.[3]

THE FOUR YOKES

The four yokes are the yoke of lust, the yoke of becoming, the yoke of views and the yoke of ignorance.[4] These are destroyed as it was taught before.

THE FOUR CLINGINGS

The four clingings are the clinging of lust, of views, of addiction to rites and ceremonies and of the theory of self.[5] Here, three clingings are destroyed in the Path of Stream-entrance. The clinging of lust is destroyed in the Path of Saintship.

---

1. ~~D. III, 216: *Tayo āsavā. Kāmāsavo, bhavāsavo, avijjāsavo*~~. See correction - last page.
2. Ibid. 230: *Cattāro ganthā. Abhijjhā kāya-gantho, vyāpādo kāya-gantho, sīlabbata-parāmāso kāya-gantho, idaṁ-saccābhiniveso kāya-gantho.* (=*Ganthana-vasena ganthā. Vaṭṭasmiṁ nāma-kāyañ c'eva rūpa-kāyañ ca ganthati bandhati palibuddhatī ti kāya-gantho. Idaṁ saccābhiniveso ti: Idam eva saccaṁ mogham aññan ti, evaṁ pavatto diṭṭhi-niveso*— Sv. III, 1024).
3. Ibid. : *Cattāro oghā. Kāmogho, bhavogho, diṭṭhogho, avijjhogo.*
4. Ibid. : *Cattāro yogā. Kāma-yogo, bhava-yogo, diṭṭhi-yogo, avijjā-yogo.*
5. Ibid. : *Cattāri upādānani. Kāmūpādānaṁ, diṭṭhūpādānaṁ, sīlabbatūpādānaṁ, attavādūpādānaṁ.*

THE FOUR WRONG COURSES OF ACTION

The four wrong courses of action are the wrong course of action of desire, the wrong course of action of anger, the wrong course of action of fear and the wrong course of action of delusion.[1] These four are cut in the Path of Stream-entrance.

THE FIVE KINDS OF MEANNESS

The five kinds of meanness are, namely, meanness as to dwelling, family, gain, colour and doctrine.[2] These five are destroyed through the Path of Non-return.

THE FIVE HINDRANCES

The five hindrances are sense-desire, ill will, rigidity and torpor, agitation and anxiety, and uncertainty.[3] Here uncertainty is destroyed through the Path of Stream-entrance; sense-desire, ill will and anxiety are destroyed through the Path of Non-Return; rigidity and agitation are destroyed through the Path of Saintship. Torpor goes together with the form.

THE SIX ROOTS OF CONTENTION

The six roots of contention are quarrelsomeness, envy, jealousy, craft, evil desires and infection of views.[4] Here, craft, evil desires and infection of views are destroyed in the Path of Stream-entrance. Quarrelsomeness, envy and jealousy are destroyed through the Path of Non-Return.

---

1. D. III, 228: *Cattāri agati-gamanāni. Chandāgatiṁ gacchati, dosāgatiṁ gacchati, mohāgatiṁ gacchati, bhayāgatiṁ gacchati.*
2. Ibid. 234: *Pañca macchariyāni. Āvāsa-macchariyaṁ, kula-macchariyaṁ, lābha-macchariyaṁ, vaṇṇa-macchariyaṁ, dhamma-macchariyaṁ.*
3. Ibid. : *Pañca nivaraṇāni. Kāmacchandha-nivaraṇaṁ, vyāpāda-nivaraṇaṁ, thīna-middha-nivaraṇaṁ, uddhacca-kukkucca-nivaraṇaṁ, vicikicchā-nivaraṇaṁ.*
4. Ibid. 246-47: *Cha vivāda-mūlāni. Idh' āvuso bhikkhu kodhano hoti upanāhī. Yo so āvuso bhikkhu kodhano hoti upanāhī, so Satthari pi agāravo viharati appaṭisso, Dhamme pi agāravo viharati appaṭisso, Saṁghe pi agāravo viharati appaṭisso, sikkhāya pi na paripūra-kāri hoti. Yo so āvuso bhikkhu Satthari agāravo viharati appaṭisso, Dhamme agāravo viharati appaṭisso, Saṁghe agāravo viharati appaṭisso, sikkhayā na paripūra-kārī, so Saṁghe vivādaṁ janeti. Yo so hoti vivādo bahujana-ahitāya bahujana-asukhāya bahu-janassa anatthāya ahitāya dukkhāya deva-manussānaṁ. Evarūpañ ce tumhe āvuso vivāda mūlaṁ ajjhataṁ vā bahiddhā vā samanupasseyyātha, tarta tumhe āvuso tass' eva pāpakassa vivāda-mūlassa pahānāya vāyameyyātha. Evarūpañ ce tumhe āvuso vivāda-mūlaṁ ajjhattaṁ vā bahiddhā vā na samanupasseyyātha, tatra tumhe āvuso tass' eva pāpakassa vivāda-mūlassa āyatiṁ anavassavāya paṭipajjeyyātha. Evam etassa pāpakassa vivāda-mūlassa pahānaṁ hoti, evam etassa pāpakassa vivāda-mūlassa āyatiṁ anavassavo hoti. Puna ca paraṁ āvuso bhikkhu makkhī hoti paḷāsī . . . issukī hoti maccharī . . . saṭho hoti māyāvī . . . pāpiccho hoti micchā-diṭṭhi . . . sandiṭṭhi-parāmāsī hoti ādhāna-gāhī duppaṭinissaggī. Yo so āvuso bhikkhu sandiṭṭhi-parāmāsī hoti ādhāna-gāhī duppaṭinissaggī, so Satthari pi agāravo viharati appaṭisso, Dhamme pi agāravo viharati appaṭisso, Saṁghe . . . pe . . . sikkhāya na paripūra-kārī hoti. Yo so āvuso bhikkhu Satthari agāravo viharati appaṭisso, Dhamme . . . Saṁghe . . . sikkhāya na paripūra-kārī, so Saṁghe vivādaṁ janeti. Yo so hoti vivādo*

THE SEVEN LATENCIES

The seven latencies are the latency of sense-desire, the latency of anger, the latency of conceit, the latency of views, the latency of uncertainty, the latency of the desire for becoming and the latency of ignorance.[1] Here, the latencies of views and uncertainty are destroyed through the Path of Stream-entrance. The latency of sense-desire and the latency of anger are destroyed through the Path of Non-Return. The latency of conceit, the latency of desire for becoming and the latency of ignorance are destroyed through the Path of Saintship.

THE EIGHT WORLDLY CONDITIONS

The eight worldly conditions are gain, loss, disgrace, fame, praise, blame, pain and pleasure.[2] Here, the resentment produced by the four kinds of places one dislikes, is destroyed through the Path of Non-Return. The inclination for the four kinds of places one likes, is destroyed through the Path of Saintship.

THE NINE CONCEITS

One produces the conceit: "I am superior to others who are superior"; or one produces the conceit: "I am equal to the superior ones"; or one produces the conceit: "I am inferior to the superior ones;" or one produces the conceit: "I am superior to others who are like me;" or one produces the conceit: "I am inferior to others who are like me;" or one produces the conceit: "I am superior to those who are inferior;" or one produces the conceit: "I am equal to those who are inferior;" or one produces the conceit: "I am inferior to others who are inferior".[3] These nine conceits are destroyed through the Path of Saintship.

---

bahujana-ahitāya bahujana-asukhāya bahujanassa anatthāya ahitāya dukkhāya deva-manussānaṁ. Evarūpañ ce tumhe āvuso vivāda-mūlaṁ ajjhattaṁ vā bahiddhā vā samanu-passeyyātha, tatra tumhe āvuso tass' eva pāpakassa vivāda-mūlassa pahānāya vāyam-eyyātha. Evarūpañ ce tumhe āvuso vivāda-mūlaṁ ajjhattaṁ vā bahiddhā vā na samanupas-seyyātha, tatra tumhe āvuso tass' eva pāpakassa vivāda-mūlassa āyatiṁ anavassavāya paṭipajjeyyātha. Evam etassa pāpakassa vivāda-mūlassa pahānaṁ hoti, evam etassa pāpa-kassa vivāda-mūlassa āyatiṁ anavassavo hoti.

1. D. III, 254: Satta anusayā. Kāmarāgānusayo, paṭighānusayo, diṭṭhānusayo, vicikicchā-nusayo, mānānusayo, bhavarāgānusayo, avijjānusayo.
2. Ibid. 260: Aṭṭha loka-dhammā. Lābho ca alābho ca yaso ca ayaso ca nindā ca pasaṁsā ca sukhañ ca dukkhañ ca.
3. Vbh. 389-90: Tattha katame navavidhā mānā?

   Seyyassa seyyo 'ham asmīti māno.
   Seyyassa sadiso 'ham asmīti māno.
   Seyyassa hīno 'ham asmīti māno.
   Sadisassa seyyo 'ham asmīti māno.
   Sadisassa sadiso 'ham asmīti māno.
   Sadisassa hīno 'ham asmīti māno.
   Hīnassa seyyo 'ham asmīti māno.
   Hīnassa sadiso 'ham asmīti māno.
   Hīnassa hīno 'ham asmīti māno.

THE TEN DEFILEMENTS

The ten defilements are greed, hatred, delusion, conceit, views, uncertainty, rigidity, agitation, immodesty, indecorum.[1] Here, views and uncertainty are destroyed through the Path of Stream-entrance. Hatred is destroyed through the Path of Non-return. The other seven are destroyed through the Path of Saintship.

(And again, there are these) ten defilements: Here one thinks: "This man opposed me, opposes me, will oppose me"; or one thinks: "This man opposed those who are dear to me, is opposing them, will oppose them"; or he thinks: "This man supported my enemy, is supporting him, will support him"; and he produces what is improper. These ten defilements are destroyed by the Path of Non-return.

THE TEN COURSES OF UNSKILFUL ACTIONS

The ten courses of unskilful action are: Taking the life of beings, taking what is not given, fornication, lying, slanderous talk, harsh talk, frivolous talk, covetousness, ill will, wrong views.[2] Here, the taking of life, of what is not given, fornication, lying and wrong views are destroyed by the Path of Stream-entrance. Slanderous talk, harsh talk, ill will are destroyed by the Path of Non-return. Frivolous talk and covetousness are destroyed by the Path of Saintship.

THE TEN FETTERS

The ten fetters are sensuous-desire, ill will, conceit, self-illusion, uncertainty, addiction to rites and ceremonies, desire for existence, envy, avarice and ignorance.[3] Here, self-illusion, uncertainty, addiction to rites and ceremonies are destroyed through the Path of Stream-entrance. Sensuous-desire, ill will, envy, and avarice are destroyed through the Path of Non-return. Conceit, desire for existence and ignorance are destroyed through the Path of Saintship.

THE TEN ERRORS

The ten errors are wrong view, wrong thought, wrong speech, wrong action, wrong, livelihood wrong exertion, wrong mindfulness, wrong con-

---

1. Vbh. 341: *Katame te sattā mahārajakkhā?*
Dasa kilesavatthūni: lobho doso moho māno diṭṭhi vicikicchā thīnaṁ uddhaccaṁ ahirikaṁ anottappaṁ. Yesaṁ sattānaṁ imāni dasa kilesavatthūni āsevitāni bhāvitāni bahulīkatāni ussadagatāni: ime te sattā mahārajakkhā.
2. D. III, 269: *Dasa akusala-kammapathā. Pāṇātipāto, adinnādānaṁ, kāmesu micchācāro, musā-vādo, pisuṇā vācā, pharusā vācā, samphappalāpo, abhijjhā, vyāpādo, micchādiṭṭhi.*
3. Dhs. 197, par. 1113: *Dasa saññojanāni—kāmarāgasaññojanaṁ paṭighasaññojanaṁ mānasaññojanaṁ diṭṭhisaññojanaṁ vicikicchāsaññojanaṁ sīlabbataparāmāsasaññojanaṁ bhavarāgasaññojanaṁ issāsaññojanaṁ macchariyasaññojanaṁ avijjāsaññojanaṁ.*

centration, wrong knowledge, wrong emancipation.[1] Here wrong view, wrong speech in the sense of lying, (wrong) action, wrong livelihood, wrong knowledge and wrong emancipation are destroyed through the Path of Stream-entrance. Wrong thought, wrong speech in the sense of slanderous talk and harsh talk are destroyed by the Path of Non-return. Wrong speech in the sense of frivolous talk, wrong exertion, wrong mindfulness, wrong concentration are destroyed through the Path of Saintship.

THE TWELVE REVERSALS

The twelve reversals are perception-reversal, thought-reversal, and view-reversal by which one regards the impermanent as permanent, the ill as well, the foul as fair and the not-self as self.[2]

Here, the three reversals by which one regards the impermanent as permanent, the three reversals by which one regards the not-self as self, the reversal of view by which one regards the foul as fair and the reversal of view by which one regards ill as well are destroyed through the Path of Stream-entrance. The reversal of perception and the reversal of thought, by which one regards the foul as fair, are destroyed through the Path of Non-return. The reversal of perception and the reversal of thought, by which one regards ill as well, are destroyed by the Path of Saintship.

THE TWELVE ARISINGS OF UNSKILFUL THOUGHT

The twelve arisings of unskilful consciousness are arisings of consciousness without external stimulus and arisings of consciousness with external stimulus, associated with views and accompanied by joy; arisings of consciousness without external stimulus and arisings of consciousness with external stimulus, not associated with views and accompanied by joy; arisings of consciousness without external stimulus and arisings of consciousness with external stimulus, associated with views and accompanied by indifference; arisings of consciousness without external stimulus and arising of consciousness with external stimulus, not associated with views and accompanied by indifference; arisings of consciousness without external stimulus and arisings of consciounsess with external stimulus associated with hatred and accompanied by grief; arisings of consciousness accompanied by excitement; and arisings of consciousness accompanied by uncertainty.[3] Here the four arisings of con-

---

1. Vbh. 391-2: *Tattha katamā dasa micchattā?*
Micchādiṭṭhi micchāsaṁkappo micchāvācā micchākammanto micchā-ājīvo micchāvāyāmo micchāsati micchāsamādhi micchāñāṇaṁ micchāvimutti. Ime dasa micchattā.
2. Pts. II, 80: *Anicce Bhikkhave 'niccan' ti saññāvipallāso cittavipallāso diṭṭhivipallāso, dukkhe Bhikkhave 'sukhan' ti saññāvipallāso cittavipallāso diṭṭhivipallāso, anattani Bhikkhave 'attā' ti saññāvipallāso cittavipallāso diṭṭhivipallāso, asubhe Bhikkhave 'subhan' ti saññāvipallāso cittavipallāso diṭṭhivipallāso.*
Ime kho Bhikkhave cattāro saññāvipallāsā cittavipallāsā diṭṭhivipallasā.
3. (*a*) Dhs. 234, par. 1369: *Katame dhammā akusalā? Dvādasa akusalacittuppādā—ime dhammā akusalā.*

sciousness associated with views and the arisings of consciousness accompanied by uncertainty are destroyed through the Path of Stream-entrance. The two arisings of consciousness which are accompanied (by grief) are thinned out in two Paths and destroyed without remainder through the Path of Non-return. The four arisings of consciousness not associated with views and the arising of consciousness accompanied by excitement are thinned out in three Paths and are destroyed without remainder through the Path of Saintship.

THE TWO ENJOYMENTS

There are two enjoyments. They are the enjoyment of the essence of the Fruit and the enjoyment of the attainment of dissolution which the commoner cannot acquire.

Q. What is the enjoyment of the Fruit? Why is it called enjoyment? Who enter upon it? How does one emerge? Why does one enter upon it? How does one enter upon it? How does one attend? Through how many conditions is it fulfilled? Conditioned by what does it stand? What conditions cause it to arise? Is this enjoyment mundane or supramundane?

ENJOYMENT OF THE FRUIT

A. "What is the enjoyment of the Fruit?": This is recluse Fruit.[1] It is the pacification of the mind in *Nibbāna*. This is called "enjoyment of the Fruit".

Why is it called enjoyment of the Fruit? Because it is the effect of the supramundane Path which is neither skilful nor unskilful. It is not an object. This is enjoyment of the Fruit. Here the Consummate One and the Non-returner enter this concentration.

A SECOND POINT OF VIEW

Again, there is another teaching: All Noble Ones can develop it as taught in the *Abhidhamma* thus: "For the sake of attaining the Path of

---

(*b*) Dhs. 239, par. 1409: *Katame dhammā hīnā? Dvādasa akusalacittuppādā—ime dhammā hīnā.*

(*c*) Vis. Mag. 684: *Akusalacittuppādā ti lobhamūlā aṭṭha, dosamūlā dve, mohamūlā dve ti ime dvādasa.*

(*d*) Abdhs. 1 Ch. 1, par. 2-3: *Tattha cittaṁ tāva catubbidhaṁ hoti kāmāvacaraṁ rūpāvacaraṁ arūpāvacaraṁ lokuttarañ ceti. Tattha katamaṁ kāmāvacaraṁ? Somanassa-sahagataṁ diṭṭhigata-sampayuttaṁ asaṅkhārikam ekaṁ sasṅkhārikam ekaṁ, somanassa-sahagataṁ diṭṭhigata-vippayuttaṁ asaṅkhārikam ekaṁ sasaṅkhārikam ekaṁ, upekkhā-sahagataṁ diṭṭhigata-sampayuttaṁ asaṅkhārikam ekaṁ sasaṅkhārikam ekaṁ, upekkhā-sahagataṁ diṭṭhigata-vippayuttaṁ asaṅkhārikam ekaṁ, sasaṅkhārikam ekan ti, imāni aṭṭha pi lobha-sahagatacittāni nāma. Domanassa-sahagatam paṭigha-sampayuttaṁ asaṅkhārikam ekaṁ sasaṅkhārikam ekan ti, imāni dve pi paṭigha-sampayutta-cittāni nāma. Upekkhā-sahagataṁ vicikicchā-sampayuttam ekaṁ upekkhā-sahagataṁ uddhacca-sampayuttam ekan ti, imāni dve pi momūha-cittāni nāma. Icc evaṁ sabbathā pi dvādasākusala-cittāni samattāni.*

Aṭṭhadhā lobhamūlāni dosamūlāni ca dvidhā
Mohamūlāni ca dve ti dvādasākusalā siyuṁ.

1. *Sāmaññaphala.*

Stream-entrance, it overcomes up-springing. This is called adoption".[1] In the same way the others should be understood.

A THIRD POINT OF VIEW

Again, it is said: "Only those Noble Ones who have extirpated (the cankers) attain to (this) concentration". It is as has been stated in the utterance of the Venerable Elder Nārada to the bhikkhus: "Venerable sirs, it is as if in a forest mount there were a well, with no rope beside it for drawing water. A man sore stricken by the heat of the sun, thirsty and tired, coming there, would merely see the water without reaching it. Even so am I [461] venerable sirs; I know well that the destruction of becoming is *Nibbāna*, but I am not a Consummate One because I have not yet done with the cankers".[2]

THE SIGNLESS CONCENTRATION OF MIND

Why is it entered upon? Having seen the Law, one enters upon it for the sake of dwelling in bliss, as the Blessed One declared to the Venerable

---

1. Pts. I. 68: *Sotapattimaggaṁ paṭilābhatthāya uppādaṁ pavattaṁ nimittaṁ āyuhanaṁ paṭisandhiṁ gatiṁ nibbattiṁ uppattiṁ jātiṁ jaraṁ byādhiṁ maraṇaṁ sokaṁ paridevaṁ upāyāsaṁ bahiddhāsaṅkhāranimittaṁ abhibhuyyatīti gotrabhū.*
2. S. II, 117-18: *Aññatreva āvuso Nārada saddhāya aññatra ruciyā aññatra anussavā aññatra ākāraparivitakkā aññatra diṭṭhinijjhānakkhantiyā aham etam jānāmi aham etam passāmi bhavanirodho nibbānanti.*

   Tenāyasmā Nārado arahaṁ khīṇāsavo ti.

   Bhavanirodho nibbānanti kho me āvuso yathābhūtaṁ sammappaññāya sudiṭṭhaṁ na camhi arahaṁ khīṇāsavo.

   Seyathāpi āvuso kantāramagge udapāno, tatra nevassa rajju na udakavārako. Atha puriso āgaccheyya ghammābhitatto ghammapareto kilanto tasito pipāsito, so taṁ udapānaṁ olokeyya, tassa udakanti hi kho ñāṇaṁ assa na ca kāyena phassitvā vihareyya.

   Evam eva kho āvuso bhavanirodho nibbāṇanti yathābhūtaṁ sammappaññāya sudiṭṭhaṁ na camhi arahaṁ khīṇāsavo ti.

   (=*Aññatr'evā ti, ekacco hi parassa saddahitvā 'yaṁ esa bhaṇati, taṁ bhūtan' ti gaṇhāti. Aparassa nisīditvā cintentassa 'yaṁ kāraṇaṁ ruccati, so atthi etan' ti ruciyā gaṇhāti. Eko cira-kālato paṭṭhāya evaṁ anussavo atthi: 'bhūtam etan'ti anussavena gaṇhāti. Aññassa vitakkayato ekaṁ kāraṇaṁ upaṭṭhāti. So 'atth' etan'ti ākāra-parivitakkena gaṇhāti. Aparassa cintayato ekā diṭṭhi uppajjati. Yassa hi kāraṇaṁ nijjhāyantassa khamati so 'atth' etan' ti diṭṭhi-nijjhāna-khantiyā gaṇhāti. Thero pana pañca pi etāni kāraṇāni paṭikkhipitvā paccāvekkhaṇena paṭividdhabhāvaṁ pucchanto aññatr' eva, āvuso Musīla, saddhāyā ti ādīni āha.*

   Tattha aññatrā ti, saddhādīni kāraṇāni ṭhapetvā. Vinā etehi kāraṇehi ti attho. Bhavanirodho nibbānan ti, pañcakkhandha-nirodho nibbānaṁ....

   Samma-ppaññāya sudiṭṭhan ti, sammā vipassanāya maggaṁ paññāya suṭṭhu diṭṭhaṁ. Na c' amhi arahan ti, anāgāmimagge ṭhitattā arahaṁ na homī ti dīpeti. Yaṁ pan' assa idaṁ bhavanirodho nibbānan ti ñāṇaṁ, taṁ ekūnavīsatiyā paccavekkhaṇa-ñāṇehi vimuttaṁ paccavekkhaṇa-ñāṇaṁ.

   Udapāno ti, vīsa-tiṁsa-hatthā-gambhīro pānīya-kūpo. Udaka-vārako ti, udaka-ussiñcana-vārako. Udakan ti kho ñāṇaṁ assā ti, tīre ṭhitassa olokayato evaṁ ñāṇaṁ bhaveyyā. Na ca kāyena phassitvā ti, udakaṁ pana nīharitvā, kāyena phassitvā, viharituṁ na sakuṇeyya. Udapāne udaka-dassanaṁ viya hi anāgāmino nibbāna-dassanaṁ. Ghammābhitatta-puriso viya anāgāmi. Udaka-vārako viya arahatta-maggo. Yathā ghammābhitatta-puriso udapāne udakaṁ passati, evaṁ anāgāmi paccavekkhaṇa-ñāṇena upari arahatta-phalābhisamayo nāma atthī ti jānāti. Yathā pana so puriso udaka-vārakassa n'atthitāya udakaṁ nīharitvā kāyena phassituṁ na labhati, evaṁ anāgāmī arahatta-maggassa n'atthitāya, nibbānaṁ ārammaṇaṁ katvā, arahatta-phala-samāpattiṁ appetvā nisīdituṁ na labhati ti—Spk. II, 122-23).

Elder Ānanda: "At this time, Ānanda, the Tathāgata does not attend to any sign; he destroys sensation only and dwells developing the concentration of signless consciousness. At this time, Ānanda, the body of the Tathāgata is at peace".[1]

"How does one enter upon it?": *A*. If that yogin wishes to get the enjoyment of Fruition, he enters into a place of solitude, views the formations by way of rise and fall and proceeds to adoptive-knowledge. Adoptive-knowledge brings the enjoyment of the Fruition of *Nibbāna* immediately. The Fruition that arises is of that meditation, *jhāna*, by which he attains to the Path. This is called the enjoyment of Fruition.

"How does one attend?": *A*. The unconditioned element of the Sublime is attended to through tranquillity.

"Through how many conditions is it fulfilled?", "Conditioned by what does it stand?", Through what conditions does one emerge?: *A*. The yogin enjoys it through two conditions: the non-attending to all signs and the attending to the element of the signless.[2] Three are the conditions of persistence: non-attention to all signs; attention to the signless element; previous preparation.[3] Two are the conditions of emergence: attention to all signs and non-attention to the signless element.[4]

"Is this enjoyment mundane or supramundane?": *A*. This enjoyment is supramundane and not mundane.

Q. The Non-returner experiences the enjoyment of Fruition. Why does not adoption develop the Path of Saintship immediately? *A*. Because it does not reach the vision of insight and (that which is present) is of little strength.

The enjoyment of Fruition has ended.

THE ENJOYMENT OF THE DISSOLUTION OF PERCEPTION AND SENSATION

Q. What is the enjoyment of the dissolution of perception and sensation? Who enter upon it? Through the fulfilment of how many kinds of strength is it entered upon? Through the tranquillizing of how many activities is it entered upon? What are the preliminary duties? How is it entered upon? How does it persist? How does the mind emerge from it? Towards what is the mind inclined? By how many kinds of contact is it experienced? What are the activities aroused at first? What is the difference between a dead man

1. D. II, 100: *Yasmiṁ Ānanda samaye Tathāgato sabba-nimittānaṁ amanasikārā ekaccānaṁ vedanānaṁ nirodhā animittaṁ ceto-samādhiṁ upasampajja viharati, phāsukato Ānanda tasmiṁ samaye Tathāgatassa kāyo hoti.*
2. M. I, 296: *Dve kho, āvuso, paccayā animittāya cetovimuttiyā samāpattiyā sabbanmittānañ ca amanasikāro animittāya ca dhātuyā manasikāro ti.*
3. Ibid. 296-97: *Tayo kho, āvuso, paccayā animittāya cetovimuttiyā ṭhitiyā: sabbanimittānañ ca amanasikāro, animittāya ca dhātuyā manasikāro, pubbe ca abhisaṅkhāro.*
4. Ibid. 297: *Dve kho, āvuso, paccayā animittāya cetovimuttiyā vuṭṭhānāya: sabbanimittānañ ca manasikāro, animittāya ca dhātuyā amanasikāro.*

and a man who enters into the concentration of the dissolution of perception and sensation? Is this concentration conditioned or unconditioned? *A.* The not-proceeding of states of mind and mental properties—this is called the concentration of the dissolution of perception and sensation.

"Who enter upon it?": *A.* The Consummate One and the Non-returner enter upon this attainment. Who do not enter upon it? The commoner, the Stream-entrant, the Once-returner and he who is born in the formless element. Here, the commoner cannot enter upon it, because he is not of that plane. The Stream-entrant and the Once-returner cannot, because they have not yet cut off the bondage of the defilements. He who enters the formless element cannot, because it is not its plane.

"Through the fulfilment of how many kinds of strength is it entered upon?": *A.* It is entered upon through the fulfilment of two kinds of strength: serenity-strength and insight-strength. Here "serenity" means: "mastery gained in the eight attainments".[1] "Insight" means: "mastery gained in the seven insights, namely, impermanence-reviewing, ill-reviewing, not-self-reviewing, repulsion-reviewing, dispassion-reviewing, cessation-reviewing, abandonment-reviewing. Serenity-strength develops the factors of the meditation, *jhāna*, of dissolution and develops immovable emancipation. Through insight-strength one is able to see the tribulations of birth, and acquire the Freedom of the Unborn.

"Through tranquillizing how many activities is it entered upon?": *A.* One attains to concentration through the tranquillizing of three activities. They are verbal formations, bodily formations and thought formations. Here, entering into the second meditation, *jhāna*, one tranquillizes the verbal formations of initial and sustained application of thought. Entering into the fourth meditation, *jhāna*, one tranquillizes the bodily formations of inhalation and exhalation. Entering into the concentration of the dissolution of perception and sensation, one removes the thought-formations of perception and sensation.

"What are the preliminary duties?"[2]: *A.* There are four preliminary duties: Non-destruction of others' property, discerning the time, non-disturbance, honouring the Community of Bhikkhus. He resolves as regards bowl, robe and other requisites. He resolves as regards non-disturbance of this body in every way. He reflects on the strength of his body and resolves after discerning the time. Here, he should consider the remote past. Discerning that it is not the time for the meeting of the Community of Bhikkhus, he sits and resolves: "I shall emerge, when I am called". And here the non-destruction of others' property is for the sake of protecting the robes (of others). The second and third are for the sake of protecting the body.

1. *Aṭṭha-samāpatti*
2. Cp. Vis. Mag. 705: *Catubbidhaṁ pubbakiccaṁ karoti: nānā-baddha-avikopanaṁ, saṅghapaṭimānanaṁ, satthu pakkosanaṁ addhānaparicchedan ti.*

The fourth is for the sake of not obstructing the meeting of the Community of Bhikkhus. Thus attaining to the sphere of nothingness and emerging therefrom, he performs the preliminary duties and enters the first meditation, *jhāna*.

Why is it developed? For the sake of happiness in the present. This is the Noble Individual's last immovable concentration. And again, for the sake of supernormal magical power, one enters the whole range of concentration like the Arahant Sañjīva.[1] It is (entered also) for the sake of protecting the body as in the case of the Venerable Elder Sāriputta[2] and in the case of the Venerable Elder Tissa, the son of the Snowy Heron.

---

1. M. I, 333-34: *Bhūtapubbaṁ pāpima āyasmā Sañjīvo aññatarasmiṁ rukkhamūle saññāvedayitanirodhaṁ samāpanno nisinno hoti. Addasāsuṁ kho pāpima gopālakā pasupālakā kassakā pathāvino āyasmantaṁ Sañjīvaṁ aññatarasmiṁ rukkhamūle saññāvedayitanirodhaṁ samāpannaṁ nisinnaṁ, disvāna nesaṁ edatahosi. Acchariyaṁ vata bho, abbhutaṁ vata bho, ayaṁ samaṇo nisinnako va kālakato, handa naṁ dahāmāti. Atha kho te pāpima gopālakā pasupālukā kassakā pathāvino tiṇañ ca kaṭṭhañ ca gomayañ ca saṅkaḍḍhitvā āyasmato Sañjīvassa kāye upacinitvā aggiṁ datvā pakkamiṁsu. Atha kho pāpima āyasmā Sañjīvo tassā rattiyā accayena tāya samāpattiyā vuṭṭhahitvā cīvarāni papphoṭetvā pubbanhasamayaṁ nivāsetvā pattacīvaraṁ ādāya gāmaṁ piṇḍāya pāvisi. Addasāsuṁ kho te pāpima gopālakā pasupālakā kassakā pathāvino āyasmantaṁ Sañjīvaṁ piṇḍāya carantaṁ, disvāna nesaṁ etad ahosi: acchariyaṁ vata bho, abbhutaṁ vata bho, ayaṁ samaṇo nisinnako va kālakato svāyaṁ patisañjīvito ti. Iminā kho etaṁ pāpima pariyāyena āyasmato Sañjīvassa Sañjīvo Sañjīvo tveva samaññā udapādi.*
2. Ud. 39-41: *Tena kho pana samayena āyasmā ca Sāriputto āyasmā ca Mahāmoggallāno Kapoṭakandarāyaṁ viharanti. Tena kho pana samayena āyasmā Sāriputto juṇhāya rattiyā navoropitehi kesehi abbhokāse nisinno hoti aññataraṁ samādhiṁ samāpajjitvā. Tena kho pana samayena dve yakkhā sahāyakā uttarāya disāya dakkhiṇaṁ disaṁ gacchanti kena cid eva karaṇīyena. Addasaṁsu kho te yakkhā āyasmantaṁ Sāriputtaṁ juṇhāya rattiyā navoropitehi kesehi abbhokāse nisinnaṁ, disvā eko yakkho dutiyaṁ yakkhaṁ etad avoca: paṭibhāti maṁ samma imassa samaṇassa sise pahāraṁ dātun ti. Evaṁ vutte so yakkho taṁ yakkhaṁ etad avoca: alaṁ samma, mā samaṇaṁ āsādesi. Uḷāro so samma samaṇo mahiddhiko mahānubhāvo 'ti. Dutiyam pi kho so yakkho . . . dātun ti. Dutiyam pi kho so yakkho taṁ yakkhaṁ etad avoca: alaṁ samma . . . mahānubhavo 'ti. Tatiyam pi kho so yakkho taṁ yakkhaṁ etad avoca: paṭibhāti . . . dātun ti. Tatiyam pi kho so yakkho taṁ yakkhaṁ etad avoca: alaṁ samma . . . mahānubhāvo 'ti. Atha kho so yakkho taṁ yakkhaṁ anādiyitvā āyasmato Sāriputtatherassa sise pahāraṁ adāsi. Api tena pahārena sattaratanaṁ vā aḍḍhaṭṭharatanaṁ vā nāgaṁ osādeyya mahantaṁ vā pabbatakūṭaṁ padāleyya. Atha ca pana so yakkho ḍayhāmi ḍayhāmi 'ti vatvā tatth' eva mahānirayaṁ apatāsi. Addasā kho āyasmā Mahāmoggallāno dibbena cakkhunā visuddhena atikkantamānusakena tena yakkhena āyasmato Sāriputtassa sise pahāraṁ dīyamānaṁ, disvāna yena āyasmā Sāriputto ten' upasaṅkami, upasaṅkamitvā āyasmantaṁ Sāriputtaṁ etad avoca: kacci te āvuso khamanīyaṁ kacci yāpanīyaṁ kacci na kiñci dukkhan ti. Khamanīyaṁ me āvuso Moggallāna yāpanīyaṁ āvuso Moggallāna, api ca me sise thokaṁ ḍukkhan ti. Acchariyaṁ āvuso Sāriputta, abbhutaṁ āvuso Sāriputta, yaṁ tvaṁ mahiddhiko āyasmā Sāriputto mahānubhāvo. Idha te āvuso Sāriputta aññataro yakkho sise pahāraṁ adāsi, tāva mahāpahāro ahosi. Api tena pahārena sattaratanaṁ . . . padāleyyā'ti. Atha ca pan' āyasmā Sāriputto evam āha: khamanīyaṁ me āvuso Moggallāna, yāpanīyaṁ me āvuso Moggallāna, api ca me sīse thokaṁ dukkhan ti. Acchariyaṁ āvuso Moggallāna, abbhutaṁ āvuso Moggallāna, yāva mahiddhiko āyasmā Mahāmoggallāno mahānubhāvo, yatra hi nāma yakkham pi passissati; mayaṁ pan' etarahi Paṁsupisācakam pi na passāmā 'ti. Assosī kho Bhagavā dibbāya sotadhātuyā visuddhāya atikkantamānusikāya tesaṁ ubhinnaṁ mahānāgānaṁ imaṁ evarūpaṁ kathāsallāpaṁ. Atha kho Bhagavā etam atthaṁ viditvā tāyaṁ velāyaṁ imaṁ udānaṁ udānesi:*

   Yassa selūpamaṁ cittaṁ ṭhitaṁ n' ānupakampati
   virattaṁ rajanīyesu kopaneyye na kuppati,
   yass' evaṁ bhāvitaṁ cittaṁ, kuto taṁ dukkham essatī 'ti.

   (—*Aññataraṁ samādhiṁ samāpajjitvā ti tattha aññātaraṁ samādhin ti, upekkhā-brahmavihāra-samāpattiṁ. Keci saññā-vedayita-nirodha-samāpattin ti vadanti. Apare panāhu āruppa-pādakaṁ phala-samāpattin ti. Imā eva hi tisso kāya-rakkhaṇa-samatthā samā'*

"How is it entered upon?": That yogin enters into a solitary dwelling, and sitting down, or lying down, enjoys the consciousness of dissolution. He enters the first meditation, *jhāna*, and merging from it peacefully, sees the impermanence, ill and not-self of that meditation, *jhāna*, immediately. Possessed of the knowledge of equanimity towards the formations,[1] he enters into the second, the third and the fourth meditations, *jhānas*, the sphere of the infinity of space, the sphere of the infinity of consciousness and the sphere of nothingness. Then emerging therefrom peacefully, he sees the impermanence, ill and not-self of Right Concentration immediately, and being possessed of the knowledge of equanimity towards the formations, he enters into the sphere of neither perception nor non-perception immediately. Then passing beyond two or three turns of consciousness, he causes the perishing of mind and enters into the Unborn and the Unmanifest. This is called the entry into the attainment of the dissolution of perception and sensation.

"How does one persist?": Here one does not consider thus: "I shall emerge". In the performance of the preliminary duties, one discerns.

"How does the mind emerge (from it)?": The Non-returner emerges on the attainment of the Fruit of Non-returning. The Consummate One emerges on the attainment of the Fruit of Saintship.

Q. "Towards what is the mind inclined?": *A*. The mind inclines towards peace only.

Q. "By how many kinds of contact is it experienced?": *A*. Through three contacts, namely, the contact of the void, the signless and the unhankered-after.

Through what formations does he emerge? With his bodily formations and his verbal formations.

"What is the difference between a dead man and a man who enters into the attainment of the dissolution of perception and sensation?": In the dead man, not only are three formations stilled, but vitality is cut off, heat is cut off, the faculties are cut off. In the man who has entered the attainment of the dissolution of perception and sensation, although the (three) formations are stilled, vitality, heat and the faculties are not cut off. This is the difference.[2]

"Is this attainment conditioned or unconditioned?": One should not say that this attainment is conditioned or unconditioned. *Q*. Why should it not be said that his attainment is conditioned or unconditioned? *A*. There is no

---

pattiyo. Tattha nirodha-samāpattiyā samādhi-pariyāya sambhavo heṭṭhā vutto yeva. Pacchimass' eva pana ācariyā vaṇṇenti—Ud.-a. 245.).

1. *Saṅkhārupekkhā.*

2. M. I, 296: *Yvāyaṁ āvuso mato kālakato, yo cāyaṁ bhikkhu saññāvedayitanirodhaṁ samāpanno, imesaṁ kiṁ nānākaraṇan ti? Yvāyaṁ āvuso mato kālakato, tassa kāyasaṅkhārā niruddhā paṭippassaddhā, vācisaṅkhārā niruddhā paṭippassadhā, cittasaṅkhārā niruddhā paṭippassaddhā, āyu parikkhīṇo, usmā vūpasantā, indriyāni viparibhinnāni: yo cāyaṁ bhikkhu saññāvedayitanirodhaṁ samāpanno tassa pi kāyasaṅkhārā niruddhā, paṭipassaddhā, vacisaṅkhārā niruddhā paṭippassaddhā, cittasaṅkhārā niruddhā paṭippassaddhā, āyu aparikkhīṇo, usmā avūpasantā, indriyāni vippasannāni. Yvāyaṁ āvuso mato kālakato yo cayaṁ bhikkhu saññāvedayitanirodhaṁ samāpanno, idaṁ tesaṁ nānākaraṇanti.*

put-together state in this attainment. The entry into and exit from the unconditioned state cannot be known. Therefore it cannot be said that this attainment is conditioned or unconditioned.

The Attainment of the Concentration of Dissolution has ended.

The Twelfth Fascicle of the Path of Freedom has ended.

Here the chapters are as follows:—

Introductory Discourse
On Distinguishing Virtue
On Austerities
On Distinguishing Concentration
On Approaching a Good Friend
The Distinguishing of Behaviour
The Distinguishing of the Subjects of Meditation
Entrance into the Subjects of Meditation
Five Kinds of Higher Knowledge
On Distinguishing Wisdom
The Five Methods
The Discernment of Truth

Thus is the sequence of the twelve chapters in the Path of Freedom.

Vast, boundless, past all thought and praise,
are the good words and knowledge set forth here
and none but the yogin knows and grasps
the essence of the Doctrine full and clear.
Best is this Path for skilful deeds;
for it away from ignorance does steer.

INDEX

COMPILED BY Mr. R. D. PIYASENA

PALI INDEX

(*Words and Subjects in Notes*)

aṁsu, 173.
Akaniṭṭha, 112; 309; °gāmi, 5; 309.
akālika, 149.
akuppa, 17; vimutti, 226.
akusala, 37. °kammapatha (*ten*), 318.
°citta (*twelve, in detail*), 320.
°cittuppāda, 319.
°mūlāni (*three*), 279, 314.
agati-gamana (*four*), 316.
agga, 37; 307; °ñña (*etc.*), 188.
aggi, °kkhanda, 299. n'atthi rāgasamo, 281; -homa, 21.
agocara (*in detail*), 19.
Agon, Chu (*Chinese*), 104; 112.
Aggivessana, 145; 189.
aṅga-samatikkama, 121.
acakkhukaraṇa, 80
accāraddha, °viriya, 77; 225-26.
acci, 287-88.
accha, 222.
ajapadadaṇḍa, 290-91.
ajjhupekkhanatā, 81.
añjalikaraṇīya, 151.
aññathā, 278.
aññāpaṭivedha, 65.
aṭṭha, -purisa-puggalā, 151.
aṭṭhi, 204; (*in detail*), 137ff.
aṭṭhika, 63.
aṭṭhita, 37.
aḍḍha, 87. °aṭṭharatana, 324.
aṇḍa, 26; kukkuṭ°, 174.
aṇṇava, mahā udaka°, 276.
Atappā, 112; 309.
ati, °nijjhāyitatta, 226; °līnaviriya, 225-26.
atta, °to 295; 305. °vāda, 294; °saññā, 186; °bhāva, 170; -hita, 289.
attha, 250. °veda, 148;
adinnādāna, 10; 188.
adukkha, 47.
adukkhamasukha, 111.
addhāna-magga-paṭipanna, 219.
adhika, vāta°, semha°, 58.
adhicitta, °sikkhā, 3; 161.
adhiṭṭhāna, 9; (*the four*), 190.
adhipaññā, °sikkhā, 3; 161.
adhipateyya, (*the three*), 13.
adhimutta, tad-, 41.
adhimokkha, 298.
adhivāsana, °sīla, 183.
adhisīla, °sikkhā, 3; 161.
anatta, °ato, 288; 310.
anabhisambuddha, 225.
anamatagga, 204; 261.
anagāriya, 227.
anācāra, kāyika°, vācasika°, 18.
Anāthapiṇḍika, 289.
anācariyaka, 140.
anāgāmi, (*the five*), 309; °magga, 307.
anāvila-saṁkappa, 307.
anicca, °ato, 288; 310.
anibbatta, 170.
animitta, 300; 313.
anukampā, 186.
anuttara, 1; 143.
anudayā, 186.
anupabbajjā, 178.
anupassanā, anatta°, anicca°, dukkha°, 313.
anupassati, (*as* nicca *etc.*), 295.
anupassi(n), anicca°, virāga°, nirodha°, paṭinissagga°, 157.
anupādisesanibbāna, 2.
anupubbavihāra, nava, 40.
anumodanā, 300.
Anuruddha (*Ven. Elder*), 131; 225.
anulomapaṭiloma, jhāna°, 132.
anulomika khanti, 300.
anusaya, 143; 307. 310. (*the seven*), 280; vicikicchā°, diṭṭhi°, 305.
anussati, 178.
anussava. aññatra anussavā *etc.*, 321.
anottappa, 7.
ankura, 261.
anta, 5; (*the two*), 149.
antaravāsaka, 29.
antima. ayam antimā jāti, 226.
andu, 74.
andhakāra, 303; tibb°, 172.
andhakaraṇa, 80.
anna, 173.
apacaya, 234.
aparimāṇa, 188.
aparihīna, 41.
apāna, 156.
apāya, 5; 186; 227.
appanā, 94.
appaṇihita, 313.
appamañña, 194. (*the four*), 63;
appamāda, °ena sampādetha, 131.
appamāṇa, citta, 63.
appameyya, 72.
abhaya, 188.
Abhayagirivāsin, 94.
abhijjhā-domanassa, 78.
Abhidharmakośa, 169.
abhiññā, °vosānapāramippatta, 223.
Abhibhū (sāvaka), 217.
abhisamaya, pahāna°, pariññā°, bhāvanā°, sacchikiriya°, 303.
amata, 147. °ogadha, °pariyosāna, 281; °dvāra, 306.
amba, 18.
Ambaṭṭha, 142.
ayoghana, 309.
arañña, 187; °gata, 157.
arati, 249.
araha, 321.
arahad-dhaja, surattaṁ, 183.
arahatta, 264; -phala, 312; 321; -phala-samāpatti, 321; °magga, 307; 321.
ariya, °sāvaka, 154; 188. -saccāni (*the four*), 5; °dhamma (*the four*), 1.
ariyā, 105.

gati, dug°, 186; 224. su°, 224; 227. (*the five*), 279; 289; 299.
gatta, aru°, pakka°, 174.
gantha (*the four*), 315.
gandhabba, °nagara, 297.
gabbhaseyyaka, 243.
gamana, vipassanā°, magga°, 312.
gambhīra, 49; 263. °avabhāsa, 263.
garu, 49.
gahapati, 25; °cīvara, 28. -parisa 25.
gāma, 185; 206; 207. (*sim*)., 223.
gāvī (*sim.*), 99.
gijjha, 136.
gilāna, bāḷha°, 275.
gihin, 16.
gehasita,
go, °ghātaka, 264. °pālaka, 324.
gocara, 19; 34. ārakkha°, upanibandha°, upanissaya°, 19.
gotrabhū, 302. ñāṇa, 302. (*definition*), 321.
gomaya, 299; 324.
ghosa, parato°, 2; 312.
Ghosita gahapati, 212.

cakkavatti, rājā, 212.
cakkhu, 239. °ndriya, 78. dibba°, 142; 227. °viññāṇa, 239.
cakkhumant, 248.
caṇḍāla, 36. °kumāraka, 25.
caturāpassena, 307.
candima, °suriya, 216.
camara, 26.
cariyā, (*three*), (*fourteen*), 54.
caraṇa, 142.
calana, 161.
cāga, 154. °anussati, 63. mutta°, 154.
cāṭukamyatā, 18.
cātummahāpatha, 81.
citta, aduṭṭha°, 183. (iddhipāda), 44. uddhaccānupatita, 158. rāga-dosa-moha-pariyuṭṭhita, 148. selūpamaṁ cittaṁ, 324. līna°, 158. °visuddhi, 4; 161. samāhita, 142.
cuṇṇa, 18. (*ref. dhātus*), 199.
Cunda (*Ven. Elder*,) 264.
Cunda (*novice*,) 16.
Cullpanthaka (*Ven. Elder*), 215.
ceto, animitta °vimutti, 322. animitta °samādhi, 322. °vasippatta, 201; 215. °vimutti, 275-76. °samādhi, 227. °vivaraṇasappāya, 19.
cela, ādittа°, 283.
cora, 283. °ghātaka, 300
Channa (*Ven. Elder*), 264.
chanda, 283. (iddhipāda), 44.
chambitatta, 225-26.
chaḷanga-samannāgata, 307.
chavi, 204.
Chu Agon (*Chinese*), 48.

janghapesanika, 18.
jacchanda (*sim.*), 250; 284-85.
Jaṭila gahapati, 212.
jarā, 191; 270.
jalati, 281; 303.
jātaveda, 309.
jāti, 270. °dhammato, 300.
jiyā (*sim.*) 204.
jivhā, 240.
jīvikā. parapaṭibaddhā me j., 23.
jegucha, adhimatta°, 172.
Jetavana, 289.
Jotika gahapati, 212.
jhāna, 24. paṭhama°, 2; 41; 83; 100; 114; 189; 311. dutiya°, 47; 101. tatiya°, 47; 90; 105. catuttha°, 47; 110; 120. appanā, 79. °vimokkhapaccavekkhanatā, 81. °visesa, 91. (*the fourfold formula*), 229.

ñāṇa, 298. anāgataṁsa°, 227. anuppāde, 312. anuloma°, 301. anvaye°, 233. āsavakkhaya°, 142. kammavipāka°, kammassakata°, 227. khaye-, 312. cutūpapāta°, 142. cetopariya°, 209. ñāṇesu°, 235. -dassana, 142. dibbacakkhu°, 209; 227. dibbasota°, 209. dukkhe°, dukkhasamudaye°, dukkhanirodhe°, dukkhanirodhagāminiyā paṭipadāya°, 235. dhamme°, 233. dhammaṭṭhiti°, 266; 286. pakati°, 190. paccavekkhaṇa-, 321. paricce°, 233. pubbenivāsānussati°, 142; 209. phalasamaṁgissa°, 233. °paripāka, 215. maggasamaṁgissa°, 233. yathākammūpaga-, 227. saccānulomika°, 233. saṅhkārupekkhā°, 301. sabbaññuta-, 190. sammasane°, (*in detail*), 287. sammuti-, 233. sekha°, 306. hetuphale°, 235. (*various*), 146.

ṭhiti, 162. avaṭ°, 162. °bhāgiya, 15; 97. saṇ°, 162.

ḍahati. ḍayhāmi ḍayhāmī'ti vatvā tath'eva mahānirayaṁ apatāsi, 324.

taca, 204.
taṇhā, 191; 249; 300. (*the three*), 277. rasa°, 22; 279. °kāya (*the six*), 279.
tathā 278.
Tathāgata, 142; 214; 322.
tadaṅgappahāṇa, 311.
tad-adhimuttatā, 81.
tama, 145.
tārakā, osadhi°, 127.
tiṇa, 206; 324. °āgarā (*sim.*), 311.
tiṇṇa, 144.
tipu, vinīla-, 174.
tiro, °kuḍḍa, °bhāva, °pākāra, °pabbata, 215.
Tivarā, 223.
Tissa (*Ven. Elder*), 250.
tīra, orima°, 276; 302; 303. pārima°, 276; 302; 303; 307.
tulādhāra, 249.
Tusita, °pura, °vimāna, 300.
tūlapicu, 214.
tecīvarikaṅga, 27.
teja, 284.
Temiya (Jātaka), 144.
tela, 18. -bindu, 173.
thapati, 17.
thīna, 25.
thīnamiddha, °adhikaranañ ca pana me samādhi cavi, 225.

ratha, 93; 218.
rasa, eka°, 83. rasesu anugiddhassa jhāne na ramatī mano, 205. loṇa°, 83; 294. vimutti°, 83.
rāga, 249. °citta, 97. (*with* dosa, moha) 308. vīta°, 234.
rukkha, 158; 207. °mūlagata, 157. °mūlikaṅga, 27.
ruci. aññatra ruciyā, 321.
rūpa, 275-76. upādā°, 238. -kalāpasantati, 242. piya-, 272. middha°, 238. -saṁgaha (*threefold*), 245. sāta-, 272.
roga (*the two*), 275.
Rohitassā, 223.

lakkhaṇa, 6; 274. °to, 159. sabhāva°, 290.
lajjin, 10.
lapanā, 20.
lava, 169.
lahutaro (*etc.*), 214.
leyya, 205.
loka, °dhammā (*the eight*), 106; 280. °vidū, saṁkhāra-, satta-, 143.
lokuttara, 188.
loma, 171; 174.
loha, °kumbhī, 265.
lohitaka, 63.

Vaṅkaka (*former name of* Vepulla), 223.
Vaṅkatā, 20.
vacana, °kkhama, 49.
vaccha, dhenūpaga (*sim.*), 107.
vaṭṭa, 188.
vaṭṭi, 303.
vaṇṇa, 265. odāta-, 127. nīla-, 124. pīta-, 125. lohitaka-, 126. °to, 159. (*various of* vikubbanā iddhi), 218. (*the four*), 307.
vata, 6; 9.
vatta, 9; 49.
vatthu, °visadakiriyatā, 81.
vadhaka, 299.
vaya, 296. °ato, 161.
varāha, 206.
vasī (*the five*), 100. °bhāva, 140.
vassāna, 38.
vassikasāṭikā, 36.
vācā. Tathāgatassa pacchimā vācā, 131.
vāta, °dhārā, 159. (*various*), 198.
vāri, 296.
vāladhi, 26.
vāsin, Abhayagiri°, 238.
vāyāma, 283.
Vāseṭṭha, 307.
vikkhambana, °ppahāna, 311.
vikkhāyitaka, 63.
vikkhittaka, 63.
vikkhepa, °assa pahānāya, 69; 166.
vicāra, 87-8. anu°, upa°, 87.
vicikicchā, 84; 225. (*in detail*), 305.
vijjā, 142; 145; 262; 276. -caraṇa-sampanna, 227. °vimutti (*perfected through* sambojjhagas), 165. sekha° 306.
vicchiddaka, 63.
viññāṇa,° āhāra, 283. °ṭṭhiti, 143; (*the seven in detail*), 280. °paccayā nāmarūpaṁ, 243. paccudāvattati kho idaṁ viññāṇaṁ, 265. paṭisandhi-, 173; 266. saṁvattanika°, 265.
vitakka, 87-8. °upaccheda, 166.
vinipāta, 186; 227.
vinipātika, 280.
vinīlaka, 63.
vipallāsa, (*the three*), 247 (*the four sets of three each*), 319. diṭṭhi°, 289. °vatthu (*the four*), 279.
vipariṇata. na c'eva no cittaṁ vipariṇataṁ bhavissati, 249.
vipassanā, 92; 190; 264; 275-76; 279; 311; 321. °upekkhā, 291. °kkhaṇa, 161. °ñāṇa, 290. taruṇa-, balava-, 229. °pubbaṅgama samatha, 310.
vipubbaka, 63.
vimāna, 281.
vimutta, sammadaññā°, 307. sammā°, 309.
vimutti, 276; 289. ceto°, 48; 179; 181. °ñāṇa-dassana, 4; 229. tadaṅga-, nissaraṇa-, paṭippassaddha-, vikkhambhana-, samuccheda-, 2. paññā°, 179. °sampanna, 178.
Vimuttimagga, 1; 57.
vimokkha, 130. aṭṭha, 40. (*the three*), 288; 312. subha-, 195.
virāga, 47; 111; 163.
viriya, 9. āraddha°, 21. accāraddha°, atilīna°, °samatā, 77. (iddhipāda), 44.
vivara, 186.
vivāda-mūla (*six in detail*), 316-17.
viveka, °jaṁ pīti-sukhaṁ, 47; 83; 229. *threefold*), 83. tadaṅga°, nissaraṇa°, paṭippassddhi°, vikkhambhana°, samuccheda°, 84.
visa, āsi°, ghora°, 250. 299. visena saṁsaṭṭho, 248.
visaya, pettika°, 19.
visesabhāgiya, 15; 97.
vihāra, ariya°, Tathāgata°, 157. diṭṭhadhamma sukha°, 188. phāsu°, 136. brahma°, 157.
vītikkamapaṭipakkha, 4.
vīmaṁsa (iddhipāda), 44.
vūpakāsa, kāya°, citta°, 178.
vūpasanta, 325.
vedanā, °upekkhā, 194. (*two to thirty-six*), 246.
Vepulla, 223.
vemajjha, 172.
vesārajja, 190. (*the four*), 147.
Vehapphala, 112.
vehāsa, 214.
vossagga, °rato, 154. °ārammaṇatā, 310-11.
vyādhi, °dhamma, 271.
vyāpada, 84.

Saṁkha (rājā), 227.
saṁyoga. jaheyya sabba saṁyogaṁ, 21.
saṁyojana, 305. kāmarāga°, paṭigha°, 307. pañcannaṁ orambhāgiyānaṁ saṁyojanānaṁ parikkhayā, 5; 179. (*the ten*), 281; 312; 318. (*the last five*), 308. tiṇṇaṁ °parikkhayā, 5; 179. (*the last five*), 307. taṇhā°, 204; 261.
saṁvara, 1. °aṭṭhena sīlavisuddhi, 161.
saṁvega, °vatthu (*the eight*), 248.
saṁsāra, 204; 261.
sakadāgāmin, 5; 179. 308. °magga, 307.

APPENDIX

CONTEMPLATION IN THE DHAMMA*

BY

SOMA THERA

Nibbāna the goal of contemplation in the Buddha's teaching is reached with the attainment of knowledge (*aññārādhanā*), through gradual training, gradual work, and gradual practice (*anupubbasikkhā, anupubbakiriyā, anupubbapaṭipadā*). Says the Master, 'Truly, the penetration of knowledge occurs not abruptly' (*na āyataken' eva aññāpaṭivedho*). Step by step, and not in the manner of a jumping frog, does a person progress on the Noble Path. Having fulfilled virtue first, then concentration, and after that wisdom, does one attain full sanctitude in the Buddha's doctrine.[1]

The order and method of development of the Path is shown in the *Rathavinīta Sutta* of the *Majjhima Nikāya*. There are seven purifications taught there. They are: purification of virtue, purification of mind, purification of view, purification of transcending doubt, purification of knowledge and vision of what is and is not the Path, purification of knowledge and vision of practice, purification of knowledge and vision.

These seven have to be developed one by one, in the order given in the *sutta* mentioned above, because of the dependence of concentraction on virtue, and of wisdom on concentration. The purifications have been set forth with an illustration of seven carriages arranged for Pasenadi, the king of Kosala, from Sāvatthi to Sāketa. No carriage takes the king beyond the one next to it on the road to Sāketa, and the last carries him to his destination. The carriages arranged for the yogi going to *Nibbāna* are the seven purifications. No purification takes the yogi beyond the one next to it on the road to *Nibbāna*, and it is by the last that he reaches his bourne.

Virtue is fulfilled by the first purification, concentration, by the second, and wisdom that precedes the Supramundane Path by the next four purifications. The last purification is attained in the Supramundane Path-moment when all the factors of the Noble Path occur together. The purifications

* *Bosat*, July, 1959.

1. A. IV, 201: *Yam pi Pahārāda imasmiṁ dhammavinaye anupubbasikkhā anupubbakiriyā anupubbapaṭipadā na āyataken'eva aññāpaṭivedho.* (*—na āyatakena aññāpaṭivedho ti maṇḍūkassa uppatitvā gamanaṁ viya āditova sīlapūraṇādiṁ akatvā arahattapaṭivedho nāma natthīti paṭipāṭiyā pana sīlasamādhipaññāyo pūretvā va sakkā arahattaṁ pattunti attho* — Mp. p. 762, *Ven. Ratmalāne Dharmārāma Nāyaka Sthavira's Sinhalese ed.*)

cannot function out of place. Each of the purifications has to work in its proper place, and do what it should to aid the others in fulfilling the yogi's aim. None of these can be ignored as they are all vital parts of single system.[1]

The gradualness of the Path of the Buddha is also taught in the following passage: 'The attainment of knowledge at once, bhikkhus, I do not make known; still the attainment of knowledge occurs by gradual training, gradual work, and gradual practice. How bhikkhus, does the attainment of knowledge occur, by gradual training, work, and practice? Here, a man imbubed with faith draws near; drawing near, he sits down near by; sitting down near by, he pays attention; paying attention, he hears the doctrine; having heard the doctrine, he remembers it; of what he remembers, he examines the meaning; while he examines the meaning, the teachings become intelligible to him; when to him the teachings become intelligible, ardour is born in him; when he is with ardour, he becomes energetic; having become energetic, he investigates the nature of things; having investigated the nature of things, he strives to reach the Path; while striving to reach the Path, he realises truly by his mental body the highest truth and sees it, having penetrated it with wisdom'.[2]

---

1. M. I, 148-50 (*Rathavinīta Sutta*): *Tena h' āvuso upaman-te karissāmi, upamāya p' idh' ekacce viññū purisā bhāsitassa atthaṁ ajānanti. Seyyathā pi āvuso rañño Pasenadissa Kosalassa Sāvatthiyaṁ paṭivasantassa Sākete kiñcid-eva accāyikaṁ karaṇīyaṁ uppajjeyya, tassa antarā ca Sāvatthiṁ antarā ca Sāketaṁ satta rathavinītāni upaṭṭhapeyyuṁ. Atha kho āvuso rājā Pasenadi Kosalo Sāvatthiyā nikkhamitvā antepuradvārā paṭhamaṁ rathavinītaṁ abhirūheyya, paṭhamena rathavinītena dutiyaṁ rathavinītaṁ pāpuṇeyya; paṭhamaṁ rathavinītaṁ vissajjeyya dutiyaṁ rathavinītaṁ abhirūheyya, dutiyena rathavinītena tatiyaṁ rathavinītaṁ pāpuṇeyya; dutiyaṁ....pāpuṇeyya; tatiyaṁ....pāpuṇeyya; catutthaṁ pāpuṇeyya; pañcamaṁ rathavinītaṁ vissajjeyya chaṭṭhaṁ rathavinītaṁ abhirūheyya, chaṭṭhena rathavinītena sattamaṁ rathavinītaṁ pāpuṇeyya; chaṭṭhaṁ rathavinītaṁ vissajjeyya sattamaṁ rathavinītaṁ abhirūheyya, sattamena rathavinītena sāketaṁ anupāpuṇeyya antepuradvāraṁ. Tam-enaṁ antepuradvāragataṁ samānaṁ mittāmaccā ñātisālohitā evaṁ puccheyyuṁ: Iminā tvaṁ mahārāja rathavinītena Sāvatthiyā Sāketaṁ anuppatto antepuradvāran-ti. Kathaṁ byākaramāno nu kho āvuso rājā Pasenadi Kosalo sammā byākaramāno byākareyyāti.—Evaṁ byākaramāno kho āvuso rājā Pasenadi Kosalo sammā byākaramāno byākareyya: Idha me Sāvatthiyaṁ paṭisavantassa Sākete kiñcid-eva accāyikaṁ karaṇīyaṁ uppajji. Tassa me antarā ca Sāvatthiṁ antarā ca Sāketaṁ satta rathavinītāni upaṭṭhapesuṁ. Atha kvāhaṁ Sāvatthiyā nikkhamitvā antepuradvārā paṭhamaṁ rathavinītaṁ abhirūhiṁ, paṭhamena rathavinītena dutiyaṁ rathavinītaṁ pāpuṇiṁ: paṭhamaṁ rathavinītaṁ nissajiṁ dutiyaṁ rathavinītaṁ abhirūhiṁ, dutiyena rathavinītena tatiyaṁ rathavinītaṁ pāpuṇiṁ, dutiyaṁ....pāpuṇiṁ; tatiyaṁ... pāpuṇiṁ; catutthaṁ....pāpuṇiṁ; pañcamaṁ rathavinītaṁ nissajiṁ chaṭṭhaṁ rathavinītaṁ abhirūhiṁ, chaṭṭhena rathavinītena sattamaṁ rathavinītaṁ pāpuṇiṁ; chaṭṭhaṁ rathavinītaṁ nissajiṁ sattamaṁ rathavinītaṁ abhirūhiṁ, sattamena rathavinītena Sāketaṁ anuppatto antepuradvāran ti. Evaṁ byākaramāno kho āvuso rājā Pasenadi Kosalo sammā byākaramāno byākareyyāti.— Evam-eva kho āvuso sīlavisuddhi yāvad-eva cittavisuddhatthā, cittavisuddhi yāvad-eva diṭṭhivisuddhatthā, diṭṭhivisuddhi yāvad-eva kaṅkhāvitaraṇavisuddhatthā, kaṅkhāvitaraṇavisuddhi yāvad-eva maggāmaggañāṇadassanavisuddhatthā, maggāmaggañāṇadassanavisuddhi yāvad-eva paṭipadāñaṇādassanavisuddhatthā, paṭipadāñāṇadassanavisuddhi yāvad-eva ñāṇadassanavisuddhatthā, ñāṇadassanavisuddhi yāvad-eva anupādā parinibbānatthā. Anupādā parinibbānatthaṁ kho āvuso Bhagavati brahmacariyaṁ vussatīti.*
2. M. I, 479-80 (*Kīṭāgiri Sutta*): *Nāhaṁ bhikkhave ādiken'eva aññārādhanaṁ vadāmi, api ca bhikkhave anupubbasikkhā anupubbakiriyā anupubbapaṭipadā aññārādhanā hoti. Katthañ ca bhikkhave anupubbasikkhā anupubbakiriyā anupubbapaṭipadā aññārādhanā hoti? Idha bhikkhave saddhājāto upasaṅkamati, upasaṅkamanato payirupāsati, payirupāsanto sotaṁ odahati, ohitasoto dhammaṁ suṇāti, sutvā dhammaṁ dhāreti, dhatānaṁ dhammānaṁ atthaṁ upaparikkhati, atthaṁ upaparikkhato dhammā nijjhānaṁ khamanti. dhammanijjhānakhantiyā sati chando jāyati, chandajāto ussaha.i, ussahitvā tuleti, tulayitvā padahati, pahitatto samāno kāyena c'eva paramaṁ saccaṁ sacchikaroti paññāya ca naṁ ativijjha passati.*

Further the Buddha says in this connection that if that man had no faith, he would not have drawn near, sat down near by, and while paying attention, heard the doctrine and realised the truth.

Conscientiousness and the fear of doing evil are called the world-protecting qualities.[1] These must be strong in one who, by faith in the Jewels, wishes to purify his virtue.[2] These world-protecting qualities make for the refinement of mind essential for the purification of virtue, the first stage in the orderly progress of the Buddhist yogi.

One who observes the precepts carefully is never callous in regard to others' good. He acts in a way that does not harm, injure, or distress others. The yogi bent on reaching the first stage of purity wants to be entirely free from any sense of guilt or remorse,[3] as they are not helpful to tranquillity, which he wants to acquire, and which has to be supported by strong virtue. Until a man has penetrated the meaning of virtue and appreciated fully its importance for the attainment of *jhāna*, which has been described by the Buddha as a state that is separate from sense-desires and other mental conditions that hinder the development of insight,[4] he does not produce the sensitiveness necessary for the purification of the first stage of progress on the Path.

One who is established in the purity of virtue has to guard his senses so that he may not be overwhelmed by evil thoughts. This is done by making the mind see things in the way leading to right understanding. Such a one trains himself in the practice of detachment, neutrality, or indifference, to all that he contacts.

As earth, water, fire, and air, are not affected, and not worried, repelled, or vexed, by what is cast on them, so the yogi must be possessed of unshakable serenity and calm, in all circumstances. Then the things that flow into his mind through the senses will not be able to inflame him.[5]

Control of the sense-faculties, abandoning of thoughts of sense-desires, bringing into being the factors of enlightenment, and protecting the sign of

1. A. I, 51: *Dve'me bhikkhave sukkā dhammā lokaṁ pālenti. Katame dve? Hiri ca ottappañ ca.*
2. A. IV, 336: *Hirottappe sati hirottappasamāpannassa upanisampanno hoti indriyasaṁvaro, indriyasaṁvare sati indriyasaṁvarasampannassa upanisampannaṁ hoti sīlaṁ.*
3. A. V, 1: *Ekamantaṁ nisinno kho āyasmā Ānando Bhagavantaṁ etad avoca 'kimatthiyāni bhante kusalāni sīlāni kimānisaṁsānī' ti? 'Avippaṭisāratthāni kho Ānanda kusalāni sīlāni avippaṭisārānisaṁsānī'ti.*
4. A. II, 211: *So ime pañca nīvaraṇe pahāya cetaso upakkilese paññāya dubbalīkaraṇe vivicc' eva kāmehi....pe....catutthaṁ jhānaṁ upasampajja viharati.*
5. M. I, 423-24 (*Mahā-Rāhulovāda Sutta*):*Paṭhavīsamaṁ Rāhula bhāvanaṁ bhāvehi, paṭhavīsamaṁ hi te Rāhula, bhāvanaṁ bhāvayato uppannā manāpāmanāpā phassā cittaṁ na pariyādāya ṭhassanti. Seyyathā pi Rāhula paṭhaviyā sucim pi nikkhipanti asucim pi nikkhipanti gūtagatam pi nikkhipanti muttagatam pi nikkhipanti khelagatam pi nikkhipanti pubbagatam pi nikkhipanti lohitagatam pi nikkhipanti, na ca tena paṭhavī aṭṭīyati vā harāyati vā jigucchati vā, evam eva kho tvaṁ Rāhula paṭhavīsamaṁ bhāvanaṁ bhāvehi... cittaṁ na pariyādāya ṭhassanti.*
   Āposamaṁ Rāhula bhāvanaṁ bhāvehi .... Tejosamaṁ .... Vāyosamaṁ .... Ākāsasamaṁ Rāhula bhāvanaṁ bhāvehi,....cittaṁ na pariyādāya ṭhassanti.

concentration, are aspects of right effort to which the yogi has to pay attention. The practice of contemplation however, is born with the effort to control the sense-faculties. It may be rightly said that the long journey to peace and immunity from mental ill through the Path does not really begin until the restraint of sense-faculties, which stops the arising of thoughts useless for release from ill, become habitual to the yogi. When control of the sense-faculties becomes strong and a habit, it makes for the maturing of the qualities necessary for intuition of highest freedom. The value of constant practice of restraint of the sense-faculties is brought out in the story given below of the Elder Mahātissa who dwelt on Cetiya Hill (Mihintale).

The Elder was once going for alms to Anurādhapura. A woman who had quarrelled with her husband having thought, 'Remaining alone in the house is better than this unpleasant marriage', got on to the road early in the morning, fully trimmed up and decked out like a divine nymph, to go towards Mihintale. And she who was going to the house of her relatives saw on the way the worshipful Elder of calm demeanour and broke out into wanton laughter with low intent of making him look at her. The Elder, who was walking with attention on his basic contemplation subject, wondering 'What is it?' looked up. And because of his seeing the row of bones of her teeth, his own contemplation subject of bones became clear to his mind. Developing insight then and there, he attained the Fruit of Arahatship. So it is said:

Having beheld the bones that were her teeth,
And called back to mind his first perception,
The elder, who was standing in that place,
Indeed, arrived at the consummate state.

The husband, who was going in search of her, saw the Elder and asked him, 'Venerable sir, did you see a woman going?'. The Elder replied:

I know not whether what passed
Through this place was a man or woman,
But I know that on this highway
There is going a frame of bones.[1]

One who is devoted to control of the senses should keep all evil thoughts out of his mind and be unremitting in his effort to be on the alert remembering the teaching of the Buddha on diligence (*appamāda*), and also keep his thoughts directed on grasping the meaning of the *Dhamma*, by study of, and reflection on, it. In that way the ardent disciple makes use of all his contacts to help

1. *Vis. Mag.* 21: *Tassā dantaṭṭhikaṁ disvā pubbasaññaṁ anussari;*
Tatth' eva so ṭhito thero arahattaṁ apāpuṇī ti.
...
Nābhijānāmi itthī vā puriso vā ito gato,
api ca aṭṭhisanghāṭo gacchat' esa mahāpathe ti.

the ripening of his wisdom. For bringing about that state of wisdom the yogi has to give attention to the practice of mindfulness and full awareness. Mindfulness is required in all effective contemplation. Through full awareness one learns to do everything with deliberation and not on the spur of the moment. Mindfulness belongs to the aggregate of concentration of the Noble Path; it has to be highly developed before success in *jhāna*, meditation, that is aloof from sense-desires, and other evil states of mind, can be achieved. When contemplatives are weak in remembering what should be remembered at the proper time their mindfulness is ineffective and full awareness of what is fit to be done, is not present. Then they also lack wise consideration, which is necessary for overcoming adventitious defilements, and are assailed by passion.[1] The story of the Elder Tissabhūti, given in the commentary to the *Sabbāsava Sutta*, illustrates what happens, when through lack of mindfulness and full awareness, one considers an object unwisely. It is said that this Elder was overcome by passion for an object of the opposite sex, while he was collecting alms in a village, but by means of immediate reflection on the danger of such a mental state, he abandoned the defilement by suppression, and returned to his monastery. The object, however, came up to him in a dream. Seeing danger in it, he was strongly moved to rid himself of the disturbing thought. He visited a teacher of contemplation. Having got from him a contemplation subject connected with the foulness of the body and opposed to lust, he practised contemplation in a jungle, and attained the third Path of Sanctitude after destroying lust.[2]

Mindfulness may also be likened to the driver of the yogi's car,[3] which travels to *Nibbāna*, because it is mindfulness that keeps the mind to the right path, does not let the mind fall into any state of excess or deficiency, and makes for the smooth working of all other mental qualities. In this sense mindfulness may also be called a protector and a refuge of the mind. Mindfulness prevents the arising of mental discord; who practises mindfulness applies himself to every action in the right way and is circumspective, planful, scrutinising, and bright of mind.

All kinds of contemplation for the production of serenity (*samatha*) and of insight (*vipassanā*) are in a sense forms of mindfulness. Mindfulness is

---

1. Cp. A. I, 10: *Pabhassaram idaṁ bhikkhave cittaṁ tañ ca kho āgantukehi upakkilesehi upakkiliṭṭhaṁ. Taṁ assutavā puthujjano yathābhūtaṁ nappajānāti. Tasmā assutavato puthujjanassa citta-bhāvanā natthī ti vadāmī ti.*
   Pabhassaraṁ idaṁ bhikkhave cittaṁ tañ ca kho āgantukehi upakkilesehi vippamuttaṁ. Taṁ sutavā ariyasāvako yathābhūtaṁ pajānāti. Tasmā sutavato ariyasāvakassa citta-bhāvanā atthī ti vadāmī ti.
2. Ps. I, 66: *Maṇḍalārāmavāsi-Mahā-Tissabhūtittherassa viya. So kira tasmiṁ yeva vihāre uddesaṁ gaṇhāti. Ath'assa gāme piṇḍāya carato visabhāgārammaṇe kileso uppajji. So taṁ vipassanāya vikkhambhetvā vihāraṁ agamāsi. Tassa supinante pi taṁ ārammaṇaṁ upaṭṭhāsi. So, ayaṁ kileso vaḍḍhitvā apāyasaṁvattaniko hotī ti saṁvegaṁ janetvā ācariyaṁ āpucchitvā vihārā nikkhamma Mahā-Sangharakkhitattherassa santike rāgapaṭipakkhaṁ asubhakammaṭṭhānaṁ gahetvā gumbantaraṁ pavisitvā paṁsukūlacīvaraṁ pattharitvā nisajja anāgāmimaggena pañcakāmaguṇarāgaṁ chinditvā, uṭṭhāya ācariyaṁ vanditvā punadivase uddesamaggaṁ pāpuṇi.*
3. S. V, 6: *Sati ārakkhasārathi.*

the central factor in the development of amity (*mettā*), which is a contemplation subject of serenity and in pondering on things (*dhammānupassanā*), which is a contemplation subject of pure insight (*suddhavipassanā*); so mindfulness is wanted in all wholesome activities of the yogi, and has been compared to a salt-tempering required for all curries.[1]

Mindfulness is above all the quality chiefly instrumental in organising mental activity generally, making it useful and coherent, producing mental catharsis (*cittavodāna*).[2] and perfecting sense-faculty restraint. In connection with control of the sense-faculties it has been compared to a rope that restrains a rebellious elephant.[3] Pure intellectual activity cannot come to be unless the mind is freed of the dirt of false imaginings, judgment and views, through mindfulness, which produces right understanding through its ability to discriminate, choose what is good, and eliminate what is ill.

The development of mind (*cittabhāvanā*) takes place through serenity (*samatha*), which eliminates obstructions to clear thinking. Without such elimination clear vision due to analysis that is to say, insight (*vipassanā*) can never arise. Serenity has been described thus, 'What extinguishes, destroys, the hostile things beginning with sense-desire is serenity; it is a name for concentration'. Insight has been explained thus, 'What sees things in different ways, according to impermanence and the like, is insight; it is a name for wisdom'. These two, serenity and insight, are essential factors of the Supramundane Path. But they are also necessary to the antecedent part of the Path leading to the highest. In the antecedent part of the Path these two are mundane factors. Thus they have first to be developed as mundane qualities before they can become supramundane.[4]

Of the great *suttas* in which both serenity (*samatha*) and insight (*vipassanā*) have been combined, the most popular are the *Satipaṭṭhāna Sutta* of the *Majjhima Nikāya*, and the *Mahā Satipaṭṭhāna Sutta* of the *Dīgha Nikāya*. Now both these discourses on the foundations of mindfulness lay more stress on the development of insight, but the aim of these *suttas* is to lead the yogi to the realisation of the highest according to the inevitable method of attainment

---

1. S. V, 115: *Satiñ ca kvāhaṁ bhikkhave sabbatthikaṁ vadāmīti.* (= *Satiñ ca kvāhaṁ bhikkhave sabb' atthikaṁ vadāmī ti, loṇa-dhūpanaṁ viya sabbattha icchitabbaṁ vadāmī ti attho*—Spk. III, 171).
2. S. III, 151: *Cittasaṁkilesā bhikkhave sattā saṁkilissanti, cittavodānā sattā visujjhanti.* (= *citta-sankilesā ti, sunahātāpi hi sattā citta-sankilesen' eva sankilissanti. Mala-ggahita-sarīrāpi cittassa vodanattā visujjhanti. Ten' āhu porāṇā:*
   Rūpamhi sankiliṭṭhamhi sankilissanti māṇavā,
   Rūpe suddhe visujjhanti anakkhātaṁ Mahesinā.
   Cittamhi sankiliṭṭhamhi sankilissanti māṇavā,
   Citte suddhe visujjhanti: iti vuttaṁ Mahesinā —Spk. II, 327).
3. Th. 1141: *Ārammaṇe taṁ balasā nibandhisaṁ nāgaṁ va thambhamhi dalhāya rajjuyā,*
   taṁ me suguttaṁ satiyā subhāvitaṁ anissitaṁ sabbabhavesu hehisi.
4. Pts.-a. I, 125: *Samatho ca vipassanā cā 'ti kāmacchandādayo paccanikadhamme vināsetī 'ti samatho, samādhiss' etaṁ nāmaṁ. Aniccatādivasena vividhehi ākārehi dhamme vipassatī 'ti vipassanā, paññāy' etaṁ nāmaṁ. Ime pana dve Dasuttarapariyāye pubbabhāgā 'ti vuttā, Sangītipariyāye ca lokiya-lokuttara-missakā ti.*

taught in the Noble Eightfold Path, that is, by following the order of the seven purifications.

The yogi who wishes to train himself in contemplation, that is, in the higher training of the mind (*adhicittasikkhā*), and of wisdom (*adhipaññāsikkhā*), should be one who, having perfected his purity of virtue and exercised himself in the control of the sense-faculties (*indriya saṁvara*), has well established himself in mindfulness and full awareness (*satisampajañña*). Concentrating on a contemplation subject of serenity (*samatha kammaṭṭhāna*) at first, he should labour to suppress the hindrances and stop distraction.[1] In the *Paṭisambhidā Magga* (I, 27), it is said that the abandoning of the hindrances by suppression occurs in him who develops the First *Jhāna* (*vikkhambhanappahānañ ca nīvaraṇānaṁ paṭhamajjhānaṁ bhāvayato*).[2] Of no state before the First *Jhāna* has it been said by the Blessed One that it is separate from sense-desires and separate from other evil states, that is to say, aloof from the hindrances that obstruct clear vision, by being far from the plane of the sensuous (*kāmāvacara bhūmi*).[3]

The whole teaching of the two main *Satipaṭṭhāna Suttas* on inner development belongs to the antecedent (mundane) part of the way (*pubbabhāgamagga*) or the antecedent (mundane) part of progress (*pubbabhāgapaṭipadā*).[4] The teaching of these two *suttas* comprises the preparatory training in contemplation, the development of mundane concentration and insight. It has already been

---

1. D. I, 71: *So iminā ca ariyena sīlakkhandhena samannāgato iminā ca ariyena indriyasaṁvarena samannāgato iminā ca ariyena sati-sampajaññena samannāgato imāya ca ariyāya santuṭṭhiyā samannāgato vivittaṁ senāsanaṁ bhajati, araññaṁ rukkha-mūlaṁ pabbataṁ kandaraṁ giri-guhaṁ susānaṁ vana-patthaṁ abbhokāsaṁ palāla-puñjaṁ. So pacchābhattaṁ piṇḍapāta-paṭikkanto nisīdati pallaṅkaṁ ābhujitvā ujuṁ kāyaṁ panidhāya parimukhaṁ satiṁ upaṭṭhapetvā.*

   So abhijjhaṁ loke pahāya vigatābhijjhena cetasā viharati, abhijjhāya cittaṁ parisodheti. Vyāpāda-padosaṁ pahāya avyāpanna-citto viharati, sabba-pāṇa-bhūta-hitānukampī vyāpāda-padosā cittaṁ parisodheti. Thīna-middhaṁ pahāya vigata-thīna-middho viharati, āloka-saññī sato sampajāno thīna-middhā cittaṁ parisodheti. Uddhacca-kukkuccaṁ pahāya anuddhato viharati, ajjhattaṁ vūpasanta-citto uddhacca-kukkuccā cittaṁ parisodheti. Vicikicchaṁ pahāya tiṇṇa-vicikiccho viharati, akathaṁkathī kusalesu dhammesu vicikicchāya cittaṁ parisodheti.

2. Pts.-a. I, 122: *Pañcasu pahāṇesu yaṁ sasevāle udake pakkhittena ghaṭena sevālassa viya tena tena lokiyasamādhinā nīvaraṇādīnaṁ paccanīkadhammānaṁ vikkhambhanaṁ dūrīkaraṇaṁ, idaṁ vikkhaṁbhanapahāṇaṁ nāma. Vikkhambhanappahāṇañ ca nīvaraṇānaṁ paṭhamajjhānaṁ bhāvayato 'ti nīvaraṇānaṁ yeva pahāṇaṁ pākaṭattā vuttan, 'ti veditabbaṁ. Nīvaraṇāni hi jhānassa pubbabhāge 'pi pacchābhāge 'pi na sahasā cittaṁ ajjhottaranti; ajjhotthaṭesu ca tesu jhānaṁ parihāyati.*

3. D. I, 73: *So vivicc' eva kāmehi vivicca akusalehi dhammehi savitakkaṁ savicāraṁ vivekajaṁ pīti-sukhaṁ paṭhamajjhānaṁ upasampajja viharati.*

4. Ps. I, 230-31: *Keci pana, "Na pāraṁ diguṇaṁ yantī" ti* (Sn. 714) *āgatanayena, yasmā ekavāraṁ nibbānaṁ gacchati, tasmā ekāyano ti pi vadanti. Taṁ na yujjati. Imassa hi atthassa sakiṁ ayano ti iminā byañjanena bhavitabbaṁ. Yadi pana ekaṁ ayanam assa, ekā gati pavattī ti evaṁ atthaṁ yojetvā vucceyya, byañjanaṁ yujjeyya; attho pana ubhayathā pi na yujjati. Kasmā? Idha pubbabhāgamaggassa adhippetattā. Kāyādi-catu-ārammaṇappavatto hi pubbabhāgasatipaṭṭhānamaggo idhādhippeto; na lokuttaro. So ca anekavāram pi ayati, anekañ c' assa ayanaṁ hoti....Thero* (*Tipiṭaka-Culla-Nāgatthera*) *cintesi: Amahākaṁ ācariyo sabbapariyattiko tepiṭako sutabuddho. Evarūpassāpi nāma bhikkhuno ayaṁ pañho ālulati. Anāgate mama bhātikā imaṁ pañhaṁ ālulissanti. Suttaṁ gahetvā imaṁ pañhaṁ niccalaṁ karissāmī ti Paṭisambhidāmaggato, "Ekāyano maggo vuccati pubbabhāgasatipaṭṭhānamaggo.*

said that the teaching of the discourses on the foundations of mindfulness, the *Satipaṭṭhāna Suttas*, is a combination of serenity and insight and that it lays stress on insight. But the practice of serenity in these *suttas* on mindfulness is not something that can be ignored. The *Satipaṭṭhāna Suttas* do not permit of restriction only to the development of insight. In short the practice of serenity (*samatha*) in these *suttas* is not optional. It is necessary for the cultivator of mindfulness to bring into being both serenity and insight, because the first leads to the second, and the practice of the first, that is, serenity is unavoidable for the beginner in the practice of the Foundations of Mindfulness, according to the pattern of the standard *suttas* on the subject. The insight taught in these *suttas* can be developed only by those who have the purity of virtue (*sīlavisuddhi*) and the purity of mind (*cittavisuddhi*), which is always taught in the books as the product of serenity, mental purity, which must be in existence before one begins to purify one's views.[1] So the Buddha begins his instruction in the two standard *Satipaṭṭhāna Suttas* by setting forth the way of producing serenity through mindfulness on breathing (*ānāpānasati*), for purification of mind through the meditation, *jhāna*, by which he himself attained full enlightenment, *sambodhi*, and of which he said, 'This truly is the way to enlightenment (*eso va maggo bodhāya*).[2]

The placing of the first tetrad of the *Ānāpānasati Sutta* at the very beginning of the two main *Satipaṭṭhāna Suttas* is clear indication of the necessity of at least the First *Jhāna*, the first meditaion of the plane of form, for getting rid of the hindrances and coming to the proper ground for the development of insight, the ground that is aloof from sense-desires and other evil states. It is certain that, from the structure of the *Satipaṭṭhāna Suttas*, the testimony of other *suttas*, and the whole architecture of the Noble Eightfold Path seen from different angles, there is no getting away from the fact that the development of insight is impossible to one who has not brought into being the antecedent part of the Path, at least, the First *Jhāna*. This is because it is admitted on all hands that the lowest *jhāna* needed in the Supramundane Path is the First *Jhāna*.

Maggān' aṭṭhangiko seṭṭho saccānaṁ caturo padā
virāgo seṭṭho dhammānaṁ dipadānañ ca cakkhumā.
Eso va maggo n'atth'añño dassanassa visuddhiyā
etasmiṁ tumhe paṭipajjatha Mārass'etaṁ pamohanaṁ
etasmiṁ tumhe paṭipannā dukkhass'antaṁ karissathā" ti

suttaṁ āharitvā ṭhapesi.

1. Vis. Mag. (a) 436: *Sīle patiṭṭhāya naro sapañño cittaṁ paññañ ca bhāvayan ti ettha cittasīsena niddiṭṭho samādhi sabbākarena bhāvito hoti, tad anantarā pana paññā bhāvetabbā.*

(b) 443: *Ettha pana yasmā imāya paññāya khandh'-āyatana-dhātu-indriya-sacca-paṭiccasamuppādādibhedā dhammā bhūmi. Sīlavisuddhi ceva cittavisuddhi cā ti imā dve visuddhiyo mūlaṁ. Diṭṭhivisuddhi kankhāvitaraṇavisuddhi maggāmaggañāṇadassanavisuddhi paṭipadāñāṇadassanavisuddhi ñāṇadassanavisuddhī ti imā pañca visuddhiyo sarīraṁ. Tasmā tesu bhūmisu tesu maggesu uggahaparipucchāvasena ñāṇaparicayaṁ katva mūlabhūtā dve visuddhiyo sampādetvā sarīrabhūtā pañcavisuddhiyo sampādentena bhāvetabbā.*

(c) 587: *Idāni yā imesu bhūmi-bhūtesu dhammesu uggahaparipucchāvasena ñāṇaparicayaṁ katvā: sīlavisuddhi c'eva cittavisuddhi cā ti dve mūlabhūtā*

It should be clear to those who know the Texts that there is no way of avoiding the practice of serenity and the development of at least the First *Jhāna*, in the antecedent part of the Noble Path according to the facts mentioned below. The Buddha placed the first tetrad of the *Ānāpānasati Sutta*, an exercise in serenity, at the very beginning of the two main *Satipaṭṭhāna Suttas*; the *Paṭisambhidā* passage cited above attributes the abandoning of the hindrances by suppression to one who develops nothing less than the First *Jhāna*; the Buddha does not apply the words, 'having separated himself from sense-desires, having separated himself from evil states', namely, from the hindrances, to a winner of a lower state than the First *Jhāna*; and the Buddha has defined Right Concentration, *Sammāsamādhi*, as the four *jhānas*, and not anything lower than them.[1]

No progress in contemplation leading towards the Supramundane Path is possible without at least getting the First *Jhāna*. The practice of insight is unfruitful, ineffective, and obstructed when it is attempted without going away from thought-proximity to the sensual plane, *kāmabhūmi*. In one who has attained the First *Jhāna* a proper environment is created internally for the intuition of the highest as well as for progress in the antecedent part of the Path that is connected with insight-development.

Of the First *Jhāna*, from the time of coming to which a yogi undergoes the first great transformation of consciousness, it is said that it is the escape from sensuality. That escape is due to the factor of unification in the *jhāna* brought about by concentration on what is not connected with sense-desire. With the escape into the consciousness of the First *Jhāna* the sensuous realm is not in being for the yogi, since attainment of this *jhāna* is only possible with abandoning the sensuous realm. As the light of a lamp is not in being when there is full darkness, so *jhāna* is not in being when sense-desires, which are contrary to it, are present. As by leaving the hither bank the reaching of the thither bank takes place, so by giving up sense-desires the First *Jhāna* is reached. The First *Jhāna*, owing to its transcension of the element of the sensuous (*kāmadhātu samatikkamanato*) and its being opposed to sensuous lust (*kāmarāga paṭipakkhabhāvato*), is truly free from sense-desires. In the sense of escape from sense-desires this *jhāna* is renunciation according to the Venerable Sāriputta Thera's words. This is the escape from sense-desires, namely, renunciation.[2]

---

visuddhiyo sampādetabbā ti vuttā, tattha sīlavisuddhi nāma suparisuddhaṁ pātimokkhasaṁvarādi catubbidhaṁ sīlaṁ, tañ ca Sīlaniddese vitthāritam eva, cittavisuddhi nāma sa upacārā aṭṭha samāpattiyo, tā pi cittasīsena vutta-Samādhiniddese sabbākārena vitthāritā eva. Tasmā tā tattha vitthārita-nayen'eva veditabbā. Yaṁ pana vuttaṁ: diṭṭhivisuddhi....imā pañca visuddhiyo sarīran ti tattha nāmarūpānaṁ yāthāvadassanaṁ diṭṭhivisuddhi nāma.

2. See n. 1, p. 189.

1. Pts. I, 41-2; D. II, 313: See n. 1 (d), p. 229.

2. As. 164: *Kāmadhātusamatikkamanato hi kāmarāgapaṭipakkhato ca idaṁ jhānaṁ kāmānam eva nissaraṇaṁ.* See n. 1 (b), 310.

In the *Dantabhūmi Sutta* of the *Majjhima Nikāya,* the Blessed one says that it is not possible for one who is given to a life of pleasure, who indulges himself in sensual delights, who is devoured by sensual thoughts, who is consumed with the fever of sensual enjoyment, and who is eager in the pursuit of the sensually pleasant, to experience, see, or realise, what has to be experienced, seen, and realised by renunciation of sense-desires.[1] Now sense-desires and the other hindrances to the First *Jhāna* are not conducive to the penetration of things and seeing them as they are. So, for the development of insight (*vipassanā*), the bringing into being of the First *Jhāna* is indispensable according to the Buddha's teaching, that is to say, the words of the Buddha in the Pali Texts.[2] There is no doubt that according to the Bodhisatta's words repeated by the Buddha in conformation, the First *Jhāna* is truly the way to enlightenment, and so this *jhāna* has a specially important place in the Buddha's scheme of salvation.

---

1. M. III, 129-30: *Yan taṁ nekkhammena ñātabbaṁ, nekkhammena daṭṭhabbaṁ, nekkhammena pattabbaṁ, nekkhammena sacchikātabbaṁ, taṁ vata Jayaseno rājakumāro kāmamajjhe vasanto kāme paribhuñjanto kāmavitakkehi khajjamāno kāmapariḷāhena pariḍayahamāno kāmapariyesanāya ussukko ñassati vā dakkhati vā sacchi vā karissatīti n'etaṁ ṭhānaṁ vijjati.*
2. A. V, 1-2: *Ekamantaṁ nisinno kho āyasmā Ānando Bhagavantaṁ etad avoca 'kimathtiyāni bhante kusalāni sīlāni kimānisaṁsāni'ti? 'Avippaṭisāratthāni kho Ānanda kusalāni sīlāni avippaṭisārānisaṁsāni'ti. 'Avippaṭisāro pana bhante kimatthiyo kimānisaṁso' ti? 'Avippaṭisāro kho Ānanda pāmujjattho pāmujjānisaṁso' ti. 'Pāmujjaṁ pana bhante kimatthiyaṁ kimānisaṁsan' ti? 'Pāmujjaṁ kho Ānanda pītatthaṁ pītānisaṁsan' ti. 'Pīti pana bhante kimatthiyā kimānisaṁsā' ti? 'Pīti kho Ānanda passaddhatthā passaddhānisaṁsā' ti. Passaddhi pana bhante kimatthiyā kimānisaṁsā' ti? 'Passaddhi kho Ānanda sukhatthā sukhānisaṁsā' ti. 'Sukhaṁ pana bhante kimatthiyaṁ kimānisaṁsan' ti? 'Sukhaṁ kho Ānanda samādhatthaṁ samādhānisaṁsan' ti. 'Samādhi pana bhante kimatthiyo kimānisaṁso' ti? 'Samādhi kho Ānanda yathābhūtañāṇadassanattho yathābhūtañāṇadassanānisaṁso' ti. 'Yathābhūtañāṇadassanaṁ pana bhante kimatthiyaṁ kimānisaṁsan' ti? 'Yathābhūtañāṇadassanaṁ kho Ānanda nibbidāvirāgatthaṁ nibbidavirāgānisaṁsan' ti? Nibbidāvirāgo pana bhante kimatthiyo kimānisaṁso' ti? Nibbidāvirāgo kho Ānanda vimuttiñāṇadassanattho vimuttiñāṇadassanānisaṁso' ti.* (= *Yathābhūtañāṇadassanattho ti ādisu yathābhūtañāṇadassanaṁ nāma taruṇavipassanā; nibbidā nāma balavavipassanā; virāgo nāma maggo; vimutti nāma arahattaphalaṁ; ñāṇadassanaṁ nāma paccavekkhanañāṇaṁ*—Mp. V, 1).

APPENDIX

(INDEX OF PALI WORDS IN FOOTNOTES)

aññā. °ārādhanā, 345. °paṭivedha, 344.
anupubba, °kiriyā, °paṭipadā, °sikkhā, 344-45.
antepura, °dvāra, 345.
ayana. ekāyano maggo vuccati pubbabhāgasatipaṭṭhānamaggo, 350.
arahatta, °paṭivedha, 344.
ariya. ariyena sīlakkhandhena samannāgato (*etc.*), 350.
Ānanda (*Ven. Elder*), 346.
upakkilesa, āgantuka, 348.
upaparikkhati, 345.
upasaṅkamati, 345
ussahati, 345.
ottappa, 346.
kāma, °rāgapaṭipakkhato, °dhātusamatikkamanato, 352. °pariyesanā, °pariḷāha, °majjhe vasanto, °vitakkehi khajjamāno, 353.
citta, °saṁkilesa, °vodāna, 349.
chanda, °jāto, 345.
tuleti, 345.
danta, °aṭṭhikaṁ, 347.
dhammavinaya, 344.
nāga, 349.
nijjhāna, khamanti, 345.
nekkhamma, 353.
paccanīka, °dhamma, 349; 350.
pañca, °kāmaguṇarāga, 348. pahāna, 350.
paññā. °paññāya dubbalīkaraṇe, 346.
paṭhavī, °samaṁ bhāvanaṁ bhāvehi (*etc.*), 346.
pabhassara, 348.
payirupāsati, 345.
Pasenadi Kosala (*the king*), 345.
Pahārāda, 344.
puthujjana, 348.
bhūmi. khandh'-āyatana-dhātu.... paṭiccasamuppādabhedā dhammā b., 351.
magga, uddesa°, 348. pubbabhāga°, 350.
Maṇḍalārāmavāsī Mahā-Tissabhūtitthera, 348.
maṇḍūka, 344.
mahā, °patha, 347.
mitta, °amaccā ñātisālohitā, 345.
mūla. dve visuddhiyo mūlaṁ, 351.
yathābhūta, 348.
rathavinīta, 345.
Rāhula (*Ven. Elder*), 346.
loṇa, -dhūpana, 349.
vipassanā, 349. taruṇa°, balava°, 353.
virāga, 353.
visuddhi, (*the seven*), 345; 351-52.
saṃvara, indriya°, 346.
sacca, parama, 345.
sati, 349.
saddhā, °jāto, 345.
sabbatthika, 349.
samatha, 349.
sarīra. imā pañca visuddhiyo sarīraṁ, 352.
Sāketa, 345.
Sāvatthi, 345.
sikkhā, anupubba°, 344.
sīla, 346. °pūraṇa, 344. °samādhipaññāyo pūretvā va sakkā arahattaṃ pattunti, 344. sīle patiṭṭhāya naro sapañño, 351. (sīla, avippaṭisāra,....vimuttiñāṇadassana), 353.
sukka, dhamma, 346.
suṇāti. ohitasoto dhammaṁ suṇāti, 345.

ADDITIONS AND CORRECTIONS

P. 6, n. 3: read *paccupaṭṭhāna*
P. 13, n. 3, for *achiddehi* read *acchiddehi*
P. 17, last line but one for (In his) read (In this)
P. 21, n. 4, line 3: for *saraṇattamo* read *saraṇattano*
P. 25, n. 5, line 2: read *brāhmaṇa-parisaṁ*
P. 27, n. 10: read *Khalupacchābhattika-°*
P. 41, n. 2: read Manopubbaṅgamā
P. 44, n. 5: alter 5 to 4; n. 4: alter 4 to 5
P. 49, n. 2: read vacanakkhamo ca, *gambhīrañ ca*
P. 72, n. 3: delete black
P. 78, n. 1, line 3: read *paṭipajjati*
P. 91, n. 2, line 3: read *thīnamiddhaṁ*
P. 124, n. 1, last line: read *pañcamaṁ*
P. 132, n. 1 (b) continued from previous page, line 1: read *paṭipāṭiyā*
P. 145, n. 5, par. 3, line 2: read *yathābhūtaṁ*
P. 161, n. 2: read *kāyasaṅkhārehi*
P. 183, n. 3: read *Surattaṁ*
P. 187, n. 2, line 4: read *appamāṇena*
P. 195, n. 1, par. 5, line 1: read *kimphalā*
P. 208, n. 1: read *Pāliputta*
P. 227, n. 3, line 2: read *vijjā-caraṇa-sampanno*
P. 233, n. 2, line 6: read *taṇhā-samudaya-saccaṁ*
P. 243, n. 1: read *Gabbhaseyyaka-sattassa;* n. 2: read *Abhāva-gabbhaseyyānaṁ*
P. 244, line 10 from bottom: substitute kinds for hinds
P. 290, n. 4 (a) continued from previous page, line 1: read *attho*
P. 302, n. 4, line 4: read *dukkhaṁ*
P. 315, n. 1: substitute—(a) D. II, 81, 84, 91, 98, 123, 126: *Paññā-paribhāvitaṁ cittaṁ sammad eva āsavehi vimuccati, seyyathīdaṁ kāmāsavā bhavāsavā diṭṭhāsavā avijjāsavā ti.*

(b) Dhs. 195, par. 1096: *Cattāro āsavā — kāmāsavo bhavāsavo diṭṭhāsavo avijjāsavo.*

(c) Netti. 116: *Tassa evaṁ gandhitā kilesā āsavanti. Kuto ca vuccati āsavantī ti? Anusayato vā pariyuṭṭhānato vā. Tattha abhijjhākāyagandhena kāmāsavo, byāpādakāyagandhena bhavāsavo, parāmāsakāyagandhena diṭṭhāsavo, idaṁ-saccābhinivesakāyagandhena avijjāsavo.*

(d) Pts. I, 94, 117: *'Āsavā' ti. Katame te āsavā? Kāmāsavo, bhavāsavo, diṭṭhāsavo, avijjāsavo.*

P. xxxii, line 8 read ask the
P. xlii, line 3 from bottom delete to